TITLE PAGE

Harrison & Lee

Basic Appraisal Procedures

based on the

2008

Appraisal Foundation
Core Curriculum

Henry S. Harrison & Burton S. Lee

MAI, ASA, IFSA, DREI　　　　　　**MAI, MBA**

Published by the New Collegiate Publishing Co. LLC.

100 York Street

New Haven, CT 06511

Phone: (203) 562-3159

henrysharrison@gmail.com

COPYRIGHT

Basic Appraisal Procedures
based on the
2008 Appraisal Foundation
Core Curriculum

by

Henry S. Harrison & Burton S. Lee
MAI, ASA, IFAS, DREI   **MAI, MBA**

ISBN # 1547216522
ISBN # 9781547216529

©2006 & 2017 by New Collegiate Publishing Co., LLC

1st	Printing	Edition 1	July	2006
1st	Printing	Edition 2	June	2017

For permission, write:
New Collegiate Publishing Company, LLC
100 York Street Unit 3D
New Haven, CT 06511

Edited by Ruth Lambert

FOREWORD

When the Appraisal Foundation announced its new education, license and certification requirements going into effect January 1, 2008 it became clear that all of the traditional educational material was going to have to be replaced.

Burton Lee and I have both been active in appraisal education for many years. Burton is a principle of an online education company and I had been writing appraisal books for over 40 years. It became apparent to us that by combining our talents we would be in a better position to fill the need for this new material.

This book, *Basic Appraisal Procedures* and its companion book Basic Appraisal Principles, are designed to cover all the material (except the Standard of Professional Practice (USPAP)), needed to become a qualified Appraisal Trainee.

These books exactly track the "Real Property Appraiser Qualifications Criteria Education Requirements" adopted by the Appraiser Qualifications Board (AQB) of The Appraisal Foundation that will became effective January 1, 2008. The AQB has announced that these topics will also "be used for developing examination content outlines...."

In addition to this required material we have included additional material to provide the appraisal trainee with practical information covering how to make an acceptable residential appraisal on the Uniform Residential Appraisal Report (URAR) and the Exterior-Only Inspection Residential Appraisal Report. This additional material includes two complete model appraisals and a line-by- line guide on how to fill out the new URAR.

Our goal is to develop courses based on these new books that will be approved by The Appraisal Foundation. Instructors who use our books will be provided with course outlines and other teaching materials to help them provide the best appraisal education possible.

Finally, we will soon release four more text books that will also follow The Appraisal Foundation's education requirements for obtaining a Residential Appraisal License. We are also developing courses that will help the appraisal trainee become a licensed residential appraiser.

Henry S. Harrison
Burton S. Lee
June 2017

CHAPTER 1

Overview of Approaches to Value

"Upon the sacredness of property civilization itself depends."

Wealth, 1889
Andrew Carnegie

Important Words and Key Concepts

Words on this list are highlighted in this chapter.
They are also defined in the Glossary at the back of this text.

Appraisal
Appraisal Report
Assumptions
Comparable Sale
Cost Approach
Depreciation
Effective Date of the Appraisal
Extraordinary Assumptions
Fannie Mae
Final Estimate of Value
Fractional Interests
Freddie Mac
General Data
Gross Monthly Rent Multiplier (GMRM)
Highest and Best Use
Hypothetical Conditions
Improvements
Income Capitalization Approach

Intended Use
Intended User
Land
Limiting Conditions
Lot and Block System
Market (Economic) Rent
Market Value
Metes and Bounds
Narrative Appraisal Report
Opinion of Value
Oral Report
Personal Property
Planned Unit Development (PUD)
Plottage
Property Rights
Purpose of the Appraisal
Real Estate
Real Property
Reconciliation

Rectangular (Government) Survey
Replacement Cost
Reproduction Cost
Restricted Use Appraisal Report
Rights of Ownership
Sales Comparison Approach
Self-Contained Appraisal Report
Scope of Work
Site
Specific Data
Specific Date
Subject Property
Summary Appraisal Report
Uniform Residential Appraisal Report (URAR)
Uniform Standards of Appraisal Practice (USPAP)
Valuation Process

INTRODUCTION TO APPRAISAL & VALUE

THE IMPORTANCE OF THE APPRAISER

The role of a professional appraiser is to provide an **opinion of value** to help their client make a decision. For example, an **appraisal** helps a lender decide if a property is adequate security for a proposed loan. Some appraisals help buyers and sellers decide how much to buy or sell a property for, to determine how much to insure a property for, or the value of a piece of property is needed for estate or tax purposes. Appraisers play an important part in the process of government acquisition of real property by eminent domain, by helping to set a fair price for the property acquired. These are just a few of the many reasons appraisers estimate property value.

For over 70 years, the appraisal profession has been working to perfect a process for estimating the value of **real estate**. The process is not stagnant—it improves as time goes on. Appraisers who feel they have an improvement to the process are encouraged to write an article for one of the appraisal journals published by the professional organizations. These journals act as a way for new techniques and procedures to be peer reviewed and enter standard practice.

The appraisal process, as it is described in this textbook, has been simplified. The authors have kept in mind that the reader will be a new appraiser probably with limited or no formal appraisal training.

Chapter 15: Residential Applications & Model Appraisals provides information about the appraisal profession. It spells out the various types of appraisal assignments that comprise the daily work of a professional appraiser. It discusses the importance of the appraiser as an expert in evaluating neighborhoods as well as individual properties and explains that the public depends upon their expert opinions. It goes into detail about the growth of professionalism in real estate appraising.

An appraiser has five things to sell a client (A, E, I, O, U):

1. **A**dequate knowledge
2. **E**xperience
3. **I**ntegrity
4. **O**bjectivity
5. **U**ncompromised willingness to do the work on a timely basis for a mutually agreed upon fee.

The purpose of this book is to provide the reader with some of the knowledge needed to accomplish these goals. This is a practical book that directly addresses how to make an appraisal. It is intended to be used with its companion book, *Basic Appraisal Principles*, which introduces the theories and principles upon which appraisal practice is based. The flow chart in Figure 1-1 is entitled **The Valuation Process**. It is helpful to see the valuation process in this format, as it clearly delineates the steps involved.

Figure 1-1

THE VALUATION PROCESS

Definition of the Problem

Identification of the client and other intended users	Identification of the intended use of the appraisers opinions and conclusions	Identification of the type and definition of value	Identification of the effective date of the appraiser's opinions and conclusions	Identification of characteristics of the property (including location & property rights to be valued)	Identification of any extraordinary assumptions necessary in the assignment	Identification of any hypothetical conditions necessary in the assignment

Determine the Scope of Work

Data Collection and Property Description

MARKET AREA DATA	SUBJECT PROPERTY DATA	COMPARABLE PROPERTY DATA
General characteristics of region, city, and neighborhood	Specific characteristics of land and improvements, personal property, business assets, etc.	Sales, listings, offerings, vacancies, cost and depreciation, income and expenses, capitalization rates, etc.

Data Analysis

MARKET ANALYSIS	HIGHEST AND BEST USE ANALYSIS
Demand studies Supply studies Marketability studies	Site as though vacant Ideal improvement Property as improved

Land (Site) Value Opinion

Application of the Approaches to Value

COST	SALES COMPARISON	INCOME

Reconciliation of Value Indications & Final Opinion of Value

Report of Final Opinion of Value & Conclusions

THE VALUATION PROCESS

DEFINITION OF THE PROBLEM

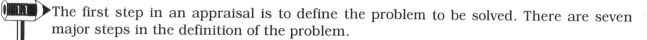The first step in an appraisal is to define the problem to be solved. There are seven major steps in the definition of the problem.

- Identification of the client and other intended users
- Identification of the intended use of the appraiser's opinions and conclusions
- Identification of the type and definition of value
- Identification of the effective date of the appraiser's opinions and conclusions
- Identification of the characteristics of the property
    (including location and property rights to be valued)
- Identification of any extraordinary assumptions necessary in the assignment
- Identification of any hypothetical conditions necessary in the assignment

Identification of Client and Other Intended Users

The identification of the client and other **intended users** is important as it affects the appropriate level of reporting and who has status in a professional liability suit against the appraiser. The **Uniform Standards of Appraisal Practice (USPAP)** require that the intended user(s) of the appraisal be identified in the appraisal report. **Freddie Mac** and **Fannie Mae** also require that the appraisal report identify all intended users.

Identification of the Intended Use of the Appraiser's Opinions and Conclusions

The USPAP requires that the **intended use** be reported in every appraisal. It is helpful for the appraiser to know the purpose of the appraisal so that the report will provide the reader with all of the information required to make a decision. The objective of most appraisals is to estimate the value of a property as of a specific date.

Identification of the Type and Definition of Value

The type of value must be identified. Typically market value is the type of value, but often other types of value are possible. For example investment value, insurable value, auction value, etc.

Once the type of value has been identified the appraiser is obligated to determine which definition for the type of value is being relied upon for assignment.

It is required that appraisals that are made for loan purposes base their **opinion of value** on market value. The current accepted definition of market value is usually attached to each appraisal or a copy is filed by the appraiser with the client and is referred to in the appraisal. Implicit in this definition is the consummation of a sale as of specified date and the passing of title from seller to buyer.

Identification of the Effective Date of the Appraiser's Opinions and Conclusions

An appraisal must be an opinion of value as of a **specific date**. The value of a property may change from day to day. For example, the sudden announcement of some event that affects the subject market will have a significant effect on the value of property. Typical announcements which affect the value of property are the expansion or contraction of business activities which are major sources of employment in the area. Other announcements that may suddenly affect value are the additions or relocation of roads and highways or anything else changing in close proximity to the **subject property**.

Sudden changes in the physical condition of the property by fire, the environment or man-made additions, demolitions or alterations all may affect the property value. It is also acceptable for an appraisal to be as of some date in the past. The appraiser then makes **assumptions** about the condition of the property and the **site** as of that date and uses data that reflect values as of the date of the appraisal.

When the **effective date of the appraisal** is the same as the date of the last inspection of the subject property, no assumptions about the future or the past are required. When the effective date of the appraisal is either before or after the date of last inspection, the appraisal must contain the assumptions the appraiser has made about the property and the market as of the effective date of the appraisal.

Identification of the Characteristics of the Property (Including Location and Property Rights to be Valued)

Every appraisal must contain an accurate description of the **real estate** (**site** and **improvements**) and any **personal property** included in the value estimate. A more precise identification, such as that provided by a legal description which can be copied from the deed or mortgage, is also required. When available, a survey helps to precisely identify a property, and may be included or cited in an appraisal report.

An appraisal of **real property** is not directly a valuation of the physical **land** and improvements; it is a valuation of the **rights of ownership**. A specific appraisal may require a value estimate of all **property rights**, while another will analyze only limited rights in property. Ownership of property may be held by an individual, a partnership, a corporation or a group of people. When ownership is vested in more than one interest, each may hold an equal or unequal share.

The property rights or interests to be appraised may be **fractional interests** such as air rights over a specified property, subsurface rights, an easement, a right-of-way, or fee simple (subject to an easement). Because the value of real property is not limited to its physical components, the appraiser cannot define the problem precisely until they are fully aware of which **property rights** are to be included in the analysis, as defined by the client. Without this knowledge, the appraiser may produce an estimate of value that is irrelevant to the problem. A clear understanding of the rights being appraised will also help the appraiser evaluate the complexity of the problem and plan appropriately for the amount of work the appraisal will require.

Identification of any Extraordinary Assumptions Necessary in the Assignment

It is important to include all *extraordinary assumptions* in every appraisal report. This precaution reduces the potential for successful professional liability suits against the appraiser, because it discloses to the users what the appraiser did and did not factually in the process of making the appraisal.

Identification of Any Hypothetical Conditions Necessary in the Assignment

Hypothetical conditions are assumptions that are known not to exist but assumed for purposes of analysis. Before you make an appraisal with a hypothetical condition, it is necessary to be familiar with all the current USPAP requirements pertaining to hypothetical conditions. Keep in mind that the 2006 USPAP states:

"Comment: A hypothetical condition may be used in an assignment only if:
  • it is required to properly develop credible opinions and conclusions;
  • the appraiser has a reasonable basis for the extraordinary assumption;
  • use of the extraordinary assumption results in a credible analysis; and
  • the appraiser complies with the disclosure requirements set forth in the USPAP for extraordinary assumptions."

SCOPE OF WORK DETERMINATION & PLANNING THE APPRAISAL

1.4 The second step of the valuation process is determination with the client what the *scope of work* will be, and making an appraisal plan. This will vary with the assignment. The following six steps are useful in planning:

1. Decide which data is needed.
2. Identify the sources of the needed data.
3. Determine what personnel are needed.
4. Make a time schedule.
5. Make a flow chart.
6. Present a fee proposal, agree upon a fee, and sign a contract.

Data Needed

The type of data required for an appraisal consists of *general data* about the market and location, and *specific data* about the subject property and the comparable properties.

GENERAL DATA
General data collection is divided into the broad categories of social, economic, governmental and environmental factors that affect the value of the property. There are a variety of ways to organize the general data. The most common way is to break the data down into regional, state, community, and neighborhood sections.

An advantage of this system is that once the data is assembled and organized, it can be used for other appraisals in the same region, state, community or neighborhood. In some areas, two of the classifications may be combined. For example, the state and regional data are often the same. When a community is small, it may contain only one neighborhood.

SPECIFIC DATA

Specific data collection is probably the most difficult aspect of performing an appraisal. This is especially true when the property is located in a territory that is unfamiliar to the appraiser. Specific data collection about the *site* and the *improvements* is described in more detail in *Chapter 9: Specific Data Analysis - Highest and Best Use*.

Data Sources

An appraiser should maintain a reliable data collection and storage system. A large bank of market data should be accumulated in the appraiser's own files and should be organized to serve the appraiser's needs most effectively. Only some of the data will be immediately pertinent; the remainder is collected, filed, and cross-indexed for future use. Sales information is usually collected and recorded on standardized sheets or cards. Many appraisers are now using computers for data storage, retrieval and analysis.

Personnel Needed

The most common configuration of an appraisal company consists of the designated appraiser, who is usually the owner or manager, and an assistant who helps gather data and/or completes on their own, with supervision, the less complex assignments. A clerical support person is usually available to staff the office, answer the phone, and do most of the typing, computer entry, filing and billing. Whether an office is a typical small appraisal company or a larger facility, a decision must be made for each assignment about how the work will be divided among the available personnel. A simple appraisal made in a one-person shop requires only one individual. An appraiser in solo practice may have to recruit outside help for a complex assignment.

Time Schedule & Flow Chart

TIME SCHEDULE

The timely production of appraisals is essential to the successful management of an appraisal practice. In many areas, the competition for single-family appraisal work requires delivery of the finished report within a few days of receiving the assignment. A schedule of how the work will be performed is a good management tool. This helps the staff begin with a clear understanding of the exact nature of the work to be done by each person, which will go a long way toward the efficient completion of an assignment.

FLOW CHART

A flow chart is commonly used to keep track of the work in an appraisal office. This can be as simple as a calendar on which the dates are marked when portions of the appraisal are due. Another common type of flow chart is a metal board on which magnetic holders are displayed indicating the steps of the appraisal and when they are due. Many offices also have computerized flow charts that help them keep track of the status of each job in progress. Many computerized offices now use e-mail notification programs to update clients about the progress on their appraisal assignments.

Fee Proposal and Contract

Some lenders and their management companies determine how much they will pay for an appraisal and the appraiser must only decide if they are willing to do the work for the fee being offered. Many other clients require the appraiser to quote a fee or a fee range in advance of a commitment to proceed with an appraisal assignment.

The relationship some appraisers have with select regular clients is so well-established that these clients permit the appraiser to proceed with an assignment without having previously agreed upon a fee. The fee an appraiser may charge for the services performed depends on the reputation of the appraiser. Appraisers who, in the view of their clients, have an established reputation for experience and sound judgment command higher fees than those appraisers who do not. This is especially true for more complex assignments.

Since appraisers are professionals, competent work is required regardless of the fee charged. An inadequate fee is not a valid excuse for inadequate work, since a professional is obliged to perform competent work regardless of the fee received. Therefore, the appraiser should be careful to correctly estimate the scope of work an assignment will require, so that a reasonable fee can be quoted. When an appraisal is performed for a regular client, such as a lending institution, mortgage broker, mortgage banker or relocation company, the appraiser often elects to work without a contract. However, even in these situations, a contract or a letter of authorization is desirable if it can be obtained. Personnel in large institutions often change jobs; what is authorized by one employee may be objectionable to their replacement. When making appraisals for the public or their representative, it is very desirable to have an appraisal contract that reflects the scope of work, time frame, and how and when the appraiser will be paid. It is also customary in many areas for the appraiser to receive a retainer.

DATA COLLECTION AND PROPERTY DESCRIPTION

Market Area Data

The market area is a geographic area in which the subject property is located and which includes the area from which a majority of demand and competition is drawn. For residential properties, it is that area in which the majority of potential buyers of the subject property would consider an alternative choice acceptable. The market area may be as small as a part of a neighborhood, a whole neighborhood or more than one neighborhood. It can be a part of a community or a whole community. Sometimes, it is as large as a part of a region or a whole region, and in some instances, market area includes more than one state.

The appraiser must describe the market area and identify is boundaries.

Appraisers should consider all the significant social, economic, governmental, and environmental influences that affect property values in their region. This information is gathered from general and specialized publications including national and local newspapers, financial magazines and real estate appraisal publications. Analysis of current economic conditions such as interest rates, effective purchasing power, construction costs, and availability of financing is included here.

GENERAL CHARACTERISTICS OF REGION, CITY AND NEIGHBORHOOD

Background data deals with the locational and economic forces outside the subject property that influence its value. This includes information about the region, community and neighborhood, such as population characteristics, price levels, employment opportunities, economic base analysis, etc.

Subject Property Data

Specific data pertaining to the **subject property** includes title and record data, the relationship of the site to general land patterns, a description and analysis of the physical characteristics of the property, and **highest and best use** analysis.

SPECIFIC CHARACTERISTICS OF THE LAND AND IMPROVEMENTS, PERSONAL PROPERTY, BUSINESS ASSETS, ETC.

-- **Title and record data:** Pertinent title data may include the identity of the owners, type of ownership, zoning, existing easements and encroachments, zoning regulations affecting the property, assessed value and taxation, and deed or other restrictions.

-- **Relationship of site to land pattern:** Descriptive data includes a complete evaluation of the site. Site features such as size, shape, topography, site and building orientation, utilities and relationship to the existing land-use patterns are also analyzed here.

CHARACTERISTICS OF THE SITE

-- **Legal description:** A parcel of **land** consists of any parcel that can be identified by a common description in one ownership. A special characteristic of real estate is that every parcel is unique. The best identification of a parcel is a legal description and a survey, which eliminates all confusion because it specifically identifies and locates a unique piece of real estate. The three methods used in the United States to legally describe land are **metes and bounds**, the **rectangular (government) survey system**, and the **lot and block system**. Details about these survey methods are provided in **Chapter 6: Property Description - Geographic & Geologic Conditions - Land/Site.**

-- **Other descriptive information:** The description of the site should also include information about the type of ownership. The property may be in fee simple ownership, **planned unit development (PUD)**, *de minimis* PUD, condominium, cooperative or some unique form of fractional ownership. (Fannie Mae and Freddie Mac permit use of the **URAR** form for single-family residences in fee simple ownership, on leased land or when there is a PUD. It may not be used for multi-family residences, or cooperative or condominium ownership.) The appraiser should check for any apparent rights that may affect the value such as surface or subsurface rights, easements, restrictions, air rights, water rights, beach rights mineral rights, obligations for unique lateral support, easements for common walls, etc.

The appraiser is not responsible for reporting rights that are not apparent. The appraiser is responsible for researching these issues to a level this is necessary to develop a credible appraisal result. This standard has two components: (1) the expectations of the intended users for similar assignments; and (2) the amount of research an appraiser's peers would conduct for a similar assignment.

The description of the property also includes information about the applicable zoning regulations and other environmental regulations that affect the use of the property. It is the responsibility of the appraiser to determine and report if the improvements are a non-conforming (legal or illegal) use based on the local ordinances.

-- Assessment and taxes: How a property is taxed affects its value. Real estate taxes are based on *ad valorem* assessments. At a minimum, the appraiser should report the current taxes and whether there are any special assessments. If they are not typical, the appraisal should compare them with typical taxes and estimate the effect of atypical taxes on the value of the subject property.

-- Physical characteristics of the site: The important physical characteristics to be described consist of the size and shape, corner influence, *plottage*, surplus land, excess land, topography, utilities, site improvements, location, environment and pollution. Details about these methods of describing property are provided in *Chapter 6: Property Description - Geographic & Geologic Characteristics Land/Site.*

-- Physical characteristics of the improvements: Most appraisal forms provide room for a comprehensive description of the improvements. A mandatory part of every appraisal is an accurate and adequate description of the property including the improvements. When the form is insufficient to describe the subject *property* adequately, for any reason, an appropriate addenda is required.

Comparable Property Data

-- Sales, listings, offerings and vacancies: Sufficient specific data must be collected in the market to apply the *sales comparison approach*.

-- Cost and depreciation: To develop the *cost approach*, the appraiser collects information on what it would cost to reproduce the subject property, as of the effective date of the appraisal.

-- Income and expenses, capitalization rates, etc.: To develop both the *income capitalization approach* and the **GMRM** income approach (*gross monthly rent multiplier*), it is necessary to obtain information about rentals in the subject market area. This data is used to estimate a *market rent* for the subject property, and to develop an appropriate GMRM and capitalization rates.

DATA ANALYSIS

Data analysis has two components: market analysis and highest and best use analysis. Every appraisal assignment, including single-family house appraisals, must be based on an understanding of the market conditions that affect the subject property and must include a highest and best use analysis of the property.

Market Analysis

The type of market analysis performed by an appraiser depends upon the type of subject property. ***The Appraisal of Real Estate, 12th edition*** outlines a six step process that serves as the foundation for all market analysis.

1. Property productivity analysis
2. Market delineation
3. Demand analysis and forecast
4. Competitive supply analysis and forecast
5. Supply and demand study
6. Capture estimation

PROPERTY PRODUCTIVITY ANALYSIS

First the appraiser identifies which features of the subject property shape productive capabilities and potential uses of the property. Those attributes can be physical, legal, or locational, and are the basis for the selection of comparables.

MARKET DELINEATION

Given the potential uses of the subject property, the appraiser identifies a market for the defined use (or more than one market, if the property has alternative uses.)

DEMAND ANALYSIS AND FORECAST

Economic base analysis considers existing and anticipated market demand. An appraiser studies population and employment data to analyze and forecast demand. The scope of work required by the assignment (as well as time and budgetary constraints) will dictate to what extent demand side variables must be investigated.

COMPETITIVE SUPPLY ANALYSIS AND FORECAST

Marginal demand is established through analysis of existing and anticipated supply of the subject property type.

SUPPLY AND DEMAND STUDY

The appraiser investigates the interaction of supply and demand to determine if marginal demand exists and if the market is out of equilibrium.

CAPTURE ESTIMATION

By comparing the productive attributes of the subject property to those of competitive properties, the appraiser can judge the market share the subject is likely to capture given market conditions, demand, and competitive supply.

"The data and conclusions generated through market analysis are essential components in other portions of the valuation process. Market analysis yields information needed for each of the three approaches to value. In the cost approach, market analysis provides the basis for adjusting the cost of the subject property for depreciation, i.e., physical deterioration and functional and external obsolescence. In the income capitalization approach, all the necessary income, expenses, and rate data is evaluated in light of market forces of supply and demand. In the sales comparison approach, the conclusions of the market analysis used to delineate the market and thereby identify comparable properties." [1]

[1] The Appraisal of Real Estate, 12th Edition, Appraisal Institute, Chicago, IL 2001

Highest and Best Use

Two separate highest and best use analyses are made: highest and best use as though vacant, and highest and best use as improved. Some appraisers think this is the most important part of the appraisal process.

ELEMENTS IN HIGHEST AND BEST USE ANALYSIS

To estimate the highest and best use of a site, the appraiser utilizes four tests. The projected use must meet all four of these tests:

1 . Physically possible
2 . Legally permissible
3 . Financially feasible
4 . Maximally productive

Each potential use of a property is considered by the appraiser in terms of all four tests. If a proposed use fails to meet any of the tests, it is discarded and another use is reviewed. The highest and best use meets all four tests.

-- Physically possible (suitable): The use of a site must be physically possible. Uses might be limited by the physical characteristics of a site, such as size, frontage, topography, soil and subsoil conditions and climate conditions. Despite the need for single-family residential housing, an area of severe terrain with poor subsoil characteristics cannot be considered appropriate for residential development.

-- Legally permitted: Each use must be tested first to see if it is legally permitted on the site. Public legal restrictions consist of zoning regulations, building codes, environmental regulations and other applicable ordinances. Private restrictions are limitations that run with the land and are passed from owner to owner. Generally, they are imposed by the developer of the tract who attempts to preserve the value of the entire development by restricting what may be done with individual sites. Easements, encroachments, party-wall agreements, etc., also restrict the development of a site.

-- Financially feasible: A realistic assessment of market demand for a proposed use is a critical factor. For example, acreage may be available that is zoned for single-family residential use of a certain concentration, served by all utilities, and with good proximity and access; however, similar subdivisions already in the market have remained unsold for some time. There is no need for the additional sites, so that although the property meets the first two tests, it fails the test of economic feasibility. Thus, market demand acts to create highest and best use. In reviewing alternative uses, the appraiser must consider the demand for each use and the other available competitive land suitable for that use, which constitutes the supply. These factors must be weighed in the economic analysis. All physically possible and legal uses that fail to meet the test of economic feasibility are discarded. The remaining uses produce some net return to the property.

-- Maximally productive: The fourth test is essentially a test for maximum return. The appraiser is seeking the most profitable among all of the legally permitted, physically suitable, and financially feasible uses.

HIGHEST AND BEST USE AS THOUGH VACANT

1.7 Analyzing the *highest and best use* of the site as though vacant serves two functions. First, it helps the appraiser identify comparable properties. The comparable properties' highest and best use should be similar to that of the subject property.

The second reason to analyze the property's highest and best use as though vacant is to identify the use that would produce maximum income to the site, after income is allocated to the improvements. In the cost approach and some income capitalization techniques, a separate value estimate of the site is required. Estimating the highest and best use of the site as though vacant is a necessary part of deriving a site value estimate.

Because change is constantly occurring, the existing use of land is often no longer the highest and best use. If the land alone has a higher value under an alternate physically suitable, legally permitted use than the whole property as currently improved and utilized, the proposed use becomes the highest and best use. The existing improvement is at the end of its economic life but it will still be the highest and best use during the transition period.

It is not sufficient to simply state the type of improvement that is the highest and best use. The ideal improvement must be described. The answer that it is a single-family residence is not sufficient. The residence should be described in some detail, and at a minimum include its size and room configuration.

HIGHEST AND BEST USE AS IMPROVED

There are two reasons to analyze the highest and best use of the property as improved. The first is to help identify comparable properties. Comparable improved properties should have the same or similar highest and best uses as the subject property.

The second reason to analyze the highest and best use of the property as improved is to decide whether the improvements should be demolished, renovated, or retained in their present condition. They should be retained as long as they have some contributory value and the return from the property exceeds the return that would be realized by a new use, after deducting the costs of demolishing the old building and constructing a new one. Identification of the most profitable use is crucial to this determination.

LAND (SITE) VALUE OPINION

Purpose of Separate Land (Site) Valuation

Even after a property has been improved it is necessary and possible to make a separate estimate of the value of the site. Details about how to make an estimate of the value of the subject site are provided in *Chapter 10: Valuation Procedures - Specific Data Analysis - Sales and Listings.*

APPLICATION OF THE THREE APPROACHES TO VALUE

The sixth step of the valuation process is the application of the three approaches traditionally used by appraisers to estimate the value of a property. The Uniform Standards of Professional Appraisal Practice require that the appraiser consider the use of all three approaches to estimate the value of each property appraised.

However, it is recognized that all three approaches may not be necessary to do to arrive at a credible opinion of value. When an appraiser elects not to use one or two of the three approaches to value, the reasons for their elimination must be detailed in the appraisal report.

The three traditional approaches to value are:

1. Cost approach
2. Sales comparison approach
3. Income approach

Using two or three approaches to value instead of just the sales comparison approach provides the appraiser with an opportunity to corroborate their estimate of the value of the property.

Cost Approach

The cost approach starts with an estimate of the value of the site and site improvements. This first step is also required by Freddie Mac and Fannie Mae, even when the cost approach is not used to estimate the value of the improvements.

Historically, the cost approach was the only approach used by appraisers for many appraisals. After WW II, it fell out of favor. Today, some states prohibit it for condemnation cases. Many relocation companies also discourage appraisers from using it. Freddie Mac and Fannie Mae do not require the use of the cost approach. However, many lender/clients require it for insurance purposes.

Experienced appraisers know that, when correctly used, the cost approach is a valuable technique. They feel more confident when they are able to make two or three independent estimates that tend to confirm each other than when their value estimate is based solely on the sales comparison approach. Unfortunately, some appraisers misuse this approach by backing into the numbers to make them agree with the sales comparison approach.

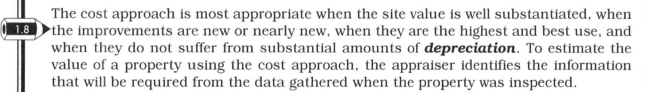

The cost approach is most appropriate when the site value is well substantiated, when the improvements are new or nearly new, when they are the highest and best use, and when they do not suffer from substantial amounts of **depreciation**. To estimate the value of a property using the cost approach, the appraiser identifies the information that will be required from the data gathered when the property was inspected.

STEPS OF THE COST APPROACH
The data is processed following the 5 steps:

1. Estimate the value of the site and site improvements.

2. Estimate the **reproduction cost** of the improvements. Some appraisers use **replacement cost** instead. When replacement cost is used, this should be noted in the comments section of the appraisal report.

3. Estimate the amount of depreciation from all causes and categorize it into the three major types of depreciation: physical deterioration, functional obsolescence and external obsolescence.

4. Deduct the total estimated **depreciation** from the reproduction or replacement cost of the improvements to derive the amount of value the improvements contribute to the property.

5. Add together the value of the site, the value contributed by the site improvements and landscaping, and the cost of all the improvements, less the applicable depreciation.

COST APPROACH SUMMARY

When used correctly, the cost approach provides the appraiser with an excellent way to support the values estimated via the other approaches to value. To be useful, it must include a supported site value estimate, an accurate estimate of the reproduction cost of the improvements, plus a complete and accurate estimate of all forms of depreciation that affect the property. Only in rare instances can the cost approach be used alone to estimate the value of a residential property. There are usually comparable sales available even for unique residences. On the other hand, the cost approach often is the only applicable approach for the valuation of special purpose, governmental and institutional properties.

Sales Comparison Approach

The sales comparison approach involves making a direct comparison between the subject property and other properties that have been sold (or listed for sale) in the same market area.

When carefully collected, analyzed, verified and reconciled, market data usually provides the best indication of **market value** for a property. The price that a typical buyer pays is often the result of a shopping process, in which many properties being offered for sale have been examined and evaluated. Buyers often base their value conclusions primarily on properties that are being offered for sale. Appraisers use this information, in addition to information about properties that have sold and were rented to reach their value estimate.

Individual sales often deviate from the market norm because of individual motivations, knowledge and/or conditions of sale. In sufficient numbers however, they tend to reflect market patterns. When information is available on a sufficient number of comparable sales, offerings and listings in the current market, the resulting pattern is the best indication of market value.

STEPS OF THE SALES COMPARISON APPROACH
The appraiser follows these five steps:

1. Finds **comparable sales**, listings, and offerings.

2. Verifies each sale including selling price, terms, motivation, and its *bona fide* nature.

3. Analyzes each comparable property and compares it to the subject property as to time of sale, location, physical characteristics and conditions of sale.

4. Makes the necessary adjustments to compensate for any dissimilarities noted between the comparables and the subject property. The adjustments are derived by comparing comparables with each other whenever possible.

5. Derives an indicated value for the subject property by comparison with the adjusted selling prices of the comparables.

SALES COMPARISON APPROACH SUMMARY

The sales comparison approach is generally considered the most applicable approach in residential appraising, since it reflects most directly the actions of buyers and sellers in the market. In order to obtain all of the information needed to use a comparable sale, the appraiser should inspect each comparable property and verify the nature of the sale with the buyer, seller or broker. These are the people who can tell the appraiser about the conditions of sale and the actual physical condition of the property at the time of sale.

New techniques using more sales are available as alternatives to the above techniques. They do not depend upon adjustments based on limited market information, but rather on statistical treatment of many comparable sales. Regression analysis and other statistical techniques are the basis of automated valuation modeling (AVMs). When the sales comparison approach is based upon a sufficient number of carefully chosen sales similar to or adjustable to the subject property, the value indication is usually persuasive.

Chapter 9: Valuation Process - Specific Data Analysis - Sales and Listing provides more detailed information about how to analyze the data collected using the sales comparison approach.

Income Capitalization Approach

In the **income capitalization approach**, appraisers measure the present value of the future benefits of property ownership. Income streams and values of property upon resale (reversion) are capitalized (converted) into a present, lump-sum value. Basic to this approach are the formulas:

Income ÷ Rate = Value

Income x Factor = Value

The income capitalization approach, like the cost and sales comparison approaches, requires extensive market research. Specific areas that an appraiser investigates for this approach are the property's gross expected income from rents and other income, the expected reduction in gross income from lack of full occupancy and collection loss, the expected annual operating expenses and the pattern and duration of the property's income stream. When accurate income and expense estimates are established, the income streams are converted into present value by the process of capitalization. The rates or factors used for capitalization are derived from an investigation of acceptable rates of return for similar properties.

Availability of alternative investments affects the market for real estate, and also helps set rates of return required. The investor in an apartment building, for example, anticipates an acceptable rate of return on the investment, in addition to return of the invested funds. The level of return necessary to attract investment capital fluctuates with changes in the money market, tax laws and with the levels of return available from alternative investments. The appraiser must be alert to changing investor requirements as revealed by demands in the current market for investment properties, and to changes in the more volatile money markets that may indicate a forthcoming trend.

GROSS INCOME APPROACH - GROSS MONTHLY RENT MULTIPLIER
The use of the income approach in valuing residential real estate is based on the assumption that value is related to the economic rent (income) that the real estate can be expected to earn.

This approach has its greatest application in areas where there is a substantial residential rental market. In neighborhoods that are predominantly owner-occupied, rental data may be too scarce to permit the use of this approach.

Where sufficient data is available, the appraiser follows these steps to derive a value indication:

1. Develop an applicable multiplier:

   a. Find houses that have recently sold in the neighborhood that are comparable and were rented at the time of sale.

   b. Divide the sale price of each comparable by the monthly rental to derive a multiplier, known as a **gross monthly rent multiplier** or **GMRM.**

   c. Reconcile the multipliers developed in step b. to obtain a single multiplier or range of multipliers applicable to the appraised property. This is not an average; it is based on the appraiser's judgment of comparability and applicability.

2. Estimate economic rent for the subject residence.

   a. Find comparable rentals in the neighborhood.

   b. Analyze each comparable rental and compare its features with those of the subject property.

   c. Estimate the adjustments required to obtain an indicated market rent for the subject property.

   d. Consider each comparable carefully, with emphasis on the need for adjustments, and formulate an opinion of the market (economic) rent of the subject house based upon the actual rents of the comparables.

3. Estimate the value of the subject residence

     a.   Multiple the estimated market rent by the estimated monthly multiplier (or range of multipliers) to obtain an indicated value of the subject property via the income approach

1.9 Even if the subject property is rented at the time of valuation, it is necessary to consider the **market (economic) rent** that would apply if the residence were available for occupancy as of the effective date of appraisal.

The market rent is defined as the rental income a property would command on the open market, as indicated by currently negotiated rentals being paid for comparable space. This may be the same as the contract rent or it may be more or less than the rent specified in an existing lease. As a lease ages, the contract rent usually differs from market rent. In the income approach, the contract rent cannot be used as the market rent, unless the competitive rents in the market substantiate its applicability.

INCOME APPROACH SUMMARY

The final estimate of value based on the value indication via the income approach will be only as good as the market data used to develop it. Therefore data used in this approach to value must be carefully sorted and selected for applicability. Care must be taken to verify the comparability of all sales and rentals, and only properties that are comparable in type, age, size, condition and location should be considered.

In using the GMRM to arrive at an indicated value of the subject property, taxes, insurance and other operating expenses of comparable properties are assumed to be similar to those of the subject property. If this is not the case, the appraiser should eliminate such sales from consideration. The appraiser should inspect both the exterior and interior of all comparable properties to adjust properly for differences. Whenever shortcuts are taken that bypass this step, the possibility of error in the final value judgment is substantially increased.

Chapter 12: Valuation Procedures - Specific Date Analysis - Income provides more detailed information about how to analyze and reconcile the data collected.

RECONCILIATION OF VALUE INDICATIONS AND FINAL OPINION OF VALUE

The seventh step in the valuation process is the **reconciliation** of the value indications obtained in each of the three approaches to derive a ***final estimate of value*** for the subject residence as of the effective date of the appraisal. Under no circumstances are these value indications merely averaged. This would be analogous to asking three people for the right time and then averaging their replies. Rather, the appraiser considers the relative applicability of each of the three approaches to the final estimate of value, and reviews the reliability of the data used in each approach.

In the reconciliation, the appraiser brings together all of the data and indicated values resulting from the three approaches and evaluates them in a logical cause-and-effect analysis which leads to a supportable value conclusion.

In this process, the appraiser must evaluate the quality and quantity of data, choose the approach or approaches that are most applicable to the specific appraisal problem, and select from among alternative conclusions or indications of value those that best represent the value of the subject property.

The final estimate should be rounded to indicate the degree of accuracy. By rounding to the nearest one hundred dollars, the appraiser indicates what they believe their estimate is accurate to the nearest one hundred dollars. With the data available for most appraisals, it would be difficult to estimate value to a one hundred dollar accuracy and therefore appraisers often round their estimates to the nearest one thousand dollars.

REPORT OF FINAL VALUE OPINION AND CONCLUSIONS

The final step of the valuation process is to produce an **appraisal report**. The report may be verbal, a letter, on a form, or a short or long form narrative report. The USPAP requires that every written appraisal report contain at a minimum the following:

- Identity of the client
- Intended user(s)
- Intended use(s) of the appraisal
- Identification of the real estate
- Interest in the property appraised
- Type of value estimated
- Effective date of the value opinion
- Date of the report
- Scope of work
- Data analyzed
- Techniques employed
- All extraordinary assumptions
- All hypothetical conditions
- Signed certificate

The 2006 USPAP states: "The USPAP Standard 2 does not dictate the form, format or style of real property appraisal report. The form, format, and style of a report are functions of the needs of the intended users and appraisers. The substantive content of a report determines its compliance.

Standard Rule 2-1

Each written or oral real property appraisal report must:

(a) clearly and accurately set forth the appraisal in a manner that will not be misleading;

(b) contain sufficient information to enable the intended users of the appraisal to understand the report properly; and

(c) clearly and accurately disclose all assumptions, extraordinary assumptions, hypothetical conditions, and **limiting conditions** uses in the assignment.

<u>Standard Rule 2-2</u>

Each written real property report must be prepared under one of the following three options and prominently state which option it uses: *Self-Contained Appraisal Report, Summary Appraisal Report, or Restricted Use Appraisal Report.*

Form Reports

Most single-family appraisals are made on forms. Many single family appraisals are now being made on the *Uniform Residential Appraisal Report (URAR)* form. Freddie Mac and Fannie Mae also have forms that are widely used for small income properties and condominiums, planned unit developments and cooperatives. The Appraisal Institute, software vendors and others also develop new forms from time to time.

Oral Reports

There are situations where an *oral report* is required because of the circumstances of the assignment. When an oral report is made, the appraiser must preserve the notes and factual records used in the appraisal process as well as complete memoranda of each analysis, conclusion and opinion contained in the oral report.

Narrative Reports

It is the responsibility of the appraiser to determine with the client what type of report will best satisfy the client's need. This is usually done as part of determining the scope of work. The appraiser is afforded the best opportunity to support opinions and conclusions and to convince the client of the soundness of their *value estimate* in a *narrative appraisal report*.

The Appraisal Institute and other appraisal organizations require the production of narrative appraisal reports as part of their requirements to obtain a designation.

Details about the methods used when preparing appraisal reports are provided in

Chapter 15: Residential Applications & Model Appraisals.

SUMMARY

The **valuation process** is the orderly step-by-step procedure an appraiser follows to produce a credible appraisal. It begins with the definition of the problem to be solved and concludes with a report of the solution in the form of an estimate of the defined value. The **purpose of the appraisal** process is to provide the outline for making a thorough, credible appraisal in an efficient and professional manner.

Most appraisers would agree that making appraisals is an art, not a science. They would further explain that the profession is constantly trying to make appraising more scientific. A big step toward this goal has been the development of the valuation process. Within this theoretical framework, a concise, logical and clearly supported value conclusion can be presented which meets the needs of clients as well as the standards of the appraisal profession. New techniques using statistical methods to abstract information from the market, such as automatic valuation models, using multiple regression analysis and other statistical techniques, are making the appraisal process more scientific.

This chapter is an overview of what is contained it rest of this text. We hope that when you have completed this text you will have enough knowledge to start making an appraisal with appropriate supervision.

REVIEW QUESTIONS

1. Step #1 of the appraisal process is:
    a. to collect the data.
    b. apply the sales comparison approach.
    c. define the problem to be solved.
    d. None of the above

2. The most common type of value estimated by appraisers is:
    a. foreclosure value.
    b. insurable value.
    c. purchase value.
    d. market value.

3. Which of the following methods of identifying a property would be most accurate?
    a. Mailing address
    b. Lot number
    c. Survey
    d. Subdivision name

4. The client has input but the appraiser must determine:
    a. the scope of work to be done.
    b. the value estimate reported.
    c. the length of the report
    d. All of the above

5. Market analysis includes:
    a. demand analysis and forecast.
    b. property productivity analysis.
    c. market delineation.
    d. All of the above

6. The highest and best use is:
    a. suitable for a very steep lot.
    b. maximally productive.
    c. an attractive design.
    d. legally not permitted.

7. Reasons to do a highest and best use analysis as though vacant are:
    a. to identify comparable sites.
    b. to identify the owner's tastes.
    c. Both a. and b.
    d. Neither a. nor b.

8. The cost approach is most applicable when:
    a. the value of the property is low.
    b. the improvements are quite old.
    c. the improvements are new.
    d. None of the above

9. When estimating the value of a rental property by the income capitalization approach, the appraiser must:
    a. multiply the cost by a factor.
    b. divide by the vacancy rate.
    c. estimate and apply a market rent in their calculations.
    d. use the contract rent in their calculations.

10. The final value estimate should be:
    a. rounded to reflect accuracy.
    b. negotiated with the client.
    c. based on the appraiser's instincts.
    d. rounded to the nearest dollar.

11. Which of the following are not acceptable types of appraisal reports?
    a. Verbal
    b. Short form narrative
    c. Form appraisal
    d. Scope of work contract.

12. Most single-family appraisal reports are:
    a. verbal.
    b. short form narratives.
    c. form appraisals.
    d. scope of work contracts.

ANSWERS

The answer to each question is indicated by the letter a, b, c or d below. The explanation of the answer is indicated by a numbered arrow that points to the appropriate paragraph on the page of the text indicated by the page number following the answer.

Q 1.1	c	Page 1-4
Q 1.2	d	Page 1-4
Q 1.3	c	Page 1-5
Q 1.4	a	Page 1-6
Q 1.5	d	Page 1-11
Q 1.6	b	Page 1-12
Q 1.7	a	Page 1-13
Q 1.8	c	Page 1-14
Q 1.9	c	Page 1-18
Q 1.10	a	Page 1-19
Q 1.11	d	Page 1-19
Q 1.12	c	Page 1-20

CHAPTER 2

Valuation Procedures - Definition of the Problem & Scope of Work

"Only free men can negotiate; prisoners cannot enter into contracts."

Nelson Mandela, Nobel Laureate
From prison in South Africa, 1985

Important Words and Key Concepts

Words on this list are highlighted in this chapter.
They are also defined in the Glossary at the back of this text.

Appraised Value
Assessed Value
Cost
Effective Date of the Value
 Opinion
Definition of the Problem
Extraordinary Assumptions
Federal Emergency
 Management Agency (FEMA)
Flood Maps
Fannie Mae

Freddie Mac
Going-Concern Value
Hypothetical Conditions
Insurable Value
Intended Use
Intended Users
Investment Value
Ordinary Assumptions and
 Limiting Conditions
Liquidation Value
Market Value

Price
Prospective Date
Retrospective Date
Scope of Work
Uniform Standards of
 Professional Appraisal
 Practice (USPAP)
Value
Value-In-Use

DEFINITION OF THE PROBLEM

2.1 The first step in an appraisal is to define the problem to be solved. There are seven major steps in the ***definition of the problem*** that are required by the 2006 USPAP in STANDARD 1-2: REAL PROPERTY APPRAISAL DEVELOPMENT which are summarized as follows:

1. Identification of client and other intended users
2. Identification intended use of the appraiser's opinions and conclusions
3. Identification of the type and definition of value
4. Identification of the effective date of the appraiser's opinions and conclusions
2.2 5. Identification of the characteristics of the property
   (including location and property rights to be valued)
6. Identification of any extraordinary assumptions necessary in the assignment
7. Identification of any hypothetical conditions necessary in the assignment

Based on the items listed above, the appraiser determines the scope of work that is appropriate to produce a credible appraisal.

IDENTIFICATION OF THE CLIENT AND OTHER INTENDED USERS

The ***Uniform Standards of Professional Appraisal Practice*** require that the ***intended user(s)*** of an appraisal be identified in the appraisal report. ***Freddie Mac*** and ***Fannie Mae*** also have guidelines about the identification of intended users. The identification of the client and intended users is important to appraisers as it affects who has status in a professional liability suit against the appraiser. Although anyone who relies on an appraisal may sue the appraiser, their position is better if they are a named client/ intended user. It is reasonable to expect that there may be changes in future editions of the USPAP as well as in future Freddie Mac and Fannie Mae Guidelines. Therefore, it is important that appraisers keep themselves current on this subject.

The client must be identified at the beginning of the appraisal process to ensure that there are no conflicts and that the appraiser understands the level of real estate experience of the client. The intended users need to be identified at the same time to ensure that they are authorized to use the report. Users who are not identified contemporaneously with the performance of the appraisal should not be permitted to use or rely upon the appraisal report for any purpose. When the client and intended users are identified, the appraiser will understand their familiarity with real estate and the local market. These and other considerations will factor into the level of explanation that should be included in the appraisal report.

IDENTIFICATION OF INTENDED USE OF THE APPRAISER'S OPINIONS AND CONCLUSIONS

The appraiser needs to know the intended use of the appraisal so that the report will provide the reader with all of the information required to make a decision. When the appraisal is made for mortgage lending purposes, the appraiser must know if it should comply with Freddie Mac, Fannie Mae, HUD/FHA, VA, or FmHA requirements. Each of these organizations has their own special appraisal requirements.

The USPAP requires that the **intended use** of the appraisal be identified in every appraisal report.

There are a variety of intended uses of an appraisal. Intended uses may include:

1. To assist with loan underwriting
2. To evaluate the collateral of an existing loan
3. For estate planning
4. For an estate tax return
5. For litigation support
6. To assist in establishing an asking price
7. To establish a transaction price.
8. To assist with *ad valorem* tax negotiations (tax appeals)

It is important to understand the intended uses of an appraisal, because it impacts the scope of work necessary to arrive at an estimated value that will be useful to the client/users, as well as the level of detail that should be included in the appraisal report.

IDENTIFICATION OF THE TYPE AND DEFINITION OF VALUE

In all cases, it is necessary that the appraisal include a clear statement as to what value is to be estimated.

Types of Value

Market value is by far the most common value that is estimated by appraisers, but there are other kinds of value estimates such as insurable value, investment value, partial interest value, etc., that are becoming a more significant proportion of the assignments available to appraisers.

Because the term value has many possible interpretations, its meaning for use in the appraisal of real property must be precisely defined. Value has been defined as the quantity of one thing that can be obtained in exchange for another or the ratio of exchange of one commodity for another. Money is the common denominator by which real property value is usually measured.

An appraisal is based on an interpretation by the appraiser of facts and value indications processed and reconciled to produce an estimate of value as of a specific date. Because the term **appraised value** is too general, the type of value must be precisely defined in the appraisal report.

The value most commonly sought in an appraisal (particularly for residences) is market value, although there are other types of value that may be considered, depending on the use for which the client requires the appraisal and the nature of the valuation problem to be solved. Obviously, the reliability and credibility of an appraisal depends on the basic competence and integrity of the appraiser and on the skill with which pertinent data is processed.

-- Need: The value of any object is not intrinsic but depends upon the relationship between supply and demand. The emphasis in appraising is on the relationship between a thing desired and the potential purchaser or consumer. The idea that need alone is responsible for the creation of value would imply that value is a characteristic inherent in the object itself. If this concept were true, bread would be intrinsically valuable because it is needed to satisfy hunger. But hunger is limited. Therefore, if bread were produced in excess of the need to satisfy all normal hunger, its value would decrease.

UTILITY AND SCARCITY

An object also cannot have value unless it has utility—that is, unless it is able to satisfy the desire for possession; but utility is relative to the satisfaction gained from the object. For example, bread has great utility to a hungry person but much less to one who is not hungry. Although utility is basic to value, utility alone does not establish value. Scarcity also must be present before significant value exists. For example, air is highly useful but because it is usually so plentiful, it has little value. No object, including a parcel of real estate, can have value unless it possesses in some degree the two factors of utility and scarcity. Yet, utility and scarcity do not by themselves create value.

PURCHASING POWER

Another necessary element for an object to have value, as defined by appraisers, is purchasing power—the ability of the individual to participate in the market in order to satisfy the desire to possess. For example, if no one has the purchasing power (money) to buy bread, bread becomes valueless,

The interpretation of value in the appraisal process can be summarized as follows:

1. Value is not a characteristic inherent in an object (real property) itself but depends on the desires of people. It varies from person to person and from time to time, as individual wants vary.

2. An object (real property) cannot have value unless it has utility. Usefulness arouses the desire for possession and has the power to give satisfaction.

3. An object (real property) must also be relatively scarce to have value.

4. The desire of a purchaser who has purchasing power to buy must be aroused for the object to have value.

Unlike rapidly consumed goods, the benefits of real property are realized over a much longer period. Land and its improvements usually have a useful life extending over decades. Therefore, the value of real property is equal to the present value of the future benefits anticipated from the property.

Estimating the market value of the highest and best use of real estate is the paramount problem in its valuation. Any such estimate must take into consideration the social, economic, government and environmental forces that may influence the property's highest and best use. A clear understanding of current and hypothetical future conditions, and the perception to recognize the forces that modify and affect these conditions, are essential.

In considering these factors, the professional appraiser should never lose sight of the fact that what must really be interpreted are the reactions of typical users and investors. Appraisers do not make value; they interpret it, chiefly from market evidence. The appraiser must sift through large quantities of data to select what has the greatest significance relative to market value.

Value Definitions for Real Estate Appraisal

2.5 ▶By far the majority of residential appraisal assignments are to estimate the market value of a residence. However, appraisers receive a wide variety of other assignments for many different purposes. It is therefore necessary that many types of value be understood. In all cases, an appraisal must include a clear statement as to what value is being estimated.

MARKET VALUE (VALUE IN EXCHANGE)
An appraisal that is made for loan purposes is based on an objective estimate of market value. The current accepted definition of market value is either attached to each appraisal or a copy is filed by the appraiser with the client and is referred to in the appraisal. Market value, or value-in-exchange, is relative. It implies a comparison of available alternative economic goods from which the potential purchaser may make a choice. It also reflects the interaction of buyers, sellers and investors.

Below is that portion of the URAR form (Freddie Mac #70-Fannie Mae #1004) which has the Freddie Mac - Fannie Mae accepted market value definition:

DEFINITION OF MARKET VALUE
2.14 ▶"The most probable price which a property should bring in a competitive and open market under all conditions requisite to a fair sale, the buyer and seller, each acting prudently, knowledgeably and assuming the price is not affected by undue stimulus. Implicit in this definition is the consummation of a sale as of specified date and the passing of title from seller to buyer under conditions whereby:

(1) buyer and seller are typically motivated;

(2) both parties are well informed or well advised, and each acting in what he considers his own best interest;

(3) a reasonable time is allowed for exposure in the open market;

(4) payment is made in terms of cash in U.S. dollars or in terms of financial arrangements comparable thereto; and

(5) the price represents the normal consideration for the property sold unaffected by special or creative financing or sales concessions* granted by anyone associated with the sale.

*Adjustments to the **comparables** must be made for special or creative financing or sales concessions. No adjustments are necessary for those costs which are normally paid by sellers as a result of tradition or law in a market area; these costs are readily identifiable since the seller pays these costs in virtually all sales transactions. Special or creative financing adjustments can be made to the comparable property by comparisons to financing terms offered by a third party institutional lender that is not already involved in the property or transaction. Any adjustment should not be calculated on a mechanical dollar for dollar cost of the financing or concession but the dollar amount of any adjustment should approximate the market's reaction to the financing or concessions based on the appraiser's judgment."

DISTINCTIONS AMONG VALUE, PRICE, AND COST

Appraisers make important distinctions among the terms value, price and cost. By tradition, in appraising, value and price are expected to be equal only under conditions of a perfect market. Since a perfect market is only conceptual, appraisers never expect value and price to be totally congruent.

▶ **Value**, as applied to real estate, represents an expected price that should result under specific conditions.

▶ **Price**, commonly referred to as sale price or transaction price, is an accomplished fact. A price represents what a particular purchaser agreed to pay and a particular seller agreed to accept under the particular circumstances surrounding their transaction. Presumptions requisite for market value - rational behavior by both the buyer and seller and no undue duress or pressure - are not implicit in any actual sale price. Neither can there be a presumption that the transaction was typical in the market. Without making an appraisal, an appraiser does not know whether a price actually paid or received represents the property's value. Although actual prices provide strong evidence of market value trends, the appraiser must analyze specific transaction prices carefully before reaching a market value conclusion.

Cost, as used in appraisal procedures, applies to production, not exchange, and is not synonymous with either value or price. Cost is the total dollar expenditure for labor, materials, legal services, architectural design, financing, taxes during construction, interest, contractor's overhead and profit, and entrepreneurial overhead and profit. Cost is either a retrospective fact or a current estimate. It may or may not have a direct relationship to the present or future utility of the property.

Consider, for instance, the classic example of a luxury hotel built in an unpopular location. The hotel might cost a great deal to build but have little value because of its poor location and resultant lack of business. Appraisal procedures provide the means to refine conclusions about whether the cost to construct a property equals the property's market value. Such market conditions as oversupply, under supply, or poor design cause market values to fall below the current cost of duplicate development. Cost will equal market value if the new building represents the highest and best use of the land as though vacant; that is, if there is no accrued depreciation. Value in this case will exceed cost only to the extent that buyers are willing to avoid the delay of constructing a duplicate property.

Other Value Definitions

In the process of solving an appraisal problem, one of the earliest decisions that must be made is what value is to be estimated. The decision is based on the problem to be solved.

-- **Value-in-use** s the value or importance of an object to a particular owner who may have no intention of exposing it on the open market. **Value-in-use** has been defined as the value of an economic good to its owner-user based on its productivity (in the form of income, utility or amenity). Value-in-use does not necessarily represent market value, unless there are a significant number of buyer-users active in the market place who are willing and able to pursue the commodity or service. If the problem is related to a proposed renovation program, then the most likely type of value sought may be value-in-use to the owner.

-- Going-concern value: For some real estate appraisals (though rarely in residential work) the value of a going business concern must be considered by the appraiser and included in the appraisal report. This is a complex matter that is beyond the scope of this book. However, all appraisers need to know the definition of *going concern value*. It can be defined as the value of a proven business operation. Included in this concept is the assumption that the business enterprise is projected to continue operation well into the future.

-- Liquidation value: The price that the owner is compelled to accept when a property must be sold with less-than-reasonable market exposure is called *liquidation value.*

-- Investment value: Closely related to value-in-use is *investment value*. As employed in appraisal assignments, investment value is the value of an investment to a particular investor based on his or her investment requirements. In contrast to market value, investment value is value to an individual, rather than value in the marketplace.

Investment value is the subjective relationship between a particular investor and a given investment. When measured in dollars, it is the highest price an investor will pay for an investment in view of its perceived capacity to satisfy a desire, need, or investment goal. In colloquial use, investment value may refer to the "reasoned value" of a given investment from the viewpoint of a typical, rather than actual, investor. In appraisals that estimate investment value, specific investment criteria must be known.

Appraisals of investment value are fairly common when the appraiser is employed by a potential purchaser of an existing investment or income-producing property, or by a developer of a new property.

-- Insurable value is based on the concept of replacement and/or reproduction cost of physical items subject to lose from hazards. *Insurable value* designates the amount of insurance that may or should be carried on destructible portions of a property to indemnify the owner in the event of a loss.

2.6 ▶ **-- Assessed value** is a value based on a uniform schedule for tax rolls in *ad valorem* taxation. The schedule may or may not conform to market value, but usually has some relation to a market value base. *Assessed value* historically has been based on cost rather than market value. In recent years, however, there has been a trend to relate assessed values to market value.

IDENTIFICATION OF THE EFFECTIVE DATE OF THE APPRAISER'S OPINIONS AND CONCLUSIONS

An appraisal must be an opinion of value as of a specific date. The value of a property may change from day to day. For example, the sudden announcement of some event

2.7 ▶ that affects all of the market will have a significant effect on the value of property. Typical announcements which affect the value of property are the expansion or contraction of business activities which are major sources of employment in the area.

Other announcements that may suddenly affect value are the additions or relocation of roads and highways or anything else in the close vicinity of the property. Sudden changes in the physical condition of the property by fire, the environment or man-made additions, demolitions or alterations all affect the property value.

-- **Effective date of the appraiser's value opinion:** (also known as the effective date of the appraisal) and the date of the appraisal report may or may not be the same date. The effective date of the appraisal is typically the same as the date of the last inspection. There are three possibilities associated with the *effective date of the appraiser's value opinion*: a current date, a retrospective date, and a prospective date.

-- **Current date:** When the effective date of the appraisal is the same date as the date of the last inspection, no assumptions about the future or past are needed. On the other hand, when the effective date of the appraisal is either before or after the date of last inspection, the appraisal must contain statements that express the assumptions the appraiser has made about the property on the effective date of the appraisal.

-- **Retrospective date:** It is sometimes required for an appraisal to be as of some *retrospective date* in the past. The appraiser then makes assumptions about the condition of the property and the site as of that date, and uses data that reflect values as of the date of the appraisal. An example of when a retrospective date of the value opinion is appropriate might be a divorce situation. If the parties to a divorce are to share in the appreciation in the value of a real estate asset during the marriage, a retrospective date for the appraiser's opinion of value as of the date of the marriage might be required. In addition, a value opinion for the current date might also be required.

-- **Prospective date:** Appraisals that attempt to estimate the value of the subject property at some *prospective date* in the future tend to be speculative. Special care must be taken by the appraiser to fully report all of the assumptions that were made (or not made) about the property, the neighborhood, the community and region, the economy (both locally and nationally), and other unknown information about the future.

Prospective dates of value opinions are used for proposed construction. The appraiser's opinion of value might be as of a prospective date, with the assumption that the improvements are completed in a professional manner, in accordance with the plans and specifications provided to the appraiser.

As a result of the uncertainty associated with future events, and the challenges of describing all of the assumptions incorporated in a prospective value analysis, some appraisers view the problem from a different perspective. Instead of a prospective value, some appraisers rely on a current date for the value opinion with a hypothetical condition that the improvement were complete as of the current date. This methodology clearly relies on current market data. The primary assumptions relate to the physical condition of the improvement once it is built.

DATE OF THE APPRAISAL REPORT
The date of the appraisal report is required for all appraisals. This is the actual date when the appraisal report is completed. The date of the report assists to clarify whether the date of the appraiser's value opinion is a current, retrospective or prospective date.

IDENTIFICATION OF THE CHARACTERISTICS OF THE PROPERTY
(including location and property rights to be valued)

Location of the Real Estate

2.8 ▶It must be crystal clear to the reader of an appraisal exactly what is being appraised. The appraisal must contain an accurate description of the real estate (site and improvements), any personal property included in the appraised value.

IDENTIFICATION OF THE SITE
The subject property is first identified by means of a mailing address or other short description such as a lot number. This is shown in the subject section of the Uniform Residential Appraisal Report (URAR). A more precise identification, such as that provided by a legal description which can be copied from the deed or mortgage, may also be required. When available, a survey helps to precisely identify a property. Whether or not a complete legal description is needed in the appraisal is a matter of judgment. When a more complete description is included, it is often attached as part of the addenda. When determining the scope of work, what will be required for a positive identification is one of the things to be established.

Identification of the site for purposes of defining the appraisal problem typically requires knowing the property address, size and zoning of the site. On occasion, particularly when the site has not been subdivided or improved, the parcel of land does not have an address. When there is no address, the appraiser must rely on the legal description or another means of describing the location of the subject property.

The site size is important in defining the appraisal problem because the appraiser needs to understand whether there might be surplus land to be valued, the types of comparables that would be relevant, and whether the appraiser has the competence to appraise the property.

Identification of the site is an important step in developing the appropriate scope of work. If there are unique conditions relative to the site that are identified after the scope of work is defined, it might need to be refined.

IDENTIFICATION OF THE IMPROVEMENTS
A required and important part of every appraisal is a complete, accurate description of all of the improvements included in the appraised value.

The improvements to be appraised must be identified as to their general age, size and use. The age is important because if it is proposed or new construction, the cost approach might be appropriate. If the improvements are older, the cost approach may not be useful. Understanding the size of the improvement is important because size plays a role in selecting comparables. If the size is particularly small or large relative to comparables in the market, additional effort might be required to identify appropriate comparables.

The use of the improvements is also important to identify the type of comparables that will be appropriate for the analysis. Additionally, the use of the improvements might be such that the appraiser does not have the expertise necessary to perform the analysis. For example, if the subject property is a full-service hotel and the appraiser has never appraised a full-service hotel, there might be additional steps that would be required for the appraiser to be able to accept the assignment.

IDENTIFICATION OF PERSONAL PROPERTY

The statutes vary from state to state as to what is personal property and what is real estate. Appraisers should be familiar with the applicable statutes in the areas where they make appraisals. One cannot always tell just by physical inspection what is real estate and what is personal property. In residential appraising, some typical items that fall into the gray area between real estate and personal property are carpeting, drapes, appliances and lighting fixtures.

Identification of personal property is required for the appraiser to incorporate the appropriate item in the analysis, For example, in some resort communities residential properties sell fully furnished. If all of the furnishings have been removed from a property that is being appraised, there could be an impact on the opinion of value. Freddie Mac and Fannie Mae do not include personal property as part of what is being appraised even when it is customary for personal property to be included in the sale. On the 2005 Fannie Mae and Freddie Mac forms the appraiser sign the certification saying that they have not included any personal property in the appraised value.

PROPERTY RIGHTS TO BE VALUED

An appraisal of real property is not directly a valuation of the physical land and improvements; it is a valuation of the rights of ownership. A specific appraisal may require a value estimate of all property rights, while another will analyze only limited rights in the property.

Ownership of property may be held by an individual, a partnership, a corporation or a group of heirs. When ownership is vested in more than one interest, each may hold an equal or unequal share. The property rights or interests to be appraised may be fractional interests such as air rights over a specified property, subsurface rights, an easement, a right-of-way, or fee simple subject to an easement. Because the value of real property is not limited to its physical components, the appraiser cannot define the problem precisely until fully aware of which property rights are involved. Without this knowledge, the appraiser may produce an estimate of value that is irrelevant to the problem. A clear conception of the rights to be appraised will also help the appraiser evaluate the complexity of the problem and the scope of work it will require.

The ownership interest to be appraised is often the fee simple interest for a single-family residences. Some other ownership interests include leasehold, leased fee, easements, sublease hold, sandwich leases, subsurface rights, and air rights. These property rights are discussed in detail later in this text. A precise understanding of the property rights to be appraised is required in order to define an appropriate scope of work.

Fannie Mae and Freddie Mac
Mandatory Assumptions and Limiting Conditions

The following are the assumptions and limiting conditions that are contained on the 2005 editions of the Fannie Mae/Freddie Mac residential appraisal forms:

"1. The appraiser will not be responsible for matters of a legal nature that affect either the property being appraised or the title to it, except for information that he or she became aware of during the research involved in performing this appraisal. The appraiser assumes that the title is good and marketable and will not render any opinions about the title.

2. The appraiser has provided a sketch in the appraisal report to show the approximate dimensions of the improvements. The sketch is included only to assist the reader in visualizing the property and understanding the appraiser's determination of its size.

3. The appraiser has examined the available **flood maps** that are provided by the **Federal Emergency Management Agency (FEMA)** (or other data sources) and has noted in this appraisal report whether any portion of the subject site is located in an identified Special Flood Hazard Area. Because the appraiser is not a surveyor, he or she makes no guarantee, express or implied, regarding this determination.

4. The appraiser will not give testimony or appear in court because he or she made an appraisal of the property in question, unless specific arrangements to do so have been made beforehand, or as otherwise required by law.

5. The appraiser has noted in this appraisal report any adverse conditions (such as needed repairs, deterioration, the presence of hazardous wastes, toxic substances, etc.) observed during the inspection of the subject property or that he or she became aware of during the research involved in performing this appraisal. Unless otherwise stated in this appraisal report, the appraiser has no knowledge of any hidden or unapparent physical deficiencies or adverse conditions of the property (such as, but not limited to, needed repairs, deterioration, the presence of hazardous wastes, toxic substances, adverse environmental conditions, etc.) that would make the property less valuable, and has assumed that there are no such conditions and makes no guarantee or warranties, expressed or implied. The appraiser will not be responsible for any such conditions that do exist or for any engineering or testing that might be required to discover whether such conditions exist. Because the appraiser is not an expert in the field of environmental hazards, this appraisal report must not be considered as an environmental assessment of the property.

6. The appraiser has based his or her appraisal report and value conclusions for an appraisal that is subject to satisfactory completion, repairs, or alterations on the assumption that the completion, repairs, or alterations of the subject property will be performed in a professional manner."

2.9

2.10

IDENTIFICATION OF ANY HYPOTHETICAL CONDITIONS EXTRAORDINARY ASSUMPTIONS AND LIMITING CONDITIONS NECESSARY IN THE ASSIGNMENT

Assumptions and limiting conditions apply to all appraisal assignments and must be a part of every appraisal report. However, **extraordinary assumptions** are only included for those assignments where they apply.

Extraordinary assumptions are those assumptions that are believed to be true for the assignment but if the assumption is incorrect, the appraisers's opinion of value could be different.   For example, if the appraiser believes that the house does not have any significant environmental problems, based on the representations of the owner, and the value is estimated on this assumption but it turns out there is a lead paint problem then the value estimated could be different. When doing work for a client that does not have rigid requirements for using the Fannie Mae/Freddie Mac underlying assumptions and limiting conditions, the appraiser should consider adding ones that pertain to the appraisal they are doing. The following are some recommendations from the Appraisal Institute [1]

"For the appraiser's and client's protection, it is often important to add additional limiting conditions. The following are seven limiting conditions which might be appropriate:

1. Any opinion of value provided in the report apply to the entire property, and any proration or division of the total into fractional interests will invalidate the opinion of value, unless such proration or division of interests has been set forth in the report.

2. Only preliminary plans and specifications were available for use in the preparation of this appraisal; the analysis, therefore, is subject to a review of the final plans and specifications when available.

3. Any proposed improvements are assumed to have been completed unless otherwise stipulated; any construction is assumed to conform with the building plans referenced in the report.

4. The appraiser assumes that the reader or user of this report has been provided with copies of available building plans and all leases and amendments, if any, encumbering the property.

5. No legal description or survey was furnished so the appraiser utilized the county tax plat to ascertain the physical dimensions and acreage of the property. Should a survey prove this information to be inaccurate, it may be necessary for this appraisal to be adjusted.

6. The forecasts, projections, or operating estimates contained herein are based upon current market conditions, anticipated short-term supply and demand factors, and a continued stable economy. These forecasts are, therefore, subject to changes in future conditions.

[1] Appraisal of Real Estate, 12th Edition, Appraisal Institute, Chicago, IL 2001.

7. The Americans with Disabilities Act (ADA) became effective January 26, 1992. This appraiser has not made a specific compliance survey or analysis of the property to determine whether or not it is in conformity with the various detailed requirements of the ADA. It is possible that a compliance survey of the property and a detailed analysis of the requirements of the ADA would reveal that the property is not in compliance with one or more of the requirements of the act. If so, this fact could have a negative impact upon the value of the property. Since the appraiser has no direct evidence relating to this issue, possible noncompliance with the requirements of ADA was not

considered in estimating the value of the property."

2.11 ▶A *hypothetical condition* is defined by the 2006 USPAP as: "that which is contrary to what exists but is supposed for the purpose of analysis:

Comment: Hypothetical conditions assume conditions contrary to known facts about physical, legal, or economic characteristics of the subject property, or about conditions external to the property, such as market conditions or trends; or about the integrity of data used in an analysis."

The 2006 USPAP Standard Rule 1-2 (g) states: "identify any hypothetical conditions necessary in the assignment.

Comment: A hypothetical condition may be used in an assignment only if:

- use of the hypothetical condition is clearly required for legal purposes, for purposes of reasonable analysis, or for purposes of comparison;

- use of the hypothetical condition results in a credible analysis; and

- the appraisal complies with disclosure requirements set forth in the USPAP for hypothetical conditions."

2006 USPAP Standard Rule 2-1 (c) "clearly and accurately disclose all ... hypothetical conditions...used in the assignment

A hypothetical condition might be an assumption that a site is annexed and zoned for development, when in fact, the site is adjacent to a municipality but not in it, and the zoning is for agricultural use. The analysis is based on the hypothetical assumption that annexation and a zoning change have occurred for the subject property, even though it is contrary to the facts.

Hypothetical conditions are only included in the appraisal report for those assignments where they apply. Any hypothetical conditions that apply to an appraisal assignment must be defined by the client and agreed to by the appraiser prior to defining the scope of work.

SCOPE OF WORK

"A clear and accurate description of the *scope of work* appropriate to the appraisal assignment is desirable to protect those persons whose reliance on the appraisal assignment may be affected. The term scope of work refers to the amount and type of information researched and the analysis applied in an assignment. The standard clearly impose a responsibility on the appraiser to determine the appropriate scope of work to develop a value opinion and prepare the report. By describing the scope of work, the appraiser signifies acceptance of the responsibility.

The appraisal report should prominently disclose the degree of precision attributable to the value opinion given the defined scope of work. When the intended use the appraisal requires the appraiser to narrow the scope of work, the value opinion may be less precise than in a more typical assignment and the value opinion is only appropriate and reliable for the intended use of the appraisal.

Discussing the scope of work in the appraisal report helps an appraiser clarify why conclusions are valid only for the intended use agreed upon by the client and the appraiser." [2]

The **2006 USPAP STANDARD RULE 1-2 (h):** defines scope of work as follows:

"An appraiser must properly identify the problem to be solved in order to determine the appropriate scope of work. The appraiser must be prepared to demonstrate the scope of work is sufficient to produce credible assignment results.

2.12 ▶ Comment: Scope of work includes, but is not limited to: • the extent to which the property is identified; • the extent to which tangible property is inspected; • the extent of data researched; and • the type and extent of analyses applied to arrive at opinions or conclusions."

The scope of work rule implementation includes the identification of the problem (or definition of the problem) and definition of what scope of work is acceptable for a particular assignment. The appraiser is obliged to disclose the scope of work in the appraisal report.

"...determine the scope of work necessary to produce credible assignment results in accordance with the SCOPE OF WORK RULE."

The Scope of Work Rule as defined in the 2006 USPAP (page 12) requires:

"For each appraisal, appraisal review, and appraisal consulting assignment, an appraiser must:
  1. identify the problem to be solved;
  2. determine and perform the scope of work necessary to develop credible assignment results; and
  3. disclose the scope of work in the report."

[2] Appraisal of Real Estate, 12th Edition, Appraisal Institute, Chicago, IL 2001.

There are three components associated with the scope of work rule: problem identification, scope of work acceptability, and disclosure obligations. The problem identification is the definition of the problem previously discussed.

To be acceptable, the scope of work must incorporate all the components associated with the identification of the appraisal problem. In determining the appropriate scope of work the appraiser must define the research and analysis that is appropriate for the assignment. The standard as to whether the scope of work is appropriate is based upon the expectation of the client and others who frequently rely on this type of analysis, and what the appraiser's peers would typically do for a similar type of assignment.

In defining the scope of work, the appraiser must ensure that the scope is adequate to produce a credible result relative to the intended use. Additionally, the appraiser must define the scope of work in such a manner that it does not result in a biased conclusion. The disclosure obligation requires the appraiser to report the scope of work in a level of detail so that the intended user(s) of the report understand the work that was performed. The disclosure should include the research and analyses performed and, where appropriate, the research and analysis that was not performed.

FREDDIE MAC/FANNIE MAE FORMS

The 2006 USPAP states that the Scope of Work will be determined by the appraiser who will take into consideration the intended users needs. Most lender/clients intend to use the appraisal as part of a portfolio of mortgages that may be sold to Freddie Mac or Fannie Mae. Therefore, the lender needs appraisals that meet Fannie Mae and Freddie Mac scope of work requirements.

The 2005 editions of the Freddie Mac/Fannie Mae appraisal forms contain specific minimum requirements for their scope of work, which does not include using the cost approach and income approach, unless the appraiser deems them necessary in order to make a credible appraisal.

When an appraiser accepts an assignment from a lender/client that the client specifies will be made on a Fannie Mae/Freddie Mac form, the appraiser can assume that the lender/client needs an appraisal that meets the Fannie Mae/Freddie Mac scope of work requirements. As a practical matter, what the appraiser needs to know from the lender/client is what in addition to the Fannie Mae/Freddie Mac scope of work requirement are the lenders additional scope of work needs.

Some examples of additions lender's need are the cost approach which they will use to determine, if the amount of insurance coverage is adequate, comparable sales in the same neighborhood to determine that there is nothing in the subject's neighborhood that is reflecting on values, or comparable sales within a time period that the lender believes will indicate value without large time adjustments.

As long as these requirements are in addition to the Fannie Mae/Freddie Mac scope of work requirements and do not violate any USPAP requirement, the lender has a right to include them in their scope of work requirements.

Before making the decision not to do anything that would normally be done to make a credible appraisal, the appraiser must be careful to comply with the current edition of the USPAP.

SUMMARY

Definition of the Problem

The first step in the valuation process is the definition of the problem to be solved. There are seven major steps in the definition of the problem: Identification of client and other intended users, intended use of the appraiser's opinions and conclusions, the type and definition of value, the effective date of the appraiser's opinions and conclusions the characteristics of the property (including location and property rights to be valued), any extraordinary assumptions necessary in the assignment and any hypothetical conditions necessary in the assignment

Each step in the valuation process helps the appraiser research, gather, organize or analyze the data required to make an appraisal. The definition of the problem helps the appraiser define what is necessary in terms of data required and time needed to produce a credible appraisal result.

Scope of Work

When the appraiser, in consultation with the client, defines the problem and determines what data is needed and what analysis of the date is required to make a credible appraisal, they have determined the scope of work.

The next step is to have the client agree with the scope of work that has been determined by the appraiser (the final responsibility of determining the scope of work is the appraiser's). When the client agrees with the scope of work, the appraiser then proceeds to make a credible appraisal.

Often, especially on more complex assignments, when the appraiser proceeds with the assignment, it become apparent to the appraiser, that in order to make a credible appraisal more data and/or analysis is required.

At this point the appraiser must get the client to agree upon the revised scope of work in order to proceed with the assignment. Knowing this is a possibility it is good business to initially explain to the client that it is possible that the scope of work will have to be revised after you start the appraisal.

You can not proceed with the appraisal unless the client agrees to the expanded scope of work which you have determined is necessary to make a credible appraisal.

Under no circumstances according to the 2006 USPAP can you produce an appraisal that is not credible.

REVIEW QUESTIONS

1. The first step of an appraisal is to:
   a. get a contract from the client.
   b. define the problem to be solved.
   c. determine what value is to be estimated.
   d. identify any hypothetical conditions.

2. The 2006 USPAP requires that:
   a. the intended user(s) be identified in the appraisal report.
   b. the intended use(s) be identified in the appraisal report.
   c. the type of value be identified in the appraisal report.
   d. All of the above

3. Which term describes what the buyer is expected to pay for a house?
   a. Cost
   b. Value
   c. Price
   d. None of the above

4. What is the common denominator by which real property value is measured in the United States?
   a. Loan to value ratio
   b. Down payment required from the typical buyer
   c. Money
   d. The amount of the loan obtainable by the typical buyer

5. Most residential appraisals are estimates of:
   a. the amount of loan available to the typical buyer.
   b. estate value.
   c. liquidation value
   d. None of the above

6. Which of the following is the basis for most *ad valorem* taxes?
   a. Value-in-use
   b. Insurable value
   c. Investment value
   d. Assessed value

7. An appraisal must be an opinion of value:
   a. as of a specific time of day.
   b. as of a specific date.
   c. as of a specific week.
   d. as of a specific month.

8. The identification of the real estate in an appraisal must include identification of the:
   a. site.
   b. improvements.
   c. personal property to be included in the appraised value.
   d. All of the above

9. Which agency produces flood maps?
   a. Freddie Mac
   b. Fannie Mae
   c. HUD/FHA
   d. FEMA (Federal Emergency Management Agency)

10. What are some typical property conditions that should be noted in the appraisal?
    a. Needed repairs
    b. Deterioration
    c. Hazardous wastes
    d. All of the above

11. A hypothetical condition is:
    a. what exists in small amounts on the property.
    b. found mostly in *de minimis* PUDs.
    c. must be contrary to know facts.
    d. never required for legal purposes.

12. Scope of work includes:
    a. the degree to which the property is inspected.
    b. the extent of research of the physical factors that could affect the value of the property.
    c. the type and extent of data analysis.
    d. All of the above

13. The amount paid for a good or service is its:
    a. price.
    b. cost.
    c. investment value.
    d. None of the above

14. Market value is:
    a. the same as insurable value.
    b. the most probable price.
    c. the same as the cost.
    d. the same as the purchase price.

ANSWERS

The answer to each question is indicated by the letter a, b, c or d below. The explanation of the answer is indicated by a numbered arrow that points to the appropriate paragraph on the page of the text indicated by the page number following the answer.

Q 2.1	b	Page 2-2
Q 2.2	d	Page 2-2
Q 2.3	c	Page 2-6
Q 2.4	c	Page 2-4
Q 2.5	d	Page 2-5
Q 2.6	d	Page 2-7
Q 2.7	b	Page 2-7
Q 2.8	d	Page 2-9
Q 2.9	d	Page 2-11
Q 2.10	d	Page 2-11
Q 2.11	c	Page 2-13
Q 2.12	d	Page 2-14
Q 2.13	a	Page 2-6
Q 2.14	b	Page 2-5

CHAPTER 3

Valuation Procedures - Collecting and Selecting Data

"...use all the quantitative data you can get; but you still have to distrust it and use your intelligence and judgment. "

Alvin Toffler
American Author

Important Words and Key Concepts

Words on this list are highlighted in this chapter.
They are also defined in the Glossary at the back of this text.

Cost Reporting Services
Cost Indices (Cost Indexes)
Capitalization Rates
General Data
Macro Data
Micro Data
Primary Data
Public Records
Quantitative Analysis
Quantitative Data
Secondary Data
Specific Data

COLLECTING AND SELECTING GENERAL DATA

TYPE OF GENERAL DATA

3.1 *General data* is useful to appraisers and can be divided into items of information that help them understand the influence of the four forces originating outside a property and their effect on the value of the property. These forces are social, economic, government and environmental. It is different from specific data which includes details about the subject property, comparable sales and rental properties, and relevant local market characteristics.

General data is classified as primary or secondary. Primary data includes original elements of information generated by an appraiser or some other group or agency. An example of primary data an appraiser can gather is the number of vacant houses and apartments in the neighborhood of the subject property.

3.2 *Primary data* becomes secondary data when it is published and made available to the public for general use. *Secondary data* that might be relied upon by an appraiser would include employment statistics, populations information, or income levels. When an appraiser relies on the research of others, they are relying on secondary data.

Macro Data

3.3 *Macro data* comprises information on aggregate phenomena, such as total employment at the national, regional and local levels; national and regional income; product growth or decline; interest rates; and the balance of trade. Macro data is typically general data obtained from secondary sources.

Micro Data

3.4 *Micro data* is more *specific data*. The supply of new apartment units in the community, the vacancy rates in a housing sub-market, the number of local households in the $50,000 to $85,000 income bracket, and the comparable properties used in the sales comparison approach are all examples of micro data. Micro data may be obtained from a primary source, such as a sample of vacant units taken from the local apartment market, or from a secondary source, such as the number of persons employed locally in manufacturing, as reported in the United States Census.

USES OF GENERAL DATA

3.5 General data is essential in the valuation process because it:

• provides a background against which to place analysis of the subject property;

• supplies information from which possible trends affecting values can be inferred and figures derived for calculations within the three approaches;

• forms a basis for judgments about highest and best use, reconciliation of value indications within the three approaches, and the final estimate of defined value.

Appraisers need an understanding of all elements that contribute to the market price and market value of real estate. An awareness of social, economic, government, and environmental trends allows an appraiser to interpret specific market phenomena.

In estimating value using sales or cost data, an appraiser uses prices and costs that have been determined in the market, which are the products of the interaction of all value determinants. Similarly, the income capitalization approach requires estimation of market-determined rents, operating expenses, capitalization rates, and financing terms. When the methodology of the income capitalization approach requires an appraiser to make explicit forecasts of future income or reversion value at the end of an assumed holding period for an investment property, these forecasts are informed by the basic determinants of value embodied in general data.

An appraiser also may do a **quantitative analysis** in which they report the level, changes, and trends in general data, then apply the **quantitative data** to the problem under consideration, and finally, show the relative importance of the data trends. For example, comparison of two local economies among markets for various types of real estate, or the analysis of comparable sales data from a given market, requires consideration of these trends.

The significance of a 2% population increase in one city, for example, depends on the population increases in other cities. The demand for apartments must be considered relative to the demand for detached single-family houses. The selection of comparables depends on their competitiveness and similarity to the subject property.

SOURCES OF GENERAL DATA

A thorough analysis of the market and market trends does not depend on technique alone; it depends heavily upon sound information.

Today there is an almost unlimited supply of data. Although good unbiased data pertaining to local communities can be difficult to find, it usually is available. Government agencies at all levels and the Federal Reserve System and its district banks around the country are excellent sources of economic data. The Federal Home Loan Bank System, which is closely related to the real estate industry, is also widely known for its economic research with application to local and state areas. Some states have online retrieval systems that provide historic and current economic, social and governmental data. Trends can be inferred from changes in data over time.

Many private organizations also serve as clearing houses for such statistics. Some real estate appraisers also make a practice of collecting pertinent statistical data as well, although it can be expensive and time consuming to update.

COLLECTING AND SELECTING SPECIFIC DATA

3.10 ▶ The entire appraisal process is dependent upon the collection and analysis of specific data from the market. All three approaches to value are really market approaches and depend upon accurate and reliable market data.

3.6 ▶ **Specific Data** is the basis of the three approaches to value. The process of extracting relevant material from the vast array of available market data helps an appraiser to develop a perception of the market. The credibility of the final opinion of value depends on the extent to which it is supported by data.

Specific data is analyzed through the process of comparison. The key task is locating data that provides the information needed to apply the correct techniques in each of the three approaches to value. A number of different data sets may be needed to extract all information pertinent to the appraisal problem. For example, if the subject property is an apartment building of three-bedroom units, the appraiser may be able to base adjustments for time of sale, location, and physical characteristics on information from comparable sales of similar apartment buildings. However, it may be necessary to analyze data on competitive properties that have not sold recently to obtain adequate income and expense data for apartment buildings in the area.

INVESTIGATIONS OF MARKET TRANSACTIONS

A study is made to find those comparable sales and listings whose costs, income and expense information are similar to the subject property. Generally, the more current the comparable sale and the more similar it is to the subject property, the better it will be as an indicator of value. Often more sales and listings and other data are considered than are finally used in the appraisal.

Collecting Data

The accuracy of the value indication via any of the approaches depends upon the quantity and quality of sales, rentals, offerings and listings data for competitive properties.

The selection of the appropriate data first depends upon a detailed description and classification of the subject property's characteristics and components. The information contained in the description of the land and improvements helps the appraiser select the data to be used in the cost, sales comparison and income approaches.

It is only after a complete analysis of the subject property that an appraiser can select the comparables that are most similar to the subject property.

In selecting market transactions for analysis, an appraiser eliminates transactions that are not pertinent to the specific market for the subject property. For example, when an appraiser considers a 10-year-old single-family residence that has three bedrooms, two baths, and 1,800 square feet of livable area, they usually eliminate two-bedroom and four-bedroom houses, if there is sufficient data concerning three-bedroom house sales. The appraiser would also probably ignore the sales of 25-30 year-old houses, and possibly the sales of new homes as well. If sufficient sales remained, sales of houses smaller than 1,600 square feet or larger than 2,000 square feet might be rejected as not similar enough to provide adequate comparability. The major determinants of the data that is ultimately used is the quantity as well as the quality of data that is available.

When comparable sales data in the area is limited, an appraiser may have to extend their search to adjacent neighborhoods and communities that are similar to that of the subject property. When the selection of data is still limited to an unacceptably narrow sample of current market activity, the appraiser may decide to use sales that are less current and may interview brokers, buyers, sellers, owners, and tenants in the area to locate data on listings and offers. These may also be used as comparables if the proper adjustments are made. However, listings and unaccepted offers are not as compelling when used as comparables in an appraisal as closed transactions. An appraiser learns broad information about the market from the pattern of sales. Important information can be revealed by the:

- Number of sales
- Period of time covered by the sales
- Availability of property for sale in the market
- Rate of absorption
- Rate of turnover (volume of sales, level of activity)
- Characteristics and motivations of buyers and sellers
- Terms and conditions of sale
- Use of property before and after the sale
- Other significant characteristics

Location of Sales Data

Through a sound collection program, a large bank of market data can be accumulated in the appraiser's own files and organized to serve the appraiser's needs most effectively. Only some of the data may be immediately pertinent; the remainder may be collected, filed and cross-indexed for future use. Many offices are using computers for data storage, retrieval and analysis.

PUBLIC RECORDS

An appraiser searches **public records** to acquire a copy of the property deed. In some areas there are services that provide electronic copies of deeds to appraisers. Deeds provide important information about the property and sales transactions. The full names of parties to a transaction and the transaction date are cited on the deed. A legal description of the property is provided, as are the property rights included in the transaction, as well as any outstanding liens against the title.

DEEDS

3.11 ▶Recorded deeds are a traditional source of sales information but their main contribution is in reflecting the existence of a sale. They usually contain only the address of the property, a legal description (this is part of a good positive identification), names of grantors and grantees, and the date of title transfer (which is sometimes a substantially different date from the actual date of the closing). In some areas, deed records also show the sales price (or have tax stamps affixed, which indicate the sales price) and the terms of the financing, but it is imprudent to rely upon this data alone as comparable sales data.

Occasionally, full names give clues as to unusual motivations for the sale. For example, a sale from John Smith to Mary S. Jones may be a transfer to a daughter, or a sale from John Smith, William Jones, and Harold Long to the SJL Corporation may not be an arms-length transaction.

TRANSFER TAX RECORDS

Some communities keep separate records of transfer taxes. The main advantage of this information is its accuracy and ease of use, particularly if it is filed by street.

Statutes in some states require that the consideration paid upon transfer of title be shown on the deed. However, it is not always dependable as a reflection of the sale price because some purchasers deduct the estimated value of personal property (e.g., in motels or resort area apartments) from the true consideration in order to reduce transfer taxes. The value of the personal property is sometimes inflated, making the recorded consideration for the real property less than the true price paid. Occasionally, the indicated consideration will be overstated in order to obtain a loan higher than is actually justifiable, or understated in order to justify a low property tax assessment. Some states require that the true consideration be reported on the deed, while other states allow the consideration to be reported as "$1.00 and other valuable consideration."

▶3.7 ASSESSMENT RECORDS

Records of the local tax assessor may include property cards for both the subject property and the comparables, with land and building sketches, areas, sale prices, and so forth. In some localities, legal or private publishing services issue information about revenue stamps and other pertinent facts about current transfers. A cooperative, knowledgeable assessor with up-to-date records can be a major asset for the appraiser. A good set of assessor's records contains an accurate description of the property. Many assessors, however, inspect properties at intervals of 10 years, and the descriptions may not include recent improvements. Many assessor's measurements are quite accurate. Although they may not use gross living area calculations, their measurements can usually be converted to such figures. Appraisers must resist the temptation, however, to depend on the assessor's description and measurements without personally inspecting the property.

REAL ESTATE NEWSPAPERS

Real estate newspapers concentrate on people making real estate news, major sales and leases and new construction; they often have information about subdivisions, condominiums and other developments that would be difficult to obtain elsewhere.

COMMERCIAL PUBLICATIONS

In some areas, special commercial publications give sales and rental information along with other business news. Although they usually report only the information available from the recorded deeds and leases, they are an excellent source for locating comparable sales.

GENERAL CIRCULATION NEWSPAPERS

Daily newspapers often publish information pertaining to real estate transfers as well as proposed developments, zoning changes and other general real estate news. Many weekend papers carry special real estate supplements or sections. The classified advertisements are a good source of information about properties for rent and for sale, and are often listed by a local known market area, neighborhood or school district.

REALTORS AND REAL ESTATE BROKERS

Realtors and real estate brokers provide a good source of data, especially in areas where other sources are not available. The appraiser may elect to use the files of individual brokers, which are often elaborate and accurate. Brokers are a particularly good source of rental data and information about listings and current offers on houses.

SHARED SALES DATA

Working with other professionals saves considerable duplication of effort and increases the quality of everyone's work. Sharing comparable data is a tradition in many areas of the country among appraisers. Some appraisers charge for exchanged sales data. New Internet-based data banks (e.g., Appraisal Data Connection) offer access to very large national databases of property information, and charge on a per use basis, or provide access free in exchange for swapped information.

PROPERTY MANAGERS

▶**3.12** ▶Property managers often have information about real estate transactions and may provide leads, especially about competitive properties. It is becoming harder to get access to specific information because of recent privacy laws. In some of the large cities, property management firms sell information.

▶**3.8** ▶MULTIPLE LISTING SERVICES (MLS)

The MLS in a community can be a bountiful source of information because they usually require a detailed description of the listed property. There can be pitfalls in using this information however. Adjectives used by brokers and salespeople to describe property conditions are often different from those used by appraisers.

"Average" to an appraiser should mean a house that is typical of its market, one whose effective age is approximately the same as its actual age, as described in ***Chapter 5: Property Description - Location Characteristics (Market Area and Neighborhood)***. A broker or salesperson might describe the condition of the same house as "good" or "very good". They may describe a substandard house is "fair", and one that is barely habitable may be called "poor" or "a fixer-upper". Houses rated by an appraiser as "above average" might be described as "like new", "excellent" or "A-l" on the MLS.

Another problem with MLS information is that functional and economic obsolescence is rarely described accurately. Square foot measurements, if shown, may prove to be inaccurate or may not be the gross living area (GLA) figure used by appraisers. Finally, conditions of sale are rarely indicated. Once the MLS is used to locate a sale, the property should be personally inspected by the appraiser.

ATLASES AND SURVEY MAPS

Atlases and survey maps give data on lot size, relate legal descriptions to street numbers, and frequently show building locations and dimensions to scale.

Verification of Sales Data

3.9 ▶ Each sale used as a comparable in an appraisal report should be personally inspected by the appraiser, and the data confirmed with the buyer, seller or broker.

The appraiser must be certain that all forms of depreciation have been considered, that the measurements are correct, and that the reported price and terms are accurate.

Verification and inspection do more than confirm the accuracy of the data gathered. They also provide for exploration of the motivating forces involved in a sale. Were both buyer and seller acting without financial pressure? Was the sale an "arms-length" transaction, or were the parties related in some way? Were both buyer and seller knowledgeable about the property and market in which the sale took place? Did the seller have reasonable time to sell and the buyer to buy? Were there any special concessions granted by either party? Was financing typical of the market, or was there a purchase money mortgage, second mortgage, assumed mortgage or other unusual situation? Were there any other special sale conditions such as the inclusion of significant personal property in the sale (furniture, above-ground pools, boats, automobiles, sports equipment, etc.)? Was there any special government program involving a subsidy, attractive financing terms or guarantee of payment?

Sometimes an owner sells for less than expected if allowed to continue to occupy the property for a substantial period of time after the transfer of title. Sometimes a sale is the result of an option granted in the past when different market conditions prevailed, resulting in a sale price that may not be typical of the current market. These are only some of the possible conditions that might make the reported sale price different from the market value. Only by personally interviewing the buyer and seller or broker can the appraiser gain knowledge about such conditions.

Filing Sales Data

A common characteristic among successful appraisers is a filing system where they collect comparable data as it becomes available and store it in an organized manner until such time as they need it for an appraisal assignment. The method of storing this data ranges from index cards to computer data banks.

Most of the stored data an appraiser keeps falls into two broad categories:

1. Data obtained from published records, MLSs and other sources which provide information about properties not inspected by the appraiser.

2. Data developed as part of the process of making appraisals which contain detailed information about properties that have been inspected.

How the data is indexed depends on the type of practice the appraiser has and the volume of data being stored. An appraiser who specializes in small residential properties and who collects large amounts of data may first divide the data by community and then by type of residential property. An appraiser with less extensive data may elect to put all the residential property together, making the initial division by property category.

One example of an office filing classification for residential property is as follows:

- Single-family residences
- Small income properties (2 to 12 family)
- Apartments (over 12 families)
- Garden-type units
- High-rise
- Individual condominiums
- Condominium projects
- Cooperatives (Co-ops)
- Mobile homes
- Timeshare units
- Residences on leased land
- Resort and recreation houses
- Housing for the Elderly
- Farm and Ranch Houses
- Mansions
- Historic Homes
- Experimental Houses
- Solar Houses

It is appropriate to cross-reference data on some properties. For example, a single family solar home would be filed both under single family residences and solar houses. Appraisers with practices that include other types of properties would establish similar classifications for commercial, industrial, agricultural and special purpose properties, dividing the data into useful categories by type or location, or both.

Additional Market Data

Investigation of the market extends beyond the determination of available comparable sales. Useful specific data is obtained by investigating properties that are similar to and competitive with the subject property, even though such properties have not sold recently. Information used in applying the cost and income capitalization approaches must often be sought from market sources other than sales. Such information may also be useful in refining adjustments made in the sales comparison approach. In the investigation of general and neighborhood data, an appraiser learns significant information on trends regarding such items as construction costs, lease terms, typical expenses, and vacancy rates. Data on these trends provides additional specific information which is used by the appraiser to derive value indications through the three approaches for the subject property.

Improvement Cost Data

Several sources are available for obtaining reliable cost data.

IN-OFFICE COST DATA FILES

The use of square foot cost estimates involves assembling, analyzing and cataloging data on actual house costs. An appraiser should have comprehensive current cost data for various types of houses and other improvements, including data on current material and labor costs. A system of grading quality of construction may also be used to refine this data further. Cost data can often be obtained from local builders, lenders, material suppliers and trade associations. A file of this kind provides a check against the costs of reproducing or replacing an existing residence, as well as against known or projected costs for existing or proposed houses of varying grades of construction. It also provides a check against the probable cost of different components of a house, which becomes important when providing a list of curable items as part of an appraisal.

COST REPORTING SERVICES

Several recognized cost data reporting services are also available to the appraiser. Some include illustrations of typical structures and provide adjustments to tailor the standard example to differently shaped or equipped residences. Some provide adjustment for individual cities or areas. Some show cubic foot costs, some square foot costs, and some are designed for unit-in-place information. New services are becoming available online, using large interactive cost databases accessible by state and region, which no longer require bulky printed guides. In addition, the data is updated regularly so that the data is current.

COST INDICES (INDEXES)

A cost data reporting service often also provides cost indexes reflecting the relative cost of construction over a period of years is also quite useful. When the actual cost of a residence constructed some years ago is known, application of the index will indicate the present construction cost (provided the actual cost was a typical figure).

For example, assume that a house cost $95,000 to build four years ago and that the cost index for that year from a national service is 284.4. The current cost index from the same cost service is 332.5. Based upon this data, the building would cost 1.169 times its original cost to build today. This is calculated by dividing the current index by the previous index from the current one, and then dividing by the previous index, to derive a factor which represents the increased cost to build the same improvement.

$$\frac{332.5}{284.4} = 1.169$$

$ 95,000 x 1.169 gives an indicated current cost to build of $111,055.

(Note: These figures are for illustration purposes only).

Income and Expense Data

In deriving pertinent income and expense data, an appraiser investigates comparable sales and rentals, as well as information on competitive income-producing properties in the same market. Current gross income estimates should be reviewed in light of average rents for several successive years. Vacancy rates, collection losses and operating expenses typical for this type of property help an appraiser to refine the forecast of income and expenses for an income-producing property.

The published information on property values for several consecutive years suggests the rate of appreciation or depreciation that is evident for various property types. Interviews with owners and tenants in the area can provide lease and expense data. Lenders are a useful source of information on current terms of available financing.

An appraiser attempts to obtain all the income and expense data for income property comparables. These figures should be derived and tabulated in a reconstructed operating statement format and filed by property type.

Rental information is often difficult to obtain. Therefore, an appraiser should take every opportunity to add rents to the data plant. Long-term leases are usually a matter of public record. A separate county index of leases may be available, which lists the parties to recorded leases and refers to the volume and page of the recorded lease. Sometimes this information is listed among the deeds and mortgages, but it is normally coded so that a lease may be spotted fairly easily. In certain cities, abstracts of recorded leases are printed by a private publishing service. Classified ads are also a source of rental information for competitive properties. Many appraisers regularly check for advertised rentals and post them to rent comparable data for a particular property type or area. The final actual rental is usually much closer to the asking rental than is the case for asking prices. Rental data is usually filed by property type and area according to the same classifications used for sales data.

The income and expense comparables should be filed chronologically and by property type. They can thus be retrieved easily to help estimate the expenses for a similar type of property. Income and expenses should be converted into units for comparison and analysis. Income may be reported in terms of rent per apartment unit, per room, per hospital bed, per square foot, and so forth. Expenses, such as insurance, taxes, painting, decorating, and other maintenance charges, can be expressed in any of the units of comparison used for income, but they may also by expressed as a percent of the effective gross rent. Any unit comparison must be used consistently throughout the analysis. Actual vacancy rate and operating expenses may also be shown as a percentage of the effective gross rent. This data is essential in the valuation of income-producing properties. Other important information includes the age and type of construction and any utilities that are provided by the owner.

Capitalization Rate Data

Market *capitalization rates* are also an essential type of market data. When income, expense, and mortgage data are available for sold properties, these indications may be used to calculate the overall capitalization rate and the equity dividend rate associated with the sale. Whenever possible, an appraiser should derive the overall and equity dividend rates of return, which are indicated by sales of comparable properties, and file the information for future reference. In the sales comparison approach, these rates would be analyzed based on the similarity of the comparable to the subject property.

Overall and equity dividend capitalization rates derived from sales may also be used as the basis from which other rates are derived. Therefore, it is important that appraisers consider these rate indications whenever this information on sales is available.

SUMMARY

GENERAL DATA

General data consists of data about the "four great forces" originating outside a property and what effect they have on the value of the subject property. They are the social, economic, governmental and environmental forces which affect property due to its fixed position in a particular location.

General data is divided into primary data which is original data collected by the appraiser or other groups and agencies. Once it becomes published and available to the public, it becomes secondary data.

Another way to classify data is macro data comprised of information on aggregate phenomena, and micro data which are more specific observations.

General data is essential to the valuation process. It provides needed background information about trends that affect property value and forms the basis for judgments about highest and best use, reconciliation and final opinion of value.

SPECIFIC DATA

Specific data includes information about the subject property and information about comparable sales, rentals, costs, expenses and other relevant data. The ability to collect specific data to consider, analyze and reconcile has a direct bearing on the credibility of the final opinion of value. Some sources of market data are real estate public records (e.g., deeds, transfer tax records, assessment records), real estate newspapers, commercial publications, general circulation newspapers. Realtors and real estate brokers, sales data shared with other appraisers, property mangers, multiple listing services, atlases and survey maps.

Improvement cost data can be obtained directly from the market and from published cost services. It can be adjusted for time with the use of appropriate cost indices.

The market is also the source of income and expense data used in the income approach and to develop capitalization rates.

Collecting data is fundamental to the valuation process. It is the selection, analysis and reconciliation of the data collected from a wide variety of sources that forms the basis for a credible opinion of value.

REVIEW QUESTIONS

1. General data can be divided into four types of information:
   a. primary, secondary, old, new.
   b. primary, secondary, social, economic.
   c. social, economic, governmental, environmental.
   d. local, regional, state, national.

2. Primary data becomes secondary:
   a. when it contains only items of secondary interest.
   b. when the government declassifies it.
   c. after it is 90 days old.
   d. when it is published and available to the public.

3. Macro data does not include:
   a. national employment trends.
   b. the number of households in the subject town,
   c. regional income levels
   d. the number of people employed locally.

4. Micro data includes which of the following?
   a. Number of apartment units in the subject's community
   b. Local vacancy rates
   c. Census data on household income.
   d. All of the above

5. General data is essential in valuation because it:
   a. provides background.
   b. supplies information about trends.
   c. forms the basis for judgments about highest and best use.
   d. All of the above

6. Specific data helps:
   a. set the fee for the appraisal.
   b. determine how long it will take to complete the assignment.
   c. the appraiser choose the computer software to use.
   d. None of the above

7. Which of the following is not usually in the assessor's records?
   a. Name of the owner
   b. Dimensions of the property
   c. The owner's occupation
   d. Last sale price of the property

8. One of the problems with MLS data is:
   a. Gross living area measurements may be incorrect
   b. The description of functional and economic obsolescence may be incorrect.
   c. The condition of the house is exaggerated.
   d. All of the above

9. It is important to verify comparable sale data:
   a. to determine if all depreciation has been considered.
   b. to determine if the measurements are correct.
   c. to determine if the price and terms are accurate.
   d. All of the above

10. The basis of the three approaches to value is:
    a. general data.
    b. specific data.
    c. tax data.
    d. site data.

11. What information about a property usually can be found on its deed?
    a. Mortgage balance
    b. Tax rate
    c. Legal description
    d. None of the above

12. What recent laws are making it harder for appraisers to obtain information?
    a. National security regulations
    b. Copyright laws
    c. Privacy laws
    d. None of the above

ANSWERS TO REVIEW QUESTIONS

The answer to each question is indicated by the letter a, b, c or d below. The explanation of the answer is indicated by a numbered arrow that points to the appropriate paragraph on the page of the text indicated by the page number following the answer.

Q 3.1	c	Page 3-2
Q 3.2	d	Page 3-2
Q 3.3	a	Page 3-2
Q 3.4	d	Page 3-2
Q 3.5	d	Page 3-2
Q 3.6	d	Page 3-3
Q 3.7	c	Page 3-6
Q 3.8	d	Page 3-7
Q 3.9	d	Page 3-8
Q 3.10	b	Page 3-3
Q 3.11	c	Page 3-5
Q 3.12	c	Page 3-7

CHAPTER 4

Valuation Procedures - General Data Analysis

"To treat your facts with imagination is one thing, but to imagine your facts is another."

John Burroughs
The Naturalist (1837-1921)

Important Words and Key Concepts

Words on this list are highlighted in this chapter.
They are also defined in the Glossary at the back of this text.

Balance of Payments

Basic Employment

Economic Base

Economic Base Analysis

General Data

Market Area

Neighborhood

Non-Basic Employment

SMSA (Standard Metropolitan
  Statistical Area)

Specific Data

ORGANIZATION OF GENERAL DATA

4.1 ▶Over the course of time an appraiser collects a great deal of data. It is very easy to get overwhelmed with all the data one soon collects. *Chapter #3* stated that the first step in organizing it is to divide the data into *general data* and *specific data* and the second step is to further divide the data into categories. This chapter covers the organization and analysis of general data.

4.2 ▶There is no single preferred way to divide general data. One popular way to organize general data is geographically. Start by sorting the data into broad categories: international and national, state and/or regional data. A method that is growing in popularity is to make the next smaller division of the data the market area which it covers. Many appraisers still use the community as a convenient category. When the community or market area is large the data can further divided by neighborhood.

INTERNATIONAL AND NATIONAL DATA

There is so much data available that it is difficult to collect meaningful international and national data files in an appraisal office. Fortunately there is so much of this type of data online that it no longer is necessary to keep this data in an office file. The exception is those items you run across that may be useful in future appraisals in your area. For example your market area is one that has automobile manufacturing as a base industry and you read an article in the Wall Street Journal that the parent company is considering closing some of their plants. You might want to save this article for future reference and refer to it if you are appraising a property who's value is dependent upon the automobile plant in your market area.

THE NATIONAL ECONOMY

The condition of the U.S. economy is very important to any real estate appraisal.
4.3 ▶Changes in interest rates, taxes on real estate profits, and the rate of inflation are just a few of the national economic trends that directly affect the value of property. Some of the national data that is helpful to keep track of is: gross national product, balance of payments to other nations, consumer price index, interest rates, employment and unemployment figures, housing starts, building permits and national home sales.

REGIONAL AND STATE ECONOMIC DATA

4.4 ▶Whether the appraiser sub-divides their data by region or state depends where they are and how directly their state's economy is tied to the economic profile of the wider region. Usually, an appraiser will collect and analyze data about housing starts, house sales, house price trends, employment and unemployment rates, plus the overall condition of the real estate market in their area.

Understanding regional and state economic trends and their impact on real estate values is an important part of an appraiser's overall grasp of market conditions which will affect properties in their area.

MARKET AREA DATA

Definition of Market Area

The term market area is used in the 2006 Uniform Standards of Professional Appraisal Practice, Standards Rule 1-3 which states:

"When necessary for credible assignment results in developing a market value opinion, an appraiser must:

(a) identify and analyze the effect on use and value of existing land use regulations, reasonably probable modifications of such land use regulations, economic supply and demand, the physical adaptability of the real estate and market area trends."

The definition provided in *The Appraisal of Real Estate* is helpful in understanding what is meant by **market area**:

> "In this edition...(the term) market area will be used for specific reference to the local market area as defined in the appraisal report as well as in the general manner the term has be traditionally used in market analysis. The term **neighborhood**, which is still used on the major residential appraisal report forms, will continue to be used for references to the concept of a specifically defined geographic area characterized by complementary land uses." [1]

The appraiser should also collect data about educational facilities, service operations, shopping facilities, health care providers, entertainment, recreational facilities, places of worship, and tourist attractions which will affect the economic health of the market area. To make a complete market area analysis it is also necessary to have data about household incomes, the relationship between home ownership and rental properties, rental levels, general property values, vacancy rates, proposed new developments and current construction.

Economic Trends

The most important category of general data is economic trends. Some of these trends have a direct effect on the value of real property. The data should provide information about economic changes that have occurred that will help the appraiser make forecasts about the probable direction of the regional and local economies as they will affect the subject property.

ANALYSIS OF GENERAL DATA

ANALYSIS OF INTERNATIONAL AND NATIONAL DATA

In today's world, the economic well-being of one nation may have a direct impact on the well-being of other nations. For example, the ability of China to produce quality

---

1 Appraisal of Real Estate, 12th Edition, Appraisal Institute, Chicago, IL 2001.

goods at low prices directly affects the American economy. The production of low cost textiles by China directly affects textile production in the United States and all industries associated with textiles, from production to fashion merchandising. Foreign automobiles are having a major effect on automobile production in the Detroit market area. The same is true of oil production and pricing by Middle Eastern countries, and the changing consumption patterns for energy in rapidly expanding economies such as China and India. The state of the national economy in terms of the global market has a direct effect on all real estate.

National Economic Policy Data

National economic policies and legislative initiatives such as changes to Federal tax laws have a significant impact on various classes of commercial property. Adoption of changes concerning the deductibility of property taxes and mortgage interest from a homeowner's income would have a significant effect on home prices. A change in the immigration laws could substantially affect the economy of those market areas that depend heavily on migrant workers.

Analysis of Regional and State Economic Data

There are many differences in the economic health of various states and regions which directly affect real estate value. Some states have little or no population growth, while others, especially in the sun belt, are growing at a fast pace. Generally, when population increases demand for real estate increases and real estate values increase. Conversely when population declines it tends to have an adverse impact on property values.

Analysis of Market Area Data

MARKET AREA ECONOMIC ANALYSIS
The principal characteristic of real estate is its fixity of location. Real property is either the benefactor or the victim of its surroundings. The economic environment of a residential property and its market area are of vital concern to the appraiser. A close relationship exists between the economic analysis of a market area and its residential market.

One major limiting factor affecting the market value of real estate is the economic potential of its market area. Just as a close relationship exists between economic development and income producing properties, such as office buildings or retail stores, there is also a high correlation between the economic potential of a specific market area and the marketability of residential properties within that area.

A growing city tends to experience increases in real estate values, while a city with decreasing population and economic resources will tend to experience a decline in property values.

DEFINITION OF MARKET AREA ECONOMIC ANALYSIS
Market area economic analysis has other names. It frequently is referred to as **economic base analysis**, regional and local economic analysis, and input-output analysis. These terms all refer to the economic health of an area and its ability to bring in income from outside the area. This is similar to international trade situations where countries seek to establish favorable trade balances. For example, if the United States sells more to Canada

than Canada sells to the United States, the ***balance of payments*** will be in favor of the United States - that is, gold or its equivalent in terms of money will flow into the United States, enhancing its economic growth.

This same concept applies to the market area. The appraiser must compare and contrast the growth potential of a particular market area with other market areas of similar characteristics, size and physical location. In which market area is it most desirable to live? Which market area has the greatest growth potential? Which has the greatest protection against unfavorable economic forces? Obviously, the market area that rates highest on each of these three questions, is the one that has the most favorable future.

IDENTIFICATION OF A MARKET AREA

4.8 ▶ The boundaries of a market area must be identified before the appraiser can do this analysis. Most simply, a market area is a geographic area that is contiguous and operates as one unit. It may be a single section of one city, or cross state boundaries, such as the greater Louisville area or the greater St. Louis area. Quite often, a market area encompasses several counties. It may be the ***Standard Metropolitan Statistical Area (SMSA)*** as defined by Bureau of the Census. Statistical data is most readily available for these standardized areas. Because substantial data is necessary to analyze the potential of a specific area, it is good practice to analyze defined areas whenever practical.

THE GROWTH OF CITIES

To understand the importance of market area economic analyses, one must understand why cities exist at all and why they grow in a particular location.

4.9 ▶ Humans are social beings. Historically, they came together for defense and self-protection or to facilitate trade among themselves and outsiders, or for religious motives, such as to escape persecution. Usually a combination of reasons bring people together into communities.

Why did people gather at a particular geographic point to develop a community? One obvious reason is location on established trade routes or other points of transportation access such as rivers. Specific points along such routes may be created by convenience For example, one day's travel distance from an established point or access to raw materials and natural resources, such as a waterfall or other source of energy. Access to markets for the products being developed also creates communities. Added to these reasons is the catalytic force that has played a significant role in recent community growth — a favorable climate. The greatest growth in the United States in the past half century has been in warmer, more moderate climates.

Economic Base Analysis

The ***economic base*** of a market area are the activities that allow local businesses, manufacturing, and institutions to generate income from outside the market area. Economic base analysis is the study of these activities.

Appraisers are concerned primarily with the economic potential of a market area as it affects the market value of the properties they will be appraising. They must therefore look at the economic potential of the entire market area as compared to competitive market areas.

Real estate markets depend on growth or the expectation of growth. Although there may be short-run market conditions that are favorable without growth, such circumstances are rare. The market for residential properties depends heavily on families and their economic capacity to purchase homes, which depends, in turn, on their jobs and the competitive position and security of those jobs. If the average family income within a specific market area is higher than the national or state average, the potential for purchase or construction of homes in that market area is greater than in other competitive market areas.

It may be helpful to understand the relationship between residential values and the market area's economic future by pointing out that certain areas in the United States are recognized for their special economic conditions, both good and bad. For example, much publicity has been given to Appalachia and its economic problems.

Certain sections of the northeastern United States are experiencing marginal economic growth because their major industries have moved to other sections of the country or have become obsolete, or are being outsourced internationally. In contrast, some geographic areas are under-going significant physical and economic growth. The Sun Belt states of Florida, Georgia, Texas, Colorado, New Mexico, Arizona and California have enjoyed spectacular growth over the past two decades.

Population increase alone does not imply sound economic growth; there must be a correspondingly strong economic base to ensure that the area can support itself and be competitive with others. Over-dependence on one industry, such as oil in the southwestern U.S., could bring about rapid destabilization of the real estate market in such areas when the economics of that industry change. Changing priorities in the defence industry dramatically impacts communities with weapons factories, military hardware production facilities, or naval bases. When these industries are replaced by similar or higher paying jobs, the economy and real estate values in the market area are stable or improved. If these industries are not replaced, a period of decline occurs.

Finally, a lack of proper planning and overuse of natural resources such as water and timber may adversely affect rapidly-growing areas in terms of future development potential. Steady growth requires adequate foresight and appropriate planning on the part of municipalities and regional governments.

BASIC AND NON-BASIC EMPLOYMENT

The economic potential of a market area is dependent on its ability to produce income. Market area economic analysis deals to a great extent with gathering and analyzing employment data. It involves the collection of statistics regarding the total basic employment within the market area plus similar statistics for non-basic employment.

4.10 ▶-- **Basic employment** is the type of employment that attracts dollars from consumers and others outside the market area being analyzed. This kind of employment is, by definition, the basis for the level of the economy in the area.

--**Non-basic employment** generates its income from within the market area. Lawyers, doctors and service employees, such as supermarket clerks or city sanitation workers, are included in this category.

Ideally, there must be both basic and non-basic employment in proper proportion to maximize the prosperity of an entire market area. A market area cannot thrive without these people and if they are insufficient in number to satisfy the needs of those in basic employment, the latter will become dissatisfied, less productive, and finally may begin to relocate to better areas with more competitive service sectors. There is no consistent standard preferred ratio of basic to non-basic employment within an economic market area. Such relationships are derived locally, and vary in accordance with the income level and nature of the basic employment. If the basic employees are primarily white-collar research and scientific personnel with extremely high levels of income, they will probably require more services; a ratio of two basic to one service employee might be appropriate. In other market areas, where basic employees have lower income levels, a ratio of three basic to one service employee might be entirely satisfactory. Certain special kinds of market areas occasionally have a ratio of one to one. The ratio itself is not important in the analysis of economic activity; however, it does affect the general social and economic climate in terms of the market area being seen by potential home buyers as a good, fair or less than satisfactory place to live.

Types of Data Collected

Data on basic employment is collected on an historical and current basis and divided into three major categories: industry; specialty, such as government and recreation; and trade, including retail, wholesale, finance and transportation. These categories are intended to include all types of basic employment and are considered to be the most critical in the estimation of the economic growth potential of the market area. They are rated according to predicted employment trends, diversification, and cyclical fluctuation. Diversification in basic employment and the need for types of basic employment that are not subject to cyclical fluctuation are important to maintain the economic viability of a market area.

INDUSTRY

The analysis of basic industry is made first and is typically given the greatest weight in an analysis of economic base. This basic employment category, also called manufacturing, includes all components of fabrication, assembly, manufacturing and extractive (mining) activities. Industry is the truly essential and fundamental area of employment for most communities, although there are some communities, such as Washington, DC that have virtually no industry. Most communities, however, still rely on industrial employment to carry the future of their economy. In some unique market areas, however, such as Silicon Valley in California, newer technologies are blurring the line between basic industry and service businesses. Is a computer, various software applications, and access to the Internet a service, a product or some combination of both? The same is true in communities, such as some university towns, where cutting-edge medical research is a major employer. Such facilities are quasi-industrial, and often produce a product, e.g., a new drug or treatment modality. However, their employment of high-level scientists and technicians, rather than semi-skilled or more traditional industrial workers, makes them a new type of basic industry.

SPECIALTY

This category includes non-industrial types of employment, such as government service, education and recreation. For purposes of economic base analysis, local government employees are not included. Only those whose salaries are paid by outside sources, such as a federal court in the market area which attracts its income from outside that market area, are considered. The fire department is paid from local tax revenue and therefore is not considered base employment. Likewise, education is limited to those institutions that attract most of their operating revenue from outside the economic area, such as a state university or a private college. Local elementary, junior and senior high schools are excluded as basic employment.

Recreational communities, such as Miami Beach, FL or Scottsdale, AZ, base their employment on providing tourist and retirement services and facilities. In such communities, the waiter employed in a hotel catering to out-of-town people is a basic employee, but the busboy in a restaurant catering primarily to local citizens is a non-basic employee. A major nationally-renowned medical facility, such as the Mayo Clinic in Rochester, MN, would be considered a basic employer.

TRADE

This category includes positions in retailing, wholesaling, finance and transportation that exist to serve users outside the economic market area. A regional shopping center that attracts those outside the market area as well as consumers inside the market area, is partially a basic employer. Major banks serving the entire state or region obviously attract some of their revenue from outside the local economic market area. The headquarters of a national bus service or moving company would be primarily a basic employer.

Local Resources

In analyzing the economic potential of a market area, the appraiser considers its primary physical and human resources. Obviously, a complete and thorough supply of data regarding the people who make up an economic area is essential. Also, information is required regarding its energy sources and physical resources, such as mineral and other types of natural resources. Favorable climate conditions may be considered a resource, especially in dealing with the recreational potential of a market area. Unfavorable factors such as smog, odors, polluted waters or hostile weather conditions are obviously a disadvantage. Capital resources that will be available are affected by the attitudes of bankers, investors, and other financial sources towards the market area.

Future Economic Activity

Economic base analysis is not merely a collection of data; it is developed so that the appraiser can project the economic potential of a defined area. It is useless to collect a mass of data and perform a thorough statistical analysis, and then fail to draw clear, concise conclusions regarding the future of the economic entity. This step is vital in the analysis of the economic potential of any market area. Concise and definitive projections regarding the competitive position of the market area, compared to other market areas and the nation as a whole, are essential. If such projections are not made, there is no justification for the economic base analysis.

Economic base analysis is not the only technique used in predicting the economic future of an area. An input/output analysis has been developed by urban economists to rate the economics of a market area on an income and expense basis. It may be further analyzed in terms similar to a profit and loss statement. Urban economists have also developed a regional accounting system that compares one part of a region or area with other parts to see which has competitive advantages.

Another type of analysis is referred to as a ***balance of payments***, which is basically a study to reveal historical, current, and future projected capacity for the favorable balance of trade in one economic market area as compared to the world, the nation, and other competitive economic areas. All economic analyses, however, are projections or estimates of future trends. The appraiser must recognize that all such projections must be used with caution.

SUMMARY

General data is frequently organized into categories such as international, national, regional/ state, and market area data. An effective organizational structure for relevant economic data will allow the appraiser to update the information with a minimum of effort.

It is important for the appraiser to to analyze the general data that has an impact on real estate value in a local market area. The relevant considerations for one market area might be materially different than the relevant general data for another market area. Which general data is relevant in a particular market area is dependent on the economic base for the market area.

Basic market area data is frequently divided into basic industry data, specialty data for non-industrial employment and trade data.

The value of a parcel of real estate reflects what surrounds it. Real property is subject to trends in its market area, state, and region, as well as its general location within the nation. The economic potential of the market area can be analyzed in a logical and orderly manner. This type of analysis emphasizes the future economic potential of the market area, not its past or present status. Future trends are paramount in such analyses.

To analyze a market area, it must be properly identified and its boundaries located. Typically, an established type of market area is chosen for which statistics are readily available, such as an SMSA.

Market area economic analysis requires identification of local resources, establishment of primary and secondary data sources, and careful consideration by the appraiser of the future economic potential of the area.

REVIEW QUESTIONS

1. The first step in organizing data is to:
    a. arrange the data into alphabetical order.
    b. enter the data into a computer.
    c. divide the data into general data and specific data.
    d. None of the above

2. The USPAP recommends that general data be organized by:
    a. social, economic, governmental and residential forces.
    b. neighborhood, community, state and national trends.
    c. climate divided into summer, winter, spring and fall.
    d. None of the above

3. Important information about the national economy for appraisers includes:
    a. interest rates.
    b. taxes on real estate profits.
    c. overall rate of inflation.
    d. All of the above

4. Important information about the regional and/or state economy includes:
    a. housing starts.
    b. house sales.
    c. house price trends.
    d. All of the above

5. The 2006 USPAP Standard Rule 1-3 states "When the value opinion to be developed is market value...the appraiser must:
    a. identify all of the liens and encumbrances."
    b. provide a map of the market area."
    c. identify and analyze market area trends."
    d. None of the above

6. A close relationship exists between the economic analysis of a market area and the analysis of:
    a. the national economic infrastructure.
    b. its residential property.
    c. state employment statistics.
    d. All of the above

7. Market area economic analysis has other names. It is also referred to as:
    a. economic base analysis.
    b. regional economic analysis.
    c. input-output analysis.
    d. All of the above

8. The _____ of a market area must be identified before an appraiser can analyze it.
    a. boundaries
    b. population
    c. topography
    d. None of the above

9. Historical reasons why people gather at a particular geographic point to develop a community are:
    a. self defense and protection.
    b. trade.
    c. religious motives.
    d. All of the above

10. Basic employment is the type of employment that:
    a. attracts dollars from outside the market area.
    b. depends upon dollars generated from within the market area.
    c. typically is employment that is not industrial.
    d. All of the above

11. Basic employment usually includes:
    a. industrial employment.
    b. specialty shop employment.
    c. retail employment.
    d. All of the above

ANSWERS TO REVIEW QUESTIONS

The answer to each question is indicated by the letter a, b, c or d below. The explanation of the answer is indicated by a numbered arrow that points to the appropriate paragraph on the page of the text indicated by the page number following the answer.

Q 4.1	c	Page 4-2
Q 4.2	d	Page 4-2
Q 4.3	d	Page 4-2
Q 4.4	d	Page 4-2
Q 4.5	c	Page 4-3
Q 4.6	b	Page 4-4
Q 4.7	d	Page 4-4
Q 4.8	a	Page 4-5
Q 4.9	d	Page 4-5
Q 4.10	a	Page 4-6
Q 4.11	a	Page 4-7

CHAPTER 5

Property Description - Location Characteristics (Market Area & Neighborhood)

"Everyone is surrounded by a neighborhood of voluntary spies"
Jane Austen
(1775-1817)

Important Words and Key Concepts
Words on this list are highlighted in this chapter.
They are also defined in the Glossary at the back of this text.

Detrimental Conditions	Market Area	Predominant Land Use
Economic Forces	Period of Decline	Rejuvenation
Gentrification	Period of Equilibrium	Special Amenities
Growth Period–	Period of Stability	Subdivision Regulations
Linkage	Planned Unit Development (PUD)	Urban Renewal

SOCIAL, ECONOMIC, GOVERNMENTAL AND ENVIRONMENTAL INFLUENCES

5.1 ▶The value of every property is determined by all the significant social, economic, governmental, and environmental influences that affect property values in the property's market area.

The appraiser gathers this information from general and specialized publications including national and local newspapers, financial magazines and real estate appraisal publications. Analysis of current economic conditions such as interest rates, effective purchasing power, construction costs, and availability of financing is included here.

This information changes on a regular basis. For example, mortgage interest rate changes have an immediate effect on the value of real estate. National news about terrorist activities, government environmental regulations, employment, etc., all affect the value of real estate. It is also incumbent upon the appraiser to keep current on both national and regional news, and to consider how current events impact the value of real estate.

REGIONAL, COMMUNITY AND MARKET AREA DATA

Events that change the **economic forces** outside the subject property influence its value. This is why an appraisal includes information about the region, community and market area, such a population characteristics, price levels, employment opportunities, economic base analysis, etc. This chapter focuses primarily on the market area and neighborhood of the subject property.

Market Area Analysis

5.2 ▶Market analysis is a relatively new term in real estate appraising. Analysis of the area in which the property is located traditionally started with an analysis of the neighborhood. Some appraisers broadened the area to encompass a district, while others used the community as the next larger area to describe and analyze. The use of the term market area for this broader area hopefully will reduce some of the confusion that has existed in the past.

Market Area Definition

Market area is a defined geographic area in which the subject property competes for the
5.3 ▶attention of market participants; the term usually broadly defines an area containing diverse land uses. The boundaries of a market area are defined by the appraiser and reasonably may vary from appraiser to appraiser.

Neighborhood Definition

"A group of complementary land uses; a related grouping of inhabitants, buildings, or business properties." [1] Similar to market area, the boundaries of a neighborhood are defined by the appraiser and they too may vary from appraiser to appraiser.

---

[1] **The Appraisal of Real Estate, 12th Edition, Appraisal Institute, Chicago, IL 2001**

THE LIFE CYCLE OF A MARKET AREA

Market areas are established when new buildings are constructed together with streets, utilities and other services. Sometimes a new and different market area is established where an old market area existed. This transition is most common where a residential neighborhood changes into a commercial or industrial neighborhood. With the help of **urban renewal**, an industrial or commercial market area can transition into a residential market area.

The first stage of a new **market area** is the **growth period**. This growth period may last for a year or so, or it may be spread over many years. It may continue until all the available land is used or it may stop when the demand for new property diminishes or acceptable financing is not available. If the market area is successfully developed, there will be active building. New construction will attract new inhabitants and businesses and usually the market area gains public recognition and favor.

When the growth period ends, the market area enters a **period of equilibrium**. Changes rarely stop completely but in this stabilizing period they may slow down considerably. New construction may continue on a limited basis as demand increases or financing terms improve and make building profitable. The **period of stability** is characterized by lack of marked gains or losses. Many market areas are stable for long periods of time. There is no pre-set life expectancy for a market area and decline is not imminent in all older market areas. The period of decline starts when the market area is less able to compete with other market areas. During this period, prices may have to be lowered to attract buyers to the area. Among the characteristics of a declining market area are properties in a poor state of maintenance, conversions to more intensive uses and a lack of enforcement of building codes and zoning regulations.

The **period of decline** may end when the market area changes to another **predominant land use** or uses, and a new market area is developed, or when it moves into a renewal period. This may be caused by a change in one or more of the economic, social, physical or governmental forces. For example, expansion of commercial activities in the community may decrease the demand for housing and increase the demand for commercial properties in the market area.

Market area **rejuvenation** can also be the result of organized community activities such as redevelopment programs, rebuilding and historical renovation. The rebirth of an older market area is often caused by a combination of these factors, some of which are a result of planning and outside aid, and some simply due to changing preferences and lifestyles.

After the rebirth of an older market area, the life cycle may be repeated in which a period of stability and eventually a period of decline may again occur unless changes in the forces that affect desirability and marketability take place.

URBAN ECONOMIC RELATIONSHIPS

The relationship of a market area to the rest of the urban community is measured in both distance and time. The same is true for the relationship between a neighborhood and the rest of the market area in which it is located. This relationship is known as the **linkage** of a neighborhood, which connects it to the origins and destinations of the people and businesses in the market area. In residential neighborhoods, this linkage is primarily to where people go to work, shop and go for recreation. For commercial neighborhoods, it is how potential customers get to the neighborhood. For industrial neighborhoods, it is how the workers get to work, how the industries get their raw materials and how they ship their finished products to their markets.

To analyze the impact of the linkage of a neighborhood, the appraiser should identify important linkages and measure their time distances by the most commonly used types of transportation. The most suitable transportation often depends on the preferences and needs of the residents in the neighborhood.

Existing and projected future linkages should be analyzed and judged in terms of how well they serve the typical resident. Much consideration should be given to transportation by automobile and trucks because these are important types of transportation for almost every neighborhood. However, in some areas, especially around larger metropolitan cities, public transportation is especially important because it is difficult to drive and park cars in the city.

When the appraiser reconciles the neighborhood analysis section of the report, the reconciliation should contain the appraiser's opinion of how the urban economic relationship of the neighborhood to its market area will affect the value of properties in the neighborhood.

NEIGHBORHOOD ANALYSIS

Every property is an integral part of its neighborhood, market area and its community. The market value of a property is substantially affected by the neighborhood in which the property is located. Therefore, the primary purpose of neighborhood analysis is to identify the geographic area that is subject to the same influences as the subject property. Prices paid for comparable properties in the defined area theoretically reflect the positive and negative influences operating in that particular neighborhood. Two houses with similar physical characteristics may have significantly different market values due to their locations in different neighborhoods, even when they are in the same market place.

In the appraisal process, neighborhood analysis provides the background for valuation. Information that has no bearing on value is irrelevant and may mislead the reader who can rightfully assume everything in the appraisal report is related to the appraisal process and the final estimate of value. Incorrect use of neighborhood analysis can lead to double counting and false conclusions.

Assume, for example, that after complete neighborhood analysis, the appraiser delineates the neighborhood and obtains an indication of value based on recent prices received for similar properties in the same neighborhood. In such a case, it is incorrect to adjust value for neighborhood influences because these influences are assumed to already be reflected in the observed market prices.

The depth of analysis varies according to the need, but a neighborhood must be defined in terms of some common characteristics and trends in order to interpret market evidence properly. The appraiser should avoid reliance on the racial, religious or ethnic characteristics of the residents. Racial and other ethnic factors are not reliable predictors of value trends and use of such factors by the appraiser in neighborhood analysis can be misleading. People's reactions and preferences are so diverse and variable that they are not readily quantifiable in the course of the appraisal process.

Consideration of observable neighborhood conditions and trends is an important aspect of neighborhood analysis and typically includes observation of factors that enhance or detract from property values.

Objectivity in Neighborhood Analysis

Objectivity is essential in identifying and discussing neighborhood conditions, trends or factors. For instance, general reference to a presumed *pride of ownership* (or lack thereof) may be too vague and too subjective to be indicative of an actual contribution to or detraction from property values. The presence of **special amenities** or **detrimental conditions** should be noted and described clearly and carefully.

The appraiser's findings with respect to neighborhood conditions and the effects of these conditions on property values are considered by buyers, sellers, brokers, lenders, courts, arbiters, public officials and other decision-makers or advisors. Because of this broad influence, the appraiser is often called upon to provide specific evidence of neighborhood conditions and trends and to elaborate the findings in a written appraisal report. The use of photographs and detailed field notes enables the appraiser to recall important evidence and verify the facts considered in the analysis.

The appraiser should avoid generalizations with respect to the desirability of particular neighborhoods. Older urban neighborhoods, as well as newer suburban subdivisions, can attract a wide range of residents. Neighborhood trends do not necessarily depend upon the age of the neighborhood or the income of neighborhood residents.

Neighborhood Definition

What constitutes a neighborhood is difficult to describe precisely. In fact, its meaning has been changing. Neighborhoods historically were defined as a segment of a community that gave a noticeable impression of unity. This unity might have been based on similar uses of the properties within the neighborhood such as mostly industrial plants, retail stores or multiple or single family housing. It also might have been a unity of structural appearance, such as mostly colonial or contemporary style buildings. It sometimes was a unity based on the economic, religious, racial or ethnic status of most of the residents of the neighborhood. For example, some neighborhoods would be occupied predominantly by workers from a local industry or by persons of a particular national origin, race or religion. Appraisers should avoid the description of a neighborhood that could violate the Federal Fair Housing Act.

Neighborhoods that can be described based on one homogeneous factor are becoming less common. Often industrial, commercial and residential uses all exist in the same neighborhood. Likewise, people with a variety of economic, ethnic, racial and religious backgrounds now often live compatibly together in the same neighborhood.

The criteria for neighborhood analysis are clearly changing, reflecting changes in our social structures and attitudes. Obsolete standards of conformity have no place in modern neighborhood analysis. Broad federal and state fair housing laws have made discrimination on the basis of racial, religious or ethnic factors unlawful in the sale, rental and financing of housing. These laws, and changing social norms, have contributed to the establishment and maintenance of many stable, integrated, heterogeneous residential areas.

Today a neighborhood tends to be any separately identifiable cohesive area within a community with some commonality of interest shared by its occupants. Some neighborhoods may have recognizable natural or man-made boundaries. Neighborhoods sometimes have their own names, such as Old Town or Pigeon Hills, but frequently large neighborhoods actually consist of many sub-neighborhoods with different characteristics. A neighborhood may be as large as an entire community, or as small as a one-block or two-block area.

Neighborhood Boundaries

The first step in the study of a neighborhood is to identify its boundaries. Sometimes these are natural physical barriers such as lakes, rivers, streams, cliffs, swamps and valleys. They also can be highways, main traffic arteries, railroad tracks, canals and other man-made boundaries. The boundary of a residential neighborhood may also be a change of land use to commercial, industrial, institutional or a public park. Some boundaries are clearly defined, while others are more difficult to identify precisely.

1. Inspection of the area's physical characteristics: The appraiser should drive around to develop a sense of the area, particularly the degree of similarity in land uses, types of structures, architectural styles, maintenance and upkeep. On a map of the area, an appraiser should note points where these characteristics show perceptible changes and should note any physical barriers, such as major streets, hills, rivers, and railroads, that coincide with such changes. New software such as Google Earth - www.google.com provide another effective means of making this determination.

2. Drawing preliminary boundaries on a map: The appraiser should draw lines that connect the points where physical characteristics change. The appraiser should identify the streets, hills, rivers, railroads, and so forth, that coincide with or that are near the shifts in physical characteristics.

3. Testing preliminary boundaries against socioeconomic characteristics of the area's population. If possible, the appraiser should obtain accurate data concerning the ages, occupations, incomes and educational levels of the neighborhood occupants. The Bureau of the Census, U.S. Department of Commerce, collects such data every 10 years. Data that pertain to population and housing characteristics, employment, and income are also available.

Reliable data may also be available from local chambers of commerce, universities, and research organizations. In unusual cases, the appraiser may also consider sampling the population of the area to obtain an indication of the relevant characteristics.

The appraiser may informally interview neighborhood occupants, businesspeople, brokers, and community representatives to determine their perceptions about how far the neighborhood extends, and its current boundaries.

Neighborhood Change

The analysis of the neighborhood continues with a description of the properties within the neighborhood. In addition to single-family housing, a typical residential neighborhood may contain multi-family dwellings, retail stores, service establishments, schools, houses of worship, theaters, municipal buildings, health institutions and sometimes industrial and commercial buildings.

Part of this analysis is the consideration of discernible patterns of urban growth that will influence the neighborhood. Careful analysis can reveal the general trends in the surrounding community area and the patterns of growth, decay and renewal that will affect the subject neighborhood.

Few neighborhoods are fixed in character. Most are dynamic in nature and are changing at various rates of speed. What is happening in one neighborhood in a community often affects other neighborhoods in the same and nearby communities. As new neighborhoods in a community are developed, they compete with existing neighborhoods. An added supply of new homes also tends to induce shifts from old to new. New neighborhoods may have the advantage of new housing stock. Older neighborhoods may have the advantage of closer location to places of work and proximity to cultural activities. A community's historic significance, and access to parks, recreational facilities and shopping also affect the competitive position of a neighborhood. All things being equal, however, a new house usually has an advantage over an older one in the same market.

EVIDENCE OF NEIGHBORHOOD CHANGE

An appraiser often detects neighborhood change, or transition, by variations within the neighborhood. For example, a neighborhood in which some homes are well maintained and others are not, may indicate that the neighborhood is in the process of decline or conversely of revitalization. The introduction of different uses, such as rooming houses or offices, into a single-family residential neighborhood indicates a possible change. These new uses may indicate potential increases or decreases in neighborhood property values.

The changes in one neighborhood are usually influenced by changes occurring in others and in the larger market area. In any relatively stable city, for example, the rapid growth of one neighborhood or district may adversely affect a competitive neighborhood or district. A city's growth may reach the point where accessibility to the center from the more remote districts is difficult. In such instances, the establishment of new, competing business centers may better serve the needs of the outlying neighborhoods. Thus, commercial sub-centers come into being and a city's pattern becomes complex.

GENTRIFICATION AND DISPLACEMENT

A relatively recent neighborhood phenomenon is called **gentrification**, where middle-income and upper-income buyers purchase properties in rundown areas, and renovate or rehabilitate them. Gentrification appears to be the result of an increase of smaller families and singles in metropolitan areas who prefer living in proximity to urban cultural activities and central business district employment opportunities.

5.8

When gentrification occurs, existing residents often become displaced. The existing residents are often lower-income families, who moved into certain older neighborhoods in various cities that middle and upper-income residents have either left or did not move into because they found the neighborhoods unappealing and unattractive. Often as a result, two or more households occupy what was formerly a single-family residence. Some neighborhoods became blighted due to these influences.

ANALYSIS OF VALUE INFLUENCE FORCES

To understand these life cycles and how market areas and neighborhoods change requires knowledge of the relevant physical, social, economic and governmental factors that affect value. The following outline covers these factors. After the outline, each of the considerations is developed in more detail.

PHYSICAL OR ENVIRONMENTAL FORCES

1.   Location within the market area
2.   Barriers and boundaries
3.   Topography
4.   Soil, drainage and climate
5.   Services and utilities
6.   Proximity to supporting facilities
7.   Street patterns
8.   Patterns of land use
9.   Conformity of structure
10. Appearance
11. Special amenities
12. Nuisances and hazards
13. Age and condition of residences and other improvements

ECONOMIC FORCES

1.   Relation to community growth
2.   Economic profile of residents
3.   New construction and vacant land
4.   Turnover and vacancy rates

GOVERNMENTAL FORCES

1.   Taxation and special assessments
2.   Public and private restrictions
3.   Schools
4.   Planning and subdivision regulations

SOCIAL FORCES

1.   Population characteristics
2.   Community and neighborhood associations
3.   Crime rates

Physical or Environmental Factors

These factors cover conditions of the natural and man-made environment that physically define and limit the neighborhood.

LOCATION WITHIN THE MARKET AREA AND COMMUNITY

The location of a neighborhood in relation to the larger market area is important. A neighborhood adjacent to the central business district, for example, may benefit from the convenience of local shopping and municipal services, or it may suffer from exposure to a higher crime rate and heavy traffic. Locations in the direction of growth may benefit, while those away from growth may suffer.

BARRIERS AND BOUNDARIES

Both natural and man-made boundaries can effectively protect and define a neighborhood. These boundaries frequently help to reinforce the neighborhood identity, particularly when they are prominent landmarks such as a large park, super highway or river. Explicit boundaries are usually a favorable characteristic.

TOPOGRAPHY

Like barriers and boundaries, topography may be natural or man-made conditions of terrain. Typically, the desirability of various topography depends upon the nature of the residential development. For large-lot, high-value properties, hillside or wooded sites are often at a premium; tract developers, however, usually seek a level area or plateau which is more conducive to subdivision construction. Proximity to a lake, river, swamp or salt marsh may constitute a topographical advantage or disadvantage. Good topography can contribute protection from wind, fog or flood as well as provide an attractive view. The preferred topography is a rolling terrain at a slightly higher elevation than surrounding neighborhoods. Values tend to rise with the elevation of the land in many areas. Values are penalized where the land is very flat or excessively rugged without reasonable access.

SOIL, DRAINAGE AND CLIMATE

The natural quality of the soil directly affects the cost to build and the value of residences. Its bearing quality, ability to support landscaping and lawns, and the absorption rate for water disposal must be considered.

Drainage of surface water and susceptibility to flooding also affect value. Flood maps are available for most communities and the appraisal report should indicate if the neighborhood and subject residence are subject to flooding. Even in neighborhoods not subject to flooding, the disposal of storm water is an important consideration. Sometimes because of proximity to water, mountains or other natural conditions, a neighborhood has a different climate than nearby neighborhoods which affects its competitive position, either positively or negatively.

SERVICES AND UTILITIES

The availability of services and utilities such as electricity, city water, sanitary sewers and natural gas affect the relative desirability of a neighborhood. Large price differentials for obtaining these services would also be detrimental to values.

PROXIMITY TO SUPPORT FACILITIES

In analyzing a neighborhood, the appraiser must consider the proximity of and accessibility to major support facilities, such as public transportation, places of worship, schools, shopping areas, recreational facilities and centers of employment. Some people prefer to live within reasonable walking distance of convenience stores and service establishments, yet such support facilities may inflict a commercial atmosphere on a residential neighborhood. Convenient access to these facilities often adds to the desirability of a neighborhood and to the values of homes in the area.

STREET PATTERNS
Streets are an important man-made physical element which can affect value. They are the entrances and exits of a neighborhood. The physical plan of a neighborhood is strongly influenced by its street pattern. The attractiveness of individual settings depends on the effective use of natural contours, wooded areas, ponds and other features. Contemporary planned neighborhoods make use of curving streets, cul-de-sacs with generous turn-around space, and circular drives. These act as deterrents to through traffic, which can be a hazard in older neighborhoods. Where well-planned streets reduce such traffic hazards, they make a neighborhood more aesthetically attractive, and help to preserve the unity of the area.

Ideally, expressways and boulevards should be outside the immediate residential neighborhood but should offer easy access from local streets. Traffic within the neighborhood should move easily and slowly.

PATTERNS OF LAND USE
The pattern of land use within a neighborhood often helps an appraiser estimate the stage in the life cycle of that neighborhood. A stable neighborhood has clearly defined areas for various uses, well-buffered areas between uses, and respect for zoning and deed restrictions which helps maintain neighborhood integrity.

CONFORMITY OF STRUCTURES
The character of a neighborhood is partially set by its typical house. The class of ownership, structural nature of the average house and its architectural style, combined with its age and condition are physical considerations that have an important impact on the desirability of the neighborhood. Widely diverse styles and levels of care often indicate a transitional period within a neighborhood.

APPEARANCE
Maintenance of individual homes and their architectural compatibility influence the general appearance of a neighborhood. Landscaping, plantings and open space preservation also directly affect the appearance of a neighborhood. Neatly kept yards, houses and community areas reflect on-going care by owners and residents.

SPECIAL AMENITIES
In neighborhood analysis, the consideration of amenities is of major importance. People tend to live in the best housing they can afford, and a major factor in higher priced housing is amenity value. The homebuyer in the lowest income group purchases shelter level housing that provides only the bare necessities. The more prosperous can afford to pay for external amenities such as parks, beaches, pools, tennis courts, country clubs and libraries. Amenities strongly improve a neighborhood's competitive position in attracting new residents.

NUISANCES AND HAZARDS
Noise, traffic congestion, smoke and other nuisances directly affect the desirability of a

neighborhood. Tolerance of nuisances and hazards tends to be inversely related to the income level of the residents. Values of properties tend to be higher in neighborhoods that have higher standards of public health, comfort and safety. A nearby factory complex or the flight path of an adjacent airport usually have a marked negative affect on the property values in a residential neighborhood.

AGE AND CONDITION OF IMPROVEMENTS

The age and condition of all residences in a neighborhood can affect the marketability of a house located in that neighborhood. Age alone may not be an indication. Buildings do eventually wear out even with good maintenance or they may become obsolete and therefore less marketable, or their location in relation to community growth may cause economic obsolescence. Regardless of age, delayed building maintenance may cause rapid loss of marketability. Several neglected houses in a neighborhood may not cause the entire neighborhood to decline in attractiveness, but as the percentage of neglected houses increases, there is a tendency for the entire neighborhood to follow the same pattern. Community and neighborhood associations often spur maintenance and repair programs, thereby preserving market value and preventing decline among residences in the neighborhood.

Economic Considerations

Economic considerations are those factors that are the result of **economic forces** affecting a market area and neighborhood.

RELATION TO COMMUNITY GROWTH

Property values in a neighborhood are directly affected by the growth pattern of the surrounding community. Houses in the path of an expanding community are usually marketable and tend to increase in value. Other neighborhoods that are less accessible to newly developing community centers or places of employment may be less desirable.

ECONOMIC PROFILE OF RESIDENTS

The income and employment profile of the residents of a neighborhood, and the corresponding price levels and rents these support, are important economic parameters in the analysis of a neighborhood. The type, stability and location of employment have a strong impact on the value of residential property, since employment determines, to a large degree, the ability of individuals to purchase or rent in a particular area. Income levels tend to set a value range for a neighborhood. The influence of neighborhood is often obvious; a superior house will be penalized for its location in a neighborhood that does not support its value.

Changes in purchasing power result in changes in property values. Therefore, substantial change affecting the incomes of people living in the area, as well as of those who constitute the market for property in the neighborhood, must be considered. A downward trend in the average income available for shelter usually previews a dip in property values.

NEW CONSTRUCTION AND VACANT LAND

Vacant land suitable for the construction of additional houses within a neighborhood may exist simply because the owners, for personal reasons, do not wish to develop or sell the land. It may forecast additional future construction activity or indicate a lack of effective demand.

If only a few vacant lots remain in a neighborhood, residential construction on them usually will not substantially affect values in the neighborhood. However, if they are zoned non-residential, or if variances are granted permitting non-residential construction, the non-conforming uses may have a direct adverse effect on the surrounding properties.

Proposed construction for the larger parcels of vacant land may substantially affect values in the neighborhood. Available information about proposed future development of these parcels is an integral part of the neighborhood analysis, and should be included in the appraisal.

TURNOVER AND VACANCY RATE

The rate and duration of vacancies is another statistical indicator of the economic health of a neighborhood. Some turnover of properties within a neighborhood is usually a sign of a healthy market. At the same time, a neighborhood that is stable and attractive continues to hold a majority of its residents. High rates of long-term vacancy may signal decline or the necessity of changes in use. A large number of *For Sale* signs may be a warning that the neighborhood is experiencing a downturn in stability. Reviewing newspaper ads offering available rentals and properties for sale helps the appraiser estimate the strength of housing demand and the extent of the supply.

Governmental Factors

These are based on the activities of government, including taxation, restrictions, schools, planning and building regulations.

TAXATION AND SPECIAL ASSESSMENTS

Neighborhoods are competitive with one another and the level of taxation can be an important deciding factor for potential residents. Taxation is often a significant variable in making comparisons from one neighborhood to another. Special assessments should be directly related to the extra services or advantages they provide, such as private beach association fees or extra fire protection costs. When special assessments become high compared to other houses in the market, they may seriously reduce the value of the highly taxed house. An unpaid special assessment lien will often reduce the value of the house by approximately the amount of the lien. This value reduction may be offset by the enhancement that results from the special improvement or service that is the basis of the assessment.

PUBLIC AND PRIVATE RESTRICTIONS

Zoning regulations and building codes are important guardians of stability for a neighborhood. They provide legal protection against adverse influences, nuisances and hazards. When special exceptions or variances are easily obtained without consideration for their effect on surrounding properties, the value of all houses in the neighborhood may be decreased. A breakdown in the enforcement of existing zoning and building regulations may also cause a decrease in value. Such violations often start with illegal signs, uses for businesses, and conversion to higher density uses than permitted by zoning.

Deed restrictions can protect properties from the negative impact of incompatible uses; breakdown of their enforcement may lead to lower values. Some deed restrictions written years ago, however, may be obsolete or unenforceable. For example, deed restrictions setting the minimum cost of construction may be meaningless based on today's costs.

The courts have also ruled that deed restrictions based on race, religion, or national origin are not enforceable. Generally, any deed restriction that is against the public interest is not enforceable.

SCHOOLS
Educational facilities may be a strong attraction for prospective home buyers. Families may be attracted to a neighborhood, at least in part, by its schools. Schools are of immediate interest to all families with children. Even homeowners with no children may consider the availability and quality of educational facilities when purchasing a house, because future buyers of their home may have children. Neighborhood schools may be of less importance where children are bussed to schools outside the area.

PLANNING AND SUBDIVISION REGULATIONS
Planning for the future development of a community is an important task of government. Such planning should include protection of the integrity and character of existing neighborhoods, while providing for anticipated future uses of undeveloped areas. Poor planning for recreational facilities, schools, service areas, and other needs of residents may lead to neighborhood disintegration and blight.

Requirements imposed on developers and sub-dividers called **subdivision regulations** influence the types and quality of basic services available to homeowners in the neighborhood and have a strong affect on the value of existing structures. The legal protection of open space areas such as wetlands acts as a deterrent to developers who may otherwise sacrifice the special character of a neighborhood's natural environment in order to build the maximum number of units.

One way communities can control development is by using Planned Unit Developments (PUDs). Special zoning districts are created in which developers can present to the community planning authority plans for developments that make use of the features of the land the community wishes to preserve. The developer is rewarded for this type of planning by being allowed to increase the density of the development.

Social Forces

Social factors include population characteristics, community and neighborhood organizations and crime level.

POPULATION CHARACTERISTICS
Population trends and characteristics indicated by U.S. Census figures or statistics compiled by local agencies are important tools in estimating the trend of a neighborhood.

It was once common practice by some appraisers to examine the racial composition of a neighborhood in an effort to detect signs of change that were assumed to be indications of a trend toward lower values. Such an approach is now regarded as illegal. This evolution in appraisal practice reflects a corresponding evolution in social attitudes and public policy. The old applications of the principle of racial or ethnic conformity have no place in current neighborhood analysis techniques. Changing social standards, supported by broad federal and state Fair Housing laws, have made it possible for the racial or ethnic composition of a neighborhood to change without values decreasing. They have also encouraged the establishment and maintenance of many stable, integrated residential areas. There is no factual support for the outdated assumption that racial or ethnic homogeneity is a requirement for maximum value.

Changing social standards and lifestyles now support a growing preference on the part of many people for social heterogeneity in their neighborhoods. In these areas, traditional social groupings are changing to reflect these social preferences. Analysis based on traditional, outdated and arbitrary social groupings has no relevance in current appraisal process. Some of the most desirable and dynamic urban neighborhoods reflect wide diversity in all parameters, from income level to racial and ethic make-up.

COMMUNITY AND NEIGHBORHOOD ASSOCIATIONS

A wide variety of community and neighborhood associations exist. Some are legal entities formed by the original developers of an area, with membership including all the owners within defined boundaries. Some of these organizations started before World War II, often in coastal communities, around lakes or other recreational areas. The developer might deed the beach, lake front or other desirable natural area to the association, which in turn maintains and controls it for the benefit of its members.

Associations are also formed to maintain and preserve exclusive subdivisions having common grounds, parks, courts and limited access. In addition to maintenance of common facilities, a major function of the association is to hire guards to keep uninvited guests off the association property. Some of the typical functions of this type of homeowners' association are:

- Maintaining commonly owned land, beaches, courts, pools, golf courses, etc.
- Collecting rubbish and garbage, removing snow, and sweeping streets.
- Providing and maintaining sewer disposal systems and water supply systems.
- Providing police and fire protection.
- Providing lifeguards on beaches, waterfronts and pools.

These groups often try to exercise considerable control by enforcing private covenants and restrictions that give them the right to approve the transfer of title or rental of property and to approve the style and size of any new buildings. They are also empowered to:

- establish an annual charge to be paid by the association members.
- put a lien on the property of owners who do not pay their charges.
- borrow money on behalf of the members.
- buy and sell property.

▶ **5.12** ▶ After World War II, the ***planned unit development (PUD)*** became popular. The developer of a PUD deeded to the local community the common land. When the community accepted the common land, it incurred a financial obligation to maintain it and also lost tax revenue on it. Because of these reasons and also because the land became usable by the whole community, many municipalities refused to accept such common land. Developers then formed private homeowners' associations to accept the land and maintain it. They found this was a good way to provide recreational facilities and often constructed swimming pools, tennis courts and golf courses on the common land as an added inducement to potential purchasers.

Other types of neighborhood organizations are formed on a voluntary basis by the residents in a neighborhood or segment of a neighborhood (for example, a block association). The purposes of these organizations are usually neighborhood preservation and enhancement, social interaction among the residents, and political lobbying efforts to prevent zoning changes the community believes to be detrimental to the neighborhood. Such groups also maintain contact with community officials to obtain services, facilities and improvements within the neighborhood. They may also become involved in political activities, supporting local candidates and parties. Neighborhood improvement projects with the members doing all or some of the work themselves, social gatherings, block parties, fairs, parades, etc., are sponsored by such community groups. Membership is voluntary and usually open to everyone living within the neighborhood.

Some associations have little or no effect on the value of property; they have limited functions, few activities and low dues or assessments. Other associations have a substantial impact on the value of property in their areas. Often they define a whole neighborhood. Houses that are in the association may have higher values than nearby houses that are not in the association. These associations usually control important recreational facilities and/or provide substantial needed services, security and other amenities.

The appraiser must investigate such associations to determine the facilities or services provided and the additional costs to individual property owners. When these services appear to be substantial or their cost is high, it is usually best to select comparables from within the association. It is often difficult to make a location adjustment to reflect the difference in value between houses in the association and those outside.

CRIME RATE

Unfortunately, the crime rate in many communities and neighborhoods continues to increase and the appraiser must consider the impact of crime level as part of the neighborhood analysis. When a neighborhood obtains the reputation of having an excessively high crime rate, some residents may leave and potential new residents are discouraged from buying homes there. Increased street lighting and police protection as well as vigilance on the part of residents in reporting suspicious activities to the police may help reduce the crime rate.

MARKET AREA AND NEIGHBORHOOD STABILITY

The stability of a market area and neighborhood is largely determined by the reasons why its residents (residential, commercial and industrial) want to live and work in the market area and neighborhood. Occupants are attracted to and choose to remain in a locale for its status, physical environment, services, affordability, convenience and a variety of other reasons that are particular to a specific neighborhood.

When making a market area and neighborhood analysis, the appraiser attempts to identify the social, economic, governmental, environmental and other influences that attract people and businesses to that neighborhood, versus competitive areas.

The identification and description of these influences is not simple. Some characteristics have greater influence than others. Also, as these characteristics change, the desirability of the neighborhood to its population may change.

When considering the relative importance of these characteristics, the appraiser should be aware that they tend to overlap. Thus, in the final analysis, it is how the subject market area and neighborhood compares to other competing neighborhoods, which matters the most. All of these factors have a bearing on the relative price levels of the sites in different competing market areas.

To project the future stability of a market area and neighborhood, the appraiser first considers the current characteristics and then considers how these may change in the future. The predictions of future change should be based on facts and not conjecture. If a large employer in the market area announced a major expansion, it would be reasonable for the appraiser to project that this may have a beneficial effect on the market area. The introduction of announced land use changes may have a significant effect on the stability of the neighborhood. For example, the building of a highway may decrease its desirability as a residential neighborhood and increase its desirability as a commercial neighborhood.

SOURCES OF MARKET AREA AND NEIGHBORHOOD DATA

Large amounts of data must be gathered in the field through close observation and analysis of existing conditions. However, other sources of information are needed for population statistics, income and employment profiles, and vacancy information. In addition to census data, local utility companies and community-level government organizations frequently have pertinent data available. Other sources include real estate brokers, lending institutions, appraisers and the residents of a neighborhood.

SUMMARY

An appraiser's description and opinion of a market area and neighborhood are an important part of an appraisal report. This places a special responsibility upon the appraiser to be objective. The analysis of a market area and neighborhood starts with a description of the market area, the neighborhood and the properties it contains. It also describes the growth pattern around the neighborhood.

A neighborhood today tends to be any separately identifiable area of a community, usually having recognizable natural or man-made boundaries. Sometimes neighborhoods are clearly defined and other times they are difficult to precisely identify.

Old concepts of unity and conformity no longer apply. Most neighborhoods are changing at various rates. What happens in one neighborhood affects surrounding neighborhoods. An added supply of new houses tends to induce a shift from older houses to the new ones. However, other factors such as location, community facilities, educational and cultural facilities, and access to parks also influence the rate of change. Most neighborhoods have more than one type of use within their boundaries.

Market areas and neighborhoods go through life cycles that start when the market area and neighborhood are developed. This is called the growth period. When construction slows down or stops, a period of stability follows. This period ends either because the housing stock deteriorates or changes occur in the economic, social, physical and governmental forces that affect the market area and neighborhood. This results in a period of decline. Decline may cease when these forces change again or when there is an organized effort to rejuvenate the market area and neighborhood. This renewal period is comparable to the original growth period. The life cycle is then repeated with another period of stability and a delayed period of decline. If the period of decline is not reversed, the market area and neighborhood will come to the end of its economic life and usually will change to another use.

To understand market areas and neighborhood cycles, the appraiser must analyze the relevant physical, social, governmental and economic forces that affect value. Information about the factors that make up the four great forces must be gathered in the field by close observation and interviewing of informed sources and local residents. This information is reconciled to determine what effect it has on the value of the subject house. It must always be objective, be supported by facts, and be based on current social standards.

Most data about a market area and neighborhood is gathered by the appraiser based on observations and interviews. Published data is useful but must be carefully reviewed as it often pertains to areas larger than the market area in which the subject property is located.

REVIEW QUESTIONS

1. The value of a property is determined by all of the following significant influences:
   a. Social, economic, educational, environmental
   b. Economic, governmental, population, social
   c. Social, economic, governmental, environmental
   d. Governmental, population, social, educational

2. Market area analysis:
   a. is an old traditional appraisal term.
   b. was invented by the USPAP.
   c. was coined by Fannie Mae.
   d. is a relatively new appraisal term.

3. Market area:
   a. is usually more than three communities.
   b. is a defined geographic area.
   c. usually contains only one land use.
   d. None of the above

4. The first stage of a new market area is:
   a. the growth period.
   b. the period of stability.
   c. the period of equilibrium.
   d. All of the above

5. Pride of ownership is a poor phrase to use in an appraisal because:
   a. its meaning is vague.
   b. it is too subjective.
   c. it may be misunderstood.
   d. All of the above

6. The first step in the analysis of a neighborhood is to:
   a. determine its age.
   b. determine its name.
   c. determine its boundaries.
   d. None of the above

7. Every 10 years, the U.S. Census Bureau collects information about people's:
   a. ages.
   b. incomes.
   c. occupations.
   d. All of the above

8. When the gentrification of a neighborhood takes place:
   a. older people displace younger people.
   b. rich people usually displace poorer people.
   c. poorer people usually displace richer people.
   d. None of the above

9. Which of the following is not a physical or environmental factor that affects value?
   a. Topography
   b. Service and utilities
   c. Special amenities
   d. Taxation

10. Special assessments should be:
    a. directly related to the extra services they provide.
    b. be the same for everyone in the market area.
    c. be the same for everyone in the neighborhood.
    d. None of the above

11. A deed restriction is:
    a. a private restriction.
    b. a public restriction.
    c. enforced by the zoning enforcement officer.
    d. None of the above

12. Planned unit developments (PUDs) became popular after:
    a. the Vietnam War.
    b. World War I.
    c. World War II.
    d. the Korean War.

13. When it comes to market area analysis, the appraiser must be:
    a. careful not to offend anyone.
    b. objective.
    c. conservative.
    d. liberal.

14. Today, a neighborhood usually:
    a. has no identifiable boundaries.
    b. contains less than three uses.
    c. contains more than one use.
    d. None of the above

ANSWERS TO REVIEW QUESTIONS

The answer to each question is indicated by the letter a, b, c or d. The explanation of the answer is indicated by the page number and on an arrow that points to the appropriate paragraph on the page of the text.

Q 5.1	c	Page 5-2
Q 5.2	d	Page 5-2
Q 5.3	b	Page 5-2
Q 5.4	a	Page 5-3
Q 5.5	d	Page 5-5
Q 5.6	c	Page 5-6
Q 5.7	d	Page 5-6
Q 5.8	b	Page 5-7
Q 5.9	d	Page 5-8
Q 5.10	a	Page 5-12
Q 5.11	a	Page 5-13
Q 5.12	c	Page 5-14
Q 5.13	b	Page 5-16
Q 5.14	c	Page 5-16

CHAPTER 6

Property Description - Geographic & Geologic Characteristics Land/Site

"Knowest thou the land where the lemon trees bloom,
Where the gold orange glows on the deep thicket's gloom;
Where a wind ever soft from a blue heaven blows,
And the groves are laurel and myrtle and rose."

Johann Wolfgang von Goethe (1749-1832)

Important Words and Key Concepts
Words on this list are highlighted in this chapter.
They are also defined in the Glossary at the back of this text.

Artesian Well	Plottage Value
Base Lines	Principle Meridian
Contour Line	Septic System
Cul-de-sac	Shallow Well
Excess Land	Site
Flood Hazard Area	Site Improvements
Flood Plains	Subsoil
Footing Drains	Surface Water
Frontage	Surplus Land
Geodetic Survey Program	Swale
Geographic Characteristics	Township Lines
Geologic Characteristics	Topographical Study
Land	Wetland
Percolation Test	

RESIDENTIAL SITE DESCRIPTION AND ANALYSIS

6.1 ▶ According to tradition, when an appraiser is asked to name the three most important factors affecting value, the answer is: "Location, location, location." More specifically, the answer might be stated: "Community location, neighborhood location and site location."

Because of the fixed nature of real estate, location contributes more than any other single factor to wide variations in value among similar sites. Therefore, good appraisal practice requires that the exact location of the subject property be clearly and definitively established. An accurate description of the legal boundaries and a detailed review of the physical features are combined with a thorough analysis of the site's location in the neighborhood and community. A deed description, copied from the deed or mortgage, and a survey, together with a neighborhood and community map, is a good way to provide this information.

In the specialized vocabulary of the real estate professional, land and site are not synonymous. **Land** means the surface of the earth, which is unimproved by man, plus a wedge-shaped subsurface piece that theoretically extends to the center of the globe and air rights extending upward to the sky. In practice, the use of air rights is limited in the United States by an act of Congress, which holds that navigable air space is public domain. In some areas of the country, subsurface mineral rights are owned by the government or someone other than the owner of the rest of the fee. All natural resources in their original state are also considered to be part of the land, including mineral deposits, fossil fuels, wildlife and timber. In the appraisal definition, everything that is natural and within the property boundaries is part of the land.

6.2 ▶ **Site** is the land plus improvements that make it ready for use, including streets, sewer systems and utility connections.

Many appraisers include such items as the cost of clearing the site, grading and landscaping, drainage, water and sewer connections (or septic systems), electric and gas service, private access streets, alleys, drives and sidewalks as part of the site analysis. Occasionally, local custom dictates that some of these items be treated as building improvements rather than site improvements. It is important in making an appraisal to indicate this distinction clearly, and treat the comparable market data in a consistent manner.

Proper appraisal terminology states that improvements *to* the site are those described above, while improvements *on* the site are the house, garage and other outbuildings and structures.

GEOGRAPHIC & GEOLOGIC CHARACTERISTICS

Every appraisal must contain an accurate description of the **geographic characteristics** and **geologic characteristics** of the subject site. Although much of the data can be obtained easily, some of it may prove to be more difficult to find or be totally unavailable. The appraisal report must state the assumptions that have been made about the nature of the site in the absence of precise information. For example, in the case of an unimproved site, a soil test is usually desirable. In the absence of such a test, the appraiser should carefully point out that assumptions have been made as to the physical characteristics of the soil, and that the value estimate may be substantially different if these assumptions do not reflect the actual conditions of the site.

SIZE AND SHAPE

Width and Frontage

Although width and *frontage* are often used synonymously, they have two distinct meanings. Width is the distance between the side lines of a site. When a site is irregular in shape, average width is often used. Another important measurement is width at the building line. Many zoning regulations specify a minimum width at this point, which is required in order to permit the use of the site for construction of a particular type of improvement. Frontage refers to the length of boundaries that abut a thoroughfare or access way. In the valuation of residential sites, front feet are often used as units of comparison, but the importance of frontage varies widely from one location to another. Care must be exercised in using front footage as the unit of comparison for residential sites. Once a site meets the standard size acceptable in a neighborhood, excess frontage does not always add proportionately to the value of the site.

Depth

Depth is always considered together with the width and frontage of a site. Most residential neighborhoods have a standard acceptable site depth, so that sites with less depth sell for less, and sites with excess depth sell at a premium. The penalty or premium paid for depth is rarely directly proportionate to the actual footage involved.

The problem of varying and disproportionate increases or decreases in value relative to changes in depth may be analyzed by constructing a table to reflect these value changes. These depth tables are popular with assessors and other mass appraisers who staunchly defend their use, claiming that the tables can be constructed and adjusted to work in different neighborhoods. Theoretically, this may be possible; nevertheless, depth tables have been so widely misused and misunderstood in the past that most professional appraisers avoid using them unless absolutely convinced that a particular table applies to the neighborhood of the subject property. Some rules do apply to many residential sites, which the appraiser should be aware of when considering the influence of depth:

1. As the depth of a site decreases from that of a typical site in the neighborhood, its value per front foot decreases, but its value per square foot or per acre increases.

2. As the depth of a site increases beyond that of a typical site in the neighborhood, the value per front foot increases, but its value per square foot or per acre decreases.

Shape

The shape of a site affects the value of the site differently from one neighborhood to another. In some areas, irregularity of shape may decrease value; in other areas, as long as the site is suitable for a house, little difference appears to exist between the value of regularly and irregularly shaped sites. If the irregular site shape results in increased construction costs, however, it would probably decrease the value of the site. The value of irregularly shaped parcels is usually indicated in dollars per square foot of area or in dollars per acre.

Size

If value were directly related only to size, the unit of comparison for site values would always be value per square foot or value per acre. However, frontage, width, depth and shape interplay with size to affect value.

Topography

The study of a piece of land that provides information about its contour, grading, natural drainage, soil condition, view and general usefulness is called a **topographical study**. Two sites that are otherwise similar may have substantially different highest and best uses, and value, because of their difference in topography. For example, steep slopes often make it economically unprofitable to develop a site. Water drainage either onto or off of a site can affect its suitability for a specific use.

Typically, the most desirable residential site is one that slopes up gently from the street to where the house is located, and then slopes downward steeply enough so that there can be a walkout basement door leading directly to the rear yard and recreation area. Again, what is true for one neighborhood is not necessarily the case for other areas. Sites tend to have lower value if they are costly to improve because of extreme topographical conditions. A site higher or lower than the abutting street level may create additional costs to correct poor drainage, erosion, or accessibility problems. Frequently, however, difficult conditions are offset by advantages recognized in the market, such as a scenic view or extra privacy. Another factor to be considered is the amount of site work required to make the site buildable. If there is bedrock, excess excavation costs may be incurred. In some cases, a site may require fill, or it may have excess fill that can be sold. These conditions all affect site value.

GEODETIC SURVEY PROGRAM

The U.S. Geological Survey is the agency in charge of the **geodetic survey program** that prepares topographical maps for most of the United States. These maps provide useful information about the height of the land by means of **contour lines**. They also show **base lines, principle meridians**, and **township lines**, as well as principle man-made features.

More information is available online about these useful maps at: *http://www.usgs.gov/pubprod/maps.html*

This website has a section called the Business Partner Program. It lists state by state the location of stores that sell the maps in each state.

The site also provides information about how to obtain their products by mail.

PLOTTAGE VALUE

Plottage value is the increase in unit value resulting from improved utility when two or more small sites are combined to form a larger one. To accommodate a substantial building development, small sites may be assembled from different owners. This procedure usually entails extra costs, and key parcels may need to be purchased for more than their individual land value, either because they are already improved or because of a negotiating disadvantage.

After assembly, the project must support the excess costs of the land acquisition in addition to other capital costs involved. It is not the cost of assembly that creates plottage value. Size itself is no guarantee of a plottage increment in value. For plottage value to be realized, there must be the potential of a higher and more profitable use. Otherwise, the whole could not be worth more than the sum of its parts.

The area of a site can also be divided into effective area and excess land. Usually the ***excess land***—particularly if it cannot be used—is worth substantially less per unit of measurement than that part of the site within the effective (usable) area.

CORNER INFLUENCE

Historically, because a corner location provides more light and air and may afford more prominence on a particular street, it was thought to have more value. However, a corner site also has less privacy and is often taxed at a higher rate. It also may be subject to more noise and more passing traffic. The appraiser must make a judgment, based on the specific site and its market, if a corner location adds or detracts from the site value when the subject property is compared with other sites in the neighborhood.

CUL-DE-SAC INFLUENCE

Sites located at the end of dead-end streets that have a ***cul-de-sac*** for a turnaround also may have different values from similar sites without the cul-de-sac influence. Again, no universal rule applies, and the appraiser must look to the market for evidence of the effects of a cul-de-sac location on value.

SURFACE AND SUBSOIL ANALYSIS

Surface Soil

In many areas the ability of the soil to support a lawn and landscaping is an important factor in the marketability of the property. An appraiser should note whether the soil appears to be suitable and typical of the surrounding neighborhood. When appraising a new subdivision, the appraiser should determine if the natural surface soil (topsoil) will be replaced at the end of the construction process or whether it is being stripped during site preparation. A trend today among developers is to disturb the natural growth and topsoil as little as possible during the building process. A naturally sandy or rocky soil may require the extra expense of purchased topsoil to support future lawns and landscaping.

Subsoil

The character of **subsoil** definitely affects the cost of preparing a site for building; it can also influence the design of the structure that can be erected on the site. If bedrock must be blasted, or if the soil is unstable, the cost to build the improvements is increased. Soil conditions are usually determined by an engineering study of the bearing quality of the soil and its suitability for foundations. Extra expense is incurred for foundation walls and the sinking of pilings if a site must be filled in. Underground tunnels can present a hazard in mining districts, and may prevent a site from being suitable for development. The appraiser must include a consideration of such possibilities in a thorough site analysis.

LANDSCAPING

Value of Landscaping

Naturally occurring trees and shrubs are usually considered part of the land itself. Landscaping is treated separately by most appraisers as a site improvement. Lawns, shrubbery, gardens and other plantings generally improve the appearance and desirability of residential properties. However, because plantings are a matter of individual taste and will deteriorate rapidly without good care, typical buyers are inclined to discount the cost of replacing such plantings, especially if they are very elaborate. Although such improvements are usually regarded as an asset, their contribution to the value of a property will vary with location and character, and may not reflect their actual cost.

DRAINAGE

Surface and Storm Water Disposal

Some method must be provided to drain the site of surface and storm water. It may be a simple **swale** that channels the water off the surface of the site to the street or into some natural drainage area. When the site is level or slopes away from the water disposal area, storm sewers must be constructed. In some areas, the leaders or downspouts that collect rain falling on the house may be connected to the storm water disposal pipes. When a house has a basement, **footing drains** are needed to carry the water from under the basement to prevent leaks from developing. When the house is built on a slope, special care must be taken to keep the **surface water** away from the sides of the house.

UTILITIES

Water

Every house requires an adequate supply of water of acceptable quality. Water can be obtained from a municipal or private company or from a well. Common sense and the FHA Minimum Property Standards require that when a public water supply is available, it should be used. Some houses still obtain water directly from rivers, streams, lakes and even rain water collected from the roof and stored in tanks. None of these systems

[6.11] is considered satisfactory, since they will not consistently supply an adequate quantity of safe water. When water is supplied by a public or publicly- regulated company, the appraiser usually need only check on its availability at the site, including whether there is sufficient pressure. When the water is supplied by a smaller, unregulated company, this must be reported and the dependability of the supply must be analyzed. Wells, either **artesian wells** or **shallow wells,** should be capable of delivering a sustained flow of five gallons per minute. The water should meet the standard bacteriological and chemical safety requirements of local health authorities.

When appraising vacant land that is not on a public water supply, the appraiser should check surrounding properties where wells have been dug to determine the probability of an adequate water supply being found on the subject site.

Sewers

Few will argue the substantial advantage of being connected to a municipal sewer system. It is estimated, however, that almost 50 million people in 15 million homes [6.12] depend on **septic systems** for their waste disposal and that 25% of new houses under construction do not connect to municipal systems. If no public sewer exists, a **percolation test** must be made on the site to determine if the soil can absorb the runoff from a septic system.

Installation of Public Utilities to the Site

Included in the value of a site is the cost of bringing water, electricity, gas, telephone, and storm and sanitary sewers to the site. Recent additions to this list are cable television and high speed computer lines. The site may have additional value because of the availability of these utilities even if they are not connected to the subject house. It is not unusual to find a house still using a well or septic system even where public water and sanitary sewers are available.

ACCESS

Streets and Alleys

A site cannot be used unless there is some type of usable access. It may be a right-of-way over abutting property or a private driveway or street. Access may also take the form of a public street or alley. When access is not by public street, special attention should be given to who maintains the street and if lending institutions servicing the neighborhood will make mortgages on houses without public access.

Street Improvements

The description of a site should include information about street improvements, such as the width of the street, how it is paved, and the condition of the pavement. In some areas, lenders require substantial details about private streets when they represent the only access to a property. Details about the sidewalks, curbs, gutters and street lighting should also be reported.

OTHER SITE IMPROVEMENTS

In addition to utility connections, which are sometimes classified as *site improvements*, a variety of other site improvements are typically found on an improved residential site. These include fences, walls, sidewalks and driveways, pools and patios, tennis courts and other recreational facilities. These all must be described in the appraisal report, and an analysis must be made as to their contribution to the value of the property.

VIEW

The view enjoyed from a property may substantially affect its value. Sites in the same neighborhood, identical in all respects except location and orientation, have markedly different values which are directly attributable to the effect of superior views. The most popular views are of water, mountains and valleys. A poor view reduces value.

HAZARDS AND NUISANCES

Flooding and Floodplains

The awareness of flood hazards has become quite important in many parts of the country now that most lenders cannot issue a mortgage in a *flood hazard area* without flood insurance. Whenever there is any water in the vicinity of the subject property it is necessary to check flood maps. An appraiser must learn whether the site is in an identified flood plain or flood hazard zone, and if so, if flood insurance is available and at what cost. The effect on value must also be considered and reported in the appraisal. Official flood maps can be obtained from the Federal Emergency Management Agency (FEMA), P.O. Box 1038, Jessup, MD 20794-1038. Ph: (800) 358-9616 or online at: *http://www.fema.gov/business/nfip/mscjumppage.shtm*

Hazards

Sometimes hazards exist in the subject neighborhood that reduce the value of property. The most common hazard is heavy traffic; the market usually will recognize and penalize for this problem. Other hazards that should be investigated include potential mud slides, earthquakes, dangerous ravines and bodies of water, or any unusual fire danger.

Nuisances

A variety of services contribute to the value of a site when they are in the neighborhood but detract from value when they are too close. For example, a firehouse, public school, stores, restaurants, hospital, medical offices and gas stations are desirable nearby but not immediately adjacent to residential property. Industries, large commercial buildings and offices, noisy highways, utility poles and high tension wires, motels and hotels, funeral parlors and vacant houses all generally detract from property values when they are located in a residential neighborhood.

ENVIRONMENT

Climatic or Meteorological Conditions

Generally, climate affects the whole region or community and should be reported and analyzed in that section of the appraisal report. Sometimes these conditions specifically affect the value of the subject site. In some regions there may be an increase in the value of sites that face a certain direction. For example, if prevailing winds are consistent, sites may be favorably or adversely affected by their relation to the direction of the wind.

Wetlands

 Unlike flood plains which are mapped by the Federal Government and use terminology determined by the Federal Government, **wetlands** are mapped and defined by both the federal and local governments.

The major federal legislation that controls the use of wetlands is Section 404 of the *Clean Water Act*. In general it defines **wetlands** as land that is inundated or saturated by surface or groundwater at a frequency and duration sufficient to support, and under normal circumstances does support, a prevalence of vegetation typically adapted for life in saturated soil conditions.

EXCESS LAND

The portion of land area that provides a typical land-to-building ratio with the existing improvements may be considered an economic unit. Excess land is the portion of a property that is not necessary to serve existing improvements. Assuming that the excess land is marketable or has value for future use, its market value as vacant land constitutes an addition to the estimated value of the economic entity. Therefore, excess land is typically valued separately.

SURPLUS LAND

Surplus land is land that is not needed to support the existing improvements. Typically it cannot be separated and sold off. It does not have any highest and best use except to be left undeveloped as no use can be made of it that will produce a profit.

RELATIONSHIP TO SURROUNDINGS

Because the location of a site is fixed, its surroundings have a significant effect on value. Much of this locational effect has been covered in the region, community and neighborhood analysis. The relationship of the specific site to its immediate environment is considered in the site valuation section.

Use of Nearby Sites

The use of the immediately adjacent sites is of great importance to the value of a property.

The principle of conformity states that to obtain maximum value, the improvements of the subject property should reasonably conform to those on surrounding sites. For example, if neighboring sites are improved with medium-value, colonial-style, multi-story houses, the appraiser might seriously question the appropriateness of plans for construction of a high-priced, extremely contemporary, split-level on the subject site. However, it is not always necessary for improvements to conform to obtain maximum value.

Orientation of Improvements

Again, the principle of conformity applies in the orientation of the improvements. If the abutting houses are set back 75 feet from the street and face out towards it, it will probably be difficult to orient the house on the subject site differently, even if such orientation—with the living/social zones facing towards the rear yard, for example—would seem preferable, without decreasing the market value of the subject.

Abutting and Nearby Streets and Traffic Flow

Abutting and nearby streets may be in the older grid pattern or the newer style of dead-end or limited-access streets. Some streets in a neighborhood will become thoroughfares and suffer from heavy traffic flow. Access by a back alley or a special service road may add to or detract from value, depending on the market.

Public Transportation

The value of a residential site is affected by the availability of public transportation. Most important is the availability of such transportation to places of work and shopping, and to recreational areas. Changes in the availability of public transportation can affect the value of property. Modern systems, such as San Francisco's BART rapid transit system, increase values in the area but deteriorating systems tend to decrease values. The quality and quantity of public highways leading from the subject property to places of work, shopping and recreation also have an effect on property values.

Access by Car

Automobile access to work, shopping and recreation areas substantially affects value. Sites that slope steeply downward from the street are less desirable than level sites or sites that slope upwards, as it is dangerous to have to back into traffic or be forced to enter on a curve or hill where visibility from oncoming cars is limited. The market will penalize a site for these problems.

Safety of Children From Traffic

The sheer volume of traffic is not the only safety consideration of parents with smaller children. Traffic and speed controls and sidewalks from the site to places such as schools and parks are also important factors. Another important point is the availability of places away from the streets for children to play.

ECONOMIC FACTORS

Many economic factors have already been discussed in the regional, community and neighborhood analyses. Some economic factors apply specifically to the individual site under appraisal rather than to larger areas.

INDIVIDUAL SITE CONSIDERATIONS

Prices of Nearby Sites

The price of nearby sites offered for sale has at least a short-term effect on the value of a site. The principle of substitution limits the price paid for the subject site to that paid for similar sites in the neighborhood at least until the supply was exhausted.

Tax Burden Compared to Competitive Sites

If assessments are not uniform, sites with excessive tax burdens are depressed in value, at least temporarily, by the excess levy. The reverse would also be true; sites that are under assessed might be expected to bring a premium.

Utility Costs

If location necessitates incurring extra costs to bring utilities to a site, the market may recognize a parallel decrease in the value of the site.

Service Costs

Some sites are not eligible for municipal services such as garbage collection or snow plowing because they are not on public streets. These services must be purchased privately, which could decrease the value of the site, if competitive sites had such municipal services.

SUMMARY

The site data and analysis portion of the appraisal should first positively identify and describe the subject property. A deed description, copied from the deed or mortgage, and a survey, together with a neighborhood and community map, is a good way to provide this information. Other shortcut methods are acceptable only if the subject property is positively identified.

Appraisers use the words "land" and "site" to distinguish between undeveloped land and land that has been improved sufficiently to make it an acceptable building site.

Every appraisal must contain an accurate description of the geographic and geological characteristics of the land or site that is the subject property. This description should include the land or site's physical characteristics including its size, shape and typography. The U.S. Government Geological Survey agency is a good source of typographic maps.

The description and analysis should consider any corner influence or cul-de-sac influence. There should be a description of the landscaping, surface and subsurface soil conditions, surface and storm water disposal as part of a complete site analysis.

Other important factors are the availability of utilities, access to streets and access to the whole market area. Other factors to be described are hazards and nuisances and any detrimental environmental conditions.

Finally, the description and analysis should include economic factors such as prices of nearby sites, availability of employment, public transportation, etc.

REVIEW QUESTIONS

1. The three most important things that affect value according to tradition are: _____ location, _____ location and _____ location:
   a. land, site, improvement.
   b. sales, cost, income.
   c. community, neighborhood, site.
   d. None of the above

2. Site is defined as land plus:
   a. streets.
   b. utility connections.
   c. sewer systems.
   d. All of the above

3. The width of a lot is synonymous with the:
   a. frontage of the lot.
   b. average distance between the front and rear lines.
   c. Both of the above
   d. None of the above

4. As the depth of a residential lot increases, the value per sq. ft. foot usually:
   a. increases.
   b. stays the same.
   c. decreases.
   d. None of the above

5. A topographical study of a tract of land provides information about its:
   a. contour lines.
   b. soil conditions
   c. water supply
   d. All of the above

6. The U.S. Geological Survey Topographical Maps provide information about the elevations of the land by means of:
   a. contour lines.
   b. base lines.
   c. township lines.
   d. All of the above

7. Plottage is when extra value is created when:
   a. a large lot is split into to parcels.
   b. two or more small plots are combined into one large plot.
   c. Both of the above
   d. None of the above

8. A cul-de-sac is usually located:
   a. in the middle of a dead end street.
   b. at the end of a dead end street.
   c. between two dead end streets.
   d. None of the above

9. Large trees are considered by appraisers to be:
   a. personal property.
   b. improvements.
   c. part of the land.
   d. None of the above

10. A swale is a depression in the land that:
    a. holds storm water until it can evaporate.
    b. channels water off the land.
    c. blocks storm water from flowing onto adjoining land.
    d. None of the above

11. Water that is safe to drink:
    a. must come from a municipal water supply.
    b. must not contain any fluoride.
    c. must not come from a surface well.
    d. None of the above

12. What type of test is made to the land to determine if it is suitable for the construction of a septic system?
    a. Septic system size test
    b. Water purity test
    c. Percolation test
    d. None of the above

13. When a house is in an identified flood hazard area:
    a. Freddie Mac will not buy the mortgage.
    b. most lenders will not make the mortgage.
    c. most lenders require flood insurance.
    d. All of the above

14. Wetlands are mapped by:
    a. state governments.
    b. the Federal Government.
    c. Both of the above
    d. None of the above

15. Surplus land typically:
    a. cannot be sold off.
    b. can be sold off without harming the site's value.
    c. can be separately developed.
    d. None of the above

ANSWERS TO REVIEW QUESTIONS

The answer to each question is indicated by the letter a, b, c or d. The explanation of the answer is indicated by the page number and on an arrow that points to the appropriate paragraph on the page of the text.

Q 6.1	c	Page 6-2
Q 6.2	d	Page 6-2
Q 6.3	d	Page 6-3
Q 6. 4	c	Page 6-3
Q 6.5	a	Page 6-4
Q 6.6	a	Page 6-4
Q 6.7	b	Page 6-5
Q 6.8	b	Page 6-5
Q 6.9	c	Page 6-6
Q 6.10	b	Page 6-6
Q 6.11	d	Page 6-7
Q 6.12	c	Page 6-7
Q 6.13	c	Page 6-8
Q 6.14	c	Page 6-9
Q 6.15	a	Page 6-9

CHAPTER 7

Land/Site Considerations for Highest and Best Use

"A right to property is founded in our natural wants..."

Thomas Jefferson
Letter to Samuel Kercheval, 1816

Important Words and Key Concepts

Words on this list are highlighted in this chapter.
They are also defined in the Glossary at the back of this text.

Assessors Map
Assisted Living
Beneficial Interests
Building Codes
Bundle of Rights
Census Tract Maps
Cooperatives
Cul-de-Sacs
Easements
Egress
Elderly Housing
Encroachments

Environmental Regulations
Environmental Restrictions
Financially Feasible
Highest and Best Use
Homeowners' Association
Ingress
Legally Permitted.
Maximally Productive
Mini-Warehouses
Mobile Homes
Party-Wall Agreements
Plottage Value

Physically Possible
Police Power
Private Restrictions
Public (Legal) Restrictions
Riparian Rights
Site
Subsurface Rights
Timeshare Ownership
Vacant Land
Wetland Controls
Zoning Regulations

HIGHEST AND BEST USE: LAND/SITE

This chapter covers how to determine the **highest and best use** of a parcel of **vacant land**. If the property is in an undeveloped area with few, if any, surrounding improvements in appraisal terminology it is called land. **Site** is the land plus improvements that make it ready for use, including streets, sewer systems and utility connections.

USPAP Standards Rule 1-3 (b) directs the appraiser to "develop an opinion of highest and best use of the real estate." The Comment to this Standard explains:

> "An appraiser must analyze the relevant legal, physical, and economic factors to the extent necessary to support the appraiser's highest and best use conclusion(s). The appraiser must recognize that land is appraised as though vacant and available for development to its highest and best use..."

The highest and best use of the land or site as though vacant may be the existing use, a projected development, a subdivision, or an assemblage; alternatively, it may involve holding the land as an investment. [1]

IDENTIFICATION OF SUBJECT PROPERTY

When appraising land or sites it is important to make a positive identification of what is being appraised. The ideal situation is when the appraiser has a class A-1 survey and the surveyor has staked out the boundaries of the property. Unfortunately, these are not always available.

Other ways a parcel of land can be identified is by finding the assessor's parcel number on the **assessors map**. These maps often will indicate the street address.

Census tract maps are also useful in identifying the parcel of land that is part of the subject property.

The complete identification should also include a postal zip code and an RFD # or any other identifier that is available.

The following is quoted from an article entitled: *"Vacant Land: Special Problems for Appraisers"* by Robert C. Wiley and Claudia Gaglione, Esq., who are recognized national experts on appraiser's professional liability insurance:

> "For many appraisers, the biggest nightmare of their career begins when someone requests a vacant land appraisal. Far too many appraisers accept vacant land assignments when they lack the experience to approach these assignments correctly....
>
> ...It may be surprising to learn that most E & O claims arising from vacant land appraisals are caused by the appraiser appraising the wrong property." [2]

---

[1] The Appraisal of Real Estate, 12th Edition, Appraisal Institute, Chicago, IL 2001
[2] Real Estate Valuation Magazine-Online, Spring 2006, www.revmag.com

PROPERTY RIGHTS APPRAISED

Part of the determination to be made by the appraiser is what property rights are to be included in the highest and best use analysis. Here is a brief review of the subject of property rights as they pertain to vacant land.

BUNDLE OF RIGHTS AND INTERESTS

The bundle of rights theory holds that the ownership of real property may be compared to a bundle of sticks where each stick represents a distinct and separate right or privilege of ownership. These rights, inherent in ownership of real property and guaranteed by law but subject to certain limitations and restrictions, include the right to occupy and to use real property, to sell it in whole or in part, to bequeath it, to lease it, or to transfer by contract for specified periods of time the benefits to be derived by occupancy and use (**beneficial interests**) or to do nothing at all with it. It is not enough to just consider the ownership of the property in **fee simple**. If any of the full **bundle of rights** is not in the appraised value, this must be prominently disclosed in the appraisal report.

ELEMENTS IN HIGHEST AND BEST USE ANALYSIS

To estimate the highest and best use of a site, the appraiser utilizes the **four tests of highest and best use**. The projected use must meet all four of these tests:

1. Physically possible
2. Legally permissible
3. Financially feasible

4. Maximally productive

Each potential use of a property is considered by the appraiser in terms of these four tests. If a proposed use fails to meet any of the tests, it is discarded and another use is

reviewed. The highest and best use meets all four tests.

When you fly over the United States, you will observe great tracts of vacant land. Vacant means that there is nothing on the land. It is not timberland or farm land. Most likely, if you were to appraise this land, you would conclude that it is not ready to be developed and nothing can be done that will meet the four tests of highest and best use. The reality is that most vacant land is not ready to be developed and the highest and best use is to hold it as an investment for future development.

Physically Possible

The use of a site must be **physically possible**. Uses might be limited by the physical characteristics of a site, such as size, frontage, topography, soil and subsoil conditions and climate.

PHYSICAL CHARACTERISTICS
Every appraisal of vacant land/site must contain an accurate, physical description of the site being appraised. The appraisal report must state the assumptions that have been made about the physical characteristics of the property in the absence of precise

information. Because of the importance of physical characteristics as part of the land/site highest and best use analysis, it is repeated here in condensed form.

SIZE AND SHAPE OF PARCEL OF LAND (SITE)

-- **Width.** Although width and frontage are often used synonymously, they have two distinct meanings. Width is the distance between the side lines of a lot. When a lot is irregular in shape, the term average width is often used. Another important measurement is width at the building line. Many zoning regulations specify a minimum width at this point, which is required in order to permit the use of the site for construction of a particular type of improvement.

-- *Frontage.* The length of boundaries that abut a thoroughfare or access way is called the frontage. In the valuation of residential lots, Care must be exercised in using front footage as the unit of comparison for residential lots. Once a lot meets the standard size acceptable in the neighborhood, excess frontage does not always add proportionately to the value of the lot. Frontage usually a key factor in the value of waterfront properties, such a beach front or lake front homes or residential lots.

-- **Depth** is considered together with the width and frontage of a lot. Most residential neighborhoods have a standard acceptable lot depth so that lots with less depth sell for less, and lots with excess depth sell at a premium. The penalty or premium paid for extra depth, however, is rarely directly proportionate to the actual square footage involved.

-- **Shape:** The shape of a lot affects the value of the lot differently from one neighborhood to another. In some areas, irregularity of shape may decrease value; in other areas, as long as the lot is suitable for a house, little difference appears to exist between the value of regularly and irregularly shaped lots. If the irregular lot shape results in increased construction costs, however, it would probably decrease the value of the lot. The value of irregularly shaped parcels is usually indicated in dollars per square foot of area or in dollars per acre.

-- **Size:** If value were directly related only to size, the unit of comparison (such as square feet or acre) for lot values would always be value per square foot or value per acre. However, frontage, width, depth, corner influence, and shape interplay with size to affect value.

PLOTTAGE

Plottage value is the increase in unit value resulting from improved utility when several plots are combined to form a larger one. To accommodate a substantial building development, several plots may be assembled, often from different owners. This procedure usually entails extra costs, and key parcels may need to be purchased for more than their individual land value, either because they are already improved or because of a buyer's negotiating disadvantage. Once assembled into a single ownership, the land is said to have plottage value.

CORNER INFLUENCE

Historically, because a corner location provides more light and air and may afford more prominence on a particular street, it was thought to have more value. However, a corner lot also has less privacy and often is taxed at a higher rate. It also may be subject to more noise and passing traffic. The appraiser must make a judgment, based on the specific lot and its market, if a corner location adds or detracts from the value.

7.3

CUL-DE-SAC INFLUENCE

Lots located at the end of dead-end streets that have **cul-de-sacs** for turnarounds also may have different values from similar lots without the cul-de-sac influence. Again, no universal rule applies, and the appraiser must look to the market for evidence of the effects of a specific location on value.

CONTOUR AND TOPOGRAPHY

Sites tend to have lower value if they are costly to improve because of extreme topographical conditions. A lot higher or lower than the abutting street level may create additional costs to correct poor drainage, erosion, or accessibility problems. Frequently, however, difficult conditions are offset by advantages recognized in the market, such as a scenic view or extra privacy. Another factor to be considered is the amount of site work required to make the site buildable. If there is bedrock, excess excavation costs may be incurred. In some cases, a site may require fill, or it may have excess fill that can be sold.

SURFACE SOIL

In many areas, the soil's ability to support a lawn and landscaping is an important factor in the marketability of the property. The appraiser should note whether the soil appears to be suitable and typical of the market area. Naturally sandy or rocky soil may require the extra expense of purchased topsoil to support future lawns and landscaping. A soil test is often desirable. Without one, the appraiser should point out that they did not have the results of a soil test and that the value estimated in the appraisal is based on assumptions made as to the physical characteristics of the soil, and that the value estimate as given may be substantially different if these assumptions do not reflect the actual conditions of the site.

SUBSOIL

The character of subsoil definitely affects the cost of preparing a site for building; it can also influence the design of the structure that can be erected on the site. If bedrock must be blasted, or if the soil is unstable, the cost of improvements is increased. Soil conditions are usually determined by an engineering study of the bearing quality of the soil and its suitability for foundations. Extra expense is incurred for foundation walls and the sinking of pilings, if a site must be filled in.

SUBSURFACE HAZARDS

Underground tunnels can present a hazard in mining districts. The appraiser must include a consideration of such possibilities in a thorough site analysis.

LANDSCAPING

Natural trees and shrubs are usually considered part of the land itself. Landscaping is treated separately by most appraisers as a site improvement.

DRAINAGE

Some method must be provided to drain the site of surface and storm water. It may be a simple swale that channels the water off the surface of the lot to the street or into some natural drainage. When the lot is level or slopes away from the water disposal area, storm sewers must be constructed.

AVAILABLE UTILITIES

-- **Water:** Every property requires an adequate supply of water of acceptable quality. Water can be obtained from a municipal or private company or from a well. Common sense and the FHA Minimum Property Standards require that when a public water supply is available, it should be used. When water is supplied by a public or publicly regulated company, the appraiser usually need only check on its availability at the site, including whether there is sufficient pressure. When the water is supplied by a smaller, unregulated company, this must be reported and the dependability of the supply must be analyzed.

When appraising vacant land not on a public water supply, the appraiser should check surrounding properties where wells have been dug to determine the probability of an adequate water supply being found for the subject property. It must be clear in the appraisal report that the value estimate is based on the assumption that an adequate safe water supply will be available.

-- **Sewers:** Few will argue the substantial advantage of being connected to a municipal sewer system. If no public sewer exists, a percolation test must be made to determine if the soil can absorb the runoff from a septic system. It must be made clear in the appraisal that the value estimate is based on the assumption that an adequate sewerage disposal will be possible.

-- **Installation of public utilities to the site:** Included in the value estimate of a site is the cost of bringing water, electricity, gas, telephone, and storm and sanitary sewers to the site. Recent additions to this list of services which are important in many markets is cable television, and high-speed Internet access.

ACCESS

-- **Streets and Alleys:** A site cannot be used unless there is some type of usable access. It may be a right-of-way over abutting property or a private driveway or street. Access may also take the form of a public street or alley. Substandard access detracts from a site's value.

-- **Street Improvements.** The description of a site should also include information about street improvements, such as the width of the street, how it is paved, and the condition of the pavement.

VIEWS

The view enjoyed from a property may substantially affect its value. Lots in the same neighborhood identical in all respects except location and orientation, have markedly different values which are directly attributable to the effect of superior views.

HAZARDS

Sometimes hazards exist in a neighborhood that reduce the value of a property. An appraiser must learn whether the site is in an identified flood hazard area. The effect on value must also be considered and reported in the appraisal. Other hazards that should be investigated include potential mudslides, earthquakes, dangerous ravines and bodies of water, or any unusual fire danger.

NUISANCES

A variety of services contribute to the value of a site when they are in the neighborhood but detract from value when they are too close to the property. For example, a fire house, public school, stores, restaurants, hospital, medical offices and gas stations are desirable nearby but not immediately adjacent to residential property. Industries, large commercial buildings and offices, noisy highways, utility poles and high tension wires, motels and hotels, funeral parlors, and vacant houses all generally detract from property values when they are located in a residential neighborhood.

EXCESS LAND
Excess land is that portion of a property that is not necessary for the proposed improvements. Assuming that the excess land is marketable or has value for future use, its market value as vacant land constitutes an addition to the estimated value of the economic entity. Therefore, excess land is typically valued separately.

USE OF NEARBY LOTS
The use of the immediately adjacent lots is of great importance to the value of a property. Economic obsolescence may be caused by neighboring uses.

ABUTTING AND NEARBY STREETS - TRAFFIC FLOW
Abutting and nearby streets may be in the older grid pattern or the newer style of dead-end or limited access streets. Some streets in a neighborhood will become thoroughfares and suffer from heavier traffic flow, which is usually a negative factor. Access by a back alley or a special service road may add to or detract from value.

TRANSPORTATION
The value of a property is often affected by the availability of public transportation. Access to systems such as San Francisco's BART rapid transit, increase values in the area. Easy access by automobile and trucks is considered normal.

Legally Permitted

Each use must be tested first to see if it is **legally permitted** on the site. **Public (legal) restrictions** consist of **zoning regulations**, **building codes**, **environmental regulations** and other applicable ordinances. **Private restrictions** are limitations that run with the land and are passed from owner to owner. Generally, they are imposed by the developer of the tract who attempts to preserve the value of the entire development by restricting what can be done with individual lots. **Easements**, **encroachments**, **party-wall agreements** and the like also restrict the development of a site.

A gas station, for example, may appear to be the highest and best use for a level corner lot at the intersection of two major traffic arteries. The appraiser cannot consider this to be the highest and best use of this site unless it is legally permitted by the zoning regulations currently in effect, or there is a high degree of probability that existing zoning can be changed within the near future to permit such development.

PUBLIC AND PRIVATE RESTRICTIONS
The following is a summary of the public and private restrictions that must be considered when testing a proposed highest and best use to determine if it is the highest and best use of the land/site:

-- **Zoning** is part of the **police power** of the government. Zoning gives the public the right to control the uses of private property for the benefit of the entire community.

Any reasonable probability of a zoning change must be considered. If the highest and best use of a site requires a zoning change, an appraiser must investigate the probability of such a change. An appraiser may obtain pertinent information by interviewing planning and zoning staff or elected officials. An appraiser may also consult a study of patterns of zoning changes to draw conclusions about the likelihood of a change in a particular instance. If a highest and best use recommendation relies on the probability of a zoning change, that probability must be supported by three elements. These are physical practicality, economic feasibility, and political probability.

-- **Building codes** are specific restrictions that, like zoning regulations, are based on the police power. They provide design control of permitted buildings and delineate the types of materials that may be used. In addition to a general building code, many communities have separate electric and plumbing codes.

-- **Deed restrictions** are limitations placed on the use of land by a property owner and will run with the title to the land as it passes on to future owners. Deed restrictions are contractual and are usually imposed by the deeds used to convey title. It usually takes a civil court action to enforce or remove a deed restriction.

-- **Easements** are rights extended to non-owners of the fee for *ingress* and *egress* over property usually for specific purposes, such as access to a roadway or beach. Other easements give non-owners the right to use the air over the property or *subsurface rights* for utility installations, soil removal, flood control or mineral deposits.

-- **Encroachments:** There are two types of *encroachments*. Either the improvement may extend over the property line onto abutting properties, or the improvements on abutting properties may encroach onto the subject site.

The appraiser is not expected to make a survey to determine if there are any encroachments. Normally, a statement in the limiting conditions section of the report declares that the assumption is that there are no encroachments. However, as with easements, if an encroachment is evident, it must be reported in the appraisal and care must be taken not to mislead a potential user of the appraisal as to the effect of such encroachment.

-- **Environmental restrictions** are controls on land use are becoming more common and more important to appraisers. *Environmental restrictions*, like zoning regulations, appear to be based on the police power of government, although some of the laws are still being tested in the courts. Appraisers must be familiar with current environmental developments that affect value, including *wetland controls*, flood hazard area designations and other land use restrictions.

-- **Riparian rights** are the rights of owners whose land abuts a body of water (lake, river, stream, ocean, etc.) with respect to the use of the water. *Riparian rights* may include the right to construct piers, boathouses and other improvements over the water or may be for use of the body of water for fishing and recreational purposes or for irrigation. Riparian rights may have a significant effect upon the value of the land and must be carefully considered where they apply.

7.4

Financially Feasible

A realistic assessment of market demand for a proposed use is a critical factor. For example, acreage may be available that is zoned for single-family residential use of a certain concentration, served by all utilities and with good proximity and access; however, similar subdivisions already in the market have remained unsold for some time. There is no need for the addition of such lots; even though the property meets the first two tests, it fails the test of financial feasibility.

Thus, market demand acts to create highest and best use. In reviewing proposed alternative uses, the appraiser must consider the demand for each use and the other available competitive land suitable for that use, which constitutes the supply. These factors must be weighed in the **economic analysis**. All physically possible and legally permitted uses that fail to meet the test of being **financially feasible** are discarded. The remaining uses must produce some net return to the property.

Many economic factors have already been discussed in the regional data section, market area, and neighborhood analyses. Some economic factors apply specifically to the individual land/site under appraisal rather than to larger areas.

PRICES OF NEARBY LOTS
The price of nearby lots offered for sale has at least a short term effect on the value of a site. The principle of substitution would limit the price paid for the subject land/site to that paid for similar lots in the neighborhood, at least until the supply is exhausted.

TAX BURDEN COMPARED TO COMPETITIVE LOTS
If assessments are not uniform, lots with excessive tax burdens are depressed in value, at least temporarily, by the excess levy. The reverse would also be true. Land/sites that are under assessed might be expected to bring a premium.

UTILITY COSTS
If location necessitates incurring extra costs to bring utilities to a land/site, the market may recognize a parallel decrease in the value of the land/site.

SERVICE COSTS
Some parcels of undeveloped land are not eligible for municipal services, such as garbage collection or snow plowing, because they are not on public streets. The fact that these services must be purchased privately would decrease the value of the land, if competitive land had such municipal services.

Maximally Productive

The fourth test is essentially a test for maximum return. The appraiser is seeking the **most profitable** (**maximally productive**) among all physically possible, legally permitted, and financially feasible uses. *The Appraisal of Real Estate, 12th Edition*, summarizes the process of determining the highest and best use as follows:

"The test of maximum productivity is applied to the uses that have passed the first three tests. Additional analysis of the market forces of supply and demand may aid in the process of elimination. The test addresses not only the value created under the maximally productive use but also the costs to achieve the value, if any, such as demolition and removal of structures, environmental remediation costs, and zoning changes. Of the financially feasible uses, the highest and best use is the use that produces the highest residual land value consistent with the market's acceptance of risk and with the rate of return warranted by the market for that use. To determine the highest and best use of land as though vacant, rates of return that reflect the associated risks are often used to capitalize income from different uses into their respective values. The use that produces the highest residual land value is the highest and best use…

The potential highest and best use of the land is usually a long-term land use that is expected to remain on the site for the normal life of the improvements. Normal life expectancy depends on building type, quality of construction, and other factors. The stream of benefits (income and amenities) produced by buildings reflects a careful consideration, and usually very specific land use programs."[3]

THE IDEAL IMPROVEMENT

7.5 ▶The final goal of a highest and best use analysis of the land/site usually is to determine if there is an ideal improvement to be built on the land/site at this point in time, or whether the highest and best use is to continue to leave it vacant and to hold it for future development.

The following section lists a variety of potential improvements to be tested for being the highest and best use of the land/site. It is not an all-encompassing list. It is intended to be a starting point for the appraiser's search for the most productive use of the property.

The list is broken into two categories, residential and other. The authors have added guidelines for appraisers to consider whenever they use one of these improvements as the proposed highest and best use of the subject land/site.

---

[3] The Appraisal of Real Estate, 12th Edition, Appraisal Institute, Chicago, IL 2001

TYPES OF IMPROVEMENTS TO BE CONSIDERED

FIG. 7-1 Types of Improvements to be considered for potential highest and best use

Residential Improvements	Other Types of Property
• Condominiums • Cooperatives • Colonial reproductions • Contemporary design houses • Elderly housing • Energy efficient/solar homes • Experimental houses • Farm and ranch houses • Log cabins • Mansions • Manufactured houses • Mobile homes • Multifamily dwellings & apartment houses • Planned unit developments • Residences on leased land • Second homes • Ski lodges and homes in ski areas • Timesharing • Waterfront houses	• Hotels, motels and inns • Commercial buildings • Industrial properties • Storage buildings • Institutional and government buildings • Special purpose properties • Mixed-use buildings

Residential Improvements

CONDOMINIUMS

The biggest change in American home ownership since World War II is the condominium, which did not exist prior to that time.

-- Types of condominiums: A condominium is a form of ownership that is used for a variety of different types of residences. There are no official categories of the different types of condominiums; however, the following is a general breakdown.

- In-town residences with few amenities
- Suburban residences with few amenities
- Suburban residences with recreational facilities
- Resort and vacation homes
- Retirement housing
- Student housing
- Large projects and new towns

Each of these types of potential condominiums require different highest and best use analysis. Condominiums can be new units or units in existing buildings that have been converted to condominium ownership. Either new or old, they can take the form of a high-rise, townhouse, small grouping of party-wall units or be free-standing units. An in-depth study as to what people like and dislike about condominium living has been made by the Urban Land Institute.

Among the favorable factors cited were:

1. Building up equity
2. Lower cost than single family housing
3. Freedom from house and yard maintenance
4. Better environment
5. Recreational facilities
6. No rent

People were found to dislike:

1. Living too close together
2. Noisy or undesirable neighbors and children
3. Neighbors' pets
4. Trouble with parking
5. Poor association management
6. Poor construction
7. Dishonest salespeople who sold units
8. Negligent builders
9. Renters in other units, rather than owners
10. Thin party-walls
11. Long identical rows of houses
12. Poor visual screening between units

In spite of the problems some condominiums have faced, this form of ownership continues to play an important role in the housing market. Any multifamily zoned residential land/site must be analyzed to determine if a condominium development is the highest and best use.

The key to the projected highest and best use is the analysis of the market data, supported by the income projections. It is not sufficient to assume that the highest density permitted is the highest and best use. The market area should be studied to see what condominium characteristics, i.e., size, price, and amenities appear to be marketed most successfully. Many lenders (and good appraisal practice) require an analysis of the whole condominium project in any estimate of the value of a single condominium unit.

COOPERATIVES

New York City is the location of most of the **cooperatives** in the United States. In the past 10 years, this form of ownership has increased in popularity for a variety of reasons. Probably the most common reason is that in some jurisdictions it is possible to convert a building into cooperative ownership without having to comply with complex condominium laws.

Very few cooperative apartments are being built on undeveloped land/sites. Before an appraiser determines that a cooperative apartment is the potential highest and best use, they should be certain they have the knowledge and experience to make this projection.

COLONIAL REPRODUCTIONS

Colonial reproductions are a popular group of single family house styles in most areas. For example, Cape Cod, Massachusetts, is filled with houses that are reproductions of the original cape cod style. Even the builders of tract developments often decorate standard houses with style features from colonial house styles such as bow windows or gambrel roofs.

In Santa Fe, New Mexico, there are many excellent reproductions of adobe houses, many of them constructed with synthetic adobe materials, but styled and shaped to historic aesthetics. Other examples of popular reproductions of regional historic styles can be found throughout the United States.

It is insufficient in a highest best use projection to simply state that the highest and best use of the property is for a single-family house. At a minimum, the appraiser must consider and test different sizes, types and configurations to determine the most productive use. In areas where there is a preference for colonial reproductions, or another clearly defined style, the appraiser must consider this market preference in their projected use analysis.

CONTEMPORARY DESIGN HOUSES

Modern design is popular in many market areas and neighborhoods. Modern designs can range from nondescript styles created by the builder to handsome houses designed by architects. Many are characterized by special amenities such as solar heat and hot water, state-of-the-art integrated entertainment systems, and custom lighting and security systems. At a minimum, the appraiser should test different sizes, types and configurations to determine the most profitable use. In areas where there is a preference for contemporary design, the appraiser should consider this in their projected use. They should also render an opinion as to how important good design is in the particular market area.

ELDERLY HOUSING (SENIOR HOUSING, 55+ HOUSING)

7.8 ▶ One of the fastest growing sectors in the housing market. One segment of this market is composed of people in the 55 to 75 year old age group. Some of these individuals are still employed, yet they find their housing needs changing as their children leave home. Many people in this age group choose to be less burdened with the care and cost of a large home. Townhouses, condominiums, and cooperatives located in affluent neighborhoods, often near their place of work and in the more culturally diverse and active areas of the city, rather than the suburbs, are more appealing to them. New federal regulations uphold the legality of restricting the sale of some property to the elderly without children. However, it is still illegal to restrict sales on the basis of sex, race or religion.

Retirement communities are another form of **elderly housing**. Here the emphasis is in leisure activities and the accompanying required facilities, such as tennis courts, golf courses and heated swimming pools. These owners tend to be in their 60's and 70's and older.

Continuum of care housing and **assisted living** facilities are other alternatives available to seniors. These tend to consist of relatively small individual apartments with the emphasis on extensive public areas, including a common dining room that provides one or more meals daily, on-site recreational programs, and staff available to provide extra services. Often the facility also includes a nursing home, and some facilities are marketed together with an extensive health care plan.

This is probably the fastest growing new housing segment in many parts of the country. Most vacant land that is suitable for housing is also suitable for one of the variety of housing types that is designed for retired and/or physically impaired occupants. At minimum, an appraisal of the vacant land should state that various elderly housing concepts were tested as a potential highest and best use.

ENERGY EFFICIENT & SOLAR HOMES

Energy efficient and solar houses are often built with extensive insulation—often double the thickness of traditional insulation. They usually are tightly sealed and have small windows. As fuel costs increased in the 2000s, so did the popularity of this type of house. The appraiser must compare the cost of adding energy efficient and solar items to the projected house, with the value they will add. Only if the extra investment in these technologies is recognized by strong response in the market would the test of financial feasibility be met. In some areas, special tax incentives and other rebate programs must be considered as well, when reviewing the actual costs to build.

EXPERIMENTAL HOUSES

A variety of experimental houses, which use new material such as plastic, fiberglass, foams and other unconventional building products exist in the United States. The number of vacant land/sites that have experimental houses as their highest and best use is currently very limited. This is because they rarely are the maximally productive use of the site.

FARM AND RANCH HOUSES

The recent economic problems of the small farmer increase the need of appraisers to have special skills and experience when appraising farm land. Rural appraising takes special skills. The appraisal of rural acreage is based on the market data approach when most of the value is in the land. The appraiser must keep in mind that there are vast amounts of agricultural land available for alternative development if it is financially feasible. Timing is very important. As soon as a few available parcels are developed locally, the market may become saturated. Therefore, what appears to be the highest and best use on the date of the appraisal may change rapidly if surrounding parcels are developed first.

LOG CABINS

The log cabin market has carved itself a unique niche. These homes appear all over the country, usually integrated into an area with few or no other log cabins. Some are authentic reproductions but many are contemporary in design. Most have modern heating and mechanical systems. Since there are usually few, if any, sales of log cabins in the same neighborhood as the subject tract, the appraiser must decide if additional log cabins are the highest and best use, which usually is not the case for vacant tracts of land. Other more conventional houses may be better received in the market area, as might other potential residential uses.

MANSIONS

Mansions or estates used to be synonymous with gracious living for those who could afford their high cost. With many extra rooms for recreation, entertaining, guest suites and servant quarters, they are usually individually designed to reflect the special tastes of the owner, whose goal is often to enhance family prestige, as well as live on a lavish scale. Some mansions may have historical value.

7.11 ▶ Now the term mansion is used to describe any large house. In some communities houses, as small as 3,000 square feet are called mansions.

The highest and best use analysis is an important part of any parcel of land or site that is suitable for a mansion. Vacant land or sites in a neighborhood where many other mansions exist must be analyzed to determine if there is a market for additional new mansions. The appraiser must consider whether the site would best utilized for a mansion or if there is excess land that can be otherwise developed to be maximally productive.

MANUFACTURED HOUSES (MODULAR HOUSES - PREFABS)

The term *manufactured house* means that substantial portions of the house were assembled in a factory and then delivered to the site, usually by truck. Some units are assembled almost totally off the site. There is little difference between a small modular house and a large mobile home. Larger modular houses consist of several segments, which are shipped to the site by rail and/or truck and joined on the site. Prefabricated houses are shells that are factory-built and then shipped to the site for assembly. They usually have less mechanical equipment as part of the package than modular homes.

Modular houses and *prefabs* are used for a variety of reasons. The construction of single family houses has changed less than almost any other major item manufactured in this country. Theoretically, the efficiency of the assembly line and mass production methods should be applicable to housing, and the manufacturers of modular and prefabricated homes are trying to do this. Speed of construction is another reason for this system of producing housing units. The on-site assembly of a factory-produced modular or prefabricated home is often as little as a few days.

The appraiser must be familiar with the acceptance of manufactured houses in the market area to be able to analyze whether this is the potential highest and best use that will produce more profit than conventionally-built houses.

MOBILE HOMES

Although not considered real estate in many states, *mobile homes* account for nearly 10% of all the existing single family residences in the United States. The pre-World War II trailer has evolved into today's mobile home. The most popular size is 12 feet by 60 feet, known as a "12 wide." There are also "14-wides" (which are only permitted in a few states) and "double-wides" which may run from 24 x 47 feet to 28 x 60 feet. There are also smaller units, but they are rarely used for year-round housing. Once settled on a pad or foundation, a mobile home is rarely moved and experienced mobile home owners claim a unit should never be moved off the original location. Special appraisal skills are needed to determine if the land/site will make a suitable mobile home development.

MULTIFAMILY DWELLINGS & APARTMENT HOUSES

Most small income properties (2-4 family) are either built on a small lot in an urban area that becomes available for a variety of reasons or result from the conversion of single family dwellings. One exception to this rule is the four-plex, which enjoys popularity in many western states and other areas too. They are often built in the suburbs on large tracts of undeveloped land.

If the subject land/site is in a market area that is active for this type of development, then it is necessary to see if they are legally permitted on the subject property. If so, they will need to be tested as a possible highest and best use. The same is true for apartment houses. Throughout the country, new apartment houses are being built in both urban and suburban areas. If they are common in the subject's market area, and if they are legally permitted on the subject site, then they must be tested as a possible highest and best use. It is not sufficient to merely determine that the highest and best use is for an apartment house. The appraiser must test the optimum number of units, the best configuration, the size of the units, and the amenities and other facilities that will bring the maximum productivity due to the market response.

PLANNED UNIT DEVELOPMENTS (PUDS)

Planned unit developments (PUDs) are a zoning alternative, not a type of housing. Houses built in PUDs can be in fee simple or condominium ownership in the form of single-family residences, townhouses or multifamily buildings. PUDs may also include commercial and industrial uses. In essence, the PUD concept permits the grouping of housing units on lots smaller than are usually permitted for residential construction. As a trade-off for being allowed to build on smaller lots, the developer sets aside some unused land to be dedicated to the community or to a *homeowners' association*.

PUD developments can provide for a more flexible and sensible design for streets, landscaping and public facilities than are possible in conventional neighborhoods. Many communities have special regulations for land/sites that are going to be used for planned unit developments. These regulations encourage this type of development in some communities and discourage it in others. Therefore, that appraiser must be familiar with the regulations and their intention. An interview with the community planner or a building official will usually help the appraiser decide if this type of development will be the highest and best use of the property.

RESIDENCES ON LEASED LAND

7.12 ▶ With the exception of the state of Hawaii and a few other places, residences on leased land are relatively scarce. In Hawaii, however, residences have long been built on leased land. Leases may be for as long as 99 years or for 50 years or less. To protect the mortgage, some leases provide that the interest of the fee owner is subordinate to the interest of the mortgagee or lender. However, most leases give the mortgagee the right to take over the land rent if the mortgagor defaults. Usually the mortgagee also has the right to find a new mortgagor to continue the lease payments. When the lease expires, the improvements become the property of the landowner, who traditionally have extended the lease after modifying it to reflect current market conditions.

An appraiser would rarely conclude that using a tract of vacant land for leased residences is the highest and best use of a property, unless there were strong evidence in the market area that this type of arrangement would be acceptable, and maximally productive.

SECOND HOMES & SKI LODGES

Several million houses in the United States are second homes, occupied by their owners on a seasonal basis. Some of these homes are large, expensive mansions, more valuable than many primary homes. Such homes are found in communities like Newport, Rhode Island, and Palm Beach, Florida. However, the majority of second homes tend to be simpler, often located near a body of water or other recreation area.

Prior to World War II, these houses tended to be developed individually or in small groups. By the early 1960s, many large corporations went into the second home business, developing large tracts of land and many houses at the same time. Recreational facilities serving the site also were constructed.

The second home market can be very volatile. Economic and weather conditions, gas shortages, and competitive developments may have a greater effect on the value of a second home than on a primary residence. One apparent trend in many areas is that properties on or near water tend to increase in value faster than similar properties without the water amenity.

In many areas where there are recreational homes, it takes experience and skill to decide if a vacant residentially-zoned parcel of vacant land will be more profitably developed as second homes than as one of the other traditional types of residence.

TIMESHARE OWNERSHIP

The essence of **timeshare ownership** is that it allows one property to be purchased by many owners, each of whom has the right to use the property for a predetermined period of time. For example, 50 owners may buy a home. Each owner shares the cost of the property equally, and each has the right to use the property for one week per year (2 weeks are often reserved for maintenance). Other devices may be used, but the goal of all of these methods is to allocate the time equally among shareholders or proportionately to what each owner pays.

In market areas where time-shares are popular their development is often the highest and best use of any parcel of vacant land that is suitable. Without special skills or knowledge of this specialty market, or the help of someone with these skills, it is difficult to make this highest and best use determination.

WATERFRONT HOUSES

 Waterfront property has probably increased in value at a greater rate than almost any other type of property. Unlike some other recreational properties, waterfront properties have held their value. There has also been a national trend for commercial property in cities on the water to increase in value. Many city renewal programs are focused on the waterfront of the city. Often these redevelopment programs include residential units.

When vacant land is on or near water, the obvious highest and best use test is for some type of development that takes advantage of the water amenity. To prevent wasting a lot of time, the appraiser should explore first what is legally permitted on the land. This usually will limit the number of relevant highest and best use projections. Assuming that a single-family house is the only permitted development, then the highest and best use study must go into detail to determine what type of single-family house will be the maximally productive use to develop.

Other Types of Properties

Most of the material in this chapter pertains to residential property. However, the appraiser cannot do an adequate highest and best use analysis of a site that is zoned for non-residential uses unless they consider other types of property development. This does not mean that if the land/site is zoned for non-residential uses, that these uses would necessarily be the highest and best use. On the other hand, in this situation it would be incumbent upon the appraiser to test the site for non-residential highest and best uses.

It is quite likely that such an analysis is beyond what is permitted by a residential license or certification. Certainly it is beyond the skill of the typical trainee. However, the authors have decided to round out this chapter by providing some useful information about some of the non-residential uses, that if legally permitted, may be the highest and best use of the subject land/site. Again, as with the above residential section of this chapter the list of possible uses is not all inclusive. Only a study of the needed additional facilities in the market area would lead the appraiser to all the potential highest and best uses.

HOTELS, MOTELS & INNS

Facilities to house people away from their home can range from large metropolitan hotels and convention centers to small inns in outlying areas of the country. In addition to the actual guest rooms, support spaces may range from small public areas in an inn all the way up to the vast exhibition and meeting areas of large hotels and convention centers. These may also include banquet, entertainment and recreational facilities.

Location plays a very important part in the success of all lodging facilities. Changing climate, availability of nearby recreation and cultural attractions, municipal facilities, ease of access and parking are just a few of the factors that have an influence on the success of a facility.

COMMERCIAL BUILDINGS

Commercial buildings include buildings used for retail and wholesale outlets, offices, lending institutions, restaurants and other service businesses. Frequently, two or more commercial uses are combined on a single property.

Current standards of design and structural features are changing all the time. Commercial property developers are constantly looking for ways to make their development more attractive to the public than their older competition. New projects often have to overcome the superior location of older competitive buildings. New materials and construction methods make it possible to design and construct buildings that are more efficient than those using old techniques, and offer commercial tenants "more bang for their buck" in the way of specialty services from wi-fi Internet to state-of-the-art fitness facilities on the premises.

When it is legally permitted to develop the land/site with a commercial building, the highest and best use analysis must include a test of many different kinds of commercial buildings. Additional tests are needed for the use, size, type of construction, etc., that will produce the maximally productive use.

INDUSTRIAL PROPERTIES

Industrial properties range from small manufacturing and assembly facilities to giant industrial complexes. Some industrial building are built on speculation, while others are custom built to the specifications of the future tenant or owner. It is not likely that an appraiser would get an appraisal assignment of vacant land that is zoned industrial without having the scope of work include a detailed study of the type of industrial development that would be most profitable

STORAGE BUILDINGS

Storage structures range from simple cubicles, known as mini warehouses, to huge regional warehouses with one million square feet of area. Functional utility and location have a major impact on the market value of storage buildings; obsolescence usually occurs before the structures deteriorate physically. The functions of warehouses are:

- to store materials in a protected environment.
- to organize materials so that they can be easily inventoried and removed.
- to provide facilities for efficient delivery.
- to provide facilities for efficient access and shipping.

Mini-warehouses are usually combined in one- or two-story rectangular structures located near business and residential customers that will use them. They should be visible, accessible, and surrounded by enough land for parking and maneuvering. The sizes of individual units within mini-warehouses vary; they usually include small storage units, which have passage doors, and larger units, which have roll-up truck doors.

Mini warehouses are springing up everywhere. When the land/site the appraiser is considering legally permits this type of development, the highest and best use tests must include it. Each market area can only support a limited number of mini-warehouses, so that existing competition must be considered in this analysis.

INSTITUTIONAL & GOVERNMENT BUILDINGS

Institutional and government buildings are types of special purpose buildings characterized by their design and construction for a single use. The buildings of great metropolitan hospitals and educational facilities are typical institutional buildings. Many government buildings including state and federal legislative houses, courts and post offices are copies of classic Greek styles introduced in this country for government buildings by Thomas Jefferson in the late 1700s. However, today most new construction is no longer built in this neoclassical style.

Expert knowledge of the market is important to determine if there is any possibility that this type of development is practical on the land/site being appraised. If so, the possibilities must be pursued, as this type of development is often the highest and best use when a need exists in the market area. Non-profit uses such as cultural centers and museums may also be suitable institutional buyers of the property.

SPECIAL PURPOSE PROPERTIES

When the subject property being appraised is a type that is not commonly exchanged or rented, it may be difficult to determine whether an opinion of market value can reasonably support enough to produce a credible appraisal. Such limited-market appraisals can cause special problems for appraisers. Keep in mind before you accept an assignment for such a property that you are confident that you have the skills and experience necessary to make the appraisal or you have the resources to obtain the help you will need to make a credible appraisal.

MIXED-USE BUILDINGS

A mixed-use building is one that combines two or more revenue producing uses. The most common one that new appraisers encounter are retail stores with living quarters on the upper floors. Many commercial, industrial and other types of buildings combine two or more uses. How to make these complex appraisals is beyond the scope of this book.

SUMMARY

7.15 ▶ The USPAP requires that the appraiser develop an opinion of the highest and best use of the subject as though vacant. The appraiser must include support for their opinion of highest and bet use as part of the appraisal report. Every appraisal requires a highest and best use analysis of the land/site as though vacant.

The highest and best use of the land/site as though vacant may be the existing use, a projected development, a subdivision, or an assemblage; alternatively, it may involve holding the land as an investment, to await a time in the future when development will become financially feasible.

This chapter starts with information about how to make a positive identification of the site. The techniques and methods explained are essential because the most frequent appraisal error made is the appraisal of the wrong parcel of vacant land.

The appraiser must also make clear which of the **bundle of rights** are included in the highest and best use analysis, and which (if any) are excluded.

The four tests of highest and best use are the core of a highest and best use analysis. Each potential use of a property is considered by the appraiser in terms of these four tests. If a proposed use fails to meet any of the tests, it is discarded and another use is reviewed. The highest and best use meets all four tests. It will be that use which is:

1. physically possible;
2. legally permitted;
3. financially feasible; and
4. maximally productive.

The final section of the chapter is devoted itself to a list of potential types of building and uses that should be considered as potential highest and best uses. The list is not complete and is very limited in detail. It is intended to round out the subject of highest and best use and to emphasize the complexity of many vacant land appraisal. Many appraisers, including the authors, think that they are the most difficult type of appraisals.

REVIEW QUESTIONS

1   What is the final test for highest and best use?
    a.   Maximally productive
    b.   Profitable
    c.   Both of the above
    d.   None of the above

2.   When a proposed use fails to meet the four tests of highest and best use:
    a.   it indicates the highest and best use is to hold the property for future use.
    b.   a different proposed use should be tested.
    c.   the highest and best use becomes one that passes three of the tests.
    d.   None of the above

3.   The special value of a group of parcels brought into a single ownership is:
    a.   plottage.
    b.   eminent domain.
    c.   comparable selectivity.
    d.   None of the above

4.   Riparian rights are the rights of the owner of a property that _____ a body of water.
    a.   is farthest from
    b.   is within two miles of
    c.   abuts
    d.   None of the above

5.   The final goal of highest and best use analysis of the land/site is:
    a.   to determine if it is ready for development.
    b.   to identify the ideal improvement.
    c.   to compare potential improvements for maximal productivity.
    d.   All of the above

6.   A survey of condominium owners found that many people disliked:
    a.   living in high rise apartments.
    b.   sharing recreation areas.
    c.   trouble with parking.
    d.   All of the above

7.   The key to the projected highest and best use:
    a.   is surveying people's preferences.
    b.   is analyzing market data.
    c.   is to build something similar to neighboring properties
    d.   is to set the selling price at the lowest possible level.

8.   Elderly or senior housing is_____ sectors of the housing market:
    a.   one of the slowest growing
    b.   the most profitable
    c.   one of the fastest growing
    d.   Both b. and c.

9.   The insulation of an energy efficient house is:
    a.   often twice as thick as traditional insulation.
    b.   made of special shingles.
    c.   made of organic materials.
    d.   None of the above

10. Log cabins are:
    a.   found mostly in Illinois and Ohio.
    b.   usually grouped together in a special sub-division.
    c.   rarely found in the U.S.
    d.   None of the above

11. The term mansion is used now to refer to any home which is:
    a.   more expensive than usual to build.
    b.   equipped with a guest suite.
    c.   at least 6,000 square feet in size.
    d.   None of the above

12. Residences on leased land are:
    a.   usually found in Hawaii.
    b.   a common zoning alternative.
    c.   hard to appraise properly.
    d.   None of the above

13. Residences which have waterfront or beach front locations:
    a.   are very rarely transferred.
    b.   are in condominium ownership.
    c.   have appreciated more than almost any other type of property.
    d.   All of the above

14. Older office buildings cannot:
    a.   offer condominium ownership.
    b.   compete at the same price with more modern offices.
    c.   obtain proper financing.
    d.   None of the above

15. USPAP requires the appraiser to determine the highest and best use of the land/site:
    a.   in fee simple with restrictions.
    b.   using three or more alternatives.
    c.   based on nearby uses.
    d.   as though vacant.

ANSWERS TO REVIEW QUESTIONS

The answer to each question is indicated by the letter a, b, c or d. The explanation of the answer is indicated by the page number and on an arrow that points to the appropriate paragraph on the page of the text.

Q 7.1	a	Page 7-3
Q 7.2	b	Page 7-3
Q 7.3	a	Page 7-4
Q 7.4	c	Page 7-8
Q 7.5	d	Page 7-10
Q 7.6	c	Page 7-12
Q 7.7	b	Page 7-12
Q 7.8	c	Page 7-13
Q 7.9	a	Page 7-14
Q 7.10	d	Page 7-14
Q 7.11	d	Page 7-15
Q 7.12	a	Page 7-16
Q 7.13	c	Page 7-17
Q 7.14	b	Page 7-18
Q 7.15	d	Page 7-19

Property Description - Improvements - Architectural Styles & Types of Construction

"If you invest in beauty, it will remain with you all the days of your life."

Frank Lloyd Wright
1868-1959

Important Words and Key Concepts

Words on this list are highlighted in this chapter
They are also defined in the Glossary at the back of this text

Automatic Diverter

Balloon Framing

Basement

Bat Insulation

Blanket Insulation

Bridging

BTU

Casement Windows

Cesspool

Circuit Breaker

Concrete Slabs

Condominium

Conversation Circle

Crawl Space

Double Hung Windows

Downspouts

Duplex Receptacle

Flashing

Foil Insulation

Footing

Gross Building Area

Gross Living Area

Gypsum

Heat Pump

Hollow Masonry Walls

Horizontal Sliding Windows

Hydronic Water System

Jalousie Windows

Leaders

Loose Insulation

Masonry Veneer Siding

Modernization

Orthographic Projection

Percolation Test

Plank and Beam Framing

Platform Frame
    Construction

Rehabilitation

Remodeling

Roof Sheathing

Septic System

Shake

Sheathing

Slab-on-Ground

Sprayed On Insulation

Stair Riser

Subterranean Termite

Veneer Siding

Wallboard Insulation

Winder

Work Triangle

IMPROVEMENT DESCRIPTION AND ANALYSIS

Every appraisal must contain an accurate and adequate description of the improvements. It is also customary to include photographs of the property and a building sketch. The description is based on a physical inspection of the property by the appraiser or information obtained from third parties who are familiar with the subject property.

This chapter presents details on residential construction and components to guide the appraiser in making the inspection. The assumption is that the appraiser makes a complete inspection of the exterior and interior of the property unless the appraisal report prominently states:

- that complete inspection was not made by the appraiser; and
- cites the reasons for this omission; and
- states how the information about the property was obtained and verified.

There are a variety of ways to organize a property description and analysis. The following outline works well for many residential properties:

- Site improvements
- Placement of improvements on site
- Classification (CTS System - Architectural Style and Type)
- Size of residence
- Number of rooms
- Car storage
- Description of exterior construction
- Description of interior construction
- Mechanical systems and equipment
- Items requiring immediate repair
- Deferred maintenance items
- Overall condition of the improvements
- . Interior design and layout (functional utility)
- . Renovation: rehabilitation, modernization and remodeling

This chapter also includes information about graphic aides, sketches, photographs and how to read a house plan.

SITE IMPROVEMENTS

The term "land" implies no improvements of any kind and that "site" refers to land plus those improvements which make it ready for use. In the typical appraisal some of these improvements are included as part of the site value while other improvements are valued separately. Because there is no universally accepted way to treat site improvements, the appraiser must be familiar with local customs. The appraisal report must indicate clearly which items are included in the site value and which are treated as site improvements.

The following allocation of improvements between site value and site improvements is common in many areas:

Improvements Included in the Site Valuation:

- Clearing
- Grading
- Draining
- Landscaping (often valued separately)
- Installation of public utilities to the site
- Access (streets and alleys)
- Lighting
- Sidewalks and curbs (often valued separately)

Site Improvements Valued Separately:

- Septic system (often included in site valuation)
- Utility connections
- Well (often included in site valuation)
- Driveways and parking spaces
- Patios
- Pools and courts
- Fences and walls
- On-site lights and poles

It is customary on the URAR and other appraisal forms to skip the step of estimating the reproduction cost of the site improvements. Instead, the appraiser estimates directly how much they contribute to the value of the property.

PLACEMENT OF THE IMPROVEMENTS ON THE SITE

A site, like a house, should be divided into zones for good planning. There are three zones: the public zone, the private zone and the service zone.

The public zone is the area visible from the street. The service zone consists of sidewalks and driveways plus trash storage areas. The private zone is where children play, the patio or family porch is located, and the vegetables grow.

A well-designed house takes advantage of the fact that during the summer the sun rises in the northeast, travels in a high arc across the sky and sets in the northwest. In the colder winter months, it rises southeast, travels in a low arc and sets in the southwest. As a result, the south side of the house, when protected by a large roof overhang, will receive much more sun in the winter than in the summer. The opposite is true of the east and west sides of such a house. All other factors being equal, such as street location, topography and view, the best direction in which to face a house is with the broad side containing large windows towards the south.

Another consideration is the location of the garage. Figure 8-1 illustrates a placement of the garage, both attached and detached, that are preferred in many markets.

Many architects believe it is better design if an attached garage has the entrance on the side and that a detached garage be set behind the house.

FIG. 8-1 PLACEMENT OF THE HOUSE ON THE LOT

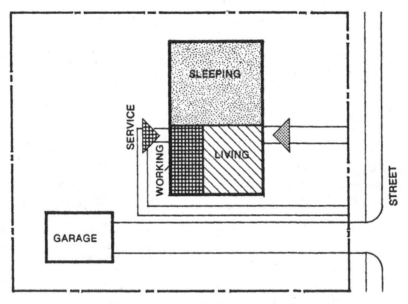

OLD WAY TO PLACE HOUSE ON INSIDE LOT

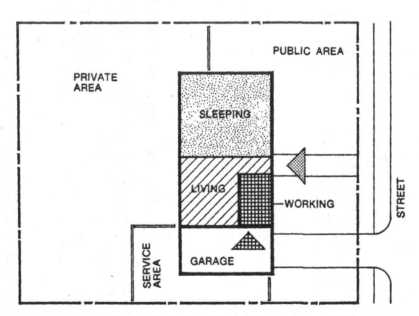

GOOD HOUSE PLACEMENT AND LAYOUT FOR INSIDE LOT

CLASSIFICATION SYSTEM (CTS) SYSTEM

The Realtors National Marketing Institute of the National Association of Realtors, developed a standard method of describing residences known at the CTS System (Class, Type, Style). This system is described and illustrated in detail in the book *Houses: The Illustrated Guide To Construction, Design and Systems.* The following material and illustrations which describes the CTS System are taken from that book.

Figure 8-2 is a chart that summarizes the CTS System. It shows illustrations of the most common house types. Next is a brief history of architectural styles in the USA and illustrations of the most common styles. In addition to the common; national types and styles there are many others found mostly locally in one part of the country or another.

FIG. 8-2 PLACEMENT OF THE HOUSE ON THE LOT

THE CTS SYSTEM
(CLASS, TYPE, STYLE)
A UNIFORM METHOD FOR DESCRIBING HOUSES

#CODE	DESCRIPTION	ABBREVIATION
	CLASS	
1	One-family, detached	1 FAM D
2	Two-family, detached	2 FAM D
3	Three-family, detached	3 FAM D
4	Four-family, detached	4 FAM D
5	One-family, party wall	1 FAM PW
6	Two-family, party wall	2 FAM PW
7	Three-family, party wall	3 FAM PW
8	Four-family, party wall	4 FAM PW
9	Other	OTHER
	TYPE	
1	One-story	1 STORY
2	One-and-a-half story	1 1/2 STORY
3	Two-story	2 STORY
4	Two-and-a-half story	2 1/2 STORY
5	Three-or-more Stories	3 STORY
6	Bi-level	BI-LEVEL
6	Raised ranch	R RANCH
6	Split entry	SPLT ENT
7	Split-level	SPLT LEV
8	Mansion	MANSION
9	Other	OTHER
	STYLE	
100	COLONIAL AMERICAN	COL AMER
101	Federal	FEDERAL
102	New England Farm House	N E FARM
103	Adams	ADAMS CO
104	Cape Cod	CAPE COD
105	Cape Ann	CAPE ANN
106	Garrison Colonial	GARR CO
101	New England	N E COL
108	Dutch	DUTCH CO
109	Salt Box	SALT BOX
109	Catslide	CATSLIDE
110	Pennsylvania Dutch	PENN DUT
	Pennsylvania German Farm House	GER FARM
111	Classic	CLASSIC
112	Greek Revival	GREEK
113	Southern Colonial	SOUTH CO
114	Front Gable New England	F GAB NE
114	Charleston	CHARLES
114	English Colonial	ENG COL
115	Log Cabin	LOG CAB
200	ENGLISH	ENGLISH
201	Cotswold Cottage	COTSCOT
202	Elizabethan	ELIZ
202	Halt Timber	HALFTIM
203	Tudor	TUDOR
203	Jacobean	JACOBEAN
204	Williamsburg	WILLIAMS
204	Early Georgian	E GEORG
205	Regency	REGENCY
206	Georgian	GEORGE

#CODE	DESCRIPTION	ABBREVIATION
300	FRENCH	FRENCH
301	French Farm House	FR FARM
302	French Provincial	FR PROV
303	French Normandy	FR NORM
304	Creole	CREOLE
304	Louisiana	LOUISIA
304	New Orleans	NEW OR
400	SWISS	SWISS
401	Swiss Chalet	SWISS CH
500	LATIN	LATIN
501	Spanish Villa	SP VILLA
501	Italian Villa	IT VILLA
600	ORIENTAL	ORIENT
601	Japanese	JAPAN
700	19th CENTURY AMERICAN	19th CTY
701	Early Gothic Revival	E GOTH
702	Egyptian Revival	EGYPT
703	Roman Tuscan Mode	RO TUSC
704	Octagon House	OCTAGON
705	High Victorian Gothic	HI GOTH
706	High Victorian Italianate	VIC ITAL
707	American Mansard	MANSARD
707	Second Empire	2nd EMP
708	Stick Style	STICK
708	Carpenter Gothic	C GOTH
709	Eastlake	EAST L
710	Shingle Style	SHINGLE
711	Romanesque	ROMAN
712	Queen Anne	Q ANNE
713	Brownstone	BROWNS
713	Brick Row House	BR ROW
713	Eastern Townhouse	E TOWN
714	Western Row House	WEST ROW
714	Western Townhouse	W TOWN
715	Monterey	MONTEREY
716	Western Stick	W STICK
717	Mission Style	MISSION
800	EARLY 20th CENTURY AMERICAN	EARLY20C
801	Prairie House	PRAIRIE
802	Bungalow	BUNGALOW
803	Pueblo	PUEBLO
	Adobe	ADOBE
804	International Style	INTERNAT
805	California Bungalow	CAL BUNG
806	Shotgun	SHOTGUN
807	Foursquare	F SQUARE
808	Art Deco	A DECO
808	Art Moderne	A MOD
900	POST WORLD WAR II AMER	POST WW2
901	California Ranch	C RANCH
902	Northwestern	NORTH W
902	Pudget Sound	P SOUND
903	Functional Modern	FUN MOD
903	Contemporary	CONTEMP
904	Solar House	SOLAR
905	"A" Frame	A FRAME
906	Mobile Home	MOBILE
907	Plastic House	PLASTIC
909	Contemporary Rustic	C RUSTIC
910	Postmodern	P MODERN

FIG. 8-3 HOUSE TYPES

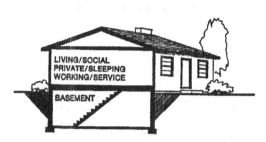

One-Story, Ranch, Rambler (1 Story - 1)

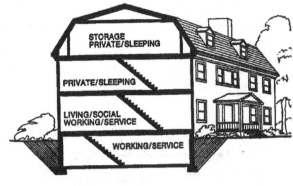

Three or More Stories (3 Story - 5)

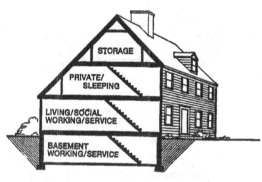

Two and One-Half Story (2½ Story - 4)

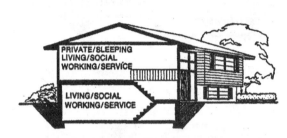

Bi-Level, Raised Ranch, Split Entry, Split Foyer
(Bi Lev or R Ranch or Split Ent or Split Foy-6)

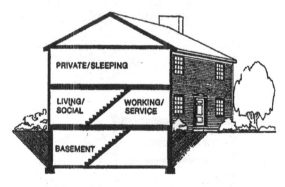

Two-Story (2 Story - 3)

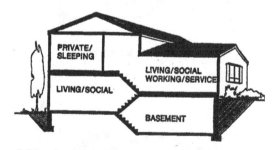

Split Levels — Side To Side, Back To Front, Front To Back (Split Le

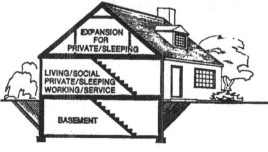

One and One-Half Story (1½ Story - 2)

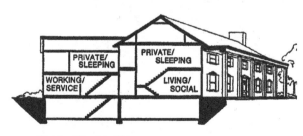

Mansion (Mansion - 8)

FIG. 8-4 HOUSE TYPES

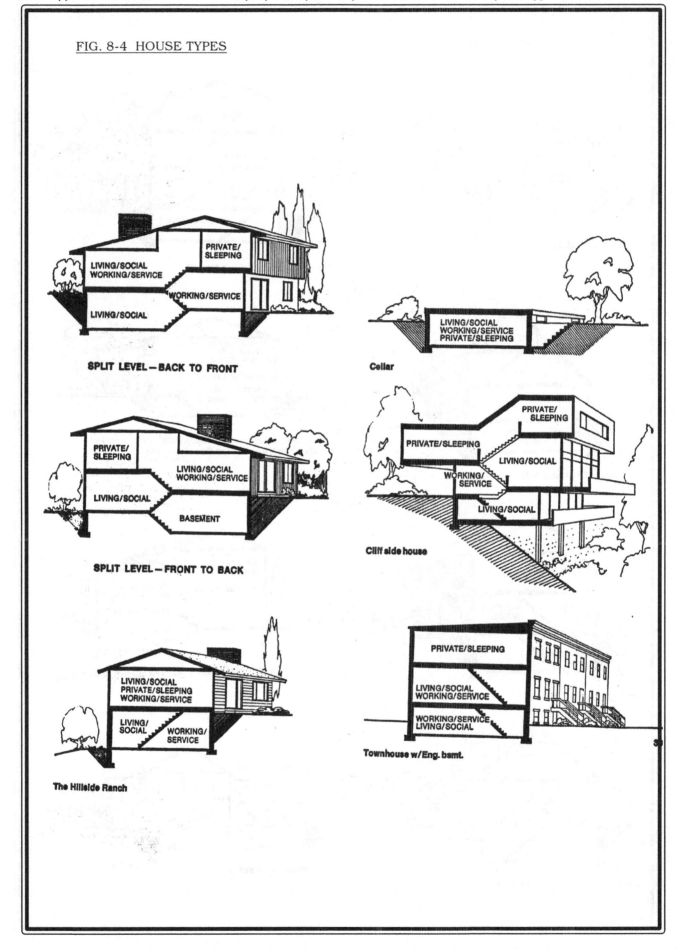

SPLIT LEVEL — BACK TO FRONT

PRIVATE/SLEEPING

LIVING/SOCIAL
WORKING/SERVICE

WORKING/SERVICE

LIVING/SOCIAL

Cellar

LIVING/SOCIAL
WORKING/SERVICE
PRIVATE/SLEEPING

SPLIT LEVEL — FRONT TO BACK

PRIVATE/SLEEPING

LIVING/SOCIAL
WORKING/SERVICE

LIVING/SOCIAL

BASEMENT

Cliff side house

PRIVATE/SLEEPING

PRIVATE/SLEEPING

LIVING/SOCIAL

WORKING/SERVICE

LIVING/SOCIAL

The Hillside Ranch

LIVING/SOCIAL
PRIVATE/SLEEPING
WORKING/SERVICE

LIVING/SOCIAL

WORKING/SERVICE

Townhouse w/Eng. bsmt.

PRIVATE/SLEEPING

LIVING/SOCIAL
WORKING/SERVICE

WORKING/SERVICE
LIVING/SOCIAL

HOUSE STYLES

It is not the purpose of this book to add wood to the fire of controversy that now rages about whether it is good or bad architecture to build houses using the traditional styles of the past.

It is only realistic to recognize that more than 60 million American homes reflect these traditional styles. They range from original colonials to authentic colonial reproductions and painstakingly restored victorian villas to cheap tract speculation houses being constructed today that adopt one or more style features of the past.

Much confusion has existed regarding the identification and the origin of these styles. On the following pages is an attempt to illustrated many of the styles found throughout the country.

The division among styles made here is very arbitrary and some of the styles are not nearly so simple to identify as these pictures may imply.

BRIEF HISTORY OF ARCHITECTURAL STYLES

In December, 1620, 102 Pilgrims landed at Plymouth Massachusetts. In spite of cold weather, they immediately started to build their first house. Shortly after it was completed, the house burned down, forcing the Pilgrims to live much of that first winter in holes in the ground that were covered with timbers, canvas and sod. Over half of them died of exposure and illness.

By the middle 1660's, there were thousands of houses in the Colonies. They ranged in type and style from small wood thatched roof cottages to large stone, brick and frame houses. Many of these houses were constructed by craftsmen who formerly built houses in the large European cities. With this imported expertise and some imported materials, they were able to construct houses that were equal in quality to those being built in Europe. Many of the colonial styles developed in this early period of our history. At the same time, the fad of copying styles from builders' handbooks and architectural design books was developing. At first, only portions of the exterior designs were taken from the books. Then, whole houses were constructed exactly like their European counterparts, built from designs in the same books.

Different styles developed in various regions of the country. Many of the early colonists copied styles from their homelands. Others copied classic Gothic, Greek and Roman designs while yet others developed truly indigenous American styles.

On the following pages are pictures of many of the house styles found all over the country.

All of these pictures are from **Houses - The Illustrated Guide to Construction, Design and System, 3rd Edition** by Henry S. Harrison, Real Estate Education Company & Residential Sales Council, Chicago, IL 60611. It is available from Forms and Worms:
1-800 243-4545 or www. formsandworms.com

FIG. 8-5 HOUSE STYLES - COLONIAL

SOUTHERN COLONIAL

CAPE ANN COLONIAL STYLE

NEW ENGLAND FARM HOUSE STYLE

DUTCH COLONIAL STYLE

ENGLISH COLONIAL STYLE

LOG CABIN

CLASSIC COLONIAL STYLE

GREEK REVIVAL STYLE

GARRISON COLONIAL STYLE

ADAMS COLONIAL STYLE

PENNSYLVANIA DUTCH COLONIAL STYLE

CAPE COD COLONIAL STYLE

NEW ENGLAND COLONIAL STYLE

SALTBOX COLONIAL STYLE

FEDERAL STYLE

FIG. 8-6 HOUSE STYLES - 19TH CENTURY AMERICAN

EARLY GOTHIC REVIVAL STYLE

EGYPTIAN REVIVAL STYLE

ROMAN TUSCAN MODE

OCTAGON HOUSE

HIGH VICTORIAN GOTHIC STYLE

HIGH VICTORIAN ITALIANATE STYLE

CARPENTER GOTHIC STYLE

SHINGLE STYLE

EASTLAKE STYLE

MONTEREY STYLE

QUEEN ANNE STYLE

BROWNSTONE

WESTERN ROW HOUSE

ROMANESQUE STYLE

MISSION STYLE

AMERICAN MANSARD STYLE

WESTERN STICK STYLE

FIG. 8-7 HOUSE STYLES - ENGLISH, FRENCH, ITALIAN. SPANISH & ORIENTAL

COTSWOLD COTTAGE

ELIZABETHAN STYLE

MASONRY TUDOR OR JACOBEAN

WILLIAMSBURG GEORGIAN

REGENCY STYLE

GEORGIAN STYLE

FRENCH FARM HOUSE STYLE

FRENCH PROVINCIAL STYLE

CREOLE

SWISS CHALET

SPANISH VILLA STYLE

FRENCH NORMANDY STYLE

JAPANESE HOUSE

ITALIAN STYLE VILLA

ENGLISH TUDOR

FIG. 8-8 HOUSE STYLES - 20TH CENTURY AMERICAN

PRAIRIE HOUSE

BUNGALOW

PUEBLO STYLE

INTERNATIONAL STYLE

CALIFORNIA BUNGALOW STYLE

PLASTIC HOUSE

CALIFORNIA RANCH STYLE

NORTHWESTERN STYLE

CONTEMPORARY STYLE

SOLAR HOUSE

"A" FRAME STYLE

MOBILE HOME

ART DECO OR ART MODERNE

FOURSQUARE

POST MODERN

CONTEMPORARY RUSTIC OR
CALIFORNIA CONTEMPORARY

SHOTGUN

MEASURING THE SIZE OF THE RESIDENCE

It is only recently that standard methods of measuring residential properties were required by Fannie Mae and Freddie Mac. These standard methods, unfortunately, are still not used by Realtors and assessors. Therefore, whenever an appraiser uses size figures supplied by other sources, there is a high probability that if the appraiser had measured the property him or her self, a different size figure would result.

Measuring Single Family Residences

The standard method for measuring single-family residences is to calculate the Gross Living Area.

8.2 ▶**GROSS LIVING AREA (GLA)**

The following are the rules for determining the *Gross Living Area (GLA):*

1. Measure around the outside of the house above the foundation to determine the GLA per floor.

2. In multi-floor houses, count each floor above grade.

3. Include all of the above grade habitable living area.

4. Do not include the basement (even when finished and heated).
    Do not include any basement area unless it is 100% above grade.

5. Garages are never included in the GLA.

6. Porches are included only when they are heated and finished in a manner similar to the rest of the house.

7. Upper stories are divided into two areas:
    a.   Attic - unfinished or having low ceilings (below 5 feet) does not count in the GLA.
    b.   Habitable area - finished and heated substantially like the rest of the house with normal ceiling height - is included in GLA.

The Fannie Mae guidelines recognize that these gross living area rules will not work for all houses in all markets. When the appraiser elects to deviate from this system, they should clearly spell out what system is used and how they deviated from the GLA system.

Measuring Individual Condominiums and Cooperative Units

How to measure a **condominium** is carefully spelled out by Fannie Mae. Their system seems to be acceptable to Freddie Mac too.

The rules are the same as the gross living area rules, with one exception for condominiums, that the interior perimeter unit dimensions are used rather than the exterior dimensions.

Only rooms that are 100% above-grade are included regardless of the quality of their finish. Garages and basements (including those that are partially above-grade) should not be included.

Real Estate Valuation Magazine interviewed Mark Simpson, Director of Mortgage Underwriting Standards for Fannie Mae, who confirmed that the best way to obtain the necessary interior dimensions for a condominium unit is from their plans, which are often available to the appraiser. Of course, the plans should be field checked to be sure that they appear to conform with the actual unit being appraised.

Measuring Small Income Properties (2-12 Families)

8.3 ▶ The rules established by Fannie Mae for what is acceptable to Fannie Mae & Freddie Mac for measuring *gross building area (GBA)* are substantially the same as the rules for calculating *gross living area (GLA)*, except for the exclusion of the basement in the GLA system and different rules for interior hallways in the GBA system.

NUMBER OF ROOMS

The HUD/FHA guidelines state "room design and count should reflect local custom". Since the reader of the appraisal may not be familiar with local custom, the appraisal should contain information about which rooms are included and excluded from the reported room count. Room count has become more important as the 2005 Freddie Mac/Fannie Mae forms no longer contain a room grid on which to conveniently report this information.

The HUD/FHA guidelines go on to state: "A dining area built as an L-shape off the kitchen may or may not be a room depending upon the size. A simple test which may be used to determine whether one or two rooms should be counted is to hypothetically insert a wall to separate the two areas which have been built as one. If the residents can utilize the resulting two rooms with the same or more utility and without increased inconvenience, the room count should be two. If the existence of the hypothetical wall would result in a lack of utility and increased inconvenience, the room count should be one."

CAR STORAGE

A majority of families owning houses also own two or more cars. Americans like their cars and they like to keep them under cover in garages and in carports. Their desire to do this varies from area to area. In many northern parts of the country any house without a two-car garage is substandard. In parts of the west and south, the demand for garages and carports is more flexible and often a one-car carport with an additional parking area for a second or third car is acceptable

A garage that is built to minimum property standards (FHA- MPS) serves only to shelter the car. These standards call for a one-car garage or carport to be 10 feet wide and 20 feet long, measured from the inside of the studs and door to the edge of the opposite wall, stair platform or any obstruction, whichever is the narrowest dimension. To build a garage to these minimum standards is false economy. For only a small additional amount of money, the garage can be built about 3 feet longer and wider. It then becomes a truly functional area of the house providing needed storage for a wide variety of materials, tools, parts and junk.
The choice between a carport or a garage is mainly influenced by local custom and climate. Some carports are so elaborate that they cost almost as much as a garage. Others are very simple and consist only of a roof extended from the house supported on a few columns or a simple wall. A carport is a good choice when it fits into the neighborhood and the prime purpose will be to shelter the automobile from the sun and rain. It is also desirable when the house is so located on the site that a garage would tend to block the breeze or appear to crowd the house.

DESCRIPTION OF EXTERIOR CONSTRUCTION

A detailed description of the exterior includes information about the major construction details, including:

- Footings and foundations
- Framing
- Insulation
- Ventilation
- Exterior wall coverings
- Masonry walls
- Windows
- Storm doors and windows
- Weather-stripping
- Screens
- Gutters and downspouts
- Roofs
- Flashing
- Chimneys

The condition of these items and any needed repairs or modernization should also be reported in this section of the report.

Footing and Foundations

The three basic design types are **slab-on-ground**, **basement** and **crawl space**. Slabs are constructed by first building footings for support, although some slabs (known as "floating slabs") are built without them. The excavation is then covered with gravel, and a vapor barrier and insulation are installed around the edge. A basement floor is constructed similarly to a slab. Crawl spaces are constructed similarly to basements except that the distance from the floor to the joists is 3 to 4 feet. They provide flooding protection and also a convenient place to run heating ducts, plumbing pipes and wires that must be accessible for repairs.

The objective of the **footing** is to provide support for the building without excessive differential or overall settlement or movement. It is the base of concrete on top of which all foundation walls are poured or laid. Block foundations walls must be properly laid and well-mortared, then filled with concrete and made watertight with cement plaster or other waterproofing compounds.

FIG. 8-9 FOOTINGS AND FOUNDATION WALL

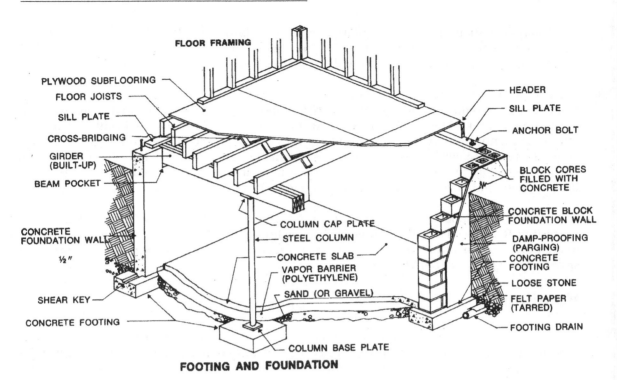

FOOTING AND FOUNDATION

Framing

8.4 Most houses built in the United States are of wood frame construction. This includes many homes that have brick veneer siding. ***Platform frame construction*** is the most common type. ***Balloon framing*** was popular for multi-story brick veneer houses, but because of poor fire resistance, it does not comply with many current building codes. ***Plank and beam framing*** was used for barns and colonial houses; it is used today for contemporary designs where the framing members are left exposed (as in exposed beam ceilings). Panelized construction, the newest methods of framing, is becoming more popular.

Many multi-family buildings are now being constructed of masonry, especially in the south and west. It is becoming difficult to construct a frame multi-family building that will comply with the building and fire codes without installing a sprinkler system.

It is harder to spot poor construction in a new building. After a building ages, visible defects become more apparent.

Bulging exterior walls can often be detected. Window sills that are not level are a sign of settling, defective framing or original sloppy carpentry. A careful inspection should include opening and closing windows. Sticking windows may be a sign of settling or defects in framing. Doors should be checked, including a look at their bottoms to detect if they have been resawed. Sagging and sloping floors may be detected visually or by putting a marble on the floor and watching if it rolls. Other signs of defective framing include large cracks developing on the outside of the house between the chimney and exterior wall or cracks running outward at an angle from the upper corners of windows and door frames.

Cracks in the walls other than these may be cause for concern but in themselves are not conclusive evidence of a serious problem. All buildings settle unless built upon solid rock; it is a rare building that doesn't develop some wall and ceiling cracks. If defects are suspected, professional consultants or engineers may be called in to confirm this opinion.

Insulation

Any building without adequate insulation is substandard today. Insulation is as important in warm climates to keep the heat out as it is in cold climates to keep heat in. Prior to World War II, many buildings were constructed without insulation.

8.5 ▶ The two primary benefits of insulation are fuel economy and occupancy comfort. Its secondary benefits are the reduction of noise transmission and of fire hazard since insulation will impede fire from spreading. The difference between fuel costs for an uninsulated building and for an otherwise identical one with storm windows and doors and good insulation can be 50%. The standard measurement for the effectiveness of insulation is its "R value" (resistance to heat flow). The higher the "R value" the better the insulation. Over-the-ceiling or under-the-roof insulation should have an R rating from R-20 to R-24 or higher.

Exterior wall insulation ranges from R-8 to R-11. Floor insulation should be at least R-9 and preferably R-13. Many of these homes, built without insulation have since been insulated. Insulation falls into the following five categories: ***loose insulation***, ***blanket*** and ***batt insulation***, ***sprayed-on***, ***foil***, and ***wallboard***.

Ventilation

8.6 ▶ To prevent water condensation, a flow of air is necessary in the attic, behind the wall covering, and through the basement or crawl space. When water condensation collects in unventilated spaces, it promotes rot and decay. Air flow will also reduce attic heat in the summer. Ventilation can be accomplished by providing holes ranging in size from one inch to several feet in diameter; these holes should always be covered with screens to keep out vermin. The use of fans also is part of many ventilation systems.

Exterior Wall Covering

The construction of an exterior wall on a frame building starts with the attachment of sheathing to the wall framing studs. Next the ***sheathing*** is covered with waterproof sheathing paper (often asphalt-saturated felt). A wide variety of wall finishes and exterior wall coverings are available. Many buildings have more than one type of siding.

MASONRY VENEER
Masonry veneer is built by attaching the masonry (clay or concrete bricks, split blocks or stone) to the sheathing. In buildings with masonry veneer walls, all the structural functions of the walls are performed by the framing and not by the masonry. When the walls are constructed, three-quarters to one-inch air spaces are left between the masonry and the sheathing, and weep holes are installed at the base to allow moisture to escape.

A variety of other types of siding materials are available, including aluminum, stone, hardboard, gypsum board, fiberglass and metals.

Masonry Walls

Masonry walls are either solid or hollow. Solid masonry walls, if well constructed, are durable and easily maintained. They should be insulated and require a larger foundation than a wood frame wall. Such walls can be either one or two units thick. Single-unit masonry walls are constructed of either two layers of brick, tile or cement block or of a combination of materials, with the higher grade material on the outside and the cheaper unit as the back-up.

FIG. 8-10 BASIC TYPES OF FRAMING

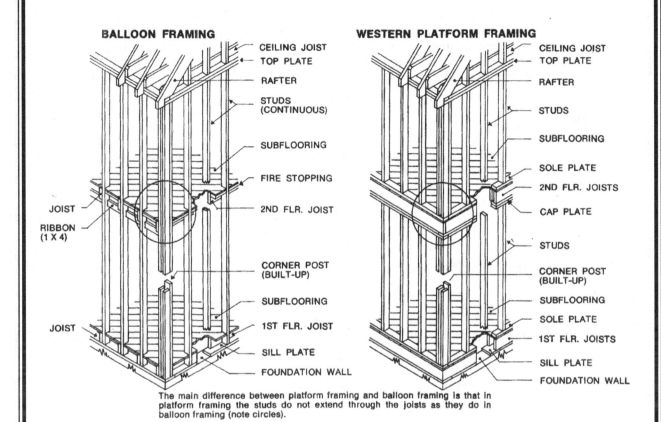

The main difference between platform framing and balloon framing is that in platform framing the studs do not extend through the joists as they do in balloon framing (note circles).

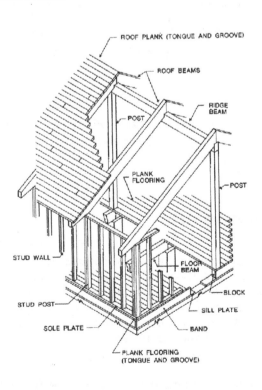

PLANK AND BEAM FRAMING

Hollow Masonry Walls

Hollow masonry walls have two wall units separated by a two-to four-inch air space and bonded together with metal ties for joint reinforcement. These cavity walls are used mainly in northern sections of the United States for protection against severe outside temperature and storms. Masonry bonded walls are similar to cavity walls. Although they are economical to construct, their insulation qualities are inferior to cavity walls and they are used primarily in the Southwest.

Windows

Among window types commonly found are single and *double hung windows, casement windows, horizontal sliding (traverse) windows* and *jalousie windows.*

During the inspection, dust streaks or water stains around the windows may be noticed, which can be evidence of leakage. Missing locks, window lifts or counter balance weights also may be discovered.

Storm Doors and Windows

Storm doors and windows serve as a means of insulation and may provide a fuel savings of between 10% and 20%. Today, they are often made of aluminum and permanently installed, together with screens. The wooden type, which are removed and stored during the summer, are becoming obsolete.

Weather-Stripping

The purpose of weather-stripping on windows and doors is to provide a seal against drafts and dust. A common kind of weather-stripping used today is the "spring tension" type made of bronze, aluminum, rigid vinyl, stainless or galvanized steel or rigid plastic steel. Other types are woven felt, compression sash guides and compression bulbs.

Screens

Most screens today have aluminum frames and screening material and are combined with storm windows. Screens are needed in almost every part of the country. The old-fashioned wood frame is becoming obsolete.

Gutters and Downspouts

Gutters and downspouts provide the means for controlling water runoff from the roof to prevent property damage and unsightly exterior wall stains where roof overhangs are not provided. Gutters or eve troughs carry rainwater off the roof to downspouts or leaders. Metal gutters of aluminum, copper or galvanized iron, which are attached with various types of metal hangers, are the common types of gutter now in use. Another common gutter material is vinyl. Built-in gutters are set into the deeply notched rafter a short distance up the roof from the eaves. Pole gutters consist of a wooden strip nailed perpendicular to the roof and covered with sheet metal.

Downspouts or *leaders* are vertical pipes that carry the water from the gutter to the ground, and into sewers or dry wells. The junction of the gutter and downspout should be covered with a basket strainer to hold back leaves and twigs.

Roofs

The roof must be constructed to support its own weight, plus that of snow, ice and wind, and also act as a base for the application of the roof finishing materials. The most common systems of roof construction found are trusses, joists and rafters, joists alone, plank and beam roofs, and panelized construction.

ROOF SHEATHING

Roof sheathing provides support for roof loads and a backing for the attachment of roofing materials.

A majority of house roofs consist of shingles and **shakes** made of wood, asphalt, asbestos, cement, slate or tile. Metal, clay tile and built-up or membrane roofs can also be found. Many multi-family buildings have flat built-up roofing systems. Since the roof covering rarely lasts to the end of the building's economic life, the appraiser should carefully observe the roof and reports its condition, age and estimated remaining life.

Water may leak through the roof for a variety of reasons. Asphalt shingle roofs may leak in a high wind if light-grade shingles are used. As these shingles get older, they curl, tear and become pierced with holes. Wood shingles may curl, split, loosen, break and fall off the roof, and asbestos shingles may crack and break. Metal roofs can rust, become bent and pierced with holes. Rolled and built-up roofs may loosen, tear, and become patched and worn through.

Flashing

Flashing is needed whenever a roof is intersected by two different roof slopes, adjoining walls or projections through the surface by chimneys, pipes or vents. Flashing is a process by which metal stripes, impregnated felt or a combination of both are nailed across or under the intersecting point; a waterproofing compound or cement is then applied and finally the roofing or siding materials are applied over the edges to hold the flashing in place permanently.

Chimneys

The efficiency of any heating system (except electric) depends upon the chimney or vent. A good chimney is safe, durable and smoke tight. Defective chimneys and vents may constitute serious fire hazards. A chimney may be a simple flue or an intricate masonry construction consisting of heater flues, ash pits, incinerators, ash chutes, fireplaces and fireplace flues. Whatever its construction, the chimney must be supported by its own concrete footings, which must be designed so that it will not settle faster than the rest of the building.

Masonry chimney walls should be eight inches thick whenever they are exposed to the exterior of the house, and must be separated from combustible construction. A two-inch air space filled with fireproof material is recommended. The chimney must extend at least two feet above any part of the roof, roof ridge or parapet wall within 10 feet of the chimney.

The heart of the chimney is the vertical open shaft, called a flue, through which smoke and gas pass to the outside air. A rough surface retards this outward flow of smoke or warm air; a flue lining will overcome this problem. The flue should extend out a few inches above the top of the chimney wall, (which should be capped with concrete, metal, stone or some other noncombustible waterproof material), that slopes from the flue to the outside edge.

The furnace and hot water heater are connected to the chimney by a smoke pipe, which, for fire safety, should be at least 10 inches below the floor joists. The joists should be further protected with plaster or a shield of metal or other fire retardant material.

FIG. 18-11 ROOF CONSTRUCTION AND COVERING

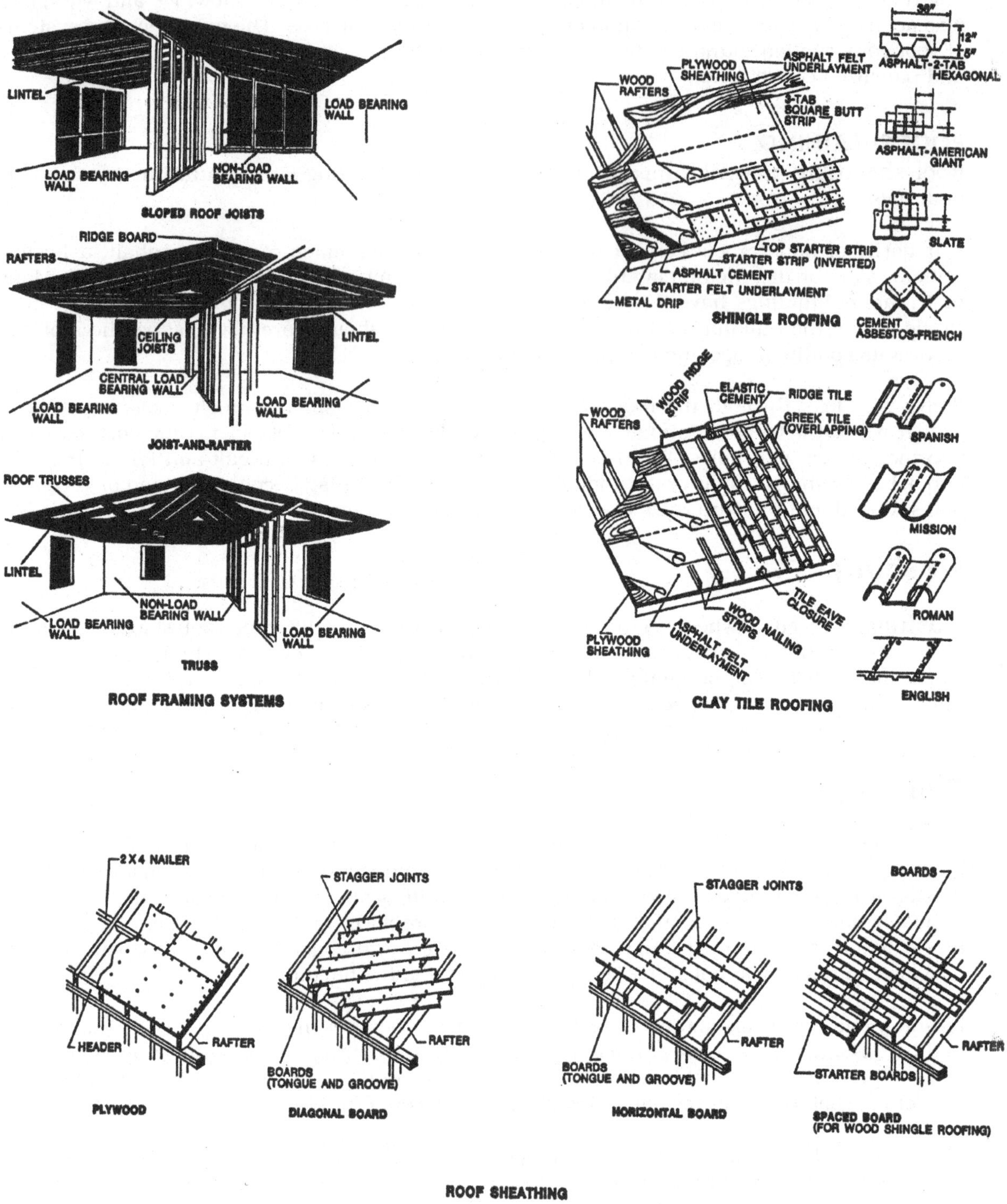

ROOF FRAMING SYSTEMS

SLOPED ROOF JOISTS

JOIST-AND-RAFTER

TRUSS

SHINGLE ROOFING

CLAY TILE ROOFING

ROOF SHEATHING

PLYWOOD

DIAGONAL BOARD

HORIZONTAL BOARD

SPACED BOARD
(FOR WOOD SHINGLE ROOFING)

Prefabricated chimneys that are assembled off the premises are now available. Many of these units consist of a flue liner encased in a concrete wall.

INTERIOR CONSTRUCTION DESCRIPTION

The description of the interior rooms should provide information about their location, individual size, number of closets, and floor, wall, and ceiling coverings or finishes. Special features should also be described and any needed repairs or modernization should be reported. Typical items included in a description of the general interior construction (exclusive of the mechanical systems and equipment, which are described separately) are:

- Basement construction and finishing
- Main bearing beam and columns
- Sub flooring
- Floor covering
- Interior walls and ceilings
- Stairs
- Doors
- Molding and trim
- Cabinets
- Fireplaces
- Termite protection

Basement Construction and Finishing

Basement construction and finishing: The basic construction of the basement consists of the footings and foundation walls previously described; a basement floor, which usually is poured concrete over a vapor barrier and gravel; and the ceiling, which often is the unfinished underside of the first floor sub flooring. Dirt floors are obsolete.

Basements can be finished in a variety of ways. There is a trend to raise the basement part way out of the ground to provide better natural light and ventilation and direct access to the outside. In raised ranch and hillside ranch-type houses the basement often is finished so as to be an integral part of the house.

A main problem with basements is dampness, which may be caused by poor foundation wall construction, excess ground water not properly carried away by drainage tiles, poorly fitted windows or hatch, a poorly vented clothes dryer, gutters and downspouts spilling water too near the foundation wall, or a rising ground water table. A basement that is wet or damp only part of the year can usually be detected any time by the presence of a powder white mineral deposit a few inches off the floor. Stains along the lower edge of the walls and columns and on the furnace and hot water heater are indications of excessive dampness, as is mildew odor.

MAIN BEARING BEAM AND COLUMNS
Main bearing beam and columns: Most buildings are too large for the floor joists to span between the foundation walls. Bearing beams resting on columns are used for support. Steel beams, because of their high strength, can span greater distances than wood beams of the same size. Most beams are supported by wood posts, brick or block piers or metal lally columns, which are concrete-filled steel cylinders.

SUB FLOORING AND BRIDGING

Sub-flooring provides safe support of floor loads without excessive deflection and adequate under layment for the support and attachment of finished flooring materials. Plywood is the most common material now being used for residential sub-flooring. Bridging is used to stiffen the joists and prevent them from deflecting sideways.

Floor Covering

Floor covering made of strips of hardwood was the residential standard in many markets for over 50 years. Before that time, planks of hard and soft woods were used.

Carpeting, installed over either finished flooring or sub flooring, is a popular floor covering. Carpeting, however, tends to depreciate very rapidly and often does not add value equal to its cost, especially when it is laid over hardwood floors or another floor covering. Hard wood floors continue to be popular. Ceramic tile is still popular for bathrooms and lavatories, and quarry tile is becoming more common in kitchens.

Concrete slabs may be used as a floor covering with no further treatment, painted with special concrete paint or covered with other flooring materials. Resilient tile, glued with special adhesives, must not be installed directly over a board or plank sub-floor; a suitable under layment must first be installed. Terrazzo flooring is made of colored marble chips mixed into cement; it is ground to a smooth surface after being laid.

Interior Walls and Ceilings

Most interior walls and ceilings are made of wood studs or metal studs, covered with a variety of materials. The materials most commonly used include plaster, gypsum, plywood, hardboard, fiberboard, ceramic tile and wood paneling.

Gypsum and other wood composition walls are installed directly onto studs or masonry, eliminating the drying time needed for plaster walls. Ceramic tile walls are installed similarly to ceramic tile floors, either by cement plaster or special adhesives.

Stairs

A well-planned stairway provides safe ascent, adequate headroom and enough space for moving furniture and equipment. A simple check for adequate design includes noting: headroom, width clearance between handrails, stair run, *stair riser*, stair winders, landings, handrail and railings. Railings should be installed around the open sides of all interior stairwells, including those in the attic and basement.

Doors

There are seven basic types of doors: batten, sliding glass, folding, flush solid, flush solid core, flush hollow core, and stile and rail doors. Batten doors, consisting of boards nailed together in various ways, are used where appearance is not important, such as for cellar and shed doors. Flush solid core doors are made with smooth face panels glued to a core that is made of either a composition material, glued-together wood blocks or glued-together wood pieces. Solid doors are often used as exterior doors. Flush hollow core doors are also perfectly flat. They have a core that consists mainly of crossed wooden slats. These doors are light and are used for interior doors. Stile and rail doors consist of a framework of vertical boards (stiles) and horizontal boards (rails). Hanging of doors is difficult. If the door is improperly hung, it will stick. Pre-hung doors are now available.

Molding and Trim

Molding is made from a variety of hard and soft woods that are cut, planed and sanded into desired shapes. A general rule is that the thicker the molding, and the more intricate the design, the more expensive it is.

Cabinets

Prior to World War II, most cabinets were made of wood. Factory-made cabinets are often used today. They are made of a variety of materials.

Fireplaces

In most American homes a fireplace is an amenity rather than a primary source of heat. There is no rule of thumb as to how much value one adds, and it is a mistake to assume, without market evidence, that a fireplace adds value equal to its cost.

 Fireplaces are usually constructed of masonry, but metal ones are becoming more common. They must be well-designed and constructed to work properly. Many fireplaces allow smoke to back up into the house, especially when it is windy outside. For fire safety, the hearth should extend at least 16 inches from the front and eight inches beyond each side of the opening. In some areas wood burning fireplaces are no longer permitted. An alternative is a gas burning fireplace.

Termite Protection

The **subterranean termite** (see Fig. 8-12) is becoming common in most parts of the United States. Termites live in the moist earth, not in wood; they travel from the ground into the wood only to feed. They do not like light and will travel above ground through cracks in masonry foundations, through wood or in mud tunnels they construct on masonry surfaces.

Termite protection is provided by (1) controlling the moisture content of the wood used; (2) providing effective termite barriers, and (3) using naturally durable or treated wood. Most appraisers are not qualified to make a complete termite inspection; however, they can make a preliminary examination which should report the following:

- Wood that is not at least six inches above ground (Joists, sills and girders should have even more clearance)

- Soft wood that may be termite infested

- Cracks in masonry that could be termite pathways

- Mud termite tubes that are signs of termites

- Insects that appear to be termites

- Termite shields and other special termite protection

Inspection by a professional termite inspector should be recommended in the appraisal report.

FIG. 8-12 DIFFERENCES BETWEEN TERMITES AND ANTS

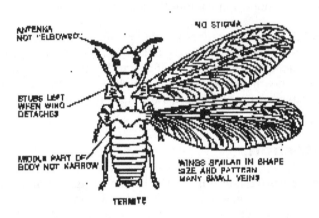

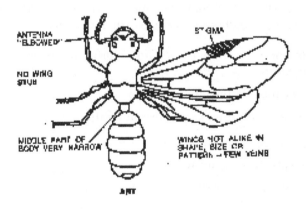

MECHANICAL SYSTEMS AND EQUIPMENT

A building does not function satisfactorily unless its mechanical systems are in good working order. Each system must be inspected by the appraiser and described in the appraisal report. There is no standard way to categorize the mechanical systems and equipment. The following is a summary of the major systems described in this chapter:

- Heating systems
- Cooling systems
- . Plumbing & waste disposal systems
- Domestic hot water systems
- Electrical systems
- Miscellaneous systems and equipment

Heating Systems

Heating systems are based on warm air, water, steam or electricity. Warm (or hot) air heating systems utilize either the natural force of gravity or some type of pressure blower to push heated air through the ducts. Filters can be installed to clean the air and a humidifier is often added to increase the moisture content. All the air systems distribute the heated air into the rooms through registers. Most gravity systems are old and obsolete and ready for replacement; however, gravity floor furnaces are still being installed in small houses. A space heater is another type of low-quality system.

Hot Water Systems

Hot water systems, are also known as **hydronic systems**, hold heated water in a cast iron or steel boiler. Some old systems depend on gravity to circulate the water through the radiators. Most modern systems use one or more electric circulators to pump the heated water through pipes into either baseboard panels or convectors, radiators or tubes embedded in the floors, walls or ceilings. These units depend on both convection (air being warmed as it passes over the heated metal and then circulated into the room) and radiation (heat waves being transferred directly from the heated metal to the object being heated by radiant energy). There are also combination systems in which the heat is brought to the radiator by warm water. A fan in the radiator blows air over the radiator fins, heating the room by convection.

Steam Heat

Steam heat is produced by a furnace that is a boiler with a firebox underneath it. As the water boils, steam is created that is forced by its pressure through pipes into radiators.

Electricity

Electricity may be considered as either a fuel to heat air or water in a furnace or as a source of heat itself. Its use with resistance elements produces heat at the immediate area to be heated. These resistance elements, which convert electricity into heat, are embedded in the floors, walls and ceilings to provide radiant heat. The advantages claimed for electric radiant heat are the lack of visible radiators or grilles and its ability to maintain adequate air humidity levels. Electric heat also provides the advantage of individual room temperature control using thermostats in each room.

ELECTRIC HEATING PANELS
Electric heating panels, also with individual resistance elements, are often used for auxiliary heat.

FIG. 8-13 BASIC TYPES OF HEATING SYSTEMS

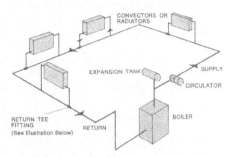

SINGLE PIPE INDIVIDUAL TAKE-OFF HOT WATER SYSTEM

Looking up at the area of the basement ceiling that is directly under the first floor radiators, one wide-diameter pipe will be seen under each radiator. Each of these pipes will be connected to its radiator by two smaller feeder pipes.

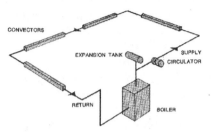

ONE-PIPE SERIES CONNECTED HOT WATER SYSTEM

This system may be identified by looking up at the part of the basement ceiling that is directly under the first floor radiators. In a one-pipe series connected hot water system, one wide-diameter pipe will be seen going in and out of each radiator. There will be no small-diameter feeder pipes.

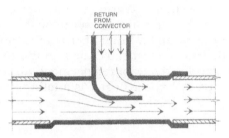

ONE-PIPE RETURN TEE FITTING

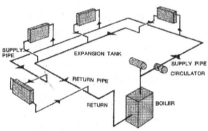

TWO-PIPE REVERSE RETURN HOT WATER SYSTEM

Looking up at the part of the basement ceiling that is directly under the first floor radiators, two wide-diameter pipes will be seen under each radiator. Each will be connected to its radiator by a smaller feeder pipe.

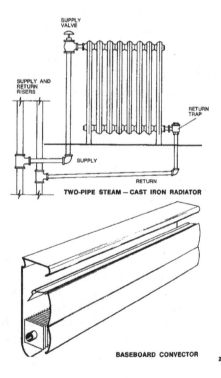

TWO-PIPE STEAM — CAST IRON RADIATOR

BASEBOARD CONVECTOR   295

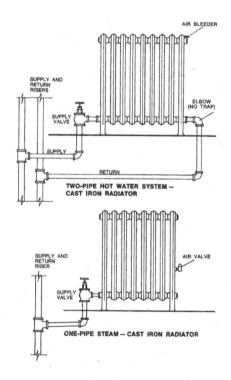

TWO-PIPE HOT WATER SYSTEM — CAST IRON RADIATOR

ONE-PIPE STEAM — CAST IRON RADIATOR

FIG. 8-14 BASIC TYPES OF HEATING SYSTEMS

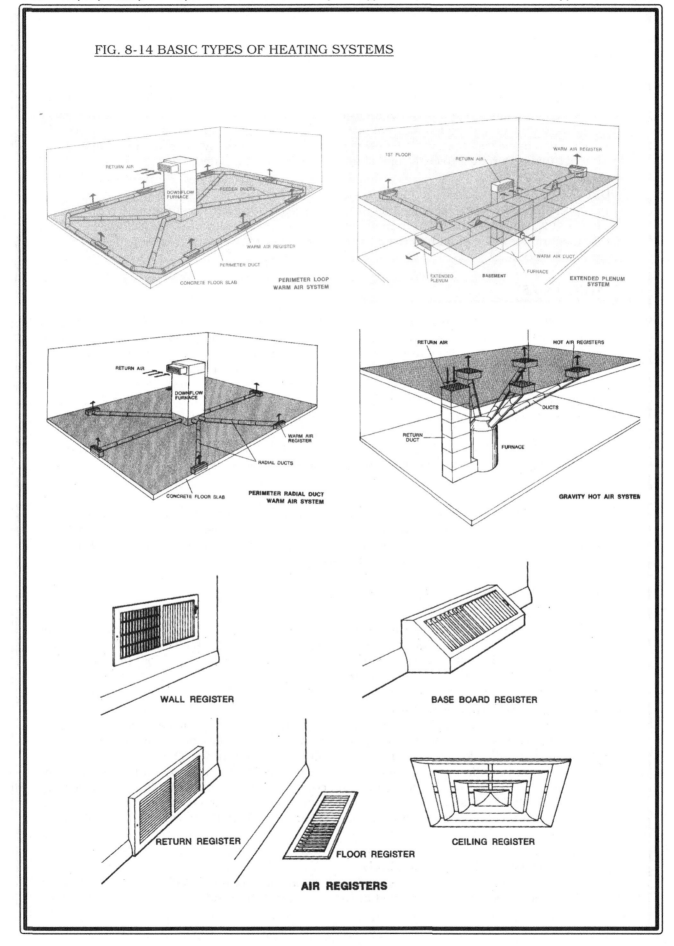

Type of Fuel

The type of fuel used in any heating system must be considered as world fuel markets and prices change from day to day. Fuel needs and supplies have become a major factor in international economics and politics. Each fuel has its own significant advantages and disadvantages which change from time to time and differ from one region to another. Coal was once the most popular fuel but most home coal systems are now obsolete; however, new systems are once again being manufactured as a return to coal from oil and gas is being suggested.

FUEL OIL
Fuel oil is often the least expensive fuel in the northeast and northwest sections of the United States and is competitively priced in many other areas as well. However, this all maybe a thing of the past as the price of oil has risen in the 2000s and shows no sign so far of return to its traditional price level.

NATURAL GAS
Natural gas offers the convenience of continuous delivery to the house via a pipeline, without the necessity of storage tanks. In most areas of the country (the major exceptions being the northeast and northwest), gas has been the most economical fuel. Liquid petroleum gas, is used in many rural areas. It requires on-premises storage tanks and is usually more expensive than natural pipeline gas. In other respects, it is similar to natural gas.

ELECTRICITY
Electricity might be the fuel of the future. Electric systems are the least expensive to install since they require no furnace, furnace room, ducts, flue or plumbing. They do require, however, a much larger electric service into the house and wiring to each unit. To date, in spite of advertising to the contrary, electric heat costs remain high, except in lower-cost power areas.

SOLAR
Solar is the least developed source of heat to date. It comes directly from the sun. Solar heat is still in the experimental stages. Many homes have at least some solar energy system. A variety of solar heating systems are on the market today and appraisers will have to stay current on solar heat developments to appraise a house with a solar system.

Cooling Systems

Until the late 1940's, most cooling was done with fans. In some areas of the west, where the humidity is low even in periods of high heat, a simple system which blows air across wet excelsior or some other water-absorbing material is used to cool the air. Most buildings being currently built have some type of air conditioning system.

WINDOW (OR SLEEVE) AIR CONDITIONING
Window (or sleeve) air conditioning units are sold by the millions each year. Small 5,000-**BTU** units usually can be self-installed and plug into a regular duplex outlet. New units gaining popularity are those no longer requiring a sleeve or window mounting. The unit is split into two parts; the compressor hangs or stands on the outside and the fan is hung on the interior wall. Only a small hole in the wall is needed for the connecting tube and wire. The appraiser must determine whether by custom or law air conditioners are classified as real or personal property in the subject market, and the appraisal report should clearly indicate which case applies.

DUCTED CENTRAL AIR-CONDITIONING
Ducted central air-conditioning systems may be custom made or pre-wired, pre-charged, factory-assembled packages that are connected at the home site. The condenser portion is set outside

the house or on the roof. It is connected by pipe to the evaporator air-handling unit inside the house. The air-handling unit, consisting of the evaporator and a fan, is connected to a system of ducts that distributes cool air to the various areas of the house. If the house has a warm forced-air heating system, the air-conditioning system can use the same fan, filter and duct work. However, the ducts may not be suitable for air conditioning because cooling generally requires double the duct size of heating, and the cooling system works much better if the registers are high on the wall or are the type that direct air steeply upward.

HEAT PUMPS

Heat pumps are used for both heating and cooling. The heat pump is actually a reversible refrigeration unit. In the winter, it takes heat from the outside air or ground or well water and distributes it inside. Its efficiency decreases when it is very cold outside and it must be supplemented with resistance heating. In the summer, the system cools by extracting heat from the inside of the house like a typical air-conditioning unit. Heat pumps constitute only a small percentage of systems being installed.

8.9 ▶

Plumbing Systems & Waste Disposal Systems

The plumbing system is an integral part of any building. The materials used for this system determine its ability to supply adequate clean water and remove wastes over a long period of time. Fig. 8-15 is a representation of a basic plumbing system

The pipes carrying clean water should work without leaking, making noise, reducing pressure or imparting any color or taste to the water. Brass was used for many years, but is now expensive. Older brass pipes tend to crystallize and become coated inside in areas where the water is corrosive. Galvanized steel is used in some areas. Like brass, it is easy to work and is connected with threaded joints and fittings, but it is easily attacked by corrosive water. Galvanized wrought iron is similar to steel but more resistant to corrosion. Copper and lead were also used. Lead until recently was used for the pipe from the water main to the house. Plastic is the newest material for pipes and is gaining acceptance. There is strong evidence that lead in water is very dangerous especially to infants. Having your water tested for lead is a wise investment especially if there is going to be an infant in the house. If the water is not lead free the source of the lead should be determined if possible and it should be removed. If this is not possible, it is a good idea to use bottled drinking water especially for babies.

WATER PIPES

Water pipes must be strong enough to withstand the pressure necessary for water to flow through them. Because there is no pressure in a waste drain line, the pipes must be slanted so that waste will flow from each fixture through the main lines into the sewer or sewage disposal system. Pipes for the drainage system are made of cast iron, copper, plastic, tile, brass, lead or fiber. Special fittings are often used, especially on cast iron pipes, to aid the flow of sewage.

8.10 ▶

STANDARD BATHROOM FIXTURES

Standard bathroom fixtures consist of lavatories (wash basins), bathtubs, showers, and toilets (water closets). The best material for lavatories is cast iron covered with acid-resistant vitreous enamel. Newer units are made of fiberglass. Bathtubs are the most expensive bathroom fixture. The most common materials are ceramic tile, steel or cast iron covered with vitreous enamel or fiberglass. The standard size for bathtubs is 5 1/2 feet long by 16 inches deep. Large bathtubs are becoming more popular. Many tubs also have a shower unit because they are less expensive to build than a separate tub and shower stall. Separate shower stalls are often prefabricated steel or fiberglass units.

RESIDENTIAL TOILETS

Residential toilets mostly consist of a bowl and a tank that stores sufficient water to create proper flushing action. The toilet can be rated by its self-cleaning properties, its flushing action, the amount

FIG. 8-15 BASIC TYPES OF PLUMBING SYSTEMS

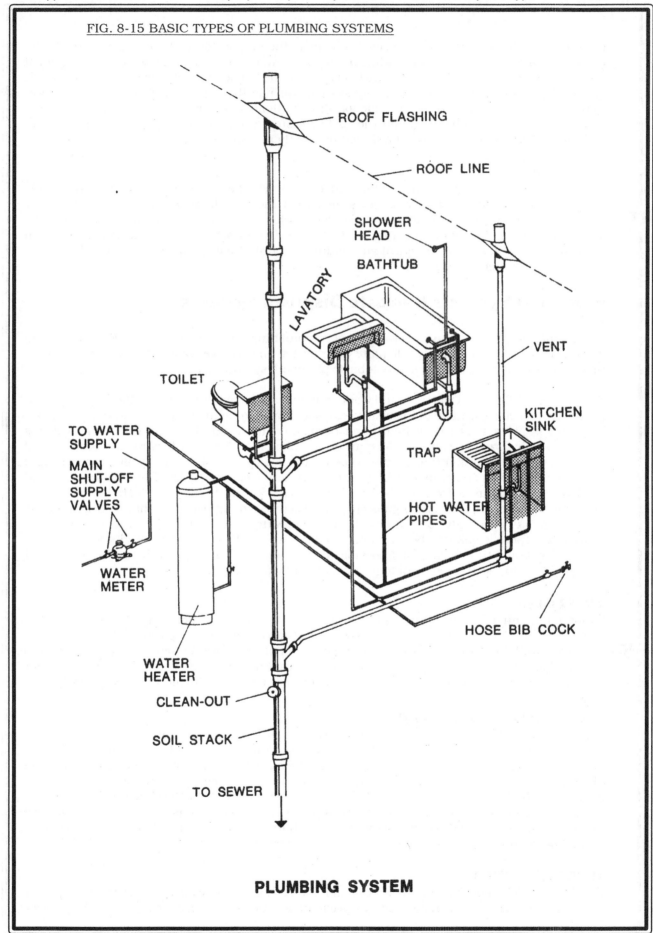

PLUMBING SYSTEM

of noise during flushing, and the ease of cleaning around the exterior. Federal regulation now regulate the amount of water that can be used for each flush. For old toilets, putting a few bricks in the tank will effectively reduce the amount of water used per flush.

KITCHEN PLUMBING FIXTURES
Kitchen plumbing fixtures include a single or double sink, generally installed in a counter. The sink drain should have a removable crumb cup or combination crumb cup and stopper. Kitchen sinks may be made of acid-resistant enameled cast iron, enameled steel, stainless steel or Monel metal. A garbage disposal unit and/or a dishwasher are often connected to kitchen plumbing.

BATHROOM AND KITCHEN FITTINGS
Bathroom and kitchen fittings both include a series of faucets, spigots and drains, which require occasional repair or replacement. The most common type of faucet arrangement has two separate valves, one each for hot and cold water. Most faucets now being installed feed into a single spout and a further refinement is a single control valve that controls both the water temperature and volume. A shower should have an **automatic diverter** control that switches the flow of water back to the tub after each shower so that the next user will not accidentally get wet or scalded. Most modern kitchen sinks have a combination faucet with a swing spout. A separate spray on a flexible tube is also common. Another attachment now available for a kitchen sink provides boiling water instantly.

SPECIALIZED PLUMBING FIXTURES
Specialized plumbing fixtures, such as laundry tubs or a wet bar, may also be found in laundry and family recreation rooms.

Domestic Hot Water System

An adequate supply of hot water is essential. Buildings with inadequate hot water systems suffer from functional obsolescence. The supply is usually generated in a hot water heater, with optional supplementary storage tanks. The heater may be powered by electricity, gas or oil as a separate unit; or hot water may be supplied from furnace heat. The latter system supplies only a small amount of hot water, which may be exhausted too quickly. Another disadvantage is the need to run the furnace all year.

▶ The recovery rate (the time it takes to heat water) determines the tank size needed. Standard gas hot water tanks range from 30 to 100 gallons. Because the recovery rate of an oil hot water heater is faster than gas or electricity, a 30-gallon tank provides enough hot water. They are not popular, however, because of the initial high cost and installation, especially if no flue or oil storage tank is already available.

In many areas of the country, large amounts of minerals such as calcium, magnesium, sulfates, bicarbonates, iron or sulphur are found in the water. These minerals react unfavorably with soap, forming a curd-like substance which is difficult to rinse from clothing, hair and skin. A water softening system can be installed to eliminate these mineral deposits and may be standard in many market areas.

Sewers, Septic Tanks and Cesspools

Few will argue the substantial advantage of being connected to a municipal sewer system by a single outlet or separately into the sanitary and storm water disposal system. Freddie Mac and Fannie Mae require that, when available, the municipal sewer system be used. With increasing awareness of the damaging effects of pollution on our environment, rapid improvement and expansion of these systems can be expected in the near future. Health experts estimate that

50 percent of the septic systems now in use are not working properly. Still, it is estimated that almost 50 million people in 15 million homes, especially in suburban and rural areas, depend upon a septic system for their waste disposal and that 25 percent of new houses being constructed do not connect to municipal systems.

SEPTIC SYSTEMS

A septic system typically consists of a large concrete tank with a capacity of 900 gallons (about 8' by 4' by 4') buried in the ground. One end accepts the waste material from the house drain line. Once inside the tank, the waste tends to separate into three parts. The solid waste materials (only about 1 percent of the total volume) sink to the bottom. The grease (also less than 1 percent of the total volume) rises to the top. The rest is liquid. Bacteria in the tank decompose the solid wastes and grease and a relatively clear liquid flows from the opposite end through the drain line either into a distribution box that directs the liquid into a network of buried perforated pipes called a leaching field or into a seepage pit. From here the liquid runs off into the ground to be absorbed.

8.13 ▶ The required capacity of the tank depends upon the size of the house and usage. The size of the leaching field depends on the soil's capacity to absorb water. The rate at which the soil will absorb water can be measured by making a **percolation test**. A hole at least 12 inches deep is dug in the ground and filled with water. Each hour the depth of the water is measured. Anything less than an inch decrease in depth each 30 minutes is substandard. This test should be carried out in the wettest season of the year and preferably by an expert. Usually the local health department will make the test at no cost or for a nominal charge. Also, it is likely that the local health authorities will have previous knowledge of the individual system.

Septic tanks must be checked frequently to make sure they are not clogged and that the bacterial action is working properly. Chemicals must be used with care as they can kill bacteria. Often the tank must be pumped out and the cycle started anew.

CESSPOOLS

A **cesspool** is similar to a septic system except that instead of a tank there is a covered cistern of stone, brick or concrete. The liquid seeps out through the walls directly into the ground rather than into a leaching field or seepage pit. It is important to learn about a house's particular system, including the location of the clean-out main, which is often buried in an unmarked spot, so that inspections and repairs can be made as required. A properly working system should produce no odor which is one of the first signs of trouble. Learning the location of the clean-out main from the current owner saves a lot of digging and searching if it is buried.

Anyone wishing to gain information on septic systems should find out how often the system has to be pumped out. In many towns the local health officer is very knowledgeable about many systems in the jurisdiction and of problems in a particular neighborhood.

Septic system problems may sometimes be corrected by simply pumping out the tank. Sometimes new leaching fields are required. Unfortunately, there are situations when the soil absorption rate is poor or the water table is close to the surface and little can be done to make the system function properly

Electrical System

8.12 ▶ Most electrical services begins at a "service entrance" which brings power from outside utility wires through an electric meter to a distribution panel. The service entrance may be designed to bring in 30, 60, 100, 150, 200, 300, or 400 amperes of electricity. In smaller and older houses, 30 or 60 ampere service may still be found. A 100-ampere service is the standard today for each dwelling unit that does not have electric heat or central air conditioning. It provides 23,000 watts of power. A typical panel box has 12 to 16 fuses or circuit breakers. In larger units, and where electric heat, central air conditioning or a large number of appliances are used, 150 to 400 ampere service is necessary.

THE DISTRIBUTION BOX

The distribution box has a switch that cuts off all electric service in the house when manually pulled in the event of an emergency. It also must contain either a master fuse or circuit breaker that will automatically disconnect the entire system if the system overloads. A fuse is a piece of wire that will melt when more than the prescribed amount of electricity flows through it. A circuit breaker is a special type of automatic switch that switches off when excess electricity passes through it. The distribution box divides the incoming electric service into separate branch circuits. Each individual circuit must also be protected by a fuse or a circuit breaker. If an overload or short circuit occurs on one line, it automatically shuts off without tripping the main fuse or circuit breaker.

WIRING

Wiring comes in a variety of types. The most preferred type of wiring is through rigid steel pipe, which looks like water pipe. It is also the most expensive method. Wires are pulled through the pipe after it is installed. A less expensive system that has code approval in most cities makes use of armored (BX) cable which consists of insulted wires wrapped in heavy paper and encased in a flexible, galvanized steel covering, wound in a spiral fashion. Surface raceways made of metal or plastic are sometimes used. Flexible steel conduit is constructed like BX cable except that it is installed without the wire, which is drawn through the conduit after installation.

NONMETALLIC CABLE

Nonmetallic cable is made of wire which is wrapped with a paper tape and then encased in a heavy water-and fire-resistant fabric. A similar system has cable with a thermoplastic insulation and jacket; the cables are attached to the joists and studs with staples. A now obsolete system involves running two parallel exposed wires from the panel box to outlets and fixtures. The wires are attached to the house with white porcelain insulators, called "knobs." When the wire passes through a wall or joist, It is placed through a white porcelain tube - hence the name "knob and tube wiring." This type of system should be replaced.

TELEPHONES AND DOORBELLS

Telephones and doorbells use low voltage wiring that does not present a safety hazard and therefore can be run loose throughout the walls and along the joists. Intercoms, central music and burglar alarm systems also use low voltage wiring.

DUPLEX RECEPTACLE

The *duplex receptacle* was until 1960 the most common household outlet used. It accepts a two-prong plug, the type most often found on lamps and small appliances. In 1960 the National Electric Code required that all receptacles be of the grounding type, designed to accept a three-prong plug, to reduce shock hazard. Special waterproof receptacles with caps for outside use and other special purpose outlets are also available.

WALL SWITCHES

Wall switches control permanently installed light fixtures and wall outlets. The simplest and most common switch is a two-way snap switch. Three-way switches are used to control a fixture or outlet from different locations, which is useful, for example, for a light in a stairwell.

LOW-VOLTAGE SWITCHING SYSTEMS

Low-voltage switching systems are used for control in some buildings. Instead of the switch directly opening and closing the circuit, it controls a relay, which in turn, operates the switch. The advantage of this system is that many lights and outlets can be controlled from one place.

ADEQUATE SWITCHING ARRANGEMENTS

Adequate switching arrangements allow one to walk anywhere in a building, turning on a path of light and then being able to turn it off without having to retrace steps or walk in the dark.

FIG. 8-16 SEPTIC SYSTEM

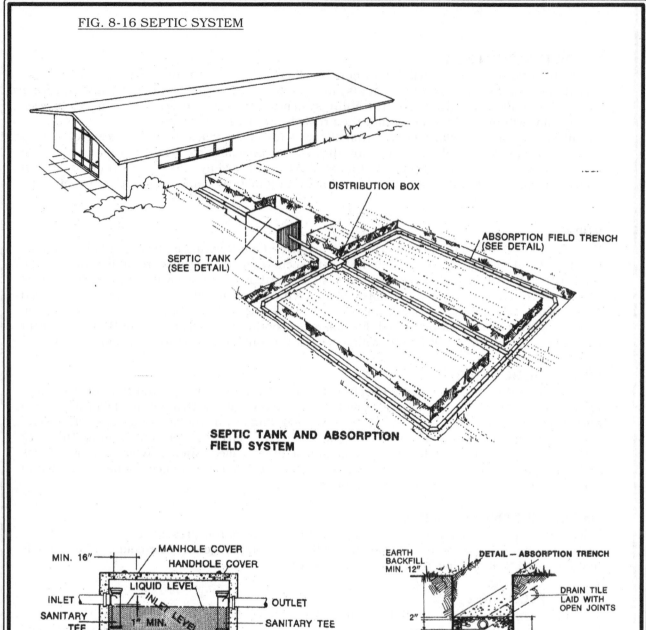

SEPTIC TANK AND ABSORPTION FIELD SYSTEM

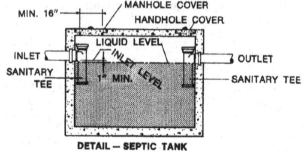

DETAIL — SEPTIC TANK

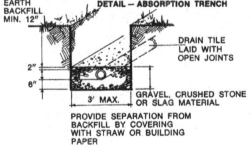

DETAIL — ABSORPTION TRENCH

Miscellaneous Systems and Equipment

A variety of mechanical systems and special equipment is being installed today. Many reflect fads or the special interests of the owner. They include such items as intercoms and sound systems, burglar and fire alarms, automatic doors, elevators, incinerators, laundry chutes, and central vacuum cleaners. The appraiser must judge each situation to determine how much value these specialized items add. A further consideration in some cases is whether the items are real estate or personal property.

ITEMS REQUIRING IMMEDIATE REPAIR
(Deferred Maintenance)

Except for buildings in an exceptional state of maintenance, there will almost always be items needing repair as of the date of the appraisal. The repair of these normal maintenance items should add more value to the property than they cost. In the cost approach these items are classified as curable physical deterioration. The repair list should include conditions observed by the appraiser that constitute a fire or safety hazard.

Many clients request that these deferred maintenance items be listed separately in the report. Sometimes the appraiser is requested to estimate the cost of each repair (cost to cure). The following is a list of the most commonly items most commonly needing immediate repair:

- Touching up exterior paint
- Minor carpentry repairs to stairs, molding, siding, trim, floors, porches
- Redecorating interior rooms
- Fixing plumbing leaks and noisy plumbing
- Freeing stuck doors and windows
- Repairing holes in screens and replacing broken windows or other glass
- Re-hanging loose gutters and leaders
- Replacing missing roof shingles and tiles
- Fixing cracks in pavements
- Making minor electrical repairs
- Replacing rotted floor boards
- Exterminating vermin
- Fixing cracked or loose bathroom and kitchen tiles
- Repairing septic system
- Eliminating all fire and safety hazards

PHYSICAL DETERIORATION INCURABLE - SHORT LIVED ITEMS

Although the paint, roof, wallpaper, etc., may show some signs of wear and tear, it may not be ready for replacement on the date of the appraisal. The test is whether its immediate repair or replacement will add more value to the property than its cost.

For example, if a building has an exterior paint job that is three years old in an area where this type of paint lasts five years, the paint has suffered some depreciation. Repainting, however, probably would not add value to the property equal to its cost if it were done at the end of three

FIG. 8-17 ELECTRIC SYSTEM

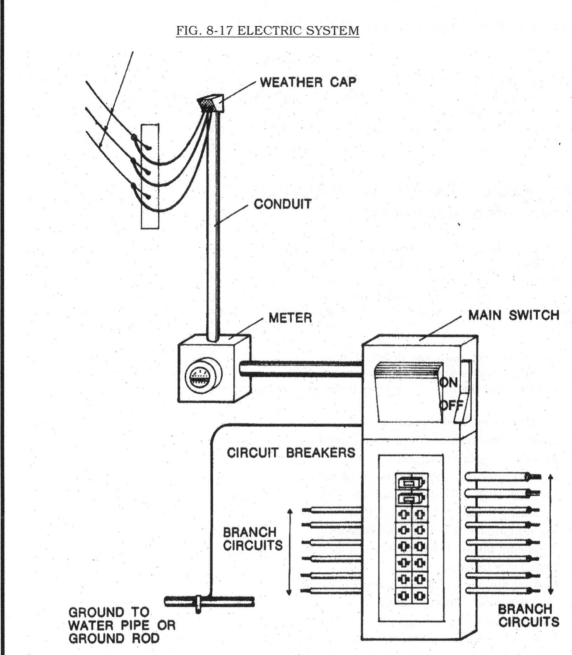

Here is the usual relationship between ampere service, number of circuit breakers and maximum number of watts:

Size of Service	No. of Branch Circuits (fuses or circuit breakers)	Maximum No. of Watts
30 ampere	4	6,900
60 ampere	6 to 8	13,800
100 ampere	12 to 16	23,000
150 or more amperes	20 or more	30,000 or more

ELECTRIC SERVICE ENTRANCE

years. This is an example of Physical Deterioration Incurable - Short lived item. If the value of the property would increase the value of the property by more than the cost of painting, the exterior paint job would be classified as physical deterioration curable - deferred maintenance.

The following items normally have to be repaired or replaced before the end of the economic life of the building. They are known as short-lived items:

- Interior paint and wallpaper
- Exterior paint
- Floor finishes
- Shades, screens and blinds
- Waterproofing and weather-stripping
- Gutters and leaders
- Storm windows
- Roof covering and flashing
- Hot and cold water pipes
- Plumbing fixtures
- Domestic hot water heater
- Electric service entrance
- Electric wiring
- Electric switches and outlets
- Electric fixtures
- Furnace
- Ducts and radiators
- Air conditioning equipment
- Carpeting
- Kitchen appliances
- Kitchen counters and cabinets
- Well pump
- Water softener system
- Laundry appliances
- Ventilating fans
- Fences and other site improvements

The appraiser should note any of these or other short-lived items whose condition is better or worse than the overall condition of the building of which they are a part.

OVERALL CONDITION OF IMPROVEMENTS

This section of the report is substantially complete when all items requiring immediate repair and all deferred maintenance are described. One last step, however, is to report the condition of items that should last the normal economic life of the building. Their condition is affected by abnormal wear and tear, and they can be damaged accidentally. They also may have been poorly made or installed. It would be a very unusual property where all the long-lived items were in exactly the same condition. For example, the clapboard siding may show signs of warping because of a roof leak; the condition may not be bad enough to warrant replacing the siding now. This case is a form of "physical deterioration-incurable."

INTERIOR DESIGN AND LAYOUT (FUNCTIONAL UTILITY)

The perfect residence is one that is the exact size, shape and design to produce the maximum profit. It would be the theoretical highest and best use of the site. Most residences are not the perfect or ideal improvements. Room sizes, their number and type, and the design and layout differ from the idealized highest and best use. In fact, many things could be improved in the design and layout of a typical house. The appraiser is not on a quest for the perfect building, but is trying to identify design elements that adversely affect value. These items constitute functional obsolescence in the cost approach.

Since most appraisers have little or no training in design, they tend to rely on their own likes and dislikes as a basis for making design judgments, an inappropriate basis on which to make such judgements. It is better to learn what is generally accepted in the market as good design.

HOUSE ZONES

A good way to consider the interior layout of a house is to divide it into zones. The private/ sleeping zone contains the bedrooms, bathrooms and dressing rooms. The living/social zone consists of the living room, dining room, recreation room, den and enclosed porch. The working/ service zone consists of the kitchen, laundry, pantry and other work areas. In addition to these three zones are circulation areas consisting of halls and stairs plus guest and family entrances (see Fig. 8-18).

NOTES

FIG. 8-18 ZONING - ONE STORY HOUSE

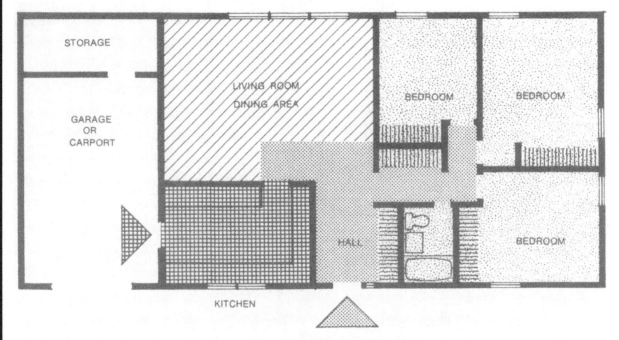

ZONING: ONE-STORY HOUSE

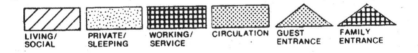

The three zones should be separated from one another so that activities in one zone do not interfere with those in another. The private/sleeping zone should be located so that it is insulated from noise in the other two zones, and it should be possible to move from the bedrooms to the bathrooms in this zone without being seen from other areas of the house. The working/service zone is the nerve center of the house; from here the household activities are directed. From the kitchen, it should be possible to control both guest and family entrances, activities in the private/sleeping zone and living/social zone, plus activities in the porch, patio and backyard areas.

The guest entrance should lead into the center of the house. From here there should be direct access to the living areas, guest closet and guest lavatory. A noise and visibility barrier should exist between the guest entrance and the private/sleeping zone.

Ideally, the family entrance should be from the garage, carport, or breezeway into the kitchen or from a circulation area directly connecting to the kitchen. Traffic from this entrance should not have to pass through the **work triangle** of the kitchen to enter the other rooms of the house. Circulation should be such that one may move from working/service zone to the private/sleeping zone without going through the living/social zone.

If the house has a basement, it may have a separate outside entrance. The inside basement entrance should lead into a circulation area that has access to the private/sleeping zone, the living social zone and both the guest and family entrances, without going through the living room or the kitchen work triangle.

COMMON FLOOR PLAN DEFICIENCIES

According to a national survey of homeowners, some of the most common floor plan deficiencies include the following items. These will vary depending on the geographic region and the size and value of the residence.
- Front door entering directly into the living room
- No front hall closet
- No direct access from front door to kitchen, bath or bedroom without passing through other rooms
- Rear door not convenient to kitchen and difficult to reach from the street, driveway and garage
- No comfortable area in or near the kitchen for family to eat

- A separate dining area or room not easily accessible from the kitchen
- Stairways off a room rather than in a hallway or foyer
- Bedrooms and baths that are visible from the living room or foyer
- Recreation or family room poorly located (not visible from kitchen)

- No access to the basement from outside the house
- Walls between bedrooms not soundproof (separation by a bathroom or closet accomplish soundproofing)

- Outdoor living areas not accessible and/or not visible from kitchen

Living Room

Until World War II, the living room was the living center of the house. In the past several decades, the status of the living room has undergone a change. Today, the family room, patio and kitchen are more likely to be the locations for relaxing, socializing and entertaining. As these areas have grown and developed, the size and the importance of the living room has diminished. Sometimes two or more rooms are combined together and called a great room.

The location of the living room may be in the traditional front of the house or, if view or access to outdoor living area is better, in the back or on a side of the house. The room should be positioned to supplement the dining and outdoor entertainment areas in the house. Often one end of the living room is the dining area, so it must have good juxtaposition with the kitchen/service areas as well. The living room should not be a traffic-way between other rooms. The following are some guidelines for judging the size of the living room compared with the rest of the house.

In a three-room house, the living room should have minimum dimensions of 11 by 16 feet, or at least 176 square feet. The recommended dimensions are 12 by 18 feet. If a dining area is at one end of the room, dimensions may go up to 16 by 26 feet or more. A maximum width of 8 feet is recommended for proper furniture arrangements around the room. Where traffic is necessary through the room, a width of 15 or 16 feet could conceivably be used to advantage by routing the traffic outside the **conversation circle** created by the furniture (see Fig. 8-19).

FIG. 8-19 CONVERSATION CIRCLES

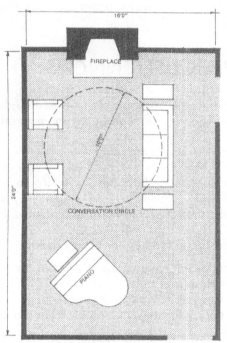

LONG AND WIDE LIVING ROOM

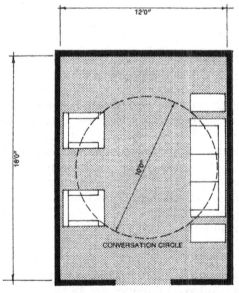

MINIMUM SIZE LIVING ROOM

Kitchen

Traditionally, the kitchen was located at the back of the house. Today it can be located wherever it best fits into the overall design and a current trend is to locate it at the front of the house. The kitchen should not be a main thoroughfare.

The size of the kitchen depends on the space available, the number of people in the family, the kind of equipment desired and what activities other than those directly associated with food preparation are carried on there. The minimum size for a kitchen in a small house is 8 by 10 feet. Better sizes are 10 by 10 and 10 by 12 feet. As the size of the house increased often the size of the kitchen also increases.

Ten percent or more of the cost of a new home is spent on the kitchen. A functional kitchen should have adequate storage space, appliance space, counter and activity space, all arranged for maximum efficiency. The term triangle has become fashionable to describe the essential work zone of the kitchen, since there are three key work areas of use and activity: the refrigerator area, sink/wash/preparation area, and range/serving area. They can be arranged in any logical way, determined by the space available and the personal preference for one particular center over another (see Fig. 8-20).

FIG. 8-20 KITCHEN LAYOUTS

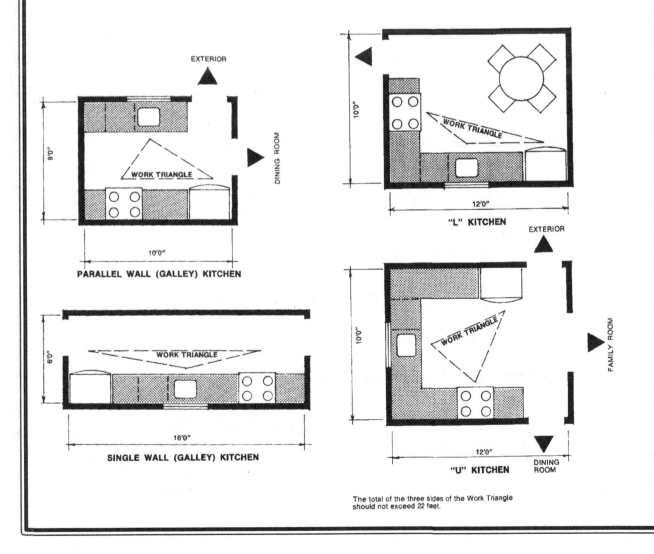

PARALLEL WALL (GALLEY) KITCHEN

SINGLE WALL (GALLEY) KITCHEN

"L" KITCHEN

"U" KITCHEN

The total of the three sides of the Work Triangle should not exceed 22 feet.

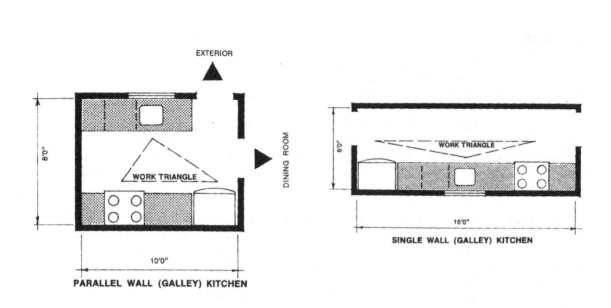

However the kitchen is arranged, work should flow in a normal sequence from one center to another. Ideally, no traffic should move through the triangle in the main kitchen work area. Properly establishing the location of windows and doors will help to ensure a traffic pattern that does not interfere with efficient use of the kitchen. Most building standards require that the window area should equal at least 10% of the floor area of the room. At least one section of a work counter should have a window over it with provision for controlling direct sunlight. Many people prefer to have a window located over the sink. (For reasons of both safety and good housekeeping, the range should never be located under a window.)

Many kitchens suffer from one or more of the following inadequacies (listed in order of most common occurrence):

- Insufficient base cabinet storage
- Insufficient wall cabinet storage
- Insufficient counter space
- No counter beside the refrigerator
- Not enough window area
- Poorly placed doors that waste wall space
- Traffic through the work triangle
- Too little counter space on either side of the sink
- No counter beside the range
- Insufficient space in front of cabinets
- Distance between sink, range and refrigerator too great
- Range under a window

Dining Rooms and Dining Areas

A dining room was included in most pre-World War II homes. Now many houses have dining areas that are part of another room. The traditional space requirements for dining rooms probably no longer apply to many markets. A minimum size dining room is 9 by 11 feet, with 12 by 12 being preferable. In some markets an acceptable alternative to the dining room or area is an extra large "eat-in" kitchen. The appraiser must determine what the market wants and judge if the appraised house meets the requirements.

Bedrooms

The number of bedrooms in a house is an important design consideration. Three bedrooms is most common today. Houses with only two bedrooms are often constructed at the direction of an owner who does not need the third room; however, many markets do not accept only two bedrooms without a substantial discount. A fourth bedroom is appealing to many families, but in many markets the additional price a four-bedroom house brings is not as great as the cost of the extra bedroom. Of course, luxury homes may have five or more bedrooms. One bedroom homes are usually substandard in any market, except for recreational homes.

Two key factors in the location of bedrooms are that they should be isolated from the noise generated in the rest of the house, and that one should be able to get from each bedroom to a bathroom without being seen from the living/social zone of the house. The minimum size bedroom for a single bed is 8 by 10 feet; this size is satisfactory only if the layout is good and no space is wasted. The minimum size room for a double bed is 10 by 11-1/2 feet. Some markets expect bedrooms to be more than minimum size; other markets will not pay the extra cost for the larger space. Each bedroom should have at least one closet with a minimum depth of two feet, a width of three feet and a height sufficient to allow five feet clear hanging space.

Bathrooms and Lavatories

Houses with only one bathroom are obsolete in many markets; 1-1/2 baths is becoming a minimum standard, except in low-priced and recreation homes. The older minimum standard for two-story houses of one bath upstairs and a lavatory downstairs is being replaced in many markets with a standard of two baths. The minimum size for a bathroom containing a five-foot tub/shower combination, basin and toilet is 5 by 7 feet. This allows for the toilet to be on the wall opposite the tub rather than between the tub and basin, which is unsatisfactory; it also allows the door to swing in without hitting a fixture (see Fig. 12-21). A bathroom should not be located between two bedrooms with a door leading directly into the bathroom from each bedroom. (This is, however, a common feature of many Victorian homes).

The terminology used to describe bathrooms and lavatories varies around the country. In most areas a full bath consists of a room with a toilet (also known as a water closet), wash basin (also known as a sink, lavatory or vanity) and a tub. A 3/4 bathroom has a toilet, wash basin and stall shower (called a full bath in some areas). A half-bath (also known as a lavatory, or powder room) has a toilet and wash basin.

The bathroom requires the most heat and the best ventilation of any room in the house. A bathroom or lavatory with or without a window is equally acceptable, but ventilation of an interior bathroom or lavatory is essential. A ventilation fan, ducted to the outside, should be wired to the light switch so that it goes on automatically when the room is in use and turns off automatically when the lights are turned off.

Family and Recreation Rooms

Before World War II attics, dens and finished basements generally were used as additional recreation space. Today, the family room is used as a den, study, guest room, nursery, library, TV room, or hobby entertainment center. The key to the successful location of this room is to have it visible from and easily accessible to the kitchen. It also should be accessible to the outdoor living area, such as the backyard or patio. A good size for the recreation room in a small house is 12 by 16 feet. Appraisers should remember that many family or recreation rooms are over improved or too large for a particular market.

FIG. 8-21 BATHROOM LAYOUTS

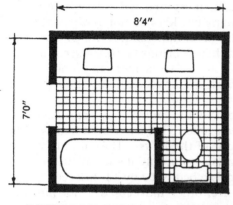

BATHROOM WITH TWO LAVATORIES

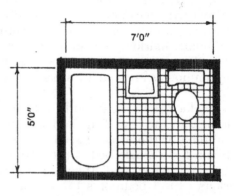

MINIMUM SIZE BATHROOM

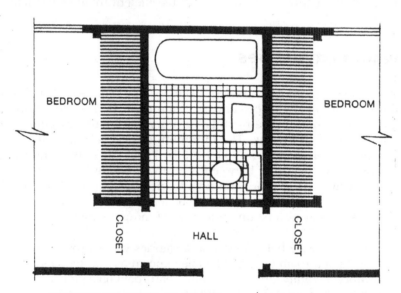

BATHROOM WITH CLOSETS AS SOUND BARRIERS

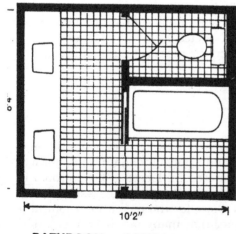

BATHROOM — COMPARTMENTED

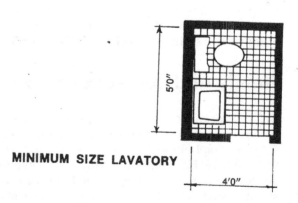

MINIMUM SIZE LAVATORY

Patios, Porches and Decks

In some areas patios are very elaborate and an integral part of the house. They can be described as part of the improvements rather than a site improvement. Porches have been decreasing in popularity and importance for many years except in a few areas of the country. The exceptions seem to be sun porches and side porches on more expensive homes, the Hawaiian "lanai" (a covered or open porch) and screened-in porches in beach and summer homes. Some styles have special porch features, such as the Victorian wrap-around porch, which will usually add value.

Laundry Rooms and Storage Areas

A growing trend has been to bring the washing machine and clothes dryer out of the basement. These appliances are being installed in the kitchen, a separate laundry or utility room, the garage, or even in hallways or closets on the first or second floors. Anyone who has lived in a house with a basement finds it hard to understand why they are not more universally accepted. A house without a basement may suffer from a lack of adequate storage space, and it will be penalized by the market. Alternate acceptable storage areas are attics, closets, storage rooms, garages, storage sheds, etc.

RENOVATION: REHABILITATION, MODERNIZATION AND REMODELING

Often the appraiser finds that substantial renovations are necessary if the existing improvement is to achieve the highest and best use of the site. These alterations and improvements go beyond the normal curable physical deterioration and functional obsolescence. The owner of the property may have come to a similar conclusion before the appraisal and may already have done some or all of the work.

These substantial changes can be described by the terms rehabilitation, modernization and remodeling. Each term has a specific meaning with which the appraiser should be familiar.

Rehabilitation

The restoration of a property to satisfactory condition, without changing the plan, form or style of a structure is called rehabilitation. In urban renewal, the restoration to good condition of deteriorated structures, neighborhoods, and public facilities. Neighborhood rehabilitation encompasses structural rehabilitation and in addition may extend to street improvements and provision of such amenities as parks and playgrounds.

A growing trend in many cities throughout the country is the restoration of older neighborhoods and homes. People are moving back into city neighborhoods, and older homes in center city locations are now attracting young professionals, business people and white-collar workers. Some older homes are not much more than four good walls and sturdy ceilings; more often the interior floors and walls are usable. The woodwork can be restored and although the mechanical systems usually have to be replaced, some parts of the original systems may be usable. The appraisal of this type of property often requires the appraiser to help plan the rehabilitation.

Modernization

Taking corrective measures to bring a property into conformity with changes in style, whether exterior or interior, or additions necessary to meet standards of current demand is called modernization. It normally involves replacing parts of the structure or mechanical equipment with modern replacements of the same kind.

Modernization implies replacement or remodeling specifically designed to offset the effect of obsolescence or making additions necessary to meet current design standards. The replacement of old radiators and lighting or plumbing fixtures with new items of fundamentally the same type, is nothing more than improving the condition of the old installation. However, the substitution of convectors for cast-iron radiators, of built-in bathtubs for tubs on legs, or of modern lighting fixtures for old-fashioned types would not necessarily reflect on the physical condition of the items being replaced and therefore would constitute an improvement of the property. These expenditures offset obsolescence and may be classified as modernization. Modernization may cost more than simple renewal but can be economically justified where it offsets the obsolescence inherent in the older equipment.

Modernization usually extends the economic life of property. To be justified, a modernization is done because the owner desires the convenience it creates. The installation of a modern kitchen at a cost of $20,000 may add only $10,000 in value. This is an example of a super adequacy or over improvement.

Remodeling

Changing the plan, form or style of a structure to correct functional deficiencies is called remodeling. Studies have shown that kitchen and bathroom remodeling are the most popular project.

Remodeling becomes practical when the use of part of the house can be changed. Common examples are finishing a basement or attic or adding a bathroom to an existing room. Considerable remodeling is often done to suit the needs of a specific owner without much thought given what the market in general expects and will pay for. The expenditure of $12,000 to finish a basement playroom may add only $6,000 to the property value in some markets.

Renovation Costs

It is much more difficult to estimate renovation or rehabilitation costs than that of new construction. Unit-in-place costs for new work, plus an additional allowance for the normally higher cost of repair work, make renovation estimates difficult. Rehabilitation estimates frequently may be based upon actual recent costs for the same or equivalent work performed in the property or in similar properties. Management records may even include bids for specific rehabilitation items that have not yet been accomplished, such as exterior painting, roof repair, or interior decorating.

The cost of some rehabilitation work may approximate that for similar work in new construction. However, the cost of modernization or remodeling work is almost invariably higher than that for new construction, for several reasons. Although the quantity of materials may be the same as for new work, more labor is involved and the conditions are different. The alteration of a structure usually involves tearing out old work and performing small portions of new work under conditions not conducive to the degree of efficiency attainable on new construction. If the estimate made by the contractor is on a flat-fee basis, the charge may be substantially higher than the cost of identical work in new construction, so the contractor can be protected against complications that may develop as the remodeling progresses. Such unforeseen complications may involve the placement of existing conduits, pipes, and structural load bearing members. Other costs to be considered are those that may be incurred by the owner rather than the contractor. These include the architect's fee, the owner's cost of supervision and loss of the use of the house while the work is being done.

Feasibility of Renovation

Whether rehabilitation, modernization or remodeling is involved, the justification for any renovation program depends on what constitutes the highest and best use of the property. The study that the appraiser gives to this question produces the cost estimates necessary for a program to achieve such use, which in turn provide the basis for a decision as to its economic justification.

If the property is old but in sufficiently sound condition for remodeling, if the neighborhood standards and trends are materially higher than the property's present status, and if the prospective value increase is substantial, a comprehensive program may be feasible. A wide range of potential programs may justify consideration, but there is only one satisfactory way to select the final plan. This is to explore the alternatives, estimate the cost and potential value increases, and then be guided by the results of a comparison of the data.

Assume that a brownstone townhouse is available in a neighborhood going through a period of redevelopment. The house can be purchased for $120,000. It is estimated that it will take about $80,000 to rehabilitate the house to meet the minimum code requirements. The estimated value when the rehabilitation is completed is $240,000. Based on these figures, the rehabilitation to meet minimum standards is feasible. A second possibility is to restore the house to its original historical appearance and do a much more elaborate renovation. The estimated cost of this renovation would be $240,000, but the final value would be $480,000. See Fig. 8-22.

FIG. 8-22 EXAMPLE OF RENOVATION FEASIBILITY

Renovation Example 1:	Acquisition price	$120,000
Rehabilitation cost	80,000	
Total Cost	$200,000	
	Estimated value after renovation	240.000
	Estimated profit	$40,000

Renovation Example 2:	Acquisition price	$120,000
	Renovation cost	240,000
	Total cost	$360,000
	Estimated value after renovation	480,000
	Estimated profit	$120,000

Both the above programs are feasible. Example 2 represents the highest and best use of the property, since it produces the maximum profit. In some cases where the profit potential, due to a program of rehabilitation, modernization and modeling is substantial, the as is value estimate for the subject property should be modified upward. In many cities, properties have been purchased at relatively low prices by imaginative investors who have undertaken programs of selective modernization, sometimes involving new exterior ("skin") treatment and other major expenditures. Modernized and attractive properties thus created have become marketable at levels substantially higher than the investments involved. Whether this is practical in any specific situation can be ascertained only by completion of a before-and-after feasibility analysis.

The appraiser's estimate of a renovation program is part of the process used to arrive at a value estimate for the property. Whether or not the owner actually carries out such a program, the value of the property in its existing state may be influenced by its potential for increased value under a feasible renovation program.

GRAPHIC AIDS

Photography

Use of photographs has become an important part of the appraisal report. Out-of-focus, over- or under-exposed amateur photos are no long acceptable.

It is just a question of time before all appraisers are using digital cameras. They allow the appraiser to take many pictures for their work file without incurring virtually any expense. Most form-fill programs seamlessly incorporate digital pictures into the form and either print them out for hard copy reports or transmit them electronically together as part of an electronically transmitted appraisal.

There is no absolute rule as to what the photographs should include. However, at a minimum, photographs of all sides of the improvements and any major site improvements, plus a shot of the street in both directions showing the subject in the foreground, may be required. When the assignment warrants the extra expense, photographs of construction details and of the interior may also be included.

Plot Plan

A plot plan shows the lot boundaries, important topographical features and the location of the improvements. A well-drawn plot plan is made to scale, with lot dimensions indicated on the boundary lines. In addition to the house and garage or carport, it should show the position of sidewalks, driveways, patios, pools, etc. Any abutting rights-of-way, known easements or apparent encroachments should also be shown. An appraiser is not expected to be a professional drafts person but the plot plan should be neat and carefully drawn. There are software programs now available to assist the appraiser in making a plot plan.

Sketch of the Building

Often a simple sketch of the exterior walls of the buildings (and garage or carport, If any) or a more complete drawing showing the location of doors, windows and interior walls is included as part of the report. Many appraisers take special pride in their ability to produce professionally drawn sketches. Such drawings are not required for a typical appraisal; a simple, neatly drawn sketch to approximate scale, showing the important dimensions, will usually suffice. The dimensions that appear on the sketch should be the same ones used to calculate the gross living area. There are good software programs available that draw sketches of the house using dimensions and other information entered by the appraiser.

Reading a House Plan

8.15 The appraiser who is appraising a house planned for construction, under construction or being considered for a program of renovation must be able to read the plans that detail the proposed construction. Architects use *orthographic projections* to picture the proposed work rather than perspective drawings. An orthographic projection permits proportional reduction of the drawing while maintaining the size and spatial relationships of the completed house. Lines drawn parallel in an orthographic projection represent walls that are parallel in the finished house.

A complete set of house plans consists of:

- Orthographic projections of each floor and the basement
- Electric plans
- Plumbing plans
- Wall sections
- Elevations of all sides
- Plot plan
- Door and window schedules
- Specifications

The dimensions of an actual house may not appear to agree with those indicated on the house plans. It is impossible to tell from looking at the plans what the actual points of measurement are. An actual measurement read on the tape measure may be from one inch to more than five inches less than the dimensions indicated on the plan. Architects seldom indicate dimensions from one wall surface to another. On drawings of frame houses, they prefer to indicate the dimensions between the surface of the studs of opposite walls or from the center of the opposite wall studs.

When stud-surface-to-stud-surface is used, the actual tape measurements are about one inch less than the indicated dimension line measurement, which is the thickness of the gypsum wall board. When the center of the stud is used as the point of measurement, the tape reading is about five inches less, since half the thickness of the stud is usually two inches plus the thickness of the gypsum wall board.

The techniques for dimensioning masonry construction are different from those for frame construction. Dimension lines on masonry construction plans usually run from one masonry surface to another, rather than to the surface of the gypsum wall board or other wall coverings.

To read house plans, it is necessary to know the many symbols architects use to represent the materials, electric switches and outlets, plumbing fixtures and pipes.

SUMMARY

The description of the improvements is an important part of the appraisal report. It provides the information used in the three approaches to value. It includes a description of all the improvements to the site as well as a complete description of the residence and any ancillary improvements. Information about all the physical components including their design, quality and condition is included. A list of items requiring immediate repair, plus a list of items that will require repair in the near future, should also be provided. When appropriate, any feasible renovations should be specified.

REVIEW QUESTIONS

1. In the summer the sun travels in a:
    a. high arc in the sky.
    b. low arc in the sky.
    c. from northwest to northeast.
    d. None of the above

2. When measuring the GLA of a house:
    a. include all the above grade habitable living area.
    b. include all the finished basement area that is 50% or more above ground.
    c. exclude laundry rooms.
    d. none of the above

3. When measuring a small income property (2-4 family) use the:
    a. gross living area measuring system.
    b. use the gross building area measuring system.
    c. Either of the above
    d. None of the above

4. The most common type of house wood framing in the United States is?
    a. Platform construction.
    b. Plank and beam construction.
    c. Balloon construction.
    d. None of the above

5. The primary benefits of insulation are fuel economy and:
    a. structural integrity.
    b. fire protection.
    c. wind resistance.
    d. water proofing.

6. The primary reason for ventilating an attic is:
    a. to prevent water condensation.
    b. to make it cool in the summer.
    c. to increase heating efficiency.
    d. None of the above

7. For safety, the hearth in front of a fireplace should extend at least _____ inches into the room.
    a. six
    b. twelve
    c. sixteen
    d. twenty four

8. An effective way to control termites is:
    a. controlling the moisture content of the wood.
    b. constructing effective termite barriers.
    c. using natural or treated termite resistant wood.
    d. All of the above

9. A heat pump?
    a. Is a device for both heating and cooling.
    b. In the winter takes heat from the water in the ground or outside air.
    c. In the summer it removes heat from inside the house.
    d. All of the above

10. A waste drain line must:
    a. be strong enough to withstand water pressure.
    b. never be made of metal.
    c. slant to provide a natural flow.
    d. None of the above

11. Which type of hot water heater has the fastest recovery rate?
    a. Electric
    b. Gas
    c. Oil
    d. Solar

12. In most areas, the minimum acceptable electric service is:
    a. 60 amperes.
    b. 90 amperes.
    c. 100 amperes.
    d. 150 amperes.

13. A percolation test is used to:
    a. test the amount of water flowing from an artesian well.
    b. test the quality of well water.
    c. test the rate soil will absorb water
    d. None of the above

14. A conversation circle is a planning device used for:
    a. designing kitchens.
    b. designing recreation rooms.
    c. arranging furniture placement.
    d. All of the above

15. What type of projection do architects usually use for house plans?
    a. Three dimensional
    b. Orthographic
    c. 25:1 scale drawings
    d. None of the above

ANSWERS TO REVIEW QUESTIONS

The answer to each question is indicated by the letter a, b, c or d. The explanation of the answer is indicated by the page number and on an arrow that points to the appropriate paragraph on the page of the text.

Q 8.1	a	Page 8-3
Q 8.2	a	Page 8-12
Q 8.3	b	Page 8-13
Q 8.4	a	Page 8-16
Q 8.5	b	Page 8-16
Q 8.6	a	Page 8-18
Q 8.7	c	Page 8-24
Q 8.8	d	Page 8-24
Q 8.9	d	Page 8-29
Q 8.10	c	Page 8-31
Q 8.11	c	Page 8-32
Q 8.12	c	Page 8-35
Q 8.13	c	Page 8-33
Q 8.14	c	Page 8-42
Q 8.15	b	Page 8-51

CHAPTER 9

Valuation Procedures - Specific Data Analysis and Highest & Best Use

"I paid too much for it, but it was worth it."

Samuel Goldwyn - Movie Producer
(1882-1974)

Important Words and Key Concepts

Words on this list are highlighted in this chapter
They are also defined in the Glossary at the back of this text

Excess Land
Highest and Best Use
Interim Use
Legal Non-Conforming Use
Modernization
Rehabilitation
Remodeling
Specific Data
Special Purpose Use
Surplus Land
Theory of Consistent Use

HIGHEST AND BEST USE ANALYSIS

9.1 The entire appraisal process is dependent upon the collection and analysis of data from the market. The **highest and best use** analysis as well as the three approaches to value are actually market approaches, and depend upon the quality of the market data the appraiser chooses to analyze.

This chapter presents methods by which **specific data** is screened and analyzed and applied to an analysis of the highest and best use of the property. The process of extracting relevant material from the vast array of available data helps an appraiser to **9.2** develop a perception of the market. The credibility of the final opinion of value depends on the extent to which it can be supported by data.

This chapter discusses the highest and best use analysis of the two major elements of a property - the site and its improvements. Appraisal theory has long supported the concept of the highest and best use of the site. Recently the concept and practice has been developed of also determining the highest and best use of the improvements on the site.

For a site to have value, it must have utility and be in demand. In highest and best use analysis, the appraiser considers that use, among all the various options, that most fully develops a site's potential utility. Highest and best use analysis forms the basis upon which the appraiser builds all the three traditional approaches to value, and is therefore a crucial step in the valuation process.

DEFINITION OF HIGHEST AND BEST USE

Highest and best use is defined as: "The reasonably probable and legal use of vacant land or an improved property that is physically possible, appropriately supported, and **9.3** financially feasible and that results in the highest value."[1]

Simply stated, the highest and best use of a site is the perfect improvement that could be constructed on the site which would produce the maximum rate of return on the capital invested. This definition applies specifically to the highest and best use of the land or site as though vacant.

9.4 When a site contains improvements, the highest and best use may be determined to be different from the existing use. The existing use - also called the **interim use** when a property is nearing the end of its economic life - will continue until land value in its highest and best use exceeds the value of the entire property in its existing use, plus the cost to remove the improvements. The existing use will continue until an owner decides to convert the improvements to the highest and best use. For example, a single-family residence on an arterial street might have more value if it were converted to an office use rather than remaining a single-family house. In this example, the highest and best use would be for proposed office use; the estimate of value should reflect this fact, be based upon a highest and best use analysis for a clearly described alternative use as an office, minus all costs necessary to convert it to office use.

---

1 The Appraisal of Real Estate, 12th Edition, Appraisal Institute, Chicago, IL 2001.

A determination of highest and best use is based on the appraiser's judgment and analytical skill. The highest and best use determined in the appraiser's analysis represents an opinion, not a fact. In appraisal practice, highest and best use is the premise upon which value is based.

TWO TYPES OF HIGHEST AND BEST USE

The definitions of highest and best use indicate that there are two types of highest and best use. The first type is highest and best use of land or a site as though vacant. The second is highest and best use of a property as improved. Each type requires a separate analysis. Moreover, in each case, the existing use may or may not be different from the site's highest and best use.

When potential buyers contemplate purchasing real estate for personal use or occupancy, their principal motivations are benefits as enjoyment, prestige, or security. Such motivations are particularly evident in the purchase of residential properties. User benefits also apply to commercial and industrial property ownership. Benefits to the owner-occupant include assured occupancy, low management costs, control and potential enhancement of the facility during the ownership period, as well as future value, from appreciation of the property realized upon reversion.

The benefits of investment properties that are not owner-occupied relate to net income potential and to eventual resale or refinancing. The highest and best use decision for investment property is often influenced by taxation on the existing or proposed improvements. Determination of the type and intensity of the improvements which will be the highest and best use of an investor's land requires an "after-tax return" analysis of all reasonable alternatives.

Land or improved property that has resale profit as its principal potential benefit is purely speculative land or speculative improved property. The price such land or improved property commands in the market reflects the real motivation of the typical purchaser, which is speculation. This type of market demand is especially volatile and hard to predict under future conditions.

9.5 ▶ Highest and best use analysis for improved sites is always done with two analyses. First the site is analyzed as though vacant and thn to analyze the property as improved.

Highest and Best Use of Land (or a Site) as Though Vacant

The highest and best use of the site, if there is no improvement, is known as the highest and best use "as is". If there is an improvement, the highest and best use of the site analysis is said to be the highest and best use "as though vacant'. The highest and best use, as though vacant determination for a site, is always made without regard to existing improvements.

In contrast, the highest and best use "as improved" is determined by an analysis of the site with its current improvements. Highest and best use as improved does not represent independent analysis of the site and the improvements, but rather is an analysis of their value in combination.

9.6 For purposes of this analysis, it is assumed that the site has no building improvement. In other words, the problem the appraiser considers is if the site were vacant, what would the best potential use of the site be? What improvements would provide the maximum return in terms of money and amenities? The appraiser then describes the type of building or buildings which could be constructed on the land if it were vacant that would maximize its utilization.

Not every parcel of land (even those already improved) is economically ready to be developed. In fact, the majority of vacant land falls into this category. In these cases, the correct conclusion is that the highest and best use is to leave the parcel vacant until some time in the future, when it may become economically feasible to develop.

If the conclusion is that the site is economically feasible to develop, the appraiser must conclude which type of improvement, with which specific characteristics, should be constructed.

The current use on the site may not be the highest and best use. The land may be suitable for a much higher (more intense) use than the existing use. For instance, the highest and best use of the land as though vacant may be a five story office building, whereas the building contains only two stories, and includes some residential rental units.

Highest and Best Use of Property as Improved

9.7 The appraiser also considers the use that should be made of the property as it exists. Should the 100 year-old home be maintained as is, renovated, expanded, partially demolished, or any combination of these actions? Should it be replaced with a use different in type or intensity?

In this context, the use that maximizes the investment property's net operating income (NOI) on a long-term basis is considered to be its highest and best use. For uses that require no capital expenditures for **remodeling**, the net operating incomes estimated for various uses can be compared directly. However, for uses that would require capital expenditures to convert the structure from its existing use to another use, a rate of return must be calculated for the total investment in the property, including capital expenditures. This rate of return can then be compared with rates of return for uses that do not require capital expenditures.

An appraiser's conclusions regarding highest and best use for owner-occupied properties also reflect consideration of **rehabilitation** or **modernization** that is consistent with the motivation of owner-occupants. For example, highest and best use determinations for a luxury residence would include the amount and type of rehabilitation required for maximum enjoyment of the property.

Purpose of Highest and Best Use Analysis

The purpose of highest and best use analysis is different for each type of highest and best use. An appraiser should clearly separate the two types in the appraisal analysis. An appraiser's report should clearly identify, explain and justify the purpose and conclusion for each type.

The value of land is always estimated as though vacant. For land that is, in fact, vacant, the reasoning is obvious: an appraiser values the land as it exists. For land that is not vacant, land value is dependent on the uses to which it can be put. Therefore, highest and best use of land, as though vacant, must be considered in relation to a variety of uses, including its existing and all potential future uses. One of the uses of the highest and best use analysis as though vacant is to select comparable land sales for the site value analysis.

There are two reasons for analyzing the highest and best use of a property as improved. The first is to identify the use of property that is expected to produce the highest overall return per dollar of invested capital. The second reason is to help in identifying comparable properties.

Relation to Economic Theory

Even though modern economic theory holds that land may be as entitled to a return as the other three "agents of production" (e.g., labor, capital, and entrepreneurship), buildings can be changed, while the essential characteristics of sites cannot. This means that the income potential of any particular site is highly dependent on the use to which it is put.

From an overall economic point of view, however, the fact that one site can be substituted for another means that generally their returns are established in the market. For a specific site, however, the land value is a direct function of the income that remains after all returns to the improvements are calculated.

Highest and best use of land as though vacant is an old concept. Highest and best use of a property as improved is a much newer concept. It has evolved since the 1960s to answer two important questions that the older concept does not address. How should the property as improved be used? Should the existing improvement be continued in use, or should it be demolished and a new improvement constructed. The older concept of highest and best use of land as though vacant addresses only the question of how the land should be used if it were vacant; it is primarily a tool for land valuation.

ELEMENTS IN HIGHEST AND BEST USE ANALYSIS

The Four Tests of Highest and Best Use

To do a highest and best use analysis of a site, the appraiser utilizes the *four tests of highest and best use*. The projected use must meet all four of these tests:

1. Physically possible
2. Legally permitted
3. Financially feasible
4. Maximum productivity

Each potential use of a property is considered by the appraiser in terms of these four tests. If a proposed use fails to meet any of the tests, it is discarded and another use is reviewed. The highest and best use is that proposed use of the site that meets all four tests.

PHYSICALLY POSSIBLE

9.10

The use of a site must be physically possible. Uses are limited by the physical characteristics of a site, such as size, frontage, topography, soil and subsoil conditions and climate conditions. Despite the need for single-family residential housing, an area of severe terrain with poor subsoil characteristics cannot be considered appropriate for such development. For example, sites along earthquake fault lines in California are not considered safe for house construction. Flood plains are also considered unsuitable for house construction. A corridor in the Palm Springs, CA, area is considered undesirable for residential construction because prevailing winds carry smog and fog to the area.

LEGALLY PERMITTED

Occasionally a site is clearly not being utilized to its highest and best use, not because of any lack of market demand or physical suitability, but solely due to legal restrictions. Since land is usually zoned according to a political/social scheme, rather than an economic one, zoning frequently does not conform to current market requirements. In such cases, the land remains economically under-utilized until the prescribed limitations are lifted. When the land manifests more valuable potential use than allowed by law, and there is a reasonable probability that a change in use will be permitted at some point in the near future, the appraiser must consider that use in their highest and best use analysis.

In such a situation, the appraiser must be extremely careful that the value estimate is not speculative, but rather that the market would widely recognize the strong possibility of a zoning change. Since future predictions are by their very nature speculative, the appraiser must feel that there is a very high degree of probability that the zoning can be changed within the very near future to include this prospect in their analysis.

FINANCIALLY FEASIBLE

It must be possible to make some profit on any proposed use for it to be considered as a possible highest and best use. The market creates highest and best use. The review by the appraiser must end with the question of whether the proposed use will at least produce some profit. If the answer is no, than the proposed use must be discarded and other potential uses analyzed. It is common that more than one proposed use will produce some profit.

MAXIMUM PRODUCTIVITY (MOST PROFIT)

The fourth test of highest and best use is essentially a test for maximum profit. The appraiser is seeking the most profitable use among those potential uses that have passed the first three tests.

As market conditions change, the existing use of land is often no longer its highest and best use. If the land alone has a higher value under an alternate physically suitable, legally permitted use than the whole property as currently improved and utilized, the proposed use becomes the highest and best use. The existing improvement is at the end of its economic life, but it still will be the highest and best use during the transition period. The existing use is an interim use for the duration of the transition period.

EXAMPLE #1: MARKET VALUE OF A SITE ZONED FOR COMMERCIAL USE

Highest and best use, as though vacant	$400,000
Market value as currently improved for residential use	$400,000
Contribution of improvement	None

The highest and best use of this property is no longer the existing use, except during the transition period, while development of an alternate use is considered by the owner. The existing use is called an **interim use.**

Testing Highest and Best Use as Though Vacant

To test highest and best use for the land as though vacant, an appraiser analyzes all logical, feasible alternatives. Usually, the appraiser can reduce the number of such alternatives to three or four uses. Alternative uses must first meet the tests for physical possibility and legal permissibility. The number of uses meeting the first two tests can then be analyzed logically to limit the number of financially feasible alternatives that must be analyzed. Similarly, development of housing for the elderly might be permissible for a site, but if most residents of the area are under 40 years old, such development might not be logical, and probably would not satisfy the criterion of financial feasibility.

TESTING HIGHEST AND BEST USE OF LAND AS THOUGH VACANT

The following examples illustrate the testing of highest and best use for land as though vacant.

EXAMPLE #2: ANALYZING SIZE OF SINGLE FAMILY RESIDENCE TO BE CONSTRUCTED

Size of proposed house	Cost per/sq. ft.	Total cost of construction
2,000 sq. ft. version	$96.00 per sq. ft.	$192,000
2,250 sq. ft. version	$92.00 per sq. ft.	$207,000
2,500 sq. ft. version	$88.00 per sq. ft.	$220,000

The estimated value of the site is $70,000.

It is estimated that the sale prices of the houses would be as follows:

Size of proposed house	Estimated selling price
2,000 sq. ft. version	$280,000
2,250 sq. ft. version	$310,000
2,500 sq. ft. version	$320,000

The calculations to test which proposed house is the highest and best use are:

House size	2,000 sq. ft.	2,250 sq. ft.	2,500 sq. ft.
Market value	$280,000	$310,000	$320,000
Cost to construct	-192.000	-207,000	-220,000
Site value	- 70.000	- 70,000	- 70,000
Anticipated profit	$ 18,000	$ 33,000	$ 30,000

It appears that a 2,250 sq. ft. house is the highest and best use among the alternatives being considered. By constructing the 2,250 sq. ft. house, the maximum potential profit can be realized. Both the bigger and small houses would produce less profit.

Another consideration the appraiser must take into account is whether the total profit on the investment is high enough to warrant the risk that is incurred whenever new houses are built on speculation.

In the example above, the builder must invest $277,000 ($207,000 construction costs plus the $ 70,000 cost of the site) to earn $33,000. This is a return on the investment of 11.9% ($33,000 ÷ $277,000). If higher rates of return are available with similar or lesser risks than the proposed development, it is not the highest and best use.

EXAMPLE #3: ANALYSIS OF A SMALL INCOME PROPERTY

Unlike the first example, where the highest and best use is a single-family house and the site value is known, highest and best use in this example is an income producing property, and the value of the site is unknown. (Often one purpose of conducting the highest and best use analysis is to estimate the land value.)

Various permitted uses must be tested to determine which will produce the most residual income after deducting return that is allocated to the improvements for total net operating income (NOI) under each use.

There is a half acre site zoned residential, multi-family. It is located in a neighborhood with an active rental market. Investigation of the rental market develops the following comparable rental data:

Size of apartment	# of bedrooms/unit	Estimated rental/month
600 sq. ft.	1 Bedroom	$1,000 per month
800 sq. ft.	2 Bedroom	$1,300 per month
1,100 sq. ft.	3 Bedroom	$1,450 per month

It will cost the following to construct the buildings:

Size of apartment	# of bedrooms/unit	Cost per sq. ft. to build
600 sq. ft.	1 Bedroom	$90 per sq. ft.
800 sq. ft.	2 Bedroom	$80 per sq. ft.
1,100 sq. ft.	3 Bedroom	$70 per sq. ft.

In this market, it is estimated that all expenses (fixed, operating and reserves) total 40% of gross rental income. There is enough parking on the site for 12 cars. Zoning requires one parking space per bedroom.

Fig. 9-1 shows how the three configurations under consideration may be tested to determine which is the highest and best use. The appraiser reduces the choices to some logical alternatives and then assembles data on construction costs, market rates of return and income that can be expected for each alternative use, along with the market capitalization rate for the improvements.

This data is best presented in a grid to show how each alternative compares with the others under consideration. For various types of properties, a reasonable review of viable alternatives is part of a typical highest and best use analysis.

FIG. 9-1 Highest and Best Use Analysis

	12 One-Bedroom Apartments	6 Two-Bedroom Apartments	4 Three-Bedroom Apartments
Cost to Construct	600 sq. ft. x $ 90 per sq. ft. = $ 54,000 ea. x 12 = **$648,000**	800 sq. ft. x $80 per sq. ft. = $ 64,000 ea. x 6 = **$384,000**	1100 sq. ft. x $70 per sq. ft. = $ 77,000 ea. x 4 = **$308,000**
Gross Income Estimate (Potential)	$1,000/mo. x 12 months x 12 apartments) **$144,000**	$1,300/mo. x 12 months x 6 apartments **$93,600**	$1,450/mo. x 12 months x 4 apartments **$69,600**
Estimated Expenses @ 40% of Gross	$144,000 x 40% -$57,600	$93,600 x 40% -$37,440	$69,600 x 40% -$27,840
NOI	$ 86,400	$56,160	$41,760
Allocated Return to Improvements @12%	-$77,760	−$46,080	-$36,960
Return to Land	$8,640	$10,080	$4,800
Land Value at 10% Capitalization Rate	$8,640 ÷ 0.10 = $86,400	$10,080 ÷ 0.10 = $100,800	$4,800 ÷ 0.10 = $48,000

According to this analysis, it appears that the 6 two-bedroom apartment development is the highest and best use, offering a potential land value under this use of $100,800.

It is possible that a mixed use building in this example would produce an even higher rate of return to the land. With the use of a computer program such as Excel, many alternative possible combinations could be readily tested.

In addition, the calculations indicate that the highest and best use is not determined by any single item, such as cost, size, total income, or rate of return. Highest and best use is the relationship among these items that determines the income remaining to the land after the other agents of production are allocated their appropriate market value. These items are compensated before land.

Testing the Highest and Best Use of a Property as Improved

An analysis of the property as improved should be made to determine if its current use is the highest and best use, or if alternate uses would produce a greater rate of return. When an alternate use produces a higher NOI, it does not automatically mean that this use will produce a higher value. The element of risk must also be considered. Sometimes an alternate use can be accomplished with little or no capital expenditures. Others may require substantial expenditures such as rehabilitation or remodeling.

EXAMPLE #4: HIGHEST AND BEST USE DETERMINED WITH NO CAPITAL EXPENDITURES

In a college town, many of the property owners are converting their multi-family units from unfurnished apartments rented with one year and two year leases to furnished apartments rented to students on an eight month lease. Usually these apartments remain vacant for the balance of the year. Furniture is rented from a local store for $1,200 per year, per unit, and the tenant assumes the risk of loss or damage to the furniture. Expenses run about 40% of gross income. The vacancy and collection loss is estimated to be 5% for the unfurnished apartments and 10% for the furnished apartments. The six apartments in the subject building currently rent for $800 per month year round, which is estimated to be their market rent. It is estimated that the market rent of the apartments to be rented furnished would be $1,600 per month for eight months out of the year. The calculations for the highest and best use are as follows in Fig 9-2:

FIG. 9-2 Highest and Best Use Analysis

Comparison of Proposed Use	6 Unfurnished Apartments 12 month rentals	6 Furnished Apartments 8 month rentals
Gross Income	$800/mo. x 12 months x 6 units = $57,600	$1,600/mo. x 8 months x 6 units = $76,800
Vacancy & Collection Loss	5% of Gross Income x $ 57,600 = $2,880	10% of Gross Income x $ 76,800 = $7,680
Effective Gross Income	$54,720	$69,120
Less Cost of Furniture Rental	- 0 -	$1,200/mo. x 12 months = -$14,400
Operating Expenses	$57,600 x 40% of Gross Income = -$23,040	$76,800 x 40% of Gross Income = -$30,720
Net Operating Income	$31,680	$24,000

It appears from these calculations that the highest and best use of the property as improved is to continue to rent it as unfurnished apartments for full year terms.

Highest and Best Use Statements in Appraisal Reports

All appraisal reports should contain statements that explain the analyses and conclusions for highest and best use of the land or a site as though vacant, or of a property as improved, or both if a separate land valuation is included. When the highest and best use conclusion is the primary objective of an assignment, the income and return calculations and reasoning should be included. If the determination of the highest and best use of an improved property is different from the existing use, similar justification should be included in a market value appraisal report. Whenever the highest and best use conclusions are based on an application of techniques to discover the highest and best use among two or more potential uses, the full analysis should be included.

In appraisals in which land value is estimated separately, it is appropriate to discuss in the report the highest and best use of the land as though vacant, as well as the highest and best use of the property as improved. When land value is not estimated separately and a condition of the appraisal assignment is continued use of the property as improved, the appraiser typically discusses only the highest and best use of the property as improved.

Each parcel of real estate may have one highest and best use of the land or site as though vacant, and a different highest and best use of the property as improved. In cases in which an appraiser analyzes both the highest and best use of the land as though vacant and the property as improved, each highest and best use must be identified separately in the highest and best use section of the appraisal report.

First, the highest and best use of the land or site is presented, along with a statement that the determination was made under the hypothetical condition that the land is vacant and available for development. Second, the highest and best use of the property as improved is determined, along with a statement that the analysis was made according to the future potential of the land and improvements as they exist. If the land is already improved to its highest and best use, the two statements may be combined. Nevertheless, the report should state specifically that the determination is the same for both the land as though vacant and the property as improved, or that the land is currently improved to its highest and best use.

The report should also identify the highest and best uses, both vacant and improved, of the comparable sales. If the improved comparables have different highest and best uses of the land if theoretically vacant and of the improved properties as they exist, this must also be explained. The difference could affect value, especially in the sales comparison approach.

The following examples, of a single-family residence and for an income-producing property, illustrate typical highest and best use statements as they are used in appraisal reports. (Obviously, the actual statements for any particular appraisal would need to be tailored to the specific situation.)

EXAMPLE #5: TYPICAL STATEMENTS IN AN APPRAISAL REPORT - SINGLE FAMILY RESIDENCE - HIGHEST AND BEST USE OF LAND AS THOUGH VACANT

The highest and best use as though vacant is employed to estimate the value of land separately from improvements. It recognizes that any significant elements of accrued depreciation would not be replicated if the land were vacant and a new building were constructed on the site. It is also helpful in identifying comparable properties, which is why it is used in this appraisal.

The existing structure is not the highest and best use of the land as though vacant. The house was constructed approximately 10 years ago and contains measurable elements of physical deterioration and functional obsolescence, as do most structures after they are two or three years old. If the site were vacant, a new single-family residence would be its highest and best use. The new house would be more architecturally compatible with other houses in the neighborhood. It would contain approximately 2,000 square feet and would include three bedrooms and two baths. The living room would be larger. The house would have more electrical outlets. All elements of physical deterioration would be eliminated.

Accordingly, the highest and best use of the site is still a single family residence. However, the highest and best use as a single family residence would meet current market design standards.

EXAMPLE #6: TYPICAL STATEMENTS IN AN APPRAISAL REPORT -
SINGLE FAMILY RESIDENCE - HIGHEST AND BEST USE OF PROPERTY AS IMPROVED

The highest and best use as improved recognizes that existing improvements should be continued in use until it becomes financially advantageous to demolish the structure and build a new one or to remodel the existing one. The existing use of the property, as a single-family residence, is the highest and best use of the property as improved. No other use of the property would be so beneficial or profitable.

The existing structure is well-maintained and in good repair. It has an effective age of about 8 years and a remaining economic life of approximately 50 years. The structure fits well in the neighborhood, which is zoned for single-family residential occupancy only. The structure was designed as a single-family residence, and no other use would be legally permitted or financially feasible.

EXAMPLE #7: TYPICAL STATEMENTS IN AN APPRAISAL REPORT -
INCOME PRODUCING PROPERTY - HIGHEST AND BEST USE OF LAND AS THOUGH VACANT

The existing structure is not the highest and best use of the land as though vacant. The highest and best use recognizes that any significant elements of accrued depreciation would not be replicated if the site were vacant and a new building were constructed. The income allocated to the land under highest and best use is capitalized to estimate the value of the land separately from the improvements.

If the site were vacant, a new apartment building would be its highest and best use. It would contain 12 apartments, the maximum number permitted by zoning for this site. Each apartment would contain a living room, dining room, kitchen, bathroom, lavatory and two bedrooms and have 1,025 sq. ft. of GLA. The building would be cement block construction with brick veneer exterior walls, frame sub-floors, and flat, built-up roof. The building would be two stories with 6 apartments on each floor. It would be set in the middle of the site allowing for an attractive front yard, parking on both sides for 30 cars and a rear yard with recreational facilities for children. All physical deterioration would be eliminated in a new building, and its functional layout and design would be consistent with modern apartments of this type.

EXAMPLE #8: TYPICAL STATEMENTS IN AN APPRAISAL REPORT-
INCOME-PRODUCING PROPERTY - HIGHEST AND BEST USE OF PROPERTY AS IMPROVED

The existing use of the property as rental units should be eliminated and the building should be converted into 10 condominium dwelling units. The property currently contains 10 apartments that have had a high vacancy rate during the past five years.

The units require renovation and remodeling to remain competitive in the local housing market. However, the amount of money necessary to make these renovations and remodeling will make the property uneconomical to maintain as rental units as the rent that would be required is above what can be obtained for this type of property in this market. The following calculations in Table 9-3 show the existing capital investment and additional capital investment required for the existing use and for conversion into condominiums. It shows the return estimated for the current use and the profit anticipated from a condominium conversion.

FIG. 9-3 Highest and Best Use Analysis

Type of Use	Present Use 10 Rental Units	Proposed Conversion 10 Condominium Units
Present Capital Investment	$600,000	$600,000
Renovation and Modernization	+ 500.000	+ 650,000
Total Capital Investment	$1,100,000	$1,250,000
Net Operating Income	$80,000	N/A
Overall Rate of Return	$80,000 ÷ $110,000 = 7.3%	N/A
Selling Costs & Legal Expenses	$ 60,000	$150,000
Total Investment	$1,160,000	$1,400,000
Estimated Selling Price	$970,000	10 units @ $160,000 each = $1,600,000
Profit (Loss)	($190,000)	$200,000

The figures indicate that continuing the use of the property as rental units would not produce a satisfactory return on the investment, with the required renovation and remodeling costs. The investment produces 7.3% in a market that expects at least 10% return for this type of property. Conversion into a condominium would produce an estimated $200,000 profit, which is considered satisfactory for this type of project, and would provide a return on the total investment of 14.3% which is almost double the rate of return of the present use.

SPECIAL SITUATIONS IN HIGHEST AND BEST USE ANALYSIS

Unique considerations in identifying and testing highest and best uses are required when the properties being considered are any of the following: *single use,* interim uses, legal non-conforming uses, non highest and best uses, multiple uses, *special purpose uses*, speculative uses, and excess and surplus land. The special requirements for highest and best use analysis in each of these situations are discussed in the following sections.

Single Use

The highest and best uses of land or sites as though vacant and properties as improved are generally consistent with and similar to surrounding uses. For example, single-family residential uses are usually not appropriate in an industrial neighborhood. Nevertheless, highest and best use may be an unusual or even a unique use. For example, demand may be adequate to support one large multi-story office building in a community, but inadequate to support more than one. A special purpose property, such as a museum, may be unique and highly beneficial to the site, but not justifiable for surrounding land uses or comparable properties. The land value would be based on its highest and best use as though vacant.

Interim Use

Often an appraisal is made of an existing house that appears to be nearing the end of its economic life, but not yet reached it. It may be an older house, in an established neighborhood of older homes, conforming substantially to the houses in the neighborhood. As with the analysis of the site as though vacant, the appraiser must determine and describe the perfect improvement for the site. However, the appraiser must also consider utilization of the existing improvements to obtain the maximum profit. If there is a house on the site, the appraiser must estimate what can be done to make it the most profitable use of the site. Any improvement that will add more value than the cost to produce it should be considered in the analysis. These improvements might range from simple repairs to major remodeling, modernization or rehabilitation to extend the remaining economic life of the existing structure.

An existing use may be nearing the end of its economic life but still be the highest and best use of the site at this point in time. If the existing house still contributes to the overall value of the total property, it continues to have utility.

EXAMPLE #9: HIGHEST AND BEST USE AS IMPROVEMENTS NEAR END OF ECONOMIC LIFE

Market value of property as currently improved for residential use	$152,000
Market value of the site zoned for commercial use (Highest and best use, as though vacant)	- 146,000
Contribution of the structure	$ 6,000

Although the highest and best use of this property as though vacant is different from the existing use, the old residential structure continues to add to the total value of the property. Thus, the existing residential use is the best use of the site for the remaining economic life of the structure. Frequently, a site is improved with a building that is at the extreme end of its economic life. A downtown property utilized as a residence may not appear to be the highest and best use of the land, but it may still contribute enough additional income to the owner to justify its continuation as a "tax payer" while plans and financing arrangements are completed for more profitable development. In an area where demand has not created an active market, an interim use may be necessary to hold the property until a more favorable market response is noted. A parcel of land suitable for a residential subdivision, for example, may be marginally farmed, until such time as the residential housing market will support the cost of its conversion to several new building lots.

Legal Non Conforming Uses

A *legal non-conforming use* is a use that was lawfully established and maintained, but no longer conforms to the use regulations of the zone where it is located. This kind of use frequently results from a change in the zoning ordinances. Zoning changes may create under-improvements or over-improvements.

A single-family residence located in an area that is subsequently rezoned for commercial use is an under-improvement. In this case, the residence will most likely be removed so that the site can be improved to its highest and best use, or the house will be considered an interim use until it can be converted to commercial use, such as a doctor's office or mixed-used building.

Non-conforming, over-improved property results when zoning changes reduce the permitted intensity of property use. For example, an old country store may be included in a neighborhood that is zoned for low-density residential use. Non-conforming uses may also result from changes in the permitted density of development and changes in development standards that affect features such as landscaping, parking, setbacks, and access. Zoning ordinances vary with the jurisdiction; they usually permit a pre-existing use to continue, but prohibit expansion or major alterations that support the older legal non-conforming use. If the non-conforming use is discontinued for a variety of reasons, it usually may not be re-established.

When valuing land with a legal non-conforming use, an appraiser must recognize that the current use may be producing more income, and thus have more value, than the property could produce with a conforming use. It may also produce more income and have a higher value than comparable properties that conform to the zoning. Therefore, to estimate the value of a non-conforming property by comparing it with similar, competitive properties in the sales comparison approach, the appraiser should consider making an adjustment to reflect the higher intensity of use allowed for the subject property, and find comparable uses in similar areas.

In most non-conforming use situations, the value estimate reflects the non-conforming use. Land value, however, is based on the legally permissible uses, assuming that the land is vacant. Once its highest and best use as though vacant is estimated, this value can be deducted from the total property value. The remaining value reflects the contribution of the existing improvements and any possible bonus for the non-conforming use.

The appraiser may find it helpful to allocate value separately to the non-conforming improvements and the bonus created by the non-conforming use. Usually, any bonus resulting from a non-conforming improvement and use is directly related to the existing improvements. Therefore, the extra income or benefit should be capitalized over a time period that is consistent with the remaining economic life of those improvements.[2]

Non Highest and Best Uses

The *theory of consistent use* is basic to appraisal practice and highest and best use analysis. A property nearing transition to a new use cannot be valued on the basis of one use for land and another for improvements. The improvements must add to the value of the land in order to have value attributed to them. The land is always valued first, and as though vacant. If the buildings existing on the site add to the value of the overall property, even if their presence restricts it to a less intensive use, the existing use often continues to be the highest and best use, even as it is nearing the end of its economic life. Only when no value may be attributed to such improvements or they represent a negative value (burden) to the property, does an alternative use become the highest and best use.

An illustration of the violation of the consistent use theory in valuing a site is shown in the following example.

---

[2] **The** Appraisal of Real Estate, 12th Edition, Appraisal Institute, Chicago, IL 2001.

EXAMPLE #10: HIGHEST AND BEST USE WHEN CONSISTENCY OF USE IS AN ISSUE

A 60 year old house is located on a corner lot, where both main thoroughfares are moving to nonresidential uses. Recent rezoning permits business use and the corner property is classified to permit the construction of a fast food restaurant. The house, which has been converted into rental apartments, is still being used. The value of the house as a rental property is estimated at $ 180,000.

An uninformed appraiser learns from the market that corners like that enjoyed by the subject property have been selling as fast food restaurant sites for $200,000. In violation of the consistent use theory, the appraiser adds to this estimated site value of $200,000 a value for the existing building of $30,000 — for a total combined property value estimate of $230,000. The correct procedure is to accept the $200,000 estimate for the site "as though vacant." However, to make it vacant, demolition costs of $5,000 are estimated. Therefore, the market value of the site in its highest and best use would be $200,000 - $5,000 in demolition costs, or a correct value estimate of $195,000.

Multiple Uses

Highest and best use often includes more than one use for a parcel of land or for a building. A larger tract of land may be suitable for a planned unit development, with a shopping center in front, condominium units around a golf course, and single-family residential sites on the remaining portions of the land. Industrial parks often have sites for retail stores in front and warehouse and light manufacturing structures in the rear. Farms often have family homes, storage areas for crops and equipment, and facilities for raising animals and crops.

Moreover, the same land may serve multiple functions. Land for timber or pasture may also provide space for hunting, recreation and mineral exploration. Land that serves as a right-of-way for power lines can double as open space or a park.

Buildings may have multiple uses. A hotel may contain a restaurant, a bar, and retail shops as well as guest rooms. A multi-story building may contain offices, apartments, and retail stores. An office building may contain retail stores and a restaurant, as well as offices. A single-family, owner-occupied home may contain an extra apartment upstairs, or a professional office with a side entrance.

An appraiser can often estimate the contributory value of each use on a multiple use site or in a multiple use building. For example, if the market value of a timber tract that can be leased for hunting is compared on a unit basis with another timber tract that cannot, the difference should be the value of the hunting rights. In oil-producing areas, a common problem for appraisers is to segregate the value of mineral rights from the value of other uses of the land. Certain properties may have mineral rights value; others may not. In all such appraisals, an appraiser must make sure that the sum of the values of the separate uses does not exceed the value of the total property.

Special Purpose Uses

Special purpose properties are appropriate for one use or for a very limited number of uses. Thus, an appraiser may encounter practical problems of specifying the highest and best uses of such properties. The highest and best use of a special purpose property as improved is probably its current use. For example, the highest and best use of a plant currently used for heavy manufacturing is usually to continue in heavy manufacturing. The highest and best use of a grain elevator probably is to continue as a grain elevator.

In certain cases, if the existing uses of special purpose properties are physically or functionally obsolete and no alternative uses are feasible, the highest and best use of the property as improved may be as scrap or salvage.

Sometimes an appraiser needs to make two appraisals of the same special purpose property: one on the basis that a purchaser could be found who would use the property for its existing use, and the other on the basis that a purchaser would use the property for an alternate purpose. This type of analysis may be required because the owner of a large, special purpose property decides to abandon the property to consolidate operations. In such cases, it is usually not possible to determine, in advance, whether a purchaser can be found who has a need for the special purpose features of the improvements.

Speculative Uses

Land that is held primarily for future sale may be regarded as speculative land. The purchaser or owner may believe that the value of the land will appreciate, but there may be considerable risk that the expected appreciation will not occur within the time the speculator intends to hold the land. Nevertheless, the current value of the land is a function of its future highest and best use. In such cases, an appraiser should discuss potential future highest and best uses. The exact future highest and best use may not be predictable, but often the future type of highest and best use (such as a shopping center or industrial park) is known or predictable because of zoning or surrounding land use patterns. In addition, there may be several potential highest and best uses, such as single-family or multi-family residential developments. Appraisers usually cannot identify future highest and best uses with much specificity, but they can discuss logical alternatives and general levels of projected incomes and expenses.

Excess Land and Surplus Land

Many parcels of land are too large for their principal highest and best uses. Land area beyond that which is necessary to accommodate a site's highest and best use is called **excess land** when the site can be legally divided and the extra land sold separately, or held for an additional use. If the site cannot be divided and the extra land sold the extra land is called **surplus land.** Such parcels may have two highest and best uses: the primary highest and best use, and the highest and best use of the remaining or excess land.

In many cases, the highest and best use of excess land is for open space, or non-development. In other cases, the highest and best use may be for some less intensive use. In any event, an appraiser should treat parcels having excess land as two separate parcels. The land that supports the site's primary highest and best use usually has a higher unit value than the excess land, which should be valued separately. Land that is required to support the primary use, such as a parking lot for an office building or a playground for a school, is not considered to be excess land. Only land beyond the normal needs of a particular use, as determined in the market, can be considered excess land.

Some atypically large sites cannot be considered as having excess land because the acreage that is beyond the normal needs of the particular use cannot be separately used. For instance, an overly large lot in an area that is 100% built up or a site that cannot be divided because of the location of its buildings are not considered to have excess land. An appraiser should clearly identify any excess land and indicate a separate unit value. The appraiser should then add the value of the excess land to the value of the primary parcel to obtain the value of the entire parcel.

SUMMARY

To determine highest and best use, the appraiser first analyzes the site as though vacant and determines what the perfect improvement for such a site would be. The four tests of highest and best use are applied to the proposed uses. Only the use that meets all four tests (physically possible, legally permitted, financially feasible and has the maximum productivity) is the highest and best use.

Next the appraiser analyzes the property as improved. If the value of the site and its improvements, maintained in its present use, is less than the value of the site as though vacant and available for alternative use, the present improvements are no longer the highest and best use. If the present improvement, in its existing use produces a higher value for the property than if the site were vacant, it may be the highest and best use even as it nears the end of its economic life. The current use is potentially the highest and best use. The appraiser must analyze the existing improvements to see what rehabilitation, modernization or remodeling could be undertaken to produce the maximum profit. The improvements, when fully renovated, would be the highest and best use of the property as improved.

Finally, several special situations may necessitate unique considerations when identifying and testing highest and best use. Single use, interim uses, legal non-conforming uses, non highest and best uses, multiple uses, special purpose uses, speculative uses, and excess and surplus land are all possible uses to be considered.

REVIEW QUESTIONS

1. What do the highest and best use, cost approach and income approach all have in common?
   a. All must be used in every appraisal.
   b. At least two must be used in every appraisal.
   c. They all are really market approaches.
   d. None of the above

2. The credibility of the final value estimate depends upon:
   a. how it is supported by data.
   b. the number of comparable sales used.
   c. the education of the appraiser.
   d. None of the above

3. The highest and best use is:
   a. usually the cheapest improvement.
   b. usually the most expensive improvement.
   c. the largest improvement that will fit on the site.
   d. None of the above

4. The highest and best use of the land as though vacant is:
   a. always the same as the highest and best use as improved.
   b. never the same as the highest and best use as improved.
   c. sometimes the same as the highest and best use as improved.
   d. none of the above

5. The highest and best use analysis for improved sites is always done in:
   a. one analysis.
   b. two analyses.
   c. three analyses.
   d. four analyses.

6. What is assumed for purposes of highest and best use analysis of the land as though vacant?
   a. The zoning will permit the land to be improved.
   b. The land is economically ready to be improved.
   c. There are no improvements on the land.
   d. All of the above

7. The highest and best use analysis of property as improved considers the question:
   a. should the existing improvements be razed?
   b. should the existing improvements be renovated?
   c. should the existing improvements be expanded?
   d. All of the above

8. Which of the following is the final test of highest and best use?
   a. Maximum productivity use
   b. Very profitable use
   c. Unprofitable use
   d. None of the above

9. Which of the following are among the tests for the highest and best use?
   a. Legally permitted
   b. Physically possible
   c. Financially feasible
   d. All of the above

10. Which of the following may make a site physically impossible to use for a legally permitted use?
    a. The site is too small.
    b. The site has a deed restriction.
    c. The site is too expensive.
    d. None of the above

11. An interim use may be:
    a. a building with a short remaining economic life.
    b. an older home on a busy street corner zoned commercial.
    c. farm land in an area not ready for development.
    d. All of the above

ANSWERS TO REVIEW QUESTIONS

The answer to each question is indicated by the letter a, b, c or d below. The explanation of the answer is indicated by a numbered arrow that points to the appropriate paragraph on the page of the text indicated by the page number following the answer.

Q 9.1	c	Page 9-2
Q 9.2	a	Page 9-2
Q 9.3	d	Page 9-2
Q 9.4	c	Page 9-2
Q 9.5	b	Page 9-3
Q 9.6	c	Page 9-4
Q 9.7	d	Page 9-4
Q 9.8	a	Page 9-5
Q 9.9	d	Page 9-5
Q 9.10	a	Page 9-6
Q 9.11	d	Page 9-14

CHAPTER 10

Specific Data Analysis - Sales and Listings

"Whatever you can do,
Or dream you can, begin it.
Boldness has genius, power
And magic in it."

Johann Wolfgang von Goethe
German poet & philosopher
(1749-1832)

Important Words and Key Concepts

Words on this list are highlighted in this chapter
They are also defined in the Glossary at the back of this text

Adjusted Sale Price	Elements of Comparison	Qualitative Adjustments
Amenities	Extraction Method	Quantitative Adjustments
Base Sale	Gross Rent Multiplier	Sales Comparison Approach
Confirmation	Market Data Approach	Scope of Work
Cumulative Percentage Adjustments	Matched Pairs of Sales	Sequence of Adjustments
Dollar Adjustments	Percentage Adjustments	Unit of Comparison
	Principle of Substitution	Verification

LAND (SITE) VALUE OPINION

PURPOSE OF A SEPARATE SITE VALUATION

It has been argued that once the site is improved, a separate site valuation is difficult, if not impossible and unnecessary. The claim is that only a total property valuation is possible in such cases and that the value of the site and the value of the real estate are inseparable. In spite of the theoretical merits of this argument, however, there are many practical reasons for making separate site valuations, even when the property is already improved.

 Separate site valuations are required by statute in most states for *ad valorem* real estate tax purposes. The assessed value is almost universally split between the land (or site) and the improvements. Special assessments for public improvements, such as streets, water lines, sewers, etc., are often based on their estimated effect on land or site values. Income tax preparation also requires that the cost of a property be split between its improvements and its site. The first step of the cost approach is to estimate a separate market value for the site. Separate site value estimates are also commonly used for establishing condemnation awards, adjusting casualty losses, deciding whether to raze existing improvements to use the site for new development, and for establishing site rentals.

PROCEDURES FOR ESTIMATING SITE VALUE

There are six basic procedures for estimating the market value of individual sites:

1. Sales comparison approach
2. Allocation procedure
3. Extraction method
4. Subdivision development method
5. Land residual technique
6. Capitalization of ground rental

Sales Comparison Approach

The **sales comparison approach** is based on comparing and contrasting pertinent data about comparable sites that have actually sold, with data about the subject site. It is the most popular and practical site valuation procedure. The appraiser may also consider offering and listing prices and other market information, but primary attention is given to actual sales of like sites, consummated under typical market conditions, as close to the date of the appraisal as possible. Sellers may offer a property at any price they choose, and potential purchasers may bid any price they like, but the actual selling price of a site —a figure acceptable to both buyer and seller—best reflects market conditions.

Within any market, there is a relevant range of value for each property. The actual sale price will depend on the specific negotiations of the transaction. The relevant range associated with a particular market is directly related to the degree of accuracy of an opinion of value.

This point is illustrated by a tendency in some markets to list the property high and allow room for negotiation to reach the transaction price. Compare this marketing strategy to a strong market where offers start at the asking price, or above the asking price to encourage a buyer to enter into a contract. The transaction price associated with each of these scenarios indicates a range of reasonable value for each property.

SALES COMPARISON APPROACH: STEPS FOR SITE VALUE ESTIMATES

In applying the sales comparison approach to estimate the value of the site, the appraiser takes five steps:

1. Studies the market and selects the sales and listings of sites most comparable to the subject property.

2. Collects and verifies data on each selected site's selling and listing prices, dates of transaction, physical and locational characteristics and any special conditions.

3 Analyzes and compares each site with the subject site as to time of sale, location, physical characteristics, and conditions of sale.

4. Adjusts the sale or listing price of each comparable site for dissimilarities between it and the subject site. Adjustments are derived from the market whenever possible. These adjustments are positive (if the comparable site is less desirable than the subject) or negative (if the comparable site is more desirable than the subject.)

5. Reconciles the adjusted sale prices of the comparable sites into an indicated value of the subject site.

In the next section of this chapter that covers estimating the value of the whole property more information about the sales comparison approach is developed. It includes how to make adjustments for any significant differences between the comparable sale and the subject property.

The Allocation Procedure

There is a relationship between the application of the agents of production and the market value of a site, based on the principles of balance, contribution, surplus productivity, and increasing and decreasing returns. Therefore, site value can be estimated by allocating the total sale price of a comparable between its two utilitarian and productive parts - the site and the improvements. The appraiser determines what portion of a property's sale price typically may be allocated between the site and the improvements, estimating the market value of the house and other improvements first. The balance or residual is then allocated to the site.

10.3 ►

To estimate the value of unimproved property in an area where vacant land sales are lacking, the appraiser allocates from the total sale price of a comparable property that part which can reasonably be attributed to the value of the improvements. The remainder, except for intangibles, is the site value.

Assume that a property with a 1,500 square foot house sold for $200,000. The appraiser estimates the value of the house at 75% of the total value, or $150,000. The remainder 25% of the sale is $50,000 which is the residual value of the site, assuming that the house represents the typical or highest and best use, and that no extraneous considerations were involved in the transaction.

The advantage of this procedure is that a sense of proportion is retained. If a neighborhood is typically improved with certain types of properties that can justify only a certain land value, the typical vacant site probably will not be improved to a higher and better use. Where no vacant site sales are available, this method can support an indication of site value. However, the results may sometimes be inconclusive and require collateral **confirmation**. Estimating the contributory value of the improvement tends to be more reliable when the improvements are relatively new.

Extraction Method

10.4 ▶ The **extraction method** also involves an analysis of improved properties, but is most applicable where the improvements contribute only a small percentage of the total property value. The contribution of the improvements is estimated and deducted from the total sale price of the comparable property to arrive at a comparable sale price attributable to the land. For example, this method would be suitable for older cottage type properties situated on prime beach front lots, where the majority of the value is clearly in the land.

The distinction between the allocation procedure and the extraction method depends on the relative contributory value of the improvements. When the improvement contributes a larger part of the value it is best to use the allocation method and when the improvements contributory value is a smaller part of the total value the technique usually used is known as the extraction method. For example if the total sale price of an improved property is $250,000 and the depreciated cost of the improvements is $25,000, the extracted value of the site is $225,000.

Subdivision Development Method

The subdivision method can be used when the highest and best use of the land is for a subdivision. The first step is to estimate the total number of sites that would be obtained from the proposed subdivision. Next, estimate the total sale price of the property. From this is deducted all the costs of development and marketing:

- Development costs:
     grading, clearing, paving, waste disposal, utility services,
     design and engineering
- Management and supervision
- Contractors overhead and profit
- Sales expenses
- Taxes
- Developer's entrepreneurial profit
- Cost of carrying the investment to when the individual lots are sold

The figure that results is the estimated value of the site.

Land Residual Technique

In the land residual technique, the site is assumed to be improved to its highest and best use, and the net operating income attributable to the site is capitalized by the land capitalization rate into an indication of land value. This technique works best for commercial and industrial sites.

Capitalization of Ground Rent

The ground rent attributable to a property can be capitalized into an indication of the value of the site. This procedure is useful when comparable rents, rates, and other factors can be developed from an analysis of sales of leased land. It is common in some areas, particularly Hawaii.

Reconciliation of Adjusted Site Sales Prices

The reconciliation process involves analyzing the quality and quantity of comparables available for analysis. The final step in the valuation process is to reconcile all the adjusted comparable sales prices into an indicated value of the subject site. Use of a simple arithmetic average of value indications is not acceptable appraisal practice. Averaging small groups of numbers produces a meaningless measure of central tendency, which may or may not reflect actual market value. The accepted procedure is to review each sale and judge its comparability to the subject property. The final value is based on all the information available to the appraiser, with greater weight given to particular comparables for well-explained reasons.

IMPROVED PROPERTY VALUE OPINION

SALES COMPARISON APPROACH - IMPROVED PROPERTY

10.5 ▶ The *sales comparison approach*, which used to be called the *market data approach*, involves making a direct comparison between other properties that have been sold (or are listed for sale) and the subject property. All three approaches to value are based on market data, but the cost and income approaches depend on a less direct comparison than does the sales comparison approach.

10.6 ▶ When carefully collected, analyzed, verified and reconciled, market data usually provides the best indication of market value for a property. The price that a typical buyer pays is often the result of a shopping process, in which many properties are examined and evaluated. Buyers often base their value conclusions primarily on properties that are being offered for sale. Appraisers use this information plus information about properties that have sold and rented.

The *principle of substitution* states that when several commodities or services with substantially the same utility are available, the one with the lowest price attracts the greatest demand and the widest distribution. It is important to understand how this principle specifically applies to the theoretical framework of the sales comparison approach. In single-family residential markets, this means that when a residence is replaceable in the market (which it usually is), its value tends to be set by the cost of acquiring an equally desirable substitute residence. The assumption is that there will be no costly delay encountered in making the substitution. Experienced real estate brokers know that most buyers will accept more than one house in the market in which they are shopping and will accept only a short delay in negotiating the purchase of any specific house.

10.7 ▶A popular myth is that one can sell a house at almost any price if one is willing to wait long enough for the one buyer who wants only that particular house and will pay substantially above its market value to obtain it. Houses that are listed substantially above market value generally remain unsold no matter how long they are offered for sale. The principle of substitution provides the basis for the premise that the market value of a house is the value indicated by active and informed buyers in the market for comparable houses offering a similar quality of shelter, **amenities** and other considerations characteristic of that market.

Individual sales often deviate from the market norm because of individual motivations, knowledge and/or conditions of sale; but in sufficient numbers, they tend to reflect market patterns. When information is available on a sufficient number of comparable sales, offerings and listings in the current market, the resulting pattern is the best indication of market value.

Sales Comparison Approach:
Steps For Improved Property Estimates

In applying the sales comparison approach, the appraiser takes five steps:

1. Studies the market and selects the sales and listings of houses most comparable to the residence being appraised. Generally, the most current and similar comparable sales prove to be the best indicators of the value of the subject.

2. Collects and verifies data on each selected property's selling and listing prices, date of transaction, physical and locational characteristics and any special conditions.

3. Analyzes and compares each comparable house with the subject as to time of sale, location, physical characteristics and conditions of sale.

4. Adjusts the sale or listing price of each comparable for dissimilarities between it and the subject. Adjustments are derived from the market whenever possible, using matched pairs, regression analysis and other adjustment techniques.

5. Reconciles the adjusted prices of the comparable properties into an indicated value of the subject residence.

STUDYING THE MARKET

A market study of the market area is made to find those comparable sales and listings that are most similar to the subject property. Generally, the more current the comparable sale **10.8** ▶and the more similar it is to the subject property, the better it will be as an indicator of the value of the subject property. More sales and listings are usually analyzed than are finally used in the appraisal. The best comparables are selected and used in the final calculations and value estimate.

COLLECTING THE DATA

Accuracy of the value indication via the sales comparison approach depends heavily upon the quantity and quality of sales and listings of competitive properties. Through a sound collection program, a large bank of market data can be accumulated in the appraiser's own files and should be organized to serve the appraiser's needs most effectively. The accuracy of the analysis depends upon the quantity and quality of data available to be analyzed.

VERIFYING THE DATA

The confirmation process should include all information about a sale that will be considered in the sales comparison analysis.

Among the data about each comparable property to be verified are:

> Address of the property
> Date of sale
> Date of contract
> Date of listing
> Sale price
> Financing terms
> Conditions of sale
> Physical characteristics:
>> Size
>> Configuration
>> Quality
>> Condition
>> Amenities (within the improvements and on the site)
> Financial characteristics
>> Lease rate
>> Lease term

10.9 Each sale used as a comparable in an appraisal report should be personally inspected and the data confirmed with the buyer, seller or broker. The appraiser must be assured that all of the facts about each comparable sale are accurate, that all depreciation has been considered, the measurements are correct and the reported price and terms are accurate.

Verification and inspection processes do more than confirm the accuracy of the data gathered. They also provide for exploration of motivating forces involved in a sale, such as: were both buyer and seller acting without financial pressure? Was the sale an arms-length transaction, or were the parties related in some way? Were both buyer and seller knowledgeable about the property and market in which the sale took place? Did the seller have a reasonable time to sell and the buyer to buy? Were there any special concessions granted by either party? Was financing typical of the market, or was there a purchase money mortgage, second mortgage, assumed mortgage or other unusual situations? Were there any special sale conditions such as inclusion of personal property in the sale (furniture, above-ground pools, boats, automobiles, sports equipment, etc.)? Was there any special government program involving a subsidy, attractive financing terms or guarantee of payment?

Sometimes an owner sells for less than expected if allowed to occupy the property for a substantial period of time after the transfer of title. Other times a sale is the result of an option granted in the past when different market conditions prevailed, resulting in a sale price that may not be typical of the current market. These are only some of the possible conditions that might make the reported sale price different from the market value. Only by personally interviewing the buyer and seller or broker can the appraiser gain knowledge about such conditions.

Clients - as part of their **scope of work -** do not always require that the appraiser visually inspect each comparable sale. When this process is skipped *only* because the client did not require it, the appraiser must decide if it is necessary to verify the information in order to make a credible appraisal.

ANALYZING AND COMPARING THE DATA

Comparison of sales and listings provides a basis for estimating the market value of the subject property. When comparable properties are similar to the subject property, have sold very recently and have few if any physical, locational and conditions of sale adjustments, such information is helpful to the appraiser in reaching a market value estimate. On most assignments, however, the appraiser recognizes substantial differences between the subject property and the comparable sales and listings. Two analytical tools used by appraisers are elements of comparison and units of comparison. Each of the **elements of comparison** (date of sale, physical characteristics, location, and conditions of sale) must be considered. Often there is more than one physical characteristic that requires adjustment. The **units of comparison** provide a means for making these adjustments.

ADJUSTING THE COMPARABLES

Once all of the elements of comparison between the comparable sales and property being appraised are described in the appraisal report, they must be analyzed and adjustments must be made to reflect the dollar or percentage value of the dissimilarities noted.

When a comparable sale is better than the subject property, a minus adjustment is made to the comparable sale. When a comparable sale is inferior to the subject property, a plus adjustment is made to the comparable sale. All adjustments are made to the comparable sale or listing, and never to the subject property.

-- **Elements of comparison** represent the components with which the comparable property is compared to the subject property. There are many possible elements of comparison, including location, size, condition of the improvements, amenities, etc.

-- **Units of comparison** represent the unit of measure associated with the appraisal analysis. Examples include by the entire property (acreage), by the square foot or front foot, by the number of bedrooms, by the number of apartment units, etc.

-- **Qualitative adjustments** are those comparisons that are non-numerical. Instead, they are a series of relative ratings, such as superior, inferior, larger, smaller, etc., that are applied to each element of comparison. Some appraisers believe that this type of analysis is more reflective of actual market participants than quantitative (measurable) adjustments.

-- **Quantitative adjustments** are numerical. There are two types of quantitative adjustments: dollars adjustments and percentage adjustments. When quantitative adjustments are used in the sales comparison analysis, a **dollar adjustment** or percentage adjustment is applied to each element of comparison.

Matched Pairs of Sales

In the past, many adjustments were based on nothing more than educated guesses. Good appraisal practice requires that adjustments be supported with data from the market. The best technique is to extract the amount of the adjustment from the market by using **matched pairs of sales**. This is often the only technique acceptable to many sophisticated purchasers of appraisals. It involves the selection of two sales in the market, one with the item for which the adjustment is sought and the other without that item. The theory behind this technique is that if a single item is the only difference between two sales, the difference in sale price can be attributed to that item. Although generally reliable where only one difference is present, the technique may still be used where there are several differences.

The following is an example of an adjustment based on only one difference between the matched pair. Each of the comparable sales used in the following illustrations is assumed to be very similar to the house being appraised and to each other, except as noted. They are also assumed to have sold recently so that no time adjustments are needed.

EXAMPLE #1: USING A MATCHED PAIR OF SALES TO EXTRACT THE VALUE OF ONE ITEM

Comparable Sale 1　　　　　　　　　Sale Price: $ 228,000
　1- acre lot
　1- car attached garage

Comparable Sale 2　　　　　　　　　Sale Price: $240,000
　1- acre lot
　2- car attached garage

　$ 240,000 - $ 228,000 = $ 12,000   Difference attributable to larger garage

The only significant difference between these two sales is the garage size. From this information, it appears that the market recognizes a $12,000 difference between one-car and two-car garages. The indicated adjustment for this item is $12,000.

EXAMPLE #2: USING A MATCHED PAIR OF SALES TO EXTRACT THE VALUE OF TWO ITEMS

Usually, more than one difference exists between two sales. In such cases, adjustments can be made for each of the differences. The final remaining difference in sale price, after all other adjustments have been made, is attributed to the item for which adjustment is being sought.

Continuing the problem in Example #2 above:

Comparable Sale 3   Sale Price: $210,000
    1- acre lot
    1- car attached garage
    Near gasoline service station

This sale can be directly paired with Comparable Sale 1. The $18,000 difference in sale price between Comparable Sale 1 and Comparable Sale 3 can be attributed to the nearby gas station. Comparable Sale 3 can be paired with Comparable Sale 2. There is a $30,000 difference between the sale prices of Comparables 2 and 3 of which $12,000 is caused by the difference in value between a one-car and two-car garage (based on calculation in Example #1). When there are two or more differences between the matched pairs, the differences may affect the sales in the same or opposite ways. In this example, they both affect the sales in the same way.

Comparable Sale 3 is $30,000 less valuable than Comparable Sale 2 because it has a smaller garage ($12,000) and is affected by the gas station next door ($18,000).

Because it is difficult to tell if the difference affects the sales in the same way or opposite ways just by looking at them, it is necessary to estimate the effect from the market. This is done by designating one comparable sale the **base sale** and then adjusting the other sale for all the differences between it and the base sale, except for the one being analyzed. When all the adjustments have been made, the remaining difference between the base sale and the other sale is attributed to the one difference left between them.

EXAMPLE #3: USING A BASE SALE TO EXTRACT THE VALUE OF SPECIFIC DIFFERENCES

Pairing Comparable Sale 2 and Comparable Sale 3 illustrates how this works.

Comparable 2 (Base Sale)   Sale Price: $240,000
    1- acre lot
    2- car attached garage

Comparable 3   Sale Price: $210,000
    1- acre lot
    1- car attached garage
    Adverse influence from nearby gas station

Adjustment for difference between 1- car and 2- car garage	+ $ 12,000
Adjusted sale price of Comparable 3	$222,000

Abstraction for remaining difference: adverse influence of nearby gas station:

Comparable Sale 2 (Base Sale)	Sale Price:	$240,000
Adjusted sale price, Comparable 3		- 222,000
Amount attributable to the adverse influence of nearby gas station		$18,000

Abstracting market data in this manner will produce reliable results, especially when a series of comparisons reveal the same or nearly the same adjustment for the item in question.

This process can be extended still further. Comparable Sale 4 is also similar to the other sales and sold recently for $270,000.

> **Comparable Sale 4**   Sale Price: $270,000
>   2- acre lot
>   2- car garage
>   Adverse influence from nearby gas station

This sale cannot be compared directly with any of the other sales to extract an adjustment for the two-acre lot. In each case, there is at least one other difference:

> **Comparable Sale 1**:   1- acre lot, 1- car garage, away from gas station
> **Comparable Sale 2:**   1- acre lot, away from gas station.
> **Comparable Sale 3:**   1- acre lot, 1- car garage, has nearby gas station

Even though there is more than one difference in each matched pair, Comparable Sale 4 can be paired with each of the others by first adjusting for the other differences.

Pairing Comparable Sale 4 with Comparable Sale 1 works out as follows:

> **Comparable Sale 1 (Base Sale)**   Sale Price: $228,000
>   1- acre lot
>   1- car garage

> **Comparable Sale 4**   Sale Price: $270,000
>   2- acre lot
>   2- car garage
>   Adverse influence from nearby gas station

Adjustment of Comparable Sale 4 to Base Sale 1 for difference between 1- car and 2- car garage	-12,000
Adjustment of Comparable Sale 4 to Base Sale 1 for adverse influence of nearby gas station	+18.000
Adjusted Sale Price of Comparable Sale 4	$276,000

Abstract remaining difference: lot size

Adjusted Sale Price of Comparable Sale 4	$276,000
Sale Price 1 (Base Sale)	-228.000
Amount attributable to difference between 1- acre and 2- acre lot	$48,000

Pairing Comparable Sales 4 and 3 works out as follows:

Comparable Sale 3 (Base Sale)   Sale Price: $210,000

    1- acre lot
    1- car attached garage
    Adverse influence from nearby gas station

Comparable Sale 4   Sale Price: $270,000
    2- acre lot
    2- car garage
    Adverse influence from nearby gas station

Adjustment of Comparable Sale 4 to Base Sale 3
   for difference between 1- car and 2- car garage   <u>-12.000</u>

Adjusted Sale Price for Comparable Sale 4 $258,000

Abstraction for remaining difference: lot size

Adjusted Sale Price for Comparable Sale 4 $258,000

Sale Price Comparable 3 (Base Sale)   <u>-210,000</u>

Amount attributable to lot size difference $ 48,000

Fig. 10-1 summarizes the data analyzed in the preceding examples in chart form. This type of chart is a useful way to organize a series of similar comparable sales.

FIG. 10-1 COMPARABLE SALES GRID

Item	Subject House	Comp. Sale 1	Comp. Sale 2	Comp. Sale 3	Comp. Sale 4
Sale Price	——	$228,000	$240,000	$210,000	$270,000
Time of Sale	Date of the Appraisal	Recent	Recent	Recent	Recent
Physical Lot/size Adjustment	1- acre -0-	1- acre -0-	1- acre -0-	1- acre -0-	2- acre – $48,000
Car Storage Adjustment	1- car attached -0-	1- car attached -0-	2- car attached – $12,000	1- car attached -0-	2- car attached – $12,000
Adverse location influence Adjustment	None -0-	None -0-	None -0-	Next to a gas station + $18,000	Next to a gas station + $18,000
Conditions of Sale Adjustment	None -0-	None -0-	None -0-	None -0-	None -0-
Net Adjustment	-0-	-0-	– $12,000	+ $18,000	– $42,000
Indicated value of subject house	$ 228,000	$228,000	$228,000	$228,000	$228,000

10.11 In actual sales analysis, calculations would rarely work out as precisely as in this example, due to two major factors. First, even active, informed markets produce different buyer and seller opinions of the value of each comparison item considered by the appraiser. Thus for each property, there may be a range of prices considered reasonable for its market. Second, the adjustment for one item of difference may already include a partial adjustment for another item of difference.

To illustrate, in the above example, the price per acre may differ for locations near service stations. For example, the market might require a larger lot to better buffer against the adverse influence, yet not pay more for the extra land. Adjustment for both the adverse influence and lot size may overstate the actual difference because an adjustment for location near the service station may already include a partial adjustment for lot size. Unless aided by properly applied adjustment processes such as regression analysis, the appraiser should generally make the least number of adjustments possible and should address the uncertainties of multiple adjustments in the final reconciliation of the opinion of value. This is particularly true when making multiple adjustments for physical differences.

10.12 Likewise, the appraiser should avoid the temptation to use cost estimates as a basis for market adjustments. While relationships between cost and value contributions of components may exist, they may be supported only by market data. Thus, comparison of market data should be used to support the adjustment used.

In the sales comparison approach, each comparable property is analyzed and compared to the subject property based on the elements of comparison. A rating grid may be used to record information about the subject property and the comparable sales and show adjustments for each difference between them. Figure 10-2 shows this process.

Each comparable sale is adjusted so that its sale price is converted to an indicated value of the subject property. For example, the only difference between the subject property and Comparable Sale 1 is that the subjext has no porch and the comparable sale has an open porch. This difference contributes $9,000 additional value to the comparable in this market. To adjust the comparable to the subject, $ 9,000 must be subtracted.

FIG. 10-2 Comparable Sale Rating Grid

	House Being Appraised	Comparable Sale 1
Sale price		$270,000
Porch	none	-9,000
Indicated value of subject property		$261,000

In the following example, the property being appraised has an in-ground swimming pool and the comparable has none. In-ground swimming pools add $24,000 value in this market, making the subject property superior to the comparable house. The comparable is less valuable than the subject property, so a plus adjustment is made.

FIG. 10-3 Comparable Sale Rating Grid

	House Being Appraised	Comparable Sale 2
Sale price		$240,000
In-ground swimming pool	yes	none
Sale Price		+24,000
Indicated value of subject property		$264,000

Types of Adjustments

The differences between comparable sales and the subject property can be adjusted for in either dollars or percentages. The manner in which the adjustment is derived for the market determines whether it is expressed as either a percentage or a dollar amount.

For residential properties, **percentage adjustments** are often converted to dollar adjustments to comply with the format of Freddie Mac and Fannie Mae forms such as the URAR, Small Income Property Report and Condominium Appraisal Report. These forms are designed to display the adjustments as dollar amounts either added to or subtracted from each comparable sale price to arrive at adjusted sales prices for all of the comparables, which can then be reconciled into a market value estimate of the subject property.

There is no rigid procedure for making adjustments.

"Adjustments can be applied in several ways, depending on how the relationship between the properties—subject and comparable, comparable and subject, or comparable and comparable—is expressed or perceived by the market. This relationship is expressed as an algebraic equation which is solved to determine the amount of adjustment to be made for the differences between the properties.

An appraiser uses logical calculations to make an adjustment, but the mathematics should not control the appraiser's judgment. Using computer and software technology an appraiser can effectively apply mathematical techniques that were prohibitively time-consuming. These techniques can be used to narrow the range of value, but a market value estimate is not determined by a set of precise calculations. Appraisal has a creative aspect in that appraisers use their judgment to analyze and interpret quantitative data."[1]

PERCENTAGE ADJUSTMENTS

10.13 ▶ Percentages are often used to express the differences between a subject property and a comparable sale, especially for time, special conditions and location adjustments. For example, time adjustments are easily expressed as a percentage per month or year. The difference in value between one location and another is also easily expressed as a percentage. For example, the subject neighborhood is 10% better

---

1 The Appraisal of Real Estate, 12 Edition, Appraisal Institute, Chicago IL, 2001

than the neighborhood where the comparable is located. When necessary, percentages can be converted to dollar adjustments for particular appraisals or appraisal report formats that require dollar adjustments.

The 5 possible relationships between the subject and comparable sales are shown below:

1. Subject and comparable are equal: no adjustment is needed.

2. The subject is 10% superior to the comparable: the price of the comparable must be increased to reflect the difference.

    This can be expressed as follows where 'x' equals the unknown value of the subject and 1 equals the known sale price of the comparable:

    $$x = 1.0 \text{ (sale price of comparable)} + 10\% \text{ (value adjustment)}$$
    $$= 1 + 0.1$$
    $$= 1.10$$

    In this situation, the sale price of the comparable is multiplied by 1.10 to determine the dollar amount that will be the indicated value of the subject. The resulting percentage adjustment to the price of the comparable is plus 0.1, or plus 10%.

    For example, if the sale price of the comparable is $ 160,000 and it is multiplied by 1.10, the indicated value of the subject property will be $ 176,000.

3. The subject is 10% inferior to the comparable: the price of the comparable must be decreased to reflect the difference.

    $$x = 1.0 \text{ (sale price of comparable)} - 10\% \text{ (value adjustment)}$$
    $$x = 1.0 - 0.1$$
    $$x = 0.9$$

    Here, we must multiply the sale price of the comparable by 0.9 to estimate the value of the subject. The resulting percentage adjustment to the price of the comparable is minus 10%.

    For example, if the sale price of the comparable is $ 160,000 and it is multiplied by .90, the indicated value of the subject property will be $ 144,000.

The appraiser must be consistent in stating the relationship between the subject and each of the comparables and the relationship should reflect as much as possible the appraiser's sense of the way the market perceives it. The comparable sale is always adjusted to reflect the indicated value of the subject property

DOLLAR ADJUSTMENTS

Many appraisers prefer when possible to compute adjustments in dollars. For example, the appraiser may conclude that the favorable location of a comparable sale resulted in a $50,000 premium paid by the buyer as compared with the subject location. There are many other adjustments, especially those for physical characteristics, which may be estimated in dollars and which are then simply added or subtracted from the sale price of the comparable to provide an indicated value for the subject property. Most people find simple addition and subtraction much easier to grasp and explain than more complicated percentage adjustment formulas.

SEQUENCE OF ADJUSTMENTS

One of the advantages of plus and minus dollar adjustments is that the **sequence of adjustments** does not matter. Similar, if all adjustments are percentage adjustments all the results will always be the same. However, when some adjustments are dollar adjustments—for example, $ 50,000 for a direct waterfront location—and others are percentage adjustments, such as 10% for a superior school district, the sequence of adjustments does affect the outcome.

There is no rigid order in which the appraiser must make the adjustments. The following order is suggested by the Appraisal Institute. [2]

1. **Property rights conveyed**
   This adjustment takes into account differences in legal estate between the comparable property and the subject property. When made first, it is applied directly to the reported sale price.

2. **Financing terms**
   This adjustment converts the transaction price of the comparable into its cash equivalent, or modifies it to match the financing terms of the subject property.

3. **Conditions of sale**
   This adjustment reflects the difference between the actual sale price of the comparable and its probable sale price if it were sold in an arm's-length transaction.

4. **Market conditions = time**
   An adjustment for the difference in the market at the time the comparable sale took place and the date of the appraisal.

5. **Location**
   The location of a property is an important factor in its value. Consider any value differences between the comparable and the subject locations as adjusted.

6. **Physical Characteristics**
   There is often more than one adjustment needed for physical characteristics.

Obviously, there will not be an adjustment made in every one of these categories for each comparable, unless there is a difference between the comparable sale and the subject. If there are special financing terms—for example, no points paid at closing— and this matches the financing terms of the subject, no adjustment would be made.

---

[2] The Appraisal of Real Estate, 12 Edition, The Appraisal Institute, Chicago, 2001

Sequential Percentage Adjustments

When applying percentage adjustments, it is important to note that it is the **adjusted sale price** which is used in subsequent percentage adjustments. Whatever adjustment is selected first is multiplied by the comparable sale price, giving an adjusted sale price that reflects this characteristic. The next adjustment is multiplied by the first adjusted price, *not* the unadjusted original reported price. This sequence is followed until all of the adjustments have been accounted for.

EXAMPLE #4: SEQUENTIAL PERCENTAGE ADJUSTMENTS

For example, if a comparable sale which sold for $ 125,000 has a location that is 10% better than the subject property's, and also the comparable has a 5% larger lot, the calculations would be as follows: $ 125,000 x 0.90 (location) = $ 112,500 x 0.95 (lot size) = $ 106,900 (r).

Unit Basis Adjustments

Adjustments may also be applied on a unit basis. A good technique is to work in units, such as square feet of gross living area, which are most commonly used for single-family residences. If this unit is chosen, the sale price of each comparable is converted into a price per square foot, before the adjustments are applied. The adjustments are then made to the unit figures.

EXAMPLE 5: UNIT BASIS ADJUSTMENTS

A comparable sale sold for $ 175,000 and had 1,850 sq. ft. of GLA. The unit value per square foot of the comparable is $ 94.59. An adjustment for the comparable sale's superior condition might be -$4.50 per square foot.

$ 94.59 - $ 4.50 = $ 90.09 per sq. ft. (adjusted sale price of the comparable)

The subject has 1,950 sq. ft. of GLA

1,950 sq. ft. x $ 90.09 = $175,700 (r) (value indication of the subject property)

The final value indication would be a reconciled value per square foot of gross living area based on analysis of each comparable using unit basis adjustments.

Reconciliation of Sales Comparison Approach

After the best comparable sales have been selected and each one is adjusted to give an indicated value of the subject property, the indications must be reconciled to produce a final estimate of value via the sales comparison approach. It is not acceptable appraisal practice to use a simple arithmetic mean of the value indications. Averaging small groups of numbers produces a meaningless measure of central tendency, and may or may not reflect actual market value.

The accepted procedure is to review each sale and judge its comparability to the subject property. Generally, the fewer and smaller the adjustments used on a comparable sale to produce an indicated value estimate, the more weight the sale is given in the final reconciliation. However, consideration should also be given to the basis for the adjustments, and overall similarity of the comparables to the subject property.

The final value selected is a judgment made by the appraiser based on all the information available. It is not always necessary to select a single figure at this point in the appraisal process. Some appraisers believe that the use of a range is more helpful. The use of such a range to describe market value is becoming more common, most likely as a result of greater awareness of statistical techniques on the part of appraisers. A range may more accurately reflect the market than a single point opinion of value.

OTHER ADJUSTMENT TECHNIQUES

Adjustments Based on Depreciated Cost

Another commonly used indirect technique for adjusting a comparable sale is to estimate the cost new, less depreciation, of the item for which an adjustment is needed. The accuracy of this technique depends on the relationship of the cost less depreciation estimates and value in terms of market recognition. Depreciation is especially difficult to estimate, because the market may recognize only a small portion of the cost of an item, and substantial functional obsolescence may have to be deducted to obtain the actual value which is contributed by a specific item to the sale price.

Regression Analysis Derived Adjustments

In recent years, attention has been given to methods of analyzing market data through use of regression analysis and other mathematical or computer-assisted techniques. Step-wise multiple regression routines, like more traditional methods, are based upon the concept that certain identifiable characteristics of residential markets (called independent variables) may each be studied for their individual and joint contributions to value.

A major contribution of these newer techniques has been to focus attention on the adjustment process in sales analysis. Where more than one set of matched pairs is used to extract adjustment factors, the possibility exists of doubling up on adjustments. This is due to the interdependence or interaction of many elements of comparison, something the scientists call "co-linearity". Traditional comparison methods have generally overlooked these relationships and do not provide a means for measuring interdependence of data.

For example, adjustments made for both square footage of living area and number of bedrooms are not independent. Either variable is likely to include some consideration of the other. Regression techniques can serve to reduce this problem and provide a means of measuring where significant interdependence is a factor. Regression techniques also permit a measure of reliability and significance to be determined for both the data used and the results produced.

Another reason for the growing use of regression analysis and similar techniques is that they often allow an appraiser to analyze considerably more market data and provide a better understanding of markets than traditional methods.

SUMMARY

The sales comparison approach to value is generally the preferred approach for estimating the market value of residences. The use of the **gross rent multiplier** for an income approach, as well as the cost approach, usually improves the accuracy of the value estimate. Residential appraisals that depend primarily upon the cost or income approaches rather than the sales comparison approach, have a strong possibility of substantial error. Overall, the quality and quantity of data used in the analysis will impact the reliability and credibility of the conclusions. The key to the sales comparison approach is good data, market abstraction of adjustments and the use of appropriate units of comparison. Typically, in the appraisal of single family houses, the unit of choice is square feet of gross living area or adjusting the entire sale price.

Each comparable sale is compared with the subject property. Adjustments are made to the comparable sales prices to reflect significant differences between them and the subject.

Traditionally, the elements of comparison are divided into the four categories: date of sale, physical characteristics, location and conditions of sale. Recently, special conditions and special financing have been added as elements of comparison.

In order to obtain all of the information needed to use a comparable sale, the appraiser should personally inspect each comparable property and verify the relevant characteristics of the sale with either the buyer, seller or broker. These are the people who can tell the appraiser about the conditions of sale, special financing and the actual physical condition of the property at the time of sale. Appraisers who do not inspect and verify comparable data must recognize that the chance of a significant error in the value estimate is substantially increased.

New techniques are available to appraisers with the advent of advanced computers. For example, regression analysis using more sales, does not depend upon adjustments based on limited market information, but rather on statistical treatment of many comparable sales. The use of regression analysis for appraising requires specialized training as well as data of sufficient quantity and quality to make the technique work in the subject's market area.

When the sales comparison approach is based upon a sufficient number of carefully chosen sales similar to the subject property, with appropriate adjustments derived from careful consideration of the market, the value indication is usually persuasive, and results in a credible appraisal report credible.

REVIEW QUESTIONS

1. Separate site valuations are required:
   a. by statute for ad valorem real estate tax purposes.
   b. in assessed value to split value between land and improvements.
   c. to calculate special assessments for public improvements.
   d. All of the above

2. The sales comparison approach is based on:
   a. comparing data about comparable sales with the subject property.
   b. analyzing resale trends.
   c. determining if the subject offers special financing terms.
   d. None of the above

3. After the appraiser determines how to allocate the sale price between land and improvements:
   a. the residual goes to the value of the improvements.
   b. the taxes affect only the land.
   c. the residual is considered to be the value of the land.
   d. All of the above

4. The extraction method is most suitable when:
   a. housing starts are very high.
   b. house sales are slowing in the subject market area.
   c. most of the value is in the house.
   d. where improvements contribute only a small percentage of value.

5. The sales comparison approach used to be called:
   a. the market reciprocal approach.
   b. the market area approach.
   c. the market data approach.
   d. All of the above

6. When carefully collected, analyzed, verified and reconciled:
   a. national economic data provides the best evidence of market value.
   b. market data provides the best indication of market value.
   c. Both a. and b.
   d. Neither a. or b.

7. Houses that are listed substantially above their market value:
   a. will sell just as well as long as the owner is willing to wait.
   b. will rarely sell at that price.
   c. will not sell even when their price is drastically reduced.
   d. None of the above

8. A _____ of the market area seeks to find comparables most similar to the subject property.
   a. market study
   b. comparable adjustment
   c. geographical survey
   d. regional review

9. Each sale chosen as a comparable in an appraisal report:
   a. should be inspected.
   b. should have its data verified.
   c. should be reviewed for comparability to the subject.
   d. All of the above

10. Good appraisal practice requires that adjustments be:
    a. made in terms of whole dollars.
    b. supported with data from the market.
    c. made only for large ticket items.
    d. None of the above

11. In actuality, sales analysis calculations:
    a. rarely work out precisely.
    b. usually show no variation.
    c. are not correlated to value.
    d. None of the above

12. The appraiser should avoid using cost estimates:
    a. to calculate residual land value.
    b. as a basis for increasing rentals.
    c. as a basis for market adjustments.
    d. None of the above

13. Percentages are often used to express:
    a. differences between a subject property and a comparable sale.
    b. time, special conditions and location adjustments.
    c. Both a. and b.
    d. Neither a. or b.

ANSWERS TO REVIEW QUESTIONS

The answer to each question is indicated by the letter a, b, c or d below. The explanation of the answer is indicated by a numbered arrow that points to the appropriate paragraph on the page of the text indicated by the page number following the answer.

Q 10-1	d	Page 10-2
Q 10-2	a	Page 10-2
Q 10-3	c	Page 10-3
Q 10-4	d	Page 10-4
Q 10-5	c	Page 10-5
Q 10-6	b	Page 10-5
Q 10-7	b	Page 10-6
Q 10-8	a	Page 10-6
Q 10-9	d	Page 10-7
Q 10-10	b	Page 10-9
Q 10-11	a	Page 10-12
Q 10-12	c	Page 10-13
Q 10-13	c	Page 10-14

CHAPTER 11

Specific Data Analysis - Cost Data

"Not everything that can be counted counts, and not everything that counts can be counted."

Albert Einstein
Physicist

Important Words and Key Concepts

Words on this list are highlighted in this chapter.
They are also defined in the Glossary at the back of this text.

Actual Age	Matched Pairs of Sales
Age Life Method	Physical Deterioration - Curable
Cost	Physical Deterioration - Incurable
Cost to Cure	Physical Life
Depreciation	Principle of Substitution
Direct Costs	Quantity Survey Method
Economic Life	Remaining Economic Life
Effective Age	Replacement Cost
Entrepreneurial Profit	Reproduction Cost
External Obsolescence	Short Lived Items
Functional Obsolescence - Curable	Square Foot Method
Functional Obsolescence - Incurable	Superadequacy
Indirect Costs	Unit-in-Place Method

COST DATA ANALYSIS

11.1 ▶ The Cost Approach, is based on the assumption that the **cost** to produce a building plus the cost to acquire and improve the site to make it suitable for building, is a good indication of what a property is worth.

Every real estate parcel is different, so location is a very important component of value. Unlike other commodities where suitable substitutes are easily found, the cost of a property is not as perfect an indicator of its value as it is for these other commodities, i.e., automobiles, diamonds, gold, etc.

There are some appraisers and some important buyers of appraisals who do not believe the Cost Approach is useful in residential appraising. Fannie Mae and Freddie Mac do not require the cost approach. Others (including the authors) believe it works well on residences, especially if the reproduction cost is obtained from a reliable source such as a computerized cost service and the depreciation is taken from the market by the abstraction process, which is explained later in this chapter.

11.2 ▶ Cost is not necessarily or automatically the equivalent of market value. The procedure for developing the estimated value of the improvements requires the conversion of cost to construct figures to market value figures. The process of making such a conversion requires care, caution and skill.

A separate valuation of the improvements is often needed for a variety of reasons, and the cost approach is one of the ways to obtain it. These reasons include tax purposes (where *ad valorem* tax laws dictate this separation in value), accounting (where it is used to report the depreciation of buildings), and to obtain the value of the land by the land residual method. The cost approach is especially useful when estimating the value of special purpose properties where there is no market data.

STEPS OF THE COST APPROACH

11.3 ▶ 1. Estimate the value of the site and site improvements (this technique is described elsewhere in this text).

2. Estimate the **reproduction cost** of the improvements (some appraisers use replacement cost; when **replacement cost** is used, it should be noted in the comments section together with a description of which items were substituted for those that actually exist in the subject property).

3. Estimate the amount of depreciation from all causes and categorize it into the three major types of depreciation: physical deterioration, functional obsolescence and external obsolescence.

4. Deduct the total estimated depreciation from the reproduction or replacement cost of the improvements to derive the amount of value that the improvements contribute to the property.

5. Add together the value of the site, the value contributed by the site improvements and landscaping, and the cost of all the improvements, less applicable depreciation.

ESTIMATE THE VALUE OF THE SITE

11.4 The value of the site is normally estimated assuming it is unimproved and ready to be used for its highest and best use.

In some circumstances, the appraisal of a property may require that the site be considered in terms other than its highest and best use. In an appraisal to estimate the use value or legal, non-conforming use value of an improved site, an appraiser may need to value the site according to its specified use or the existing improvements, not its highest and best use. In this case, the appraiser should value the site both in terms of its highest and best use and its conditional use.

In the past, the estimate of site value was part of the cost approach in the valuation process. Now it is considered to be a separate step.

ESTIMATE THE COST NEW OF THE IMPROVEMENTS

Reproduction Cost versus Replacement Cost

REPRODUCTION COST
The dollar amount required to construct an exact duplicate of the subject building, at current prices.

REPLACEMENT COST:
The cost of creating a structure and other improvements having the same or equivalent utility, using current standards of material and design, based on current prices for labor and materials.

Theoretically, reproduction cost is easier to use but as a matter of practicality, it becomes quite difficult to estimate for older buildings, because identical materials are not always available and construction methods and design are constantly changing. The use of replacement cost provides a practical alternative. It represents the funds required to build an equally desirable substitute building, not necessarily with identical materials or to the same specifications.

For example, reproduction cost for an older house erected with solid brick walls would be computed on the basis of identical construction today. On the other hand, an estimate of replacement cost would not necessarily imply a structure with solid brick walls. Quite possibly current design and construction standards in the neighborhood for a house of this type, style and value would be frame construction with brick veneer walls. Accordingly, by using replacement cost instead of reproduction cost, some of the obsolescence or "inutility" present in the house with solid masonry walls would be eliminated from the estimate, before deductions for accrued depreciation are made.

Care must be exercised not to take double depreciation. In the above example, the solid masonry walls have already been treated by using the replacement cost of a frame house with brick veneer walls. A penalty should not be deducted again under functional obsolescence.

Types of Costs

For both reproduction cost and replacement cost estimates, costs can be broken down into direct or *hard costs* and indirect or *soft costs*. The developer's entrepreneurial profit is added to these costs.

DIRECT (HARD) COSTS

These are the costs of labor, materials, and contractors' and subcontractors' overhead and profit. It does not include the hoped for profit of the developer - who may or may not be the contractor.

Typically **direct cost**s consist of the following:

- Labor
- Materials
- Equipment
- Contractor profit and overhead
- Security during construction
- Temporary construction building
- Temporary fencing and walls
- Utilities used during construction
- Storage of materials during construction
- Contractor's performance bond

INDIRECT (SOFT) COSTS

These are all the other costs associated with the construction of a building that are not included in the direct costs.

Typical **indirect costs** consist of the following:

- Professional services:
    - Architect's fees
    - Engineer's fees
    - Surveyor's fees
    - Legal fees and expenses
    - Appraisal fees
- Developer's overhead
- Building permits and licenses
- Insurance premiums
- Interest
- Taxes
- Selling expenses (commissions, advertising, promotion)
- Carrying costs from time of completion to sale or occupancy

ENTREPRENEURIAL PROFIT

Many appraisers feel that an additional amount should be added to the direct and indirect costs to represent **entrepreneurial profit**. Since not all developers make profit, this figure should represent the typical anticipated developer profit.

ESTIMATING REPRODUCTION OR REPLACEMENT COST

11.6 ▶There are three methods for estimating the reproduction cost or replacement cost of a building:

1. Square foot or cubic foot method (comparative-unit method), in which the cost per square foot or cubic foot of a recently built comparable structure is multiplied by the number of square feet in the subject property.

2. Unit-in-place method (segregated cost method), in which the construction cost per square foot or other appropriate measure of each component part of the subject building (including material, labor, overhead, and builder's profit) multiplied by the number of square feet or other appropriate measure of the component part in the subject building.

3. *Quantity survey method*, in which the cost of erecting or installing all the component parts of a new building are added. Indirect costs (building permit, land survey, overhead expenses such as insurance and payroll taxes, and builder's profit) are totaled, and added to the direct costs (site preparation and all phases building construction, including fixtures).

The quantity survey method is the one generally used by cost estimators, contractors, and builders. Of the three methods, the quantity survey method results in the most accurate cost estimate, since all of the building components are analyzed. The square foot and unit-in-place methods are generalized cost figures for either comparable building types (square foot method) or specific building components (unit-in-place method). Of the two methods, the unit-in-place method is more exact, since it allows for more variables in the subject building.

Square Foot Method

To begin the *square foot method* of estimating reproduction cost, the appraiser must determine the dimensions of the subject building, to compute the number of square feet of ground area the building covers. In collecting cost data to use in the square foot method, the appraiser must find the cost of a comparable new building. Since a comparable new building may not be available, the appraiser usually relies on cost manuals or cost data services for basic construction prices.

The typical cost manual provides information about many types of property. The subject's type of building is located where construction features are itemized, with utilities (mechanical features) listed separately. If the closest example in the cost manual still has significant differences from the subject building, a cost differential could be added to (or subtracted from) the cost per square foot given in the cost manual. Computer services are also available which produce cost data for appraisers. An example is shown in Fig. 11-1.

Figure 11-1 Computer Produced Cost Estimate

REPRODUCTION COST

The reproduction cost of the house was obtained using a cost service, Information about the subject house was inputted in an office computer. The cost calculations were printed on our printer as shown below;

City, State, ZIP: Bloomville, IL 60611
Surveyed by   :   Henry S. Harrison & Burton S. Lee
Date of Survey: _____200_

Single Family Residence   Floor Area: 1,888 square feet
Effective Age: 30 years   Quality: Average
Cost as of:_____200_   Condition: Average

Style: One Story
Heating & Cooling: Baseboard, Hot Water
Exterior Wall: Face Brick
Roofing: Composition Shingle
Floor Structure: Wood Sub floor
Floor Cover: Standard Allowance
Plumbing: Standard Allowance
Appliances: Standard Allowance
Other Features: Single Fireplace

	Units	Costs	Total
Basic Structure Cost.............	1,888	106.70	201,450
Garage:			
Attached Garage...................	506	32.30	16,344
Extras:			
Roofed Porch w/steps.........	144	26.88	3,871
Domestic Solar Hot Water Unit			7,000
Subtotal			10,870
Replacement Cost New...............	1,888	126.87	239,535
Less Depreciation			
Physical Deterioration...............	(40.0%)		(95,814)
Functional Obsolescence............	(7.9%)		(18,923)
Locational Obsolescence............	(5.0%)		(11,976)
Subtotal.................................	(52.9%)		(126,713)
Depreciated Cost........................	1,888	59.76	112,822
Miscellaneous:			
Land..			40,000
Site Improvements...................			6,000
Subtotal..................................			46,000
Total..	1,888	84.12	158,822

Unit-in-Place Method/Segregated Cost Method

The **unit-in-place method** is also called the segregated cost method. It employs unit costs for various building components as they are normally installed.

A unit-in-place cost estimate is made by breaking a building into its components and estimating the cost of the material and labor required to install that component or unit into the subject building assuming it was being built on the date of the appraisal. Unit-in-place cost estimates are made in terms of standard costs for each of the building components as installed.

FIG. 7-2 ESTIMATED COSTS OF HOUSE CONSTRUCTION COMPONENTS*

Component	Unit	Quantity	Unit Cost	Total
General Expense (Engineering, Plans, Survey, Site)	Sq. ft./GLA	1,442 sq. ft.	$2.76	$4,000
Foundation	Sq. ft./GLA	1,442 sq. ft.	4.44	6,400
Basement	Sq. ft./GLA	1,442 sq. ft.	6.64	9,600
Floors	Sq. ft./GLA	1,383 sq. ft.	7.52	10,400
Exterior walls & insulation (including windows & exterior doors)	Sq.. ft./wall	1,451 sq. ft.	12.96	18,800
Roof	Sq. ft./GLA	1,442 sq. ft.	8.32	12,000
Roof Dormers	Lin. ft. across face	None	–	–
Interior walls, ceilings, doors, cabinets, trim, & accessories	Sq. ft./GLA	1,442 sq. ft.	13.04	18,800
Stairways	Each	2 Outside	800.00	1,600
Attic Finish	Sq. ft./fin. Area	None	–	–
Heating	Sq. ft./GLA	1,442 sq. ft.	4.44	6,400
Cooling Electric System	Sq. ft./GLA	1,442 sq. ft.	5.56	8,000
Plumbing System	Sq. ft./GLA	1,442 sq. ft.	11.08	16,000
Fireplaces & Chimneys	Each	1 Chimney	3,200.00	3,200
Built-in Appliances	Each	2	1,200.00	2,400
Porches	Sq. ft./porch	None	–	–
Patios	Sq. ft./patio	144 sq. ft.	5.56	800
Other	Doors & Windows	22	72.72	1,600
Site improvements (not included in land value)	Lump Sum	–	2,400.00	2,400
Garage	Sq. ft./garage	460 sq. ft.	17.39	8,000
Indirect Costs**	Sq. ft./GLA	1,442 sq. ft.	20.53	29,600
TOTAL				**$160,000**

*These are *not* actual costs but an illustration of how costs might be approximately allocated in a $160,000 house.

**May be added to each component (rather than shown separately, as in this example).

Quantity Survey Method

This comprehensive method is used by many contractors. It requires the preparation of a detailed inventory of all the materials and equipment used to build the house. The cost of each item installed assuming the building was built, on the date of appraisal, is estimated. The amount of labor in hours needed to install each item, using current labor rates is also estimated. Finally, the indirect costs, overhead and profit are added to the cost of materials, equipment and labor.

FIG. 11-3 SECTION OF CONTRACTOR'S COST BREAKDOWN

		MATERIAL	LABOR			TOTALS		
Items	Units	Price	Subtotal	Hours	Rate	Subtotal	Total Costs	
Cabinet work base-finished w/Formica top	16	$88	$1,408	14	$14.60	$204.40	$1,612.40	
Plumbing 60-gal. hot water heater	1	$1,300	$1,300	30	$30.80	$924.00	$2,224.00	

To prepare this breakdown using the quantity survey method, the contractor first lists all the material and equipment, and estimates the amount of labor required to install each item. Then the material, equipment and labor are priced out per unit and extended to give the total cost of installing each item.

Except for an unusual appraisal, this type of breakdown is beyond the scope usually required. When such a breakdown is required, the services of a trained cost estimator should be obtained. Appraisers often use a summary of the contractor's cost breakdown; Fig. 11-4 shows typical cost breakdowns for a house. The specifications and general description of the house used for this example are as follows:

-- **General Description:** One-family, one-story, ranch-style, seven rooms (living room, family room, dining room, kitchen, three bedrooms, two full baths), full unfinished basement. no porches. gross living area: 1,422 square feet. two-car, attached garage.

-- **General Construction:** Concrete footings and foundation walls; exterior walls cedar shingled. Roof covering: cedar shingles; wood double-hung windows, combination aluminum storm windows and screens, aluminum gutters and downspouts, Batt type insulation; wood platform framing, plywood sub floors, oak floors except kitchen (vinyl tile) and bathrooms (ceramic tile wainscot).

-- **Mechanical Systems:** Plumbing: copper water and PVC waste pipes connected to municipal services in street. Electric 60-gal. domestic hot water heater. One double stainless steel kitchen sink. Each bathroom has standard water closet, lavatory and tub with shower. Laundry tub in basement and washer/dryer hook-up; heating: oil-fired, hot water furnace; two circulators; baseboard radiators. Electrical: 100-amp service; 16 circuits protected with circuit breakers: BX cable; adequate outlets and features. Built-in Appliances: gas oven and range, hood with exhaust fan in kitchen.

Work Provided by Sub-Contractor

Many contractors use numerous subcontractors who have special expertise in certain areas and can often do the work better and cheaper than a general contractor. Typically, general contractors who use a substantial number of subcontractors figure the cost of a building by breaking it down into components corresponding to the work done by the various subcontractors. Popular cost services also use the technique and call it the segregated cost method. The technique is based on the use of unit prices for the various building components, using workable units such as square foot or linear foot or some other appropriate basic unit.

Fig. 11-4 shows a typical list of house construction components. The cost estimates for these components are made in terms of standardized unit costs for installation. Providing that the units accurately reflect costs, this estimate is a short-cut to an actual quantity survey. The resulting figure should correspond in accuracy with that derived from a quantity survey.

Based on the summary in Fig. 11-4, an appraiser would estimate the reproduction cost new at $160,000. Note that this example is not in itself a complete quantity survey breakdown, but represents a recapitulation of the cost estimator's quantity survey analysis.

The distinction between a quantity survey analysis and a segregated cost analysis is the level of detail. The quantity survey analysis has the lowest level of detail including material quantities and cost, labor quantity and costs and costs for each component. The segregated cost method relies on one amount per component.

FIG. 11-4   EXAMPLE OF A COST BREAKDOWN FOR A SINGLE FAMILY HOUSE

Component	% of Total	Cost
Survey & Financing	.5	$ 800
Plans & Plan Checking	.5	800
Site Preparation	.5	800
Excavation	1.0	1,600
Footings & Foundation	.4	6,400
Basement	6.0	9,600
Framing	7.5	12,000
Interior Walls & Ceiling	3.5	5,600
Exterior Siding	3.0	4,800
Roof Covering & Flashing	5.0	8,000
Insulation	2.0	3,200
Fireplaces & Chimneys (no fireplace)	2.0	3,200
Leaders & Gutters	1.0	1,600
Exterior & Interior Stairs	1.0	1,600
Doors, Windows & Shutters	2.0	3,200
Storm Windows, Doors & Screens	1.0	1,600

Main Floor Covering (Carpeting)	3.0	4,800
Kitchen Flooring	.5	800
Bathroom & Lavatory Floors	.5	800
Hardware	.5	800
Water Supply	1.0	1,600
Waste Disposal	1.0	1,600
Heating	4.0	6,400
Cooling (no central air conditioning)	–	–
Domestic Hot Water	1.0	1,600
Piping	4.0	6,400
Plumbing Fixtures	3.0	4,800
Kitchen Cabinets & Counters	3.0	4,800
Built-in Appliances	1.5	2,400
Shower Doors	.5	800
Bathroom Accessories	.5	800
Vanities, Medicine Cabinets & Counters	.5	800
Electric Service	2.0	3,200
Electric Wires & Outlets	2.0	3,200
Lighting Fixtures	1.0	1,600
Painting & Decorating	4.0	6,400
Porches (none)	–	–
Patios	.5	800
Finish Grading	.5	800
Landscaping	1.0	1,600
Garages & Carports	5.0	8,000
Clean Up	.5	800
Interest, Taxes & Insurance	1.0	1,600
Contractor's Overhead & Temporary Facilities	4.0	6,400
Professional Services, Permits & Licenses	1.0	1,600
Selling Expenses, Carrying Costs	5.0	8,000
Contractor's Profit	7.5	12,000
TOTAL COST	100	$160,000

SOURCES OF COST FIGURES

11.7 ▶Several reliable sources for obtaining cost data are available.

-- Cost data files: The use of square foot cost estimates involves assembling, analyzing and cataloging data on actual house costs. An appraiser should have available comprehensive current cost information for various types of houses and other improvements, including data on current material and labor costs. A system of grading quality of construction may also be used to refine the data further. This data can often be obtained from local builders, lenders, material suppliers and trade associations.

A file of this kind provides a check against costs of reproducing or replacing an existing residence, as well as against known or projected costs for existing or proposed houses of varying grades of construction. It also provides a check against the probable cost of different components of a house and of the various trades or work involved.

-- Cost services: Several recognized cost reporting services are also available to the appraiser. Some include illustrations of typical structures and provide adjustments to tailor the standard example to differently shaped or equipped residences. Some provide adjustments for individual cities or areas. Some show cubic foot or square foot costs, and some provide unit-in-place information.

-- Cost indices: A cost index service reflecting the relative cost of construction over a period of years is also useful. When the actual cost of a residence constructed some years ago is known, application of the index will indicate the present construction cost (provided the actual cost was a typical figure). For example, assume that a house cost $53,000 to build in 1955 and that a 1955 cost index, obtained from a national service, was 284.4. The current year cost index was 863.2. Based upon this data, in the current year the building would cost 3.035 times its January 1955 cost to build: 863.2 ÷ 284.4 = 3.035. This ratio gives an indicated cost to build in the current year of $160,855. ($53,000 x 3.035).

Building Cost Estimates

Building cost estimates should include all materials, equipment and labor. The contractor's overhead and profit, architect's fees and other outside professional service fees, taxes, insurance, administration and interest on borrowed funds during the construction is applied proportionately across the direct costs; others estimate and report them separately. Some appraisers also add developer's profit.

For example, assume as a benchmark house a two-story, brick residence that costs $150,000 to build, exclusive of a detached garage or other site improvements. The quality of construction is roughly comparable to that of an average mass-produced home with asphalt shingle roofing, 1/2-inch drywall, good/average finish and equipment, with combination forced-air heat and air conditioning, plus a dishwasher, disposal and fireplace. Included are three bedrooms, 2-1/2 baths and a full basement. This residence contains 1,496 square feet, thus costing approximately $100 per square foot of gross living area ($ 150,000 ÷ 1,496 = $ 100.26).

Assume that the appraiser is preparing a cost estimate for a house roughly comparable to the above example. In contrast to the benchmark house, the subject house has a concrete block foundation *in lieu* of poured concrete, no fireplace, and a good grade of wood siding instead of brick exterior walls. The appraiser makes downward adjustments for these differences: $5.00 per sq. ft. of GLA for wood siding; $1.00 per sq. ft. of GLA for the block foundation; and $3.00 per sq. ft. of GLA for the lack of a fireplace. The adjusted unit cost is now $91.00 per square foot. ($100 - $9 = $91). If indirect costs are not included in these unit cost adjustments, their total may be increased by an additional 15% to 20%.

DEPRECIATION

A simple definition of depreciation is the difference between the cost of an improvement and the value of the improvement on the date of the appraisal. More formally, it has been defined as follows:

A loss of utility and hence value from any cause. An effect caused by deterioration and/or obsolescence. Deterioration or physical depreciation is evidenced by wear and tear, decay, dry rot, cracks, encrustations, or structural defects. Obsolescence is divisible into two parts, functional and external. Functional obsolescence may be due to poor plan, mechanical inadequacy or over adequacy, functional inadequacy or superadequacy due to size, style, age, etc. It is evidenced by conditions within the property. External obsolescence is caused by changes external to the property. Depreciation begins immediately upon construction of the improvements. Components begin to age physically and to suffer from functional obsolescence in their design. Negative environmental forces cause immediate external obsolescence.

When the improvements are constructed, their economic life begins. During this period, they should contribute value to the property. If they are the "perfect improvement", the amount of value they contribute would be their total cost. Since few, if any, perfect improvements are constructed, a difference usually exists between their total cost and their value, which represents some form of depreciation. At the point when an improvement cannot be profitably utilized or when it no longer contributes to the value of the property as a whole, it is at the end of its economic life and depreciation has reached 100%.

Generally, if the house is of average condition and design and conforms to the other houses in a neighborhood and it is not subject to unusual economic influences, its effective age and chronological age will be about the same. If the house has had better than average maintenance, rehabilitation or modernization, its effective age probably will be less than its chronological age. If it is in poorer condition than typical houses of the same age or has not been modernized or rehabilitated as other similar houses in the neighborhood have or if some off-site economic or environmental factor is negatively affecting the value, the effective age will be greater than the chronological age.

TECHNIQUES FOR ESTIMATING ACCRUED DEPRECIATION

Accrued depreciation may be estimated directly through observation and analysis of the components of depreciation affecting the property or through use of a formula based on physical or economic age-life factors. It may also be estimated indirectly by use of the income or sales comparison approach.

Three techniques are used by the appraiser to measure depreciation:

1. The breakdown method separates charges on the basis of origin for cause of loss: physical deterioration, curable and incurable; functional obsolescence, curable and incurable; and external obsolescence. Each component is estimated separately, using the engineering method or observation techniques.

2. The age-life method is accomplished by estimating the typical economic life of the

improvements and their effective age.

3. The abstraction or market method extracts depreciation directly from the market, using matched pairs of properties with different rates of depreciation.

The Breakdown Method

The breakdown method is accomplished by dividing depreciation into its three separate components: physical deterioration, functional obsolescence and external (environmental) obsolescence. Physical deterioration and functional obsolescence may be further broken down into curable and incurable types. A grasp of these underlying principles is essential to an overall understanding of depreciation.

PHYSICAL DETERIORATION - CURABLE (DEFERRED MAINTENANCE)

These are all the items of maintenance that a prudent owner should accomplish as of the date of the appraisal to maximize profit (or minimize loss) if the property is sold. Almost any item of physical deterioration can be corrected at a price. However, to be classified as curable, the cure normally must contribute more value than it costs. Items of deferred maintenance usually fall into the category, including paint touch-ups and minor carpentry, plumbing and electric repairs (leaking faucets, squeaking or tight doors and windows, etc.). Interior and exterior painting and redecorating may also be included.

The ultimate test is whether the market will recognize as additional value at least the cost of the repair. Realtors® have long recognized that minor repairs do add value equal to or in excess of their cost and they try to have an owner make these repairs before a house is offered for sale. The measure of *physical deterioration-curable* is the *cost to cure*. Many appraisal clients require that an itemized list of the curable items be part of the appraisal report, together with an estimate of the cost to cure.

PHYSICAL DETERIORATION - INCURABLE

As soon as a house is constructed, it begins to age and suffer from wear and tear. *Physical deterioration-incurable* is based on the physical condition of the components of the house. The total physical life of the house would equal its total economic life if other forms of depreciation were not present. One of the practical problems in estimating the percentage of physical deterioration-incurable is estimating the physical life of the components. There is a tendency to assign too much depreciation to physical deterioration-incurable by using estimates of 50 to 100 years for items such as footings, foundations, framing, wall and ceiling coverings, etc. Some of these items may last hundreds of years.

To measure physical deterioration-incurable, items are divided into two categories: long-lived and *short-lived*. Long-lived items, such a footings, foundations, etc., can be depreciated as a group by making an estimate of their effective age and remaining physical life based on their condition. The engineering method, in which items are separately listed and their reproduction cost estimated, can also be used (see Fig. 11-5). By observation, a percentage of depreciation is estimated and extended into a dollar estimate for each component. Indirect costs must be either allocated proportionately to each component or listed separately, and depreciation for them must also be estimated.

FIG. 11-5 COMPONENT PHYSICAL LIFE (ENGINEERING METHOD)

House Component	Reproduction Cost New	Estimated % Deterioration	Accrued Depreciation
Survey & engineering	$800	20%	$160
Foundation	3,200	20%	640
Plumbing	4,000	30%	1,200
Electrical system	8,000	15%	1,200
Heating system	6,000	30%	1,800
TOTAL	$160,000		$88,000

Short-lived items are components whose remaining physical life is shorter than the total estimated remaining economic life of the house. Typically these include the roof, gutters and downspouts, kitchen cabinets and counters, painting and decorating. Sometimes these items are classified as physical deterioration-curable (deferred maintenance).

Again, the technique for estimating depreciation is to make a list of components, estimating the reproduction cost of each as well as a percentage of depreciation, based on the appraiser's observations of their current physical condition. These estimates are extended into a dollar estimate for each component and totaled. The process may be shortened by estimating a total reproduction cost of all the short-lived items, and using an average percentage of depreciation; this may, however, decrease the accuracy of the estimate.

FUNCTIONAL OBSOLESCENCE - CURABLE

Most *functional obsolescence-curable* in residential properties is caused by some kind of deficiency. In other types of properties, some superadequacy would also be considered curable, but this is rare in residential properties. Typical items that fall into this category are kitchens that need new counters, cabinets, fixtures and floor coverings; inadequate electrical service and hot water systems; and need of an additional bath or powder room where adequate space exists. Again, the test is whether the value added by correcting the obsolescence is greater than the cost to cure as indicated in the market.

The measure of functional obsolescence-curable is the difference between what it would cost on the date of the appraisal to reproduce the house with the curable item included and to reproduce the house on the same date without it. Only the excess cost of adding the item to the existing structure above the cost of incorporating the item as part of a total house construction process represents the measure of accrued depreciation. It is neither proper nor logical to deduct accrued depreciation from the reproduction cost of an item that has not been included in the reproduction cost estimate for the existing house.

For example, assume that in light of current market expectations, the subject house lacks a second bath where room exists to install one. The estimated cost to include this bath as part of the total house construction program as of the date of the appraisal is $8,000. The estimated cost to do it as a separate job as of the same date would be more, because it generally costs more to build parts of a house separately as compared to building the whole house at one time. If it would cost $10,000 to build the extra bath as a separate job, the measure of depreciation would be only the $2,000 excess cost.

FUNCTIONAL OBSOLESCENCE—INCURABLE

These items can be divided into two categories: loss in value caused by a deficiency or by an excess or superadequacy. Deficiencies are caused by exterior or interior design that does not meet current market expectations. This can be measured by the rent loss attributable to the deficiency, multiplied by the gross monthly rent multiplier (GMRM) applicable to the property as shown in Fig. 11-6.

FIG. 11-6 ESTIMATING INCURABLE FUNCTIONAL OBSOLESCENCE BY CAPITALIZING RENT LOSS

Monthly rental, House A with 3 bedrooms	$1,140
Monthly rental, House B with 2 bedrooms	1,060
Difference attributable to deficiency	$ 80
GMRM for the neighborhood	x 130
($80 monthly rent loss x 130 GMRM)	$10,400

FUNCTIONAL OBSOLESCENCE - SUPERADEQUACY

 A second type of *incurable functional obsolescence* is caused by *superadequacy*. Probably only a small percentage of houses exist that do not have some such obsolescence. The number of superadequacy items tends to increase as a house gets older and the occupants improve it with features suited for their individual living style. Superadequacy are not only improvements made after construction, but also anything initially built into the house that does not add value at least equal to its cost. For example, a builder elects to install in a new house an intercom system, central air conditioning, stainless steel kitchen sink and vinyl kitchen floor, the cost of which might be $20,000 total. If these items only add $16,000 value to the house, the lost $4,000 would be functional obsolescence-superadequacy, assuming no other forms of depreciation were involved.

Another example is a master bedroom, 16 x 18 feet, which costs $2,000 more to build than a bedroom 14 x 16 feet. If the extra size only adds $1,200 value, the lost $800 is functional obsolescence-superadequacy (again, assuming there are no other forms of depreciation).

Almost all superadequacy is incurable in houses. (In commercial and investment properties it sometimes pays to remove them because of excess operating costs saved). For example, a new house suffering from no physical deterioration or external obsolescence has a swimming pool that cost $40,000 to install. It adds only $25,000 value, so $15,000 is functional obsolescence-superadequacy.

Superadequacy are measured in the same manner as deficiencies, by finding a matched pair of sales from the market. If a rent differential can be attributed to the superadequacy, it can be capitalized to indicate the value of the superadequacy. The difference between this value and the cost of the item, less other forms of depreciation, would be classified as functional obsolescence-superadequacy.

EXTERNAL OBSOLESCENCE

Also called locational or environmental obsolescence by some appraisers, external obsolescence is the loss of value to the improvements caused by factors outside the property boundaries. It is unique to real estate, caused by its fixed location. The value of a house is directly affected by the neighborhood, community and region in which it is located. In analyzing the location and environment of the property, the appraiser must consider government actions, economic forces, employment, transportation, recreation, education services, taxes, etc.

Consideration must also be given to factors in the immediate vicinity that detract from value. Unattractive natural features such as swamps, polluted waterways and obstructed views are examples of items that will detract from value. Poorly maintained non-conforming houses and uncollected junk in nearby yards are indications of possible economic obsolescence.

Although facilities such as fire stations, schools, stores, restaurants, hospitals and gas stations are advantageous to have nearby, they may detract from the value if they are too close to the house. Nearby industry, highways and airports may be another type of nuisance, especially if they are unattractive, noisy or emit smoke and odors. External obsolescence can also be caused by factors that affect the supply or demand of houses competitive with the subject house, such as an unusual number of houses for sale in the area.

The list of factors causing economic obsolescence is almost endless; the appraiser should carefully search for and evaluate anything off the property that detracts from its value.

External obsolescence, like functional obsolescence, can also be measured by the rent loss attributable to the factor causing the obsolescence. However, a different method is used because part of the rent loss caused by detrimental external factors must be allocated to the land. For example, the market indicates that houses next to gasoline stations rent for $40 less than other houses. The GMRM for the neighborhood is 130. The land-to-improvement ratio in this neighborhood is typically land 15%, and improvements 85%. Some of the rent loss must be allocated to the land, which in this case is 15%. The calculations are shown in Fig. 11-7.

FIG. 11-7 ESTIMATING ECONOMIC OBSOLESCENCE USING THE RENT LOSS METHOD

Total rent loss	$40.00
Loss portion allocated to land ($40 x 15%)	- 6.00
Loss allocated to improvement	$34.00
Economic obsolescence ($34.00 x GMRM 130)	$4,420

External obsolescence can also be calculated by finding **matched pairs of sales**. The pair must consist of one sale that is affected by the influence causing economic obsolescence and another sale that is not so affected. First, all other differences are adjusted for, so that any remaining difference may be attributed to economic obsolescence. For example. House E is a new, one-story, ranch-style house with a two-car garage. It is two blocks from the local school. House F is very similar to House E, except that it has a one-car garage and is next door to the school. House E sold for $192,000. House F sold for $178,000. Two-car garages in this market add $12,000 value to houses and one-car garages add $4,000 value. Lots in this neighborhood represent about 20% of the total value of a typical property, and improvements represent 80% of value. Fig. 11-8 shows how to make this calculation.

FIG. 11-8 ESTIMATING ECONOMIC OBSOLESCENCE USING A MATCHED PAIR OF SALES

Sale price, House E with 2-car garage, away from school	$192,000
Sale price, House F with 1-car garage, next to school	-178,000
Difference	$ 14,000
Difference between the value of a 2-car garage and a 1-car garage	- 8,000
Indicated difference in value cased by proximity to school	$ 6,000
Obsolescence allocated to improvements ($6,000 x 80%)	$ 4,800

Age Life Method

DEFINITION OF TERMS

11.12 -- **Economic life:** The time period over which a house may be profitably utilized. It is the total period of time that the improvements contribute value to the entire property. As soon as the site alone is worth as much as the site and the improvements combined, the improvements have reached the end of their *economic life.*

-- **Physical life:** The time period during which the house may be expected to remain physically in existence. Since over 90% of the houses ever built in the United States are **11.13** still in existence and since houses in Europe have lasted hundreds of years, it is almost impossible to forecast the actual physical life of a house. Caution must be exercised in the use of tables that purport to estimate total *physical life* for different types of houses. They are of limited use to appraisers.

-- **Effective age:** How old the house appears to be, based on observation, considering its condition, design and the economic forces that affect its value. To paraphrase an old saying, "If it has the physical condition and design of a 13-year-old house, then for appraisal purposes it should be treated as a 13-year-old house, (effective age - 13 years), even if it is 10 or 20 years old." The chronological age or *actual age* of the house should be noted in the appraisal (if known) but it normally has little application in arriving at the final value estimate. The *effective age* can be less than, equal to, or more than the actual age.

-- **Remaining economic life:** The period of time from the date of the appraisal to the end of the house's economic life. It is that period of time during which the house will continue to contribute value to the property. This is the period the appraiser attempts to estimate. The assumption should not always be that the property will continue to deteriorate at its present rate. Often rehabilitation, modernization or remodeling will extend the life of the property; lack of normal maintenance will shorten its economic life. Changing economic conditions and public tastes will also affect the remaining economic life. The estimate must be based on the assumption there will be no significant changes in the house or neighborhood, and be qualified to recognize that any changes may extend or shorten the **remaining economic life**.

The relationships between effective age, remaining economic life and total economic life are shown in Fig. 11-9.

FIG. 11-9 LIFE SPAN OF A HOUSE

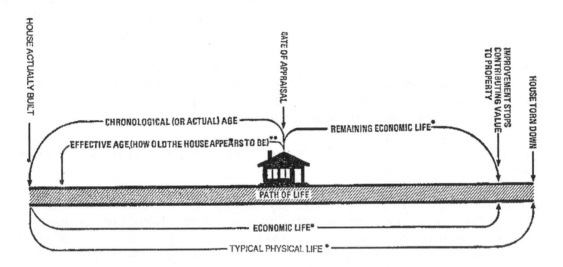

*MAY BE EXTENDED BY REHABILITATION, REMODELING OR MODERNIZATION OR CHANGING CONDITIONS.
**MAY ALSO BE GREATER THAN ACTUAL AGE.

AGE/LIFE CALCULATIONS
This method of estimating depreciation using the **age life method** is based primarily upon observation. The basis is that the percentage that the effective age represents of the typical economic life of the property is the same percentage that the accumulated depreciation represents of total reproduction cost.

Effective Age ÷ Typical Economic Life = % Depreciation of Reproduction Cost

Example 1:
A house has an estimated typical economic life of 50 years. Its chronological age is 20 years. Its effective age, based on its condition, design, and environment, is 25 years because it is in poor condition and is located near a gasoline service station.

25 years (effective age) ÷ 50 years (typical economic life) = .50 or 50% depreciated

Example 2:
Another house in the same neighborhood also has an estimated typical economic life of 50 years. Its chronological age is also 20 years. Its effective age, based on its condition, design and environment, is 20 years because it is in average condition and there are no unusual adverse environmental influences.

20 years (effective age) ÷ 50 years (typical economic life) = .40 or 40% depreciated

Example 3:
Still another house in the same neighborhood has an estimated economic life of 60 years. This longer economic life is forecast because of its superior design and construction. Its chronological age is 20 years. Its effective age, based on its superior construction, modernization and lack of negative environmental influences, is 12 years.

12 years (effective age) ÷ 60 years (typical economic life) = .20 or 20% depreciated

These examples show how three houses in the same neighborhood, all of which are the same chronological age, can suffer from substantially different amounts of depreciation. All of these estimates incorporate the effect of all three forms of depreciation.

When the estimate of effective age considers only one form of depreciation, for example, physical deterioration, the result is the amount of depreciation caused by physical deterioration. For example, a house has an estimated typical physical life of 75 years. The effective age, based only on the physical condition of the house, is 25 years.

25 years (effective age) ÷ 75 years (typical economic life) = .333 or 33.3% physical depreciation

The age/life method is an easy-to-understand, simple-to-use method based primarily upon the appraiser's observations, research and judgment. Therefore, its accuracy is heavily dependent upon the appraiser's knowledge and experience. It is an effective way to estimate the depreciation accumulated up to the date of the appraisal, but has proven to be a poor way to estimate the rate of depreciation that a property will suffer in the future.

For example, if by the age/life method it is estimated that a 25-year old residence has depreciated at the rate of 2% per year and is now 50% depreciated, it is incorrect to say that the remaining economic life is 25 years. This will only be true if:

1. The present rate of depreciation continues into the future on a straight line basis.
2. There are no changes in the forces that affect the value of the property.
3. There is no modernization, rehabilitation or remodeling.
4. The property is "normally" maintained through its remaining economic life.

A forecast that is based on a series of assumptions that most likely will not all be true serves a limited purpose. This kind of forecast has been misused by lenders to limit the terms of mortgages. If an estimate of remaining economic life is required, it must be made considering all of the above factors, and it must be clear that any changes in conditions may extend or shorten the remaining economic life.

Abstraction Method

This method involves the use of market data to obtain an indication of the amount of depreciation affecting the property being appraised. An analysis of current sales indicates the amount of depreciation with which the market has penalized each sale. By analyzing sales of residential properties similar to and in the same neighborhood as that being appraised, the amount and annual rate of depreciation can be calculated. The assumption is that residential properties of similar age, construction, size, condition and location depreciate at about the same rate.

The following steps are used to analyze the sales of comparable houses to obtain an indication of depreciation:

1. Select recently sold houses that are comparable to the one being appraised and obtain all the data necessary to estimate their reproduction cost.

2. Estimate the value of the site (land) for each comparable. Use the sales comparison approach if sales data is available.

3. Deduct the site (land) value from the comparable sales price and obtain an indicated depreciated value of the improvements.

4. Estimate the reproduction cost new of each comparable sale as of the date of the appraisal. Use any of the appropriate techniques described in this chapter.

5. To obtain the total amount of depreciation indicated for each of the sold properties, subtract the depreciated value of the improvements (Step 3) from the reproduction cost of the improvements (Step 4).

6. Estimate the effective age of the comparable property.

7. To obtain the average annual amount of depreciation indicated by each of the sold properties, divide the total depreciation by the effective age.

8. To obtain the average annual rate of depreciation, divide the annual amount of depreciation by the reproduction cost of the improvements.

9. Convert the rate to a percentage (multiply by 100 and add a percent sign).

The process outlined above should be performed for several comparable sales in the neighborhood. As in the sales comparison approach, the more sales that are used and the closer they are in similarity to the subject property, the more accurate the estimate of depreciation will be.

FIG. 11-10   ESTIMATING ACCRUED DEPRECIATION BY ABSTRACTION - EXAMPLE A

Step 1: Select a comparable house that has sold and obtain the needed
data to estimate its reproduction cost new.   Sale Price: $165,000

Step 2: Estimate the value of the comparable house's site (land) from the market.
Subtract site value: -36,000

Step 3: Depreciated value of the comparable improvements: $129,000

Step 4: Reproduction cost of comparable sale as of the date of the
appraisal: $207,000

Step 5: Less depreciated value of improvements   -129,000
Total depreciation indicated by the market $ 78,000

Step 6: Estimated effective age   13 years

Step 7: Depreciation $78,000 ÷ effective age 13 = $6,000 average annual
           amount of depreciation $6,000

Step 8: Annual depreciation $6,000 ÷ reproduction cost $207,000 = .029
           Average annual rate of depreciation   .029

Step 9: Average annual percentage of depreciation (.029 x 100)   =   2.9%

FIG. 11-11 ESTIMATING ACCRUED DEPRECIATION BY ABSTRACTION — EXAMPLE B

Step 1: Sale Price $136,500

Step 2: Less site (land) value (from the market)   -27,000

Step 3: Depreciated value of the house and other improvements $109,500

Step 4: Reproduction cost
              House (2,200 sq. ft. x $81.75)   179,850
              Garage   9,900
              Site improvements   3,600
              Total reproduction cost $193,350

Step 5: Less depreciated value of improvements   -109,500
           Total depreciation indicated by market $83,850

Step 6: Effective age   20 years

Step 7: Total depreciation $83.850 ÷ effective age 20 = $4,192
           Annual amount of depreciation $4,192

Step 8: Annual depreciation $4,192 ÷ reproduction cost $193,350 = .0217
           Average annual rate of depreciation   .0217

Step 9: Average annual percentage of depreciation (.0217 x 100) =   2.17%

In the example below, Fig. 11-12 the reproduction or replacement cost of the site improvements, such as stone walls, fences, driveways, landscaping, etc., is difficult to estimate. Under these circumstances an alternate acceptable method is to deduct the estimated value these items contribute to the sale price first, and then proceed to abstract the depreciation of the improvements.

Fig. 11-10 provides a more specific example. Assume there is a 20-year-old (actual and effective age), two-story colonial-style house, with 2,200 sq. ft. of gross living area, including living room, dining room, kitchen, recreation room, four bedrooms and two full baths. This house also has a two-car garage, with an estimated reproduction cost of $9,900 and site improvements with an estimated cost of $3,600. Lots are estimated to be worth $27,000 from market data available. The estimated reproduction cost of the house is $81.75 per sq. ft. of gross living area. The house sold for $136,500.

FIG. 11-12 ESTIMATING ACCRUED DEPRECIATION BY ABSTRACTION — EXAMPLE C

Step 1: Sale Price $180,000

Step 2: Site value: 45,000
     Contribution of site improvements   13,500
        Total value of site and improvements $58,500

Step 3: Depreciated value of the house and other improvements = $121,500

Step 4: Reproduction cost:
     House (3,000 sq. ft. x $87,00) $261,000
     Garage   + 18,000
     Total reproduction cost $279,000

Step 5: Less depreciated value of the house and other improvements   -121,500
     Total depreciation = $157,500

Step 6: Effective age   15 years

Step 7: Total depreciation $157,500 ÷ effective age 15 = $10,500
     Annual amount of depreciation = $10,500

Step 8: Annual depreciation $10,500 ÷ reproduction cost $279,000 = .0376
     Average annual rate of depreciation   =.0376

Step 9: Average annual percentage of depreciation (.0376 x 100)   =3.76%

A single category of depreciation can also be calculated by the abstraction method. This is done by first calculating the total depreciation as in the above examples. Then two of the three categories of depreciation (physical, functional and economic) are estimated by observation and subtracted from the total depreciation. What remains is the amount attributable to the remaining form of depreciation.

Total Accrued Depreciation by Abstraction
     Less: Physical Deterioration and Functional Obsolescence
     Gives: Economic Obsolescence

Total Accrued Depreciation by Abstraction
     Less: Functional and Economic Obsolescence
     Gives: Physical Deterioration

Total Accrued Depreciation by Abstraction
     Less: Physical Deterioration and Economic Obsolescence
     Gives: Functional Obsolescence

To estimate economic obsolescence, follow this example:

FIG. 11-13 HOW TO ESTIMATE THE THREE FORMS OF DEPRECIATION BY ABSTRACTION

Total depreciation estimated by abstraction	$ 83,850
Estimated physical deterioration	$ 49,500
Estimated functional obsolescence	+ 21,900
Total	$ 71,400
Less total of physical deterioration and functional obsolescence	- 71,400
Depreciation attributable to economic obsolescence	$ 12,450

This technique is limited by the accuracy of the observed estimates of physical deterioration and functional obsolescence. Care must be taken by the appraiser not to attribute to economic obsolescence what is actually an error in estimating physical and functional obsolescence, land value or cost new. The possibility of error is reduced when a number of properties is used.

SUMMARY

The cost approach is based on the **principle of substitution**. It holds that value tends to be set by the cost of a reasonable substitute improvement that could be built without undue delay. The steps of the cost approach are:

1. Estimate the value of the site (land) in its highest and best use, as if vacant.

2. Estimate the reproduction cost (or replacement cost) new of all the improvements.

3. Estimate accrued depreciation from all sources.

4. Deduct the accrued depreciation from all causes from the cost new of the improvements to derive the depreciated value of the improvements.

5. Add the site (land) value to the depreciated value of the improvements to derive an indicated value of the property by the cost approach.

Site (land) value is estimated in its highest and best use as if vacant from data found in the market.

Reproduction cost is the cost of creating a replica of the house and other improvements. Replacement cost is the cost of certain improvements with the same or equivalent utility using current design and materials. Estimating reproduction/replacement cost can be done using the quantity survey, unit-in-place or comparative methods. Accrued depreciation is the difference between the reproduction/replacement cost new of the improvements and their value as of the date of appraisal. It represents the loss of value from all causes: physical deterioration, functional obsolescence and economic (external) obsolescence.

There are three principal methods used to measure accrued depreciation. The abstraction method uses sales from the market to indicate the depreciated value of the improvements. The breakdown method divides depreciation into three categories: physical deterioration, functional obsolescence and economic (external) obsolescence. Each type of depreciation is estimated by whichever technique is most applicable with regard to the subject property. The age/life method is based on observation, in which estimates of economic life and effective age are converted into percentages of depreciation. The accuracy of the cost approach depends on the appraiser's accuracy in estimating the value of the land, as of the date of the appraisal, the reproduction cost new of all the improvements, and all forms of depreciation. Without market data to support these estimates, the possibility of significant error is great.

Extreme caution should be practiced when the cost approach is used alone or as the most significant indicator of value. The report should contain valid justification as to why the appraiser has elected to do so.

REVIEW QUESTIONS

1. The cost approach is based on the assumption that:
   a. the cost to produce a building plus the cost of the site are in indicator of its value.
   b. the cost to produce a building is often more than its value.
   c. there is little relationship between cost and value
   d. None of the above

2. Cost is:
   a. always the same as value.
   b. always the same as price.
   c. never exceeds value.
   d. None of the above.

3. The first step of the cost approach is to:
   a. estimate the reproduction cost of the improvements.
   b. estimate the cost of the site improvements.
   c. estimate the builders profit.
   d. None of the above.

4. The value of the site is normally estimated assuming:
   a. it has an adequate water supply.
   b. it is unimproved and ready to used.
   c. it will be improved with the biggest house possible.
   d. All of the above

5. Entrepreneurial profit is the profit made by the:
   a. mortgage lender.
   b. contractor.
   c. real estate agent.
   d. None of the above

6. The following are methods of estimating reproduction or replacement cost?
   a. Cubic foot, segregated cost and comparative unit
   b. Square foot, cubic foot and unit in place
   c. Square foot, unit in place and quantity survey
   d. All of the above.

7. Which of the following are sources of cost data?
   a. Cost data files
   b. Cost services
   c. Cost indices
   d. All of the above

8. A simple definition of depreciation is:
   a. the difference between the cost of the improvements and their value.
   b. a loss of utility and hence value from any cause.
   c. both of the above.
   d. None of the above

9. Techniques for analyzing accrued depreciation are the:
   a. breakdown method.
   b. age life method.
   c. abstraction method.
   d. All of the above

10. Depreciation can be analyzed by dividing it into:
    a. one or two separate components.
    b. three or five separate components.
    c. six or seven separate components.
    d. an infinite number of separate components.

11. Which of the following is not a form of functional obsolescence?
    a. A gasoline station next door.
    b. Damage done by termites.
    c. Broken window screens
    d. All of the above

12. Economic Life is:
    a. the time period over which a house maybe profitability utilized.
    b. the time period in which the house is expected to remain physically in existence.
    c. the period of time from the date of the appraisal to the end of the house's economic live.
    d. None of the above

13. Physical Life is:
    a. the time period over which a house maybe profitability utilized.
    b. the time period in which the house is expected to remain physically in existence.
    c. the period of time from the date of the appraisal to the end of the house's economic live.
    d. None of the above

ANSWERS TO REVIEW QUESTIONS

The answer to each question is indicated by the letter a, b, c or d below. The explanation of the answer is indicated by a numbered arrow that points to the appropriate paragraph on the page of the text indicated by the page number following the answer.

Q 11.1	a	Page 11-2
Q 11.2	d	Page 11-2
Q 11.3	d	Page 11-2
Q 11.4	b	Page 11-3
Q 11.5	d	Page 11-4
Q 11.6	d	Page 11-5
Q 11.7	d	Page 11-10
Q 11.8	a	Page 11-12
Q 11.9	d	Page 11-12
Q 11.10	b	Page 11-13
Q 11.11	d	Page 11-14
Q 11.12	a	Page 11-17
Q 11.13	b	Page 11-17

CHAPTER 12

Specific Data Analysis - Income

*"There's no such thing as a good tenant.
Some are just worst than others."*

*Rochelle R. Lambert, Real Estate Investor
& mother of the editor*

Important Words and Key Concepts
Words on this list are highlighted in this chapter
They are also defined in the Glossary at the back of this text

Band of Investment Method

Capitalization Rate

Direct Capitalization Rate

Effective Gross Income (EGI)

Fixed Expenses

Gross Rent Multiplier (GRM)

Gross Income Multiplier (GIM)

Gross Monthly Rent Multiplier (GMRM)

Income Capitalization

Market Rent

Mortgage Constant

Mortgage Debt Service

Net Operating Income

Operating Expenses

Overall Capitalization Rate

Potential Gross Income

Reconstructed Operating Statement

Reserves

Vacancy and Collection Allowance

ANALYSIS OF RENTAL DATA

Often when people buy residential property, they consider the amount of rent the property is generating or has the potential to generate.

 There are two techniques appraisers use to analyze income potential for a property: gross monthly rent multiplier (GMRM) and income capitalization. This chapter will focus on the GMRM income approach as it is the approach that is frequently used for one-four family residences and small income properties, and demonstrate how rental data is analyzed and utilized via this method to develop an indicated value of the subject property. The direct capitalization of net operating income is also covered at the end of this chapter.

ONE - FOUR FAMILY RESIDENCES

 The most common income approach, when applied to one-four family residences is also called the gross rent multiplier (GRM) or gross income multiplier (GIM).

The gross rent multiplier (GRM)income approach used for one-four family residences is based on the assumption that there is a direct relationship between what residences sell for and their monthly rental income. Buyers consider rental income in addition to location, size, condition, etc.

By custom, monthly rents are used for one-four family residences and small income properties. Frequently these rentals are for residences that are unfurnished and do not include utilities. The reliability of the analysis is increased when the terms of the rentals are similar to the subject property. For example, the residences are all unfurnished and the rent does not include utilities.

Steps of the GMRM Income Approach

When sufficient data is available, the appraiser follows these steps to analyze the data to derive an indicated market value via the GMRM income approach:

1. Calculate the gross monthly rent multiplier.

   a. Find residences that have recently sold and were rented at the time of sale, comparable to the subject property, and that are in the same or similar neighborhoods.

   b. Divide the sale price of each property by their monthly rental to derive the gross monthly rent multiplier (GMRM). For example, if a sale price is $150,000 and the monthly rent is $1,000, the GMRM is 150 ($150,000 ÷ $1,000).

   c. Reconcile the multipliers developed to obtain a single multiplier or a range of multipliers that are applicable to the subject property. This is not an average; it is a judgment, made by the appraiser, of comparability and applicability.

2. Estimate the market rent of the subject residence.

a.   Find comparable rentals in the neighborhood.

b.   Analyze each rental, comparing its features with those of the subject residence.

c.   Estimate the adjustments required to obtain an indicated market (economic) rent for the subject residence being appraised.

d.   Consider each comparable carefully, and formulate an opinion of the market rent of the subject residence, based upon the actual rents of the comparables. If the subject property is rented as of the effective date of value, the rent should be analyzed as part of the market rent analysis.

12.4 ▶ 3. Develop an indicated value of the subject property.

12.8 ▶ a.   Multiply the estimated market rent of the subject residence by the estimated monthly multiplier (or range of multipliers) to obtain its indicated market value via the income approach.

The multiplier is relied on as an indicator of market value because it tends to express a constant relationship between the monthly rental income of a residence and its sale price.

12.5 ▶ The multiplier is usually a whole number. The number is produced by dividing the monthly rental income into the sale price of a comparable property. For example, if the sale price of a residence were $120,000 and it had been rented for $1,200 a month, $120,000 is divided by $1,200 and the multiplier is 100. The technique is used by practicing appraisers because it is straightforward and simple. Its reliability, of course, rests on the dependability of the data used and the skill with which it is analyzed.

Most appraisers believe that no adjustments can or should be made in the development of the multiplier. They feel that if comparable sales are not reasonably similar, they should be dropped from consideration. A few appraisers still feel that under some circumstances, adjustments can be made in the data collected, on the same basis as in the sales comparison approach, using the four elements of comparison. This process is not recommended.

GMRM Limitations

The multiplier, like any other approach, can produce excellent results if the data used is reliable and it is applied appropriately. However, it can be misleading and produce indefensible conclusions if the analysis used or the information and method applied is inappropriate. The situations under which the results are most desirable include:

12.6 ▶ 1. The properties from which the multiplier is developed have common characteristics   (e.g., size, age, physical condition, neighborhood, etc.) with the subject residence.

2. The multiplier is extracted using properties for which there is an active market. If there is not an active market (that is, one that includes many recent sales), the information upon which to base a conclusion will be inadequate.

3. The market information is correct and rentals have been verified. When verification develops significant special conditions or special financing, the data should either not be used or given little weight.

GMRM Calculations

The following example illustrates how a GMRM is derived from the market. It is based on using actual sales figures which are divided by the actual rentals of these comparables at the time of the sale, without making any adjustments. The multipliers extracted from the market in this manner are shown in Fig. 12-1.

The indicated GMRM ranges from 106.4 to 112.3 with 110 as the most common multiplier. It is also the multiplier for properties that appear to be most similar to the subject property. Therefore, 110 was selected as the appropriate GMRM. The GMRM is frequently expressed as a whole number.

FIG. 12-1 FINDING THE GMRM WITHOUT ADJUSTMENTS

Comparable Property	Verified Sale Price	Monthly Rent	Indicate Gross Monthly Rent Multiplier
1	$119,700	$1,125	106.4
2	123,600	1,150	107.5
3	127,500	1,150	110.9
4	1212,1250	1,200	107.4
5	132,000	1,200	110.0
6	133,500	1,250	106.8
7	133,350	1,200	111.1
12	134,700	1,200	112.3
9	132.000	1,200	110.0
10	133,500	1,200	111.2
11	132,500	1,200	110.4
12	123,600	1,100	112.4

ESTIMATING MARKET RENT OF THE SUBJECT RESIDENCE

The following section shows how to estimate a market rent for the subject residence from the market:

Example One - Estimating Market Rent Without Adjustments

If the subject property is rented, the monthly rental can be used as an indication of the market rent. It is not acceptable appraisal practice, however, to use this contract rent without checking it against other rents in the market. In this illustration, the subject property is rented for $1,200 per month. Based on information obtained from the owner and tenant, it appears to be an arms-length arrangement, with both parties believing the rent is what the property should be generating. This is a good indication that the market rent for such a property is $1,200. However this should be verified by checking other rented houses that are similar to the subject property. When the owner occupies one of the units market rent should be used for that unit.

Based on the array shown in Fig. 12-2, and considering the reported contract rent of the subject residence, its market rent appears to be about $1,200. Some appraisers would consider this to be sufficient data on which to base the estimate of market rent. Other appraisers feel it is better to adjust the rental of each of the residences and then make the estimate, especially when the comparables differ to a certain extent from the subject property.

FIG. 12-2 ESTIMATING MARKET RENT WITHOUT ADJUSTMENTS

Comparable Property	Monthly Rental
1	$1,185
2	1,200
3	1,215
4	1,200
5	1,200
6	1,170
7	1,230
8	1,200

The market rent comparables range from $1,170 to $1,230 When this data was analyzed and reconciled, an estimated market rent of $1,200 was indicated for the subject property, based on those comparables found to be most similar to the subject.

EXAMPLE TWO - ESTIMATING MARKET RENT WITH ADJUSTMENTS
In this example, the property being appraised has one bathroom, a one-car garage, no central air conditioning and is rented without utilities included. Some comparable rentals have two bathrooms, two-car garages, central air conditioning and/or are rented with utilities included. Adjustments may be needed to reflect the rental differences. When more than one difference exists, one rental is designated as the base rental which is adjusted for all known differences except the one being sought. Then it is compared with the other rental in the pair and any remaining difference in rent is attributed to the remaining element of comparison. This technique is illustrated in Fig. 15-3.

FIG. 12-3 ESTIMATING MARKET RENT WITH ADJUSTMENTS

Comparable Rental #1 - The same neighborhood and similar to the subject property. It has one bathroom, no central air conditioning, and a one car garage. It was recently rented unfurnished and without utilities for $1,215 per month. There were no reported special conditions.

Comparable Rental #2 - The same neighborhood and similar to the subject property. It has two bathrooms, no central air conditioning, and a one car garage. It was recently rented unfurnished and without utilities for $1,275 per month. There were no reported special conditions.

Comparable Rental #3 - The same neighborhood and similar to the subject property. It has two bathrooms, no central air conditioning, and a two car garage. It was recently rented unfurnished and without utilities for $1,320 per month. There were no reported special conditions.

Comparable Rental #4 - The same neighborhood and similar to the subject property. It has two bathrooms, central air conditioning, and a two car garage. It was recently rented unfurnished and without utilities for $1,395 per month. There were no reported special conditions.

Comparable Rental #5 - The same neighborhood and similar to the subject property. It has one bathroom, no central air conditioning, and a one car garage. It was recently rented unfurnished and with owner-supplied utilities for $1,410 per month. There were no reported special conditions.

Adjustments		Monthly Rent
BATHROOM ADJUSTMENT		
Comparable Rental #1 (base) -	one bathroom, one car garage	- $ 1,215
Comparable Rental #2 -	two bathrooms, one car garage	+1,275
Difference attributable to a second bathroom:		$60

GARAGE ADJUSTMENT

Comparable Rental #1 (base) -	one bathroom, one car garage-	$1,215
Comparable Rental #3 -	two bathrooms, two car garage+	1,320

Adjustment to Comparable Rental #3 to reflect difference in number of bathrooms based on Comparable Rentals #1 and #2	-60	
Adjusted Comparable Rental #3		$1.260
Monthly rental difference attributed to size of garage: $1,215 [base Comp. #11- $1,260 [Adjusted Comp. #3]		$45

CENTRAL AIR CONDITIONING ADJUSTMENT

Comparable Rental #1 (base) -	one bathroom, one car garage, no central air conditioning -	$1,215
Comparable Rental #4 -	two bathrooms, two car garage, central air conditioning	+1,395
Adjustment to Comparable Rental #4 to reflect difference in number of bathrooms	-60	

Adjustment to Comparable Rental #4
to reflect difference in garage size
(based on Comparable Rentals #1 and #3)   -45

Adjusted Comparable Rental #4 $1,290

Difference attributable to central air conditioning: $75

INCLUSION OF UTILITIES ADJUSTMENT
Comparable Rental #1 (base) -   one bathroom,
                                 one car garage,
                                 no central air,
                                 no utilities   -$1,215

Comparable Rental #5 -   one bathroom,
                               one car garage,
                               no central air,
                               utilities paid by owner   +1410

Difference attributable to inclusion of utilities: $195

Each comparable rental is adjusted to give an indication of the market rental of the appraised property. If an element of comparison in the comparable rental results in a higher rental than what the property being appraised would rent for, a minus adjustment is made. For example, if the only difference is that the appraised property has three bedrooms and a comparable rental has four bedrooms, with the extra bedroom contributing $250 to the monthly rental, then a minus $250 adjustment is made on the comparable rental. These adjustment techniques are identical to those used in the sales comparison approach.

Actual data would rarely work out this precisely. Often both plus and minus adjustments would be made and the indicated rents for the house being .appraised would vary, requiring reconciling into a final indicated rental value.

It is not practical or possible to prove every adjustment from data in the market, but an attempt should be made to do so whenever possible. Once a matched pair is developed for an adjustment in a market, it can often be used for more than one appraisal. When an adjustment cannot be supported by market data, the appraiser has no choice but to estimate the adjustment. Large, unsupported market rent adjustments are one of the major contributing factors to the lack of credibility of the income approach in appraisal reports.

ESTIMATING THE VALUE OF THE SUBJECT PROPERTY
The third step of the income approach is to estimate the indicated market value of the subject residence. This is accomplished by multiplying the estimated market rent of the subject residence by the GMRM selected from the market.

For example, if the GMRM selected were 110 based on market data, and the estimated market rent of the subject residence were $1,200 per month (unfurnished and without utilities), its indicated market value would be calculated as follows:

FIG. 12-4 ESTIMATING THE VALUE OF THE SUBJECT PROPERTY

1. Estimated market rent of the subject residence $1,200

2.   Gross monthly rent multiplier   x   110

3.   Indicated value of the subject residence
      via the GMRM income approach $132,000

SMALL INCOME PROPERTIES

Many people buy property for the income it will produce and the increase in value that they hope will take place over the period of time that they hold the property. The income approach covered in this section of Chapter 12 will focus on the income motivation and other techniques as to how the appraiser can analyze the income a property produces and use it as an indication of the value of the property.

The income a property produces flows to the owner in a variety of ways:

- Current Cash Flow
- Current Tax Savings
- Deferred Income from Rents
- Capital Gains from the Sale or Gift of the Property in the Future
- Tax Savings from the Gift or Trade of the Property in the Future

The definition of market value assumes the buyer and seller to be well informed. Therefore it is also assumed that the buyers and sellers consider all of the potential benefits of property ownership.

Income Capitalization

In the income capitalization approach, appraisers measure the present value of the future benefits of property ownership. Income streams and values of property upon resale (reversion) are capitalized (converted) into a present, lump-sum value. Basic to this approach are the formulas:

Income ÷ Rate = Value
Income x Factor = Value

The income capitalization approach, like the cost and sales comparison approaches, requires extensive market research. Specific areas that an appraiser investigates for this approach are the property's gross income expectancy, the expected reduction in gross income from lack of full occupancy and collection loss, the expected annual operating expenses, the pattern and duration of the property's income stream, and the anticipated value of the resale or other real property interest reversions. When accurate income and expense estimates are established, the income streams are converted into present value by the process of capitalization. The rates or factors used for capitalization are derived by the investigation of acceptable rates of return for similar properties.

Research and analysis of data for the income capitalization approach are conducted against a background of supply and demand relationships. This background provides information on trends and market anticipation that must be verified for data analysis by the income capitalization approach.

The investor in an apartment building, for example, anticipates an acceptable return on the investment in addition to return of the invested funds. The level of return necessary to attract investment capital fluctuates with changes in the money market and with the levels of return available from alternative investments. The appraiser must be alert to changing investor requirements as revealed by demand in the current market for investment properties, and to changes in the more volatile money markets that may indicate a forthcoming trend.

TWO SIMPLE STEPS

Many appraisers make the income approach more complex than it need be for the types of property they are appraising. Appraisers who are just starting to appraise investment properties should start by using the simple process described below and then, as their assignments become more complex, apply the more advanced techniques when they feel they are necessary.

The two simple steps of the income approach produce an estimate of the anticipated net operating income (NOI) of the subject property, which is then converted to a value estimate using the capitalization process.

INCOME ANALYSIS

Net Operating Income (NOI)

Net operating income is a phrase developed and used by real estate appraisers. It has special meaning to them and is not regularly used by owners, accountants, tax people, etc. Therefore, whenever you develop the NOI of a property for appraisal purposes, you should consider defining the word in your appraisal report. NOI is based on the assumption that all the property will be rented at the market rent. It is based on what is projected for the first year after the date of the appraisal.

12.12 Estimating the NOI starts by estimating the potential gross income (PGI). It is the anticipated total market rent and other income for the first year after the date of the appraisal.

Anticipated loss due to non-occupancy, turnover and non-payment of rent by tenants, commonly called a vacancy and collection allowance, is deducted from the PGI. This produces the effective gross income (EGI).

From the projected annual EGI all of the annual projected stabilized expenses are deducted (fixed expenses, operating expenses and reserves). The result is the projected NOI.

To develop the NOI, the appraiser creates a special reconstructed operating statement. Information used on this statement is obtained for a variety of sources. The information cannot simply be obtained from the owner, agent, accountant, attorney or tax person though all of these people are potential sources for some of the information that must be assembled in order to create a reconstructed operating statement. This process requires the judgment and expertise of an experienced appraiser.

POTENTIAL GROSS INCOME (PGI)

The estimated total gross rental income is combined with other income available from the property to give the potential gross income (PGI).

The potential gross income estimate is the foundation upon which the income approach is built. A small error in this estimate will be mathematically compounded as it is processed in the income approach and will become a large error in the final value estimate.

It is advisable that the rents being paid by the current tenants also be considered. However, more often than not, the contract rent will not be the current market rent of the property. This is often true because the property was leased prior to the date of the appraisal. In addition, the owner or management of the property may not be typical for this property and their skills or lack of skill will produce a difference between market and contract rent. However, the appraiser should report in the appraisal a rental history including information on the current rents being received. In spite of everything, the actual rents being received for a property should be given serious consideration by the appraiser when estimating the potential gross income.

The PGI for the year following the effective date of the value opinion should incorporate a market rent analysis for the current year as well as consideration of the contract rents being paid of the date of the value opinion as well as for the following year.

Besides rents from the tenants, there is often other available income to the property owner. Some typical sources of other income are the following:

• Coin-operated washers and dryers
• Other vending machines
• Parking and garage fees
• Advertising signs

Since this is usually only a fraction of the total rent most appraisers just add it to potential gross rental. Some appraisers put "other income" after the "vacancy and collection allowance" because their "other income" estimate already includes a collection loss.

VACANCY AND COLLECTION ALLOWANCE

No matter how good a tenant is, there is a potential that some of the rent over a projected ownership period will not be collected. Since the estimate of market rent is based on the assumption that the property is vacant and ready to be rented to a typical tenant, it would not be correct to assume it was rented to a tenant who would never be a credit risk and would remain a tenant throughout the projected ownership period. There is no standard figure for a vacancy and collection allowance. The best way to develop figures is to take properties where you can obtain a rental history over an extended period of time and analyze the actual historical results. Property management companies are good sources of this type of information. Analyzing the actual current vacancies in the subject's market area is another basis for estimating a vacancy and collection allowance.

EFFECTIVE GROSS INCOME (EGI)

The effective gross income (EGI) is calculated by deducting from the potential gross income (PGI) the estimate vacancy and collection allowance and adding any projected other income that was not included in the PGI.

Expense Analysis

The expenses incurred by the owner of a property are divided into three groups: fixed expenses, operating expenses and reserves. Again, these are special appraisal terms used to classify expenses on the reconstructed operating statement and normally will not be available from any one source. It will be necessary to adjust the information received from a variety of sources before using it.

FIXED EXPENSES

Fixed expenses are the property taxes and casualty insurance. They are classified as fixed expenses because they vary little (if at all) with the occupancy of the property.

Property taxes are a matter of public record. A trip to the tax collector's office will develop accurate information about the taxes. If the tax rate has not been set for the community, an estimate is made considering the current taxes and the trend in the community. In many areas, the property tax consists of more than one tax and may include school taxes, sewer taxes, special assessments, etc. In some jurisdictions this information is available on line.

Casualty insurance is normally a combination of fire insurance, boiler insurance, general liability, and flood insurance. It does not include mortgage life insurance. The owner's actual cost is often misleading. Owners sometimes pay for more than one year at a time and they often do not carry the amount or all the kinds of insurance typical owners of the property would carry.

Fig. 12-5 COMPOSITE LIST OF FIXED EXPENSES OF MANY PROPERTIES

Property taxes
Insurance

OPERATING EXPENSES (VARIABLE)

These are sometimes called variable expenses and include expenses incurred in a typical year to maintain the property, provide services for the tenants and maintain the income stream. These expenses vary based on the occupancy of the property. Shown is a list of typical expenses that should be considered when making a reconstructed operating statement. It is recommended that a checklist be used so when you are gathering expense data you will not skip an item that does not appear on the operating statement provided by the owner or the management of the property. Fig. 12-6 is a list of operating expenses of a composite of many properties (for small income properties some of these categories are frequently combined):

Fig. 12-6 COMPOSITE LIST OF OPERATING EXPENSES OF MANY PROPERTIES

Management fees

Utilities:
  Electricity
  Gas
  Oil
  Coal
  Telephone
  Water
  Sewer charges

Employee payroll:
  Janitor
  Manager
  Grounds keeper
  Bookkeeper
  Elevator operator
  Lifeguard
  Engineer
  Security
  Telephone operator
  Maintenance
  Cleaning
  Other
Payroll taxes & employee benefits
Maintenance and repairs

Service contracts:
  Sprinkler system
  Elevator
  Intercom & telephone
  Lawn & landscaping
  Pool expenses & supplies
  Rubbish & garbage removal

Painting and decorating
Supplies - office, cleaning & other
Magazines and newspapers
Snow removal
Travel and entertainment
Exterminating
Bank charges
Legal fees
Advertising
Accounting fees
Automobile expense

Variable expenses are frequently summarized as:
1. Management fees
2. Utilities
3. Repairs and Maintenance
4. Payroll (if not included in the other items)

Not every property will have all the expenses on this list, and some properties will have other expenses which do not appear on this checklist.

The figures the appraiser use are not the actual expenses as reported by the owner. It is a forecast of what the expenses would be for the following year, assuming it was a typical year.

For example, for a property that requires fuel oil, you obtain a 5 year history of oil consumption which is:

Last year	3,200 gallons
Year before	3,300 gallons
2 years before	3,100 gallons
4 years before	3,100 gallons
5 years before	3,300 gallons

The appraiser forecasts that consumption for a typical year is 3,200 gallons and that the price of fuel next year will be $3.25. Therefore, the forecasted fuel oil expense will be $10,400 ($3.25 x 3,200).

RESERVES (REPLACEMENT ALLOWANCE)
Some expenses vary considerably from year to year and others occur once or twice over a period of many years. A decision must be made as to where in the reconstructed operating statement to include these expenses. Some of these expenses, such as plumbing repairs, may be included in the maintenance and repair item in the operating expenses. Even though a particular plumbing repair may occur only infrequently, as a group they appear quite regularly; and it is possible to estimate what, as a group, they would be in a typical year. Those infrequently occurring items that are not included in the operating expenses are included in the reserve section.

For example, if the typical life of a refrigerator was estimated to be 20 years and the cost of a new refrigerator was $1,200, a reserve of $60 for each refrigerator in the property might be established yearly ($1,200 + 20 = $60).

Reserves are typically deducted for short lived items which are those components of the improvements that have a useful life that is less than the economic life of the improvement.

The use of reserves must be carefully explained in the appraisal report because the word reserve implies that the money is being put aside. Most owners do not actually set aside these monies. Some of the items that are traditionally included in the reserve section of the reconstructed operating statement are listed in Fig. 12-7

Fig. 12-7 COMPOSITE LIST OF RESERVE EXPENSES OF MANY PROPERTIES

Built in refrigerators
Built in dishwashers
Garbage disposals
Hoods and vent fans
Pool equipment
Short-lived building components
Elevators
Roof covering
Boilers
Security systems
Fire alarm systems
Carpeting
Air conditioning
Grounds equipment
Telephone systems

Again, this is a composite list from many types of properties. It is unlikely that any one property will include all of these items. Also, some properties will require reserves for items that are not on this list.

A common mistake that appraisers make is to include the same item in both the operating expense and the reserve sections of the reconstructed operating statement or to leave out items from both sections which should have been included.

Later in this chapter, the development of capitalization rates will be discussed. Here again the fact that any operating statement used to develop a capitalization rate must include reserves, will be pointed out. The analysis of reserves must be consistently applied in the reconstructed statement and when developing a capitalization, or an incorrect rate will be developed.

OTHER EXPENSES (NOT INCLUDED)

Some expenses which are a part of an income and expense statement used for income tax purposes are not included in the reconstructed operating statement. This is because these items are either reflected in the capitalization rate and to include them as expenses or reserve, would have the effect of including them twice, or they are not considered to be a cost directly related to operating the property. Included in this group are:

Fig. 12-8 EXPENSES NOT INCLUDED IN THE RECONSTRUCTED OPERATING STATEMENT

Mortgage interest	Income tax
Mortgage amortization	Corporate taxes
Mortgage life insurance	Corporate directors' fees
Depreciation	Franchise taxes

SUMMARY - ESTIMATED NET OPERATING INCOME (NOI)

The first step of the income approach is to estimate the net operating income (NOI) of the property. This is an appraisal technique that is accomplished by making a reconstructed operating statement for the property. This statement uses information gathered by the appraiser from the owner, management, accountant, tax person and a variety of other sources. It usually cannot be obtained from a single source in the format that is required.

The potential gross income (PGI) is estimated using market data and the rental history of the property being appraised. A vacancy and collection allowance is deduced from this figure. Any other income is added, and the result is a projection of what the effective gross income (EGI) of the property would be if it were vacant on the date of the appraisal, and were then rented to a typical tenant in the market at current rental rates.

Next, the typical expenses are projected for the coming year after being divided for clarity into fixed expenses, operating expenses and reserves. Other expenses such as interest, amortization, depreciation and expenses, not directly related to the running of the property, are not included.

All of the fixed expenses, operating expenses and reserves are subtracted from the effective gross income (EGI), to produce the net operating income (NOI).

Fig. 12-9 EXAMPLE OF A RECONSTRUCTED OPERATING STATEMENT (12 UNIT APARTMENT HOUSE)

INCOME ANALYSIS

Potential gross income

6 two bedroom unit w/o air conditioning @$750/mo. =		$54,000
(750 x 12 = 9,000 x 6 = 54,000)		
2 two bedroom units w/air conditioning @$800/mo. =		19,200
(800 x 12 = 9,600 x 2 = 19,200)		
2 three bedroom units w/o air conditioning @$1,000/mo. =		24,000
(1,000 x 12 = 12,000 x 2 = 24,000)		
2 three bedroom units w/air conditioning @$1,100/mo. =		26,400
(1,100 x 12 = 13,200 x 2 = 26,400)		

Total:	$123,600
Vacancy and collection loss (6%)	(7,416)

Other Income
Laundry machines (concession)	2,400
Vending machines	1,250

EFFECTIVE GROSS INCOME	$119,834

EXPENSES

Fixed Expenses

Insurance (apartment package including rents	5,600
Flood insurance	600
Property tax	14,846
School district tax	8,480
Total fixed expenses:	$29,526

Variable (operating) expenses

Management fees	8,080
Utilities	
Electricity (halls (only)	1,646
Gas	16,600
Telephone	250
Water	3,200
Sewer charge	320
Rubbish removal	770
Employee payroll:	
Part-time janitor	8,000
Payroll taxes	240
Employee benefits	690
Worker's compensation insurance	240
Lawn care	690
Maintenance supplies	500
Maintenance & repairs	2,400
Painting & decorating	1,200
Snow removal	240
Exterminating	480
Legal fees	300
Accounting	600
Bank charges	160
Total operating expenses:	$46,606

Reserves

Kitchen appliances	1,200
Lobby furniture	200
Carpeting	2,000
Air conditioning	600
Roof	1,000
Total reserves:	$5,000
Total expenses:	($81,132)

NET OPERATING INCOME PROJECTION: $38,702

Note: Some appraisers do not use a reconstructed operating statement that is as detailed as this example. They reduce the size (often to one page) by combining some of the items.

CAPITALIZATION

The second step of the income capitalization approach is to convert the net operating income (NOI) projection into an estimate of the value of the property on the date of the appraisal. This process is called **capitalization** and is usually done by dividing the NOI by the capitalization rate.

$$\frac{\text{NOI}}{\text{Capitalization Rate}} \quad = \quad \text{Value of Property}$$

Many investors and some appraisers use a capitalization process by which they estimate the value of an investment property by multiplying either the gross income, net income (or some other income figure they rely upon) by a multiplier to produce the value of the property. It is not unusual for investors to say a particular property is worth so many times its current or projected gross rental income.

This multiplier is derived by taking properties one is familiar with and dividing the sale price by the rent or net income. This relationship can be expressed in a formula as follows:

$$\frac{\text{Sales Price}}{\text{Income}} \quad = \quad \text{Rent Multiplier}$$

The GMRM, GRM and GIM were discussed in detail earlier in this chapter.

Direct Capitalization

There are a variety of ways to develop a direct capitalization rate directly from the market using data collected in the market. If the above formula converts NOI into value, then the following formula would convert value into a direct capitalization rate (assuming the NOI is also known).

$$\frac{\text{NOI}}{\text{Value of Property}} \quad = \quad \text{Overall Capitalization Rate}$$

The type of rate developed in this way is called an overall capitalization rate. For example, assume there is information available about a property similar to the one being appraised. It shows that the comparable property sold for $370,000 and that it had an NOI of $37,000. Using the above formula, the overall capitalization rate is taken from this data as follows:

$$\frac{\$37,000 \text{ (NOI)}}{\$370,000 \text{ (Sale Price)}} \quad = \quad .10 \text{ (Overall Capitalization Rate)}$$

Like any other data being used in the appraisal process, the more similar the data source is to the property being appraised the better it is. Also, it is not good practice to develop a rate from just one set of data. Often, the best source of data to develop capitalization rates comes from other appraisals where the property was sold around the date of the appraisal. This is because all the calculations needed to reconstruct the operating statement have already been made. When you receive data about a building that has been sold, you will need to reconstruct its operating statement just as you would if you were appraising the property; otherwise the rate you develop from the property being sold will not work.

Unfortunately, there has been so much emphasis on other more complex, less direct methods of constructing capitalization rates that many appraisers gravitate to these methods rather than taking the time to develop the market data derived from the method explained above.

When rates are developed for a series of properties in a market, it will become apparent that an identifiable pattern develops. Generally, the better the quality of the property, the lower the rate will be.

Advanced Capitalization Techniques

Some appraisers have become serious students of Band of Investment - Mortgage Equity Components, Built Up Method, "Ellwood" and other capitalization techniques. However, some feel that even the more complex theories do not produce the best results in all instances.

Charles B. Akerson developed procedures that substituted arithmetic formulae for the algebraic equations used by Ellwood. He also incorporated the "J" factor into his formula which provides a tool for the appraiser to incorporate changes in the income stream and property value into the rate calculations.

One of the features that has contributed to the popularity of the "Ellwood" capitalization technique, is the ability to create a graph that displays the results and shows what alternate rates would be when some of the assumptions are changed.

Readers who are interested in these and other advanced capitalization techniques can read about them in the Appraising of Real Estate, 12th ed.. The Appraisal Institute, 1275 North Michigan Avenue, Chicago, IL 60611, 2001. Better still, they should take an advanced capitalization course.

Band of Investment - Mortgage and Equity Components

Most properties are purchased with debt and equity capital. The overall capitalization rate must satisfy the market return requirements of both investment positions. Lenders must anticipate receiving a competitive interest rate commensurate with the perceived risk of the investment or they will not make funds available. Lenders also require that the principal amount of the loan be repaid through periodic amortization payments. Similarly, equity investors must anticipate receiving a competitive equity cash return commensurate with the perceived risk or they will invest their funds elsewhere.

The capitalization rate used for the debt portion in the band of investment method is equal to the annual debt service amount (payments of principal and interest) divided by the original amount of the loan. This figure can be calculated mathematically using a financial calculator or looked on a table of mortgage constant payments. The mortgage constant is the annual debt service divided by the loan amount: it changes depending on the mortgage interest rate, loan term and the frequency of the mortgage payments.

Built-Up Method

This method of constructing a capitalization rate separates the rate into its component parts. It would be almost impossible to accurately construct a rate using only this method. However, once some of the components of the rate have been estimated from other sources, they can be assembled and together they can be analyzed and tested for reasonableness by using the built-up method of rate construction.

SUMMARY

The first part of this chapter illustrates the use of the GMRM income approach as it applies to one-four family residences and small income properties. It is also sometimes referred to as the gross monthly rent multiplier approach and is considered a reliable approach to estimating market value if sufficient data is used and properly verified, and is representative of the market. In markets where one-four family residences are rarely rented, this approach would not be appropriate due to lack of sufficient data.

The income capitalization approach is based on the theory that the value of income producing property is determined by the future income the property produces.

The first step in estimating the value of a property based on its future income stream is to estimate the amount of the income stream to be obtained by the owner in the future. The appraiser starts by estimating the potential gross income (PGI) attributable to the property, assuming it is fully rented at market rent, for the first year from the date of appraisal. Other income from the property is added. From this, an estimated income loss from vacancies and uncollected rents is subtracted, and the result is the annual projected effective gross income (EGI).

The appraiser subtracts the projected annual fixed expenses, operating expenses and reserves from the effective gross income. The result is the projected annual net operating income (NOI). This term (NOI) is unique to appraising as it does not include deductions for **mortgage debt service** and book depreciation because they are included as part of the capitalization rate.

The second step uses the projected net operating income to estimate the value of the property by dividing it by a capitalization rate which reflects the ratio between the NOI and the value of the property being appraised.

There are many ways to project an appropriate capitalization rate. The best, most simple and direct way is to abstract an overall rate from the market when market.

The formula for converting NOI into value is:

$$\frac{NOI}{Capitalization\ Rate} = Value$$

When suitable market data is not available, other advanced techniques might be appropriate.

These advanced capitalization techniques are beyond the scope of this book. Appraisers interested them should seek out courses, seminars and text books that cover these advances techniques. There is a list of suggested readings in the addenda of this book.

REVIEW QUESTIONS

1. When a typical buyer considers buying a residence they often consider its:
   a. size.
   b. condition.
   c. monthly rental income.
   d. All of the above

2. The income approach, when it is applied to a single-family residence, is sometimes called:
   a. gross monthly rent multiplier.
   b. gross rent multiplier.
   c. gross income multiplier.
   d. All of the above

3. The first step of the GMRM income approach is to:
   a. find residences that have recently sold that were rented at the time they sold.
   b. estimate the rental value of the subject property.
   c. analyze each rental.
   d. None of the above

4. A rent multiplier expresses a ratio between:
   a. old rents and new rents.
   b. high rents and low rents.
   c. mortgages and vacancy rates.
   d. None of the above

5. A rent multiplier is usually:
   a. a whole number.
   b. about 100.
   c. rounded to two decimal places.
   d. None of the above

6. It is best if the properties from which a multiplier is developed:
   a. vary in size.
   b. have common characteristics with the subject
   c. are within one mile of the subject.
   d. All of the above

7. A GMRM is derived from the market by:
   a. dividing actual sale prices by estimated market rents.
   b. dividing actual sale prices by actual rents.
   c. multiplying actual sale prices by estimated market rents.
   d. multiplying actual sale prices by actual rents.

8. To estimate the value of the subject property:
   a. multiply the estimated market rent of the subject property by the appropriate GMRM.
   b. divide the estimated market rent of the subject property by the appropriate GMRM.
   c. multiply the contract rent of the subject   property times the GMRM
   d. None of the above

9. When estimating the rent for a three family house where one of the units is occupied by the owner:
   a. ask the owner what they would ask for rent if they decided to rent the unit.
   b. check the market for comparable rents and use them to estimate the rent of the owners apartment.
   c. average the rents paid for the other units to determine the rent of the owners unit.
   d. None of the above

10 Which of the following is a fixed expense?
   a. insurance costs
   b. utility payments
   c. rubbish removal
   d. None of the above

11. Net Operating Income divided by a capitalization rate equals:
   a. return on investment.
   b. value
   c. return on equity
   d. Nothing related to appraisal

12. Net Operating Income is calculated by:
   a. PGI minus V & C minus operating expenses.
   b. EGI minus V & C minus operating expenses.
   c. PGI plus V & C minus operating expenses.
   d. EGI plus V & C minus operating expenses.

ANSWERS TO REVIEW QUESTIONS

The answer to each question is indicated by the letter a, b, c or d. The explanation of the answer is indicated by the page number and on an arrow that points to the appropriate paragraph on the page of the text.

Q 12.1	d	Page 12-2
Q 12.2	d	Page 12-2
Q 12.3	a	Page 12-2
Q 12.4	d	Page 12-3
Q 12.5	a	Page 12-3
Q 12.6	b	Page 12-3
Q 12.7	b	Page 12-4
Q 12.8	a	Page 12-3
Q 12.9	b	Page 12-4
Q 12.10	a	Page 12-16
Q 12.11	b	Page 12-17
Q 12.12	a	Page 12-9

CHAPTER 13

Reconciliation and Final Opinion of Value

"I am not one who was born in the possession of knowledge."

Confucius
(551-4137 B.C.)

Important Words and Key Concepts

Words on this list are highlighted in this chapter.
They are also defined in the Glossary at the back of this text.

Appraisal Report

Correlation

Credible Appraisal

Final Reconciliation

Insurable Value

Market Value

Opinion of Value

Reconciliation

Scope of Work

Window Dressing

SCOPE OF WORK

13.1 ▶All appraisal assignments should start with an agreement between the appraiser and the client as to the appraisal problem is to be solved. This is necessary to allow the appraiser to determine the **scope of work** required in order to develop a credible estimate of value that will meet the needs of the client for their intended use.

It is the appraiser who always makes the final determination of what the scope of work will be. The USPAP makes it clear that the appraiser must do whatever is necessary to produce a credible appraisal. Sometimes as is often the case with Fannie Mae and Freddie Mac, the client does no seem to care if the appraiser chooses to use the income or cost approach. However, they are careful to state that if the appraiser thinks one or both of these approaches are necessary for the production of a credible appraisal then they say that the appraiser should use them.

What follows is the series of steps in the valuation process that ends with a reconciliation that produces the final **opinion of value** and an **appraisal report.**

13.3 ▶In each step of the appraisal process, the appraiser collects and analyzes data and reconciles it. This results in interim reconciliations. There is also a **final reconciliation.** In the reconciliation, the appraiser considers the quantity and quality of the data collected, analyzed and displayed in the appraisal report.

In addition, the appraiser considers any other related data about which they have knowledge, as well as general knowledge of the market and the economy.

In the past, this process was known among appraisers as **correlation**. Since correlation has a different meaning in statistics and other academic disciplines, it has been replaced by the word **reconciliation**.

13.2 ▶The final opinion of value must be as of a specific day, supported and credible.

VALUATION PROCESS - RECONCILIATION STEPS

DEFINITION OF THE PROBLEM

Reconciliation starts at the very beginning of an appraisal, with the definition of the appraisal problem, the preliminary survey and the data collection plan. The appraiser must ascertain the character and quantity of work to be accomplished and begin to weigh the relative significance and applicability of various data and approaches to the problem.

Identification of the Real Estate

13.4 ▶ The report must provide a positive identification of the subject residence. Regardless of the method of identification (street name and number, metes and bounds, etc.) The location and boundaries must be specified. All significant easements, encroachments and rights-of-way must be considered. If there is a homeowners association or rights to use nearby facilities are involved, these rights must be completely identified. The appraiser must be sure the identification meets the requirements of the Uniform Standards of Professional Appraisal Practice (USPAP), which requires a clear and complete description of the property.

Identification of the Property Rights to be Valued

When the property is in fee simple, a plain statement to this effect should be sufficient. If a leasehold or a residence on leased land is involved, the terms of these leases must be described and their effect on the market value must be analyzed. Analysis of condominium or cooperative ownership rights requires a description of the entire project in which the features, both good and bad, of the entire project are related to the ownership interest being appraised. A residence that has time-sharing rights requires other considerations. For example, are the rights to use the property for December and June equal to the rights to use the same property for January and July?

The ownership rights of the subject property must be compared to those of comparable sales and offerings. Any differences will require adjustment.

Effective Date of the Opinion Of value

13.5 ▶The USPAP requires that every appraisal be as of a specific effective date. This does not have to be the same date as the date of the appraisal report. In a stable market, any time adjustments made to comparable sales, rentals, cost estimates and offerings, present few problems. However, in unstable and rapidly changing markets, any time differential is reviewed. Time adjustments are often averaged over a period of time when, in reality, the market has been moving both upward and downward during the period. Such adjustments, based on average value changes in a community, may not apply to the neighborhood or the price range of the subject property.

Large time adjustments, should be based on one or two matched pairs. They still may contain substantial error caused by an unknown factor or factors.

Identification of Client and Intended Users

The identification of the client and intended users is important as it affects who has status in a professional liability suit against the appraiser. Sometimes, during the process of making the appraisal information is received by the appraiser that the client and/or intended users of the appraisal are different than those that were identified at the time the scope of work was agreed upon between the original client and the appraiser. When the appraiser becomes aware of a change the appraiser must include their identification in the report and be sure that the scope of work does not require any changes to meet the needs of the different client or users.

Intended Use of the Appraisal

When the scope of work was agreed upon between the client and the appraiser the discussion should have included the intended use of the appraisal. It is up to the appraiser to make an appraisal that is suitable for this intended use. If the intended use changes during the process of making the appraisal it is up to the appraiser to determine if this change in intended uses requires changing the appraisal.

Type of Value

If the objective of the appraisal is to estimate the market value, the appraiser must decide if it accomplishes this objective. Is the potential error in the appraisal within boundaries that are satisfactory to the user of the appraisal? Would more data and better analysis reduce the possibility of potential error? Does the appraisal state the degree of potential error that exists, or is the implied degree of accuracy misleading?

When the objective of the appraisal is to estimate value other than market value, the data collected and analyzed must be sufficient and proper to produce a credible value estimate. For example, if the value to be estimated is insurable value, were all the items to be excluded, such as footings, underground pipes, etc., properly treated?

Finally, the most important question is whether the type of value estimated in the appraisal report is a sufficiently accurate and credible estimate for the intended use and users of the appraisal.

Definition of Value

 If the definition of value used in the appraisal is **market value** it should be the same definition that is incorporated into all eleven Fannie Mae residential appraisal forms. This definition of market value is mandated by Congress for all federally-related appraisals.

When the intended use is for some other purpose, it may be necessary to use a different definition of value.

For example, **insurable value** requires a definition that is acceptable for the intended use of setting the appropriate amount of coverage for the insurable parts of the property. This definition may exclude the value of the site, site improvements and parts of the improvements, such as the foundation. Part of the determination of the scope of work is an agreement with the client as to the appropriate definition of value.

Assignment Conditions

For the protection of appraisers and clients, it is necessary for the appraiser to set forth any, extraordinary assumptions, hypothetical conditions and limiting conditions that apply to the appraisal assignment,

PRELIMINARY SURVEY AND APPRAISAL PLAN

A step-by-step review of the preliminary survey and appraisal is made, to determine if all the necessary data has been obtained, and adequate analysis has been provided to arrive at the value estimate. Often, the initial estimate of the data needed to make the appraisal proves to be insufficient to arrive at a credible value estimate. For example, the original plan may call for only the use of comparable sales. However, when the market analysis is made, it may indicate that the shifting market is being affected by the number of competitive listings available. Therefore, information about listings should be used in the sales comparison approach.

Changing building costs, the availability of sites, and new competitive houses may indicate that a detailed application of the cost approach, based on actual costs of available sites and residences currently under construction, will provide a good value indication. The lack of current rentals and information about rented houses that have sold may require the abandonment of an original plan to include an income approach analysis.

As part of the reconciliation process, the data used in each section of the report must be carefully analyzed, with emphasis on making a final judgment about whether sufficient data has been collected, and which data should be used to make the final value estimate. It is poor practice to have inflexible rules about the type and amount of data used; this decision must be made separately for each appraisal problem.

Data Sources

After the initial data has been collected and analyzed, the data sources should be reviewed once again to determine if additional sources may be available. For example, offerings of nearby comparable properties from an MLS may not show as sales because they were sold either by a broker who was not a member of the local MLS system or by the owner without the use of a broker, or as a result of an Internet listing of the property. By tracking these particular properties in the sales records of the community, additional useful comparable sales may be found.

Brokers, lenders, and others interviewed for information often supply leads to additional data sources. All data sources should be reviewed to determine if they have been properly used.

Personnel and Time Requirements

The initial estimate of needed personnel to perform an appraisal should be reviewed to see if they will be able to obtain all the necessary data within the prescribed time. If additional data is needed, extra personnel or additional time on the part of the original personnel will be required.

Often the time originally allocated to complete an assignment will have to be revised. Only when the special requirements of a specific assignment are known can a final estimate of the time schedule be made. Other considerations such as new assignments taking priority over existing assignments, unexpected illnesses of personnel, revised requirements of the client, and personal needs of the appraiser often make scheduling revisions necessary.

The completion flow chart initially serves as a guide through the appraisal process. It can consist of simple notes on how the appraisal will be made or it may be a formal chart showing the progress of the appraisal on a step-by-step basis. Some appraisers use magnetic boards and movable pieces to plot the progress of each appraisal assignment. Whatever system is used, it should be reviewed to keep track of the progress of the assignment, and altered as needed to reflect the updated requirements to complete the assignment.

Fee Proposal and Contract

It is good practice to have an agreement with each client spelling out the **scope of** *work*, the work to be performed, when it is due, and when and how the appraiser will be paid. This contract may be verbal or it may be in writing.

DATA COLLECTION AND ANALYSIS

Ongoing decisions must be made on how much data will be collected and whether the quantity and quality of the data are sufficient to complete the appraisal assignment and to make a *credible appraisal*.

General Data

13.13 It is easy to collect masses of general data about the region, community and neighborhood in which the subject residence is located. It is very hard to cull from this mass of data that information which directly describes the environment and explains the forces affecting the value of the property.

This reconciliation is probably one of the most difficult to do properly and one that tends to be down-played in importance. **Window dressing** is an appraiser's term for unnecessary (merely decorative) figures, charts and displays. It is not appropriate in a professional appraisal report.

The use of demographic information is a good example. There is little justification for simply presenting population figures. Rather, a comparison of population increase with the availability of housing stock, vacancy rates and a forecast of the rate of growth of new housing is more valuable. Raw figures cannot tell the story. All information pertaining to the region, community and neighborhood must be carefully analyzed and reconciled to produce a meaningful presentation.

Economic data, used to prepare market, financial and economic base analyses and to project future trends, also tends to be available in great masses. A visit to the local Chamber of Commerce will often supply the appraiser with pounds of this type of information. Usually one source, no matter how good, will be insufficient to provide all the needed data. As the data is sorted and analyzed, it must be reconciled into a meaningful analysis that will be useful in making a value estimate of the subject property.

Specific Data

Information about the subject property is obtained at the community record source and at the property site. The goal is to accumulate all of the needed data during one trip to each of these places. This can be accomplished by careful planning and the use of checklists and field note forms. A careful review of the data collected on location is the beginning of the specific data reconciliation.

An appraiser is not expected to be a title searcher. However, it is necessary to acquire enough skill to be able to find and use the needed documents. Title papers are examined to produce a positive description of the property; they will also reveal easements, rights-of-way and any private deed restrictions. Sometimes these items have a substantial effect on the value of the property.

Another item to be checked at the record source is the tax assessment. If possible, the assessor's field card should be examined. It often contains useful descriptive information about the property that may affect the final value estimate.

Zoning information can also be obtained at the municipal record source. A preliminary reconciliation may reveal whether the property conforms or if a reasonable probability of a zoning change exists.

An initial reconciliation at the data source can determine whether additional record data pertaining either to the subject property or comparable properties is needed. For example is there a three year ownership history in the collected data. Later, when the data about the community, neighborhood, and subject property is reconciled, a more accurate judgment may be made.

Most of the information about the subject property is usually obtained at the site. The use of checklists or field note forms is helpful. Some clients will provide forms with their special informational requirements. Some clients require a complete list of all items of observed physical deterioration-curable, together with individual estimates of the cost to cure each item.

The final reconciliation of this information determines whether the property has been completely and accurately described and whether there is sufficient information to complete each of the three approaches to value.

Highest and Best Use

Estimating the highest and best use starts with an analysis and reconciliation of all the general and specific information collected about the property. It is done in two parts.

▶ **13.10** The first step is to estimate the highest and best use assuming that the site is vacant and ready to be built upon. This analysis is then repeated to estimate the highest and best use of the property as improved.

The appraiser starts by analyzing the site as if it was vacant. The information is reconciled using the four tests of highest and best use. Zoning information and private restrictions are reconciled to indicate what uses are currently legally permitted. Then, the community and neighborhood information is reconciled with economic information to determine if a reasonable probability of change in zoning exists. The information is further reconciled into an analysis of the reasonable and probable permitted legal uses. Next, the physical information about the site is reconciled to estimate which of the reasonable and probable legally permitted uses is also physically possible.

The community, neighborhood and economic data are again reconciled to estimate what uses would result in the production of a profit. Even if the legally permitted use is for a single-family residence and such a residence can be built and can produce a profit, this is not sufficient to conclude that the highest and best use is for a single family-residence. The type of residence, style, size, design and construction must also be determined.

If after reconciliation of the available information, it is estimated that the highest and best use is for something other than a single-family residence, this must be stated.

The final step is an estimate of the most profitable use. Again, all the information is reconciled. If additional information is needed, it is gathered and analyzed. Reconciliation produces a decision about what the most potentially profitable, physically and legally permitted use of the site is, assuming it were vacant.

This analysis is then repeated to estimate the highest and best use of the property as improved. The information about the region, community, neighborhood, site and existing improvements is analyzed to determine what renovation and repairs, if any, could be made to result in a greater potential profit (or smaller loss) by the owner if the property were sold on the effective date of the appraisal. This estimate may range from a simple list of physical and functional curable items through major renovations and proposed additional improvements to the site.

The estimation of highest and best use is based on a thorough analysis and reconciliation of all the data collected. Again, it may be necessary to collect and analyze additional data before a final reconciliation as to the highest and best use can be made. For example, the preliminary reconciliation may indicate that some renovation may be needed. At this point additional information about its cost and physical feasibility is necessary before a final determination can be made; the reconciliation process is continued after the needed information is collected and analyzed.

Information about the cost to build comparable properties, sales of comparative sites and improved properties, comparative rentals, and rented properties that have sold is initially reconciled to see if it is sufficient to produce a credible indicated value by the three approaches to value.

The preliminary reconciliation reviews the sources of cost data which will be used to estimate reproduction or replacement costs. If a cost service is used as one source, a second source should also be developed. The cost data should be subject to a preliminary reconciliation with the description of the improvements to see if material to estimate all of the costs is available.

A decision about the method of estimating depreciation, based on the available data should be made. If the abstraction method is used, comparable sales are analyzed to see if they are sufficient in number and comparable enough to the subject property to produce a satisfactory depreciation estimate. If the age-life or breakdown method is used, a preliminary reconciliation is made to determine if sufficient data has been collected.

The income approach depends upon sufficient data on comparable rented residences to estimate both the market rent of the subject property, and also to develop the GMRM. The rentals used to develop the GMRM must be of properties that have recently sold. The initial reconciliation determines if sufficient usable data has been collected to make these estimates, or whether additional rentals and sales are needed. If insufficient data regarding sales of rented properties is available, the income approach may not be usable.

Since the final value estimate of most single-family residential appraisals depends heavily on the sales comparison approach, it is necessary to reconcile the comparative sales data continuously during the appraisal process. Initial reconciliations are needed to see if sufficient comparable sales data, as well as data to make necessary adjustments, has been collected to reflect the differences between the comparable sales selected and the subject residence.

It is not good appraisal practice to claim that insufficient data has been found to develop the sales comparison approach unless a thorough search of the market has been conducted. If sales appear insufficient after the initial reconciliation, the search should begin again. This expanded search can be over a wider geographic area, wider price range or greater time frame. The process may be repeated several times, each time collecting and reconciling data to determine its usefulness, until either sufficient data is collected for the sales comparison approach or further expansion of the search will not produce any additional useful data.

All of the reconciliations done up to this point are preliminary in nature. The primary goal is to collect enough useful data to proceed through the three approaches to value.

APPLICATION OF THE THREE APPROACHES

The reconciliation process continues as the collected data is further analyzed for use in each of the approaches.

Cost Approach

The reconciliation process is applied to each step of the cost approach.

1. Estimate the market value of the site as if it was vacant and available for development to its highest and best use. The estimate of the site value typically includes all of the steps of the sales comparison approach. First, the comparable sites are reconciled, comparing their use with the estimated highest and best use of the subject site. For example, if the subject site were best suited for a house in the $180,000 to $200,000 range, sites for houses of similar value would be the best comparables, even if the subject house were in the $130,000 to $135,000 range and therefore not the highest and best use.

   The best comparables are selected and individually compared to the subject site. Differences between the comparable sites and the subject site are reported. The data is further analyzed for information on which to base adjustments for all the significant differences. A decision is then made about each comparable as to whether it can be adjusted satisfactorily or must be rejected and replaced with a better comparable. If many sales are rejected, it may be necessary to go back to the market and expand the search for more comparable site sales and/or more data on which to base the adjustments.

   When the appraiser is satisfied that the assembled data is adequate and all the needed adjustments have been made, the adjusted sales price of each of the comparables is analyzed and a final indicated value of the subject site is obtained. This estimate is not an average of the adjusted sale prices of the comparables; it is based on the results of the reconciliation.

2. Estimate the reproduction (or replacement) cost new of the improvements. This estimate can be based on data from construction cost services and/or from actual costs of similar residences constructed in the same market. The available data is reconciled to determine which method will be used. Both the description of the improvements and the data being used as a cost basis are analyzed to determine if everything needed to make the cost estimate has been gathered. The cost data is reconciled with the description of the improvements data to produce

an estimated reproduction or replacement cost of the subject residence.

3. Estimate the amount of depreciation the improvements have suffered. A decision is made as to which method will be used to estimate the accrued depreciation. When the abstraction method is used, the sales selected from which to abstract the depreciation are analyzed and processed. The range of resulting amounts of depreciation or rates of depreciation are reconciled. Reconciliation considers the comparability of the data from which the amount or rate of depreciation is abstracted. The final reconciliation considers the amount of data used, the degree of variance between the rates, and whether additional data is needed to produce a satisfactory estimate of depreciation.

If the age-life method is used, depreciation may be based entirely upon observation. To estimate the typical economic life of a residence, data about the region, community and neighborhood is considered, along with specific data about the subject residence. Each of the four great forces that affect the value and life of the residence is considered. This data is then reconciled by the appraiser, who relies heavily on personal knowledge and experience, into an estimate of typical economic life. Finally, the percentage of depreciation is calculated by dividing the effective age by the typical economic life. A final reconciliation of the results determines how good the estimate is, and how much weight it will be given in the appraisal process.

The breakdown method of estimating depreciation is done in five steps that correspond to the five types of depreciation identified by this method. First, the physical deterioration-curable is estimated by making a list of all the physical deterioration that is observed. Cost to cure these items is estimated either by the appraiser or by a local contractor who can provide the needed cost information.

Most items of routine maintenance are automatically classified as physical deterioration-curable without actually proving they add value in excess of their cost. However, it may be necessary to obtain market information to justify classifying large items of maintenance as curable. The list of items to be cured and the estimated costs to do the work are reconciled into an estimate of physical deterioration-curable.

Physical deterioration-incurable is divided into two groups. One group is items that are not ready to be cured on the effective date of the appraisal but will need to be cured before the end of the residence's economic life. A list is prepared together with cost estimates to repair or replace the items. These items are reconciled into an estimate of physical deterioration-incurable (short-lived items). The other group of items includes those that have suffered some deterioration but will not be economically feasible to repair or replace during the remaining typical economic life of the improvements. The estimate is often made based on an engineering breakdown of the components of the residence, against which percentage of depreciation estimates are applied, to produce a total estimate of the physical deterioration-incurable. This estimate depends heavily on the appraiser's knowledge and judgment. All the data used should be carefully reconciled, and the reliability of the results reported.

Items of functional obsolescence are listed and analyzed to estimate if a cure is possible. If so, it is noted whether the cost to cure is less than the value added. Reconciliation of this information may require the use of additional data to support whether the value added will exceed the cost to cure. Data is also needed to estimate the cost to cure the items as part of a total construction program, as well as the cost to do so separately on the date of the appraisal. The reliability of this estimate is considered in the reconciliation.

The loss from functional obsolescence-incurable may be based on comparison of recently sold or rented residences with and without the item or features causing the obsolescence.

The items off the premises that cause a loss in value (economic obsolescence) are listed, considered and estimated.

In the past, the breakdown method was a favorite method of many appraisers. However, it is a very difficult method to use in actual practice because of all the data needed. There is usually a high probability of error.

4. Deduct the depreciation from the reproduction (or replacement) cost new of the improvements to obtain the depreciated value of the improvements as is. If depreciation has been estimated by more than one method, the results are reconciled into a depreciation estimate. When sufficient data is available, the abstraction method usually produces the most accurate estimate because it is based directly upon market data. The age-life method usually is based primarily on the appraiser's judgment, supported more heavily by general knowledge than by specific data. Because it is easy to explain, it usually is the best method when insufficient data is available for the abstraction method. The results of the breakdown method tend to be deceiving because it is broken into five parts. Because it is not primarily based on the market, there is potential for substantial error. When used, it should be carefully reconciled to eliminate as much potential error as possible.

    When more than one method is used, the results should be compared. Reasons for differences should be sought and the estimates further refined, if possible, to reduce the discrepancies. The final depreciation estimate is deducted from the estimated reproduction or replacement cost to produce the depreciated value of the improvements.

5. Add the site (land) market value, obtained in Step 1, to the depreciated value of the improvements to obtain an indicated value of the property. After the estimated value is obtained, it is compared with the values indicated by the other approaches. A wide variance is indicative of possible weaknesses in the data, assumptions, or application of the cost approach, or its validity and applicability to the specific appraisal problem.

Sales Comparison Approach

The reconciliation process is applied to each of the steps of the sales comparison approach.

1. Find the sales, listings and offerings of properties that are similar to the subject property. When a group of sales, listings and offerings has been collected, a preliminary reconciliation is made for the purpose of deciding if enough usable data has been

obtained. The setting of arbitrary numbers of sales, listings and offerings to be used—without actually considering the quality of the data—is poor appraisal practice.

2. Verify each sale with the buyer, seller or broker to confirm the selling price, data of transaction, physical and locational characteristics and conditions of sale. The only acceptable way to find out about the conditions of sale that affected a transaction is to interview the buyer, seller or broker. Only these people will know all the terms, motivations and whether the sale was *bona fide* in nature. The results of the interviews should be reconciled. If information indicates conditions of sale that will be difficult to adjust for, the sale should be rejected and replaced with additional data, if possible, and the reconciliation process repeated.

3. Analyze the important attributes of each comparable and compare them to the corresponding features of the subject property. Use the elements of comparison such as time of sale, location, physical and other characteristics. The analysis of the important attributes of each comparable will identify differences between the comparables and the subject property. The available data is then reconciled to determine if it can serve as a basis for making the needed adjustments or whether additional data will be needed. The search continues for data until a sufficient number of sales, listings and offerings is found with differences that can be adjusted for.

4. Estimate the adjustments that will be required for the sales price of each comparable to give an indicated value for the subject property. Adjustments should be supported with data developed from the market, which is reconciled to produce an adjusted sale price for each comparable.

5. Consider each of the comparable sales and the accuracy of any and all adjustments required because of dissimilarities among these sales and the appraised property.

Formulate an opinion of market value for the subject property based on the comparable sales which have been analyzed. The reconciliation of the adjusted price of each comparable into a final value estimate for the subject property is the critical step in the appraisal process because this estimate will most likely be used as the main basis for the final value estimate. The reconciliation process considers the supporting data for each adjustment. When there is a substantial spread in adjusted prices, consideration should be given to expanding the data search and repeating the whole process to obtain better results.

In the final reconciliation of the sales comparison approach, the quantity and quality of all the data is reviewed. Generally, the older the data, the further from the subject property and the more physically dissimilar, the less accurate the adjusted sale price will be. It is particularly difficult to adjust accurately for conditions of sale and economic influences.

Again, the value obtained in the sales comparison approach is compared with values indications derived via the other two approaches. Wide discrepancies in estimated value usually suggest that further collection, refinement and analysis of pertinent data is needed.

Income Approach (GMRM)

13.12 ▶ The gross monthly rent multiplier (GMRM) technique used in the appraisal of single-family residences includes the following eight steps:

1. Find residences that have recently sold in the neighborhood that are comparable to the subject property, that were rented at the time of sale. All recent sales are reviewed and those most comparable are selected for final use. No fixed number of comparables is needed. If a large number can be found, they may lend themselves to analysis by statistical techniques.

2. Divide the sales price of each comparable by the monthly rental to derive the GMRM. The resulting GMRM figures should be arranged in order to determine if they fall into a useful range and if extremes should be dropped or additional data is needed.

3. Reconcile the multipliers to obtain a single multiplier or a range of multipliers that is applicable to the subject property. If a single GMRM is selected, it should not be an average of the multipliers. It should be a result of judgment about how comparable each of the properties that produced a multiplier was to the subject property, or the result of statistical analysis of the range of multipliers.

4. Find comparable rentals in the neighborhood. Comparable rentals are reviewed and selected for final use. Again, no fixed number is standard; however, less than three usually is not satisfactory. The reconciliation emphasizes the comparability of the rental to the subject property and the identification of the existing significant differences for which adjustments are made.

5. Analyze each of the comparable rentals by comparing them with the corresponding features of the subject house. A decision must be made on an item-by-item basis about whether the differences can be adjusted for or if the rental must be rejected. If many rentals are rejected, it may be necessary to go back to the market and expand the search to find additional useful data.

6. Estimate the required adjustments for each comparable rental property to obtain an indicated rental for the subject property. All the additional rentals needed to estimate the adjustments are analyzed. Those that will produce indications of the needed adjustments are processed. These adjustments are reconciled with the comparable sales, and data is added or eliminated as required.

7. Consider each comparable rental carefully, with emphasis on the need for adjustments, and formulate an opinion of the market (economic) rent of the subject property, based on the adjusted rentals of the comparables. Often the rentals are adjusted with the aid of a grid. The result is a group of adjusted rentals, each of which is an indication of the market rent of the subject residence. These adjusted rentals are individually compared to the subject property to estimate which are most comparable. Finally, a decision is made as to the estimated market rent of the subject property. This estimate should not be an average, but is based on the results of the reconciliation.

8. Multiply the estimated market rent of the subject property by the estimated monthly multiplier (or range of multipliers) to obtain an indicated value of the subject residence via the income approach. This result should not be accepted without another reconciliation of all the data. The appraiser must be satisfied that the data used is of adequate quantity and quality to produce a useful estimate.

FINAL RECONCILIATION

13.13 ▶The final step in the reconciliation is to check all data for accuracy, reliability and applicability. The intended use and objectives of the report are summarized and the characteristics of the property are reviewed. A decision is made regarding the most appropriate approaches to value and the reliability of each value indication obtained.

The appraiser should step away from the various indications of value and consider what the property is worth based on their experience and judgement independent of what is indicated by the analysis in the appraisal.

Occasionally, it is possible to become so focused on the data and analysis in the appraisal that good common sense is left out of the final analysis and recodnciliation.

A credible final opinion of value should be well supported with appropriate supplied appraisal techniques and fit with the appraisers and users sense of reason as well.

Advantages and Disadvantages of Each Approach

The cost approach was traditionally the favorite approach to value for many appraisers. Its advantages are that it is simple to use and usually reliable for new improvements on properties developed to their highest and best use. The disadvantages are the difficulty of accurately estimating accrued depreciation when no sales are available from which to calculate the depreciation by abstraction, and the fact that the reproduction cost estimates may not reflect actual prevailing economic and market conditions.

The sales comparison approach is usually the preferred approach in single-family residential appraising. The value indication obtained is based on actual market transactions, is easily understood by lay people, and is most applicable in court testimony. It is not particularly useful when there is a lack of recent, reliable and highly comparable sales data.

The GMRM income approach is mathematically simple and direct. It is most useful when the subject property is located in a neighborhood where houses are frequently rented. Disadvantages are that the condition of the comparables is not always reflected in rent differentials, many quality neighborhoods have few houses that are rented and subsequently sold, and a considerable volume of rental and sales data is necessary to properly estimate the market rent and appropriate multiplier for use in this approach.

Reconciliation: Additional Considerations

Appraisal practice requires all pertinent data to be reviewed during the reconciliation process. The data is reviewed for:

- quality and quantity;
- reliability of the sources;
- timeliness; and
- . conformity of the subject property to the market

Quantity and Quality of Data

The quantity and quality of the data used as a basis for making the value estimates determines the degree of accuracy of these estimates. The more confidence the appraiser has in the data, the more confidence they will have in a value estimate that is made based on the data.

Often the appraiser will have more confidence in the data used in one approach than that used in the other approaches. When this is the case, more weight should be given to the approach with the best data.
Generally, the larger and more numerous the adjustments are, the less confidence the appraiser will have in the adjusted prices that result. The accuracy of some data has a greater effect than the accuracy of other data. A difference of a few thousand dollars in an adjustment in the sales comparison approach will usually have a smaller effect on the final value estimate than a percentage difference in estimating a capitalization rate, where every percent difference has a significant effect on the final value estimate.

Reliability of the Data

There are many sources of information that are relied upon in an appraisal. Some sources are more reliable than others. As the reliability and detail of the data increases, confidence in the value opinion also increases.

For example, if a confirming source provides detailed information about a transaction, including the particulars of the negotiations, the reliability of the information would increase. Conversely, if the verifying source provides only rough generalizations without any specifics relative to the transaction being confirmed, the reliability of the information would decline.

Typically, more reliable details are associated with more recent transactions. More recent sales are also more reflective of current market conditions.

Timeliness of the Data

More recent comparable data is more reliable than older comparable data. When all of the data is within the last few months, there frequently is more detail available and the information is more reflective of current market conditions. In some markets, there are only a limited number of sales during a particular time period, however. If the majority of the information that is used in an appraisal is old, the credibility of the value conclusion suffers.

Conformity of the Subject with the Market

When the subject property represents the bottom or the top end of the market, it is more difficult to identify market data that supports the value conclusion. For example, a large custom home on a multi-acre lot that is located in an urban area will not have many direct comparables. The lack of conformity of the subject with other properties in the market reduces the credibility of the analysis. By contrast, a tract home in a tract home subdivision should have a significant amount of data from properties that are similar or even identical to the subject property, except for the location of the lot. This would result in an analysis that has more credibility.

COST APPROACH FINAL RECONCILIATION

There might be multiple reconciliations within the cost approach. There could be reconciliation of the site value, the replacement/reproduction cost new, and the depreciation. Any time there are multiple potential conclusions based on the analyses that are performed, reconciliation is required. Reconciliation allows the appraiser to show the reader of their report what considerations informed their choice of how to weight the data they have gathered. The more thoughtful a reconciliation is, the more credibility the appraiser gains for their value opinion.

Site Value

The site value could be developed with one or more of the five techniques that are available for estimating land value. If multiple techniques are used, the appraiser must reconcile the results of the various analyses to arrive at an opinion of value for the site. The reconciliation should take into consideration the applicability of the data obtained and analyzed using each technique. Ultimately the appraiser must be able to explain the basis for their opinion of the land value.

Replacement/Reproduction Cost New

There are many techniques available to estimate replacement/reproduction cost new. These include cost manuals, extraction from the market, actual historical costs, and anticipated budgeted costs. If multiple techniques are used, the appraiser must reconcile the results of the various analyses to arrive at an opinion of the replacement/reproduction cost new. The reconciliation should take into consideration the applicability of each technique in light of the quality and quantity of data that was available. The appraiser must explain the basis for their estimate of replacement/reproduction cost new.

Depreciation

There are several techniques available to estimate depreciation. They include published depreciation tables, effective age/life analysis, and component depreciation. If multiple techniques are used, the appraiser must reconcile the results of the various analyses to arrive at the depreciation figures that will be used in the appraisal. The reconciliation should take into consideration the applicability of each technique in light of the quality and quantity of data available. Ultimately the appraiser must be able to explain the basis for applying a particular level of depreciation in their appraisal.

Typically, when improvements are newer it is easier to estimate depreciation. When properties are older, the variability associated with estimating depreciation increases, and the applicability and credibility of the data is lessened.

SALES COMPARISON APPROACH FINAL RECONCILIATION

Reconciliation within the sales comparison approach requires the appraiser to critically evaluate the sales that are included in the analysis, as well as carefully review the adjustments that were applied. Generally, the higher the magnitude of the absolute adjustments, the more the reliability of the conclusion is suspect.

As part of the reconciliation process, the appraiser is not required to give all of the sales in the analysis similar consideration. There might be a two or three sales that represent the best indication of the value of the subject property. These sales should represent the primary basis for the opinion of value.

If the appraisal analysis does not have sales that bracket the lower end and the upper end of the relevant range of values for the subject property, additional sales data should be gathered and new comparable sales added to the analysis. When the sales comparison approach indicates a value of the subject property that is lower than any of the comparable sales, the adjustments become the primary focus of the analysis. If there are inadequate sales to rely upon from the sales comparison approach to reliably indicate the value of the subject, this should be noted. A lack of appropriate comparable sales is a serious problem in creating a credible appraisal.

INCOME APPROACH FINAL RECONCILIATION

The reconciliation of the income approach is dependent on the techniques that are used to develop the value indication. It is possible that both the GMRM and the direct capitalization techniques are applied. When both techniques are used, the appraiser must reconcile the results obtained from the different methodologies.

It is also possible that a range of gross monthly rent multipliers are applied. In this instance, the appraiser must select a range of indicated values from the GMRM approach to value. The appraiser should have a logical explanation for their reconciliation and subsequent opinion of value via the income approach.

Rounding

Numbers that are estimates indicate reader their degree of accuracy by how they are rounded. When the estimated value of a site is reported as $32,100 the appraiser is implying accuracy to the nearest $100. If the estimated value is reported to be $32,000 the appraiser is implying that the estimate is accurate to the nearest $1,000 dollars. Rounding helps to make an estimate more believable. Clients find it hard to believe that an appraiser can estimate the value of a house to within a hundred dollars or the value of a million dollar commercial property to within a thousand dollars.

There are three different rounding techniques that are commonly used. One rounds every estimate within an appraisal to indicate its degree of accuracy (i.e., reproduction cost, depreciation, individual adjustments, etc.). Some appraisers leave the numbers within each approach unrounded and round only the values indicated by each approach and the final value estimate. Other appraisers round only the final value estimate.

APPRAISAL REPORT

The final step of the appraisal process is the preparation of a report of the value estimate. Keep in mind that what type of report is made does not change the appraisal process and what must be done to make a credible appraisal that conforms to the scope of work determined by the appraiser.

The 2006 USPAP requires that when to give a value estimate you must prepare a report that meets at least the minimum USPAP reporting requirements.

All the data is reviewed once more so that the appraiser may select the material to be displayed in the appraisal report. Reports to be used for condemnation proceedings and other legal proceedings often must be very comprehensive, containing large amounts of the data used to make the value estimate. Photographs, maps, sketches, charts and other graphics are often included to help the reader understand the analysis and reasoning that led the appraiser to the final value estimate.

A lender who uses the services of an appraiser on a regular basis may require only a form report that displays the highlights of the data and the reasoning used to arrive at the final opinion of value.

SUMMARY

The accuracy of an appraisal depends on the appraiser's knowledge, experience, and judgment. Equally important are the quantity and quality of the available data that will be reconciled in the final value estimate. A judgment is made as to the validity and reliability of each of the value indications derived from the three approaches to value. These indications are never merely averaged. To do so is to substitute arithmetic for judgment. Rather, the appraiser reconciles the value indications, analyzes the alternatives, and selects from among them that indication of value which will be most defensible and truly representative of the subject property.

REVIEW QUESTIONS

1. What is the first thing an appraiser must do to determine the appropriate scope of work?
   a. Decide what approaches to value are needed.
   b. Determine the problem to be solved.
   c. Determine the value to be estimated.
   d. None of the above

2. The final opinion of value must be:
   a. credible.
   b. supported.
   c. as of a specific date.
   d. All of the above

3. A process of reconciliation takes place in the:
   a. sales comparison approach.
   b. income approach.
   c. cost approach.
   d. All of the above

4. Each appraisal must contain:
   a. the name(s) of the lender/client.
   b. an income approach
   c. an identification of the real estate being appraised.
   d. All of the above

5. The effective date of the appraisal can be:
   a. the same date as the date of the appraisal report.
   b. a date prior to the date of the appraisal report.
   c. a date after the date of the appraisal report.
   d. All of the above

6. Congress has mandated a definition of value for:
   a. all appraisals made by licensed and/or certified appraisers.
   b. all appraisers.
   c. verifying comparable sales.
   d. None of the above

7. Besides sales from the local MLS system, the appraiser should look for sales:
   a. directly made by the property owner.
   b. by brokers who are not members of the local MLS.
   c. through the Internet.
   d. All of the above

8. Why is it a good idea to have a written agreement with the client for an appraisal assignment?
   a. It clarifies the scope of work.
   b. It is required by the USPAP.

   c. It is required by Fannie Mae.
   d. All of the above

13. General data usually includes data about the:
   a. region.
   b. community.
   c. neighborhood.
   d. All of the above

10. The first step of the highest and best use analysis is a:
   a. reconciliation of the sales comparison approach.
   b. reconciliation of all the general data.
   c. determination of which approaches are needed in the appraisal.
   d. None of the above

11. The income approach for single-family residences:
   a. is rarely applicable.
   b. is a capitalization process.
   c. is based on the GMRM technique.
   d. None of the above

12. Which of the following data must be reconciled in the sales comparison approach?
   a. Listings
   b. Offerings
   c. MLS sales
   d. All of the above

13. The final step of the reconciliation process is to check all the data for:
   a. applicability.
   b. reliability.
   c. accuracy.
   d. All of the above.

14. Rounding indicates to the reader of an appraisal:
   a. if the appraiser used a computer to make the appraisal.
   b. how numbers are customarily rounded in the subject's market area.
   c. the degree of accuracy of the number.
   d. that the appraiser knows the final value should be rounded to the nearest one hundred dollars.

ANSWERS TO REVIEW QUESTIONS

The answer to each question is indicated by the letter a, b, c or d below. The explanation of the answer is indicated by a numbered arrow that points to the appropriate paragraph on the page of the text indicated by the page number following the answer.

Q 13.1	b	Page 13-2
Q 13.2	d	Page 13-2
Q 13.3	d	Page 13-2
Q 13.4	c	Page 13-3
Q 13.5	d	Page 13-3
Q 13.6	d	Page 13-4
Q 13.7	d	Page 13-5
Q 13.8	a	Page 13-6
Q 13.9	d	Page 13-6
Q 13.10	d	Page 13-7
Q 13.11	c	Page 13-12
Q 13.12	d	Page 13-13
Q 13.13	d	Page 13-14
Q 13.14	c	Page 13-17

CHAPTER 14

Communicating the Appraisal

"A verbal agreement isn't worth the paper it's written on."

Samuel Goldwyn
(1882-1974)

Important Words and Key Concepts

Words on this list are highlighted in this chapter
They are also defined in the Glossary at the back of this text

Appraisal Report

Assumptions

Extraordinary Assumptions

Hypothetical Conditions

Limiting Conditions

Oral Appraisal Reports

Restricted Use Appraisal Report

Self-Contained Appraisal Report

Summary Appraisal Report

Valuation Process

PURPOSE OF AN APPRAISAL REPORT

14.3

"The assignment is not complete until the conclusion is stated in a report and presented to the client. The reported value is the appraiser's opinion and reflects the experience and judgment that has been applied to the study of the appraisal data. The appraisal report is the tangible expression of the appraiser's work and the last step of the *valuation process.*" [1]

REPORTING REQUIREMENTS OF THE USPAP

14.2

The Uniform Standards of Professional Practice (USPAP) provides standards that guide the appraiser on how to communicate the results of the appraisal to the lender/client and intended user(s) who must always be identified in the *appraisal report*, either by name or type.

ORAL REPORTS

14.1

Appraisal reports may be oral or written. When the report is oral it is still necessary to make and keep a written record of the report.

The 2006 USPAP ethics rule spells out what is required in the record keeping section of the USPAP. Here are the parts of the ethics rule that apply to *oral appraisal reports*:

"An appraiser must prepare a work file for each appraisal...The work file must include:

14.4

• The name of the client and the identity by name or type, of any other intended User(s)....

14.5

• Summaries of any oral reports or testimony, or a transcript of testimony, including the appraiser's signed and dated certification; and all other data, information, and documentation necessary to support the appraiser's opinions and conclusions and to show compliance with this Rule and all other applicable Standards, or references to the location(s) of such other documentation."

The requirements for retaining these records are the same as for written appraisal reports.

The appraiser should think twice before making an oral appraisal report. In many cases it is more desirable to prepare one of the three types of written reports that are permitted by the USPAP.

Clients who request oral appraisal reports often do so for the purpose of reducing the appraisal fee. The appraiser should explain to the client the amount of written work and record retention that is required by USPAP even when the report is oral.

---

[1] The Appraisal of Real Estate, 12 edition, Appraisal Institute, Chicago, IL 2001

WRITTEN APPRAISAL REPORTS

Types of Written Appraisal Reports

14.6 ▶USPAP Standards Rule 2-2 spells out that "Each written real property appraisal report must be prepared under one of the following three options and prominently state which option is used: self-contained appraisal report, summary appraisal report or restricted use appraisal report.

Self-contained Appraisal Reports

"A *self-contained appraisal report* fully describes the data and analysis used in the assignment. All appropriate information is contained within the report and not referenced to the appraiser's files."

14.7 ▶Most self-contained appraisal reports are narrative appraisal reports. However, this is not a USPAP requirement and it is possible to make a self-contained appraisal report on a form.

USPAP STANDARDS FOR SELF-CONTAINED APPRAISAL REPORTS

USPAP Standard Rule 2-2 (a) spells out specific requirements for a self-contained appraisal report. These requirements are quoted below. In the USPAP in addition to these requirements, there are Comments for each Standard Rule, as well a references to Advisory Opinions and Statements that are not included here.

Before an appraiser attempts to make a self-contained appraisal report they must become familiar with all the parts of the USPAP that apply to self-contained appraisal reports.

The authors highly recommend that before an appraiser attempts to make a narrative appraisal report they successfully complete a course or seminar on this subject.

The following are those portions of the USPAP that specify the requirements for making a self-contained appraisal report:

"STANDARD 2: REAL PROPERTY APPRAISAL REPORTING

In reporting the results of a real property appraisal, an appraiser must communicate each analysis, opinion, and conclusion in a manner that is not misleading.

Standards Rule 2-1

Each written or oral real property appraisal report must:

(a)   clearly and accurately set forth the appraisal in a manner that will not be misleading.

(b)   contain sufficient information to enable the intended users of the appraisal to understand the report properly; and

14.8 ▶

(c)   clearly and accurately disclose all **assumptions**, **extraordinary assumptions**, **hypothetical conditions**, and **limiting conditions** used in the assignment."

"Standards Rule 2-2 (a)

(a)   The content of a self-contained appraisal report must be consistent with the intended use of the appraisal and, at a minimum;

    (i)   state the identity of the client and any intended users, by name or type;

    (ii)   state the intended use of the appraisal;

    (iii)   describe information sufficient to identify the real estate involved in the appraisal, including the physical and economic property characteristics relevant to the assignment;

    (iv)   state the real property interest appraised;

    (v)   state the type and definition of value and cite the source of the definition;

    (vi)   state the effective date of the appraisal and the date of the report;

    (vii)   describe the scope of work used to develop the appraisal;

    (viii)   describe the information analyzed, the appraisal methods and techniques employed, and the reasoning that supports the analyses, opinions, and conclusions; exclusion of the sales comparison approach, cost approach, or income approach must be explained;

    (ix)   state the use of the real estate as of the date of value and the use of the real estate reflected in the appraisal; and, when an opinion of highest and best use was developed by the appraiser, describe the support and rationale for that opinion;

    (x)   clearly and conspicuously:

        •   state all extraordinary assumptions and hypothetical conditions; and

        •   state that their use might have affected the assignment results; and

    (xi)   include a signed certification in accordance with Standards Rule 2-3."

Summary Appraisal Reports

Most form reports may be classified as **summary appraisal reports**, depending on the level of detail and the quantity of supporting documentation. Form reports often meet the needs of financial institutions, insurance companies and government agencies. They are required for the purchase and sale of most homes and for the resale of existing mortgages on residential properties in the secondary mortgage market created by government agencies and private organizations. Because these intended users review many appraisals, using a standard report form is both efficient and convenient. When a form is used, those responsible for reviewing the appraisal know exactly where to find each category or item of data in the report. By completing the form, the appraiser ensures that no item required by the reviewer is overlooked...

"...Appraisers must be very careful to ensure that a report form does not dictate the appraisal process. The methodology employed in a valuation is determined by the nature of the specific appraisal problem, not by the type of report. If a report form does not provide for adequate presentation and discussion of all the analysis and data that the appraiser believes to be pertinent, that information must be added as a supplement."

USPAP STANDARDS FOR SUMMARY APPRAISAL REPORTS
USPAP Standard Rule 2-2 (b) spells out the following requirements for a summary appraisal report. These requirements are quoted here. In the USPAP, in addition to these quoted requirements, there are Comments for each Standard Rule, as well as references to Advisory Opinions and Statements that are not included here.

Before an appraiser attempts to make summary appraisal report they must become familiar with all the parts of the USPAP that apply to summary appraisal reports.

The authors highly recommend that before an appraiser attempts to make a summary appraisal report they successfully complete a course or seminar on this subject.

The following are those portions of the USPAP that specify the requirements for making a summary appraisal report:

"STANDARD 2: REAL PROPERTY APPRAISAL REPORTING

In reporting the results of a real property appraisal, an appraiser must communicate each analysis, opinion, and conclusion in a manner that is not misleading.

Standards Rule 2-1

Each written or oral real property appraisal report must:

(a)   clearly and accurately set forth the appraisal in a manner that will not be misleading

(b)   contain sufficient information to enable the intended users of the appraisal to understand the report properly; and

 (c)   clearly and accurately disclose all assumptions, extraordinary assumptions, hypothetical conditions, and limiting conditions used in the assignment."

"Standards Rule 2-2 (b)

(b)   The content of a summary appraisal report must be consistent with the intended use of the appraisal and, at a minimum;

   (i)   state the identity of the client and any intended users, by type or name;

   (ii)   state the intended use of the appraisal;

   (iii)   summarize information sufficient to identify the real estate involved in the appraisal, including the physical and economic property characteristics relevant to the assignment;

   (iv)   state the real property interest appraised;

   (v)   state the type and definition of value and cite the source of the definition;

   (vi)   state the effective date of the appraisal and the date of the report;

   (vii)   summarize the scope of work used to develop the appraisal;

   (viii)   summarize the information analyzed, the appraisal methods and techniques employed, and the reasoning that supports the analyses, opinions, and conclusions; exclusion of the sales comparison approach, cost approach, or income approach must be explained;

   (ix)   state the use of the real estate as of the date of value and the use of the real estate reflected in the appraisal; and, when an opinion of highest and best use was developed by the appraiser, describe the support and rationale for that opinion;

   (x)   clearly and conspicuously:

   •   state all extraordinary assumptions and hypothetical conditions; and

   •   state that their use might have affected the assignment results; and

   (xi)   include a signed certification in accordance with Standards Rule 2-3."

Restricted Use Appraisal Reports

 A *restricted use appraisal report* is a very special type of report that is not intended for public use. Its most common use is when a lender wants to review their portfolio and requires specific information from the appraiser for this purpose. When determining the scope of work required for a restricted use appraisal report, the burden is on the appraiser to determine if the lender/client fully understands the limitations of a restricted use appraisal report and is sophisticated enough to be able to accomplish their intended use with this type of report.

The burden is also on the appraiser to be satisfied that the lender/client fully understands that the contents of a restricted use appraisal report if for the clients use only and cannot be communicated to the public.

Since the possibility of misunderstanding is so high when restricted use appraisal reports are used, it is a good idea to have the conditions of the assignment in writing and signed by the client.

USPAP STANDARDS FOR RESTRICTED USE APPRAISAL REPORTS

USPAP Standard Rule 2-2 (c) spells out the following requirements for a restricted use appraisal report. These requirements are quoted here. In the USPAP in addition to these quoted requirements, there are Comments for each Standard Rule, as well a references to Advisory Opinions and Statements that are not included here.

Before an appraiser attempts to make a restricted use appraisal report they must become familiar with all the parts of the USPAP that apply to restricted use appraisal reports.

The following are portions of the USPAP that specify the requirements for making a restricted use appraisal report:

"STANDARD 2: REAL PROPERTY APPRAISAL REPORTING
In reporting the results of a real property appraisal, an appraiser must communicate each analysis, opinion, and conclusion in a manner that is not misleading.

Standards Rule 2-1

Each written or oral real property appraisal report must:

(a) clearly and accurately set forth the appraisal in a manner that will not be misleading

(b) contain sufficient information to enable the intended users of the appraisal to understand the report properly; and

(c) clearly and accurately disclose all assumptions, extraordinary assumptions, hypothetical conditions, and limiting conditions used in the assignment."

"Standards Rule 2-2 (c)

(c) The content of a restricted use appraisal report must be consistent with the intended use of the appraisal and, at a minimum;

(i) state the identity of the client, by name or type; and state a prominent use restriction that limits the use of the report tothe client and warns that the appraiser's opinions and conclusions set forth in the report may not be understood properly without additional information in the appraiser's work file;

(ii) state the intended use of the appraisal;

(iii state information sufficient to identify the real estate involved in the appraisal;

(iv) state the real property interest appraised;

(v) state the type and definition of value and cite the source of the definition;

(vi) state the effective date of the appraisal and the date of the report;

(vii) state the scope of work used to develop the appraisal;

(viii) state the appraisal methods and techniques employed, state the value opinion(s) and conclusion(s) reached, and reference the work file; exclusion of the sales comparison approach, cost approach, or income approach must be explained.

(ix) state the use of the real estate as of the date of value and the use of the real estate reflected in the appraisal; and, when an opinion of highest and best use was developed by the appraiser, state that opinion;

(x) clearly and conspicuously:

• state all extraordinary assumptions and hypothetical conditions; and

• state that their use might have affected the assignment results; and

(xi) include a signed certification in accordance with Standards Rule 2-3."

The primary distinction between a self-contained appraisal report, summary appraisal report and a restricted use appraisal report is the level of detail that is included in the report.

A self contained appraisal report describes, a summary appraisal report summarizes and a restricted use appraisal report states the clients minimum requirements.

SUMMARY

The final step of the valuation process is to prepare an appraisal report. The report can be oral or written . The USPAP has very specific requirements for all types of appraisal reports. These requirements include not only how they must be prepared but also covers how they may be used and how they must be retained in the appraiser's files.

When a oral report is made the USPAP has specific requirements pertaining to the creation of written records of what was reported orally and for the retention of these records by the appraiser.

USPAP Standards Rule 2-2 spells out that there are three types of acceptable written appraisal reports: self-contained appraisal reports, summary appraisal reports and restricted use appraisal reports.

Chapter 15: Residential Applications & Model Appraisals in this text gives examples of completed Fannie Mae/Freddie Mac Uniform Residential Appraisal Reports. It is the most commonly used summary appraisal report form.

REVIEW QUESTIONS

1. The conclusions reached by the appraiser in the valuation analysis may be communicated to the client:
   a. only in a written appraisal report.
   b. first by an oral appraisal report.
   c. never first by an oral appraisal report.
   d. None of the above

2. The USPAP requires that the lender/client:
   a. are the only ones who can receive the appraisal report.
   b. must always be identified in the appraisal report by name or type.
   c. be the first ones to receive the appraisal report.
   d. None of the above

3. The appraisal assignment is not complete until:
   a. the appraiser is paid.
   b. an appraisal report is deliveredd to the client.
   c. the date of the appraisal has passed..
   d. None of the above

4. An appraiser must make and keep a work file for:
   a. a restricted appraisal report.
   b. an oral appraisal report.
   c. Both of the above
   d. Neither of the above

5. When an appraiser makes an oral appraisal report in court they must keep a record of the appraisal in their file in the form of:
   a. a transcript of the court testimony.
   b. a copy of the written appraisal report that was the basis of their court testimony.
   c. Either of the above
   d. Both of the above

6. Which of the following **is not** a type of written appraisal report permitted by the USPAP?
   a. Summary appraisal report
   b. Self-contained appraisal report
   c. Complete appraisal report
   d. Restricted use appraisal report

7. Most self-contained appraisal reports:
   a. are narrative appraisal reports.
   b. are required by the USPAP to be narrative appraisal reports.
   c. are not permitted to be used in most Federal courts.
   d. All of the above.

8. The USPAP requires that a self-contained appraisal report clearly and accurately disclose all the:
   a. assumptions.
   b. hypothetical conditions.
   c. limiting conditions.
   d. All of the above

9. The USPAP requires that a summary appraisal report clearly and accurately disclose all the:
   a. assumptions.
   b. hypothetical conditions.
   c. limiting conditions.
   d. All of the above

10. The USPAP requires that a restricted-use appraisal report clearly and accurately disclose all the:
    a. assumptions.
    b. hypothetical conditions.
    c. limiting conditions.
    d. All of the above

11. Which of the following types of appraisal reports permits the scope of work to be summarized?
    a. Complete appraisal report
    b. Summary appraisal report
    c. Restricted appraisal report
    d. None of the above

12. A restricted use appraisal report is not intended to be used by:
    a. lending institutions.
    b. mortgage brokers.
    c. the public.
    d. All of the above

13. A restricted use appraisal report must:
    a. state the real property interest appraised.
    b. state the intended use of the appraisal.
    c. state the effective date of the appraisal.
    d. All of the above

ANSWERS TO REVIEW QUESTIONS

The answer to each question is indicated by the letter a, b, c or d. The explanation of the answer is indicated by the page number and on an arrow that points to the appropriate paragraph on the page of the text.

Q 14.1	b	Page 14-2
Q 14.2	b	Page 14-2
Q 14.3	b	Page 14-2
Q 14.4	c	Page 14-2
Q 14.5	c	Page 14-2
Q 14.6	c	Page 14-3
Q 14.7	a	Page 14-3
Q 14.8	d	Page 14-4
Q 14.9	d	Page 14-6
Q 14.10	d	Page 14-7
Q 14.11	b	Page 14-6
Q 14.12	c	Page 14-7
Q 14.13	d	Page 14-7

Residential Applications & Model Appraisals

"Everything is worth what its purchaser will pay for it."

Maxim 847
Publius Syrus, 1st c. B.C.

Important Words and Key Concepts

Words on this list are highlighted in this chapter
They are also defined in the Glossary at the back of this text

Appraisal Subcommittee

Appraiser Qualification Board

Appraisal Standards Board

Condemnation

Economic Feasibility

Fee Appraiser

Independent Contractor

Narrative Appraisal Report

The Appraisal Foundation

THE APPRAISAL PROFESSION

TYPES OF RESIDENTIAL ASSIGNMENTS

15.1 Real estate appraisals are generally made by staff appraisers in the organizations requiring such appraisals or by *fee appraisers*, who are *independent contractors*. Almost anyone the appraiser meets can be a potential source of business. The list of those seeking the services of a real estate appraiser includes:

Buyers and Sellers of Homes

Appraisers assist them in setting listing and offering prices and in making final decisions to complete a sale or purchase.

Lending Institutions

Appraisers receive a substantial amount of their work from lending institutions such as savings banks, commercial banks, credit unions, insurance companies, pension funds and investment trusts. A substantial amount of work is also received from mortgage brokers and management companies. Appraisers estimate the market value of residences being accepted as loan security. The trust departments of these organizations use appraisers for estate planning and estate disposal. Real estate departments use appraisers to help manage and plan their activities.

Investors

Appraisers help them acquire and dispose of real estate investments.

Architects

15.2 Appraisers help judge the *economic feasibility* of proposed projects as well as site selection and acquisitions.

Builders and Developers

Appraisers help them to make site acquisitions, develop sites to highest and best use, test the feasibility of projects, obtain mortgages and equity financing, attract investors and assist in the sale of projects.

Lawyers

15.3 Appraisers are hired on behalf of their clients by lawyers. Lawyers recommend appraisers to help divide property between disputing heirs, partners or clients. They use appraisers for *condemnation* cases, tax appeals, estate planning and disposal of estates and a variety of other uses.

Tenants

Appraisers help tenants estimate fair rental. In condemnation proceedings, tenants need appraisers to estimate their leasehold value (leasehold interests are those of the lessee, tenant or renter).

Insurers and the Insured

Appraisers estimate the insurable value of property to aid in determining the proper amount of insurance. Appraisers also play an important role in claims adjustments.

Accountants

Appraisers are recommended to the accountant's clients to help estimate the value of assets and to establish rates of depreciation.

Business Corporations

Appraisers help business corporations acquire and dispose of residential and commercial property, assist in the transfer of employees, evaluate real estate assets, develop real estate programs and plan real estate activities.

Non-profit Organizations

Appraisers assist non-profit organizations in purchase decisions and value the organization's holdings.

Government Agencies at Federal, State and Local Levels

Appraisers are hired by many government agencies who are all large users of appraisals. Some federal agencies that use appraisals are the Veterans Administration, Federal Housing Administration, Federal Home Loan Mortgage Corporation, General Services Administration, Internal Revenue Service, Post Office Department, and Farmers Home Administration. States condemn and purchase residential land for schools and other government buildings, parks, open space programs and wetlands. Local governments depend on appraisers in the process of acquiring property for schools and other government buildings. Redevelopment programs require appraisers for both acquisition and reuse programs. Ad valorem (property) taxes are based on real estate assessments (appraisals).

Public Utility Companies

Appraisers are needed by public utility companies for the acquisition of rights-of-way for utility wires, pipelines and other real estate acquisitions.

The list of users of residential appraisals is almost endless, and the need for appraisers appears to be constantly increasing and continues to change with the refinement of automated valuation models. The field presents good opportunities for those who are willing to acquire the necessary skills to serve the public as professionals.

THE DEFINITION OF A REAL ESTATE APPRAISAL

There is no one standard accepted definition of the words appraisal or real   estate appraisal. However, most of the accepted definitions incorporate the following seven principles:

1. An appraisal is an opinion of value.

2. The opinion must be appropriately supported with general and specific data.

3. It must be as of a specific date.

4. The value estimated must be defined.

5. The property being appraised must be adequately and accurately described.

6. The person making the appraisal must be qualified by reason of adequate education and experience.

7. The person making the appraisal must be unbiased and have no undisclosed interest in the property.

An appraisal is an appropriately supported objective and unbiased opinion of the value, as of a specific date, of an adequately and accurately described property, made by a qualified person who has no undisclosed interest in the property.

An appraisal may include such complicated considerations as various interests, equities, retrospective and prospective values and other conditions that are present. It may be based on hypothetical conditions, provided they are clearly stated and there is a reasonable probability that the assumptions will take place some time in the near future.

PURPOSE AND INTENDED USE OF AN APPRAISAL

The fundamental purpose of an appraisal is to estimate some kind of value. The need for an appraisal of market value may arise from many situations, including:

- Transfer of ownership.
- Financing and credit.
- Just compensation in condemnation (eminent domain) proceedings.
- As a basis for taxation.
- To establish rental schedules and lease provisions.
- Feasibility analysis.

In addition to the need for estimating market value, appraisals are also made to estimate:

- Insurable value.
- Going-concern value.

- Liquidation value.
- Assessed value (which may be a percentage of market value).

Although the list does not include all the needs for appraisals, it does indicate the broad scope of the professional appraiser's typical activities.

THE IMPORTANCE OF THE APPRAISER

The appraiser is frequently regarded by lenders and the public as the expert in evaluating a neighborhood's strengths and weaknesses. Accordingly, the appraiser must exercise this responsibility with care and be certain that a considered judgment about a community's trend is supportable by objective facts. Emotional public arguments or advocacy must never affect the professional appraiser's presentation of demonstrable facts. This is especially true when the appraiser speaks at a public hearing.

GROWTH OF PROFESSIONALISM IN REAL ESTATE APPRAISING

A profession is, by definition, a vocation that involves primarily intellectual activities and requires high levels of technical competence, individual responsibility and personal integrity. Historically, the first professionals were physicians and surgeons, professors, lawyers, accountants, engineers and the clergy. Today, a professional is a member of an organized vital vocation or activity in which the membership is highly competent, thoroughly honest and devoted to the ideal of performing a service to the maximum of their capacity, regardless of compensation. A professional has a responsibility to help make the world a better place in which to live.

The need for professional real estate appraisers came into focus with the collapse of real estate values during the depression of the 1930's. Prior to that time, real estate appraising as a vocation had been unstructured and little educational material was available, although as early as 1929, the National Association of Real Estate Boards had a publication called Standards of Appraisal Practice. To the early appraiser, market price was the equivalent of market value.

THE REGULATION OF REAL PROPERTY APPRAISERS

(Quoted from A Guide for Understanding the 2008 Real Property Appraiser Qualification Criteria, The Appraisal Foundation, Washington, DC, Revised January 2006)

"In response to the failure of a large number of savings and loan institutions in the 1980s, Congress conducted several hearings to determine the root cause of the crisis and took steps to ensure that a similar crisis would not occur in the future.

During the course of their investigation, Congress was surprised to learn that appraisers, the individuals determining the value of the underlying collateral of loans, were generally unregulated. While professional licensing issues generally fall into the domain of state governments, Congress was concerned about protecting the future integrity of deposit insurance funds."

Accordingly, when passing legislation in 1989 to address the financial institution crisis (known as the Financial Institutions Reform, Recovery and Enforcement Act or FIRREA), Congress included a provision known as Title XI mandating the regulation of real estate appraisers by the states. The regulatory program contained three components:

- each state government is to establish an appraiser regulatory body to issue licenses and certificates and to address enforcement of disciplinary issues;

- *The Appraisal Foundation* provides private sector expertise regarding appraisal standards and appraiser qualification;

- a small federal government agency, the (***Appraisal Subcommittee***) was created to oversee the program to ensure it remained consistent with the original intent of Congress.

State Appraiser Regulatory Agencies

Under Title XI each state was required to put in place a regulatory system that typically includes a board of five to nine individuals and support staff. The board members are generally appointed by the governor of the state and often include one or more members of the public who are not appraisers. The regulatory agency issues licenses and certificates to individuals who meet the Real Property Appraisal Qualification Criteria established by the ***Appraiser Qualification Board (AQB)*** of The Appraisal Foundation.

The state appraiser regulatory agencies must also investigate and take appropriate action on complaints they receive regarding the actions of appraisers. Although it can vary for state-to-state, disciplinary action taken against appraisers, such as fines, suspensions or revocation of licenses is often made public.

Private Sector Expertise

Congress also mandated that all appraisals connected to federally related transactions involving financial institutions that are regulated by the federal government would have to conform to the Uniform Standards of Professional Appraisal Practice (USPAP), the generally accepted appraisal performance standards promulgated by the **Appraisal Standards Board (ASB)** of The Appraisal Foundation. The state appraiser regulators also use USPAP when addressing disciplinary issues.

Congress gave The Appraisal Foundation considerable responsibilities that are traditionally under the purview of government agencies. Congress mandated that the state appraiser regulatory agencies must use the criteria adopted by the Appraiser Qualifications Board (AQB) of The Appraisal Foundation when issuing certificates to individuals. The criteria outlines minimum requirements in the areas of education, experience and continuing education. Individuals seeking to become state licensed or certified appraisers must also pass a comprehensive state examination that has been reviewed by the AQB.

In exchange for providing USPAP and the Real Property Appraiser Qualification Criteria, The Appraisal Foundation is eligible to receive federal grants; these grants are made at the discretion of the federal appraisal oversight agency know as the Appraisal Subcommittee to the real property work of the AQB and ASB.

Federal Government Oversight

Because the issue of regulating appraisers emanated from concerns about appraisal of collateral for loans made by financial institutions, Congress entrusted federal oversight to an entity known as the Appraisal Subcommittee of the Federal Financial Institutions Examination Council. The Examinations Council is an umbrella organization for all federal financial regulatory agencies, and its primary mission is to ensure that financial institution examiners are trained in a consistent manner. The Appraisal Subcommittee is composed of representatives from six governmental agencies and meets on a monthly basis.

The responsibilities of the Appraisal Subcommittee include:

- Oversight of the state appraiser regulatory programs to ensure consistency with the intent of Congress. This oversight includes periodic "site visits" to review the operations of state programs.

- Monitoring the activities of The Appraisal Foundation and providing grants for projects specifically related to Title XI work.

- Maintaining a National Registry of Appraisers and collecting registry fees. The fees collected ($25.00 from each appraiser annually) fund the operations of the Appraisal Subcommittee and provide funds for the above referenced grants to The Appraisal Foundation; and

- Reporting on an annual basis to the U.S. Congress.

When the appraiser regulatory system was first implemented in early 1990s, there was considerable reservations about the ability of government regulators and the private sector to work together. Today, a productive working relationship has developed between state and federal regulators and The Appraisal Foundation, and the appraiser regulatory system in the United States is generally working as Congress intended.

Professional Organizations and Designations

Some lenders formerly would only use appraisers who have designations from certain appraisal organizations. They believed that such a designated appraiser would be automatically qualified. This practice is now prohibited by federal law for any federally related appraisal.

The American Institute of Real Estate Appraisers (which awarded the RM and MAI designations) and the Society of Real Estate Appraisers (which awarded the SRA, SRPA and the SREA designations) have existed since before World War II. Both have a long history of rigid standards for awarding their designations. To earn any of these designations, an appraiser must have taken several courses, have years of proven experience, produced demonstration appraisals and passed several examinations. On January 1, 1991 the A.I.R.E.A. and the Society officially merged into The Appraisal Institute.

There are many other national appraisal organizations, which award designations to their members plus some regional and state organizations too. Some of the larger of these organizations are the National Association of Independent Fee Appraisers, National Association of Realtors, American Society of Appraisers, Columbia Society of Appraisers, National Association of Master Appraisers and the National Association of Real Estate Appraisers.

There are some good appraisers who, for various reasons, have decided not to apply for any designation. Many feel that the license or certification that they have obtained is sufficient to acknowledge their level of accomplishment. Lenders who refuse to consider appraisers who do not have designations may be eliminating some well-qualified appraisers who are capable of doing their work. Also it is illegal for a lender to use designations as the criteria for selecting appraisers for federally related work assignments.

WHAT APPRAISERS HAVE TO SELL

An appraiser basically has five things to sell a client:

A.	**A**dequate knowledge
E.	**E**xperience
I.	**I**ntegrity
O.	**O**bjectivity
U.	**U**ncompromising willingness to do the work on a timely basis for a mutually agreed upon fee

Adequate Knowledge

A qualified appraiser should have a good general education, have taken a variety of appraisal courses and seminars, and be keeping current with continuing education in the field.

In a profession as complex as real estate appraising, most lenders feel that a minimum of a high school education is required. The Appraisal Institute now requires a college degree for their designations. However, this is a recent requirement and many of their older members are not college graduates. New requirements for general certification going into effect January 1, 2008 require a college education or equivalent.

Since the appraisal profession and appraisal licensing and certification requirements are changing all the time, it is necessary that the appraiser keep up with current appraisal regulations. Many feel the best way to insure this is to require appraisers to attend continuing education courses and/or seminars on a regular basis. However, it should be kept in mind that it is desirable for an appraiser to also keep current by reading the available appraisal journals and other appraisal publications.

Experience

There is an old saying that nothing is a substitute for experience. This is not what a new appraiser wants to hear. The reality is that appraising is still not a science but rather an art. Often, when it comes to making adjustments, rating the neighborhood and/or the improvements and reconciling differences throughout the appraisal, the appraiser must rely primarily upon judgment.

Since no one is born with experience, a substitute has to be found for the new appraiser. Appraisal experience can be obtained by working as an appraiser, lender, contractor or Realtor. At least some of the required experience should be obtained by actually making residential appraisals.

It is appropriate for an inexperienced appraiser to work with a seasoned appraiser who reviews their work and jointly assumes responsibility for it by signing the appraisal report as the review appraiser. It is a good policy to require that the review appraiser, who jointly signs the appraisal, also inspect the interior of the subject property when the primary appraiser is very inexperienced, when the value of the house is high, when the house is old, or when the property has some significant atypical characteristics. Many people feel that at least two years experience is a minimum requirement for an appraiser to be able to sign an appraisal without supervisory review.

Integrity

There are a variety of ways a client can check on the integrity of an appraiser. The most common is by checking personal, general business and professional references. Others include talking with other appraisers. The participation of the appraiser in community activities and in their professional association are other indicators of their reputation in the community and their standing among peers.

Objectivity

The appraiser signs a certificate with each appraisal saying that they have no present or future contemplated interest in the property being appraised. This includes making appraisals for friends and relatives.

Unfortunately, clients are sometimes their own worst enemy when it comes to appraiser objectivity. It does not take long for an appraiser to figure out whether a client is primarily interested in making loans regardless of the value of the loan security or whether they are primarily interested in obtaining the true value of the property in order to protect their loan portfolio.

The amount of pressure that some clients put on appraisers is well documented. Many people feel such pressure is a primary cause of poor appraisals. It is up to the clients to communicate to the appraiser how they really feel. If they want true value estimates, they must make it clear to the appraiser that the assignments and payments they receive in the future will not be in jeopardy if they produce appraisals where the appraised value is less than the contract price of the pending loan application.

Uncompromised Willingness To Do Work On a Timely Basis for a Mutually Agreed Upon Fee

The final step in selecting appraisers is finding those who are willing and able to do the client's work on a timely basis for a mutually agreed upon fee. The client should investigate the appraiser's capacity to produce work. If the appraiser has a one, two or three person operation, the amount of work they can turn out is limited. Usually the appraiser has other clients who also want their work done on a timely basis.

The best arrangement is when the client and appraiser agree upon the approximate number of appraisals that will be ordered in any given period of time. Unfortunately, clients cannot always control the number of appraisals they need and when they get busy, may give appraisers more work than they can handle. It seems to be a pattern that in the spring when business traditionally picks up, appraisers become swamped and get behind in their work.

Clients have different policies on how they pay appraisers. Some large lenders have a published fee schedule. Appraisers must decide whether they are willing to accept the offered fee in order to get assignments from the lender. Other lenders negotiate fee schedules with each appraiser, taking into consideration the appraiser's knowledge, experience and the length of time they have been working together. Clients should recognize that some appraisal assignments require substantially more work than others. Often the fee will be adjusted to reflect the extra work required to make an appraisal of a high value home, waterfront property, historic property, contemporary house and other houses with significant atypical characteristics.

PROFESSIONAL CONDUCT

The essence of our civilization is that people acknowledge the limited right of society to control the activities of individuals for the benefit of the public. In addition, many people conduct their own activities at a higher level than is required by the law or by their fellow humans.

Levels of Professional Conduct

There are several levels of conduct.

FIRST LEVEL OF CONDUCT
The first level of conduct deals with the laws that apply to all people. In the United States, there are federal, state and local laws. Everyone is required to obey these laws. It makes little difference if one agrees or disagrees with them. If someone does not obey a law, society has the right to punish the lawbreaker. (Of course, not all laws are enforced uniformly and many of the people who break laws are not necessarily caught or punished.)

SECOND LEVEL OF CONDUCT
The second level of conduct consists of the laws that apply to certain groups of people. These are laws and rules that regulate special activities such as those of lawyers and doctors. Often one has to obtain a license or permit to participate in such activities. For example, in the real estate field, one must have a license to sell or rent real estate for compensation. Real estate brokers are subject to special laws that control their activities. Other common examples at this level are the laws pertaining to driving automobiles, building houses, practicing medicine, or running a store. Such regulatory laws apply only when one voluntarily engages in a special activity controlled by the legislation or regulation. In all states, real estate appraising for federally related institutions will fall into this category of control.

THIRD LEVEL OF CONDUCT

The third level of conduct consists of The Uniform Standards of Professional Appraisal Practice and the various codes of ethics that have been developed by the professional organizations to control the activities of their members. The members of the organization agree to be governed by its code of ethics as one of the conditions of membership. The organization itself develops and enforces the code of ethics. Violators may be disciplined in a variety of ways. The maximum penalty usually is expulsion from the group. The American Medical Association, the American Bar Association, the National Association of Realtors as well as many other organizations have such codes governing the conduct of their members with the public, their clients and among their own members.

FOURTH LEVEL OF CONDUCT

The fourth level of conduct encompasses the personal rules people set for themselves to control their own lives according to their personal (and religious) beliefs. Many everyday decisions people make about their professional activities and conduct fall outside the scope of the three preceding levels of conduct. The decision regarding how to act must be made by the individual based on personal standards of conduct. The rewards for functioning at this higher level are personal satisfaction and approval by one's family and peers. The punishment is from one's own conscience and disapproval by others.

APPRAISAL REPORTS

The vast majority of residential appraisals are made on the forms issued by Freddie Mac and Fannie Mae. A significant number of appraisals are made on the forms required by the Employee Relocation Council. Recently the Appraisal Institute and some of the software vendors have developed forms for appraisals that do not require the use of the Freddie Mac/Fannie Mae and the ERC Forms.

The following is a summary of the nine Fannie Mae appraisal forms that were revised in March 2005. HUD/FHA, the VA and other governmental organizations have also approved many of these forms for use. Any of these forms with prior revision dates can no longer be used. From time to time Fannie Mae revises their forms. The best way to be certain you are using the most current version is to check on the Fannie Mae web site: www.efanniemae.com

FANNIE MAE/FREDDIE MAC APPRAISAL REPORT FORMS

When Fannie Mae revised all of their appraisal forms in March 2005 they issued Fannie Mae Announcement 05-02, which is the source of this information:

Uniform Residential Appraisal Report

Uniform Residential Appraisal Report (Fannie Mae form 1004) for an appraisal of a one-unit property (including an individual unit in a PUD project) based on an interior and exterior property inspection.

Exterior-Only Inspection Residential Appraisal Report

Exterior-Only Inspection Residential Appraisal Report (Fannie Mae form 2055) for an appraisal of a one-unit property (including a individual unit in a PUD project) based on an exterior-only property inspection.

Manufactured Home Appraisal Report

Manufactured Home Appraisal Report (Fannie Mae form 1004C) for an appraisal of a one-unit manufactured home (including a manufactured home in a PUD), condominium or cooperative project) based on an interior and exterior property inspection.

Individual Condominium Unit Appraisal Report

Individual Condominium Unit Appraisal Report (Fannie Mae form 1073) for an appraisal of an individual condominium unit based on an interior and exterior property inspection.

Exterior-Only Inspection
Individual Condominium Unit Appraisal Report

Exterior-Only Inspection Individual Condominium Unit Appraisal Report (Fannie Mae form 1075) for an appraisal of an individual condominium unit based on an exterior only property inspection.

Individual Cooperative Unit Appraisal Report

Individual Cooperative Unit Appraisal Report (Fannie Mae form 2090) for an appraisal of an individual cooperative unit based on an interior and exterior property inspection.

Exterior-Only Inspection
Individual Cooperative Unit Appraisal Report

Exterior-Only Inspection Individual Cooperative Unit Appraisal Report (Fannie Mae form 2095) for an appraisal of an individual cooperative unit based on an exterior only property inspection.

Small Income Property Appraisal Report

Small Income Property Appraisal Report (Fannie Mae form 1025) for an appraisal of a two-unit to four-unit property (including an two unit to four unit property in a PUD project) based on an interior and exterior property inspection.

Appraisal Update and/or Completion Report

Appraisal Update and/or Completion Report (Fannie Mae form 1004D) for appraisal updates and/or completion reports for all one-unit to four-unit appraisal reports.

There are also two new Review Appraiser forms in this series.

Uniform Residential Appraisal Report (URAR) Model Appraisal

On the following pages are examples of a completed Fannie Mae/Freddie Mac 2005 Uniform Residential Appraisal Report and Exterior Only Appraisal Report of the same property. The forms have been cut up to permit a larger and easier to read display of the form.

URAR Model Appraisal: Subject & Contract

The purpose of this summary appraisal report is to provide the lender/client with an accurate, and adequately supported, opinion of the market value of the subject property.

SUBJECT	Property Address 420 Gladville Ave. City Bloomville State IL Zip Code 60611
	Borrower Will N. Buyer Owner of Public Record County Lake County
	Legal Description see attached addenda sheet
	Assessor's Parcel # 7/63 Tax Year 200_ R.E. Taxes $ 5,320.00
	Neighborhood Name Wrightville Map Reference Census Tract
	Occupant [X] Owner [ ] Tenant [ ] Vacant Special Assessments $ none [ ] PUD HOA $ [ ] per year [ ] per month
	Property Rights Appraised [X] Fee Simple [ ] Leasehold [ ] Other (describe)
	Assignment Type [X] Purchase Transaction [ ] Refinance Transaction [ ] Other (describe)
	Lender/Client Easy Money Institution Address Center City, USA
	Is the subject property currently offered for sale or has it been offered for sale in the twelve months prior to the effective date of this appraisal? [X] Yes [ ] No
	Report data source(s) used, offerings price(s), and date(s). offering price $180,000 Lake County MLS updated 1 month ago

CONTRACT

I [X] did [ ] did not analyze the contract for sale for the subject purchase transaction. Explain the results of the analysis of the contract for sale or why the analysis was not performed. Sales price within 10% of offering price, typical financing, no personal property, special financing or sales concessions reported

Contract Price $ 170,000   Date of Contract 2/25/200_ Is the property seller the owner of public record? [X] Yes [ ] No Data Souce(s) Deed

Is there any financial assistance (loan charges, sale concessions, gift or downpayment assistance, etc.) to be paid by any party on behalf of the borrower? [ ] Yes [X] No

If Yes, report the total dollar amount and describe the items to be paid. None

URAR Model Appraisal: Neighborhood & Site

Note: Race and the racial composition of the neighborhood are not appraisal factors.

	Neighborhood Characteristics			One-Unit Housing Trends				One-Unit Housing		Present Land Use %	
Location	[ ] Urban	[X] Suburban	[ ] Rural	Property Values	[ ] Increasing	[X] Stable	[ ] Declining	PRICE	AGE	One-Unit	50 %
Built-Up	[X] Over 75%	[ ] 25-75%	[ ] Under 25%	Demand/Supply	[ ] Shortage	[X] In Balance	[ ] Over Supply	$ (000)	(yrs)	2-4 Unit	6 %
Growth	[ ] Rapid	[X] Stable	[ ] Slow	Marketing Time	[X] Under 3 mths	[ ] 3-6 mths	[ ] Over 6 mths	140 Low	30	Multi-Family	6 %
								190 High	60	Commercial	13 %
								160 Pred.	35	Other see below 25 %	

Neighborhood Boundaries Wrightville neighborhood boundaries shown on neighborhood map in addenda

Neighborhood Description Present landuse 5% industrial, 5% parks, and 15% vacant

Market Conditions (including support for the above conclusions) Typically there are about a dozen houses for sale in Wrightville. Asking prices range from $140,000 to $290,000. Sales average 4 per month. Ample conventional financing available. Loan discounts, interest buydowns, and other concessions are not common.

SITE

Dimensions 700' x 115'	Area 11,500 sq. ft. Shape rectangle View average
Specific Zoning Classification single family res.	Zoning Description single family only

Zoning Compliance [X] Legal [ ] Legal Nonconforming (Grandfathered Use) [ ] No Zoning [ ] Illegal (describe)

Is the highest and best use of subject property as improved (or as proposed per plans and specifications) the present use? [X] Yes [ ] No If No, describe. Except for physical, functional, and external obsolescence described in the Cost Approach

Utilities	Public	Other (describe)		Public	Other (describe)	Off-site Improvements—Type	Public	Private
Electricity	[X]		Water	[X]		Street	[X]	
Gas	[X]		Sanitary Sewer	[X]		Alley None		

FEMA Special Flood Hazard Area [ ] Yes [X] No FEMA Flood Zone c   FEMA Map # 095060 0003   FEMA Map Date 11/10/200_

Are the utilities and/or off-site improvements typical for the market area? [X] Yes [ ] No If No, describe.

Are there any adverse site conditions or external factors (easements, encroachments, environmental conditions, land uses, etc.)? [X] Yes [ ] No If Yes, describe.

Typical utility easements for electricity, sewer, and telephone. No effect on market value. No apparent adverse easements, encroachments, special assessments, slide areas, etc.

URAR Model Appraisal: Improvements

General Description	Foundation	Exterior Description materials/condition	Interior materials/condition
Units ☒ One ☐ One with Accessory Unit	☐ Concrete Slab ☒ Crawl Space	Foundation Walls Concrete	Floors Hardwood/Ave.
# of Stories	☐ Full Basement ☐ Partial Basement	Exterior Walls Brick Veneer	Walls Plaster/Ave.
Type ☒ Det. ☐ Att. ☐ S-Det./End Unit	Basement Area N/A sq. ft.	Roof Surface Asph. Shingle.	Trim/Finish Wood/Ave.
☒ Existing ☐ Proposed ☐ Under Const.	Basement Finish N/A %	Gutters & Downspouts Aluminum	Bath Floor Cer. Tile/Ave.
Design (Style) Ranch	☐ Outside Entry/Exit ☐ Sump Pump	Window Type Wood/D.H.	Bath Wainscot Cer. Tile/Ave.
Year Built 197	Evidence of ☐ Infestation	Storm Sash/Insulated Comb. Alum	Car Storage 2 ☐ None
Effective Age (Yrs) 30 Yrs	☐ Dampness ☐ Settlement	Screens Comb. Alum	☐ Driveway # of Cars
Attic ☒ None	Heating ☐ FWA ☒ HWBB ☐ Radiant	Amenities ☐ Woodstove(s) #	Driveway Surface Paved
☐ Drop Stair ☐ Stairs	☐ Other Fuel Gas	☒ Fireplace(s) # ☐ Fence	☒ Garage # of Cars 2
☐ Floor ☐ Scuttle	Cooling ☐ Central Air Conditioning	☐ Patio/Deck ☐ Porch	☐ Carport # of Cars
☐ Finished ☐ Heated	☐ Individual ☒ Other	☐ Pool ☐ Other	☐ Att. ☐ Det. ☐ Built-in

Appliances ☒ Refrigerator ☒ Range/Oven ☐ Dishwasher ☒ Disposal ☐ Microwave ☐ Washer/Dryer ☒ Other (describe)   Hood with Fan

Finished area above grade contains: 7   Rooms   3   Bedrooms   2   Bath(s) 1,888   Square Feet of Gross Living Area Above Grade

Additional features (special energy efficient items, etc.) Domestic solar hot water system (50 gal.) adds $2,500 value, based on matched pairs of sales. They cost new (Continued in Addenda)

Describe the condition of the property (including needed repairs, deterioration, renovations, remodeling, etc.). There are no significant repairs needed not. There is a general lack of storage space. No eating area in kitchen and no basement. The market recognizes these deficiencies. Nearby railroad and industrial area estimated to cause 5% external obsolescence. (Continued in addenda)

Are there any physical deficiencies or adverse conditions that affect the livability, soundness, or structural integrity of the property? ☐ Yes ☒ No If Yes, describe
Based on my careful inspection of the exterior and interior of the subject property I found no evidence of apparent physical deficiencies or adverse conditions that effect the livability, soundness or structural integrity of the property.

Does the property generally conform to the neighborhood (functional utility, style, condition, use, construction, etc.)? ☒ Yes ☐ No If No, describe

URAR MODEL APPRAISAL - Sales Comparison Approach Grid (1)

There are **10** comparable properties currently offered for sale in the subject neighborhood ranging in price from $ **130,000** to $ **200,000**				
There are **25** comparable sales in the subject neighborhood within the past twelve months ranging in sale price from $ **135,000** to $ **185,000**				

FEATURE	SUBJECT	COMPARABLE SALE # 1		COMPARABLE SALE # 2		COMPARABLE SALE # 3	
Address	420 Gladville Ave. Bloomville, IL 60611	341 Pine Road Bloomville, IL		413 Cedar Street Bloomville, IL		210 Hoover Road Bloomville, IL	
Proximity to Subject		1 Block south		1 Block west		7 Blocks south	
Sale Price	$ 170,000	$ 140,000		$ 146,000		$ 164,000	
Sale Price/Gross Liv. Area	$ 90.04 sq. ft.	$ 76.92 sq. ft.		73.92 sq. ft.		86.32 sq. ft.	
Data Source(s)		MLS Service		MLS Service		Appraiser's File	
Verification Source(s)		Listing Agent		Buyer		Seller	
VALUE ADJUSTMENTS	DESCRIPTION	DESCRIPTION	+(-) $ Adjustment	DESCRIPTION	+(-) $ Adjustment	DESCRIPTION	+(-) $ Adjustment
Sale or Financing		None		None		None	-10,000
Concessions		Equal		Equal		Equal	
Date of Sale/Time		1/0 - 2/0		11/0 - 1/0		12/0 - 1/0	
Location	Average	Avg./Equal		Avg./Equal		Avg./Equal	
Leasehold/Fee Simple	Fee Simple	Fee Simple		Fee Simple		Fee Simple	
Site	11,500 sq. ft.	About equal		About equal		About equal	
View	Avg./Typical	Equal		Equal		Equal	
Design (Style)	Ranch/Avg.	Equal		Equal		Equal	
Quality of Construction	Average	Avg./Equal		Avg./Equal		Avg./Equal	
Actual Age	30 yrs	30 yrs		30 yrs		30 yrs	
Condition	Average	Avg./Equal		Avg./Equal		Avg./Equal	
Above Grade	Total / Bdrms. / Baths	Total / Bdrms / Baths		Total / Bdrms. / Baths		Total / Bdrms. / Baths	
Room Count	7 / 3 / 2.00	7 / 3 / 2.00		7 / 3 / 2.00		7 / 3 / 2.00	
Gross Living Area	1,888 sq. ft.	1,820 sq. ft.	+3,400	1,975 sq. ft.	+650	1,900 sq. ft.	-600
Basement & Finished	Crawl space	Crawl space		Crawl space		Crawl space	
Rooms Below Grade		Equal		Equal			
Functional Utility	Avg./Poor stor.	Equal/poor stor.		Equal/poor stor.		Equal/poor stor.	
Heating/Cooling	HWBB/Individual	Equal/Equal		Equal/Equal		Equal/Equal	
Energy Efficient Items	DomSolar HW	None	+5,000	None	+5,000	DomSolar HW	
Garage/Carport	2 Car Gar. Att.	2 Car Gar. Att.		2 Car Gar. Att.		2 Car Gar. Att.	
Porch/Patio/Deck	144 sq. ft. Br.	No porch	+2,000	No porch	+2,000	Open porch	
Fireplaces	1 Fireplace	None	+4,000	1 Equal		1 Equal	
Kitchen eating area	None	None/equal		None/equal		None/equal	
Net Adjustment (Total)		X + ☐ -	$ 14,400	X + ☐ -	$ 7,650	☐ + X -	$ -10,600
Adjusted Sale Price of Comparables		Net Adj: 10% Gross Adj : 10%	$ 154,400	Net Adj: 5% Gross Adj: 5%	$ 153,650	Net Adj: -6% Gross Adj: 6%	$ 153,400

URAR Model Appraisal: Sales Comparison Approach (2)

I [X] did [ ] did not research the sale or transfer history of the subject property and comparable sales (list source(s))

My research [ ] did [X] did not reveal any prior sales or transfers of the subject property for the three years prior to the effective date of this appraisal.

Data source(s): Sales recorded in county records

My research [X] did [ ] did not reveal any prior sales or transfers of the comparable sales for the year prior to the date of sale of the comparable sale.

Data source(s): Sales recorded in county records

Report the results of the research and analysis of the prior sale or transfer history of the subject property and comparable sales (report additional prior sales on page 3).

ITEM	SUBJECT	COMPARABLE SALE #1	COMPARABLE SALE #2	COMPARABLE SALE #3
Date of Prior Sale/Transfer	8 years ago	6 months ago	Over one year	Over one year
Price of Prior Sale/Transfer	$77,000	$138,000	unknown	unknown
Data Source(s)	Deed	MLS	MLS	MLS
Effective Date of Data Source(s)	Current	One month ago	One month ago	One month ago

Analysis of prior sale or transfer history of the subject property and comparable sales The subject property sold 10 years ago for $77,000. Since then, prices have approximately doubled. Comparable Sale #1 sold 2 years ago for $131,000. The owner was transferred and the house resold this year for $140,000. There were no sales within the past year of Comparable Sales #2 & #3. There is no evidence of flipping or unusual price trends in the neighborhood.

Summary of Sales Comparison Approach Subject property is typical of many houses in the neighborhood, as are all of the comparable sales. Size adjustments were based on $50 per sq. ft. of GLA difference, which is the approximate value of the comparable improvements (after deducting their site value). Fireplaces are estimated to add $4,000 value. Porches add value approximately equal to their depreciated cost, $5,000. Domestic Hot Water Heating system adjustment is taken from market by market pairs (continued in addenda).

Indicated Value by: Sales Comparison Approach $ 154,000

URAR Model Appraisal: Reconciliation

Indicated Value by Sales Comparison Approach $ 154,000   Cost Approach (if developed) $ 155,000   Income Approach (if developed) $ 156,160

The best indication of value was the Sales Comparison Approach. There was a substantial amount of good data available. It was well supported by the Cost Approach and Income Approach. The $154,000 estimated by the Sales Comparison Approach is the final estimate of value on the date of the appraisal.

This appraisal is made [ ] "as is", [ ] subject to completion per plans and specifications on the basis of a hypothetical condition that the improvements have been completed, [ ] subject to the following repairs or alterations on the basis of a hypothetical condition that the repairs or alterations have been completed, or [X] subject to the following required inspection based on the extraordinary assumption that the condition or deficiency does not require alteration or repair: Termite and home inspection is recommended because of property age and condition.

Based on a visual inspection of the exterior areas of the subject property from at least the street, defined scope of work, statement of assumptions and limiting conditions, and appraiser's certification, my (our) opinion of the market value, as defined, of the real property that is the subject of this report is

$ 154,000 , as of   200   , which is the date of inspection and the effective date of this appraisal.

URAR Model Appraisal: Additional Comments

URAR Model Appraisal: Cost Approach

COST APPROACH TO VALUE (not required by Fannie Mac)				
Provide adequate information for the lender/client to replicate your cost figures and calculations				
Support for the opinion of site value (summary of comparable land sales or other methods for estimating site value) Assessor states sites are typically 30% of total value. Typical neighborhood value 160,000 x 30% = 48,000. Last lot sold for $50,000. Developer sold nearby unlandscaped lots for $35,000 to $40,000. Subject lot is near railroad station. Estimated value of subject site: $40,000.				
ESTIMATED [X] REPRODUCTION OR [ ] REPLACEMENT COST NEW	OPINION OF SITE VALUE			=$ 40,000
Source of cost data Sheriff and Slow	Dwelling 1,888 Sq. Ft. @ $ 107			=$ 202,016
Quality rating from cost service Ave Effective date of cost data 3/12/200	144 Sq. Ft. @ $ 27			=$ 3,888
Comments on Cost Approach (gross living area calculations, depreciation, etc.)	Domestic Solar Hot Water Heater			6,000
Physical deterioration 40%	Garage/Carport 506 Sq. Ft. @ $ 32			$ 16,182
Functional obsolescence 8%	Total Estimate of Cost new			=$ 228,086
Economic obsolescence 5%	Less Physical 40 Functional 8 External 5			
	Depreciation 91,238 10,849 8,285			$ 108,482
See addenda for additional comments	Depreciated Cost of Improvements			=$ 119,614
	"As-is" Value of Site Improvements			=$ 6,000
Estimated Remaining Economic Life (HUD and VA only) 45	Years Indicated Value By Cost Approach			=$ 165,614

URAR Model Appraisal: Income Approach (GMRM)

INCOME APPROACH TO VALUE (not required by Fannie Mac)				
Estimated Monthly Market Rent $ 1,280 X Gross Multiplier 122 = $ 156,160 Indicated Value by Income Approach				
Summary of Income (including support for market rent and GRM) See addenda for additional comments				

URAR MODEL APPRAISAL: PUD Information

PROJECT INFORMATION FOR PUDs (if applicable)		
Is the developer/builder in control of the Homeowner's Association (HOA)? [ ] Yes [X] No Unit type(s) [X] Detached [ ] Attached		
Provide the following information for PUDs ONLY if the developer/builder is in control of the HOA and the subject property is an attached dwelling unit.		
Legal Name of Project Wrightville Acres PUD, Inc.		
Total number of phases 1 Total number of units 36 Total number of units sold 36		
Total number of units rented 2* Total number of units for sale 3** Data source Adam L. Clark, Pres HOA		
Was the project created by the conversion of existing building(s) into a PUD? [ ] Yes [X] No If Yes, date of conversion.		
Does the project contain any multi-dwelling units? [ ] Yes [X] No Data source.		
Are the units, common elements, and recreation facilities complete? [X] Yes [ ] No If No, describe the status of completion.		
*Rented houses are not owned by the developer. **The developer does not own the units for sale.		
Are the common elements leased to or by the Homeowner's Association? [ ] Yes [X] No If Yes, describe the rental terms and options.		
Describe common elements and recreational facilities. Small park with swings and sand box, bike paths, entrance signs and light, park lights.		

Freddie Mac Form 2055 March 2005

Fannie Mae Form 2055 March 2005

ClickFORMS Appraisal Software 800-622-8727

Page   3 of 3

URAR Model Appraisal: Page 4

Exterior-Only Inspection Residential Appraisal Report

This report form is designed to report an appraisal of a one-unit property or a one-unit property with an accessory unit; including a unit in a planned unit development (PUD). This report form is not designed to report an appraisal of a manufactured home or a unit in a condominium or cooperative project.

This appraisal report is subject to the following scope of work, intended use, intended user, definition of market value, statement of assumptions and limiting conditions, and certifications. Modifications, additions, or deletions to the intended use, intended user, definition of market value, or assumptions and limiting conditions are not permitted. The appraiser may expand the scope of work to include any additional research or analysis necessary based on the complexity of this appraisal assignment. Modifications or deletions to the certifications are also not permitted. However, additional certifications that do not constitute material alterations to this appraisal report, such as those required by law or those related to the appraiser's continuing education or membership in an appraisal organization, are permitted.

SCOPE OF WORK: The scope of work for this appraisal is defined by the complexity of this appraisal assignment and the reporting requirements of this appraisal report form, including the following definition of market value, statement of assumptions and limiting conditions, and certifications. The appraiser must, at a minimum: (1) perform a visual inspection of the exterior areas of the subject property from at least the street, (2) inspect the neighborhood, (3) inspect each of the comparable sales from at least the street, (4) research, verify, and analyze data from reliable public and/or private sources, and (5) report his or her analysis, opinions, and conclusions in this appraisal report.

The appraiser must be able to obtain adequate information about the physical characteristics (including, but not limited to, condition, room count, gross living area, etc.) of the subject property from the exterior only and reliable public and/or private sources to perform this appraisal. The appraiser should use the same type of data sources that he or she uses for comparable sales such as, but not limited to, multiple listing services, tax and assessment records, prior inspections, appraisal files, information provided by the property owner, etc.

INTENDED USE: The intended use of this appraisal report is for the lender/client to evaluate the property that is the subject of this appraisal for a mortgage finance transaction.

INTENDED USER: The intended user of this appraisal report is the lender/client.

DEFINITION OF MARKET VALUE: The most probable price which a property should bring in a competitive and open market under all conditions requisite to a fair sale, the buyer and seller, each acting prudently, knowledgeably and assuming the price is not affected by undue stimulus. Implicit in this definition is the consummation of a sale as of a specified date and the passing of title from seller to buyer under conditions whereby: (1) buyer and seller are typically motivated; (2) both parties are well informed or well advised, and each acting in what he or she considers his or her own best interest; (3) a reasonable time is allowed for exposure in the open market; (4) payment is made in terms of cash in U.S. dollars or in terms of financial arrangements comparable thereto; and (5) the price represents the normal consideration for the property sold unaffected by special or creative financing or sales concessions granted by anyone associated with the sale.

*Adjustments to the comparables must be made for special or creative financing or sales concessions. No adjustments are necessary for those costs which are normally paid by sellers as a result of tradition or law in a market area; these costs are readily identifiable since the seller pays these costs in virtually all sales transactions. Special or creative financing adjustments can be made to the comparable property by comparisons to financing terms offered by a third party institutional lender that is not already involved in the property or transaction. Any adjustment should not be calculated on a mechanical dollar for dollar cost of the financing or concession but the dollar amount of any adjustment should approximate the market's reaction to the financing or concessions based on the appraiser's judgment.

STATEMENT OF ASSUMPTIONS AND LIMITING CONDITIONS: The appraiser's certification in this report is subject to the following assumptions and limiting conditions:

1. The appraiser will not be responsible for matters of a legal nature that affect either the property being appraised or the title to it, except for information that he or she became aware of during the research involved in performing this appraisal. The appraiser assumes that the title is good and marketable and will not render any opinions about the title.

2. The appraiser has examined the available flood maps that are provided by the Federal Emergency Management Agency (or other data sources) and has noted in this appraisal report whether any portion of the subject site is located in an identified Special Flood Hazard Area. Because the appraiser is not a surveyor, he or she makes no guarantees, express or implied, regarding this determination.

3. The appraiser will not give testimony or appear in court because he or she made an appraisal of the property in question, unless specific arrangements to do so have been made beforehand, or as otherwise required by law.

4. The appraiser has noted in this appraisal report any adverse conditions (such as needed repairs, deterioration, the presence of hazardous wastes, toxic substances, etc.) observed during the inspection of the subject property or that he or she became aware of during the research involved in performing this appraisal. Unless otherwise stated in this appraisal report, the appraiser has no knowledge of any hidden or unapparent physical deficiencies or adverse conditions of the property (such as, but not limited to, needed repairs, deterioration, the presence of hazardous wastes, toxic substances, adverse environmental conditions, etc.) that would make the property less valuable, and has assumed that there are no such conditions and makes no guarantees or warranties, express or implied. The appraiser will not be responsible for any such conditions that do exist or for any engineering or testing that might be required to discover whether such conditions exist. Because the appraiser is not an expert in the field of environmental hazards, this appraisal report must not be considered as an environmental assessment of the property.

5. The appraiser has based his or her appraisal report and valuation conclusion for an appraisal that is subject to satisfactory completion, repairs, or alterations on the assumption that the completion, repairs, or alterations of the subject property will be performed in a professional manner.

URAR Model Appraisal: Page 5

Uniform Residential Appraisal Report

File #

APPRAISER'S CERTIFICATION: The Appraiser certifies and agrees that:

1. I have, at a minimum, developed and reported this appraisal in accordance with the scope of work requirements stated in this appraisal report.

2. I performed a complete visual inspection of the interior and exterior areas of the subject property. I reported the condition of the improvements in factual, specific terms. I identified and reported the physical deficiencies that could affect the livability, soundness, or structural integrity of the property.

3. I performed this appraisal in accordance with the requirements of the Uniform Standards of Professional Appraisal Practice that were adopted and promulgated by the Appraisal Standards Board of The Appraisal Foundation and that were in place at the time this appraisal report was prepared.

4. I developed my opinion of the market value of the real property that is the subject of this report based on the sales comparison approach to value. I have adequate comparable market data to develop a reliable sales comparison approach for this appraisal assignment. I further certify that I considered the cost and income approaches to value but did not develop them, unless otherwise indicated in this report.

5. I researched, verified, analyzed, and reported on any current agreement for sale for the subject property, any offering for sale of the subject property in the twelve months prior to the effective date of this appraisal, and the prior sales of the subject property for a minimum of three years prior to the effective date of this appraisal, unless otherwise indicated in this report.

6. I researched, verified, analyzed, and reported on the prior sales of the comparable sales for a minimum of one year prior to the date of sale of the comparable sale, unless otherwise indicated in this report.

7. I selected and used comparable sales that are locationally, physically, and functionally the most similar to the subject property.

8. I have not used comparable sales that were the result of combining a land sale with the contract purchase price of a home that has been built or will be built on the land.

9. I have reported adjustments to the comparable sales that reflect the market's reaction to the differences between the subject property and the comparable sales.

10. I verified, from a disinterested source, all information in this report that was provided by parties who have a financial interest in the sale or financing of the subject property.

11. I have knowledge and experience in appraising this type of property in this market area.

12. I am aware of, and have access to, the necessary and appropriate public and private data sources, such as multiple listing services, tax assessment records, public land records and other such data sources for the area in which the property is located.

13. I obtained the information, estimates, and opinions furnished by other parties and expressed in this appraisal report from reliable sources that I believe to be true and correct.

14. I have taken into consideration the factors that have an impact on value with respect to the subject neighborhood, subject property, and the proximity of the subject property to adverse influences in the development of my opinion of market value. I have noted in this appraisal report any adverse conditions (such as, but not limited to, needed repairs, deterioration, the presence of hazardous wastes, toxic substances, adverse environmental conditions, etc.) observed during the inspection of the subject property or that I became aware of during the research involved in performing this appraisal. I have considered these adverse conditions in my analysis of the property value, and have reported on the effect of the conditions on the value and marketability of the subject property.

15. I have not knowingly withheld any significant information from this appraisal report and, to the best of my knowledge, all statements and information in this appraisal report are true and correct.

16. I stated in this appraisal report my own personal, unbiased, and professional analysis, opinions, and conclusions, which are subject only to the assumptions and limiting conditions in this appraisal report.

17. I have no present or prospective interest in the property that is the subject of this report, and I have no present or prospective personal interest or bias with respect to the participants in the transaction. I did not base, either partially or completely, my analysis and/or opinion of market value in this appraisal report on the race, color, religion, sex, age, marital status, handicap, familial status, or national origin of either the prospective owners or occupants of the subject property or of the present owners or occupants of the properties in the vicinity of the subject property or on any other basis prohibited by law.

18. My employment and/or compensation for performing this appraisal or any future or anticipated appraisals was not conditioned on any agreement or understanding, written or otherwise, that I would report (or present analysis supporting) a predetermined specific value, a predetermined minimum value, a range or direction in value, a value that favors the cause of any party, or the attainment of a specific result or occurrence of a specific subsequent event (such as approval of a pending mortgage loan application).

19. I personally prepared all conclusions and opinions about the real estate that were set forth in this appraisal report. If I relied on significant real property appraisal assistance from any individual or individuals in the performance of this appraisal or the preparation of this appraisal report, I have named such individual(s) and disclosed the specific tasks performed in this appraisal report. I certify that any individual so named is qualified to perform the tasks. I have not authorized anyone to make a change to any item in this appraisal report; therefore, any change made to this appraisal is unauthorized and I will take no responsibility for it.

20. I identified the lender/client in this appraisal report who is the individual, organization, or agent for the organization that ordered and will receive this appraisal report.

URAR Model Appraisal: Page 6

Uniform Residential Appraisal Report

21. The lender/client may disclose or distribute this appraisal report to the borrower; another lender at the request of the borrower; the mortgagee or its successors and assigns; mortgage insurers; government sponsored enterprises; other secondary market participants; data collection or reporting services; professional appraisal organizations; any department, agency, or instrumentality of the United States; and any state, the District of Columbia, or other jurisdictions; without having to obtain the appraiser's or supervisory appraiser's (if applicable) consent. Such consent must be obtained before this appraisal report may be disclosed or distributed to any other party (including, but not limited to, the public through advertising, public relations, news, sales, or other media).

22. I am aware that any disclosure or distribution of this appraisal report by me or the lender/client may be subject to certain laws and regulations. Further, I am also subject to the provisions of the Uniform Standards of Professional Appraisal Practice that pertain to disclosure or distribution by me.

23. The borrower, another lender at the request of the borrower, the mortgagee or its successors and assigns, mortgage insurers, government sponsored enterprises, and other secondary market participants may rely on this appraisal report as part of any mortgage finance transaction that involves any one or more of these parties.

24. If this appraisal report was transmitted as an "electronic record" containing my "electronic signature," as those terms are defined in applicable federal and/or state laws (excluding audio and video recordings), or a facsimile transmission of this appraisal report containing a copy or representation of my signature, the appraisal report shall be as effective, enforceable and valid as if a paper version of this appraisal report were delivered containing my original hand written signature.

25. Any intentional or negligent misrepresentation(s) contained in this appraisal report may result in civil liability and/or criminal penalties including, but not limited to, fine or imprisonment or both under the provisions of Title 18, United States Code, Section 1001, et seq., or similar state laws.

SUPERVISORY APPRAISER'S CERTIFICATION: The Supervisory Appraiser certifies and agrees that:

1. I directly supervised the appraiser for this appraisal assignment, have read the appraisal report, and agree with the appraiser's analysis, opinions, statements, conclusions, and the appraiser's certification.

2. I accept full responsibility for the contents of this appraisal report including, but not limited to, the appraiser's analysis, opinions, statements, conclusions, and the appraiser's certification.

3. The appraiser identified in this appraisal report is either a sub-contractor or an employee of the supervisory appraiser (or the appraisal firm), is qualified to perform this appraisal, and is acceptable to perform this appraisal under the applicable state law.

4. This appraisal report complies with the Uniform Standards of Professional Appraisal Practice that were adopted and promulgated by the Appraisal Standards Board of The Appraisal Foundation and that were in place at the time this appraisal report was prepared.

5. If this appraisal report was transmitted as an "electronic record" containing my "electronic signature," as those terms are defined in applicable federal and/or state laws (excluding audio and video recordings), or a facsimile transmission of this appraisal report containing a copy or representation of my signature, the appraisal report shall be as effective, enforceable and valid as if a paper version of this appraisal report were delivered containing my original hand written signature.

URAR Model Appraisal: Page 6 (continued)

APPRAISER

Signature
Name   Harry Hanson
Company Name _____
Company Address _____

Telephone Number
Email Address _____
Date of Signature and Report _____
Effective Date of Appraisal _____
State Certification #
or State License #
or Other (describe)   State #
State
Expiration Date of Certification or License

ADDRESS OF PROPERTY APPRAISED
420 Mallard Ave
Bloomville, Lake County, IL

APPRAISED VALUE OF SUBJECT PROPERTY $
LENDER/CLIENT
Name   Check Loan Officer
Company Name Easy Money Institution
Company Address Centerville, IL

Email Address BMK@you.com

SUPERVISORY APPRAISER (ONLY IF REQUIRED)

Signature
Name
Company Name _____
Company Address _____

Telephone Number
Email Address _____
Date of Signature _____
State Certification #
or State License #
State
Expiration Date of Certification or License

SUBJECT PROPERTY

[X] Did not inspect exterior of subject property
___ Did inspect exterior of subject property from street
     Date of Inspection

COMPARABLE SALES

[X] Did not inspect exterior of comparable sales from street
___ Did inspect exterior of comparable sales from street
     Date of Inspection

Freddie Mac Form 2055   March 2005   Uniform Residential Appraisal Report   Fannie Mae Form 2055   March 2005

                                Page   3   of   3

URAR Model Appraisal: Addenda: Sales Contract

Approved Standard Agreement Form

AGREEMENT

This Agreement is made and entered into by and between

SELLER(S): Mae B. Zeller
ADDRESS: 420 Gladville Avenue, Bloomville, IL

BUYER(S): John W. Buyer
ADDRESS: 23 Oak Park Rd, Oakville, IL 60611

PURCHASE PRICE: $170,000

Payable as follows:

a. By Initial Deposit tendered herewith . . . . $ 1,000
b. By Additional Deposit due upon Sale's Acceptance . . . . $ 4,000
c. By Additional Deposit due upon satisfaction of financing contingency $ 5,000
d. By Proceeds of New Purchase Financing $ 160,000
e. By Proceeds of Seller Financing $
f. Balance due at closing $
   TOTAL MUST EQUAL PURCHASE PRICE: $170,000

4. REAL PROPERTY:
   a. Street Address: 420 Gladville Ave
   b. City: Bloomville, IL
   c. Approximate Lot Size: 3/4 Acre

5. PERSONAL PROPERTY, IF ANY, TO BE INCLUDED None.

6. THIRD PARTY FINANCING CONTINGENCY:
   a. Amount: $160,000
   b. Annual rate of interest: 6 % per annum Fixed
   c. Term: 30 years
   d. Loan to be obtained within: 30 days

7. SELLER FINANCING:
   a. Amount: $
   b. Interest Rate:
   c. Term:
   d. Periodic payment:
   e. Balloon payment (if any):

8. PHYSICAL INSPECTION CONTINGENCY:
   a. Inspection period: 10 days
   b. Notification period: 10 days

9. CLOSING DATE: May 25, 200—

A. TITLE SEARCH

B. LOAN ADJUSTMENT

C. UNLESS DELETED, THE FOLLOWING PARAGRAPHS ON THE REVERSE SIDE ARE HEREBY MADE A PART OF THIS AGREEMENT: A, B, C, D, E, F, J, K, L, M, N, O, P

D. LISTING BROKER: Bloomville Real Estate Co.

E. COOPERATING BROKER (IF ANY): Oak Park Realtors

F. TIME TO ACCEPT: The SELLER shall have

BUYERS SIGNATURE(S):
Will K Buyer   Date: Mar 25 200—

SELLERS SIGNATURE(S):
Mae B Seller   Date: Mar 29 200—

URAR Model Appraisal: Addenda:
Photographs of Subject Street & Comparable Sales

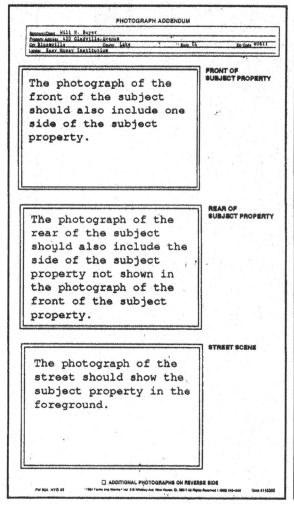

PHOTOGRAPH ADDENDUM

Borrower/Client Will N. Buyer
Property Address 420 Gladville Avenue
City Bloomville   County Lake   State IL   Zip Code 60611
Lender Easy Money Institution

FRONT OF SUBJECT PROPERTY

The photograph of the front of the subject should also include one side of the subject property.

REAR OF SUBJECT PROPERTY

The photograph of the rear of the subject should also include the side of the subject property not shown in the photograph of the front of the subject property.

STREET SCENE

The photograph of the street should show the subject property in the foreground.

☐ ADDITIONAL PHOTOGRAPHS ON REVERSE SIDE

PHOTOGRAPH ADDENDUM

Borrower/Client Will N. Buyer
Property Address 420 Gladville Avenue
City Bloomville   County Lake   State IL   Zip Code 60611
Lender Easy Money Institution

COMPARABLE SALE #1

A photograph of each comparable sale is now required by the FHLMC and the FNMA.

COMPARABLE SALE #2

A photograph of each comparable sale is now required by the FHLMC and the FNMA.

COMPARABLE SALE #3

A photograph of each comparable sale is now required by the FHLMC and the FNMA.

☐ ADDITIONAL PHOTOGRAPHS ON REVERSE SIDE

URAR Model Appraisal: Addenda: Building Sketch

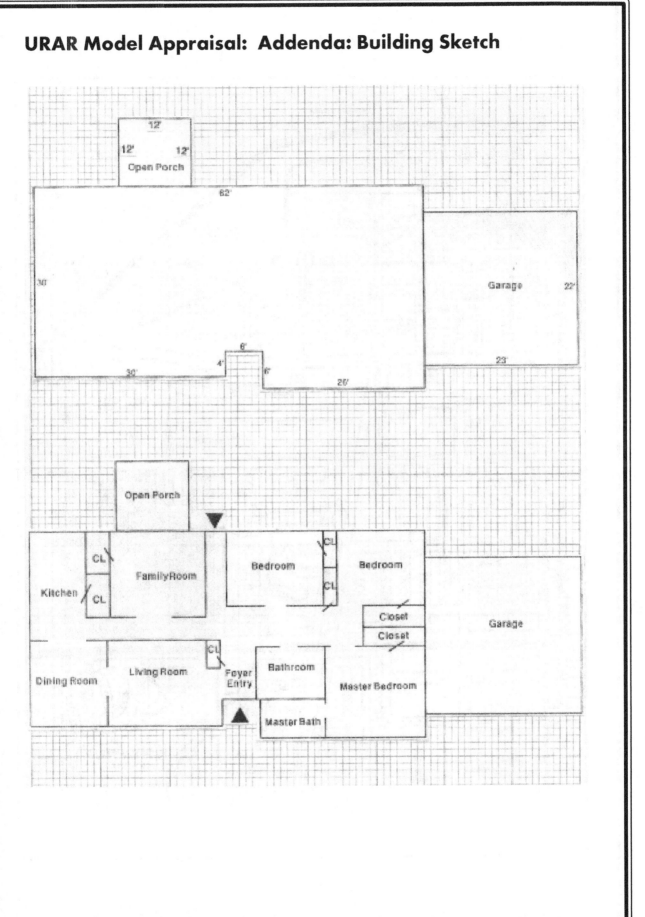

URAR Model Appraisal: Addenda: Neighborhood Map

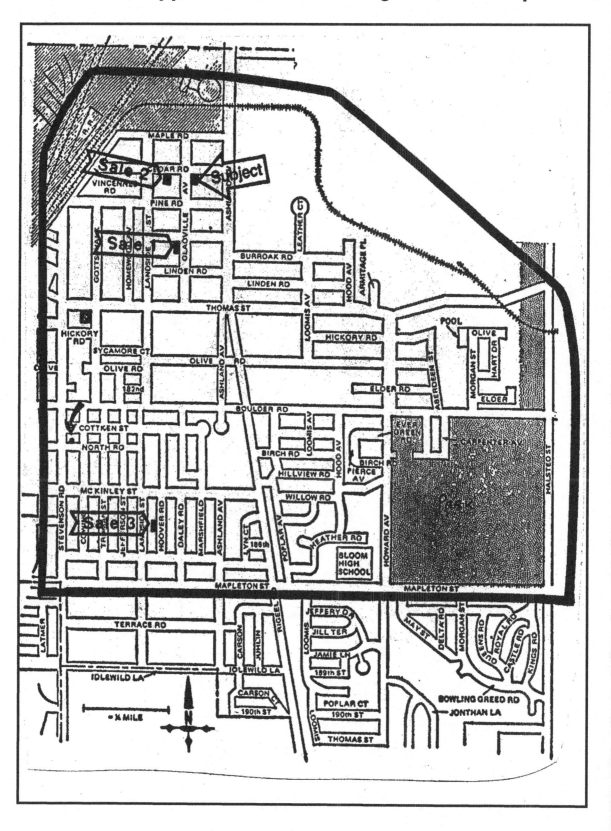

URAR Model Appraisal: Addenda: Community Map

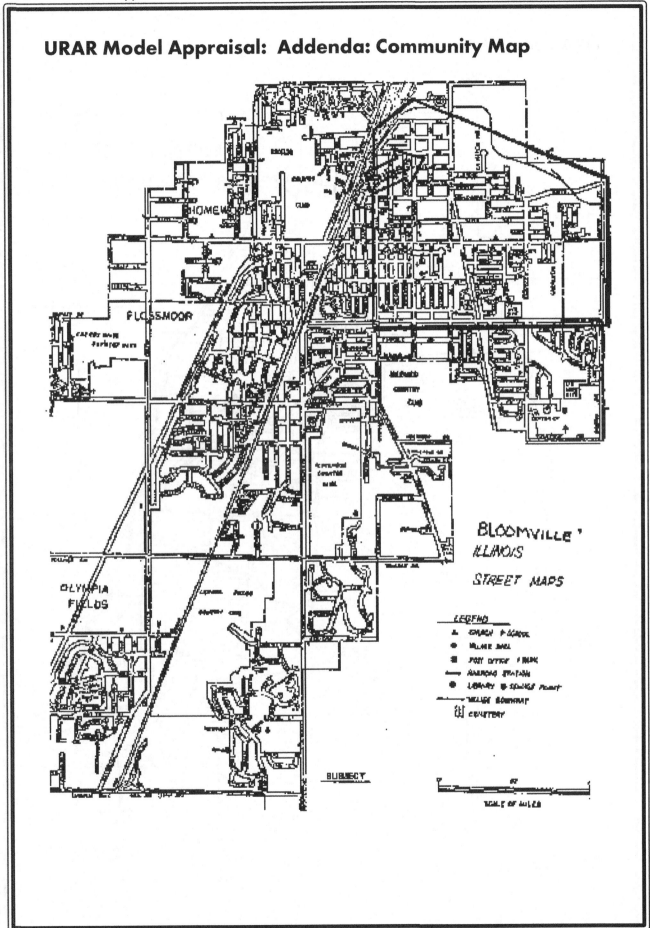

URAR Model Appraisal: Addenda: Regional Map

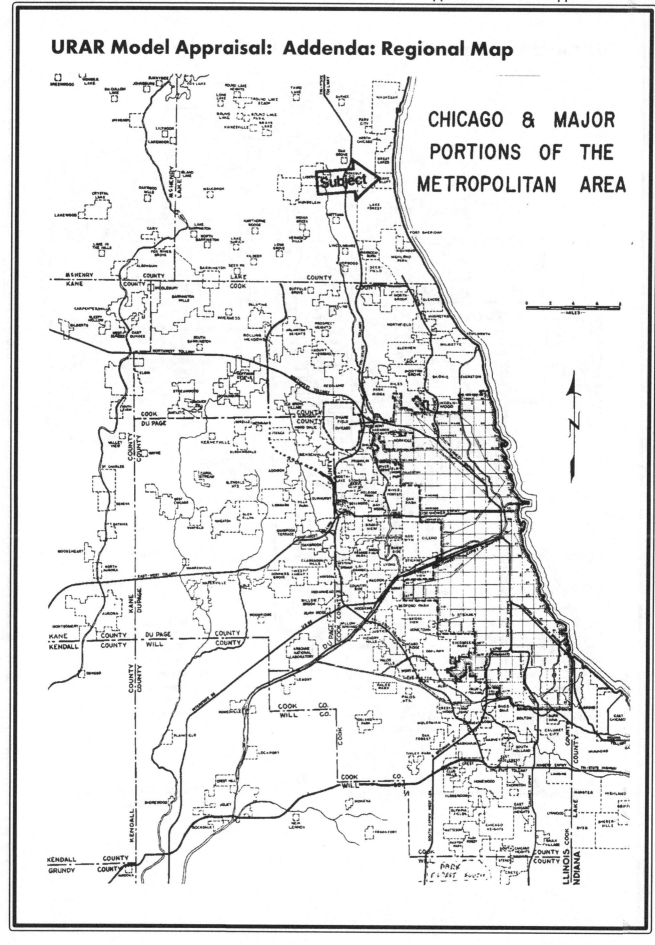

CHICAGO & MAJOR PORTIONS OF THE METROPOLITAN AREA

URAR Model Appraisal: Addenda:
Single - Family Comparable Rent Schedule

SINGLE FAMILY COMPARABLE RENT SCHEDULE

This form is intended to provide the appraiser with a familiar format to estimate the market rent of the subject property. Adjustments should be made only for items of significant difference between the comparables and the subject property.

ITEM	SUBJECT	COMPARABLE NO. 1		COMPARABLE NO. 2		COMPARABLE NO. 3	
Address	420 Gladville Bloomville, IL	341 Pine Road Bloomville, IL 60611		413 Cedar Street Bloomville, IL 60611		210 Hover Road Bloomville, IL 60611	
Proximity to Subject		3 blocks south		5 blocks south		1 block east	
Date Lease Begins Date Lease Expires	No Lease	No Lease		No Lease		No Lease	
Monthly Rental	If Currently Not Rented: $ rented	$1,150		$1,200		$1,340	
Less: Utilities Furniture	$unfurnished	$unfurnished		$unfurnished		$unfurnished	
Adjusted Monthly Rent	$not rented	$1,150		$1,200		$1,340	
Data Source	owner	owner		owner		owner	
RENT ADJUSTMENTS	DESCRIPTION	DESCRIPTION	+(–) $ Adjustment	DESCRIPTION	+(–) $ Adjustment	DESCRIPTION	+(–) $ Adjustment
Rent Concessions		None	0	None	0	None	0
Location/View	Ave/Ave	Ave/Ave	0	Ave/Ave	0	Good/Ave	–50
Design and Appeal	Ave	Ave	0	Ave	0	Ave	0
Age/Condition	30yrs/Ave	30yrs/Ave	0	30yrs/Ave	0	30yrs/Ave	0
Above Grade Room Count — Total Bdrms Baths	7 3 2	7 3 2	+60	7 3 2	+30	7 3 2	–10
Gross Living Area	1,888 Sq. Ft.	1,820 Sq. Ft.		1,875 Sq. Ft.		1,900 Sq. Ft.	
Other (e.g., basement, etc.) Fireplace	1 Masonry	None	+20	1 Masonry	0	1 Masonry	0
Other: Solar H.W.	Solar H.W.	No Solar H.W.	+50	No Solar H.W.	+50	Solar H.W.	0
Net Adj. (total)		x + – $ 130		x + – $ 80		+ x – $ 60	
Indicated Monthly Market Rent		$ 1,280		$ 1,280		$ 1,280	

Comments on market data, including the range of rents for single family properties, an estimate of vacancy for single family rental properties, the general trend of rents and vacancy, and support for the above adjustments. (Rent concessions should be adjusted to the market, not to the subject property.)

Comparable No. 1: Locaton is inferior to subject's. No domestic hot water system, no fireplace, no porch.

Comparable No. 2: Locaton is inferior to subject's. No domestic hot water system, no porch.

Comparable No. 3: Very similar to subject.

Final Reconciliation of Market Rent:
Equal weight as given to all three comparable rentals which were good indications of the rental value of the subject property.

I (WE) ESTIMATE THE MONTHLY MARKET RENT OF THE SUBJECT AS OF ____ March 1 ____ 200_ . TO BE $ 1,280

Appraiser(s) SIGNATURE Your signature

Review Appraiser SIGNATURE Review Appraiser's signature
(if applicable)

NAME Your name printed or typed

NAME Review Appraiser's Printed or Typed

URAR Model Appraisal: Addenda - Additional Comments

ADDITIONAL COMMENTS:
The interior and equipment are typical of houses in this neighborhood. The appraised value includes only those items of equipment that are considered to be part of the real estate. The house is well maintained. No significant repairs are currently needed. See Environmental Addenda for additional information on environmental hazards.

COST APPROACH:
This house is 40 years old. It does not need any modernization. The bathrooms, kitchen, mechanical equipment and other features of the house meet the current standards for houses of this age in this market.

Included in the value of the site improvements are the walks, driveways, fences, utility connections and landscaping.

The house has a general lack of storage space. $4,000 of functional obsolescence was estimated for this deficiency

There is no eating area in the kitchen which is expected in this market. $4,000 of functional obsolescence was estimated for this deficiency

There is only a crawl space under the house in a market that prefers basements. $8,000 of functional obsolescence was estimated for this deficiency. In addition the reproduction cost does not include the cost of a basement so the difference for a house with and without a basement would be greater than $4,000.

The domestic solar hot water heater (which is less than a year old) cost $7,000. It adds only $5,000 in value, and therefore it suffers $2,000 functional obsolescence.

SALES COMPARISON APPROACH:
The comparable sales were verified and no personal property was included in their sale prices.

All comparable sales are closed sales.

In order to locate these comparable sales, we checked the appraisals we previously made in the area, the SREA Market Data Center, MLS Service, and our own files.

The comparable sales were verified by the sources shown in the report, and the appraiser was able to ascertain that there were no significant sales concessions, special financing, or other special considerations.

The dates of sale reported are the closing dates. Many comparable closed sales were considered in making this appraisal. The three closed sales displayed are considered to be the most comparable and the best indicators of value for the subject property. Most weight is given to Comparable #2 because it required the fewest adjustments, is in a similar location to the subject, and has the most reliable adjustments.

INCOME:
Good rental data and information about houses that were rented when they were sold was available in this neighborhood to develop an Estimated Market Rent and Gross Rent Multiplier.

COMPETENCY:
The Appraiser and the Supervisory Appraiser, both signers of this report, believe that they are competent to make this appraisal based on their experience and educational background.

Exterior - Only Inspection Residential Appraisal Report (2055) - Model Appraisal

The following is quoted from the Fannie Mae announcement that pertains to the Exterior-Only Inspection Residential Appraisal Report dated March 2005 and available on the Fannie Mae web site: www.efanniemae.com

"USE

This report form is designed to report an appraisal of a one-unit property or a one-unit property with an accessory unit (including a unit in a planned unit development (PUD)), based on an **exterior only inspection of the subject property from the street.** This report form is not designed to report an appraisal of a manufactured home or a unit in a condominium or cooperative project.

"The appraiser must be able to obtain adequate information about the physical characteristics (including but not limited to, condition, room count, gross living area, etc.) of the subject property from the exterior-only inspection and reliable public and/or private sources to perform this appraisal. The appraiser should use the same type of data sources that he or she uses for comparable sales such as, but not limited to, multiple listing services, tax and assessment records, prior inspections, appraisal files, information provided by the property owner, etc."

Exterior-Only Inspection Residential Appraisal Report (2055) Model Appraisal Report: Subject & Contract

File No.
Case No.

Exterior-Only Inspection Residential Appraisal Report

The purpose of this summary appraisal report is to provide the lender/client with an accurate, and adequately supported, opinion of the market value of the subject property.

SUBJECT

Property Address 420 Gladville Ave.   City Bloomville   State IL Zip Code   60611

Borrower Will N. Buyer   Owner of Public Record   County Lake County

Legal Description see attached addenda sheet

Assessor's Parcel #   7/63   Tax Year   200   R.E. Taxes $ 5,320.00

Neighborhood Name   Wrightville   Map Reference   Census Tract

Occupant [X] Owner [ ] Tenant [ ] Vacant Special Assessments $ none   [ ] PUD   HOA $ [ ] per year [ ] per month

Property Rights Appraised [X] Fee Simple [ ] Leasehold [ ] Other (describe)

Assignment Type [X] Purchase Transaction [ ] Refinance Transaction [ ] Other (describe)

Lender/Client Easy Money Institution   Address Center City, USA

Is the subject property currently offered for sale or has it been offered for sale in the twelve months prior to the effective date of this appraisal? [X] Yes [ ] No

Report data source(s) used, offerings price(s), and date(s). offering price $180,000 Lake County MLS updated 1 month ago

CONTRACT

I [X] did [ ] did not analyze the contract for sale for the subject purchase transaction. Explain the results of the analysis of the contract for sale or why the analysis was not performed. Sales price within 10% of offering price, typical financing, no personal property, special financing or sales concessions reported

Contract Price $ 170,000   Date of Contract 2/25/200   Is the property seller the owner of public record? [X] Yes [ ] No Data Souce(s)   Deed

Is there any financial assistance (loan charges, sale concessions, gift or downpayment assistance, etc.) to be paid by any party on behalf of the borrower? [ ] Yes [X] No

If Yes, report the total dollar amount and describe the items to be paid. None

Exterior-Only Inspection Residential Appraisal Report (2055) Model Appraisal Report: Site

Note: Race and the racial composition of the neighborhood are not appraisal factors.

NEIGHBORHOOD

Neighborhood Characteristics			One-Unit Housing Trends				One-Unit Housing		Present Land Use %		
Location [ ] Urban	[X] Suburban	[ ] Rural	Property Values [ ] Increasing	[X] Stable	[ ] Declining	PRICE	AGE	One-Unit	50	%
Built-Up [X] Over 75%	[ ] 25-75%	[ ] Under 25%	Demand/Supply [ ] Shortage	[X] In Balance	[ ] Over Supply	$ (000)	(yrs)	2-4 Unit	6	%
Growth [ ] Rapid	[X] Stable	[ ] Slow	Marketing Time [X] Under 3 mths	[ ] 3-6 mths	[ ] Over 6 mths	140 Low	30	Multi-Family	6	%
Neighborhood Boundaries Wrightville neighborhood boundaries shown on neighborhood map in						190 High	60	Commercial	13	%
addenda						160 Pred.	35	Other see below 25		%

Neighborhood Description Present landuse 5% industrial, 5% parks, and 15% vacant

Market Conditions (including support for the above conclusions) Typically there are about a dozen houses for sale in Wrightville. Asking prices range from $140,000 to $290,000. Sales average 4 per month. Ample conventional financing available. Loan discounts, interest buydowns, and other concessions are not common.

SITE

Dimensions 700' x 115'   Area   11,500 sq. ft.   Shape   rectangle   View   average

Specific Zoning Classification single family res.   Zoning Description single family only

Zoning Compliance [X] Legal [ ] Legal Nonconforming (Grandfathered Use) [ ] No Zoning [ ] Illegal (describe)

Is the highest and best use of subject property as improved (or as proposed per plans and specifications) the present use? [X] Yes [ ] No If No, describe. Except for physical, functional, and external obsolescence described in the Cost Approach

Utilities	Public	Other (describe)		Public	Other (describe)	Off-site Improvements—Type	Public	Private
Electricity	[X]		Water	[X]		Street	[X]	
Gas	[X]		Sanitary Sewer	[X]		Alley None		

FEMA Special Flood Hazard Area [ ] Yes [X] No FEMA Flood Zone c   FEMA Map # 095060 0003   FEMA Map Date 11/10/200_

Are the utilities and/or off-site improvements typical for the market area? [X] Yes [ ] No If No, describe.

Are there any adverse site conditions or external factors (easements, encroachments, environmental conditions, land uses, etc.)? [X] Yes [ ] No If Yes, describe.

Typical utility easements for electricity, sewer, and telephone. No effect on market value. No apparent adverse easements, encroachments, special assessments, slide areas, etc. (see addenda)

Exterior-Only Inspection Residential Appraisal Report (2055)
Model Appraisal Report: Improvements

Source(s) Used for Physical Characteristics of Property		Appraisal Files		MLS		Assessment and Tax Records	X	Prior Inspection		Property Owner	
X	Other (describe)		Listing agent		Data Source(s) for Gross Living Area			Listing agent's sketch			

General Description		General Description		Heating / Cooling		Amenities		Car Storage	
Units: X One	One with Accessory Unit	Concrete Slab X Crawl Space		FWA X HWBB		X Fireplace(s) # 1		None	
# of Stories 1 Story		Full Basement Finished		Radiant		Woodstove(s) #		Driveway # of Cars	
Type X Det. Att. S-Det./End Unit		Partial Basement Finished		Other		Patio/Deck		Driveway Surface	
X Existing Proposed Under Const.	Exterior Walls Brick veneer		Fuel Gas		Porch		X Garage # of Cars 2	
Design (Style) Ranch		Roof Surface Asph shin		Central Air Conditioning		Pool		Carport # of Cars	
Year Built 198_		Gutters & Downspouts Aluminum	X Individual		Fence		X Attached Detached	
Effective Age (Yrs) 30 year		Window Type Wood/DH		Other		Other		Built-in	

Appliances	Refrigerator	Range/Oven	Dishwasher	Disposal	Microwave	Washer/Dryer	Other (describe)

Finished area **above** grade contains: 7   Rooms   3   Bedrooms   2   Bath(s)   1,888   Square Feet of Gross Living Area Above Grade

Additional features (special energy efficient items, etc.) Domestic solar hot water system (50 gal.) adds $5,000 value based on matched pairs of sales. They cost $7,000 new (continued in addenda)

Describe the condition of the property and data source(s) (including apparent needed repairs, deterioration, renovations, remodeling, etc.). There are no significant repairs known to be needed now. There is a general lack of storage space. No eating area in the kitchen. No basement. The market recognizes these deficiencies. Nearby railroad and industrial area estimated to cause 5% external obsolescence (continued in addenda)

Are there any apparent physical deficiencies or adverse conditions that affect the livability, soundness, or structural integrity of the property?   Yes X No
If Yes, describe Based on my prior inspection of the property and on information obtained from the listing agent, I am unaware of any apparent physical deficiencies or adverse conditions that affect the livability, soundness, or structural integrity of the property.

Does the property generally conform to the neighborhood (functional utility, style, condition, use, construction, etc.)? X Yes   No If No, describe

Freddie Mac Form 2055 March 2005   Fannie Mae Form 2055 March 2005

Exterior-Only Inspection Residential Appraisal Report (2055)
Model Appraisal Report: Sales Comparison Approach Grid (1)

File No.

Exterior-Only Inspection Residential Appraisal Report

There are __10__ comparable properties currently offered for sale in the subject neighborhood ranging in price from $ __130,000__ to $ __200,000__ .

There are __25__ comparable sales in the subject neighborhood within the past twelve months ranging in sale price from $ __135,000__ to $ __185,000__ .

FEATURE	SUBJECT	COMPARABLE SALE # 1	+(-) $ Adjustment	COMPARABLE SALE # 2	+(-) $ Adjustment	COMPARABLE SALE # 3	+(-) $ Adjustment
Address	420 Gladville Ave. Bloomville, IL 60611	341 Pine Road Bloomville, IL		413 Cedar Street Bloomville, IL		210 Hoover Road Bloomville, IL	
Proximity to Subject		1 Block south		1 Block west		7 Blocks south	
Sale Price	$ 170,000	$ 140,000		$ 146,000		$ 164,000	
Sale Price/Gross Liv. Area	$ 90.04 sq. ft.	$ 76.92 sq. ft.		$ 73.92 sq. ft.		$ 86.32 sq. ft.	
Data Source(s)		MLS Service		MLS Service		Appraiser's File	
Verification Source(s)		Listing Agent		Buyer		Seller	
VALUE ADJUSTMENTS	DESCRIPTION	DESCRIPTION	+(-) $ Adjustment	DESCRIPTION	+(-) $ Adjustment	DESCRIPTION	+(-) $ Adjustment
Sale or Financing		None		None		None	
Concessions		Equal		Equal		Equal	
Date of Sale/Time		1/0 - 2/0		11/0 - 1/0		12/0 - 1/0	
Location	Average	Avg./Equal		Avg./Equal		Good/Sup.	-10,000
Leasehold/Fee Simple	Fee Simple	Fee Simple		Fee Simple		Fee Simple	
Site	11,500 sq. ft.	About equal		About equal		About equal	
View	Avg./Typical	Equal		Equal		Equal	
Design (Style)	Ranch/Avg.	Equal		Equal		Equal	
Quality of Construction	Average	Avg./Equal		Avg./Equal		Avg./Equal	
Actual Age	30 yrs	30 yrs		30 yrs		30 yrs	
Condition	Average	Avg./Equal		Avg./Equal		Avg./Equal	
Above Grade	Total / Bdrms / Baths	Total / Bdrms / Baths		Total / Bdrms / Baths		Total / Bdrms / Baths	
Room Count	7 / 3 / 2.00	7 / 3 / 2.00		7 / 3 / 2.00		7 / 3 / 2.00	
Gross Living Area	1,888 sq. ft.	1,820 sq. ft.	+3,400	1,875 sq. ft.	+650	1,900 sq. ft.	-600
Basement & Finished	Crawl space	Crawl space		Crawl space		Crawl space	
Rooms Below Grade		Equal		Equal		Equal	
Functional Utility	Avg./Poor stor.	Equal/poor stor.		Equal/poor stor.		Equal/poor stor.	
Heating/Cooling	HWBB/Individual	Equal/Equal		Equal/Equal		Equal/Equal	
Energy Efficient Items	DomSolar HW	None	+5,000	None	+5,000	DomSolar HW	
Garage/Carport	2 Car Gar. Att.	2 Car Gar. Att.		2 Car Gar. Att.		2 Car Gar. Att.	
Porch/Patio/Deck	144 sq. ft. Br.	No porch	+2,000	No porch	+2,000	Open porch	
Fireplaces	1 Fireplace	None	+4,000	1 Equal		1 Equal	
Kitchen eating area	None	None/equal		None/equal		None/equal	
Net Adjustment (Total)		X + ☐ -	$ 14,400	X + ☐ -	$ 7,650	☐ + X -	$ -10,600
Adjusted Sale Price of Comparables		Net Adj: 10% Gross Adj : 10%	$ 154,400	Net Adj: 5% Gross Adj: 5%	$ 153,650	Net Adj: -6% Gross Adj: 6%	$ 153,400

Exterior-Only Inspection Residential Appraisal Report (2055) Model Appraisal Report : Sales Comparison Approach Grid (2)

I [X] did [ ] did not research the sale or transfer history of the subject property and comparable sales. If not, explain

My research [ ] did [X] did not reveal any prior sales or transfers of the subject property for the three years prior to the effective date of this appraisal.
Data source(s) Sales recorded in county records
My research [X] did [ ] did not reveal any prior sales or transfers of the comparable sales for the year prior to the date of sale of the comparable sale.
Data source(s) Sales recorded in county records
Report the results of the research and analysis of the prior sale or transfer history of the subject property and comparable sales (report additional prior sales on page 3).

ITEM	SUBJECT	COMPARABLE SALE # 1	COMPARABLE SALE # 2	COMPARABLE SALE # 3
Date of Prior Sale/Transfer	8 years ago	6 months ago	Over one year	Over one year
Price of Prior Sale/Transfer	$77,000	$138,000	unknown	unknown
Data Source(s)	Deed	MLS	MLS	MLS
Effective Date of Data Source(s)	Current	One month ago	One month ago	One month ago

Analysis of prior sale or transfer history of the subject property and comparable sales   The subject property sold 10 years ago for $77,000. Since then, prices have approximately doubled. Comparable Sale #1 sold 2 years ago for $131,000. The owner was transferred and the house resold this year for $140,000. There were no sales within the past year of Comparable Sales #2 & #3. There is no evidence of flipping or unusual price trends in the neighborhood.

Summary of Sales Comparison Approach   Subject property is typical of many houses in the neighborhood, as are all of the comparable sales. Size adjustments were based on $50 per sq. ft. of GLA difference, which is the approximate value of the comparable improvements (after deducting their site value). Fireplaces are estimated to add $4,000 value. Porches add value approximately equal to their depreciated cost, $5,000. Domestic Hot Water Heating system adjustment is taken from market by market pairs (continued in addenda).

Indicated Value by Sales Comparison Approach $ 154,000

Exterior-Only Inspection (2055) Model Appraisal Report: Reconciliation

Indicated Value by: Sales Comparison Approach $ 154,000   Cost Approach (if developed) $ 165,614   Income Approach (if developed) $ 156,160
The best indication of value was the Sales Comparison Approach. There was a substantial amount of good data available. It was well supported by the Cost Approach and Income Approach. The $154,000 estimated by the Sales Comparison Approach is the final estimate of value on the date of the appraisal.
This appraisal is made [ ] "as is," [ ] subject to completion per plans and specifications on the basis of a hypothetical condition that the improvements have been completed, [ ] subject to the following repairs or alterations on the basis of a hypothetical condition that the repairs or alterations have been completed, or [X] subject to the following required inspection based on the extraordinary assumption that the condition or deficiency does not require alteration or repair: Termite and home inspection is recommended because of property age and condition.
Based on a visual inspection of the exterior areas of the subject property from at least the street, defined scope of work, statement of assumptions and limiting conditions, and appraiser's certification, my (our) opinion of the market value, as defined, of the real property that is the subject of this report is
$ 154,000   , as of   200_   , which is the date of inspection and the effective date of this appraisal.
Freddie Mac Form 2055   March 2005   Fannie Mae Form 2055   March 2005

Exterior-Only Inspection Residential Appraisal Report (2055)
Model Appraisal Report: Additional Comments

File No.
Case No.

Exterior-Only Inspection Residential Appraisal Report

SUBJECT: Information about the pending sale was obtained from the Lender and verified by the Seller Mae B. Seller. A copy of the ratified sales contract is included as part of the addenda.

Information about any special conditions and/or loan charges to be paid by the Seller was obtained from the lender who said there were none.

The subject property has not sold within the past year. It was purchased by the present owner about 8 years ago.

NEIGHBORHOOD: In this neighborhood, there is little direct relationship between the age of houses and their values. Older homes that have been modernized sell for prices per sq. ft. of gross living area similar to newer houses.

The house being appraised is newer than the typical house in this neighborhood. It conforms sufficiently in size and value with the older homes in the neighborhood. Therefore, it does not suffer any additional functional obsolescence.

This house is within walking distance of grammar and high schools. There is good public transportation available near the subject property, including frequent train service to Center City. However, this has little effect on the value of the property because many properties in the market have similar transportation available. There are few recreation facilities available near the subject property. They consist of a swimming pool, tennis courts, and a golf course. This has little effect on the value of the property because the available facilities are similar to many houses in the same market.

This market provides an average environment for the house being appraised. There are not observed factors in the neighborhood that effect negatively the marketability of the house. All the items in the rating grid are rated good or average. The public schools, parks, view and noise levels are typical for this type of neighborhood.

The subject property is on the north side of the Wrightville neighborhood--near the railroad station and industrial area--and is effected negatively by them.

This market is stable. The community continues to grow at a steady rate.

SITE: The improvement on the property appears to conform to the current zoning regulations. In the event of a major loss by fire, it could be rebuilt without obtaining a zoning variance.

The improvements are substantially the Highest and Best Use, except for those items of depreciation which are described in the appraisal as items of functional obsolescence.

The landscaping on this site is average, which is typical of other sites in this neighborhood.

The size, shape, and landscaping of this site is typical of many sites in the neighborhood. There are no apparent adverse easements, encroachments, special assessments, slide areas, etc. that will have a negative effect on the value of the property.

IMPROVEMENTS:

This house is in average condition for a home of its age in this neighborhood. Its actual age is 40 years, and the effective age is 30 years.

There is no evidence of termites or other infestation. However, because of its age and the prevalence of termites in this area, a termite inspection is recommended.

The number of rooms, bedrooms, and baths is typical of many houses in this neighborhood. The foyer has been excluded from the room count.

ADDITIONAL COMMENTS

Exterior-Only Inspection Residential Appraisal Report (2055) Model Appraisal Report - Cost Approach

COST APPROACH TO VALUE (not required by Fannie Mae.)					
Provide adequate information for the lender/client to replicate your cost figures and calculations.					
Support for the opinion of site value (summary of comparable land sales or other methods for estimating site value) Assessor states sites are typically 30% of total value. Typical neighborhood value $160,000 x 30% = $48,000. Last lot sold for $50,000. Developer sold nearby unlandscaped lots for $35,000 to $40,000. Subject lot is near railroad station. Estimated value of subject site: $40,000.					

ESTIMATED [X] REPRODUCTION OR [ ] REPLACEMENT COST NEW	OPINION OF SITE VALUE			=$	40,000
Source of cost data Sheriff and Slow	Dwelling	1,888	Sq. Ft. @ $ 107	=$	202,016
Quality rating from cost service Ave Effective date of cost data 3/12/200_		144	Sq. Ft. @ $ 27	=$	3,888
Comments on Cost Approach (gross living area calculations, depreciation, etc.)	Domestic Solar Hot Water Heater				7,000
Physical deterioration 40%	Garage/Carport 506		Sq. Ft. @ $ 32	=$	16,192
Functional obsolescence 8%	Total Estimate of Cost-new			=$	229,000 (r)
Economic obsolescence 5%	Less Physical 40 Functional 8 External 5				
	Depreciation $ 91,600(r) $ 18,000(r) $ 11,500 (r)			=$	121,000 (r)
See addenda for additional comments	Depreciated Cost of Improvements			=$	108,000
	"As-is" Value of Site Improvements			=$	6,000
Estimated Remaining Economic Life (HUD and VA only) 45 Years	Indicated Value By Cost Approach			=$	155,000

Exterior-Only Inspection Residential Appraisal Report (2055) Model Appraisal Report - Income Approach

INCOME APPROACH TO VALUE (not required by Fannie Mae.)					
Estimated Monthly Market Rent $ 1,280	X Gross Multiplier 122	=$ 156,160	Indicated Value by Income Approach		
Summary of Income (including support for market rent and GRM) See addenda for additional comments					

Exterior-Only Inspection Residential Appraisal Report (2055) Model Appraisal Report - PUD Information

PROJECT INFORMATION FOR PUDs (if applicable)			
Is the developer/builder in control of the Homeowner's Association (HOA)? [ ] Yes [X] No Unit type(s) [X] Detached [ ] Attached			
Provide the following information for PUDs ONLY if the developer/builder is in control of the HOA and the subject property is an attached dwelling unit.			
Legal Name of Project Wrightville Acres PUD, Inc.			
Total number of phases 1 Total number of units 36 Total number of units sold 36			
Total number of units rented 2* Total number of units for sale 3** Data source Adam L. Clark, Pres HOA			
Was the project created by the conversion of existing building(s) into a PUD? [ ] Yes [X] No If Yes, date of conversion.			
Does the project contain any multi-dwelling units? [ ] Yes [X] No Data source.			
Are the units, common elements, and recreation facilities complete? [X] Yes [ ] No If No, describe the status of completion.			
*Rented houses are not owned by the developer. **The developer does not own the units for sale.			
Are the common elements leased to or by the Homeowner's Association? [ ] Yes [X] No If Yes, describe the rental terms and options.			
Describe common elements and recreational facilities. Small park with swings and sand box, bike paths, entrance signs and light, park lights.			

Freddie Mac Form 2055   March 2005   Fannie Mae Form 2055   March 2005

Exterior-Only Inspection Residential Appraisal Report (2055) Model Appraisal Report - Page 4

Exterior-Only Inspection Residential Appraisal Report   File

This report form is designed to report an appraisal of a one-unit property or a one-unit property with an accessory unit; including a unit in a planned unit development (PUD). This report form is not designed to report an appraisal of a manufactured home or a unit in a condominium or cooperative project.

This appraisal report is subject to the following scope of work, intended use, intended user, definition of market value, statement of assumptions and limiting conditions, and certifications. Modifications, additions, or deletions to the intended use, intended user, definition of market value, or assumptions and limiting conditions are not permitted. The appraiser may expand the scope of work to include any additional research or analysis necessary based on the complexity of this appraisal assignment. Modifications or deletions to the certifications are also not permitted. However, additional certifications that do not constitute material alterations to this appraisal report, such as those required by law or those related to the appraiser's continuing education or membership in an appraisal organization, are permitted.

SCOPE OF WORK: The scope of work for this appraisal is defined by the complexity of this appraisal assignment and the reporting requirements of this appraisal report form, including the following definition of market value, statement of assumptions and limiting conditions, and certifications. The appraiser must, at a minimum: (1) perform a visual inspection of the exterior areas of the subject property from at least the street, (2) inspect the neighborhood, (3) inspect each of the comparable sales from at least the street, (4) research, verify, and analyze data from reliable public and/or private sources, and (5) report his or her analysis, opinions, and conclusions in this appraisal report.

The appraiser must be able to obtain adequate information about the physical characteristics (including, but not limited to, condition, room count, gross living area, etc.) of the subject property from the exterior-only inspection and reliable public and/or private sources to perform this appraisal. The appraiser should use the same type of data sources that he or she uses for comparable sales such as, but not limited to, multiple listing services, tax and assessment records, prior inspections, appraisal files, information provided by the property owner, etc.

INTENDED USE: The intended use of this appraisal report is for the lender/client to evaluate the property that is the subject of this appraisal for a mortgage finance transaction.

INTENDED USER: The intended user of this appraisal report is the lender/client.

DEFINITION MARKET VALUE: The most probable price which a property should bring in a competitive and open market under all conditions requisite to a fair sale, the buyer and seller, each acting prudently, knowledgeably and assuming the price is not affected by undue stimulus. Implicit in this definition is the consummation of a sale as of a specified date and the passing of title from seller to buyer under conditions whereby: (1) buyer and seller are typically motivated; (2) both parties are well informed or well advised, and each acting in what he or she considers his or her own best interest; (3) a reasonable time is allowed for exposure in the open market; (4) payment is made in terms of cash in U. S. dollars or in terms of financial arrangements comparable thereto; and (5) the price represents the normal consideration for the property sold unaffected by special or creative financing or sales concessions* granted by anyone associated with the sale.

*Adjustments to the comparables must be made for special or creative financing or sales concessions. No adjustments are necessary for those costs which are normally paid by sellers as a result of tradition or law in a market area; these costs are readily identifiable since the seller pays these costs in virtually all sales transactions. Special or creative financing adjustments can be made to the comparable property by comparisons to financing terms offered by a third party institutional lender that is not already involved in the property or transaction. Any adjustment should not be calculated on a mechanical dollar for dollar cost of the financing or concession but the dollar amount of any adjustment should approximate the market's reaction to the financing or concessions based on the appraiser's judgment.

STATEMENT OF ASSUMPTIONS AND LIMITING CONDITIONS: The appraiser's certification in this report is subject to the following assumptions and limiting conditions:

1. The appraiser will not be responsible for matters of a legal nature that affect either the property being appraised or the title to it, except for information that he or she became aware of during the research involved in performing this appraisal. The appraiser assumes that the title is good and marketable and will not render any opinions about the title.

2. The appraiser has examined the available flood maps that are provided by the Federal Emergency Management Agency (or other data sources) and has noted in this appraisal report whether any portion of the subject site is located in an identified Special Flood Hazard Area. Because the appraiser is not a surveyor, he or she makes no guarantees, express or implied, regarding this determination.

3. The appraiser will not give testimony or appear in court because he or she made an appraisal of the property in question, unless specific arrangements to do so have been made beforehand, or as otherwise required by law.

4. The appraiser has noted in this appraisal report any adverse conditions (such as needed repairs, deterioration, the presence of hazardous wastes, toxic substances, etc.) observed during the inspection of the subject property or that he or she became aware of during the research involved in performing this appraisal. Unless otherwise stated in this appraisal report, the appraiser has no knowledge of any hidden or unapparent physical deficiencies or adverse conditions of the property (such as, but not limited to, needed repairs, deterioration, the presence of hazardous wastes, toxic substances, adverse environmental conditions, etc.) that would make the property less valuable, and has assumed that there are no such conditions and makes no guarantees or warranties, express or implied. The appraiser will not be responsible for any such conditions that do exist or for any engineering or testing that might be required to discover whether such conditions exist. Because the appraiser is not an expert in the field of environmental hazards, this appraisal report must not be considered as an environmental assessment of the property.

5. The appraiser has based his or her appraisal report and valuation conclusion for an appraisal that is subject to satisfactory completion, repairs, or alterations on the assumption that the completion, repairs, or alterations of the subject property will be performed in a professional manner.

Exterior-Only Inspection (2055)
Model Appraisal Report: Page 5

Exterior-Only Inspection Residential Appraisal Report   File #

APPRAISER'S CERTIFICATION: The Appraiser certifies and agrees that:

1. I have, at a minimum, developed and reported this appraisal in accordance with the scope of work requirements stated in this appraisal report.

2. I performed a visual inspection of the exterior areas of the subject property from at least the street. I reported the condition of the improvements in factual, specific terms. I identified and reported the physical deficiencies that could affect the livability, soundness, or structural integrity of the property.

3. I performed this appraisal in accordance with the requirements of the Uniform Standards of Professional Appraisal Practice that were adopted and promulgated by the Appraisal Standards Board of The Appraisal Foundation and that were in place at the time this appraisal report was prepared.

4. I developed my opinion of the market value of the real property that is the subject of this report based on the sales comparison approach to value. I have adequate comparable market data to develop a reliable sales comparison approach for this appraisal assignment. I further certify that I considered the cost and income approaches to value but did not develop them, unless otherwise indicated in this report.

5. I researched, verified, analyzed, and reported on any current agreement for sale for the subject property, any offering for sale of the subject property in the twelve months prior to the effective date of this appraisal, and the prior sales of the subject property for a minimum of three years prior to the effective date of this appraisal, unless otherwise indicated in this report.

6. I researched, verified, analyzed, and reported on the prior sales of the comparable sales for a minimum of one year prior to the date of sale of the comparable sale, unless otherwise indicated in this report.

7. I selected and used comparable sales that are locationally, physically, and functionally the most similar to the subject property.

8. I have not used comparable sales that were the result of combining a land sale with the contract purchase price of a home that has been built or will be built on the land.

9. I have reported adjustments to the comparable sales that reflect the market's reaction to the differences between the subject property and the comparable sales.

10. I verified, from a disinterested source, all information in this report that was provided by parties who have a financial interest in the sale or financing of the subject property.

11. I have knowledge and experience in appraising this type of property in this market area.

12. I am aware of, and have access to, the necessary and appropriate public and private data sources, such as multiple listing services, tax assessment records, public land records and other such data sources for the area in which the property is located.

13. I obtained the information, estimates, and opinions furnished by other parties and expressed in this appraisal report from reliable sources that I believe to be true and correct.

14. I have taken into consideration the factors that have an impact on value with respect to the subject neighborhood, subject property, and the proximity of the subject property to adverse influences in the development of my opinion of market value. I have noted in this appraisal report any adverse conditions (such as, but not limited to, needed repairs, deterioration, the presence of hazardous wastes, toxic substances, adverse environmental conditions, etc.) observed during the inspection of the subject property or that I became aware of during the research involved in performing this appraisal. I have considered these adverse conditions in my analysis of the property value, and have reported on the effect of the conditions on the value and marketability of the subject property.

15. I have not knowingly withheld any significant information from this appraisal report and, to the best of my knowledge, all statements and information in this appraisal report are true and correct.

16. I stated in this appraisal report my own personal, unbiased, and professional analysis, opinions, and conclusions, which are subject only to the assumptions and limiting conditions in this appraisal report.

17. I have no present or prospective interest in the property that is the subject of this report, and I have no present or prospective personal interest or bias with respect to the participants in the transaction. I did not base, either partially or completely, my analysis and/or opinion of market value in this appraisal report on the race, color, religion, sex, age, marital status, handicap, familial status, or national origin of either the prospective owners or occupants of the subject property or of the present owners or occupants of the properties in the vicinity of the subject property or on any other basis prohibited by law.

18. My employment and/or compensation for performing this appraisal or any future or anticipated appraisals was not conditioned on any agreement or understanding, written or otherwise, that I would report (or present analysis supporting) a predetermined specific value, a predetermined minimum value, a range or direction in value, a value that favors the cause of any party, or the attainment of a specific result or occurrence of a specific subsequent event (such as approval of a pending mortgage loan application).

19. I personally prepared all conclusions and opinions about the real estate that were set forth in this appraisal report. If I relied on significant real property appraisal assistance from any individual or individuals in the performance of this appraisal or the preparation of this appraisal report, I have named such individual(s) and disclosed the specific tasks performed in this appraisal report. I certify that any individual so named is qualified to perform the tasks. I have not authorized anyone to make a change to any item in this appraisal report; therefore, any change made to this appraisal is unauthorized and I will take no responsibility for it.

Exterior-Only Inspection Residential Appraisal Report (2055)
Model Appraisal Report: Page 6

Exterior-Only Inspection Residential Appraisal Report

20. I identified the lender/client in this appraisal report who is the individual, organization, or agent for the organization that ordered and will receive this appraisal report.

21. The lender/client may disclose or distribute this appraisal report to: the borrower; another lender at the request of the borrower; the mortgagee or its successors and assigns; mortgage insurers; government sponsored enterprises; other secondary market participants; data collection or reporting services; professional appraisal organizations; any department, agency, or instrumentality of the United States; and any state, the District of Columbia, or other jurisdictions; without having to obtain the appraiser's or supervisory appraiser's (if applicable) consent. Such consent must be obtained before this appraisal report may be disclosed or distributed to any other party (including, but not limited to, the public through advertising, public relations, news, sales, or other media).

22. I am aware that any disclosure or distribution of this appraisal report by me or the lender/client may be subject to certain laws and regulations. Further, I am also subject to the provisions of the Uniform Standards of Professional Appraisal Practice that pertain to disclosure or distribution by me.

23. The borrower, another lender at the request of the borrower, the mortgagee or its successors and assigns, mortgage insurers, government sponsored enterprises, and other secondary market participants may rely on this appraisal report as part of any mortgage finance transaction that involves any one or more of these parties.

24. If this appraisal report was transmitted as an "electronic record" containing my "electronic signature," as those terms are defined in applicable federal and/or state laws (excluding audio and video recordings), or a facsimile transmission of this appraisal report containing a copy or representation of my signature, the appraisal report shall be as effective, enforceable and valid as if a paper version of this appraisal report were delivered containing my original hand written signature.

25. Any intentional or negligent misrepresentation(s) contained in this appraisal report may result in civil liability and/or criminal penalties including, but not limited to, fine or imprisonment or both under the provisions of Title 18, United States Code, Section 1001, et seq., or similar state laws.

SUPERVISORY APPRAISER'S CERTIFICATION: The Supervisory Appraiser certifies and agrees that:

1. I directly supervised the appraiser for this appraisal assignment, have read the appraisal report, and agree with the appraiser's analysis, opinions, statements, conclusions, and the appraiser's certification.

2. I accept full responsibility for the contents of this appraisal report including, but not limited to, the appraiser's analysis, opinions, statements, conclusions, and the appraiser's certification.

3. The appraiser identified in this appraisal report is either a sub-contractor or an employee of the supervisory appraiser (or the appraisal firm), is qualified to perform this appraisal, and is acceptable to perform this appraisal under the applicable state law.

4. This appraisal report complies with the Uniform Standards of Professional Appraisal Practice that were adopted and promulgated by the Appraisal Standards Board of The Appraisal Foundation and that were in place at the time this appraisal report was prepared.

5. If this appraisal report was transmitted as an "electronic record" containing my "electronic signature," as those terms are defined in applicable federal and/or state laws (excluding audio and video recordings), or a facsimile transmission of this appraisal report containing a copy or representation of my signature, the appraisal report shall be as effective, enforceable and valid as if a paper version of this appraisal report were delivered containing my original hand written signature.

Exterior-Only Inspection Residential Appraisal Report (2055)
Model Appraisal Report: Page 6

APPRAISER

Signature
Name   Jerry Janicek
Company Name
Company Address

Telephone Number *
Email Address *
Date of Signature and Report *
Effective Date of Appraisal *
State Certification # *
or State License # *
or Other (describe) *   State = ____ *
State *
Expiration Date of Certification or License *

ADDRESS OF PROPERTY APPRAISED
400 Charlotte Ave
Scottville, Lake County, IL

APPRAISED VALUE OF SUBJECT PROPERTY $ ____ 157,000

LENDER/CLIENT
Name   Check Loan Officer
Company Name Easy Money Institution
Company Address Castle City, IL

Email Address EMI@abk.com
Freddie Mac Form 2055   March 2005

SUPERVISORY APPRAISER (ONLY IF REQUIRED)

Signature
Name
Company Name *
Company Address *

Telephone Number *
Email Address *
Date of Signature *
State Certification # *
or State License # *
State *
Expiration Date of Certification or License *

SUBJECT PROPERTY

[X] Did not inspect exterior of subject property
[ ] Did inspect exterior of subject property from street
     Date of Inspection

COMPARABLE SALES

[X] Did not inspect exterior of comparable sales from street
[ ] Did inspect exterior of comparable sales from street
     Date of Inspection

Fannie Mae Form 2055   March 2005

LK-M URAR Appraisal Software 800-123-4567   Page   4   of   5

* This information is based on the Appraiser's and Supervisory Appraiser's (only if required) personal data.

Exterior-Only Inspection Residential Appraisal Report (2055)-14

Exterior-Only Inspection (2055)
Model Appraisal Report: Addenda

The requirements for the addenda of an Exterior-Only Inspection Residential Appraisal Report (2055) are the same as for the Uniform Residential Appraisal Report (URAR).

The addenda exhibits on the URAR Model Appraisal Report are the same as the this **Exterior-Only Inspection (2055) Model Appraisal Report - Addenda**

NARRATIVE APPRAISAL REPORTS

The appraiser is afforded the best opportunity to support opinions and conclusions and to convince the client of the soundness of their value estimate in a *narrative appraisal report*. Its content and arrangement may vary. A typical report follows the table of contents shown in Fig. 15-1. Some appraisal organizations have their own specific guidelines for the preparation of narrative demonstration appraisals to be used for credit towards their designations.

FIG. 15-1 CONTENTS OF A TYPICAL NARRATIVE APPRAISAL REPORT

Part One - Introduction Title Page
Letter of transmittal
Certification
Table of contents
Qualifications of the appraiser
Photographs of the property
Summary of salient facts and conclusions

Part Two - Premises of the Appraisal
Underlying assumptions and limiting conditions
Intended use
Intended user
Client
Market value definition
Effective date of appraisal
Date of report
Property rights appraised

Part Three - Presentation of Data
Identification of the property
Identification of non-realty items
Regional map
Regional data
Community map
Community data
Neighborhood boundary map
Neighborhood data
Zoning data
Assessment and tax data
Site plan
Site data
Description of the improvements
History of the property
Ownership history
Floor plans

Part Four - Analysis of Data and Conclusions
The appraisal process
Highest and best use of the site as though vacant
Highest and best use of the property as improved
Cost approach including site valuation
Sales comparison approach
Income approach
Reconciliation and final value estimate

Part Five - Addenda
Detailed legal description
Additional regional, community, neighborhood data and statistics
Additional photographs
Additional plans
Other appropriate items

SUMMARY

The valuation process is the orderly step-by-step procedure an appraiser follows to produce a credible appraisal. It begins with the definition of the problem to be solved and concludes with a report of the solution in the form of an estimate of the defined value that is sought. The purpose of the appraisal process is to provide the outline for making thorough, accurate appraisals in an efficient manner.

Most appraisers would agree that making appraisals is an art, not a science. They would further explain that the profession is constantly trying to make appraising more scientific. A big step toward this goal has been the development of the valuation process. Within this theoretical framework, a concise, logical and clearly supported value conclusion can be presented which meets the needs of clients as well as the standards of the appraisal profession. New techniques using statistical methods to abstract information from the market, such as automatic valuations models using multiple regression analysis and other statistical techniques, are also making the appraisal process more scientific.

The final step of the valuation process is to produce an appraisal report. What type of report is produced should be determined when the appraiser and the client determine what the client's needs are, who the intended user(s) are, what the intended use(s) of the appraisal will be will there be any additional intended users? It is one of the many things to be decided as part of the process of agreeing upon the scope of work.

Appraisal reports can be oral reports, letter reports, form report or narrative reports. The USPAP has requirements for producing each of these types of report which must be strictly followed.

It is the appraiser's responsibility to produce a credible appraisal report that will satisfy the needs of the client and all identified intended users.

REVIEW QUESTIONS

1. An appraiser is usually a:
   a. fee appraiser.
   b. staff appraiser.
   c. both of above.
   d. Neither of above

2. Architects use appraisers to:
   a. help them pick suitable building materials.
   b. choose a confirming design for the house.
   c. set the asking price for the house.
   d. None of the above

3. Lawyers hire appraisers in behalf of their clients:
   a. to verify the clients credit worthiness.
   b. for condemnation proceedings.
   c. Both of above
   d. None of above

4. Appraisers help:
   a. estimate the amount to insure a house for.
   b. help settle claims.
   c. Both of the above
   d. None of the above

5. Public utility companies hire appraisers to help them with:
   a. acquisition of rights-of-ways for utility easements.
   b. acquisition of real estate.
   c. Both of the above
   d. Neither of the above

6. Which of the following is not one of the seven principles incorporated into the definition of a real estate appraisal?
   a. The appraisal must be as of a specific date
   b. The appraisal is an opinion of value
   c. The source of the value definition must be disclosed
   d. The person making the appraisal must be qualified to do so

7. The purpose of an appraisal is to:
   a. estimate some kind of value.
   b. estimate the kind of material needed to build the house.
   c. Both of the above
   d. None of the above

8. By definition a professional is:
   a. someone who is very well paid for their services.
   b. a college graduate.
   c. Brokers(s).
   d. None of the above

9. During the congressional hearings in the late 1980s concerning the collapse of the savings and loan associations:
   a. Congress put the primary blame for the collapse on bad appraisals
   b. Congress was surprised to learn that most appraisers were unregulated.
   c. Congress also recommend that Realtors be federally regulated.
   d. All of the above

10. Which if the following is a federal government agency?
    a. The Appraisal Foundation
    b. The Appraisal Subcommittee
    c. The Appraisal Standards Board
    d. The Appraiser Qualification Board

11. The responsibility to oversee the activities of the state appraisal regulators is?
    a. The Appraisal Foundation
    b. The Appraisal Subcommittee
    c. The Appraisal Standards Board
    d. The Appraiser Qualification Board

12. Who is responsible to take disciplinary action against an appraiser when a complaint of a USPAP violation is discovered to be valid?
    a. The Appraisal Foundation
    b. The Appraisal Subcommittee
    c. The State Regulatory Agency
    d. Any of the above

13. Who is responsible for running the Federal Registry of Real Estate Appraisers?
    a. The Appraisal Foundation
    b. The Appraisal Subcommittee
    c. The Appraisal Standards Board
    d. The Appraiser Qualification Board

14. Appraisers pay $25.00 _____ to run the Federal Registry:
    a. per year.
    b. per license or certification renewal period
    c. every other year
    d. none of the above

15. When using the Fannie Mae Exterior-Only Inspection form 2055 the appraiser must:
    a. not inspect the interior of the subject property even when asked the owner to do so.
    b. is not required to, but may inspect the interior of the subject property
    c. use the 2055 form only when the owner will not permit an interior inspection by the appraiser.
    d. None of the above

ANSWERS TO REVIEW QUESTIONS

The answer to each question is indicated by the letter a, b, c or d. The explanation of the answer is indicated by the page number and on an arrow that points to the appropriate paragraph on the page of the text.

Q 15.1	c	Page 15-2
Q 15.2	d	Page 15-2
Q 15.3	b	Page 15-2
Q 15.4	c	Page 15-3
Q 15.5	c	Page 15-3
Q 15.6	c	Page 15-4
Q 15.7	a	Page 15-4
Q 15.8	d	Page 15-5
Q 15.9	b	Page 15-5
Q 15.10	b	Page 15-6
Q 15.11	b	Page 15-6
Q 15.12	c	Page 15-6
Q 15.13	b	Page 15-7
Q 15.14	a	Page 15-7
Q 15.15	a	Page 15-32

A | Glossary

Actual Age
Chronological age of a structure, as opposed to its functional or economic age.

Addenda
An addition to an appraisal that contains additional information that supports the credibility of the report.

Adjusted Sale Price
The figure produced when the transaction or sales price of a comparable sale used in the sales comparison approach section of a real estate appraisal is adjusted for the elements of comparison.

(See: Elements of Comparison)

Adverse Conditions
A detrimental condition that exists on the property or in the market area of the subject property that negatively effects its value.

Age Life Method
One of several methods of estimating the amount of physical deterioration incurable. It is a percentage that reflects the ratio between the estimated effective age of the improvements and the typical economic life of the improvements.

Allocation Procedure
A procedure for estimating the value of the subject site. The sale price of an improved comparable sale is divided between the val-

ADAMS STYLE

ue if its improvements and its site. That part that is attributable to the site is an indication of the value of the subject site.

Amenities
A feature or benefit such as a tennis court or pool which materially increases enjoyment of a property, including good design, superior view, etc.

Appraisal
An appropriately supported, objective and unbiased opinion of a defined value, as of a specific date, of an adequately and accurately described property, made by a qualified person who has no undisclosed present or future interest in the property.

Appraisal Foundation
Created by appraisal trade groups for the purpose of regulating the appraisal industry. Empowered in 1989 by the Financial Institutions Reform, Recovery and Enforcement Act (FIRREA) to set minimum standards and qualifications for appraisers.

Appraisal Purpose
The type of value to be estimated

Appraisal Qualifications Board
A part of The Appraisal Foundation that is charged with developing the criteria for appraisal licenses and certifications.

A   Glossary

Appraisal Report

Written report of an appraiser's estimate of value for a particular piece of real property, as of a certain date, as well as other general and specific data concerning the property which help to support the value estimate.

Appraisal Standards Board (ASB)

A part of The Appraisal Foundation that is charged with developing standards for the appraisal profession and publishing them in the form of the Uniform Standards of Professional Practice.

Appraisal Subcommittee

A government agency created by congress in 1989 to oversee the regulation of the appraisal profession. It also maintains the Federal Registry of Licensed and Certified Appraisers.

Appraiser

Real estate professionals who estimate the value of property for a wide variety of purposes, on a fee basis.

Approaches to Value

The methods used by appraisers to estimate the value of a subject property using data taken from the market.

There are three traditional approaches to value: sales comparison approach, cost approach and income approach.

Artesian Well

A well drilled through impermeable strata deep enough to reach water that rises to the surface by internal hydrostatic pressure.

Assessed Value

A value assigned to a property by the tax assessor to be used as a basis for taxation; usually a percentage of market value.

Assessors Map

A map prepared by an assessor that show the location of each property within the jurisdiction of the assessor that will be taxed based on the assessor's valuation of the property.

Assumptions

(1) A statement made by an appraiser in an appraisal report of something they believe to be true without having verified whether it is or is not true.

(2) When a new owner agrees to take over responsibility for paying an existing mortgage and this action is permitted under the terms of the loan.

Automatic Diverter

A plumbing device that is part of a shower. Its purpose it to automatically change the flow of water from coming out of the shower head to the faucet in the tub when the shower is turned off. This prevents someone from accidently getting wet or burned when the shower is first turned on.

B | Glossary

Balance of Payments

A measure of the flow of money, goods and services between different geographic areas. When area exports more then it imports it is said to have a favorable balance of payments. When the opposite is true it has a negative balance of payments.

Balloon Framing

A type of framing system where the studs extend unbroken from the sill to the roof, popular for multi-story brick veneer and masonry veneer structures.

Band of Investment Method

A technique used in the income approach to develop a capitalization rate. It is a weighted average of each portion of the investment and its applicable interest rate.

Base Lines

1. In accordance with the rectangular survey system, base lines are east-west lines that serve as references for other parallels.

2. The topographic center line of a survey.

3. In construction, an established line from which measurements are taken when laying out building plans or other working plans.

Basement

The lowest level of a house that is usually substan-

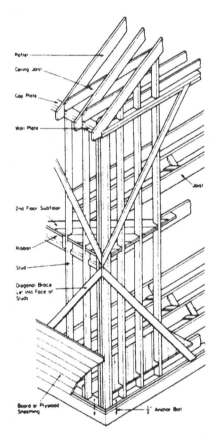

tially below ground. It is often used for storage and for large appliances such as the furnace. It sometime can be finished into usable living space.

Base Sale

A technique used when developing adjustments based on pairs of comparable sales. One sale is designated as the base sale in order to determine of the developed adjustment is plus or minus.

Basic Employment

Employment in those economic activities in a community that bring in money from outside the community.

Batt Insulation

A strip of insulation that fits closely between the studs of a wall.

Beneficial Interests

Benefits, profits or advantages resulting from a trust contract. The equitable title in a property as distinguished from the interest of the trustee who only hold title.

Blanket Insulation

A type of insulation that often is made of fiberglass with a backing material. It usually comes in rolls that are sized to fit between the studs or rafters.

Bridging

Strips of wood or metal nailed between joists or studs to give them lateral rigidity.

B-C Glossary

BTU (British Thermal Unit)
A measurement of heating and cooling capacity. It is the amount of heat required to raise the temperature of one pound of water one degree fahrenheit.

Building Codes
The set of governmental regulations that specify minimum construction standards. Often there are separate codes for the electrical and plumbing systems.

Building Cost Estimate
A detailed breakdown of all the costs that make up a building item by item. They are often prepared by builders, architects and professional cost estimators.

Bundle of Rights
A concept of property ownership from English common law.

The rights of the government include:

• The right to regulate the use of property for the good of all the people,

• The right to tax,

• The right to take property for public use and

• The right to receive property free if the chain of title ends (escheat).

The private owner has the right to:

• Use his or her property,

• Rent or lease it

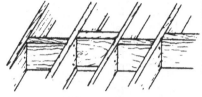

(a) Solid bridging

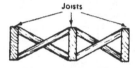

Joists

(b) 1 × 3 cross bridging

(c) Steel cross bridging

BUNDLE OF RIGHTS THEORY

• Sell it,

• Inherit it,

• Give it away.

• Do nothing with it

Capitalization Rates
A rate that reflects the relationship between the value of a property and its net operating income (NOI) in capitalization

Casement Windows
A type of window hinged to open at one of its vertical edges.

Census Tract Maps
The smallest geographic area into which the Standard Metropolitan Statistical Area (SMSA) is divided for statistical purposes. Tract boundaries are established in cooperation with a local committee and the Bureau of the Census and allowances are made for subdividing a single tract into subtracts bearing the same numerical identification. Tracts are designed to be relatively uniform with respect to demographic and economic conditions and include approximately 4,000 people.

Cesspool
Part of a waste disposal system that functions similarly to a septic tank; a covered cistern of stone, brick, or concrete block.

C | Glossary

Chronological Age
The actual number of years since a structure was built; the actual age.

Circuit Breaker
A permanent safety device used as a substitute for a fuse which automatically turns off an electric circuit when it is overloaded.

Comparable Sale
A property used in the sales comparison approach in the appraisal of real estate. Often it is compared to the subject property and adjustments are made to its sale price to reflect the differences between it and the subject property.

Comparables
An appraisal term for properties that are similar in value to the subject property and are used to indicate fair market value for the subject property.

Complete Appraisal
One of kinds of appraisals that was defined by the Uniform Standards of Appraisal Practice prior to the July 2006 edition when the use of the term was eliminated.

Concrete Slabs
(See: Slab-on-Ground)

Condemnation
The power of the government to take private property by due process of law for public use or benefit, without the owners consent. The owner is howev-

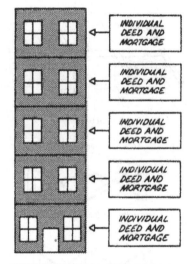

CONDOMINIUM OWNERSHIP

CASEMENT WINDOW

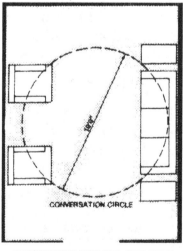

CONVERSATION CIRCLE

er entitled to receive just compensation.

Condominium
A form of ownership in which each owner owns the fee to the individual unit, and a percentage of the fee to the common areas.

Condominium Ownership
A form of ownership in which each owner holds fee simple interest to their individual unit, and also shares a percentage of the fee of the common area.

Confirmation
A contract, memorandum or deliberate act which validates a previous agreement that might otherwise have been void.

Contour
A line on a map that connects points of equal elevation or outlines a water body.

Conversation Circle
A circle that is ideally about ten feet in diameter in which furniture can be arranged for easy sit down communication. Circles for standing conversation need only be six feet in diameter.

Cooperatives
Properties in a form of ownership in which each owner owns shares in a corporation which owns the entire property. The share holder obtains the exclusive right to occupy part of the property. The

C | Glossary

property if financed by a mortgage that covers the entire property.

Correlation
(See: Reconciliation)

Cost Reporting Services (3)
A company that collects cost information from a variety of sources and publishes them in a manual or electronically. They are part of a system used to estimate the cost of properties being appraised or constructed.

Cost
The expenditure made to produce the improvements. In general use, it is often synonymous with price and value.

(See also: Reproduction Cost and Replacement Cost)

Cost Approach
One of the three traditional approaches to value used by real estate appraisers. It is based on the theory that the value of a property is the sum of the value of the land plus the reproduction cost of all the improvements, less depreciation from all causes.

Cost Indices (Indexes)
A multiplier that reflects the differences in prices or costs at different historical times.
Common real estate indexes are the cost of living index, house price and building cost indexes.

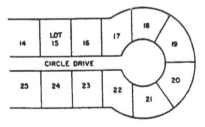

CUL-DE-SAC

Cost to Cure
The amount needed to restore an item of deferred maintenance to a new or reasonably new condition.
(See: Physical Deterioration Curable)

Crawl Space
In basement less houses, the open space between the underside of the floor joists and the ground.

Creative Financing
A type of mortgage that has an interest rate, amortization schedule, down payment requirement or some other feature that is different from conventional mortgages being offered at the time.

Credible Appraisal
An appraisal worthy of belief, The 2006 USPAP requires that every appraisal be credible.

Cul-de-sac)
A dead-end street that is at the end to allow cars to make a U turn.

Cumulative Adjustments (
In the sales comparison approach a method used when there is more than one adjustment.

D Glossary

Data
Records and information on real properties kept by appraisers, lenders, etc.

Data Sources
A variety of places that are the sources of the various kinds of General Data and Specific Data needed by an appraiser.

Date of Appraisal
(See: Effective Date of Value Opinion}

Date of Inspection
Usually the last date before the effective date of the value opinion that the appraiser inspected the subject property.

de minimus PUD
A term that used to be used by Freddie Mac and Fannie Mae to describe a PUD in which the common property has a relatively insignificant influence upon the enjoyment of the premises or has little or no effect upon the value of the property..

Definition of the Problem
The first step of the valuation process. The appraiser determines what the problem is that the client has engaged the appraiser to solve. Often it is to estimate the value of a property.

Definition of Value
A mandatory part of the appraisal report that is the exact definition of the value estimated in the report

DOUBLE HUNG WINDOW

Date of Value Opinion
(See: Effective Date of the Value Opinion)

Depreciation
The difference between the reproduction cost of improvements and their value. It is the loss in value suffered by improvements to property and personal property caused by physical deterioration, functional obsolescence, and external obsolescence.

Detrimental Condition
An adverse condition that exists on the property or in the market area of the subject property that negatively effects its value.

Direct Capitalization Rate
A capitalization rate that is extracted from market data collected in the Market Area. The net operating income of a comparable property is divided by the value of the property to produce the rate.

Direct (Hard) Costs
The costs of constructing an improvement that consist of labor, materials and the contractor's profit.

Dollar Adjustments
One of the methods used adjust for differences between a comparable sale and the subject property. The amount of the adjustment is stated in dollars not a percentage.

Double Hung Windows
A window with two sashes the move up and down independently in tracks.

D-E | Glossary

Downspouts

A pipe used for carrying rainwater from the roof of a house to the ground or into a dry well or sewer connection.

Duplex Outlet

A common type of electrical outlet used in the United States up to 1960 when it was replaced with outlets that had a ground wire.

Duplex Receptacle

(See: Duplex Outlet}

Easements (

A liberty, privilege, or right that one has to use land for a specific purpose distinct from ownership of the soil, such as the right to cross X to get to Y.

Economic Base

The major economic activities of a community that provide it support by bringing in funds form outside the community.

Economic Base Analysis

A technique for the analysis of the macro economic supports of a community. It is used as a means of predicting income and population or other variables that affect real estate value.

Economic Feasibility

A study of the projected income and expenses of a project to determine whether the project warrants the proposed cost to develop it.

Economic Forces

One of the four forces that effect the value of property. They are: relationship to Community growth,

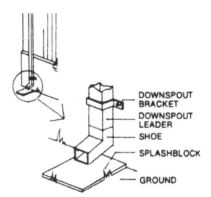

DOWNSPOUTS

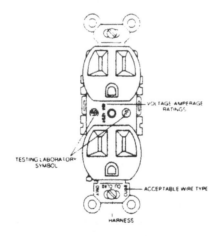

DUPLEX OUTLET

economic profile of the residents, new construction and vacant land and turnover and vacancy rates.

Economically Feasible

(See: Financially Feasible)

Economic Life

The length of time improvements can be profitably utilized, and continue to contribute value to the property. When the improvements no longer contribute any value, they have reached the end of their economic life.

Economic Rent

The rent that a property would command in the market at any given time, if it wee vacant and available for lease, even thought the actual rent may be different.

Effective Date of the Value Opinion

A mandatory date that must be stated in every appraisal report. It is the date to which the value estimate applies. It can be the date of the last inspection or any other date clearly specified in the appraisal report.

Effective Age

The age an improvement appears to be, as compared to other improvements in the market, considering its condition and design. Effective age is often different from the actual age.

E | Glossary

Effective Date of the Appraisal
(See: Effective Date of the Value Opinion)

Effective Gross Income (EGI)
The total estimated potential income for a property including rents and all other miscellaneous income, less an allowance for loss of income due to vacancy and collection losses.

Egress
The right or action of going on or off a property.

Elderly Housing
(See: Housing for the Elderly)

Elements of Comparison
In the valuation process, the factors an appraiser for similarities and differences between the subject property and the chosen comparable sales or comparable listings. There are five basic elements of comparison which many appraisers consider:

- Conditions of Sale
- Time of Sale
- Location
- Physical Characteristics
- Financing

Encroachments
An intrusion of one person's property upon the property of another. It may be a wall, a fence, or a cornice or casement window that extends upon adjoining property.

Entrepreneurial Profit
An additional amount that many appraisers feel should be added to cost of improvements in the cost approach in addition to the direct cost and indirect costs to reflect the typical profit that is made by a developer of the type of property being appraised.

Environmental Obsolescence
(See: Eternal Obsolescence)

Environmental Regulations
Local, state and federal environmental ordinances that control the use of property.

Environmental Restrictions
Restrictions on the development and use of the land based on environmental considerations. There are federal, state, and local environmental restrictions.

Excess Land
The land that is not needed to develop the property to its highest and best use.

External Obsolescence
Any loss of value suffered by a property caused by things that are off the premises. The loss can be caused by physical or economic conditions.

E-F Glossary

Extraction Method

A method of estimating the value of a site based on sales of comparable properties. The contribution of the improvements is estimated and deducted from the total sales price to arrive at a sales price for the land. This technique works best when the contribution of the improvements to the total price is small.

Extraordinary Assumptions

An assumption, directly related to a specific assignment, which, if found to be false, could alter the appraiser's opinions or conclusions. They presume as fact otherwise uncertain information about physical, legal or economic characteristics of the subject property; or about conditions external to the property, such as market conditions or trends; or about the integrity of data used in the analysis,

Fannie Mae

It was created by the federal government as a government agency called the Federal National Mortgage Association and later chartered as a private corporation now called Fannie Mae. Its stock is publicly traded. Its primary purpose is to buy mortgages from primary lenders and sell them in the secondary mortgage market. Originally it dealt primarily in FHA and VA insured mortgages. Now it buys and sells many types of mortgages.

Federal Emergency Management Agency (FEMA)

A government agency that was started to sell flood insurance, produce flood maps and regulate building in flood hazard areas. Its functions have been increased to also provide flood and other types of disaster relief.

Fee Appraiser

An appraiser who primarily acts as an independent contractor and receives appraisal assignments from multiple clients.

Fee Simple

The best and most complete title an owner can have to a piece of real estate.

Final Estimate of Value

An opinion made by an appraiser after all of the steps of the valuation process and after the final reconciliation as to what the appraiser feels is the value of a property.

Final Reconciliation

An appraisal term for the process of choosing the most appropriate data and selecting from among alternative conclusions developed in the three approaches to value in order to estimate a final indicated value for the property.

Financially Feasible

One of the four test to determine the highest and best use of a property. The use being tested must be capable of producing some profit to pass the test.

F || Glossary

Fixed Expenses
Expenses associated with managing real estate that tend to remain the same regardless of the occupancy of the property, such as taxes and property insurance,

Fixtures
Personal property accessory to the real estate and part and parcel of it, such as toilets, light fixtures, and furnaces; usually considered to be part of the real estate when the property is sold.

Flashing
Metal or composition, used to protect, cover, or deflect water in places where two materials join or form angles, such as roof valleys and chimney protrusions.

Flood Hazard Area
An area designated by FEMA where there is a of the area flooding every 100 years or less.

Flood Maps
Maps produced by FEMA that show the different flood zones in the area covered by the map.

Flood Plains
The flat surfaces on the banks of rivers and streams that are subject to flooding.

Foil Insulation
A type of insulation that has a foil backing that increases it capacity to insulate by reflecting the heat waves.

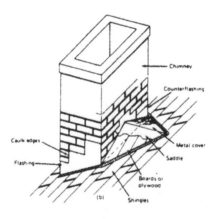

FLASHING

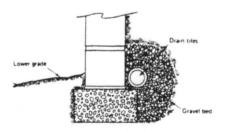

FOOTINGS & FOOTING DRAINS

Footing
A concrete support under a foundation, chimney, or column that usually rests on solid ground and is wider than the structure being supported.

Footing Drains
Drains that run around the perimeter of the footing, usually made of perforated pipes that divert the water from the footing to somewhere on the site where it can be absorbed or diverted off the site.

Fractional Interests
Ownership interests that are less than fee simple such as air rights, subsurface rights, easements, right of ways, or any other partial interest.

Freddie Mac
It was created by the federal government in 1970 as a government agency called the Federal Home Loan Mortgage Corporation and later chartered as a private corporation now called Freddie Mac.. Its stock is publicly traded. Its primary purpose is to buy mortgages from primary lenders and sell them in the secondary mortgage market. Originally it dealt primarily in mortgages written by Federal Savings and Loan Associations. Now it buys and sells many types of mortgages.

Frontage
The length of the boundary line that touches the street.

F-G Glossary

**Functional Obsolescence
- Curable**

Those impairments or defects in functional capacity or efficiency which are cost-effective to cure, i.e. that will return enough value to the property to offset the cost to correct them.

**Functional Obsolescence
- Incurable**

Those impairments or defects in functional capacity or efficiency which it is not cost-effective to cure, i.e. that will not return enough value to the property to offset the cost to correct them

**Functional Obsolescence-
Superadequacy**

Those improvements to a property that are excessive and do not contribute value equal to their cost. However, since they contribute some value it is not economically prudent to remove them.

General Data

Data that originates outside the property. It is divided into primary data which is generated by the appraiser or some agency and is not know by the public and secondary data which is published and available to the public.

Gentrification

A process of renovation and rehabilitation, usually of inner city properties, which results in increased value, and a grad-

ual increase in the socio-economic circumstances of the residents in the neighborhood, both owners and renters. The process brings increased wealth and stability to the city, it causes problems for poorer people caught in the upward rise of rents and values who can no longer afford to remain in their neighborhood.

Geographic Characteristics

Characteristics such as size, shape, width, depth and shape.

Geologic Characteristics

Characteristics such as typography, soil and subsoil composition, drainage and wetlands.

Geodetic Survey Program

A program of the U.S. Geological Agency to make typographic maps for most of the United States.

Going Concern Value

The special value that a property or business has while it is in operation, which will cease to exist when the business operation is not functioning.

Gross Building Area

A way of measuring the size of a building based on its exterior dimensions. It includes all of the building's area, regardless of how it is finished or how it is used.

Gross Income Multiplier

A figure which, when multiplied by a property's annual gross income, will produce an estimate of

G-H | Glossary

the value of that property. The figure is obtained by taking a sample of similar properties and dividing each property's selling price by its annual gross income (rent and other income). The results are reconciled into a single multiplier or range of multipliers.

Gross Living Area (GLA)

This is the interior measurement of finished, above-grade residential space. Excluded are unheated areas such as porches, balconies and any unfinished attic areas. An important figure for comparison of comparable sales with a subject property in most appraisals.

Gross Monthly Rent Multiplier (GMRM)

A version of the income approach used by appraisers mostly for estimating the value of residences. The estimated monthly rent of the property (without furniture or utilities) is multiplied by the gross rent multiplier to produce a value or range of values.

Gross Rent Multiplier (GRM)

Similar to the Gross Monthly Rent Multiplier but used in appraising larger commercial buildings where a GRM abstracted from the market is multiplied by the annual gross rental of the property to yield an estimate of its value.

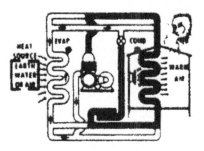

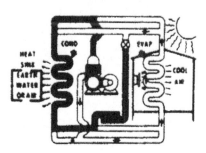

HEAT PUMP

Growth Period

A period in the evolution of a market area and neighborhood during which it is expanding. It is characterized by successful developments with the area.

Gypsum

A widely distributed mineral consisting of hydrous calcium sulfate which is used to make plaster of paris which is the primary ingredient of a popular type of wall board called drywall marketed as Sheetrock.

Heat Pump

A system employed to transfer heat into a space or substance. A condenser provides the heat while an evaporator picks up heat from air, water, etc. By shifting the flow of air or water, a heat pump system may also be used to cool the space.

Highest and Best Use

The utilization of a property to its best and most profitable use. It is that use, chosen from among reasonably probable and legal alternative uses, which is found to be physically possible, appropriately supported, and financially feasible to result in highest land value.

H-I   Glossary

Highest and Best Use Tests (four)

The four tests used to determine highest and best use for a particular property. To be the highest and best use, a proposed use must meet all four tests, and be:

1. Physically possible

2. Legally permissible

3. Financially feasible

4. Maximally productive

Hollow Masonry Walls

A hollow masonry unit that has core holes which exceed 25% of the total tile volume.

Homeowners' Association

1. An association of property owners in a residential formed for the purpose of improving the area both physically and socially. The association may own or maintain some physical facilities.

2. An association that is formed as part of the process of establishing the ownership of a property such as a condominium or planned unit development. The association is responsible for the regulation and maintenance of the commonly owned property.

Horizontal Sliding Windows

A type of window that slides open and shut on horizontal tracks.

Housing for the Elderly

A special classification of housing that is designed with features needed by elderly residents

Hydronic Water System

A type of heating system that used hot water to convey the heat from the furnace to the radiators.

Hypothetical Conditions)

That which is contrary to what exists but is supposed for the purpose of analysis. It assumes conditions contrary to known facts about physical, legal, or economic characteristics of the subject property, or about conditions external to the property, such as market conditions or trends, or about the integrity of the data used in an analysis. (Source: 2006 USPAP)

Improvements

1. Objects or structures attached to the land.

2. The site preparations required for building which include grading, landscaping, driveways, utility connections and others.

3. Additions in structure, function or utility made to a property to increase its value.

Income Capitalization

(See: Income Approach)

Glossary

Income Capitalization Approach

An approach to value used by appraisers to measure the present value of the future benefits of property ownership.

Independent Contractor

A self-employed person who performs services without being controlled by the person or organization for whom the services are rendered. For a real estate salesperson to be an independent contractor, he or she must be free to act independently and without obligations such as floor time, meeting attendance, fixed hours, etc. The independent contractor should be paid gross amounts without tax deductions for his or her services.

Indirect Costs

The cost of constructing a building that are not included in the direct costs. Typical indirect costs include: professional services, developers overhead, building permits and licenses, insurance premium, interest, taxes, selling expenses and carrying costs.

Ingress and Egress

A right to enter upon and pass through land.

Insurable Value

An estimate of the value of a property for the purpose of obtaining insurance. It includes only the value of those portions of real property that are insurable, and excludes those that are not, such as land.

Intended Use

The use or uses of an appraiser's reported appraisal, appraisal review, or appraisal consulting assignment opinions and conclusions, as identified by the appraiser based on communication with the client at the time of the assignment. (Source: 2006 USPAP)

Intended User

The client and any other party as identified, by name or type, as users of the appraisal, appraisal review, or appraisal consulting assignment opinions and conclusions, as identified by the appraiser based on communication with the client at the time of the assignment. (Source: 2006 USPAP)

Interim Use

Temporary use of a property to produce some income during the period in which development is postponed.

Investment Value

Value to an investor based on his or her individual needs and income tax bracket.

J ‖ Glossary

Jalousie Windows
Windows and doors made of movable glass louvers that can be adjusted to slope upward to admit light and air yet exclude rain or snow.

Joists
A series of parallel wood or steel beams set at even distances apart which are used to support floors and ceilings.

Land
1. The solid portion of the earth's surface substantially in its undisturbed condition.

2. Unimproved property, without site improvements such as roads, utilities, etc.

3. That portion of a real property which is not structures or other improvements.

Land Residual Technique
A five-step process that is used to estimate the value of land. It is based on the assumption that the income a property earns can be split between the land and the improvements.

Leaders
(See: Downspout)

Legal Description
A method of identifying the boundaries of a property. There are a variety of different systems approved by the laws of different states. See also Geodetic System, Metes

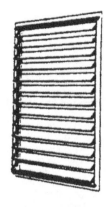

JALOUSIE WINDOWS

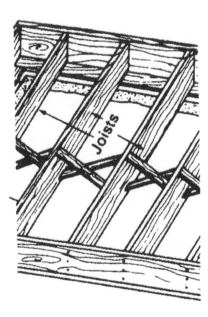

JOISTS

and Bounds, Public Land System, Recorded Map.

Legal Non Conforming Use
A use that was lawfully established and maintained, but no conforms to the use regulations in the zone where it is located.

Legally Permitted
A use that is legally permitted by the zoning ordinances, building codes, environmental regulations and any other ordinance that applies to the subject site.

Letter Reports
(See: Letter of Opinion)

Limited Appraisal
Any appraisal which does not conform to all of the requirements for a Complete Appraisal as delineated in the USPAP of the Appraisal Foundation.

Limiting Condition
A statement in an appraisal that the appraisal is subject to consummation (or elimination) of situations prior to the effective date of the appraisal (or completion of transaction) which items, if not done , may effect the value conclusion,

Linkage
The connection between a property and what supports its use. Examples are residences to places of work, and stores to their customers.

L-M | Glossary

Liquidation Value
The value of real property if it were forced to be sold quickly to raise money.

Locational Obsolescence
(See Economic Obsolescence)

Loose Insulation
A type of insulation that is not attached to a backing material. It is usually poured between rafters or blown or poured into the walls between the studs

Lot and Block System
A map that divides a parcel of land into lots and is the basis of legal descriptions. It is used in most of the United States except in the original thirteen states.

Macro Data
Information on aggregate phenomena such as employment, national & regional income, interest rates, and balance of trade.

Market (Economic) Rent
The amount of rent a property should bring if it were being currently offered for rent under competitive market conditions.

Market Area
The geographic territory within which a product being marketed can reasonably expect to find a buyer.

Market Data Analysis
A study made of general market conditions for the product proposed to be marketed. It takes into consideration the supply and demand of the product. It also considers the current attitudes of the buyers and sellers and the availability of financing.

Elements of Fair Market Value

- Buyer and seller are ready, willing and able to buy and sell
- Buyer and seller are informed
- Buyer and seller are acting under no unusual compulsion or duress
- Property is exposed to the market for a reasonable period of time
- Sale is for money with typical financing available

MARKET VALUE

Market Data Approach
(See: Sales Comparison Approach)

Market Price
The actual price paid for a property.

Market Rent
The amount of rent a property should bring if it were being currently offered for rent under competitive market conditions.

Market Value
The price (highest or most probable) that a property will sell for in a competitive market when all the conditions for a fair sale exist. These conditions include buyers and sellers who are knowledgeable of the property and the market and who are typically motivated and free of unusual stimulus and acting in their own best interest. It also assumes that there is sufficiently time available to market the property and that typical financing will be available.

Masonry Veneer Siding
A masonry facing that is placed against a wall but not bonded to it primarily for decorative purposes and for protecting the exterior surface from wear. It may also increase the insulation rating of the wall.

M | Glossary

Mass Appraisal

The process of appraising an entire area or district at the same time usually for the purpose of adjusting property taxes.

Matched Pairs of Sales

A technique which is part of the market data approach of the appraisal process, whereby the appraiser identifies highly similar properties to extract a value for a single dissimilarity. For example, using two identical condominium units, except for a fireplace in one but not in the other, an appraiser may extract the market value of a fireplace. Matched pairs are often used to extract land values or the value of excess land.

Metes and Bounds

1. The boundary lines of a property including terminal points and angles.

2. A system of property description used primarily in New England where land records predate the government survey system.

Micro Data

Specific data such as housing supply in a market area, comparable property sales and listings

Mini Warehouses

A group of small warehouses that are offered to individuals and businesses for short terms to store their business and personal property.

MOBILE HOME

Mobile Homes

The old name for a manufactured home or house trailer. A house that is manufactured off the site and then transported to the site.

Modernization

The process of bringing a property up to current standards of design and mechanical equipment. This may require changes in the exterior and interior and the replacement of mechanical equipment with current equipment.

Mortgage Constant

The total annual payment of principal and interest (annual debt service) on a mortgage with a level-payment amortization, expressed as a percentage of the initial principal amount,

Mortgage Debt Service

The annual sum of all mortgage payments.

Most Profitable

One of the original four tests of Highest and Best Use. It is now called "Maximally Productive."

Multiple Regression Analysis

A statistical technique for measuring the effect that a number of independent variables have on one dependent variable. The technique is now used by appraisers to attempt to develop adjustment from large amount of comparable sale data.

N-O   Glossary

Narrative Reports
Presentation of an estimate of value, featuring a book-type layout. Typically, a narrative report consisting of many pages and is divided into sections, including exhibits and photographs of the of the subject. This is the most complete type of appraisal presentation.

Neighborhood
Every neighborhood is constantly changing, often following a four-phase life cycle:

1. Growth: The period when active construction takes place, new inhabitants are attracted, and the neighborhood gains favor and acceptance.

2. Stability: A period of undefined length in which there are no major changes and no marked gains or losses.

3. Decline: A period that begins when a neighborhood is less able to compete with other neighborhoods. Properties may change use and be in a poor state of maintenance.

4. Renewal: A period of rejuvenation and rebirth of market demand.

Non-Basic Employment
Employment in those activities in a community that do not bring in money from outside the community.

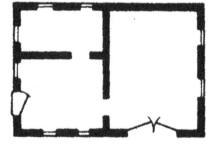

ORTHOGRAPHIC PROJECTION

Opinion of Value
The value estimated by an appraiser and reported in a appraisal report of a defined value.

Operating Expenses
The expenses resulting from the production of income from a property such as taxes, insurance maintenance, repairs. utilities and rubbish removal.

Oral Appraisal Reports
An oral report by an appraiser, usually in a court of law, which references a written real estate appraisal, but presents substantial material evidence in oral format, for use by a jury or judge in making a decision. It also can be made to a client who specifically requests it, but it must comply with the record keeping requirement of the USPAP.

Ordinary Assumptions and Limiting Conditions
Statements made by the appraiser that are part of the appraisal report about things that may or may not be as described in the report. Should they turn out not to be as described the estimated value may not be accurate.

Orthographic Projection
A drawing of building without perspective. It is the most common way that building plans are drawn. The lines that are parallel in the building are parallel on the drawing.

O-P   Glossary

Overall Capitalization Rate

The ratio between annual net operating income (NOI) and the value or sales price. It is often used by appraiser to process income into value.

Party Wall Agreements (13)

An agreement regarding a common wall in buildings that separates two units into separate ownership. It is commonly found in row houses and town houses.

Percentage Adjustment

Adjustments for differences between the subject property in an appraisal and the comparable sales, expressed in percentages and used in the market data approach of the appraisal process to reflect certain conditions in a specific market.

Percolation Test

A test made to determine the capacity of the soil to absorb water, often required to establish the location of the leaching fields of a septic system.

Period of Decline

A period in the evolution of a market area and neighborhood during which it is declining. It is characterized by little or no developments and a decreasing reputation

Period of Equilibrium

A period in the evolution of a market area and neighborhood during which expansion slows down as the availability of vacant land decreases. It is characterized by successful developments and a continued good reputation.

Period of Stability

A period in the evolution of a market area and neighborhood during which it stops expanding. This period often last a long time.

Personal Property

One of the two broad classifications of property, the other being real property, which is distinguished by its movability versus being permanently affixed. In making the distinction which varies from state to state, the manner of annexation, intent of the parties who annexed it, and the use must all be considered.

Physical Deterioration

1. Loss in value of a property caused by wear, tear, age, and use

2. An appraisal term for one of the three broad categories of depreciation.

Physical Deterioration (Depreciation)

1. Loss in value of a property caused by wear, tear, age, and use.

2. An appraisal term for one of the three broad categories of depreciation.

P | Glossary

Physical Deterioration - Curable

Items of physical deterioration in a property that should be cured by a prudent owner because the value added to the property by making the repairs is greater than the cost of the repairs.

Physical Deterioration - Incurable

Items of physical deterioration in a property that a prudent owner would not cure either because it is not physically possible to do so or because the cost of making the repair would exceed the increase in value of the property as a result of the repair.

Physical Life

Typical life of an improvement that has been correctly maintained and cared for.

Physically Possible

One of the four traditional tests for highest and best use.

Plank and Beam Framing

One of the three common methods of framing in which beams are placed up to eight fee apart and covered with planks.

Planned Unit Developments) (PUDs)

A type of land development that is specially provided for in a community's zoning regulations, allowing the developer more flexible use of the land. Part of the land is divided into lots, which are individual-ly owned. The balance is set aside for use by all the owners of lots within the subdivision and is owned either by the community or by an association formed for the lot owners in the subdivision.

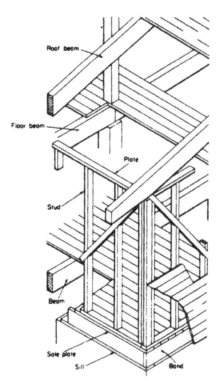

PLANK AND BEAM CONSTRUCTION

Plat Map Productivity

A map that indicates the boundary liens of real estate, usually of land that has been subdivided.

Platform Frame Construction

One of the three common methods of framing (also called Western platform framing). It is characterized by sub flooring that extends to the outside edges of the building to provide a platform upon which exterior walls and interior partitions are erected. It is the most common type of framing system used for houses.

Plottage

When two or more small lots under different ownership are assembled into one common ownership to produce a larger lot with increased utility.

Plottage Value

The increase in value created when two or more small lots under different ownership are assembled into one common ownership to produce a larger lot with increased utility.

Police Power

The power of the govern-

P   Glossary

ment to control the use of real estate for the general welfare of the public. It does this through zoning regulations, building codes, environmental regulations, etc. It also includes the government's right to acquire property by condemnation.

Potential Gross Income
The total rent that could be collected for a property if all the space was rented at market rent and all the tenants paid 100% of the rent due

Predominant Land Use (12)
The most common use of the developable land in a market area or neighborhood.

Price

1. The sum of money for which a property or other item is sold.

2. The asking or listing price of a property.

3. Historical transaction cost of property.

Primary Data
Data that is collected by the appraiser from original sources that are not generally available to the public such as the number of vacant houses in the neighborhood or the rents of various types of apartments.

Principle Meridian
Lines on a map running north to south also called longitude lines. They are

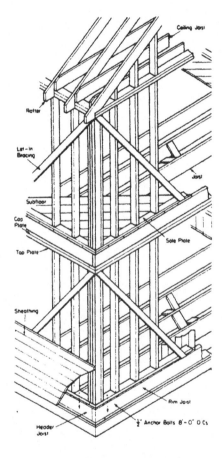

PLATFORM FRAME CONSTRUCTION

used as boundary lines in the U.S. rectangular survey system. The Principle Meridian lines shown on the maps in this system are about one mile apart.

Principle of Substitution
States that when several commodities or services are available providing substantially the same utility and benefit, the one with the lowest price will be chosen by the market.

Private Restrictions
Limitations on the use of land that are created by an owner and passed on to all future owner by means of a deed restriction.

Property

1. A broad term for an area of land under one legal ownership together with all the buildings and other improvements.

2. The rights or interests in land or chattels.

3. Anything that is owned by a person, partnership, corporation or other type of organization.

Property Rights
The rights associated with a piece of real estate are divided in the rights of the government and private property rights which consist of a bundle of rights including the rights to use the property, or transfer the rights by sale or gift.

P-R Glossary

Prospective Date
The effective date of valuation that is a date after the date of the last inspection of the property by the appraiser.

Public Legal Restrictions
The rights of the government to regulate the use of the property, the right to tax, the right to take the property for the good of the public and the right of escheat.

Public Records
Records which the government is required to keep in order for someone or some organization to give notice that is required by law such as deeds, mortgages and other real estate related documents required to be filed to satisfy a variety of statutory requirements.

Purpose of the Appraisal
A term for the type of value to be estimated by the appraiser.

Quantitative Analysis
A type of analysis that reports the changes and trends taking place to the general data used in the appraisal.

Quantitative Data
(See: General Data)

Quantity Survey Method
A method of estimating the cost of a new building or the reproduction or replacement cost of an existing building by making a detailed estimate of the quantity and quality of the necessary materials as well as the labor necessary to install the materials.

Range Lines
In the government survey land description, lines parallel to the principle meridian, marking off the land into six-mile strips known as ranges, they are numbered east or west of the principle meridian

Real Estate
Land and all attachments that are of a permanent nature; same as realty. Real Estate is distinguished from personal property. At one time real estate was the sole source of wealth, and thus achieved a special place in the law because of its importance.

Real Property
The right to use real estate as

1. fee simple estate,

2. life estate or

3. leasehold estate. Some times defined as real estate.

Reconciliation
The final step in the appraisal process, in which the appraiser combines the estimates of value received from the sales comparison, cost and income approaches to arrive at a final estimate of market value for the subject property.

R | Glossary

Reconstructed Operating Statement

A special operating statement prepared by an appraiser for use in the income approach of an appraisal. It includes only those items of income and expense that are directly related to the property, It does not include mortgage interest and amortization or depreciation.

Rectangular (Government) Survey

A system established in 1785 by the federal government, providing for surveying and describing land by reference to principal meridians and base lines.

Regression Analysis

(See: Multiple Regression Analysis)

Rehabilitation

1. Restoration of utility and appeal in deteriorating properties and public facilities in an urban renewal area

2. Restoring and renovating a property without destroying existing improvements or changing the form or style of the property,

Rejuvenation

A period in the life cycle of a market area or neighborhood after a period of decline that is often the result organized community activities such as redevelopment programs, rebuilding and historical renovation.

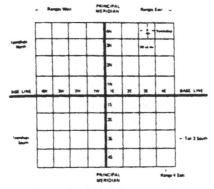

RECTANGULAR (GOVERNMENT) SURVEY SYSTEM

Remaining Economic Life

The period of time from the effective date of the value estimate to when the improvements will cease to contribute any value to the property,

Remodeling

Changing the plan, form or style of a structure to correct functional deficiencies or satisfy the special needs of the owner or tenant.

Renovation

Substantially improving a property through rehabilitation, modernization and remodeling

Replacement Cost (1)

The cost of erecting a building to take the place of or serve the functions of a previous structure. Replacement cost often sets the upper limit on value; it is often used for insurance purposes.

Reproduction Cost (1)

The normal cost of exact duplication of a property as of a certain date. Reproduction cost differs from replacement cost in that replacement requires the same functional utility for a property, whereas reproduction is an exact duplicate, using the same materials and craftsmanship.

Reserves

1. Money set aside from earnings to pay for future taxes, unusual maintenance, future claims or possible liabilities related to the ownership of a property.

R-S Glossary

2. Often the money is not actually set aside, but is a bookkeeping entry that allows the money to be an expense before the anticipated event occurs.

Restricted Appraisal Report
A special type of appraisal report, prohibited by the USPAP, for use by the public. It is most commonly used by lenders for portfolio revaluation.

Retrospective Date
The effective date of valuation that is a date before the date of the last inspection of the property by the appraiser. It is commonly used for estate valuations and tax appeals.

Rights of Ownership
The bundle of public and private rights which together make up the bundle of rights of property ownership. Ownership of all the private rights is called fee simple ownership.

Riparian Rights
Rights pertaining to the use of water on, under or adjacent to one's land. In most states, riparian rights provide that property owners cannot alter the flow of water to their downstream neighbors.

Roof Sheathing (14)
A rigid material that provides the support for roof loads and a backing for the attachment of roofing materials.

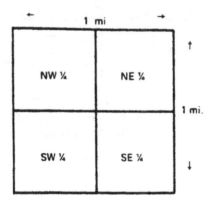

SECTIONS

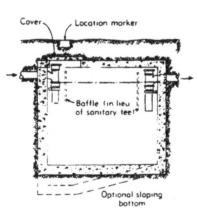

SEPTIC SYSTEM

Sales Comparison Approach
The process of estimating the value of a property by examining and comparing actual sales of comparable properties

Scope of Work
The amount and type of information researched and the analysis applied in an assignment.

Secondary Data
Data that is relied upon by that appraiser that has been published and is available to the general public.

Sections
One square mile in the government survey, containing 640 acres. There are 36 sections in a six-mile-square township.

Self-Contained Appraisal Report
An appraisal report that fully describes the data and analysis used in the assignment, All the appropriate information is contained within the report and not referenced to the appraisers files.

Septic System
A sewage system consisting of a septic tank, distribution box and leaching field, used in areas where sewers have not been installed or hooked up.

S | Glossary

Sequence of Adjustments
(The order in which quantitative adjustments are applied to the sales prices of comparable properties in the sales comparison approach of the valuation process, determined by the market and analysis of the data.

Shake
A hand-split shingle used as roofing or siding.

Shallow Well
A well that is used to supply water to a property that is dug only as deep as it necessary to supply an adequate supply of water and not deep enough to supply the pressure necessary to deliver the water from the well with out the aide of a pump.

Sheathing
A wall board or plywood covering placed over the exterior studs or rafters of a house, often over insulation materials.

Short Lived Items
Those portions of a structure that have a shorter expected economic life than the rest of the structure.

Site
A Parcel of land that is improved with grading, utilities, driveways and utility hookups and is suitable for building purposes

Site Improvements (11)
Those specific improvements to raw land that turn the parcel of raw land

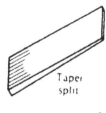

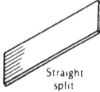

SHAKE

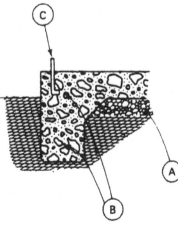

A   Firm Subbase of Crushed Rock
B   Continuous Reinforcement Rods
C   Anchor Bolt

SLAB-ON-GROUND

into a building site., such as grading, drainage, installation of utility connections, access roads, etc.

Slab-on-Ground
A type of basement less foundation made by pouring concrete directly onto an area of prepared ground surface on top of the footings.

SMSA
(See: Standard Metropolitan Statistical Area)

Special Amenities
Special features or benefits such as a tennis court or pool which materially increases enjoyment of a property, including good design, superior view, etc. that may not add value equal or greater than their cost.

Special Purpose Use
Uses that are appropriate for one user or for a very limited number of users.

Specific Data
Data which includes details about the subject property, comparable sales and rental properties, and relevant local market characteristics.

Specific Date
Every appraisal must be as of a specific date which is defined by the 2006 USPAP as a specific day.

Sprayed On Insulation
Insulation that is usually in a liquid form that is applied to the property by spraying over the surface to be insulated.

S Glossary

Square Foot Method

A method used in the cost approach to determine the replacement or reproduction cost of the subject property. The known cost per square foot of a recently built comparable structure is multiplied by the number of square feet in the subject property to determine the cost of the subject property.

Stair Riser

The part of a stair that is the vertical board between the stair threads.

Standard Metropolitan Statistical Area (SMSA)

Areas established by the U.S. Census Bureau that consisted of each city in the United States that together with its suburbs that had a population of 50,000 or more when they were established.

Subdivision Regulations

Requirements imposed on developers and sub-dividers that control the types and quality of basic services available to home-owners in the neighborhood and have a strong affect on the value of existing structures.

Subject Property

The property being appraised. It must be identified is such a way as there can be no confusion what is being appraised.

Subsoil

The layer immediately below the top soil. The quality this layer affects the ability of the site to support the intended structures. If it is rock it may have to be removed. If it too soft it may be necessary to dig deep to find soil capable of bearing the weight of the structure.

Subsurface Rights

Ownership rights in a parcel of real estate to the water, minerals, gas, oil and so forth that lie beneath the surface of the property.

Subterranean Termite

A insect that lives in the moist earth and invade above ground wood which they consume as food. They are found in most areas of the United States. When uncontrolled they can do substantial damage to a building.

Summary Appraisal Report

One of the three kinds of reports that are permitted by the USPAP. Most form appraisals are summary appraisal reports. In general they summarize the information analyzed, the appraisal methods and techniques employed, and the reasoning that supports the analyses, opinions and conclusions.

S-T | Glossary

Superadequacy

Those improvements that are made to a property that add less value than their cost because they are an over improvement to the property in the existing market,

Surface Soil

Also known a top soil. The first layer of soil that often has the ability to support lawns and other vegetation. When it is removed as part of the construction process it should be stored and replaced when the project is completed.

Surface Water

Water from any source that appears in a diffused state with no permanent, continuous source of supply nor any regular course or channel to flow along.

Surplus Land

Land that is not needed to support the existing improvements. Typically it cannot be separated and sold off.

Survey

The process by which a parcel of land is measured and its area ascertained; also, the blueprint showing the measurements, boundaries and area. A survey is needed to determine exact boundaries and any easements or encroachments.

Swale

A shallow, open channel for the collection and disposal of excess surface water.

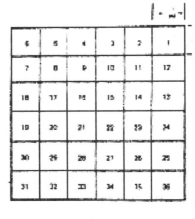

TOWNSHIP

The Appraisal Foundation
(See: Appraisal Foundation)

Theory of Consistent Use

An appraisal theory that states that a property nearing transition to a new use cannot be valued on the basis of one use for the land and another for the improvements.

Timeshare Ownership

A form of ownership interest that may include an estate interest in property and which allows use of the property for a fixed or variable time period.

Title & Record Data

Evidence that the owner of land is in lawful possession thereof; evidence of ownership. Often clarified or qualified by an adjective such as absolute, good, clear, marketable, defective or legal.

Township Lines

Lines that divide townships at their northern and southern boarders,

Townships

A six-mile-square tract delineated by government survey.

Typographical Study

A study of a piece of land that provides information about the its contour, grading, natural drainage, soil condition, view and general usefulness.

U Glossary

Uniform Residential Appraisal Report (URAR)

A widely recognized and accepted appraisal report form designed to report an appraisal of a one-unit property or a one-unit property with an accessory unit (including a unit in a planned unit development), based on an interior and exterior inspection. It is approved by Fannie Mae, Freddie Mac, FHA and others.; It carries the form numbers Fannie Mae 1004 and Freddie Mac 70.

Uniform Standards of Professional Appraisal Practice (USPAP)

A set of professional appraisal standards established by the Appraisal Standards Board of The Appraisal Foundation. The standards address the development and reportage requirements for appraisals and analyses, as well as issues of ethics and practice.

Unit in Place Method

An appraisal method of estimating construction costs by estimating the cost of each component section, including all materials, labor costs and overhead and adding the figures together for an estimated cost of the improvements.

Unit of Comparison

An appraisal technique that divides properties into units, such as front feet, square feet, dwelling units, number of beds, acres etc. A value is estimated for each unit of comparison, and the value of any similar properties in the market is estimated by multiplying the number of units by the estimated unit price.

Urban Renewal

A controlled method of redeveloping and rehabilitating urban areas by demolishing, renovating or repairing existing structure and infrastructures using, federal, state, local and private funds usually according to an established plan.

V | Glossary

Vacancy and Collection Allowance

In a reconstructed operating statement, used as part of the income approach in the valuation process, it is an amount subtracted from the potential income of the property to reflect rent that will be uncollected because of unrented space or uncollected rent.

Vacant Land

Property in an undeveloped area with few, if any, surrounding improvements in appraisal terminology it is called land as opposed to site which is land plus improvements that make it ready for use, including streets, sewer systems and utility connections.

Valuation Analysis

Estimated worth or price; also, valuing by appraisal. Valuation is the process of estimating the worth of an object.

Value

The worth of all the rights arising from ownership; the quantity of one thing that will be given in exchange for another. Price is the historic amount that was paid; value is an estimate of what it is worth. Often value is qualified as to a specific type: market, user, assessed, insurable, speculative and so on.

Value Estimate

The value estimated by an appraiser and reported in a appraisal report of a defined value. See: Opinion of value

Value-In-Use

The particular (usually additional) value which an asset for a specific owner, due primarily to a unique use or as a function of its location in combination with a use, which is not a part of the real property or personal property and may not prove to be transferable as part of a future sale.

Valuation Process

A systematic procedure an appraiser follows to provide answers to a client's question about real property value.

Verification

The process used by appraisers to confirm the validity of data about comparable properties used in the sales comparison approach.

W-Z | Glossary

Wallboard Insulation
On of the five primary categories of insulation. A wallboard that in addition to having structural strength also provide insulation.

Wetland

1. Land periodically covered by water, such as salt marshes, bogs, wet meadows, mud flats and ponds subject to environmental legislation.

2. Land containing high quantities of soil moisture where the water table is at or near the surface for most of the year.

Wetland Controls
Environmental regulation that control the use of wetlands.

Winder
Treads that are part of a curved stair case that are cut with one end wider than the other so that they make the curve in the stair case.

Window Dressing
An appraiser's term for unnecessary (merely decorative) figures, charts and displays.

Work Triangle
A triangle drawn on a plan by kitchen designers to test the design of a kitchen. The points of the triangle are the fronts of the range, sink and refrigerator. The total length of the side of the triangle should not exceed 22 ft. and traffic the flows through the kitchen should not go through the triangle.

Zoning Regulations
Law restricting, regulating and controlling the use of real estate for the general welfare , usually under the jurisdiction of a zoning board or commission.

Zygocephalum
A real estate term for any inaccurate measurement of land. Historically, it was the amount of land a yoke of oxen could plow in a single day.

How to make a
Single Family Appraisal on the

2005 Uniform Residential Appraisal Report (URAR)

Fannie Mae Form 1004 ~ Freddie Mac Form 70

Revised March 2005

Condensed and Abridged

Henry S. Harrison
MAI, SRPA, RM, ASA, IFAS, CSA, DREI

Published by the H Squared Company
315 Whitney Avenue
New Haven, CT 06511
Phone: (203) 562-3159 • FAX: (203) 562-5481
henryhsq@aol.com

How to make a Single Family Appraisal
on the 2005 Uniform Residential Appraisal Report (URAR)
Fannie Mae Form 1004 ~ Freddie Mac Form 70

Condensed and Abridged

by Henry S. Harrison
MAI, SRPA, RM, ASA, IFAS, CSA, DREI

ISBN # 0-927054-18-3

©2005 by H Squared Company
All rights reserved.
Printed in the United States of America

1st Printing	Edition 1	December	1977
38th Printing	Edition 8	December	2005
39th Printing		January	2006

Special Condensed And Abridged
Printing   April   2006

Edited and Typeset by Jason Gaines

This Condensed and Abridged version of the 2005 Illustrated Guide was prepared to help new appraisers make better use of the new 2005 Uniform Residential Appraisal Report (URAR).

In the full version of the book are the latest Fannie Mae and Freddie Mac guidelines. The 01/01/05 USPAP revisions were also considered. Suggestions are made in the appropriate places on how to make your appraisals comply with the revised 2005 USPAP. It is important that you make yourself aware of all current USPAP requirements that apply to appraising single family residences. There will be substantial changes to the next revision of the USPAP due out 7/1/06.

It is not the intent of this Illustrated Guide to make anyone an instant appraiser. Producing a satisfactory appraisal report requires education and experience. This book is for those who have completed the necessary education and have achieved the requisite experience to perform a professional appraisal and complete a professional quality appraisal report.

My thanks to Jason Gaines and my wife, Ruth Lambert, who helped me update and edit various sections of this book, based on the current instructions and regulations of the organizations and agencies noted above.

I like to hear from appraisers who use my books and have questions, suggestions, or problems. Please contact me by phone at (203) 562-3159, by FAX at (203) 562-5481, E-mail *askhenryharrison@aol.com* or by writing to: 315 Whitney Avenue, New Haven, CT 06511.

Henry S. Harrison
April 2006

P.S The full version of this book is available from Forms and Worms:

Call 1-800-243-4545

FAX 1-800-270-1075

Order Online at: www.formsandworms.comm

TABLE OF CONTENTS

TABLE OF CONTENTS

TABLE OF CONTENTS

TABLE OF CONTENTS

TABLE OF CONTENTS

Uniform Residential Appraisal Report - USE

This report form is designed to report an appraisal of a one-unit property or a one-unit property with an accessory unit (including a unit in a planned unit development (PUD)), based on an **interior and exterior inspection of the subject property**. This report form is not designed to report an appraisal of a manufactured home or a unit in a condominium or cooperative project.

MODIFICATIONS, ADDITIONS, OR DELETIONS

This appraisal report is subject to the scope of work, intended use, intended user, definition of market value, statement of assumptions and limiting conditions, and certifications contained in the report form. Modifications, additions, or deletions to the intended use, intended user, definition of market value, or assumptions and limiting conditions are not permitted. The appraiser may expand the scope of work to include any additional research or analysis necessary based on the complexity of this appraisal assignment. Modifications or deletions to the certifications are also not permitted. However, additional certifications that do not constitute material alterations to this appraisal report, such as those required by law or those related to the appraiser's continuing education or membership in an appraisal organization, are permitted.

SCOPE OF WORK

The scope of work for this appraisal is defined by the complexity of this appraisal assignment and the reporting requirements of this appraisal report form, including the following definition of market value, statement of assumptions and limiting conditions, and certifications. The appraiser must, at a minimum:

(1) perform a complete visual inspection of the interior and exterior areas of the subject property;
(2) inspect the neighborhood;
(3) inspect each of the comparable sales from at least the street;
(4) research, verify, and analyze data from reliable public and/or private sources; and
(5) report his or her analysis, opinions and conclusions in this appraisal report.

REQUIRED EXHIBITS

• A street map that shows the location of the subject property and of all comparables that the appraiser used;
• An exterior building sketch of the improvements that indicates the dimensions. The appraiser must also include calculations to show how he or she arrived at the estimate for gross living area. A floor plan sketch that indicates the dimensions is required instead of the exterior building or unit sketch if the floor plan is atypical or functionally obsolete, thus limiting the market appeal for the property in comparison to competitive properties in the neighborhood;
• Clear descriptive photographs (either in black and white or in color) that show the front, back, and a street scene of the subject property, and that are appropriately identified. (Photographs must be originals that are produced either by photography or electronic imaging.);
• Clear, descriptive photographs (either in black and white or in color) that show the front of each comparable sale and that are appropriately identified. Generally, photographs should be originals that are produced by photography or electronic imaging; however, copies of photographs from a multiple listing service or from the appraiser's files are acceptable if they are clear and descriptive;
• Any other data — as an attachment or addendum to the appraisal report form — that are necessary to provide an adequately supported opinion of market value.

Fannie Mae
2900 Wisconsin Ave. NW
Washington, DC 20016-2892

Announcement 05-02
March 24, 2005
Amends these Guides: Selling Final Appraisal Report Forms
(Note: Only parts of this announcement that pertain to the URAR form are included here)

Part XI: Property and Appraisal Analysis Guidelines

In Lender Announcement 04-07, dated November 8, 2004, we released a total of eleven test appraisal and appraisal review report forms for a comment period that ended on December 15, 2004. We received hundreds of comments on how to further improve the quality of those forms. We would like to thank the many lenders, appraisers, and organizations that took the time to share their significant recommendations with us, especially the Appraisal Institute, the Appraisal Standards Board of The Appraisal Foundation, the Manufactured Housing Institute, the Association of Appraiser Regulatory Officials, the Appraisal Subcommittee of the National Association of Realtors, the American Guild of Appraisers of the AFL-CIO, the National Association of Independent Fee Appraisers, and the state appraiser licensing and regulatory boards. With that feedback, we made several improvements and are now releasing the eleven final report forms:

These report forms are a continuation of our efforts to improve the property appraisal process that led to the development of the property valuation component of Desktop Underwriter® (DU). At that time, we developed more concise appraisal report forms, offered an exterior-only property inspection option, and reduced the amount of required appraisal report documentation. Lenders that have used the DU appraisal forms report reductions in the amount of time and costs as compared with using the standard appraisal report forms. Our focus, then and now, is to give lenders access to a streamlined property valuation process, which enables them to more efficiently manage the overall valuation process while maintaining property appraisal and underwriting quality.

In revising the forms, we consolidated the number of appraisal report forms in order to simplify our documentation requirements for lenders and appraisers. In addition, we have applied the more streamlined approach and reporting formats of the DU appraisal report forms to all of the revised forms. The more consistent presentation of the appraiser's research, analysis, and conclusions will help appraisers more clearly present the results of their valuation, and will enhance the lender's review of the appraisal.

We now have one appraisal report form for reporting an appraisal for each property and inspection type for both DU and manually processed mortgages. As a result, lenders and appraisers are now able to determine which report form should be used based on the type of property and property inspection required. The form changes also further our efforts to work with the state appraiser licensing or regulatory boards. As part of our quality assurance efforts, we refer unacceptable appraisal reports to the state boards for an investigation and any action they consider appropriate. We have received feedback from many state boards and their investigators about the types of information that would help them in their investigations. Many of those observations helped us to identify the strengths and weaknesses of the report forms and provided us with the framework for consolidating and improving the forms.

Our final appraisal report forms, dated March 2005, are required for appraisals performed on and after November 1, 2005. Lenders and appraisers may continue to use our existing appraisal report forms or the test forms released in 2004 until October 31, 2005. All of our standard applicable exhibits that are used to support an appraisal based on the particular property inspection type are required when using these report forms.

You may download a copy of each of these report forms by accessing this Announcement on our website. Once on the homepage, under Single-Family Quick Access, select Guides, then Guide Announcements, and then All 2005 Guide Announcements.

Overview of Key Modifications

The primary enhancements to the report forms are designed to help communicate our expectations for the property valuation and appraisal reporting processes, clarify the appraiser's accountability for the quality of his or her appraisal, and help ensure the appraiser's compliance with our requirements and those of the Uniform Standards of Professional Appraisal Practice.

The revised format enables the appraiser to report the results of the valuation in a brief but comprehensive manner, which will be more efficient for reviewing and processing than our existing forms. Also, the expanded areas for comments throughout the forms should help to eliminate the need for additional addenda and attachments. Direct questions have been added to the report forms that require the appraiser to report his or her analysis and conclusions on key areas in a clear and succinct yes/no format to address whether:

- the subject property is currently offered for sale or if it was offered for sale in the twelve months prior to the effective date of the appraisal;
- the appraiser analyzed the contract for sale for the subject property for a purchase money transaction;
- the subject property has any adverse physical deficiencies or conditions such as (but not limited to) needed repairs, and whether such conditions affect the livability, soundness, or structural integrity of the property;
- the subject property generally conforms to the neighborhood; and
- the appraiser researched, analyzed and reported on the sale (or transfer) history for the subject property and comparable sales.

Each of the revised appraisal report forms includes the purpose of the appraisal, scope of work, intended use, intended user, definition of market value, statement of assumptions and limiting conditions, and appraiser's certification. The appraiser's certification on each of the revised appraisal report forms was expanded to more clearly communicate our expectations of the appraisal and appraisal reporting process. In addition, new certifications were developed to:

- affirm that the appraiser has the appropriate knowledge and experience to appraise the particular type of property in the market area;
- clarify the permitted disclosure or distribution of the appraisal report and the parties that may rely on the appraisal report as part of a mortgage finance transaction; and
- acknowledge that any intentional or negligent misrepresentation may result in civil liability and/or criminal penalties including, but not limited to, fine or imprisonment or both.

Uniform Standards of Professional Appraisal Practice

The valuation analysis performed in conjunction with our appraisal report forms is based on the sales comparison approach to value because that generally is the most reliable indicator of value for one-unit to four-unit properties. In order to reduce the time and costs associated with performing the appraisal, we do not require the appraiser to develop the cost and income approaches to value for all appraisal assignments.

Appraisals reported on our report forms are considered limited appraisals that are subject to the Departure Rule of the Uniform Standards of Professional Appraisal Practice (USPAP) if the cost and income approaches to value are applicable under the USPAP and they are not developed. An appraisal reported on our forms, however, will be considered a complete appraisal when the cost and income approaches to value are not applicable because the omission of those approaches for the particular type of appraisal assignment is not a departure from the USPAP. We have identified in the appraiser's certification on certain appraisal report forms that the cost and/or income approaches to value were not developed, unless otherwise noted in the report, which is an approach that complies with the USPAP. The Appraisal Standards Board of The Appraisal Foundation has clarified that appraisers are not required to identify an appraisal as "limited" or "complete" in the report. However, the appraiser is required to disclose in the appraisal report any departures from the USPAP, such as the valuation approaches not developed, that would be applicable to the particular appraisal assignment.

Fannie Mae will continue to have its own separate appraisal requirements to supplement the minimum requirements of the USPAP to ensure that all of our specific concerns are addressed for any given appraisal. The appraisal report forms reflect our requirements, which are supplemental standards to the minimum requirements of the USPAP. An appraiser will be in full compliance with our requirements if he or she addresses all of the information on the report forms and presents the data accurately and completely.

Although the extent of the appraisal process is reflected in the appraisal report forms, the forms are not designed or intended to limit the appraisal process. As with all appraisal report forms, appraisers should go beyond any limitations of a particular form by reporting any additional research or analysis they have performed, and any additional conclusions they may have, as necessary or helpful to adequately document the valuation process and/or to support the appraisal. The extent of the appraiser's research, analysis, and reporting is determined by the complexity of the appraisal assignment.

Pamela S. Johnson, Senior Vice President
Fannie Mae

Pitfalls to Watch Out For When Using the 2005 URAR Appraisal Report

by Henry S. Harrison

*(Based on an article in the June-Aug. 2005 **Real Estate Valuation Magazine Online**)*

The new 2005 URAR, created by Fannie Mae, has been adopted by most other governmental and quasi-governmental agencies. I have expressed my feelings in several Real Estate Valuation Magazine editorials that it would have been better for a broad-based committee, such as the one which originally designed the Classic 6/93 URAR, to revise the URAR rather than Fannie Mae doing so unilaterally. I am also disappointed that the URAR has turned into a form designed specifically for mortgage appraisals, unlike the Classic URAR which is an all-purpose form. In my opinion, the Classic 6/93 URAR was not broken; all it needed was an update.

However, the reality is that the new 2005 URAR is probably here to stay for a while. Therefore, I have written an Illustrated Guide to help appraisers make professional appraisals that meet Fannie Mae's requirements, as well as the requirements of the other agencies that have adopted these forms, and the Uniform Standards of Professional Appraisal Practice (USPAP).

The 2005 URAR is **not** an all-purpose form like the Classic 6/93 URAR. Instead, it is a form which has been specifically designed to meet the need for an appraisal where the "Intended Use" is only for a mortgage finance transaction. Unlike the Classic URAR, the 2005 URAR cannot be used for condominiums or manufactured houses; it may only be used for single family residences.

The 2005 URAR has many additional requirements that are not found in the Classic URAR 6/93. Fannie Mae (and Freddie Mac, et al.) have justified adding these new requirements as part of their revised "Scope of Work" definition. This change permits them to require things that are not required by the Uniform Standards of Professional Practice (USPAP). It also restricts appraisers from accepting assignments that are permitted under USPAP, but not allowed by Fannie Mae and Freddie Mac when using this new form.

Below are highlights of the Fannie Mae Announcement 05-02 that pertain to the 2005 URAR:

Overview of Key Modifications
The primary enhancements to the report forms are designed to help communicate our expectations for the property valuation and appraisal reporting processes, clarify the appraiser's accountability for the quality of his or her appraisal, and help ensure the appraiser's compliance with our requirements and those of the Uniform Standards of Professional Appraisal Practice...

Direct questions have been added to the report forms that require the appraiser to report his or her analysis and conclusions on key areas in a clear and succinct yes/no format to address whether:

PITFALLS TO WATCH OUT FOR

- the subject property is currently offered for sale or if it was offered for sale in the twelve months prior to the effective date of the appraisal;
- the appraiser analyzed the contract for sale for the subject property for a purchase money transaction;
- the subject property has any adverse physical deficiencies or conditions such as (but not limited to) needed repairs, and whether such conditions affect the livability, soundness, or structural integrity of the property;
- the subject property generally conforms to the neighborhood; and
- the appraiser researched, analyzed and reported on the sale (or transfer) history for the subject property and comparable sales.

The appraiser's certification on each of the revised appraisal report forms was expanded to more clearly communicate our expectations of the appraisal and appraisal reporting process. In addition, new certifications were developed to:

- affirm that the appraiser has the appropriate knowledge and experience to appraise the particular type of property in the market area;
- clarify the permitted disclosure or distribution of the appraisal report and the parties that may rely on the appraisal report as part of a mortgage finance transaction.

HIGHLIGHTS OF IMPORTANT CHANGES

HIGHEST AND BEST USE

The Highest and Best Use Line is reworded:

"Is the highest and best use of the subject property as improved (or as proposed per plans and specifications) the present use? ☐ Yes ☐ No   If No, describe"

USPAP Standards Rule 2-2 (a)(x) Page 25: (This Standards Rule contains binding requirements from which departure is not permitted.) "When reporting an opinion of market value, describe the support and rationale for the appraiser's opinion of the highest and best use of the real estate."

The appraiser must provide a rationale for his or her opinion of Highest and Best Use.

PHYSICAL DEFICIENCIES OR ADVERSE CONDITIONS

"Are there any physical deficiencies or adverse conditions that affect the livability, soundness, or structural integrity of the property? ☐ Yes ☐ No   If Yes, describe"

ADVERSE SITE CONDITIONS

"Are there any adverse site conditions or external factors (easements, encroachments, environmental conditions, land uses, etc.)? ☐ Yes ☐ No   If Yes, describe"

A significant change on the URAR is the elimination of the word "apparent." I don't see how you can answer this question without checking the deed for easements, land use restrictions, etc.

This is a very broad question which should be carefully answered. If a Disclosure Form is part of the sales transaction, it should be examined to see if anything disclosed falls into the category of what is being asked for in this question. Most likely, the Lender is going to require these deficiencies to be corrected. Therefore, the appraiser must be prepared to support his or her opinion when it is questioned by the homeowner.

SALES COMPARISON APPROACH GRID

"Age" has been changed to "Actual Age."

In the past, the appraiser could estimate the effective age of the subject property and report it on the age line. Now, the appraiser must determine the actual age of the property.

PUD INFORMATION

The PUD INFORMATION section has been redesigned and expanded. The appraisal of a unit in a PUD requires special skills and experience. Keep in mind that if you accept one of these appraisal assignments, you will be certifying that you have the necessary skill and experience (without getting help from anyone) to do the assignment.

ADEQUATE KNOWLEDGE AND EXPERIENCE

The Appraiser's Certification states that the Appraiser has adequate knowledge and experience to make the appraisal. It does not recognize that USPAP permits the appraiser several other alternatives.

This is not a USPAP requirement. It is a Fannie Mae and Freddie Mac requirement. In the past, it was common to obtain the help of someone who had the prerequisite knowledge and experience when:

1. The subject is in a market outside of the appraiser's usual territory and he or she is not familiar with the market.
2. The dwelling is an historic house.
3. The dwelling is a mansion.

This is no longer permitted by Fannie Mae and Freddie Mac, even though it is permitted by the USPAP.

APPRAISER RESPONSIBLE THAT TRAINEE IS QUALIFIED

It is no longer sufficient to just name whoever helped you with an appraisal. You must now identify the Trainee and anyone else who helped you and specify what tasks he or she performed. You must also certify that he or she is qualified to do the tasks performed.

This certification requires the Appraiser to acknowledge work done by Trainees, and it points out that the Appraiser is responsible for the quality of the work done by the Trainee. Appraisers will have to consider how it will look to clients when they find out that a substantial part of an appraisal was done by a Trainee.

LENDER/CLIENT ONLY ONE TO RECEIVE REPORT FROM APPRAISER

The Appraiser's Certification requires that the Lender/Client identified in the report be the one who receives the report.

This section of the certification prevents the Appraiser from giving a copy of the report to the property owner, another lender, the broker, etc. These people and others may be entitled to a copy of the report. It should be supplied by the Lender/Client, however, and not the Appraiser.

ONE YEAR SALE HISTORY OF COMPARABLE SALES

The 2005 URAR has questions on it that substantially expand the amount of work necessary to complete the form. A good example is on page 2 in the SALES COMPARISON APPROACH section:

"My research ☐ did ☐ did not reveal any prior sales or transfers of the comparable sales for the year prior to the sale of the comparable sale?"

In many areas, this is difficult information to obtain. Note that the sales history required is not from the date of appraisal, but rather from one year before the date of the sale of the comparable sale. If you used a comparable sale that sold one year ago, you would have to search back two years from the date of the appraisal.

CONCLUSION

Fannie Mae and Freddie Mac seems to be rather two-faced regarding appraisals. On one hand, they are pushing for computer-made or computer-assisted appraisals, and yet at the same time, instead of making the URAR easier to complete, they have made it more complex in subtle and not-so-subtle ways.

They claim that by eliminating the Income Approach and Cost Approach, for example, they are simplifying mortgage appraising. However, this work doesn't take much time compared to how long it takes to find the sales history and actual age of the comparable sales. In reality, what they are doing is taking over the easy jobs and giving the appraisers all of the harder ones.

For the time being, the 2005 URAR is going to rule the roost, and whatever Fannie Mae wants, Fannie Mae will get. If you want to continue to do work that will end up with Fannie Mae, Freddie Mac, or the other agencies which have adopted their forms and requirements, you are going to have to do appraisals their way.

Uniform Residential Appraisal Report

File #

The purpose of this summary appraisal report is to provide the lender/client with an accurate, and adequately supported, opinion of the market value of the subject property.

SUBJECT

Property Address		City		State	Zip Code
Borrower	Owner of Public Record			County	

Legal Description

Assessor's Parcel #		Tax Year	R.E. Taxes $
Neighborhood Name		Map Reference	Census Tract

Occupant ☐ Owner ☐ Tenant ☐ Vacant   Special Assessments $ ☐ PUD   HOA $ ☐ per year ☐ per month

Property Rights Appraised ☐ Fee Simple ☐ Leasehold ☐ Other (describe)

Assignment Type ☐ Purchase Transaction ☐ Refinance Transaction ☐ Other (describe)

Lender/Client   Address

Is the subject property currently offered for sale or has it been offered for sale in the twelve months prior to the effective date of this appraisal? ☐ Yes ☐ No

Report data source(s) used, offering price(s), and date(s).

CONTRACT

I ☐ did ☐ did not analyze the contract for sale for the subject purchase transaction. Explain the results of the analysis of the contract for sale or why the analysis was not performed.

Contract Price $ Date of Contract   Is the property seller the owner of public record? ☐ Yes ☐ No   Data Source(s)

Is there any financial assistance (loan charges, sale concessions, gift or downpayment assistance, etc.) to be paid by any party on behalf of the borrower? ☐ Yes ☐ No

If Yes, report the total dollar amount and describe the items to be paid.

NEIGHBORHOOD

Note: Race and the racial composition of the neighborhood are not appraisal factors.

Neighborhood Characteristics			One-Unit Housing Trends				One-Unit Housing		Present Land Use %	
Location ☐ Urban ☐ Suburban ☐ Rural			Property Values ☐ Increasing	☐ Stable	☐ Declining		PRICE	AGE	One-Unit	%
Built-Up ☐ Over 75% ☐ 25–75% ☐ Under 25%			Demand/Supply ☐ Shortage	☐ In Balance	☐ Over Supply		$ (000)	(yrs)	2-4 Unit	%
Growth ☐ Rapid ☐ Stable ☐ Slow			Marketing Time ☐ Under 3 mths	☐ 3–6 mths	☐ Over 6 mths		Low		Multi-Family	%
Neighborhood Boundaries							High		Commercial	%
							Pred.		Other	%

Neighborhood Description

Market Conditions (including support for the above conclusions)

SITE

Dimensions		Area	Shape	View

Specific Zoning Classification   Zoning Description

Zoning Compliance ☐ Legal ☐ Legal Nonconforming (Grandfathered Use) ☐ No Zoning ☐ Illegal (describe)

Is the highest and best use of the subject property as improved (or as proposed per plans and specifications) the present use? ☐ Yes ☐ No If No, describe

Utilities	Public	Other (describe)		Public	Other (describe)	Off-site Improvements—Type	Public	Private
Electricity	☐	☐	Water	☐	☐	Street	☐	☐
Gas	☐	☐	Sanitary Sewer	☐	☐	Alley	☐	☐

FEMA Special Flood Hazard Area ☐ Yes ☐ No FEMA Flood Zone   FEMA Map #   FEMA Map Date

Are the utilities and off-site improvements typical for the market area? ☐ Yes ☐ No If No, describe

Are there any adverse site conditions or external factors (easements, encroachments, environmental conditions, land uses, etc.)? ☐ Yes ☐ No If Yes, describe

IMPROVEMENTS

General Description		Foundation		Exterior Description materials/condition		Interior materials/condition	
Units ☐ One ☐ One with Accessory Unit		☐ Concrete Slab ☐ Crawl Space		Foundation Walls		Floors	
# of Stories		☐ Full Basement ☐ Partial Basement		Exterior Walls		Walls	
Type ☐ Det. ☐ Att. ☐ S-Det./End Unit		Basement Area sq. ft.		Roof Surface		Trim/Finish	
☐ Existing ☐ Proposed ☐ Under Const.		Basement Finish %		Gutters & Downspouts		Bath Floor	
Design (Style)		☐ Outside Entry/Exit ☐ Sump Pump		Window Type		Bath Wainscot	
Year Built		Evidence of ☐ Infestation		Storm Sash/Insulated		Car Storage ☐ None	
Effective Age (Yrs)		☐ Dampness ☐ Settlement		Screens		☐ Driveway # of Cars	
Attic ☐ None		Heating ☐ FWA ☐ HWBB ☐ Radiant		Amenities ☐ Woodstove(s) #		Driveway Surface	
☐ Drop Stair ☐ Stairs		☐ Other Fuel		☐ Fireplace(s) # ☐ Fence		☐ Garage # of Cars	
☐ Floor ☐ Scuttle		Cooling ☐ Central Air Conditioning		☐ Patio/Deck ☐ Porch		☐ Carport # of Cars	
☐ Finished ☐ Heated		☐ Individual ☐ Other		☐ Pool ☐ Other		☐ Att. ☐ Det. ☐ Built-in	

Appliances ☐ Refrigerator ☐ Range/Oven ☐ Dishwasher ☐ Disposal ☐ Microwave ☐ Washer/Dryer ☐ Other (describe)

Finished area above grade contains: Rooms   Bedrooms   Bath(s)   Square Feet of Gross Living Area Above Grade

Additional features (special energy efficient items, etc.)

Describe the condition of the property (including needed repairs, deterioration, renovations, remodeling, etc.)

Are there any physical deficiencies or adverse conditions that affect the livability, soundness, or structural integrity of the property? ☐ Yes ☐ No If Yes, describe

Does the property generally conform to the neighborhood (functional utility, style, condition, use, construction, etc.)? ☐ Yes ☐ No If No, describe

Freddie Mac Form 70 March 2005	Page 1 of 6	Fannie Mae Form 1004 March 2005

NOTES

Uniform Residential Appraisal Report
File #

The purpose of this summary appraisal report is to provide the lender/client with an accurate, and adequately supported, opinion of the market value of the subject property.

Property Address	City	State	Zip Code
Borrower	Owner of Public Record	County	
Legal Description			
Assessor's Parcel #	Tax Year	R.E. Taxes $	
Neighborhood Name	Map Reference	Census Tract	
Occupant ☐ Owner ☐ Tenant ☐ Vacant	Special Assessments $	☐ PUD	HOA $ ☐ per year ☐ per month
Property Rights Appraised ☐ Fee Simple ☐ Leasehold ☐ Other (describe)			
Assignment Type ☐ Purchase Transaction ☐ Refinance Transaction ☐ Other (describe)			
Lender/Client	Address		
Is the subject property currently offered for sale or has it been offered for sale in the twelve months prior to the effective date of this appraisal? ☐ Yes ☐ No			
Report data source(s) used, offering price(s), and date(s).			

Introduction

It is the clear intention of Fannie Mae and Freddie Mac that the Uniform Residential Appraisal Report (URAR) be a Summary Appraisal Report. It is also their intention that the purpose of the appraisal is to "provide the lender/client with an accurate, and adequately supported, opinion of the market value of the subject property."

Type of Report – Purpose of the Appraisal

This statement, printed on the first page at the top of the report, makes it difficult (if not impossible) to use the form for any other purpose. The statement satisfies the requirements of the USPAP STANDARD I (Introduction), Standards Rule 1-2 (f), and Standards Rule 2-2 (b).

Property Address

Often, the above data does not completely and unambiguously identify the subject property. If that is the case, then further information, such as additional unit letters or numbers, should be included here or in an addendum. A Legal Description may also be used to better identify the subject.

Borrower – Owner of Public Record

Often the **Borrower** is the Buyer or the current owner who is refinancing. However, there are exceptions. To be 100% safe, you should not guess. The best source of this information is your client (who is often the lender) who will make the mortgage loan.

The appraiser is now required to research who is the **Owner of Public Record**. This is because Fannie Mae and Freddie Mac are concerned about "flipping." It is a good policy to ask the parties identified by the Lender/Client as the seller if they are the current owners of the property.

Another source for this information is found recorded in the public records. When what is reported by the seller and what is found in the public records do not agree, further investigation is necessary.

The **Current Owner** of the property is always named on this line. This information is on the ratified sales contract which is supplied to the appraiser if the appraisal is for a Fannie Mae loan. A simple title check at the record source will also reveal this information accurately.

Legal Description

USPAP requires that every appraisal must accurately identify the property being appraised. Often, the appraiser decides that the street address number alone does not provide the required positive identification. In such cases, a **Legal Description** of the subject must be obtained from the mortgage, deed or other land record sources in the community. This information may be attached as an addendum if the space provided is insufficient.

Assessor's Parcel

The **Assessor's Parcel #** line requires that the appraiser report the Assessor's parcel number when applicable. Enter "not available" if none exists.

Tax Year – R.E. Taxes $

The total of all current year real estate taxes is shown in the **R.E. Taxes $** blank, whenever this information is available. When current tax data is not available, space is provided to indicate for which **Tax Year** the reported information applies. Sometimes a property is subject to more than one property tax (i.e., school district tax, fire district tax, etc.). The total of all such taxes should be indicated.

The appraiser should consider whether the taxes on the subject property are comparable to the taxes on similar properties in this market. Excessive taxes may negatively affect the value of the property. When the appraiser concludes that the taxes on the subject property are excessive as compared to similar properties, this must be reported and analyzed on either a comments line or in the addenda.

Neighborhood Name

Fannie Mae and Freddie Mac have placed new emphasis on the correct identification of the neighborhood and/or project. In addition to the neighborhood name, it is now also required that the appraiser either describe all the boundaries of the neighborhood and/or project or indicate them on a neighborhood/ project map that is part of the addenda of the report.

Map Reference

This is an optional space available to indicate an additional **Map Reference**. It is good practice to show subdivision map numbers or any other available map number that will make a more positive identification of the property.

NOTE: Any Census Tract map numbers and SMSA numbers should not be included here. They are listed on the Census Tract line.

Census Tract

The appraiser must indicate, in the applicable space, the **Census Tract** number for all properties located within an area with assigned numbers. For properties located in an area without assigned tract numbers, "N/A" is entered on the **Census Tract** line to indicate there is no applicable number.

A complete census tract designation has two to six digits. The first 4 indicate the Census Tract. When the tract number is less than 4 digits, e.g. 22, add zeros (example 0022). Sometimes there are two more numbers called the Census Tract suffix (example 1426.02).

This information is provided by the U.S. Bureau of Census. Here are the instructions on how to use the U.S. Bureau of Census web site which provides all the information and maps free:

Sign on: www.census.gov

Click (in blue box on left of screen) "American Fact Finder" then
Click (in blue box on left of screen) "Maps and Geography" then
Click (in text section of screen) "Reference Map"
Enter "Zip Code" or " Street Address & State" (in pop up box) and click "GO"

You will get a Census Tract Map of the area you want with all the Census Tract Numbers.

Follow the instructions on how to zoom in and out and move around the map.

Occupant

Fannie Mae and Freddie Mac now require appraisers to indicate when a property is vacant at the time of the inspection. If a vacant property does not appear to be properly closed up and protected, this should be noted.

Property Occupant (on date of inspection) is now indicated by a check in the "Owner," "Tenant" or "Vacant" check box.

Special Assessments $

The **Special Assessment $** line is for reporting special assessments such as sewer assessments. Enter "none" if there aren't any. Do not confuse association fees with special assessments. Report association fees on the HOA $_____ line.

PUD – HOA $

The URAR is used for some PUD appraisals. It is no longer approved for Condominium or Cooperative appraisals.

When the subject property includes ownership of some common property which is maintained by a Home Owners' Association (HOA), the monthly or annual association dues are reported in the   HOA $_____ space. The appropriate box is checked to indicate whether it is a monthly or annual charge.

A regular PUD (the only PUD recognized by Fannie Mae and Freddie Mac) is usually created by formal documents filed in the land records. Common property does contribute additional value, because it is usually a recreational facility or a large tract of vacant land. The homeowners' association is formally constituted with duly elected officers and directors, charges significant dues, and has the right to place liens or restrict the common property use of owners who do not pay the assessed dues.

Property Rights Appraised

Property Rights Appraised is divided into two parts. First, by checking the appropriate box, the appraiser indicates if the ownership is "Fee Simple," "Leasehold," or "Other."

Assignment Type

It is incumbent upon the appraiser to determine what type of transaction is the basis of the assignment.

A sale of the property being financed by a new mortgage is indicated by checking the box next to **Purchase Transaction**.

A refinancing of the property by the current owner is indicated by checking the **Refinance Transaction** box.

The **Other (describe)** box is used for unusual transactions where the Lender/Client is usually not a traditional lending institution. The appraiser must be careful to amend the wording of the URAR to cover these situations.

Lender/Client – Address

The URAR requires that the user(s) of the report be identified. When the Lender/Client is the user (as they almost always will be), this can be indicated by filling in his or her name on this line.

USPAP STANDARDS RULE 1-2 (a) "Identify the client and other intended users"

When the appraisal is for mortgage lending purposes, the **Lender's** name and address is entered on this line.

Unless otherwise indicated, it is assumed that the lender is also the client. When the client is not the lender, the client's name should also be indicated. If the client is the owner, it is now sufficient to state "Client is the Owner and User." If the lender is also going to be a user, that too must be stated somewhere.

When the **Borrower** is also a user, that must be stated (usually on the line that contains the name and address of the **Borrower**).

It is required that appraisers indicate the name(s) of all of the following somewhere in the **SUBJECT** section or in the addendum: **Owner, Occupant, Lender, Client, Borrower.** Indicate which of these are **Users** of the report. These may be five different people, but often one person has more than one role.

History of Property Being Offered For Sale

Direct questions have been added to the report forms that require the appraiser to report his or her analysis and conclusions on key areas in a clear and succinct yes/no format to address whether:

• the subject property is currently offered for sale or if it was offered for sale in the twelve months prior to the effective date of the appraisal.

Data Sources Used, Offering Prices(s), and Date(s)

Whenever possible, the current owner and/or seller should be interviewed and asked for a 12 month listing and 3 year sale history. MLS data is also useful, but it will not include offerings of the owner without the use of a real estate agent.

Use this line, comment lines, and/or the addenda to fully report the results of the 12 month history search and what data sources were used, together with the dates they were checked.

CONTRACT

|---|---|
C O N T R A C T	I ☐ did ☐ did not analyze the contract for sale for the subject purchase transaction. Explain the results of the analysis of the contract for sale or why the analysis was not performed.
	Contract Price $ Date of Contract Is the property seller the owner of public record? ☐Yes ☐No Data Source(s)
	Is there any financial assistance (loan charges, sale concessions, gift or downpayment assistance, etc.) to be paid by any party on behalf of the borrower? ☐ Yes ☐ No If Yes, report the total dollar amount and describe the items to be paid.

Introduction

This is a new section that was not previously on the URAR. It is used when there is a contract to sell the subject property to a new owner.

It is clearly the intent of USPAP, Fannie Mae, and Freddie Mac that whenever possible the appraiser obtain a copy of any sales contract that is in effect on the date of the appraisal, report its contents, and provide an analysis of these contents.

In order to be considered a valid Contract for Sale, it must be signed by both the Buyer(s) and Seller(s).

This section provides space for the following information:

Analysis of Subject Contract for Sale

Here, the appraiser indicates whether he or she did or did not analyze any Contract for Sale of the subject property in effect on the date of the appraisal.

If you did not analyze the Contract for Sale, the most common reason is that you were unable to obtain a copy of it and, as explained on the previous page, you have reported the steps taken to obtain it.

Though it is not required, it is a good idea to obtain written authorization from the Lender/Client to proceed without the Contract for Sale, in order to avoid having to redo the appraisal (without being paid) when, at a later date, a Contract for Sale is obtained and provided. This happens often.

The purpose of the analysis of the Contract for Sale is to determine if the reported sales price reflects the true value of the real estate being sold.

The following are some of the things that may cause the price reported on the Contract for Sale not to be the market value of the real estate:

- Parties to the sale are related to each other
- Personal property is included in the sale
- Occupancy by the Seller continues after the closing
- Occupancy by the Buyer starts before the closing date
- Time between the signing of the Contract for Sale and the closing date is unusually long or short
- Mortgage points are paid by the Seller
- An interest rate buy down exists
- Commission is paid by Buyer
- Financing is by a purchase money mortgage
- Sale is conditional upon non-traditional financing
- Sale is conditional upon Seller making repairs or alterations

It is unlikely the one line provided on the form will be adequate for this analysis. It is best to use the line to indicate where in the report the analysis is found.

Contract Price $_____ – Date of Contract

The Contract Price $_____ is used to report the price shown on the signed Contract for Sale that was in effect on the date of the appraisal.

When the analysis of the Contract for Sale indicates that the reported Contract Price does not reflect only the value of the real estate (but that it also includes other considerations), the blank line in this section should report this and indicate where in the appraisal the analysis of the Contract for Sale is found.

The Date of Contract is the final date on which both the Buyer(s) and Seller(s) sign the contract, unless the Contract for Sale indicates another effective date.

Is the property seller the owner of public record? – Data Source

This is a very specific question that requires some research to answer. It is asked because Fannie Mae and Freddie Mac are concerned about property "flipping," and they want the appraiser to help them identify those situations.

The best way to obtain this information is to examine a copy of the deed and compare the Owner's name on the deed with the Seller's name on the Contract for Sale.

When the deed is not available, alternate sources of information must be used. The easiest ones are asking the Seller(s), real estate agent(s), or attorney(s). If any of them indicate that the Seller(s) are not the Owner(s), the problem is solved.

When you are in a situation where you suspect flipping, you may wish to investigate further as a service to your Lender/Client and Fannie Mae/Freddie Mac.

Financial assistance paid by anyone on behalf of the borrower?

The lender must disclose to the appraiser any and all information about the subject property that it is aware of, if the information could affect either the marketability of the property or the appraiser's opinion of the market value of the property. Specifically, the lender must make sure that it provides the appraiser with all appropriate financing data and sales concessions for the subject property that will be, or have been, granted to anyone associated with the transaction. Generally, this can be accomplished by providing the appraiser a copy of the complete, ratified sales contract for the property that is to be appraised. If the lender is aware of additional pertinent information that is not included in the sales contract, it should inform the appraiser. Information that must be disclosed includes:

* settlement charges;
* loan fees or charges;
* discounts to the sales price;
* payment of condominium/PUD fees;
* interest rate buy downs, or other below-market rate financing;
* credits or refunds of the borrower's expenses;
* absorption of monthly payments;
* assignment of rent payments; and
* non-realty items that were included in the transaction.

Note: Race and the racial composition of the neighborhood are not appraisal factors.									
Neighborhood Characteristics				**One-Unit Housing Trends**				**One-Unit Housing**	**Present Land Use %**
Location ☐ Urban	☐ Suburban	☐ Rural	Property Values	☐ Increasing	☐ Stable	☐ Declining	PRICE AGE	One-Unit %
Built-Up ☐ Over 75%	☐ 25–75%	☐ Under 25%	Demand/Supply	☐ Shortage	☐ In Balance	☐ Over Supply	$ (000) (yrs)	2-4 Unit %
Growth ☐ Rapid	☐ Stable	☐ Slow	Marketing Time	☐ Under 3 mths	☐ 3–6 mths	☐ Over 6 mths	Low	Multi-Family %
Neighborhood Boundaries							High	Commercial %
							Pred.	Other %
Neighborhood Description									
Market Conditions (including support for the above conclusions)									

Introduction

The foundation of a good appraisal is a well documented analysis of the **NEIGHBORHOOD**.

The URAR is designed to permit the appraiser to report the social and economic characteristics of the neighborhood to the extent that they are likely to affect the value of the subject property.

The reporting of detrimental neighborhood conditions is not optional. Failure to report these conditions, if they exist, is poor appraisal practice and may violate the Uniform Standards of Professional Appraisal Practice.

The **NEIGHBORHOOD** section was modified to reinforce the appraiser's purpose for performing a neighborhood analysis, which is to identify the area – based on common characteristics or trends – that is subject to the same influences as the subject property. The sales prices of comparable properties in the identified area should reflect the positive and negative influences of the neighborhood. The results of the neighborhood analysis will enable the appraiser to define the area from which to select comparables, to understand market preferences and price patterns, to reach conclusions about the highest and best use of the subject property site, to examine the effect of different locations within the neighborhood, to determine the influence of nearby land uses, and to identify any other value influences affecting the neighborhood.

One of the more important modifications to this section was the elimination of the neighborhood analysis rating grid. This change should result in the appraiser focusing on describing the various components of a neighborhood and reporting the factors that have an impact on value in the space provided for narrative comments in the report, rather than trying to develop a "relative" rating for the neighborhood.

The following are the parts of the **NEIGHBORHOOD** section:

Race and Racial Composition – not appraisal factors

The URAR contains the statement, "**Race and the racial composition of the neighborhood are not appraisal factors.**"

Previous editions of the form stated that the above was the policy of Fannie Mae and Freddie Mac. It remains the policy of these two agencies as well as the other organizations represented on the committee that produced the URAR. The committee recognized the universal acceptance of this principle and therefore deemed it unnecessary to list the individual organizations who subscribe to it.

Neighborhood Characteristics

Location

The first step in the study of a neighborhood is to identify its boundaries. Sometimes they are natural, physical barriers such as lakes, rivers, streams, cliffs, swamps and valleys. They also can be highways, main traffic arteries, railroad tracks, canals and other man-made boundaries. The boundary of a residential neighborhood may also be a change of land use to commercial, industrial, institutional or public park. Some boundaries are clearly defined and others more difficult to identify precisely.... A neighborhood may be as large as an entire community, but it may be as small as a one or two block area.

Appraisers should think twice before classifying the **Location** of a **Rural** area as **Suburban**. The following Fannie Mae guidelines make it clear what is necessary for an area to be classified as Suburban.

Built-Up

Built-Up refers to the percentage of available land that has been improved. For example, assume there are 10 available lots out of a total of 100 lots in a neighborhood where 50% of the land is a state park. The **Over 75%** box would be checked because 90% of the _available_ land has been developed, even though substantial vacant park land still exists.

Growth

When a neighborhood is fully developed, its **Growth** rate has ended (at least for the present), and the **Stable** box should be checked. A neighborhood can be fully developed even if there are vacant lots, provided they are few, scattered, and unavailable for sale at their present value. If there are many lots available, the growth rate may be **Rapid**, **Stable** or **Slow**.

One-Unit Housing Trends

Property Values

The **Property Values** in the neighborhood are analyzed to see if they are **Increasing**, **Stable** or **Declining**. The best method is to find houses that have sold and then resold recently and to compare the two selling prices. Adjustments should be made for any improvements to the property between sales.

Demand/Supply

Demand/Supply refers to the balance between the number of houses sold and the number of new listings available for sale. It does not refer to market activity. One market may have 20 sales and 20 new listings in a month while another may have only 2 sales and 2 listings in the same period. Both would be characterized as **In Balance** because the number of listings equals the number of sales.

A good way to determine the **Demand/Supply** balance is to check the Multiple

Listing Service and compare the number of houses currently being offered to the number being offered three months ago.

Marketing Time

Marketing Time is the average time a similar property in the same market as the subject will take to sell when it is offered at a price close to its true market value (many appraisers use a selling price difference of 10% or less from the listing price as a guide).

The following shows a random sample of sales in the same market as the subject property, taken from an MLS comparable sale book. The average of the number of days to sell indicates the **marketing time** for that market.

Sale #	Listing Price	Selling Price	# of Days to Sell		Remarks
1	$125,000	$120,000	85		Good sale
2	149,000	141,000	121		Good sale
3	135,000	131,000	119		Good sale
4	149,000	130,000		210	* Not Used
5	129,000	125,000	45		Good sale
6	135,000	130,000	66		Good sale
7	140,000	120,000		125	* Not Used
8	160,000	151,000	133		Good sale
9	139,000	132,000	25		Good sale
10	165,000	145,000		139	* Not Used
11	119,000	115,900	85		Good sale
12	124,000	124,000	60		Good sale
13	144,000	141,500	75		Good sale
14	160,000	160,000	85		Good sale
15	129,000	111,000		120	* Not Used
16	134,500	131,000	93		Good sale
17	144,500	132,000	135		Good sale
18	144,900	141,300	75		Good sale
19	134,000	131,250	30		Good sale
20	139,900	136,300	66		Good sale
21	143,000	143,000	65		Good sale
22	134,500	132,000	70		Good sale
23	119,000	115,500	85		Good sale
24	125,000	121,000	120		Good sale

Ave. # of days to sell =   1,638   / 20 = 79.6 Days (Mean)

* These sales were not used because of the difference between their listing price and selling price exceeded 10% of the listing price.

NOTE: A good random sample will have at least 18 good sales.

One-Unit Housing

PRICE and AGE range

This section was designed to allow the appraiser to show a relationship between **One-Unit Housing**'s **PRICE** and **AGE** in the subject neighborhood. If such a relationship exists, it should be indicated by appropriate comments. To avoid confusion, it is also a good idea to comment when no relationship exists.

Present Land Use %

Enter the estimated percentage of each type of **Present Land Use** in the neighborhood. Enter a "0" or a "-" when there is no land in a specified classification. When a portion of the land is parks or another unspecified classification, enter that percent in the "Other" line and explain further in the **ADDITIONAL COMMENTS** section.

NOTE: The total of all 4 specified uses, plus any "Other" ones, must equal 100%.

Neighborhood Boundaries

Neighborhood Boundaries requires that the specific neighborhood boundaries be described in the report. (As an alternative, this line may be used to refer to the neighborhood boundary map in the addenda.)

NOTE: More and more appraisers are attaching a map to their appraisals delineating the boundaries of the neighborhood.

Neighborhood Description

A **Neighborhood Description** should start off with a general description of the neighborhood. This description could include the following:

- **Location of the neighborhood within the community**
- **Size of the neighborhood**
- **Topography**

- Other factors to be considered are **Property Compatibility.** Include the types of land uses prevalent in a neighborhood, lot sizes, price ranges, and building ages and styles. Rate the subject neighborhood on the extent to which these attributes are compatible with one another as compared to their compatibility in similar competing neighborhoods in the same market.

- **Police & Fire Protection** can be important factors affecting the value of houses in competing neighborhoods. When the buying public feels that a neighborhood has inadequate police or fire protection, home values are likely to be lower than those in competing neighborhoods with better protection.

- Consider the **general appearance of properties** in the subject neighborhood, particularly the extent to which both buildings and yards are maintained. Unmaintained properties often reduce the value of all other nearby properties in the neighborhood.

- **Proximity to employment and amenities** is a rating of the distance from the subject neighborhood to local employment sources and community amenities in terms of mileage and travel time. The cost and convenience of public transportation for commuters should also be considered and reported here.

• **Convenience to school** is determined by the distance to schools and the time it takes for a student to cover that distance. For example, when bus transportation is required, distance traveled and the student's travel time on the bus are factors which should be considered. In many areas, the market will penalize a house that is beyond safe walking distance to schools.

• Rate the neighborhood's **convenience to shopping** facilities in terms of distance, time, and required means of transportation. Consideration should be given to convenience stores, neighborhood and community shopping centers, regional malls and downtown city shopping.

A boundary map is very helpful to reviewers. Often when a reviewer compares two appraisals of the same property, he or she finds substantially different information in the **NEIGHBORHOOD** sections. This may occur because the two appraisers have used different neighborhood boundaries to develop their information. This often is a reasonable difference of opinion rather than an error made by one of the appraisers. With a neighborhood map, the reviewer knows what area is included in each appraiser's neighborhood analysis and is better able to determine which neighborhood boundaries are most appropriate.

Market Conditions

Another three lines are provided to report **Market Conditions** in the subject neighborhood.

This is a good place to comment on the trend of property values, demand/supply of houses in the neighborhood, typical marketing times for a house that is listed close to its market value, and competitive listings in the neighborhood.

When the subject property is in an area where many new houses are being constructed, the appraiser should analyze the projected effect the introduction of these new houses will have on the resale value of the existing houses in the neighborhood.

Dimensions		Area	Shape	View
Specific Zoning Classification		Zoning Description		
Zoning Compliance ☐ Legal ☐ Legal Nonconforming (Grandfathered Use) ☐ No Zoning ☐ Illegal (describe)				
Is the highest and best use of the subject property as improved (or as proposed per plans and specifications) the present use? ☐ Yes ☐ No If No, describe				

Utilities	Public	Other (describe)		Public	Other (describe)	Off-site Improvements—Type	Public	Private
Electricity	☐	☐	Water	☐	☐	Street	☐	☐
Gas	☐	☐	Sanitary Sewer	☐	☐	Alley	☐	☐
FEMA Special Flood Hazard Area ☐ Yes ☐ No FEMA Flood Zone				FEMA Map #		FEMA Map Date		
Are the utilities and off-site improvements typical for the market area? ☐ Yes ☐ No If No, describe								
Are there any adverse site conditions or external factors (easements, encroachments, environmental conditions, land uses, etc.)? ☐ Yes ☐ No If Yes, describe								

Introduction

The SITE section of the URAR requires the below information. These items are described in detail on the following pages.

Dimensions – Area

These blanks are to contain the Dimensions and total site Area. If the lot is irregular in shape, list all the boundary dimensions in the blank (for example: 100 x 120 x 205 x 150), and attach a sketch or legal description of the site.

All measurements should be in units which are standard for the subject community or market. Some conversions between commonly used units of land measurement are shown below:

Shape

Shape affects the value of lots differently from one neighborhood to another. Yet in most areas, an irregular shape resulting in increased construction costs decreases the value of the lot.

The site must have some type of drainage for surface and storm water—like a swale that channels surface water off of the lot to the street—or some natural drainage. However, when the lot is level or slopes away from the water disposal area, storm sewers are necessary.

View

The View from a property may substantially affect its value. Lots in the same neighborhood, identical in all respects except for location and orientation, will often have markedly different values directly attributable to the superior view one enjoys. The most popular views are of water, mountains and valleys. Conversely, a poor view such as a highway, railroad, alley or dump site will reduce value.

Specific Zoning Classification – Zoning Description

State the Specific Zoning Classification, Zoning Description, and major permitted uses exactly as designated by the local zoning code.

Zoning Compliance

Zoning Compliance is reported by checking one of four boxes to indicate whether the use of the property, on the date of inspection, was "Legal," "Legal Nonconforming (Grandfathered Use)," "Illegal" or in an area where there is "No Zoning." Check "Legal Nonconforming" when the existing property does not comply with all of the current zoning regulations (i.e., use, lot size, improvement size, off-street parking, etc.).

When the property is nonconforming, the appraiser must render an opinion as to what effect, if any, being nonconforming has on the value of the property. In rendering this opinion, the appraiser should consider what will happen if the property is destroyed by fire or other causes (flood, hurricane, tornado, etc.). Rebuilding may be restricted by current zoning regulations, building codes, and certain land-use regulations such as coastal tideland or wetland laws.

Several common nonconformities are described below:

Nonconforming placement on site - The improvements extend over the prescribed front, side or rear building lines.

Grandfather clause - Zoning regulations were effected after the property was constructed or the non-compliant usage began.

Variance or special exception - Zoning regulations are waived in reference to a specific property to permit construction of a nonconforming improvement.

Illegal Use - Existing improvements violate current zoning regulations, but to date the regulations have not been enforced.

An illegal or legal nonconforming zoning use must be carefully researched and reported if the property does not comply with all of the current zoning regulations (i.e., use, lot size, improvement size, off-street parking, etc.) When the property is nonconforming, the appraiser must render an opinion as to what effect, if any, being nonconforming has on the value of the property.

Highest and Best Use

USPAP Standards Rule 2-2 (a)(x)   Page 25: (This Standards Rule contains binding requirements from which departure is not permitted.) "When reporting an opinion of market value, describe the support and rationale for the appraiser's opinion of the highest and best use of the property."

The form now asks, "Is the highest and best use of the subject property as improved (or as proposed per plans and specifications) the present use?" When significant, the highest and best use of the property "as if vacant" should also be reported in an addenda of the appraisal.

"Highest & best use as improved" should not be interpreted too literally. Most major appraisal organizations teach that few if any properties are improved to their highest and best use, which implies the perfect improvement. Therefore, check Yes if the property is improved reasonably close to its highest and best use as defined below.

To determine the highest and best use, the appraiser utilizes four tests. The highest and best use is the one which meets all four of these tests: (1) Legally permitted, (2) Financially feasible, (3) Physically possible, and (4) Most profitable.

The four tests are done twice. First, the site is analyzed as improved. Then, the property is analyzed again, this time considering the best use for the site assuming it were vacant and ready to be built upon on the date of the appraisal.

If the proposed use fails to meet all four tests assuming the site is vacant, the process is repeated until a proper use is found. It is very possible that no improvement can be found to satisfy the criteria. In this event, the best use may be to leave the site vacant until some future date when development becomes feasible.

If building a single family home is determined to be the highest and best use of the site, the appraiser must then describe the perfect improvement. This residence would take advantage of all the previously considered factors about the neighborhood, community, and region. Some of the decisions to be made about the proposed house include its type, style, size, number of rooms, layout, special features, mechanical systems, and the kind and quality of construction materials.

Utilities

An analysis is then done of the existing residence to determine the highest and best use of the site and improvements. Again, as with the analysis of the site as if vacant, the appraiser must determine what the perfect utilization would be. However, the appraiser must now consider existing improvements when deciding what could be done to the property to obtain maximum profit. Any new improvement which will add more value than its production cost should be analyzed. The changes to be considered can range from minor repairs to major remodeling, modernization, or rehabilitation.

Finally, the results of the two analyses are compared to the existing improvements. When the highest and best use of the site as if vacant describes the existing property reasonably closely, the appraiser would check "Yes." If this is not the case, the appraiser must check "No" and explain further in an addendum.

The adequacy of the Utilities in the neighborhood should have already been reported in the description question of the NEIGHBORHOOD section. Here, the available utilities at the site are noted.

Public means governmentally supplied and regulated. It does not, therefore, include community systems sponsored, owned or operated by the developer or a private company not subject to government regulation or financial assistance. If such systems are found, a description thereof should be given in the ADDITIONAL COMMENTS section or in an addendum to the report.

The appraiser must also report any utilities which are available to the subject, but are not connected and not being used. In resort areas, report if the utilities are available all year long.

Off-site Improvements

These lines require the appraiser to report about the abutting and nearby streets (avenues, roads, rights of way, etc.) and alleys. When they are publicly owned and maintained, it is usually only necessary to check the appropriate box.

When they are privately owned or maintained, this must be reported together with an explanation as to how they are maintained and what effect (if any) this has on the value of the subject property.

FEMA Special Flood Hazard Area – FEMA Flood Zone – FEMA Map # – FEMA Map Date

FEMA Special Flood Hazard Area reporting is clarified by a check box that indicates "Yes" or "No" to whether any part of the property is in a "FEMA Flood Hazard Area," which is defined as "only 100-year flood plain areas." This eliminates the confusion about whether "B" zones should be included.

The Fannie Mae Guidelines do not consider "B" zones to be in FEMA 100-year flood plain areas. However, some lenders require flood insurance when properties are in a "B" flood hazard area, so some appraisers report this, when applicable, on the URAR with an explanation in the Addenda.

Space is provided for the appraiser to indicate the FEMA Flood Zone, FEMA Map #, and FEMA Map Date. To avoid professional liability suits, appraisers must be certain to use the most current FEMA maps in their determinations. Many appraisers attach a copy of the FEMA map to their appraisal reports.

When any portion of the site is in a FEMA Special Flood Hazard Area, check the Yes box and list the community panel and flood zone numbers from the appropriate Flood Insurance Rate Map (FIRM) on the FEMA Zone line. List the map number and map date on the appropriate lines.

If part of the site is in a flood hazard area, but the improvements are not, report this in the ADDITIONAL COMMENTS section.

Flood Insurance Rate Maps (FIRM) can be obtained by contacting FEMA at the address, telephone number, fax number, or web site shown below:

FEMA Map Service Center   Telephone: 1-800-358-9616   E-mail   FEMA-MSCservice@ dhs.gov
P.O. Box 1038   Fax: 1-800-358-9620
Jessup, MD 20794-1038   Website: www.fema.gov

If any part of the principal structure is located in a Special Flood Hazard Area – zones A, AE, All, AO, AR, A1-30, A-99, V VE, VO, or Vi-30 – flood insurance is required. If the principal structure is not located in the Special Flood Hazard Area, flood insurance is generally not required.

Are the utilities/off-site improvements typical for market area?

Some common situations where the utilities and/or off-site improvements are not typical for the market area are:

• Most of the streets and alleys abutting and leading to the subject property are owned by the municipality and maintained by the government, but a street or alley nearby or abutting the subject is privately owned and maintained.

• There are sewers nearby in the street, but the subject property is not connected to them and is served by a septic system (or cesspool).

• There is public water available in the neighborhood, but the subject property has only a well.

Each of these (and any other applicable conditions) must be reported and commented upon. Include what effect (if any) they have on the value of the property.

If the subject property has use of a tennis court, pool, beach, etc., it should be reported here and explained on the blank lines below.

Are there any adverse site conditions or external factors?

The most significant change on the URAR is the elimination of the word "apparent" from this line. Now, not only are you required to report what is apparent, but you may also be required to check the deed for recorded easements. Before, you were only asked for "apparent" environmental conditions; now the question asks for any environmental conditions. I think it would be prudent to add a statement on the blank lines such as the Model Comment below.

An easement is a right of non-possessing interest accorded to a non-owner to use property for a specific purpose. The three broad types of easements are surface easements, sub-surface easements and overhead easements.

Typical easements found on residential sites include:

• Party driveways
• Walks & paths leading to places off the site
• Drainage easements & sewer easements
• Telephone, cable TV and electric wire easements
• Neighbor's right to place a sign, mail box, or newspaper box on the property
• High voltage power line easements
• Gas and water line easements
• Historic & view easements

• Mineral and mining easements

An encroachment occurs when one owner's improvements extend onto the land of an abutting owner. The encroachment can be either the improvements of the property being appraised extending onto a neighboring property, or the reverse, a neighboring improvement extending onto the property being appraised.

A site in or near a slide area presents special problems which must be reported and analyzed by the appraiser (usually in an addendum).

Other adverse conditions which should be noted if they affect site value are: unusual shape or size; drainage problems; unusual topography; substandard utility supply; poor site improvements such as sidewalks, walls, fences, driveways, landscaping, pools and courts; or poor street improvements including paving, curbing, road surfaces, lighting, width and condition.

Nearby hazards including: bodies of water; earthquake, volcano or landslide areas; ravines; unusual fire hazards; and heavy traffic and pollution also need to be discussed here.

Finally, the effect that any of the above identified items have on the value of the site should be described.

NOTES

General Description	Foundation	Exterior Description materials/condition	Interior materials/condition
Units ☐ One ☐ One with Accessory Unit	☐ Concrete Slab ☐ Crawl Space	Foundation Walls	Floors
# of Stories	☐ Full Basement ☐ Partial Basement	Exterior Walls	Walls
Type ☐ Det. ☐ Att. ☐ S-Det./End Unit	Basement Area sq. ft.	Roof Surface	Trim/Finish
☐ Existing ☐ Proposed ☐ Under Const.	Basement Finish %	Gutters & Downspouts	Bath Floor
Design (Style)	☐ Outside Entry/Exit ☐ Sump Pump	Window Type	Bath Wainscot
Year Built	Evidence of ☐ Infestation	Storm Sash/Insulated	Car Storage ☐ None
Effective Age (Yrs)	☐ Dampness ☐ Settlement	Screens	☐ Driveway # of Cars
Attic ☐ None	Heating ☐ FWA ☐ HWBB ☐ Radiant	Amenities ☐ Woodstove(s) #	Driveway Surface
☐ Drop Stair ☐ Stairs	☐ Other Fuel	☐ Fireplace(s) # ☐ Fence	☐ Garage # of Cars
☐ Floor ☐ Scuttle	Cooling ☐ Central Air Conditioning	☐ Patio/Deck ☐ Porch	☐ Carport # of Cars
☐ Finished ☐ Heated	☐ Individual ☐ Other	☐ Pool ☐ Other	☐ Att. ☐ Det. ☐ Built-in

Appliances ☐Refrigerator ☐Range/Oven ☐Dishwasher ☐Disposal ☐Microwave ☐Washer/Dryer ☐Other (describe)

Finished area **above** grade contains: Rooms Bedrooms Bath(s) Square Feet of Gross Living Area Above Grade

Additional features (special energy efficient items, etc.)

Describe the condition of the property (including needed repairs, deterioration, renovations, remodeling, etc.).

Are there any physical deficiencies or adverse conditions that affect the livability, soundness, or structural integrity of the property? ☐ Yes ☐ No If Yes, describe

Does the property generally conform to the neighborhood (functional utility, style, condition, use, construction, etc.)? ☐ Yes ☐ No If No, describe

Introduction

The <u>IMPROVEMENTS</u> section is divided into twelve areas, some of which are broken up into smaller parts as shown below and described in detail on the following pages.

General Description

Number of Units and Accessory Units

The Fannie Mae URAR is acceptable for only single units with one accessory unit.

The appraiser must be familiar with local zoning ordinances in order to determine if an accessory unit makes the property a multiple-unit dwelling (and therefore ineligible to be appraised on the URAR).

General Description - # of Stories

The # of Stories line is used to more precisely describe the house.

Type

Fill in the Type line, with Det. (Detached) when the house has free standing walls, with Att. (Attached) when there is a "party wall" shared by neighboring structures, or with S-Det/End Unit when there is a semi-detached or end unit.

Existing – Proposed – Under Construction

The URAR can be used for Proposed construction and residences Under Construction, as well as Existing improvements.

When the subject is Proposed or Under Construction, the appraiser must clearly indicate, in the ADDITIONAL COMMENTS section or an addendum, what plans or specifications he or she used to make the appraisal. When the subject house is new, the appraiser should determine if a Certificate of Occupancy has been issued, and if so, he or she should ascertain that it is not contingent upon any construction being completed. If the Certificate of Occupancy requires work to be done, the appraiser should note what that work is and whether or not it has been completed in the COMMENTS or Addenda.

Design (Style)

Design (Style) is used to describe the exterior appearance of a house based on historical or contemporary fashion.

Year Built – Effective Age (Yrs)

Year Built is used to calculate the actual age of the subject.

Effective Age (Yrs.) is the age an improvement appears to be considering its design, condition, other houses in the market, and any economic forces affecting its value. To paraphrase an old saying, "If it has the physical condition and appearance of a 13-year-old house and market conditions affect it as if it were a 13-year-old house, then for appraisal purposes it should be treated as a 13-year-old house (effective age: 13 years), even if it is 10 or 20 years old."

Generally, a house of average design and condition in a neighborhood that is not subject to unusual economic forces will have the same actual and effective age. However, when a house is modernized, its effective age is reduced. It is, therefore, unusual for a renovated, remodeled, or modernized house to have an effective age as old as its actual age, unless its condition has again lapsed since the renovation. In fact, the purpose of renovation, remodeling, and modernization is to reduce effective age.

Foundation

Type of Foundation

Check the boxes that describe the type of Foundation:
- ☐ Concrete Slab
- ☐ Crawl Space
- ☐ Full Basement
- ☐ Partial Basement

Often, the FOUNDATION is some combination of Basement, Crawl Space and Concrete Slab. Check the box next to all appropriate descriptions, and then indicate the percentage of the total foundation made up of each in the ADDITIONAL COMMENTS section.

> With the exception of those being constructed in the northern portions of the country, fewer and fewer houses are being built with Basements. And, where basements are built, there is an increasing trend to gain additional living space by finishing portions into family rooms, utility areas, baths and lavatories, workrooms, kitchens and even bedrooms. In the event that the house has a basement, the height between the basement floor, which is constructed similarly to a slab, and the bottom of the joists is usually 7.5 to 8 feet.

> For basementless houses, the finish grade is a major factor in the choice between slab or crawl space as a foundation. For Slab construction, it is important that the finished ground grade fall sharply away from the house... to prevent flooding. Slabs are constructed by first building footings for support, although some..., known as "floating slabs," are built without them. The excavation is then covered with gravel and a vapor barrier and insulation is installed around the edge.

Crawl Spaces, which provide flooding protection and... a convenient place to run heating ducts, plumbing pipes and wires that must be accessible for repairs, are constructed similarly to basements except that the distance from the floor to the joists is 3 to 4 feet. The floor can be concrete, as in a basement, or it can be dirt, often covered with a vapor barrier. In northern regions, crawl spaces must be insulated or heated to prevent pipe freezing and cold floors.*

Basement Area sq. ft. — Basement Finish %

Some appraisers measure Basement Area sq. ft. inside the foundation walls. On a one-story ranch with a full basement, this produces an area smaller than the GLA. To eliminate this problem, other appraisers measure around the outside of the foundation wall. Included here are all above-grade or partially below-grade areas regardless of how the space is utilized.

Basement Finish % is the percent of total basement area which is finished, not a percent of the ground floor area. A basement that is 50% of the first floor area and completely finished is indicated as 100% finished.

Outside Entry/Exit

In many parts of the country, an Outside Entry/Exit to the basement is an unknown item. In other areas (New England, for example), a house without a basement and an outside entry (usually a wood or steel hatch leading to the rear yard) probably suffers from significant functional obsolescence. Check the box to indicate if there is an Outside Entry/Exit. If checked, note in the ADDITIONAL COMMENTS section what type of entry or exit exists.

Sump Pump

One of the ways to remove water that gets into a basement is to install a Sump Pump. A hole is cut in the basement floor into which an electric pump is installed. The water flows from the basement floor into the hole (ideally, the basement floor slants towards the hole). When the water fills the hole, it trips a float switch that turns on the pump. The water is pumped to the outside of the house or into a sewer line. Check the box to indicate if there is a Sump Pump.

Evidence of Infestation

Check this box if any type of Infestation is observed or suspected. Describe the infestation in the ADDITIONAL COMMENTS section. A professional inspection for termites and other infestations may be recommended.

Evidence of Dampness

Check this box if any type of Dampness is observed or suspected. Describe the dampness in the ADDITIONAL COMMENTS section.

Dampness is the main problem with basements. The most likely causes of dampness include: poor foundation construction; excess ground water due to improper drainage; leaky windows, hatches, or clothes dryer vents; gutters or downspouts spilling water too near the foundation; or a raising ground water table. A basement that is wet only part of the year can be detected even when dry by a white mineral deposit on the walls, usually a few inches off the floor. Stains along the lower edge of columns, the furnace, or the hot water heater are also indications of dampness, as is mild odor.

---

* Henry S. Harrison, Houses - The Illustrated Guide to Construction, Design and Systems (3rd Edition) (Chicago, IL: Residential Sales Council of the National Association of Realtors, 1999).

Mold is another problem associated with dampness, and many basements have it. However, mold can be found in many other areas of the house. Signs of mold include a strong musty odors and various dark colored stains. Whenever you find any trace of mold, it should be reported together with the recommendation that a mold inspection be obtained from an expert.

Evidence of Settlement

Cracks in the basement walls or floor indicate Settlement. Whenever the appraiser observes cracks in the basement walls or floors, this should be noted in the appraisal report. Hairline cracks normally are no problem. Medium-size cracks (up to 1/4" wide) are dangerous about 50% of the time, and as the cracks get larger the possibility of serious structural damage increases. If there is any question about a crack, it is best to recommend an inspection by a structural engineer.

Exterior Description

Foundation Walls

Specify the type of material used for the Foundation Walls (e.g., poured concrete, cinder or concrete block, brick, field stone, or treated wood).

Exterior Walls

Specify the material used for the Exterior Walls covering (e.g., clapboard, log, board and batten, wood or asbestos shingles, aluminum, vinyl, stucco, or brick). If brick, specify whether veneer (brick on some form of masonry block) or solid masonry.

Nine out of ten houses are frame construction covered with a variety of materials. Some common types of wood siding materials are bevel, bungalow, colonial, rustic, shiplap, and drop. Aluminum and vinyl siding also are very popular in some areas.

Shingles and shakes are also common siding materials. Wood shingles can be split or sawed. The most popular shingle material is cedar, while other types are made of asbestos and asphalt. Shingles come in four grades, with the best being No. 1, blue label. Stucco used to be more common around the country but is still a popular siding in warm climates. It can be applied to wood framing or directly over solid masonry walls.

There are a variety of other common masonry products which can be applied over wood framing and used as siding. These include clay bricks, concrete bricks, and split blocks and stone. In houses with masonry veneer walls, all of the structural support is from the wood framing and not the one-unit thick masonry.

Exterior walls can also be made of solid masonry. The most common types of masonry wall are 8" thick cement block, two layers of brick, and a combination of brick and block. Masonry walls can either be solid masonry or hollow walls known as cavity masonry walls.

Roof Surface

State the material used for the Roof Surface (e.g., wood shingles or shakes, asphalt or asbestos shingles, tile, etc.). The majority of houses have roofs covered with shingles and shakes made of wood, asphalt, asbestos, cement, slate, or tile. Other less frequently used materials are metal, clay tile, and built-up or membrane roofs.

Most roofs start with a layer of sheathing material that is nailed to the roof framing members. (When the roof is quite steep and covered with wood shingles, sheathing is not always required.) Asphalt felt underlayment is fastened to the sheathing. The roofing is laid on top of the underlayment.

When shingles are used, a double layer known as a starter course is attached at the bottom of the roof. Each succeeding course or row of shingles is then nailed to the sheathing so that it covers the top of the row below leaving part of the lower row exposed to the weather.

Slate is nailed over the sheathing, which has been covered with special impregnated slater's felt. Shingle tile is applied in the same manner.

Interlocking tiles known as French, Spanish, Mission, Roman, or Greek tile are designed to provide maximum coverage with minimum material. These tiles have interlocking ridges on each side to reduce the overlap needed to maintain water tightness and hold tiles together.

Roll roofing is applied by nailing it down in strips that lap and then sealing the laps with roofer's cement.

Gutters & Downspouts

Gutters and Downspouts prevent damage or unsightly stains on walls where roof overhangs are not provided.

Metal Gutters, which are attached to the house with various types of metal hangers, are the most common type of gutter now in use. Aluminum, copper, galvanized iron and other materials are used. Wood gutters should be attached to the house with non-corroding screws bedded in elastic roofer's cement to prevent leakage. Built-up gutters are made of metal and set into the deeply notched rafter a short distance up the roof from the eaves. Pole gutters consist of a wooden strip nailed perpendicularly to the roof and covered with sheet metal.

Downspouts (or leaders) are vertical pipes that carry water from gutters to the ground and into sewers, dry wells, drain tiles, splash pans, or simply off the property. Downspouts must be large enough to carry water away as fast as they receive it from the roof. The junction of the gutter and downspout should be covered with a basket strainer to hold back leaves and twigs, especially if the gutter connects to a storm or sanitary sewer, which is difficult to clean out if clogged.

Window Type

Describe the Window Type(s) (e.g., casement, sliding, double hung, etc.). Also identify the window frame material (e.g., wood, aluminum, steel, etc).

Storm Sash/Insulated

State if there are Storm Sashes and/or windows with Insulated glass and their materials.

Screens

State if there are Screens and their materials. Page 5-24 shows pictures and descriptions of the most common types of windows with an explanation of corresponding screens.

Interior Description

Floors

The Floors space is used to describe the floor finish in the major portion of the house. If this is wall-to-wall carpeting, indicate the material over which the carpet is installed. Otherwise, state the type of floor cover in an addendum or the ADDITIONAL COMMENTS section. Floor covering in the kitchen or other areas such as the foyer may also be described there.

The condition of the floors should be rated "Good," "Average," "Fair," or "Poor."

Walls

Indicate the type of Walls in the main section of the house. Most modem houses use "Drywall" construction, consisting of 2" by 4" studs (16 inches apart) covered with 3/8 inch thick gypsum board. If the studs are 24" apart, they should be covered with 1/2 inch gypsum board.

Older houses and some modern custom homes have plaster walls. Other less common interior walls are made of plywood, hardboard, fiberboard, ceramic wall tile and wood paneling.

The condition of walls should be rated "Good," "Average," "Fair," or "Poor."

Trim/Finish

The use of various items of Trim in a house enhances its beauty. In lower priced houses, trim may be limited to simple casings around doors, windows, baseboards, or ceilings. In more elaborate houses and houses in the architectural style of certain periods, extensive or elaborate moldings may be used.

Molding is made of a variety of hardwoods and softwoods for interior and exterior use. It is milled by special machines that cut, plane, and sand the lumber surfaces into desired shapes. Elaborate moldings are thicker, more intricate, and often consist of two or three pieces of wood together. Most molding used today, however, is "stock" molding in one of several standard sizes and shapes.

The use of elaborate moldings, cornices, ornamental molding around the fireplaces, wainscot, chair rails, and picture moldings are signs of above-average Trim/Finish.

The type of Trim/Finish should be indicated by 1) material (wood, plastic, metal, etc.) and 2) quality of workmanship and condition (Good, Average, Fair, or Poor, e.g., "Wood/Avg." or "Metal/Fair").

Bath Floor

The Bath Floor often has a different covering than other floors in the house. The type of bathroom floor covering should be indicated on this line. If the bathrooms have different floor coverings, this should be described either in the ADDITIONAL COMMENTS section or an addendum. Until recently, the preferred material for bathroom floors was ceramic tile. This is still an excellent material, but some others are also now equally acceptable.

Ceramic tile can be installed in two basic ways. One is to set the tile into a bed of plaster at least 1.25 inches thick, known as a "mud job." Grout is then compressed between the tiles and tooled to make it smooth. Ceramic tile can also be attached to the subflooring with special waterproof adhesives. Again, grout is compressed into the spaces between tiles and tooled smooth.

There are now many attractive vinyl, rubber and asphalt tiles that make satisfactory bathroom floors when properly installed over solid subflooring. Rolled goods of the same materials, when properly installed, are excellent, especially for rental units. Recently, carpeting the bathroom has increased in popularity, but this is often expensive as the carpet must be specially made to be waterproof and easily cleaned.

The condition of the Bath Floor should be rated "Good," "Average," "Fair," or "Poor."

Bath Wainscot

When the lower portion of a wall is finished with a different material from the upper portion, the lower portion is referred to as "wainscot." The material with which the wainscot is finished is called "wainscoting." Many people still feel that the best material for Bath Wainscot is ceramic tile. Tile is now available in many colors and designs and can be glued to gypsum board wall with special adhesive or set into a plaster wall.

There is a variety of plastic wall covering products available that are suitable for bathroom wall coverings too. New waterproof wallpapers are being used successfully. It is also quite common to leave substantial portions of the walls uncovered except for a coating of waterproof paint.

When bathrooms are of the new fiber glass prefabricated type, they should be described in the ADDITIONAL COMMENTS section.

The condition of the Bath Wainscot should be rated "Good," "Average," "Fair," or "Poor," and presented in the "materials/condition" format.

Attic

None – Drop Stair – Stairs – Floor – Scuttle – Finished – Heated

An Attic is that part of the upper levels of a house which is not counted as Gross Living Area (GLA) for one or more of the following reasons:

1) It is finished differently from the main portion of the house.

2) It is unheated.

3) It has low ceiling height (many appraisers feel that ceilings less than 5 feet are below normal).

4) It has inadequate window area (window area should be at least 10% of the floor area).

NOTE: When an area fits one of the above criteria and is described as an Attic, it must not be included in GLA calculations.

Check the None box if there is no attic. Check the appropriate box describing attic access: Drop Stair, Stairs, Floor (when the attic has a floor), or Scuttle (a hole in the ceiling leading into the attic, usually covered by an opening panel). Check the Finished box when the attic is finished and the Heated box when the attic is heated.

Use the ADDITIONAL COMMENTS section to describe how the attic is finished and how it is used.

Heating/Cooling

Type of Heat Distribution

The URAR has check boxes to identify the three principle types of heating systems: (check the appropriate box[es])

☐ FWA (Forced Warm Air): This system corrected the deficiencies of the old gravity system. A fan or blower pushes warm air from the furnace through ducts throughout the house. The distribution is balanced by opening and closing the registers in each room.

☐ HWBB (Hot Water Base Board): This system distributes hot water from the furnace by pumping it through finger-size pipes into baseboard radiators in each room. When the baseboard radiators are connected by one pipe in series, it is difficult to balance the heat. A better system is to use two pipes to be turned on or off. Another way to balance the heat in either system is with flaps that control the amount of air that flows by the hot pipe.

☐ Radiant: The pipes in a radiant system are inside the walls and floors. Unlike the above systems that depend heavily upon air flowing over the pipes to distribute the heat into the rooms, the pipes in this system distribute heat by direct radiation only.

☐ Other: This box is checked when systems other than the above (FWA, HWBB, and Radiant) exist in the house. Most fireplaces are an amenity rather than a heat system and are reported by checking the Fireplace(s) box in the Amenities section.

Common Other heating systems are heat pumps, gravity, hot air, solar (active and passive), steam, and wood stoves.

Fuel

Fuels are oil, gas, liquid petroleum gas, coal, and wood. Electricity is both a type of heat and a fuel. Fuel costs may be checked by asking for a year's bill from the homeowner or fuel supplier. Be aware that fuel costs can vary considerably according to the residents' habits.

Fuel costs are raising substantially, and the market in many areas is making choices based on the type of fuel used in a house. If one type of fuel is more popular in the area where the subject property is located, it may be necessary to make an adjustment for the different kinds of fuel used by the subject property and the comparable sales.

Air Conditioning

Central Air Conditioning is indicated by putting an "X" in the Central Air Conditioning box.

Individual Window Units are indicated by putting an "X" in the Individual box.

The Other box is used to indicate a variety of systems found in various parts of the country such as ceiling fans.

When part of the house has Central Air Conditioning and part Individual Window Units, both boxes should be checked.

Amenities

Fireplaces(s) # – Patio/Deck – Pool – Woodstove(s) # – Fence – Porch – Other

Amenities are now grouped together with check boxes for Fireplaces(s) #, Patio/Deck, Pool, Woodstove(s) #, Fence, Porch, and an Other check box.

Car Storage

Driveway – Garage – Carport

Car Storage reporting has been reorganized.

Each market has a Car Storage standard, and houses that fail to meet or exceed this standard suffer from functional obsolescence. For example, a house with a garage in a neighborhood with only carports has a superadequacy. Similarly, a house with a carport in an area where most homes have garages has a deficiency.

Detached garages have decreased in popularity in some areas of the country.

Appliances

Kitchen Equipment

As a result of Federal banking regulations, appraisals are now being rejected, or the final value adjusted, because the value of kitchen equipment (which is not part of the real estate) is included. The value of kitchen appliances, which are not classified as real estate in the subject area (or any other non-real estate equipment or appliances), should never be included in the appraised value of the real estate.

In many areas, it is customary to include some kitchen equipment as part of the sale without any division of the sales price into real estate and included equipment. Such sales prices often are recorded and reported including a substantial amount of personal property. The best way to avoid the personal property problem is to verify the sale with the Buyer, Seller, Broker or closing Attorney. The verification process also helps the appraiser learn about any other special conditions surrounding a sale.

Some lenders instruct appraisers to indicate on the URAR any personal property known to be on the premises that will be included in the sale. Items of personal property may be indicated by a letter "P" instead of an "X". To be safe, items of personal property shown on the appliances line should also be listed in the ADDITIONAL COMMENTS section or an addendum.

Keep in mind that Item #4 on page 5 of the Uniform Residential Appraisal Report says, "I developed my opinion of the market value of the real property that is subject to this report...." No mention is made of personal property being included in the estimated value.

Standard 1-2e of the 2005 USPAP states, "Identify the characteristics of the property that are relevant to the type and definition of value and intended use of the appraisal, including any personal property, trade fixtures, or intangible items that are not real property but are included in the appraisal."

Finished area above ground contains:

Rooms – Bedrooms – Bath(s) – Square Feet of Gross Living Area

The total of all above grade finished rooms is entered in the first blank space. Foyers, baths, and laundry rooms are not usually included in the Rooms count. Do not include any rooms in the basement. Include rooms in the attic only if they are furnished and heated like the rest of the house, and if they have a normal ceiling height (approximately 5' or more).

In order to make an appraisal, it is required that the appraiser obtain reliable information about the number of Rooms, Bedrooms, Bath(s), and Square Feet of Gross Living Area. Keep in mind APPRAISER CERTIFICATION ITEM #10: "I verified from a disinterested source all information in this report that was provided by parties who have a financial interest in the sale or financing of the subject property."

Additional features:

These lines and the addenda should be used to describe any special energy efficient items that exist in the subject property.

Normal insulation is not considered to be a special energy efficient item, but super insulation is. Super insulation is usually found in the walls and ceilings. Typical wall insulation is 3 1/2" thick and fits between a 2" x 4" wall stud. Super wall insulation is usually about 5 1/2" thick and fits between special 2" x 6" wall studs. Typical ceiling or attic insulation is 5 1/2" to 6" thick and is installed over the ceiling. Super ceiling insulation is 10" to 12" thick. Insulation around the hot water tank and hot water pipes is also considered special insulation.

Items that are considered special energy efficient items include:

- Super insulation (as described above)
- Special caulking and weatherstripping
- Double or triple pane window(s)
- Window shades and blinds used for solar control

- Window quilt(s)
- Landscaping used for solar control
- Roof overhang designed for solar control
- Storm fittings
- Automatic setback thermostat(s)
- Heating, cooling, lighting systems, and built-in appliances designed specifically to be energy efficient
- Solar systems (passive and active) for water heating, space heating, and cooling
- Wood-fired heating systems
- Houses with other special design features which minimize energy use, such as smaller window areas and earth shelters

Special energy efficient items, etc.

The Additional features lines may also be used to provide details about special features of the house which are not fully described elsewhere on the URAR. The appraiser should ask himself or herself whether a person reading the form will get a complete picture of the subject property. If the answer is "no," additional comments are needed here and/or on addendum sheets to complete the picture for the reader.

Describe the condition of the property

The following is a list of common repairs needed, especially as a house gets older. The appraiser must use good judgment and observation skills to recognize all the needed significant repairs, renovations and remodeling, etc.

- Floors
- Termite damage
- Walks and driveways
- Interior and exterior paint
- Roof, gutters and downspouts
- Stuck windows, broken glass
- Basement: walls and floors
- Kitchen: cabinets, counters, and equipment
- Plumbing: septic system, pipes, and fixtures
- Electrical: damaged, inadequate, or substandard wiring
- Heating/Cooling: furnace, hot water heater, air conditioning

Deficiencies or Adverse Conditions

This section includes a new entry in which the appraiser must report "any physical deficiencies or adverse conditions that affect the livability, soundness, or structural integrity of the property" (such as, but not limited to, hazardous wastes, toxic substances, etc.) that are present in the improvements, on the site, or in the immediate vicinity of the subject property. This question clarifies the appraiser's responsibility to report what he or she became aware of through the normal research involved in performing the appraisal. In states where the use of an owner's "Disclosure Statement" is part of a real estate transaction, a copy should be obtained and used to obtain this information.

Keep in mind Appraiser's Certification #14: "I have taken into consideration the factors that have an impact on value with respect to the subject neighborhood, subject property, and the proximity of the subject property to adverse influences in the development of my opinion of market value. I have noted in this appraisal report any adverse conditions (such as, but not limited to, needed repairs, deterioration, the presence of hazardous wastes, toxic substances, adverse environmental conditions, etc.) observed during the inspection of the subject property or that I became aware of during the research involved in performing this appraisal. I have considered these adverse conditions in my analysis of the property value, and have reported on the effect of the conditions on the value and marketability of the subject property."

WARNING: The answer to this question has the potential of being the basis of a lawsuit. The appraiser is being asked to report about the exterior and interior condition of the property based on their inspection and what they were aware of. It is a good idea to ask the owners if there are any problems with the property, and keep a record of who was asked and what the reply was. The problem is that the question on the URAR does not limit the answer to only apparent problems. At a minimum, I believe that in a comment section of the report, the appraiser should put the Lender/Client and Users on notice that you are not a trained home inspector and that the answer to this question is limited to what is apparent as part of a normal inspection made by a real estate appraiser in your area. It is not sufficient, in my opinion, to rely on the Appraiser's Certification to provide this information.

Does the property generally conform to the neighborhood?

The first thing the appraiser must do is answer Yes or No to this question. The form suggests the following should be considered:

- Functional utility
- Style
- Condition
- Use
- Construction
- Etc. (Size, position on lot, color, typography, landscaping, zoning, etc.)

If you answer "No" to this question you are asked to describe how the subject property does not coform to the neighborhood. This comment should include your opinion as to whether or not being nonconforming effects the value of the subject property.

NOTES

Uniform Residential Appraisal Report

File #

There are _____ comparable properties currently offered for sale in the subject neighborhood ranging in price from $ _____ to $ _____

There are _____ comparable sales in the subject neighborhood within the past twelve months ranging in sale price from $ _____ to $ _____

FEATURE	SUBJECT	COMPARABLE SALE # 1		COMPARABLE SALE # 2		COMPARABLE SALE # 3	
Address							
Proximity to Subject							
Sale Price	$		$		$		$
Sale Price/Gross Liv. Area	$ sq. ft.	$ sq. ft.		$ sq. ft.		$ sq. ft.	
Data Source(s)							
Verification Source(s)							
VALUE ADJUSTMENTS	DESCRIPTION	DESCRIPTION	+(-) $ Adjustment	DESCRIPTION	+(-) $ Adjustment	DESCRIPTION	+(-) $ Adjustment
Sale or Financing Concessions							
Date of Sale/Time							
Location							
Leasehold/Fee Simple							
Site							
View							
Design (Style)							
Quality of Construction							
Actual Age							
Condition							
Above Grade	Total Bdrms. Baths	Total Bdrms. Baths		Total Bdrms. Baths		Total Bdrms. Baths	
Room Count							
Gross Living Area	sq. ft.	sq. ft.		sq. ft.		sq. ft.	
Basement & Finished Rooms Below Grade							
Functional Utility							
Heating/Cooling							
Energy Efficient Items							
Garage/Carport							
Porch/Patio/Deck							
Net Adjustment (Total)		☐ + ☐ -	$	☐ + ☐ -	$	☐ + ☐ -	$
Adjusted Sale Price of Comparables		Net Adj. %		Net Adj. %		Net Adj. %	
		Gross Adj. %	$	Gross Adj. %	$	Gross Adj. %	$

I ☐ did ☐ did not research the sale or transfer history of the subject property and comparable sales. If not, explain

My research ☐ did ☐ did not reveal any prior sales or transfers of the subject property for the three years prior to the effective date of this appraisal.

Data source(s)

My research ☐ did ☐ did not reveal any prior sales or transfers of the comparable sales for the year prior to the date of sale of the comparable sale.

Data source(s)

Report the results of the research and analysis of the prior sale or transfer history of the subject property and comparable sales (report additional prior sales on page 3).

ITEM	SUBJECT	COMPARABLE SALE # 1	COMPARABLE SALE # 2	COMPARABLE SALE # 3
Date of Prior Sale/Transfer				
Price of Prior Sale/Transfer				
Data Source(s)				
Effective Date of Data Source(s)				

Analysis of prior sale or transfer history of the subject property and comparable sales

Summary of Sales Comparison Approach

Indicated Value by Sales Comparison Approach $

Indicated Value by: Sales Comparison Approach $ _____ Cost Approach (if developed) $ _____ Income Approach (if developed) $ _____

This appraisal is made ☐ "as is", ☐ subject to completion per plans and specifications on the basis of a hypothetical condition that the improvements have been completed, ☐ subject to the following repairs or alterations on the basis of a hypothetical condition that the repairs or alterations have been completed, or ☐ subject to the following required inspection based on the extraordinary assumption that the condition or deficiency does not require alteration or repair.

Based on a complete visual inspection of the interior and exterior areas of the subject property, defined scope of work, statement of assumptions and limiting conditions, and appraiser's certification, my (our) opinion of the market value, as defined, of the real property that is the subject of this report is
$ _____ , as of _____ , which is the date of inspection and the effective date of this appraisal.

Freddie Mac Form 70   March 2005   Page 2 of 6   Fannie Mae Form 1004   March 2005

NOTES

SALES COMPARISON APPROACH

There are	comparable properties currently offered for sale in the subject neighborhood ranging in price from $		to $	
There are	comparable sales in the subject neighborhood within the past twelve months ranging in sale price from $		to $	

FEATURE	SUBJECT	COMPARABLE SALE # 1		COMPARABLE SALE # 2		COMPARABLE SALE # 3	
Address							
Proximity to Subject							
Sale Price	$		$		$		$
Sale Price/Gross Liv. Area	$ sq. ft.	$ sq. ft.		$ sq. ft.		$ sq. ft.	
Data Source(s)							
Verification Source(s)							
VALUE ADJUSTMENTS	DESCRIPTION	DESCRIPTION	+(-) $ Adjustment	DESCRIPTION	+(-) $ Adjustment	DESCRIPTION	+(-) $ Adjustment
Sale or Financing Concessions							
Date of Sale/Time							
Location							
Leasehold/Fee Simple							
Site							
View							
Design (Style)							
Quality of Construction							
Actual Age							
Condition							
Above Grade	Total	Bdrms.	Baths	Total	Bdrms.	Baths	
Room Count							
Gross Living Area	sq. ft.	sq. ft.		sq. ft.		sq. ft.	
Basement & Finished Rooms Below Grade							
Functional Utility							
Heating/Cooling							
Energy Efficient Items							
Garage/Carport							
Porch/Patio/Deck							
Net Adjustment (Total)		☐ + ☐ -	$	☐ + ☐ -	$	☐ + ☐ -	$
Adjusted Sale Price of Comparables		Net Adj. % Gross Adj. %	$	Net Adj. % Gross Adj. %	$	Net Adj. % Gross Adj. %	$

I ☐ did ☐ did not research the sale or transfer history of the subject property and comparable sales. If not, explain

My research ☐ did ☐ did not reveal any prior sales or transfers of the subject property for the three years prior to the effective date of this appraisal.
Data source(s)
My research ☐ did ☐ did not reveal any prior sales or transfers of the comparable sales for the year prior to the date of sale of the comparable sale.
Data source(s)
Report the results of the research and analysis of the prior sale or transfer history of the subject property and comparable sales (report additional prior sales on page 3).

ITEM	SUBJECT	COMPARABLE SALE # 1	COMPARABLE SALE # 2	COMPARABLE SALE # 3
Date of Prior Sale/Transfer				
Price of Prior Sale/Transfer				
Data Source(s)				
Effective Date of Data Source(s)				

Analysis of prior sale or transfer history of the subject property and comparable sales

Summary of Sales Comparison Approach

Indicated Value by Sales Comparison Approach $

Introduction

In applying the SALES COMPARISON APPROACH, the appraiser:

1.	Studies the market and selects the sales and listings of properties most comparable to the residence being appraised, generally the most current and similar comparable sales. Often, more sales and listings are considered than are finally used.

2.	Collects and verifies data on each selected property's selling and listing prices, dates of transaction, physical and locational characteristics, and any special conditions.

3.	Analyzes and compares each property with the subject as to time of sale, location, physical characteristics and conditions of sale.

4.	Adjusts the sale or listing price of each comparable for dissimilarities between it and the subject, using matched pairs, (as described under Location), regression analysis, and other adjustment techniques.

5.	Reconciles the adjusted prices of the comparable properties into an indicated market value of the appraised residence.

Grid

Always The grid used for the SALES COMPARISON APPROACH on the URAR has been redesigned to make it easier for the appraiser to use and the reviewer to read. Figures which are intended to be added line up in a column, and other numbers are positioned to avoid confusion. Space for Sales or Financing Concessions is located at the top of the grid below Value Adjustments to emphasize its importance.

General Instructions

Always select the comparable sales with the fewest dissimilarities. Use older sales only if more recent ones are not available, and be sure to explain the reason for their use in the COMMENTS section.

The following Fannie Mae 03-05 instructions apply to the SALES COMPARISON APPROACH.

"The appraiser must report a minimum of three comparable sales as part of the sales comparison approach to value. The appraiser may submit more than three comparable sales to support his or her opinion of market value, as long as at least three are actual settled or closed sales. Generally, the appraiser should use comparable sales that have been settled or closed within the last 12 months. However, the appraiser may use older comparable sales if he or she believes that it is appropriate and selects comparable sales that are the best indicators of value for the subject property. The appraiser must comment on the reasons for using any comparable sales that are more than six months old. For example, if the subject property is located in a rural area that has minimal sales activity, the appraiser may not be able to locate three truly comparable sales that sold in the last 12 months. In this case, the appraiser may use older comparable sales as long as he or she explains why they are being used."

"The appraiser may use the subject property as a fourth comparable sale or as supporting data if the property previously was sold (and closed or settled). If the appraiser believes that it is appropriate, he or she also may use contract offerings and current listings as supporting data. However, in no instance may the appraiser create comparable sales by combining vacant land sales with the contract purchase price of a home (although this type of information may be included as additional supporting documentation)."

"For properties that are in established subdivisions, or for units in established condominium or PUD projects that have resale activity, the appraiser should use comparable sales from within the same subdivision or project as the subject property if there are any available. Resale activity from within the subdivision or project should be the best indicator of value for properties in that subdivision or project. If the appraiser uses sales of comparable properties that are located outside of the subject neighborhood, he or she must include an explanation with the analysis."

"For properties in new subdivisions, or for units in new (or recently converted) condominium or PUD projects, the appraiser must compare the subject property to other properties in its general market area as well as to properties within the subject subdivision or project. This comparison should help demonstrate market acceptance of new developments and the properties within them. Generally, the appraiser should select one comparable sale from the subject subdivision or project and one comparable sale from outside the subject subdivision or project. The third comparable sale can be from inside or outside of the subject subdivision or project, as long as the appraiser considers it to be a good indicator of value for the subject property. In selecting the comparables, the appraiser should keep in mind that sales or resales from within the subject subdivision or project are preferable to sales from outside the subdivision or project as long as the developer or builder of the subject property is not involved in the transactions."

Price Range of Comparable Current Offerings in the Neighborhood

It is not intended or necessary to report all of the properties offered for sale in the subject neighborhood. What is being asked for here is a report of what an appraiser normally does when making a sales comparison analysis. The appraiser should examine all of the comparable properties available for sale in the neighborhood and select those that are reasonably comparable to the subject property. It is the range of this group that is reported here. Usually, the final indication of value from the Sales Comparison Approach falls within the range of these listings.

Price Range of Comparable Sales in the Neighborhood

It is not intended or necessary to report all of the sales within the past twelve months in the subject neighborhood. What is being asked for here is a report of what an appraiser normally does when making a sales comparison analysis. The appraiser should examine all known comparable sales in the neighborhood. The appraiser should consider the dates of sale as well as the physical attributes of each property and then select those that are most comparable to the subject. The range of this group of sales is reported here. From this group, usually three or more sales are selected to be displayed and adjusted in a Summary (URAR) appraisal report.

Address

Under Address, identify the location of the subject and all comparables by exact street number, street name, and community name. Be sure that the address is sufficient for a review appraiser to locate each comparable sale.

Proximity to Subject

The Proximity to Subject is the distance and direction from the subject property to each comparable in terms of blocks, fractions of a mile, or miles (as the case may be).

When the distance indicated appears to be outside of the neighborhood boundaries, a comment should be made to clarify why it was necessary to go beyond the neighborhood boundaries to find the most comparable sales.

Sale Price

The Sale Price shown for the subject property is the pending contract price when the appraisal is made for lending purposes. It is not the last recorded sale price of the subject property. The sale price of the Comparable Sales are the gross prices before deductions for selling expenses.

Sale Price/Gross Liv. Area

Calculate the Sale Price/Gross Liv. Area (total sale price per square foot of gross above-grade living area [GLA]) for the subject and each of the comparable sales by dividing each Sale Price (above) by total GLA.

When measurements provided by another source are used, there is a substantial possibility that the Gross Living Area will be incorrect, either because the reported measurements are inaccurate or the area reported is not Gross Living Area as described in the IMPROVEMENTS section.

Data Source(s) & Verification Source(s)

The **SALES COMPARISON APPROACH** adjustment grid was modified to include an entry in which the appraiser reports the Data and/or Verification Source for the comparable sales (to assure compliance with the USPAP requirement that the appraiser verify comparable market data). An appraiser may use a single source for his or her data and verifications. However, multiple sources are sometimes needed to adequately verify the comparable sales. The quality of the data available for single-family residential properties varies from source to source and from one locality to another. In view of this, a single data source may be adequate if the appraiser uses a source that provides quality sales data that is confirmed or verified by closed or settled transactions. On the other hand, if the appraiser's basic data source does not confirm or verify the sales data, the appraiser will need to use additional sources. The internet can be used to verify data in many areas.

Give the data source from which the information pertaining to each comparable was obtained (e.g., deed records, recordation tax stamps, brokers, multiple listings, data bank, buyer or seller, etc.). This should be detailed enough so that a review appraiser can locate the comparable sale in the source of the data. The MLS # is helpful to reviewers when the data source is an MLS system.

For the subject property, indicate the source of data about the pending sale for which the mortgage loan has been applied. It is assumed that other information about the subject property comes from the appraiser's personal inspection.

The following is a list of some good sources of market data:

- Appraiser's own files
- Multiple Listing Services
- Deed records
- Title companies
- Assessment records
- Mortgage loan records
- Real estate brokers' files
- Government and private mortgage insurers
- Atlases and survey maps
- Other appraisers
- Real estate newspapers
- Special publications
- General circulation newspapers
- SREA Market Data Center
- Miscellaneous sources

Value Adjustments

Sale or Financing Concessions

The Sale or Financing Concessions adjustments line has no DESCRIPTION in the SUBJECT column. Concessions that are involved in the comparables but not the subject are described and adjusted for in the appropriate COMPARABLE column. Fannie Mae requires that these adjustments be negative. Any properties requiring positive adjustments cannot be considered as comparables. All adjustments should reflect the difference between the comparable's actual Sale Price and what the property would have sold for without any concessions.

Date of Sale/Time

The appraiser is now required by Fannie Mae to report both a contract date and a closing date for the comparables in the Date of Sale/Time space. If one of the dates is unavailable, the sale date reported must be identified as either the contract date or the closing date. Also, if only the contract date is reported, a comment must be added stating that the sale has, in fact, closed. It is usually only necessary to report the month and the year of the sales.

Location

Give an overall quality rating (good, average, fair, etc.) for the Location of the subject and a comparison rating (superior, equal or inferior) for the comparables. Then make the adjustment indicated by the market for any differences between the comparables and the subject property.

The best way to obtain a location adjustment is to use matched pairs. This technique involves finding a pair of houses in the area which are similar, except that one is in the neighborhood for which a location adjustment is sought while the other is in the neighborhood of the house being appraised. After adjusting the prices for any other discrepancies between the sales, the remaining price difference is attributable to their difference in location. This price difference then can be used as a location adjustment..

Leasehold/Fee Simple

When the subject property is in "fee simple" form of ownership, it is preferable to use comparable sales that are also in "fee simple" ownership. If it is necessary to use a comparable sale that is a "leasehold," a significant adjustment may be required to reflect that the site value is not part of a "leasehold" sale price.

When the subject property is a "leasehold" form of ownership, it is preferable to use comparable sales that are also in "leasehold" ownership. If it is necessary to use a comparable sale that is in "fee simple" ownership, a significant adjustment may be required to reflect that the value of the site is not included in the appraised value of the subject property.

Site

An overall quality rating of good, average, fair, or poor is to be given for the subject property. A comparison rating, as indicated under Location above, should be provided for the Site for each comparable. Factors to be considered by the appraiser under Site include size, shape, topography, drainage, encroachments, easements, or any detrimental site conditions.

Again, the best way to estimate any adjustment for the physical characteristics of the site is to use matched pairs. Find properties that have physical characteristics similar to that for which the adjustment is being sought, and which have sold. Compare these sales with other properties without these characteristics which are otherwise very similar. After adjustments are made for any other differences, the remainder can be attributed to the difference in physical characteristics.

View

An overall quality rating of good, average, fair, or poor is to be given for the subject property. A comparison rating, as indicated under Location above, should be provided for the View for each comparable.

Again, the best way to estimate any adjustment for the view of the site is to use matched pairs. Find properties that have a view similar to that for which the adjustment is being sought, and which have sold. Compare these sales with other properties without these characteristics which are otherwise very similar. After adjustments are made for any other differences, the remainder can be attributed to the difference in view

Design (Style)

The Design (Style) category considers such aspects of the property as appeal of exterior design, interior attractiveness, and special features. Also included are any other characteristics which would change the property's attractiveness to purchasers in general or otherwise alter its marketability. The appraiser is to give comparison ratings, as indicated for the preceding items above, for each of the comparables. The appropriate adjustments may then be made.

Appraisers must be careful when making the Design (Style) adjustment to reflect the standards of the market rather than their own personal standards. Many appraisers use this line to adjust for any difference the market reflects between one- and two-story houses.

The exterior design of the residence will often affect the value. This is especially true when the design is different from the majority of houses in the market. This does not mean that the style and type must conform exactly with the rest of the neighborhood. In many areas, the public's taste has changed and the old principle of uniformity no longer applies as it did in the past. In both old and new neighborhoods now, Colonial, European, and Contemporary styles, and even commercial and industrial uses, all coexist in harmony.

More important is the public's increasing awareness of good design and the rejection of poor design. The post-World War II badly designed tract house, for example, may have suffered little or no functional obsolescence in the market when it was new, but now, may be heavily penalized for inferior design. As a general rule, a well designed house will have more value and depreciate slower than a poorly designed house in the same neighborhood, in similar condition.

Quality of Construction

The Quality of Construction adjustment covers quality of materials and workmanship including exterior walls, roof covering, framing, finish flooring, interior walls, trim, doors, hardware, plumbing and electrical systems, baths, and kitchen and mechanical equipment. The appraiser should indicate an overall quality rating for the subject property and give comparison ratings for each of the comparables. Any adjustments should reflect the market's monetary reaction based on these comparisons.

When the house being appraised is constructed either better or poorer than the standard found in the market, an adjustment may be needed. Like other adjustments, the best way to obtain it is to find matched pairs of sales. When this is impossible, a judgment should be made as to the impact of the difference in quality on value. If the subject's quality of construction is substantially different, the adjustment may not actually reflect the market's reaction.

Actual Age

The Actual Age line may be used only to adjust for the actual age. This is a change of the form which used to give the appraiser the choice of using the "Age" line for either "Actual Age" or "Effective Age" adjustments.

Differences in "Effective Age" between the subject property and the comparable sales may also require adjustment. If an adjustment is needed for "Effective Age," one of the blank lines near the bottom of the grid should be used.

Condition

The Condition line includes the appraiser's opinion of the subject property's condition (whether good, average, fair, or poor), comparison ratings (superior, equal, or inferior) for the comparables, and adjustments made as indicated by the market.

The Condition adjustment should be limited to items that have not already been included in the Actual Age and Effective Age (on one of the blank lines at the bottom of the grid) adjustments. It would be a mistake to increase the effective age of a residence because of its condition and also make adjustment here for the same condition factors.

One way to prevent duplication is to restrict the Condition adjustment to items of physical deterioration-curable. The items of physical deterioration-incurable, then, are included in the Actual Age adjustment. The cost-to-cure acts as a guide to the amount of depreciation here. The reason such items are classified as curable is that they will, when taken care of, add value equal to or greater than the cost to cure them.

Above Grade Room Count – Gross Living Area

The appraiser is to report the total Above Grade Room Count including the number of bedrooms and baths. Adjustments reflective of the market may be needed for any differences between the room count of the subject property and the comparable sale. The appraiser may elect to make a separate adjustment for differences in room count or combine it with the GLA adjustment.

Adjusting for the number of rooms must be done very carefully. More than likely, most of the difference in value has already been adjusted for when the Gross Living Area adjustment is made. In contrast, the adjustment of an extra bath or a deficiency in baths is often greater than just the square foot adjustment involved.

Also, make sure that all adjustments made here are for above grade rooms. Any below grade or partially below grade rooms should not be included in GLA and are adjusted for under Basement & Finished Rooms Below Grade.

The following guidelines will help you correctly calculate the Gross Living Area of the comparable sales:

- Use the measurements around the outside of the house above the foundation.
- In multi-floor houses, count each floor above grade.
- Include all of the above grade habitable living area.
- Do not include the basement (even when it is finished and heated).
- Garages are never included in the GLA.
- Porches are included only when they are heated and finished in a way similar in quality to the rest of the house.
- Upper stories are divided into two areas:

a. Attic is the unfinished part or that part with low ceilings (below 5ft.).

b. Habitable area finished and heated substantially like the rest of the house with normal ceiling heights (5ft. is the most common height used by appraisers as normal ceiling height in attics).

Basement & Finished Rooms Below Grade

The Basement & Finished Rooms Below Grade adjustment should include any basement or other fully or partially below grade improvements found in the subject property and the comparables. If there is no basement (in a house with a slab or crawl space) or only a partial basement, this should also be indicated. Appropriate adjustments must then be made to reflect differences between the comparables and the subject property.

When the measurement system is the Gross Living Area system as required for this appraisal form, special care is needed to correctly adjust for all differences between the subject and comparables in one and only one place. Make sure that the comparables have been measured using the GLA system and that any adjustments made in the Above Grade Room Count Gross Living Area and Other sections are not duplicated here. At the same time, check to make sure all differences between the subject and comparables are adjusted for somewhere in an appropriate section.

The Basement & Finished Rooms Below Grade adjustment is really two separate adjustments combined into one. First, there is the adjustment for full basement versus partial basement versus crawl space versus slab. In many markets, there are significant value differences between similar houses with these various foundations. In areas where basements are expected by the typical buyer, houses without basements often sell for substantially less than similar houses with basements. Conversely, in markets where most houses are built on a slab or over a crawl space, there may be little or no premium paid for houses with basements.

The second adjustment is for that portion of the basement that is finished. Prior to the adoption of the Gross Living Area measurement system, many appraisals included finished, heated basement, in the overall square footage of living area. When using the GLA system, the finished basement is not included, so any adjustment must be made here. Note that using cost figures, rather than value contribution estimated from the market, will often lead to errors.

Functional Utility

Functional Utility refers to, among other things, room sizes, layout and overall livability. A rating should be given for the subject property which will summarize the ratings for these factors found on the URAR. Comparison ratings, such as those indicated previously for Location, are to be given for the comparables and appropriate adjustments made to represent the market's reaction to any differences.

The Functional Utility adjustment should take into account the size of the rooms in both the subject and comparable sales. Each room should be at least the FHA minimum required size and many markets require rooms be larger than the FHA minimum standards.

Heating/Cooling

In most parts of the country, an "average" heating system is a standard quality central system fueled by gas, oil, or electricity. In some areas, one fuel so dominates the market that the appraiser must consider whether a system using another fuel causes functional obsolescence.

Quality heat pump systems and central air conditioning add extra value in most areas. Appropriate adjustments for central air can range from the cost of installation in markets where central air is standard to almost no adjustment when it is considered to be a superadequacy.

Window units provide cooling in many homes. Appraisers must know whether or not window units are legally classified as real estate in their area. When window units are not considered real estate, they should be treated like any other item of personal property included in a sale; their value should not be included in the market value estimate.

Again, the matched pairs technique is useful in estimating the amount of Heating/Cooling adjustment required.

Energy Efficient Items

Energy Efficient Items often are installed at a cost exceeding their contribution to the value of the residence. Any difference the appraiser estimates to exist between the cost of these items and their value on the date of the appraisal should be divided between physical deterioration and functional obsolescence.

Here is a list of some of the items that are considered to be Energy Efficient Items:
- Solar heating
- Solar domestic hot water system
- Extra insulation
- Special insulated window glass
- Automatic thermostat controls
- Automatic flue opening and closing devices
- Electric use monitors
- Special furnace controls with outdoor temperature monitors
- Any wind or hydroelectric power device

Garage/Carport

Garage/Carport adjustments are based on whether the subject property and the comparables have garages or carports and, if so, their car storage capacity. The increase or decrease in value should not necessarily represent the cost of construction, but rather it should be based on the market's response.

In many areas, the market is very sensitive to the influence that garages and carports have on the value of a property. Often, there is a market standard or price range within a neighborhood, and properties which do not conform to the standard suffer substantial depreciation. For example, the market may expect a two-car attached garage. The construction cost differential between a two-car attached garage and a one-car attached garage may be about $3,000, yet matched pairs of sales will indicate a $5,000 sales price differential. In the same market, a property with a three-car attached garage may sell for only $1,000 more than one with a two-car attached garage. The use of cost as a value indication would therefore result in a substantial error.

Porches/Patios/Deck

The appraiser should indicate the presence or absence of a Porch, Patio, or Deck and make the necessary adjustments indicated by the market. Cost data may, at times, serve as a guide, but is not necessarily indicative since these improvements may not return their entire cost upon resale as added value.

In some parts of the country, porches and patios add little or no value to properties; in other areas, they add value greater than their cost. Again, matched pairs of sales are the best indication of the value of such features. When the adjustment is very small, some portion of the porch or patio cost may be used. However, it should be recognized that an adjustment made on this basis is nothing but an educated guess.

Swimming pools have become a major appraisal problem in many parts of the country. They range from simple above-ground, semi-portable pools to elaborate in-ground pools with pumping and filtering systems. Some even have pool houses with wet bars and cooking facilities (and sometimes sleeping quarters), lighting and heating systems and occasionally, year round covers or tops. Regardless, the appraiser must first decide if the pool is part of the real estate to be included in the appraised value. The status of the pool should then be clearly indicated on the report on one of the blank lines immediately below the Porch/Patio/Deck line.

As with other adjustments, the best way to estimate the value that various kinds of pools add is to use matched pairs. First find houses with pools similar to the pool of the house being appraised (that have sold) and other sales of properties that are without pools. After adjusting for other differences, the remaining difference can be attributed to the value of the pool.

Other

The following is a list of some of the items that may be adjusted for in the Other section:
- Effective Age
- Swimming pool
- Fireplace(s)
- Kitchen: Counters, Cabinets & Built-in equipment and appliances
- Plumbing systems: Special features & fixtures, Deficiencies &

Special bathroom features
- Domestic hot water system
- Electric: Service (size and age) & Wiring (type and condition)
- Water supply
- Waste disposal system
- Other special purpose rooms
- Attic finish
- Insulation
- Fire & burglar alarm systems
- Rehabilitation, modernization, & remodeling
- Any additional items which require adjustments, but did not fall under any other category

It is important to remember that a comparable sale's condition and its special features at the time of its sale may differ from what they are on the date of the appraisal. For example, a comparable may have needed painting and a new roof when it was sold and these items have been repaired since. Changes in condition and features can often be determined by interviewing the current owner, seller, broker or closing attorney. Information on the MLS card may also be helpful.

Net Adjustment (Total)

The Net Adjustment (Total) space is used to report the net total of all VALUE ADJUSTMENTS made in the + (-) $_____ Adjustment column above. The appraiser must also indicate whether, on balance, the total is positive or negative by checking the appropriate box. If the total adjustments appear excessive in relation to the sale price as outlined in the box above, the appraiser would be well advised to reexamine the comparability of that sale.

Adjusted Sale Price of Comparables

The Adjusted Sale Price of Comparables is calculated for each comparable by adding (or subtracting if appropriate) its Net Adjustment (Total) to (or from) its Sale Price.

It is good appraisal practice to round the Adjusted Sale Price of Comparables to reflect the appraiser's opinion of the accuracy of the adjusted value. When the market data is so good that the appraiser feels the estimate is within one hundred dollars, the estimate should be rounded to the nearest hundred dollars. More often the appraiser will feel that the estimate is accurate to the nearest thousand and, on more expensive homes, to the nearest five thousand dollars.

Transfer & Sale History

Subject & Comparables - Did/Did Not Research

Check the box that is appropriate. If "did not" is checked, you must provide a valid reason why you failed to do so. Keep in mind that Fannie Mae expects this to be done within the scope of work for appraisals for loans submitted to them.

This line on the URAR reflects the increasing emphasis on reporting and analyzing the sales history of both the subject property and the comparable sales.

Subject Property 3 Years Sales History Research Result

Fannie Mae, in Announcement 05-02, dated March 24, 2005 clarifies the scope of work it expects for appraisals on the URAR that are submitted to them:

Direct questions have been added to the report forms that require the appraiser to report his or her analysis and conclusions on key areas in a clear and succinct yes/no format to address whether:

• the subject property is currently offered for sale or if it was offered for sale in the twelve months prior to the effective date of the appraisal;

• the appraiser analyzed the contract for sale for the subject property for a purchase money transaction;

• the appraiser researched, analyzed and reported on the sale (or transfer) history for the subject property and comparable sales.

A grid is provided to report the date of prior sale, price of prior sale of transfers, and data source for prior sales of the subject property and comparables sales and the effective date of the data sources. A data source date might be the publication date of an MLS book that was issued two months prior to the date of the appraisal.

USPAP STANDARD RULE 1-5: This rule effective 01/01/03 requires an appraiser to report and analyze all prior sales of the subject property within the past three (3) year, if such information is available in the normal course of business.

Comparable Sales 1 Year Sales History Research Result & Data Sources

Fannie Mae requires a sales history of each comparable sale for one year from the date the comparable sale last sold, not from the effective date of the appraisal.

Fannie Mac and Freddie Mac require the appraiser to research any available sources of information that would include a record of the sale of the comparable sales up to one year before the date of sale of the comparable sale.

Check the appropriate box to indicate the results of your research, and indicate the data sources you used. The data source for the prior sales of the comparables does not have to be the same as the appraiser's data and/or verification source that was reported at the top of the adjustments grid.

It is good to include in your data sources Public Records, Lender, Seller, Owner, Occupant, Realtor, and any known closing attorney.

Your answer to this question may be closely looked at by Fannie Mae, Freddie Mac, and the lenders who want to avoid making loans where "flipping" may be involved.

I recommend you do not check the "did not" box unless you have actually tried to get this information from all of the data sources mentioned above.

Using just this grid is not sufficient to report the results of your research on the three year sales history of the subject property and the one year sales history of each comparable sale. The additional information and analysis should be reported on the blank lines on page 3 of the URAR.

When you check a data source, the information in it may not be current to the date of the appraisal. For example, the MLS may only have information up to the end of the previous month or week.

Grid: Sale/Transfer Subject Property & Comparable Sales

Using just this grid is not sufficient to report the results of your research on the three year sales history of the subject property and the one year sales history of each comparable sale. The additional information and analysis should be reported on the blank lines on page 3 of the URAR.

When you check a data source, the information in it may not be current to the date of the appraisal. For example, the MLS may only have information up to the end of the previous month.

Analysis of prior sales/transfer history of the subject property and comparable sales

The space used for providing narrative comments related to the sales comparison analysis was significantly expanded for the appraiser's analysis of any prior sales of the subject property and the comparables, as well as of any current agreement of sale, option, or listing of the subject property (to assure compliance with the Uniform Standards).

The appraiser should make a significant attempt to obtain a signed copy of the Contract for Sale. Sometimes, the agreement of sale is supplied after the appraiser has completed and delivered the appraisal to the Lender/Client. The appraiser is then asked to submit a letter or addenda to the appraisal saying that he or she has reviewed the Contract for Sale and either found that it has no effect on the appraisal or explain how it does affect the appraisal.

This supplemental letter or addenda has the potential of getting the appraiser into all kinds of trouble. I recommend that a new appraisal be made instead.

Summary of Sales Comparison Approach

The Summary of Sales Comparison Approach section has two major uses.

The first is to explain how the SALES COMPARISON APPROACH is reconciled. This should not be an averaging technique, but rather a reasoning process. Explain which comparable sales are given most weight, which adjustments seem most reliable, and how the final sales comparison estimate of value is selected.

The second use is to explain the basis for the adjustments, especially those which are significant in size. Adjustments can be based on the following:

1. Market studies made by the appraiser or made available to the appraiser.

2. Matched pairs of sales where other differences are eliminated.

3. Cost data from which the appraiser deducts appropriate estimated depreciation. (This is a good technique for small differences in physical characteristics).

4. Estimates based on the appraiser's training, experience, and knowledge of the market. (All too often, this is the only method available to make a particular adjustment).

5. Regression and other computer studies that, in the appraiser's judgment, apply to the subject market and property.

NOTE: It is a rare appraisal where all of the above will fit in the Summary of Sales Comparison Approach. Therefore, the lines on Page 3 and an addendum page are usually necessary.

Indicated Value by Sales Comparison Approach $

Fannie Mae and Freddie Mac require a single figure and not a range.

The figure given should be rounded to indicate the accuracy of the estimate. Most appraisers tend to round to a minimum of the nearest thousand dollars, unless they strongly feel that their estimate is more accurate.

Indicated Value by: Sales Comparison Approach $	Cost Approach (if developed) $	Income Approach (if developed) $

This appraisal is made ☐ "as is", ☐ subject to completion per plans and specifications on the basis of a hypothetical condition that the improvements have been completed, ☐ subject to the following repairs or alterations on the basis of a hypothetical condition that the repairs or alterations have been completed, or ☐ subject to the following required inspection based on the extraordinary assumption that the condition or deficiency does not require alteration or repair:

Based on a complete visual inspection of the interior and exterior areas of the subject property, defined scope of work, statement of assumptions and limiting conditions, and appraiser's certification, my (our) opinion of the market value, as defined, of the real property that is the subject of this report is $, as of , which is the date of inspection and the effective date of this appraisal.

Freddie Mac Form 70 March 2005   Page 2 of 6   Fannie Mae Form 1004 March 2005

Introduction

Fannie Mae has clarified that the purpose of the appraisal is to estimate the market value of the "real property" which is the subject of the report. This means that the appraiser would need to perform a separate analysis if significant personal property is included. Therefore, when a property is sold including kitchen appliances, washer and dryer, and other items of personal property, it is quite common for the appraised value to be less than the sale price, which often includes these non-realty items.

The **RECONCILIATION** section of the URAR requires the below information. These items are described in detail on the following pages.

Indicated Value by: Sales Comparison, Cost and Income Approaches

Enter the results of each of the approaches to value from Pages 2 and 3. If one or more of the approaches to value is not developed, indicate this with "—" or "N/A" or "Not Dev." or some similar notation.

If one or more of the approaches is not developed, a simple comment to this effect should be entered on the blank lines in this section, including the reason why it was not developed.

A suggested comment to use when one or more of the approaches is not developed is: "Please refer to the appropriate comments on Page 3 of this report as to why the Cost and/or Income Approach was not developed for this appraisal." Clearly, the scope of work required by Fannie Mae for the URAR (as stated on the form) when used for loans submitted to Fannie Mae does not include the development of a Cost Approach or Income Approach. However, the USPAP does not say that an appraiser should eliminate either approach just because the Lender/Client (or Fannie Mae) excludes them from their required Scope of Work.

USPAP STANDARDS RULE 1-2 (f) [p.18, 2005 USPAP]
This Standards Rule contains binding requirements from which departure is not permitted:

An appraiser must have sound reasons in support of the scope of work decision and must be prepared to support the decision to exclude any information or procedure that would appear to be relevant to the client, an intended user, or the appraiser's peers in the same or a similar assignment.

An appraiser must not allow assignment conditions or other factors to limit the extent of research or analysis to such a degree that the resulting opinions and conclusions developed in an assignment are not credible in the context of the intended use of the appraisal.

RECONCILIATION

Appraisal Made: "As Is" – "Subject to Completion" – "Subject to Inspection"

Indicate, by checking the appropriate box, whether **This appraisal is made**:

- **"as is"**

- **subject to completion per plans and specifications on the basis of a hypothetical condition that the improvements have been completed**

- **subject to the following required inspection based on the extraordinary assumption that the condition or deficiency does not require alteration or repair.**

Most lenders require that the value estimated be based on **"as is"** condition. However, if structural repairs are needed to make the property livable or saleable, they should be itemized together with an estimate of their cost. Some lenders also require a list (with costs-to-cure) of items of physical curable deterioration.

When the appraisal is made subject to **plans and specifications**, the appraisal should indicate the source, location, and exact identity of the plans and specifications.

If the appraisal is made **subject to repairs, alterations, or conditions**, the appraiser must carefully and in detail spell out exactly what the repairs, alterations, and conditions are. Often a mortgage will be made subject to a requirement that the borrower make the needed repairs or alterations and correct the reported conditions. Unless these items are precisely described by the appraiser, the lender and borrower will have trouble determining exactly what needs to be done.

NOTE: Some appraisers are now checking the "subject to the repairs, alterations, inspections, or conditions listed below" box whenever they *have not* been supplied with a Phase 1, 2 or 3 environmental inspection. They indicate in the comments that their value estimate is based on the assumption that the property does not contain any detrimental environmental conditions or hazardous substances which might be revealed by an environmental inspection.

> The reconciliation leading to a value conclusion takes place in each step of the appraisal process. There is also a final reconciliation which leads to the final value estimate. ...The accuracy of an appraisal depends on the appraiser's knowledge, experience, and judgment. Equally important are the quantity and quality of the available data that will be reconciled in the final value conclusion. A judgment is made as to the validity and reliability of each of the value indications derived from the three approaches to value.*

Final Value Estimate

The **RECONCILIATION** ends with this statement: "Based on a complete visual inspection of the interior and exterior areas of the subject property, defined scope of work, statement of assumptions and limiting conditions, and appraiser's certification, my (our) opinion of the market value, as defined, of the real property that is the subject of this report is $_____, as of _____, which is the date of inspection and the effective date of this appraisal."

Before you sign the report, you should consider the representations that are being made in this statement. **If they are not correct, you cannot sign the report**.

(a) You made a complete visual inspection of the interior and exterior areas of the subject property.

(b) **No personal property** is included in the value estimate (appliances, furnishings, above ground pool, etc.).

(c) The date of inspection and date of appraisal **are the same**

---

* George F. Bloom and Henry S. Harrison, <u>Appraising the Single Family Residence</u> (Chicago: American Institute of Real Estate Appraisers, 1978), pg. 295.

Uniform Residential Appraisal Report
File #

ADDITIONAL COMMENTS

(blank lined area)

COST APPROACH TO VALUE (not required by Fannie Mae)

Provide adequate information for the lender/client to replicate the below cost figures and calculations.

Support for the opinion of site value (summary of comparable land sales or other methods for estimating site value)

COST APPROACH	
ESTIMATED ☐ REPRODUCTION OR ☐ REPLACEMENT COST NEW	OPINION OF SITE VALUE .... = $
Source of cost data	Dwelling Sq. Ft. @ $ =$
Quality rating from cost service Effective date of cost data	Sq. Ft. @ $ =$
Comments on Cost Approach (gross living area calculations, depreciation, etc.)	Garage/Carport Sq. Ft. @ $ =$
	Total Estimate of Cost-New .... = $
	Less Physical	Functional	External
	Depreciation =$( )
	Depreciated Cost of Improvements.................=$
	"As-is" Value of Site Improvements................=$
Estimated Remaining Economic Life (HUD and VA only) Years	Indicated Value By Cost Approach ....=$

INCOME APPROACH TO VALUE (not required by Fannie Mae)

Estimated Monthly Market Rent $ X Gross Rent Multiplier   = $ Indicated Value by Income Approach

Summary of Income Approach (including support for market rent and GRM)

PROJECT INFORMATION FOR PUDs (if applicable)

Is the developer/builder in control of the Homeowners' Association (HOA)? ☐ Yes ☐ No   Unit type(s) ☐ Detached ☐ Attached

Provide the following information for PUDs ONLY if the developer/builder is in control of the HOA and the subject property is an attached dwelling unit.

Legal name of project

Total number of phases   Total number of units   Total number of units sold

Total number of units rented   Total number of units for sale   Data source(s)

Was the project created by the conversion of an existing building(s) into a PUD? ☐ Yes ☐ No   If Yes, date of conversion

Does the project contain any multi-dwelling units? ☐ Yes ☐ No   Data source(s)

Are the units, common elements, and recreation facilities complete? ☐ Yes ☐ No   If No, describe the status of completion

Are the common elements leased to or by the Homeowners' Association? ☐ Yes ☐ No   If Yes, describe the rental terms and options.

Describe common elements and recreational facilities

Freddie Mac Form 70   March 2005   Page 3 of 6   Fannie Mae Form 1004   March 2005

NOTES

Uniform Residential Appraisal Report

File #

ADDITIONAL COMMENTS

On all previous versions of the URAR, each section had some comments lines. When the 2004 test versions of the new Fannie Mae URAR were released, one of the common complaints was that there was not enough room for comments. The final solution for the URAR was to include about a half a page devoted solely to comments at the top of page 3. These comments lines are in addition to the many comment lines in other sections of the form.

Since these lines can be used for comments pertaining to any section of the URAR, it is helpful if each comment starts off with an identification as to which section the comment relates to. For example:

"Cost Approach – When measuring the house, I did not include any part of the attic in the Gross Living Area measurements because the walls were plywood and the heat was inadequate electric baseboards. The rest of the house had walls that were sheetrock and the heat was hot water baseboard heat."

COST APPROACH TO VALUE (not required by Fannie Mae)				
Provide adequate information for the lender/client to replicate the below cost figures and calculations.				
Support for the opinion of site value (summary of comparable land sales or other methods for estimating site value)				
ESTIMATED ☐ REPRODUCTION OR ☐ REPLACEMENT COST NEW	OPINION OF SITE VALUE..			= $
Source of cost data	Dwelling	Sq. Ft. @ $	....	=$
Quality rating from cost service Effective date of cost data		Sq. Ft. @ $	....	=$
Comments on Cost Approach (gross living area calculations, depreciation, etc.)				
	Garage/Carport	Sq. Ft. @ $	....	=$
	Total Estimate of Cost-New		....	= $
	Less Physical	Functional	External	
	Depreciation			=$( )
	Depreciated Cost of Improvements............................			=$
	"As-is" Value of Site Improvements...........................			=$
Estimated Remaining Economic Life (HUD and VA only) Years	Indicated Value By Cost Approach............................			=$

Introduction

Fannie Mae and Freddie Mac do not require the use of the COST APPROACH on the URAR. When the Cost Approach is not used because it is not required as part of the Fannie Mae or Freddie Mac Scope of Work, then the appraisal automatically becomes a Limited Appraisal. When the appraiser determines the Cost Approach is not needed, the appraisal may be a Complete Appraisal without the Cost Approach.

There are five basic steps to the COST APPROACH. Essentially they provide for an estimate of site value, to which is added the depreciated reproduction cost or replacement cost (new) of the improvements as of the date of the appraisal.

1. Estimate the value of the site as if vacant.

2. Estimate the reproduction cost or replacement cost (new) of all the improvements (excluding any included as part of the site value).

3. Estimate accrued Depreciation from all causes (Physical deterioration, Functional obsolescence and External obsolescence).

4. Deduct accrued depreciation from the cost (new) of the improvements to arrive at a Depreciated Value of Improvements.

5. Add the site value to the depreciated value of the improvements to obtain the Indicated Value By Cost Approach.

The following are the subsections of the COST APPROACH:

Provide adequate information for the lender/client

Fannie Mae and Freddie Mac have added an additional reporting requirement: "Provide adequate information for the lender/client to replicate the below cost figures and calculations."

In order to comply with this requirement, the appraiser must provide details on how the reproduction or replacement cost was calculated. A good way to provide this information is to attach a copy of the computer printout or worksheet used to calculate the reproduction or replacement cost.

Support for the opinion of site value

The two most common ways to estimate the value of the site are:

1. Use comparable sales of vacant sites in the same market as the subject property, making whatever adjustments are needed to reflect the differences between the subject site and the comparable site sales.

When this method is used, the appraiser should add an addendum to the appraisal report that provides information about each of the comparable sales and what adjustments were needed.

2. Obtain the Site Value using the abstraction method.

These calculations should be attached as an addendum.

ESTIMATED REPRODUCTION OR REPLACEMENT COST NEW

The ESTIMATED REPRODUCTION OR REPLACEMENT COST NEW, i.e., the cost of reproducing the subject structures using the same floor plan, materials and workmanship, is reproduced here. This section of the COST APPROACH starts with two check boxes to indicate whether REPRODUCTION COSTS or REPLACEMENT COSTS were used for the Approach.

Reproduction Cost is the cost of reproducing the subject house using the same floor plan, materials, and workmanship.

It is recognized that in some cases involving older buildings containing obsolete materials or unusual functional features, it is difficult, if not impossible, to estimate Reproduction Cost New with any reasonable degree of accuracy. Therefore, in such cases, the Replacement Cost may be used with a description of the materials used for the estimate included. When using Replacement Cost, also state the functional deficiencies that have been eliminated.

If the building is too old to estimate reproduction cost, it probably is too old for the COST APPROACH to be meaningful.

Source of cost data

The appraiser should indicate the Source of cost data. Many appraisers attach a computer printout or their worksheets that show how the cost was calculated as an addenda to the form. Include enough detail about the Cost Service used to allow a reviewer to verify the calculations.

Quality rating from cost service

This is a new question on the URAR. Most cost services base the cost estimate on the appraiser's input of a quality rating. Indicate this rating in the space provided.

The cost service often provides guidelines about selecting an appropriate Quality Rating. The Quality Ratings are not necessarily the same as are used in other parts of the appraisal report.

Effective date of cost data

This is a new question on the URAR. Cost services are updated monthly, quarterly, semi-annually, and annually, depending upon the particular cost service and the type of subscription. Therefore, the effective date of the cost service information usually is not exactly the same as the effective date of the appraisal.

Usually, if the two effective dates are within a year of each other, it is not necessary to make an adjustment for the difference, except in periods of rapidly rising or declining costs. Indicate the effective date of the cost service in the space provided.

Comments on Cost Approach

These comments lines can be used for any appropriate cost approach comments. Additional comments can be added in the ADDITIONAL COMMENTS section of the URAR or an addendum sheet. Comments on the following items are often needed:

- Site Value
- Physical determination
- Functional obsolescence
- External obsolescence
- Construction warranty

- The OPINION OF SITE VALUE basis should be explained here or on an addendum sheet.

- The square foot (size) calculation for the property may be shown on these lines or indicated on the exterior building sketch of the improvements, which Fannie Mae requires as an exhibit in the addenda section of each appraisal report.

Measurements		No. Stories		Sq. Ft.
30' x 30'	x	1	=	900
6' x 26'	x	1	=	156
26' x 32'	x	1	=	832
Total Gross Living Area		1,888		

The above is an example of the correct way to enter the measurements of the house shown in the case study in this book.

NOTE: Freddie Mac and Fannie Mae require that this space show only square foot Gross Living Area calculations and cost approach comments. The sketch of the building should be attached on a separate sheet.

OPINION OF SITE VALUE

The final estimate of the Site Value is reported on this line. Details about the basis of the estimate are explained on the Comments lines. Do not include the value of the Site Improvements in this figure, as it is entered separately below on the form.

Included in the site value should be all costs to develop the site not included on the "As-is" Value of Site Improvements line. Be careful not to duplicate items. For example, wells and septic systems are significant items that often (by mistake) are included in both the site value and the site improvement value.

When a house is on leased land and the land rent being paid is the same as the current economic (market) rent, there is no leasehold value. "0" is entered for the OPINION OF SITE VALUE. If the rent being paid is less than the economic (market) rent, the discounted value of the difference is the value of the leasehold and this figure is entered for the opinion of site value. For properties involving a leasehold, an addendum sheet should be attached with details of the lease and how leasehold value (if any) is calculated.

Site value can be estimated in built-up areas by estimating what percentage of the total property value (in the same neighborhood) the typical site is. The percentage can then be used to estimate the value of the site being appraised by multiplying the estimated total value of the property by the typical site/property ratio. Care should be exercised in using this technique as it may be subject to substantial error.

Total Estimate of Cost New: Dwelling – Garage/Carport

These lines are used to summarize the estimated Reproduction or Replacement Cost-New. Usually, these figures are derived from the Cost Service or Builder's Cost Estimates.

Remember, Fannie Mae and Freddie Mac require, if you elect to use the Cost Approach, that the appraiser provide sufficient information in the Comments lines to allow the reviewer to verify the appraiser's calculations.

Depreciation: Physical/Functional/External

There are three types of Depreciation: Physical deterioration, Functional obsolescence, and External obsolescence. The appraiser should estimate the value lost to each of the three types of depreciation and enter the dollar value in the appropriate column in this space. The total of all three types of depreciation is then entered on the blank line at the right after the $ sign.

Depreciated Cost of Improvements

On the URAR, site improvements are not included in the total Depreciated Cost of Improvements. They are shown as a separate item on the next line.

The Depreciated Cost of Improvements is their reproduction cost (or replacement cost) less all forms of depreciation.

Subtract the total Depreciation: Physical, Functional, and External from the Total Estimated Cost-New to obtain the Depreciated Cost of Improvements.

"As-is" Value of Site Improvements

There is no universal agreement among appraisers as to which improvements are classified as site improvements and which are part of the site value. Based on the SITE section of the URAR, it appears the following items should be included in the "As-is" Value of Site Improvements value. If these are included as site improvements, do not also include them as part of the OPINION OF SITE VALUE.

- Clearing, grading, or other landscaping
- Drainage systems
- Installation of public utilities
- Access driveways, streets, and alleys
- Outside lighting and poles
- Sidewalks and curbs
- Fences and walls

The appraiser must also decide whether to include the following items as site improvements or as part of the house. The custom of the area where the subject house is located should be considered.

- Septic systems and cesspools
- Utility connections
- Wells and well pumps
- Patios, pools and tennis courts

The best way to avoid confusion is to list on an addendum sheet those items which are included as part of the site, site improvement, and improvement value estimates.

NOTE: "As is" means that the items are reported at their contributory or depreciated value. This eliminates the need to estimate the reproduction cost of large trees and other site improvements.

Remaining Economic Life (HUD/FHA & VA Only)

The Estimated Remaining Economic Life is the appraiser's forecast of the number of years that the improvements will contribute to the value of the property. Often, the site itself has substantial value at the end of this period.

The URAR provides space for an estimate of remaining economic life. It is not required by Freddie Mac or Fannie Mae, but it is required by some lenders. Appraisers must take great care in making this estimate, as some lenders limit the term of the mortgage based on it.

Many appraisers believe it is impossible to estimate remaining economic life unless a property is nearing the end of that life. However, most feel the estimate can be made, provided it is qualified by projecting no substantial future changes in the four great forces (Governmental, Physical, Economic and Social) that affect value in a particular neighborhood. The problem is that the probability of these forces remaining unchanged for long periods of time is remote. Therefore, an estimate of long remaining economic life based on this assumption serves little purpose.

It is no longer considered good appraisal practice to estimate the remaining economic life by projecting an historic rate of depreciation into the future.

When forecasting remaining economic life, the appraiser must consider the quality of both design and construction of the house, along with its condition, in relation to the projected effects of the four great forces on its value and economic life. When a residence is remodeled, subjected to excessive wear and tear, or affected by forces different from those projected, the remaining economic life may also change.

Indicated Value by Cost Approach

The Indicated Value By Cost Approach is calculated by adding the "As-is" Value of Site Improvements value and the OPINION OF SITE VALUE to the Depreciated Cost of Improvements.

NOTES

INCOME APPROACH TO VALUE (not required by Fannie Mae)			
Estimated Monthly Market Rent $	X Gross Rent Multiplier	= $	Indicated Value by Income Approach
Summary of Income Approach (including support for market rent and GRM)			

Introduction

The <u>INCOME APPROACH</u> is used by very few appraisers for single family houses. This is unfortunate because when used correctly, it can be a valuable tool. There are ample rentals to develop the needed Gross Rent Multiplier and Estimated Monthly Market Rent in far more markets than most appraisers realize. The <u>INCOME APPROACH</u> works best when a large number of comparable rental/sales are used to develop the market rent and multiplier. A good source of these comparables is realtors who are active in the market where the subject property is located.

NOTE: The Uniform Standards of Professional Appraisal Practice require that all approaches to value be used unless there is a valid reason for the omission of one. If an approach is not used, the reason should be explained in the <u>ADDITIONAL COMMENTS</u> section.

Fannie Mae and Freddie Mac do not require the use of the <u>INCOME APPROACH</u> in their "Scope of Work." When the appraiser decides not to use the <u>INCOME APPROACH</u> based on the "Scope of Work," the appraisal becomes a Limited Appraisal and must comply with all the USPAP requirements for limited appraisals.

The following are the subsections of the <u>INCOME APPROACH</u>:

Estimated Monthly Market Rent

The first step of the <u>INCOME APPROACH</u> is to estimate the Monthly Market Rent for the subject property.

Find comparable rental properties in the same or a similar neighborhood to the property being appraised. Compare their monthly rent with that of the property being appraised (if it is rented) to confirm that the subject's rent is typical of the market. If the subject property is rented and the price is typical, enter the monthly rent in the Estimated Market Rent $ space. Otherwise, adjust each comparable's rent for significant differences between the comparable and the subject property. Consider the adjusted monthly rents and reconcile the data into the Estimated Market Rent $ for the subject property assuming it is vacant and available to let on the date of the appraisal.

Gross Rent Multiplier

The second step of the <u>INCOME APPROACH</u> is to develop a Gross Rent **Multiplier**.

Find residences in the same or a similar neighborhood to the property being appraised that recently sold and were rented at the time of sale. The residences themselves should also be reasonably similar to the subject. Divide the sale price of each property by its monthly rental (unfurnished & without utilities) to obtain a multiplier as shown below.

Comparable	Sale Price	Rent on Sale Date	Multiplier
1	$160,000	$1440	111 r
2	$165,000	$1550	110
3	$170,000	$1520	112 r
4	$172,500	$1540	112 r
5	$176,000	$1600	110

Reconcile the multipliers developed above to derive a Gross Rent Multiplier (GRM) applicable to the subject. This should not be an average, but rather a judgment of comparability and applicability.

Indicated Value by Income Approach

The third step of the INCOME APPROACH is to multiply the Estimated Market Rent $ by the Gross Rent Multiplier to obtain an Indicated Value by Income Approach for the residence being appraised.

Summary of Income Approach

The final step is to summarize the results and to justify why or why not the Income Approach was applicable to the property being appraised.

PROJECT INFORMATION FOR PUDs (if applicable)
Is the developer/builder in control of the Homeowners' Association (HOA)? ☐ Yes ☐ No   Unit type(s) ☐ Detached ☐ Attached
Provide the following information for PUDs ONLY if the developer/builder is in control of the HOA and the subject property is an attached dwelling unit.
Legal name of project
Total number of phases   Total number of units   Total number of units sold
Total number of units rented   Total number of units for sale   Data source(s)
Was the project created by the conversion of an existing building(s) into a PUD? ☐ Yes ☐ No If Yes, date of conversion
Does the project contain any multi-dwelling units? ☐ Yes ☐ No Data source(s)
Are the units, common elements, and recreation facilities complete? ☐ Yes ☐ No If No, describe the status of completion.
Are the common elements leased to or by the Homeowners' Association? ☐ Yes ☐ No If Yes, describe the rental terms and options.
Describe common elements and recreational facilities

Introduction

The URAR now includes a separate section that is completed if the property being appraised is located in a Planned Unit Development (PUD).

Important: Most of the information in this PUD INFORMATION section is not required by Fannie Mac and Freddie Mac for "Detached Units." However, some lenders require it for all PUD appraisals.

Is the developer/builder in control of the HOA?

The appraiser must determine who controls the Homeowners' Association (HOA). Initially, it is controlled by the developer who often has subsidized the operating cost.

At some point during the development of the project (this is often mandated by state law and based on the percentage of units sold), control of the HOA is turned over to property owners who elect a Board of Directors and officers to run the HOA.

Sometimes, property owners or realtors do not know who controls the HOA. It may be necessary to interview the developer, the project attorney, etc., to obtain accurate information about the control of the HOA.

Unit Types(s)

This question asks about all the "Unit Types" in the PUD, not just what "Unit Type" the subject property is.

When the developer/builder is in control of the HOA and the subject property is an "Attached Dwelling" unit, Freddie Mac and Fannie Mae require that the balance of the PUD INFORMATION section be completed.

Like for the COST APPROACH and INCOME APPROACH, it is up to the appraiser to decide if it is necessary to complete this section in order to make a credible appraisal as required by the USPAP.

Legal name of project

The name that appears on the signs is not always the legal name of the project. Likewise, you cannot depend upon the project name on the sales contract.

management company, HOA's attorney, any other attorney who has closed the sale of a property in the PUD and the HOA's accountant are all good sources for finding out the legal name of the PUD project.

Total number of phases – Total number of units – Total number of units sold

Some PUDs are built in more than one phase. Good sources of this information are the President of the Homeowners' Association, the developer, or the building inspector. The legal documents that are recorded will also contain this information.

The Total number of units is for all phases unless the appraiser indicates otherwise.

The Total number of units sold is for all phases unless otherwise indicated.

The developer is a good source for this information.

Total number of units rented – Total number of units for sale – Data source(s)

The Total number of units rented can be obtained from the developer (if he or she is still in control of the HOA) or the local MLS system.

When the HOA is controlled by the property owners, there often is a management company who will have this information.

Wherever you get this information must be recorded on the Data source(s) line.

Was the project created by the conversion of an existing building(s) into a PUD?

When the subject property is an attached dwelling unit, the appraiser must determine whether it was always in PUD ownership or whether it is a conversion from "fee simple" or some other form of ownership.

Whoever you got this information from (developer, manager, attorney, etc.) hopefully can give you the date of the conversion. The recorded documents will almost always indicate this information
Does the project contain any multi-dwelling units?

Usually you can tell by inspecting the development whether it contains any multi-dwelling units. Indicate on the form how you obtain this information.

Does the project contain any multiple units? Describe Source

On many projects the answer to this can be obtained by observation.

Are the units, common elements, and recreation facilities complete?

This is a complex question that is going to require some research to correctly answer.

The first things to determine are the total number of units planned for all phases of the PUD project and if they are all completed. The building inspector is an excellent source of this information. When units are completed, the building inspector issues a Certificate of Occupancy. Therefore the building inspector knows if any units have not been completed.

It is harder to obtain accurate information about incomplete common elements and recreation facilities. Sometimes, the only way to obtain this information is to read the filed PUD documents and then inspect the property to see if the promised common elements and recreation facilities in these documents actually exist and are completed.

The appraiser is required to report on the status of any incomplete or missing facilities.

Are the common elements leased to or by the Homeowners' Association?

Some states allow the developer to own some of the recreation facilities and charge the owners of the individual PUD units rent to use the facilities.

Some states even permit the developer to own the recreational facilities and rent their use to the public.

If either of these situations are permitted in your state, investigate how it works in the PUD development in which the subject property is located.

The comment lines should be used to explain the arrangement and what effect it has on the value of the unit being appraised.

Describe common elements and recreational facilities

The description of the common elements and recreational facilities should include both complete and incomplete facilities.

If there are known planned additional recreational facilities, they should also be reported.

NOTES

Uniform Residential Appraisal Report   File

This report form is designed to report an appraisal of a one-unit property or a one-unit property with an accessory unit; including a unit in a planned unit development (PUD). This report form is not designed to report an appraisal of a manufactured home or a unit in a condominium or cooperative project.

This appraisal report is subject to the following scope of work, intended use, intended user, definition of market value, statement of assumptions and limiting conditions, and certifications. Modifications, additions, or deletions to the intended use, intended user, definition of market value, or assumptions and limiting conditions are not permitted. The appraiser may expand the scope of work to include any additional research or analysis necessary based on the complexity of this appraisal assignment. Modifications or deletions to the certifications are also not permitted. However, additional certifications that do not constitute material alterations to this appraisal report, such as those required by law or those related to the appraiser's continuing education or membership in an appraisal organization, are permitted.

SCOPE OF WORK: The scope of work for this appraisal is defined by the complexity of this appraisal assignment and the reporting requirements of this appraisal report form, including the following definition of market value, statement of assumptions and limiting conditions, and certifications. The appraiser must, at a minimum: (1) perform a complete visual inspection of the interior and exterior areas of the subject property, (2) inspect the neighborhood, (3) inspect each of the comparable sales from at least the street, (4) research, verify, and analyze data from reliable public and/or private sources, and (5) report his or her analysis, opinions, and conclusions in this appraisal report.

INTENDED USE: The intended use of this appraisal report is for the lender/client to evaluate the property that is the subject of this appraisal for a mortgage finance transaction.

INTENDED USER: The intended user of this appraisal report is the lender/client.

DEFINITION OF MARKET VALUE: The most probable price which a property should bring in a competitive and open market under all conditions requisite to a fair sale, the buyer and seller, each acting prudently, knowledgeably and assuming the price is not affected by undue stimulus. Implicit in this definition is the consummation of a sale as of a specified date and the passing of title from seller to buyer under conditions whereby: (1) buyer and seller are typically motivated; (2) both parties are well informed or well advised, and each acting in what he or she considers his or her own best interest; (3) a reasonable time is allowed for exposure in the open market; (4) payment is made in terms of cash in U. S. dollars or in terms of financial arrangements comparable thereto; and (5) the price represents the normal consideration for the property sold unaffected by special or creative financing or sales concessions* granted by anyone associated with the sale.

*Adjustments to the comparables must be made for special or creative financing or sales concessions. No adjustments are necessary for those costs which are normally paid by sellers as a result of tradition or law in a market area; these costs are readily identifiable since the seller pays these costs in virtually all sales transactions. Special or creative financing adjustments can be made to the comparable property by comparisons to financing terms offered by a third party institutional lender that is not already involved in the property or transaction. Any adjustment should not be calculated on a mechanical dollar for dollar cost of the financing or concession but the dollar amount of any adjustment should approximate the market's reaction to the financing or concessions based on the appraiser's judgment.

STATEMENT OF ASSUMPTIONS AND LIMITING CONDITIONS: The appraiser's certification in this report is subject to the following assumptions and limiting conditions:

1. The appraiser will not be responsible for matters of a legal nature that affect either the property being appraised or the title to it, except for information that he or she became aware of during the research involved in performing this appraisal. The appraiser assumes that the title is good and marketable and will not render any opinions about the title.

2. The appraiser has provided a sketch in this appraisal report to show the approximate dimensions of the improvements. The sketch is included only to assist the reader in visualizing the property and understanding the appraiser's determination of its size.

3. The appraiser has examined the available flood maps that are provided by the Federal Emergency Management Agency (or other data sources) and has noted in this appraisal report whether any portion of the subject site is located in an identified Special Flood Hazard Area. Because the appraiser is not a surveyor, he or she makes no guarantees, express or implied, regarding this determination.

4. The appraiser will not give testimony or appear in court because he or she made an appraisal of the property in question, unless specific arrangements to do so have been made beforehand, or as otherwise required by law.

5. The appraiser has noted in this appraisal report any adverse conditions (such as needed repairs, deterioration, the presence of hazardous wastes, toxic substances, etc.) observed during the inspection of the subject property or that he or she became aware of during the research involved in performing this appraisal. Unless otherwise stated in this appraisal report, the appraiser has no knowledge of any hidden or unapparent physical deficiencies or adverse conditions of the property (such as, but not limited to, needed repairs, deterioration, the presence of hazardous wastes, toxic substances, adverse environmental conditions, etc.) that would make the property less valuable, and has assumed that there are no such conditions and makes no guarantees or warranties, express or implied. The appraiser will not be responsible for any such conditions that do exist or for any engineering or testing that might be required to discover whether such conditions exist. Because the appraiser is not an expert in the field of environmental hazards, this appraisal report must not be considered as an environmental assessment of the property.

6. The appraiser has based his or her appraisal report and valuation conclusion for an appraisal that is subject to satisfactory completion, repairs, or alterations on the assumption that the completion, repairs, or alterations of the subject property will be performed in a professional manner.

NOTES

Uniform Residential Appraisal Report   File

This report form is designed to report an appraisal of a one-unit property or a one-unit property with an accessory unit; including a unit in a planned unit development (PUD). This report form is not designed to report an appraisal of a manufactured home or a unit in a condominium or cooperative project.

This appraisal report is subject to the following scope of work, intended use, intended user, definition of market value, statement of assumptions and limiting conditions, and certifications. Modifications, additions, or deletions to the intended use, intended user, definition of market value, or assumptions and limiting conditions are not permitted. The appraiser may expand the scope of work to include any additional research or analysis necessary based on the complexity of this appraisal assignment. Modifications or deletions to the certifications are also not permitted. However, additional certifications that do not constitute material alterations to this appraisal report, such as those required by law or those related to the appraiser's continuing education or membership in an appraisal organization, are permitted.

Introduction

The 2005 URAR has been expanded to six pages and is now an all-inclusive report form. It is no longer necessary to attach the Freddie Mac Form 439 – Fannie Mae Form 1004B which contained a DEFINITION OF MARKET VALUE, SUMMARY OF LIMITING CONDITIONS AND APPRAISER'S CERTIFICATION, SUPERVISORY APPRAISER'S CERTIFICATION, ADDRESS OF PROPERTY APPRAISED, APPRAISER and SUPERVISORY APPRAISER [signature and license details]. All of these items are now included on pages 3 to 6 of the 2005 URAR.

The first introductory paragraph spells out Fannie Mae's and Freddie Mac's requirements that this form only be used: "to report an appraisal of a one-unit property or a one-unit property with an accessory unit, including a unit in a planned unit development (PUD)." This paragraph also spells out Fannie Mae's and Freddie Mac's requirement that specifically does not permit the use of the URAR form for appraisals of manufactured homes or units in condominium or cooperative projects. Other forms have been developed for these types of property.

The next paragraph notes that an appraisal report made on the URAR is "subject to the following: scope of work, intended use, intended user, definition of market value, statement of limiting conditions, and certifications." This paragraph also adds Fannie Mae's and Freddie Mac's requirement that, "Modifications, additions, or deletions to the intended use, intended user, definition of market value, or assumptions and limiting conditions are not permitted." [emphasis added] This paragraph further states that Fannie Mae's and Freddie Mac's scope of work requirements permit the appraiser to: "expand the scope of work to include any additional research or analysis necessary based on the complexity of this appraisal assignment." [emphasis added]

It also states, "Modifications or deletions to the certifications are also not permitted." However, appraisers are permitted to make "additional certifications that do not constitute material alterations to this appraisal report, such as those required by law or those related to the appraiser's continuing education or membership in an appraisal organization." [emphasis added

Scope of Work

SCOPE OF WORK: The scope of work for this appraisal is defined by the complexity of this appraisal assignment and the reporting requirements of this appraisal report form, including the following definition of market value, statement of assumptions and limiting conditions, and certifications. The appraiser must, at a minimum: (1) perform a complete visual inspection of the interior and exterior areas of the subject property, (2) inspect the neighborhood, (3) inspect each of the comparable sales from at least the street, (4) research, verify, and analyze data from reliable public and/or private sources, and (5) report his or her analysis, opinions, and conclusions in this appraisal report.

Fannie Mae and Freddie Mac, in their scope of work requirements, are stating that the form itself provides what their minimum requirements are and that the whole form must be completed. In addition, it may be necessary to go beyond what is required in order to just fill out the form, depending upon the complexity of the appraisal assignment.

Intended Use

> **INTENDED USE:** The intended use of this appraisal report is for the lender/client to evaluate the property that is the subject of this appraisal for a mortgage finance transaction.

This is a very limited Intended Use. It precludes the Lender/Client using the appraisal for an overall evaluation of their mortgage portfolio, for example, as that would be a more general use than "a mortgage finance transaction." It also does not include property owners or their agent using the appraisal report to determine an offering or listing price for their property or relying on the property inspection portion of the appraisal to determine the condition of the property.

Intended User

> **INTENDED USER:** The intended user of this appraisal report is the lender/client.

This paragraph spells out that if the appraisal is going to be acceptable to Fannie Mae and Freddie Mac, the Intended User is limited to the Lender/Client. This is a very limited intended user. It does not include the property owner or their agent using the appraisal for any purpose. This does not preclude the owner of the property from obtaining a copy of the appraisal. However, it does preclude them from using it for anything other than its intended use by the Lender/Client.

Definition of Market Value

> **DEFINITION OF MARKET VALUE:** The most probable price which a property should bring in a competitive and open market under all conditions requisite to a fair sale, the buyer and seller, each acting prudently, knowledgeably and assuming the price is not affected by undue stimulus. Implicit in this definition is the consummation of a sale as of a specified date and the passing of title from seller to buyer under conditions whereby: (1) buyer and seller are typically motivated; (2) both parties are well informed or well advised, and each acting in what he or she considers his or her own best interest; (3) a reasonable time is allowed for exposure in the open market; (4) payment is made in terms of cash in U. S. dollars or in terms of financial arrangements comparable thereto; and (5) the price represents the normal consideration for the property sold unaffected by special or creative financing or sales concessions* granted by anyone associated with the sale.
>
> *Adjustments to the comparables must be made for special or creative financing or sales concessions. No adjustments are necessary for those costs which are normally paid by sellers as a result of tradition or law in a market area; these costs are readily identifiable since the seller pays these costs in virtually all sales transactions. Special or creative financing adjustments can be made to the comparable property by comparisons to financing terms offered by a third party institutional lender that is not already involved in the property or transaction. Any adjustment should not be calculated on a mechanical dollar for dollar cost of the financing or concession but the dollar amount of any adjustment should approximate the market's reaction to the financing or concessions based on the appraiser's judgment.

The DEFINITION OF MARKET VALUE is the same on the 2005 URAR as the one used on the CLASSIC 6/93 URAR.

When an appraisal is made for Fannie Mae, Freddie Mac, or other federally related agencies, it must use the "Definition of Market Value" contained in federal legislation known as the Federal Institutions Reform, Recovery, and Enforcement Act of 1989 (FIRREA).

Statement of Assumptions and Limiting Conditions

#1 No Responsibility for Matters of Legal Nature and Title

> **STATEMENT OF ASSUMPTIONS AND LIMITING CONDITIONS:** The appraiser's certification in this report is subject to the following assumptions and limiting conditions:
>
> 1. The appraiser will not be responsible for matters of a legal nature that affect either the property being appraised or the title to it, except for information that he or she became aware of during the research involved in performing this appraisal. The appraiser assumes that the title is good and marketable and will not render any opinions about the title.

Number 1 in the **Statement of Assumptions and Limiting Conditions** on the URAR is similar to #1 on the CLASSIC 6/93 URAR, except that the wording "The property is appraised on the basis of being reasonable ownership..." has been eliminated.

I never understood what "reasonable ownership" *was*, much less how the appraiser was supposed to know this.

#2 Appraiser Has Provided a Sketch

> 2. The appraiser has provided a sketch in this appraisal report to show the approximate dimensions of the improvements. The sketch is included only to assist the reader in visualizing the property and understanding the appraiser's determination of its size.

This item is the same as #2 on the CLASSIC 6/93 URAR.

#3 Flood Maps – Special Flood Hazard Areas

> 3. The appraiser has examined the available flood maps that are provided by the Federal Emergency Management Agency (or other data sources) and has noted in this appraisal report whether any portion of the subject site is located in an identified Special Flood Hazard Area. Because the appraiser is not a surveyor, he or she makes no guarantees, express or implied, regarding this determination.

This item on the 2005 URAR is similar to #3 on the CLASSIC 6/93 URAR, except they add the phrase: "...*any portion* of the subject site..." [emphasis added]

This is a helpful clarification. In the past, some appraisers have taken the position that it is only necessary to report a property being in a flood area when the actual improvements are in the flood area.

#4 Testimony in Court

> 4. The appraiser will not give testimony or appear in court because he or she made an appraisal of the property in question, unless specific arrangements to do so have been made beforehand, or as otherwise required by law.

This item on the 2005 URAR is similar to #4 on the CLASSIC 6/93 URAR, except they have added the wording: "...or as otherwise required by law."

One of the advantages of having an employment contract with your Lender/Client is that you can insert a provision in it that states that if you are required to appear in court as a result of making the appraisal, the Lender/Client will pay you for your time. In any event, if you are required to appear in court, don't be afraid to ask the judge, or the attorney, to have one of the parties pay you. Many courts take the position that when an expert witness is required to appear in court, he or she should be paid by whoever demands that they be there.

No matter what you say on the appraisal, however, you have to respond when you receive a subpoena.

It is always appropriate for you to discuss a subpoena with the lawyer who issued the subpoena to try to work out how you will get paid and to try to resolve any scheduling conflicts.

Sometimes, you should consult your own attorney for advice on what do to about a subpoena.

If you are asked a question in court that you do not want to answer, you can ask the judge if you have to answer the question. You must do whatever the judge says.

#5 Adverse Conditions – Physical Deficiencies – Adverse Conditions – Environmental Hazards

> 5. The appraiser has noted in this appraisal report any adverse conditions (such as needed repairs, deterioration, the presence of hazardous wastes, toxic substances, etc.) observed during the inspection of the subject property or that he or she became aware of during the research involved in performing this appraisal. Unless otherwise stated in this appraisal report, the appraiser has no knowledge of any hidden or unapparent physical deficiencies or adverse conditions of the property (such as, but not limited to, needed repairs, deterioration, the presence of hazardous wastes, toxic substances, adverse environmental conditions, etc.) that would make the property less valuable, and has assumed that there are no such conditions and makes no guarantees or warranties, express or implied. The appraiser will not be responsible for any such conditions that do exist or for any engineering or testing that might be required to discover whether such conditions exist. Because the appraiser is not an expert in the field of environmental hazards, this appraisal report must not be considered as an environmental assessment of the property.

This item on the 2005 URAR is similar to #6 on the CLASSIC 6/93 URAR.

Because it was only used in conjunction with needed repairs, the word "depreciation" was changed to the more precise term "deterioration."

The representation about knowledge of hidden or unapparent items has been clarified to read: "The appraiser has no knowledge of any hidden or unapparent physical deficiencies or adverse conditions of the property (such as, but not limited to, needed repairs, deterioration, the presence of hazardous wastes, toxic substances, adverse environmental conditions, etc.) that would make the property less valuable, and has assumed that there are no such conditions and makes no guarantees or warranties, express or implied."

There are several other wording changes that clarify Item #5.

#6 Satisfactory completion, repairs, alterations

6. The appraiser has based his or her appraisal report and valuation conclusion for an appraisal that is subject to satisfactory completion, repairs, or alterations on the assumption that the completion, repairs, or alterations of the subject property will be performed in a professional manner.

Freddie Mac Form 70   March 2005   Page 4 of 6   Fannie Mae Form 1004   March 2005

This item on the 2005 URAR is similar to #9 on the CLASSIC 6/93 URAR, except that the wording "will be performed in a workman like manner" has been changed to "will be performed in a professional manner."

It is nice to know that Freddie Mac and Fannie Mae now consider workmen to be professionals (just like appraisers). On the other hand, it is possible that you don't have to be a professional to do "professional" work.

NOTES

Uniform Residential Appraisal Report

File #

APPRAISER'S CERTIFICATION: The Appraiser certifies and agrees that:

1. I have, at a minimum, developed and reported this appraisal in accordance with the scope of work requirements stated in this appraisal report.

2. I performed a complete visual inspection of the interior and exterior areas of the subject property. I reported the condition of the improvements in factual, specific terms. I identified and reported the physical deficiencies that could affect the livability, soundness, or structural integrity of the property.

3. I performed this appraisal in accordance with the requirements of the Uniform Standards of Professional Appraisal Practice that were adopted and promulgated by the Appraisal Standards Board of The Appraisal Foundation and that were in place at the time this appraisal report was prepared.

4. I developed my opinion of the market value of the real property that is the subject of this report based on the sales comparison approach to value. I have adequate comparable market data to develop a reliable sales comparison approach for this appraisal assignment. I further certify that I considered the cost and income approaches to value but did not develop them, unless otherwise indicated in this report.

5. I researched, verified, analyzed, and reported on any current agreement for sale for the subject property, any offering for sale of the subject property in the twelve months prior to the effective date of this appraisal, and the prior sales of the subject property for a minimum of three years prior to the effective date of this appraisal, unless otherwise indicated in this report.

6. I researched, verified, analyzed, and reported on the prior sales of the comparable sales for a minimum of one year prior to the date of sale of the comparable sale, unless otherwise indicated in this report.

7. I selected and used comparable sales that are locationally, physically, and functionally the most similar to the subject property.

8. I have not used comparable sales that were the result of combining a land sale with the contract purchase price of a home that has been built or will be built on the land.

9. I have reported adjustments to the comparable sales that reflect the market's reaction to the differences between the subject property and the comparable sales.

10. I verified, from a disinterested source, all information in this report that was provided by parties who have a financial interest in the sale or financing of the subject property.

11. I have knowledge and experience in appraising this type of property in this market area.

12. I am aware of, and have access to, the necessary and appropriate public and private data sources, such as multiple listing services, tax assessment records, public land records and other such data sources for the area in which the property is located.

13. I obtained the information, estimates, and opinions furnished by other parties and expressed in this appraisal report from reliable sources that I believe to be true and correct.

14. I have taken into consideration the factors that have an impact on value with respect to the subject neighborhood, subject property, and the proximity of the subject property to adverse influences in the development of my opinion of market value. I have noted in this appraisal report any adverse conditions (such as, but not limited to, needed repairs, deterioration, the presence of hazardous wastes, toxic substances, adverse environmental conditions, etc.) observed during the inspection of the subject property or that I became aware of during the research involved in performing this appraisal. I have considered these adverse conditions in my analysis of the property value, and have reported on the effect of the conditions on the value and marketability of the subject property.

15. I have not knowingly withheld any significant information from this appraisal report and, to the best of my knowledge, all statements and information in this appraisal report are true and correct.

16. I stated in this appraisal report my own personal, unbiased, and professional analysis, opinions, and conclusions, which are subject only to the assumptions and limiting conditions in this appraisal report.

17. I have no present or prospective interest in the property that is the subject of this report, and I have no present or prospective personal interest or bias with respect to the participants in the transaction. I did not base, either partially or completely, my analysis and/or opinion of market value in this appraisal report on the race, color, religion, sex, age, marital status, handicap, familial status, or national origin of either the prospective owners or occupants of the subject property or of the present owners or occupants of the properties in the vicinity of the subject property or on any other basis prohibited by law.

18. My employment and/or compensation for performing this appraisal or any future or anticipated appraisals was not conditioned on any agreement or understanding, written or otherwise, that I would report (or present analysis supporting) a predetermined specific value, a predetermined minimum value, a range or direction in value, a value that favors the cause of any party, or the attainment of a specific result or occurrence of a specific subsequent event (such as approval of a pending mortgage loan application).

19. I personally prepared all conclusions and opinions about the real estate that were set forth in this appraisal report. If I relied on significant real property appraisal assistance from any individual or individuals in the performance of this appraisal or the preparation of this appraisal report, I have named such individual(s) and disclosed the specific tasks performed in this appraisal report. I certify that any individual so named is qualified to perform the tasks. I have not authorized anyone to make a change to any item in this appraisal report; therefore, any change made to this appraisal is unauthorized and I will take no responsibility for it.

20. I identified the lender/client in this appraisal report who is the individual, organization, or agent for the organization that ordered and will receive this appraisal report.

NOTES

APPRAISER'S CERTIFICATION

Introduction

The following is quoted from the March 2005 Fannie Mae Instructions:

"Fannie Mae and Freddie Mac have created these 25 Certifications for a variety of reasons. Mostly it is an attempt to have the appraisal comply with the requirements of the USPAP. Modifications or deletions are not permitted. However, additional certifications that do not constitute material alterations to this appraisal report, such as those required by law or those related to the Appraiser's continuing education or membership in an appraisal organization, are permitted."

MODIFICATIONS, ADDITIONS, OR DELETIONS

"This appraisal report is subject to the scope of work, intended use, intended user, definition of market value, statement of assumptions and limiting conditions, and certifications contained in the report form. Modifications, additions, or deletions to the intended use, intended user, definition of market value, or assumptions and limiting conditions are not permitted. The appraiser may expand the scope of work to include any additional research or analysis necessary based on the complexity of this appraisal assignment. Modifications or deletions to the certifications are also not permitted. However, additional certifications that do not constitute material alterations to this appraisal report, such as those required by law or those related to the appraiser's continuing education or membership in an appraisal organization, are permitted."

The **APPRAISER'S CERTIFICATION** contains the following 25 items:

1. Scope of Work

> **APPRAISER'S CERTIFICATION:** The Appraiser certifies and agrees that:
>
> 1. I have, at a minimum, developed and reported this appraisal in accordance with the scope of work requirements stated in this appraisal report.

Freddie Mac and Fannie Mae restate here that the 2005 URAR is designed to help the appraiser comply with their unique Scope of Work requirements.

For this reason, the 2005 URAR may not be suitable for other Lender/Clients.

This description of the Scope of Work may be expanded to include anything additional the Lender/Client and the appraiser agree is necessary to accomplish the assignment.

2. Complete visual inspection — Reported physical deficiencies

> 2. I performed a complete visual inspection of the interior and exterior areas of the subject property. I reported the condition of the improvements in factual, specific terms. I identified and reported the physical deficiencies that could affect the livability, soundness, or structural integrity of the property.

Here is restated the Freddie Mac and Fannie Mae requirement that the appraiser make a complete visual inspection of the interior and exterior areas of the subject property.

Since the certificate cannot be changed, the appraiser should think twice before doing an appraisal where a visual inspection of the attic, basement, and all of the rooms of the house was not made.

It is not clear why Freddie Mac and Fannie Mae have limited what is to be reported to "physical deficiencies that could affect the livability, soundness or structural integrity of the property." It would seem that the appraiser should also report anything he or she observed that would affect the value of the property.

3. USPAP compliance

> 3. I performed this appraisal in accordance with the requirements of the Uniform Standards of Professional Appraisal Practice that were adopted and promulgated by the Appraisal Standards Board of The Appraisal Foundation and that were in place at the time this appraisal report was prepared.

This is the mandatory certification that the appraisal conforms to the requirements of the USPAP.

This certification has been rewritten to make it clear that the USPAP requirements that are effective on the date of the appraisal are the ones that apply to the appraisal. Also, all references to "Departure" have been eliminated. I believe that this is due to the anticipated probable elimination of the concept of Departure in the 2006 USPAP. As far as I can determine, nobody is going to miss Departure.

4. Opinion of market value based on sales comparision approach

4. I developed my opinion of the market value of the real property that is the subject of this report based on the sales comparison approach to value. I have adequate comparable market data to develop a reliable sales comparison approach for this appraisal assignment. I further certify that I considered the cost and income approaches to value but did not develop them, unless otherwise indicated in this report.

Freddie Mac and Fannie Mae are quite clear that as far as they are concerned, when it comes to single family dwellings, they have little or no use for the Cost and Income Approaches. They again state that belief here. However, in order to comply with the USPAP, they cannot tell appraisers not to consider the Cost and Income Approaches if the appraiser feels these approaches will be helpful in estimating the value of the subject property.

This item gets Freddie Mac and Fannie Mae off the hook about the Cost and Income Approaches. It requires the appraiser to certify that he or she doesn't need the Cost and/or Income Approaches because the Sales Comparison Approach is sufficient to make a reliable value estimate, or if this is not so, that the appraiser has used the Cost and/or Income Approach. You may want to think twice about certifying that you had adequate comparable market data to develop a reliable sales comparison approach without the support of a Cost Approach and/or Income Approach.

5. Researched, verified, analyzed, reported subject property agreements or sale for prior three years

5. I researched, verified, analyzed, and reported on any current agreement for sale for the subject property, any offering for sale of the subject property in the twelve months prior to the effective date of this appraisal, and the prior sales of the subject property for a minimum of three years prior to the effective date of this appraisal, unless otherwise indicated in this report.

By putting this certification on the form, Freddie Mac and Fannie Mae are requiring that the appraiser research, verify, analyze, and report on any current agreement for sale of the subject property. They also require a report of any offering of the subject within the past twelve months and a history of prior sales of the subject property for at least the past 36 months.

A one year sales history for each comparable is **not** a USPAP requirement. It is a Freddie Mac and Fannie Mae Scope of Work requirement. In some areas, this is relatively easy information to obtain from public records. In others, it is very difficult to obtain and Freddie Mac and Fannie Mae recognize this.

If you cannot obtain the information in the normal course of business, you are permitted to indicate this in the report.

6. Researched, verified, analyzed, reported prior comparable sales for minimum one year

6. I researched, verified, analyzed, and reported on the prior sales of the comparable sales for a minimum of one year prior to the date of sale of the comparable sale, unless otherwise indicated in this report.

This certification starts by saying that the appraiser has reported a minimum of a one year sales history for each of the comparable sales, unless it is otherwise indicated in the report. This history starts on the date of the comparable sale, and not on the effective date of the report.

If any of the above certifications are not true, you cannot certify to them. In order to sign the certification, you must provide a valid reason(s) why you were unable to obtain the information.

7. Comparable sales are locationally, physically, and functionally most similar to subject

7. I selected and used comparable sales that are locationally, physically, and functionally the most similar to the subject property.

Here, the appraiser certifies that he or she used comparable sales that are locationally, physically, and functionally the most similar to the subject property.

Although Fannie Mae does not specify date of sale as one of these factors, I think it is safe to assume that they want you to certify that you have not excluded any known sales that were more similar to the subject property, based on these parameters, that sold within a reasonable time period from the effective date of the appraisal.

8. Did not use comparable sales that were combinations of land sale and contract to purchase a home

> 8. I have not used comparable sales that were the result of combining a land sale with the contract purchase price of a home that has been built or will be built on the land.

Not using "comparable sales that were the result of combining a land sale with the contract purchase price of a home that has been built or will be built on the land" is a Freddie Mac and Fannie Mae Scope of Work requirement. Using this type of sale is not covered by USPAP.

You cannot use as a comparable sale the sale of a new house that was made in two parts (i.e., where the Buyer contracts to purchase a site at an agreed-upon price and then enters into a separate agreement to have a house built on the site based on a special set of plans and specifications).

There is a fine line between the sale of a site with a house on it based on a model home with some custom alterations and the two part contract prohibited here.

9. Adjustments to comparable sales

> 9. I have reported adjustments to the comparable sales that reflect the market's reaction to the differences between the subject property and the comparable sales.

The purpose of an adjustment is to "reflect the market's reaction to the differences between the subject property and the comparable sales."

This certification reinforces the concept that the only adjustments that should be made are ones that reflect value differences that the market recognizes.

10. Verification of information supplied by interested parties

> 10. I verified, from a disinterested source, all information in this report that was provided by parties who have a financial interest in the sale or financing of the subject property.

It is always good appraisal practice to verify information received from the Buyer, Seller, Agent, and anyone else that has a financial interest in the transaction, including the Mortgage Broker and Lender.

The appraiser's work file should contain information about how they verified the data that was obtained from anyone with a financial interest in the transaction. This is not always easy to do.

If you cannot do this, you should not make the appraisal for Fannie Mae, Freddie Mac, or the FHA.

11. Adequate knowledge and experience to make appraisal

> 11. I have knowledge and experience in appraising this type of property in this market area.

This certification states that the Appraiser has the knowledge and experience to make the appraisal. It does not recognize that USPAP permits the appraiser several other alternatives. This is not a USPAP requirement. It is a Fannie Mae and Freddie Mac requirement.

The USPAP COMPETENCY RULE states:

Prior to accepting an assignment or entering into an agreement to perform any assignment, an appraiser must properly identify the problem to be addressed and have the knowledge and experience to compete the assignment competently; or alternatively must:

1. Disclose the lack of knowledge and/or experience to the client before accepting the assignment.
2. Take all steps necessary or appropriate to complete the assignment competently; and
3. Describe the lack of knowledge and/or experience and the steps taken to complete the assignment competently in the report.

The COMPETENCY RULE goes on to suggest ways that appraisers can overcome the problem. One of the most common is to associate with someone who is competent to do the assignment. The following are the most common situations where an appraiser accepts a single family dwelling assignment which they are not competent to do:

1. The subject is in a market outside of the appraiser's usual territory and he or she is not familiar with the market.
2. The dwelling is an historic house.
3. The dwelling is a mansion.

In spite of what the USPAP permits, you must have the knowledge and experience to make the appraisal, without help, when you do it for Freddie Mac or Fannie Mae.

12. Access to data sources

12. I am aware of, and have access to, the necessary and appropriate public and private data sources, such as multiple listing services, tax assessment records, public land records and other such data sources for the area in which the property is located.

The appraiser certifies that he or she is aware of and has access to necessary data sources.

Again, this is a Freddie Mac and Fannie Mae requirement. Often an appraiser operates in a territory or area where he or she does not have access to the MLS data. Sometimes there are private data sources (this is common in New York City), but they are often very expensive to access.

If you do not have access to all of the necessary and appropriate public and private data sources, you cannot make an appraisal on the 2005 URAR for Fannie Mae, Freddie Mac, or the FHA.

13. Information from others considered reliable

13. I obtained the information, estimates, and opinions furnished by other parties and expressed in this appraisal report from reliable sources that I believe to be true and correct.

The appraiser is required to obtain data from sources that they believe are reliable.

14. Reported everything known or observed that affects the value of the property

14. I have taken into consideration the factors that have an impact on value with respect to the subject neighborhood, subject property, and the proximity of the subject property to adverse influences in the development of my opinion of market value. I have noted in this appraisal report any adverse conditions (such as, but not limited to, needed repairs, deterioration, the presence of hazardous wastes, toxic substances, adverse environmental conditions, etc.) observed during the inspection of the subject property or that I became aware of during the research involved in performing this appraisal. I have considered these adverse conditions in my analysis of the property value, and have reported on the effect of the conditions on the value and marketability of the subject property.

This is a broad certification that requires the appraiser to report and take into consideration anything he or she observes or learns about that has an effect on the value of the property.

This problem often comes up when appraising dwellings in urban areas, where often dwellings are used for purposes that are not permitted by the zoning ordinances. Reporting these uses may make the property ineligible for the loan that is being applied for. Another common problem is how to report anything in the neighborhood that may have a negative impact on the value of the subject property.

15. Not knowingly withheld significant information

> 15. I have not knowingly withheld any significant information from this appraisal report and, to the best of my knowledge, all statements and information in this appraisal report are true and correct.

This is very similar to #14.

There should be no doubt in the appraiser's mind that he or she is obligated to report anything that might have an effect on the value of the subject property, even if the result is that the loan will not be granted.

Common things that appraisers do not report are prohibited uses of the property, items in need of immediate repair, and neighborhood and community problems such as high crime, heavy traffic, poor schools, etc.

16. Personal, unbiased, professional analysis

> 16. I stated in this appraisal report my own personal, unbiased, and professional analysis, opinions, and conclusions, which are subject only to the assumptions and limiting conditions in this appraisal report.

This seems okay at first glance. However, I think it would be better if it read: "I stated in this appraisal report my own personal, unbiased, and professional analysis, opinions, and conclusions, which are subject only to the assumptions and limiting conditions in this appraisal report, *the USPAP, and other Federal and State regulations, as well as the Codes of Ethics of the Appraisal Organizations to which I belong.*"

17. No present or prospective interest in the subject property

> 17. I have no present or prospective interest in the property that is the subject of this report, and I have no present or prospective personal interest or bias with respect to the participants in the transaction. I did not base, either partially or completely, my analysis and/or opinion of market value in this appraisal report on the race, color, religion, sex, age, marital status, handicap, familial status, or national origin of either the prospective owners or occupants of the subject property or of the present owners or occupants of the properties in the vicinity of the subject property or on any other basis prohibited by law.

This is a certification stating that the appraiser has no present or future interest in the subject property. It is also a non-discrimination certification.

18. Employment and/or compensation not conditional upon a predetermined value

> 18. My employment and/or compensation for performing this appraisal or any future or anticipated appraisals was not conditioned on any agreement or understanding, written or otherwise, that I would report (or present analysis supporting) a predetermined specific value, a predetermined minimum value, a range or direction in value, a value that favors the cause of any party, or the attainment of a specific result or occurrence of a specific subsequent event (such as approval of a pending mortgage loan application).

This is very strong language stating that the Appraiser has been able to resist all pressure to conform to the Lender/Client's idea for a value that will make the loan work.

It is too bad that the Lender/Client is not required to sign a similar statement. It is not too far-fetched to imagine a URAR that included a section that the Lender/Client would have to sign upon receipt of the report that essentially said the same thing, and that Freddie Mac and Fannie Mae would require theLender/Client to sign before they would accept the report.

Keep in mind that there is nothing in the USPAP that prevents you from accepting a "phased" assignment. Theoretically, you could accept an assignment where you know the figure needed to make the loan; if as you proceed you conclude your final estimated value will be below that figure, you can stop working. Then you notify the Lender/Client and ask if he or she wants you to stop working on the appraisal or proceed to complete the appraisal. If you are instructed not to complete the appraisal, you must insist upon being paid for the work you have already done, otherwise it will appear that your payment was contingent upon reaching a predetermined value. This is prohibited by USPAP.

However, this procedure if full of problems. On the surface, it certainly could be misunderstood as coercion. Also, as soon as you render any value opinion, you have made an appraisal and therefore are required to have in your file everything you need for an appraisal even if you don't issue the report.

It is my opinion that "happiness" is not to accept a "phased" assignment.

19. Personally prepared all conclusions and opinions or acknowledged assiatence

> 19. I personally prepared all conclusions and opinions about the real estate that were set forth in this appraisal report. If I relied on significant real property appraisal assistance from any individual or individuals in the performance of this appraisal or the preparation of this appraisal report, I have named such individual(s) and disclosed the specific tasks performed in this appraisal report. I certify that any individual so named is qualified to perform the tasks. I have not authorized anyone to make a change to any item in this appraisal report; therefore, any change made to this appraisal is unauthorized and I will take no responsibility for it.

This certification requires acknowledgement of any significant help received in making the appraisal report. It also states that nobody is authorized to change the report in any way.

This certification requires the acknowledgement of work done by trainees and points out that the appraiser is responsible for the quality of the work done by the trainee

20. Identified lender/client

> 20. I identified the lender/client in this appraisal report who is the individual, organization, or agent for the organization that ordered and will receive this appraisal report.

This certification requires that the Lender/Client identified in the report be the one who receives the report.

This certification prevents the appraiser from giving a copy of the report to the property owner, another lender, the broker, etc. These people and others may be entitled to a copy of the report. It should be supplied by the Lender/Client, however, and not the appraiser.

(Certifications #21 to #25 appear on page 6 of the URAR)

21. Lender/client may disclose or distribute appraisal

> 21. The lender/client may disclose or distribute this appraisal report to: the borrower; another lender at the request of the borrower; the mortgagee or its successors and assigns; mortgage insurers; government sponsored enterprises; other secondary market participants; data collection or reporting services; professional appraisal organizations; any department, agency, or instrumentality of the United States; and any state, the District of Columbia, or other jurisdictions; without having to obtain the appraiser's or supervisory appraiser's (if applicable) consent. Such consent must be obtained before this appraisal report may be disclosed or distributed to any other party (including, but not limited to, the public through advertising, public relations, news, sales, or other media).

This certification lists a variety of people and organizations that the appraiser gives the Lender/Client permission to distribute the report to. It also lists parties that the Lender/Client is not permitted to disclose the report to without the Appraiser's permission.

I have serious doubts about the enforceability of these restrictions on the distribution of the report. However, they do get the appraiser off the hook if the appraiser is criticized because of the unauthorized use of the report. The appraiser can truly say that they did not authorize such a use. By signing the Appraiser's Certification, you are giving permission for your information to be given to a "data collection or reporting service" who probably will use the data to make AVMs. Fortunately, Lenders are still subject to privacy laws which may prevent using data in the appraisal that was provided by the property owner or their representatives.

22. Appraiser is subject to laws and the USPAP

> 22. I am aware that any disclosure or distribution of this appraisal report by me or the lender/client may be subject to certain laws and regulations. Further, I am also subject to the provisions of the Uniform Standards of Professional Appraisal Practice that pertain to disclosure or distribution by me.

The appraiser certifies that he or she is aware of USPAP restrictions on the distribution of an appraisal report.

The USPAP addresses these restrictions in USPAP – ETHICS RULE – Confidentiality: (Page 8, USPAP 2005 Edition):

"An appraiser must be aware of, and comply with, all confidentially and privacy laws and regulations applicable in an assignment. An appraiser must not disclose confidential information or assignment results prepared for a client to anyone other than the client and persons specifically authorized by the client; state enforcement agencies and such third parties as may be authorized by due process of law; and a duly authorized professional peer review committee except when such disclosure to a committee would violate applicable law and regulation."

The Gramm-Leach-Bliley Act (1999) includes appraisers in the Federal regulation of Privacy (USPAP 2005 Edition, p.8).

23. Borrower, lender, and others may rely on this appraisal

> 23. The borrower, another lender at the request of the borrower, the mortgagee or its successors and assigns, mortgage insurers, government sponsored enterprises, and other secondary market participants may rely on this appraisal report as part of any mortgage finance transaction that involves any one or more of these parties.

This certification gives the Lender/Client permission to make the appraisal part of a loan package that may be assigned and/or sold. What this is saying is that almost anyone in the lending process who gets the rightful use of the appraisal report has a right to rely on it. Unfortunately, this may also give him or her the right to make a professional liability claim against the appraiser, even if he or she is not the original Lender/Client. Unfortunately, the only alternatives you have are to accept this additional liability exposure or refuse to do Fannie Mae and Freddie Mac work, as the new 2055 Exterior-Only report form also contains this certification.

Note: As of April 2006 when this was written, there was significant controversy about Appraiser's Certification #23. You should check the web sites of Fannie Mae at www.efanniemae. com and Real Estate Valuation Magazine at www.revmag.com for the latest information about permitted changes (if any). Information is also available at www.aaro.net. Also read the Fannie Mae "Frequently Asked Questions" on the Fannie Mae web site.

24. "Electric record" and "Electronic signature"25. Subject to Title 18 of US Code, Section 1001, et seq., or similar state laws

> 24. If this appraisal report was transmitted as an "electronic record" containing my "electronic signature," as those terms are defined in applicable federal and/or state laws (excluding audio and video recordings), or a facsimile transmission of this appraisal report containing a copy or representation of my signature, the appraisal report shall be as effective, enforceable and valid as if a paper version of this appraisal report were delivered containing my original hand written signature.

If Federal and/or State laws permit electronic transmission of appraisals and signatures, then the appraiser recognizes these transmissions to be legal. The whole field of electronic transmission of legal documents (including appraisals) is changing. It is up to the appraiser to keep current as to what is and is not permissible.

25. Subject to Title 18 of US Code, Section 1001, et seq., or similar state laws

25. Any intentional or negligent misrepresentation(s) contained in this appraisal report may result in civil liability and/or criminal penalties including, but not limited to, fine or imprisonment or both under the provisions of Title 18, United States Code, Section 1001, et seq., or similar state laws.

This certification reiterates that appraisals are covered by "Title 18, United States Code, Section 1001, et seq., or similar state laws" and that the violation of these laws "may result in civil liability and/or criminal penalties including, but not limited to fine or imprisonment or both."

I am not sure what the purpose of this certification is, but it certainly is scary. There is nothing in Item #25 that would not apply without this certification.

SUPERVISORY APPRAISER'S CERTIFICATION: The Supervisory Appraiser certifies and agrees that:

1. I directly supervised the appraiser for this appraisal assignment, have read the appraisal report, and agree with the appraiser's analysis, opinions, statements, conclusions, and the appraiser's certification.

2. I accept full responsibility for the contents of this appraisal report including, but not limited to, the appraiser's analysis, opinions, statements, conclusions, and the appraiser's certification.

3. The appraiser identified in this appraisal report is either a sub-contractor or an employee of the supervisory appraiser (or the appraisal firm), is qualified to perform this appraisal, and is acceptable to perform this appraisal under the applicable state law.

4. This appraisal report complies with the Uniform Standards of Professional Appraisal Practice that were adopted and promulgated by the Appraisal Standards Board of The Appraisal Foundation and that were in place at the time this appraisal report was prepared.

5. If this appraisal report was transmitted as an "electronic record" containing my "electronic signature," as those terms are defined in applicable federal and/or state laws (excluding audio and video recordings), or a facsimile transmission of this appraisal report containing a copy or representation of my signature, the appraisal report shall be as effective, enforceable and valid as if a paper version of this appraisal report were delivered containing my original hand written signature.

Introduction

The SUPERVISORY APPRAISER'S CERTIFICATION has been expanded from one to six paragraphs on the 2005 URAR.

This certification increases the liability exposure of the Supervisory Appraiser.

The following are subsections of the SUPERVISORY APPRAISER'S CERTIFICATION:

#1. Scope of Supervision

SUPERVISORY APPRAISER'S CERTIFICATION: The Supervisory Appraiser certifies and agrees that:

1. I directly supervised the appraiser for this appraisal assignment, have read the appraisal report, and agree with the appraiser's analysis, opinions, statements, conclusions, and the appraiser's certification.

The Supervisory Appraiser asserts that he or she agrees 100% with everything in the appraisal report. Be cautious about signing such a statement unless you have carefully reviewed the report.

#2. Acceptance of full responsibility for the appraisal

2. I accept full responsibility for the contents of this appraisal report including, but not limited to, the appraiser's analysis, opinions, statements, conclusions, and the appraiser's certification.

The Supervisory Appraiser accepts full responsibility for the appraisal report.

The Supervisory Appraiser may be accepting full responsibility for a report where they have not seen the subject property or the comparable sales. This is **permitted** by USPAP, Freddie Mac, and Fannie Mae.

Why anyone would be willing to do this is hard to understand.

#3. Appraiser is sub-contractor or employee, qualified, and acceptable by state law

> 3. The appraiser identified in this appraisal report is either a sub-contractor or an employee of the supervisory appraiser (or the appraisal firm), is qualified to perform this appraisal, and is acceptable to perform this appraisal under the applicable state law.

The Supervisory Appraiser is certifying here that the appraiser is a sub-contractor or an employee of the Supervisory Appraiser (or his or her appraisal firm), and that the Supervisory Appraiser has determined that the appraiser is qualified to make the appraisal and is acceptable to do so under applicable state law.

The Supervisory Appraiser accepts full responsibility for the appraiser who has made the appraisal and certifies that the appraiser has a valid state license or certification. The Supervisory Appraiser cannot sign a report for an appraiser **who is not** a sub-contractor or employee of the Supervisory Appraiser or their appraisal firm.

In the past, Supervisory Appraisers often signed reports for trainees who did not meet these requirements.

#4. Complies with USPAP

> 4. This appraisal report complies with the Uniform Standards of Professional Appraisal Practice that were adopted and promulgated by the Appraisal Standards Board of The Appraisal Foundation and that were in place at the time this appraisal report was prepared.

The Supervisory Appraiser is certifying that the appraisal complies with the USPAP. This is stronger language than what the Appraiser has to certify.

The Supervisory Appraiser becomes equally responsible for any USPAP violations committed by the appraiser in the process of making the appraisal

#5. "Electronic Record" and "Electronic Signature"

> 5. If this appraisal report was transmitted as an "electronic record" containing my "electronic signature," as those terms are defined in applicable federal and/or state laws (excluding audio and video recordings), or a facsimile transmission of this appraisal report containing a copy or representation of my signature, the appraisal report shall be as effective, enforceable and valid as if a paper version of this appraisal report were delivered containing my original hand written signature.

If Federal and/or State laws permit electronic transmission of appraisals and signatures, then the Supervisory Appraiser recognizes these transmissions to be legal.

The whole field of electronic transmission of legal documents (including appraisals) is changing. It is up to the Supervisory Appraiser to keep current as to what is and is not permissible.

APPRAISER

Signature_____

Name _____

Company Name _____

Company Address_____

_____

Telephone Number _____

Email Address_____

Date of Signature and Report_____

Effective Date of Appraisal _____

State Certification #_____

or State License #_____

or Other (describe) _____ State # _____

State _____

Expiration Date of Certification or License _____

ADDRESS OF PROPERTY APPRAISED

_____

_____

APPRAISED VALUE OF SUBJECT PROPERTY $ _____

LENDER/CLIENT

Name _____

Company Name _____

Company Address_____

_____

Email Address_____

SUPERVISORY APPRAISER (ONLY IF REQUIRED)

Signature_____

Name_____

Company Name _____

Company Address_____

_____

Telephone Number _____

Email Address _____

Date of Signature _____

State Certification #_____

or State License # _____

State _____

Expiration Date of Certification or License _____

SUBJECT PROPERTY

☐ Did not inspect subject property

☐ Did inspect exterior of subject property from street

 Date of Inspection _____

☐ Did inspect interior and exterior of subject property

 Date of Inspection _____

COMPARABLE SALES

☐ Did not inspect exterior of comparable sales from street

☐ Did inspect exterior of comparable sales from street

 Date of Inspection _____

Introduction

The section on the left at the end of page 6 contains spaces to provide information about the APPRAISER, ADDRESS OF PROPERTY APPRAISED, APPRAISED VALUE OF SUBJECT PROPERTY and the LENDER/CLIENT. The section to the right, at the end of page 6, is headed: SUPERVISORY APPRAISER (ONLY IF REQUIRED). In addition to a signature line, there are lines to provide information about the Supervisory Appraiser.

Appraiser

Signature, Company, Address, License/Certification Info.

Some of this information is a repeat of the information in the SUBJECT section on page 1 of the URAR. The information asked for is all self-explanatory.

ADDRESS OF PROPERTY APPRAISED

Some of this information is a repeat of the information in the **SUBJECT** section on page 1 of the URAR. The information asked for is all self-explanatory.

APPRAISED VALUE OF SUBJECT PROPERTY

Some of this information is a repeat of the information in the **RECONCILIATION** – **Final Value Estimate** section on page 2 of the URAR. The information asked for is all self-explanatory.

LENDER/CLIENT

Some of this information is a repeat of the information in the SUBJECT section on page 1 of the URAR. The information asked for is all self-explanatory.

Supervisory Appraiser

Signature, Company, Address, License/Certification Info.

Some of this information is a repeat of the information in the SUBJECT section on page 1 of the URAR. The information asked for is all self-explanatory.

SUBJECT PROPERTY—Did or did not inspect subject

The check boxes under the heading **SUBJECT PROPERTY** refers to actions the Supervisory Appraiser did or did not take to inspect the subject property.

Neither the USPAP, Freddie Mac, or Fannie Mae require that the Supervisory Appraiser inspect the Subject Property.

COMPARABLE SALES—Did or did not inspect exterior

The check boxes under the heading **COMPARABLE SALES** refers to actions the Supervisory Appraiser did or did not take to inspect the subject property.

Neither the USPAP, Freddie Mac, or Fannie Mae require that the Supervisory Appraiser inspect the Subject Property.

INDEX

Q

R

S

Frequently Asked Questions

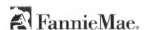

Fannie Mae's Revised Appraisal and Property Report Forms
(Forms Dated March 2005 for Appraisals Performed On/After 11/1/05)
Frequently Asked Questions

1. Why did Fannie Mae decide to revise the appraisal report forms?

The primary objectives for the revision of the appraisal report forms were to:

• more clearly communicate Fannie Mae's expectations for the property appraisal and reporting processes;
• help appraisers comply with those expectations;
• clarify appraisers' accountability for the quality of their work to those who rely on it; and
• help appraisers comply with the Uniform Standards of Professional Appraisal Practice.

2. What are the major changes to the forms?

The revised report forms clarify that the Scope of Work for the appraisal is defined by the complexity of the appraisal assignment and the reporting requirements of the appraisal report form, including the stated purpose of the appraisal to provide the Lender/Client with an accurate, and adequately supported, opinion of the market value of the subject property, based on our Definition of Market Value.

We also applied the streamlined approach and reporting formats of the Desktop Underwriter® appraisal report forms. The more consistent presentation of the appraiser's research, analysis, and conclusions will help appraisers more clearly present the results of their valuation, and will enhance the lender's review of the appraisal report. The revised format enables the appraiser to report the results of the valuation in a brief but comprehensive manner, which will be more efficient for reviewing and processing than the previous forms. Direct questions have been added to the report forms that require the appraiser to report his or her analysis and conclusions on key areas in a clear and succinct yes/no format. The expanded areas for comments throughout the forms should also help to eliminate the need for additional addenda and attachments.

The appraiser's certification on each of the revised appraisal report forms was expanded to more clearly communicate Fannie Mae's expectations of the property appraisal and reporting process. In addition, new certifications were developed to:

• affirm that the appraiser has the appropriate knowledge and experience to appraise the particular type of property in the market area;
• clarify the permitted disclosure or distribution of the appraisal report;
• acknowledge the parties that often rely on the appraisal report as part of a mortgage finance transaction; and
• acknowledge that any intentional or negligent misrepresentation may result in civil liability and/or criminal penalties including, but not limited to, fine or imprisonment or both.

3. What is the appraiser's responsibility for reporting property condition?
The appraiser is responsible for considering all factors that have an impact on value in the development of his or her opinion of market value for the subject property. Fannie Mae requires the appraiser to

express an opinion about the condition of the property improvements on our appraisal report forms. The appraiser must report the condition of the improvements in factual, specific terms. We believe that an accurate description of the physical condition of the subject property is a critical element in arriving at a supportable opinion of market value, as well as in the prudent underwriting of a mortgage loan.

4. What is expected with regard to the appraiser's inspection of a property?

Fannie Mae's expectation of the appraiser's property inspection for an appraisal based on an interior and exterior inspection is a complete visual inspection of the accessible areas of the property. The appraiser is responsible for noting in his or her report any adverse conditions (such as, but not limited to, needed repairs; deterioration; the presence of hazardous wastes, toxic substances, or adverse environmental conditions; etc.) that were apparent during the inspection of the property or that he or she became aware of during the research involved in performing the appraisal.

The appraiser is expected to consider and describe the overall quality and condition of the property and identify items that require immediate repair as well as items where maintenance may have been deferred, which may or may not require immediate repair. On the other hand, an appraiser is not responsible for hidden or unapparent conditions. In addition, we do not consider the appraiser to be an expert in all fields, such as environmental hazards. In situations where an adverse property condition may be observed by the appraiser but the appraiser may not be qualified to decide whether that condition requires immediate repair (such as the presence of mold, an active roof leak, settlement in the foundation, etc.), the property must be appraised subject to an inspection by a qualified professional. In such cases, the lender may need to ask the appraiser to update his or her appraisal based on the results of the inspection, in which case the appraiser would incorporate the results of the inspection and measure the impact, if any, on his or her final opinion of market value.

5. In what situations should a property be appraised "as-is" versus "as-repaired"?

Fannie Mae permits an appraisal to be based on the "as-is" condition of the property as long as any minor conditions, such as deferred maintenance, do not affect the livability, soundness, or structural integrity of the property, and the appraiser's opinion of value reflects the existence of these conditions. Minor conditions and deferred maintenance include worn floor finishes or carpet, minor plumbing leaks, holes in window screens, or cracked window glass. Minor conditions and deferred maintenance typically are due to normal wear and tear from the aging process and the occupancy of the property. Such conditions generally do not rise to the level of a "required repair." Nevertheless, they must be reported.

The appraiser must identify physical deficiencies that could affect the soundness, structural integrity, or livability of the property as part of his or her description of the physical condition of the property. These may include cracks or settlement in the foundation, water seepage, active roof leaks, curled or cupped roof shingles, inadequate electrical service or plumbing fixtures, etc. In situations where an adverse property condition may be observed by the appraiser but the appraiser may not be qualified to decide whether that condition requires immediate repair, the property must be appraised subject to an inspection by a qualified professional. In such cases, the lender must have the property inspected and any material conditions repaired before it delivers the mortgage loan to Fannie Mae. The appraiser may be asked to update his or her appraisal based on the results of the inspection, in which case the appraiser would incorporate the results of the inspection and measure the impact, if any, on his or her final opinion of market value.

Frequently Asked Questions

6. Why was the new appraiser's certification # 23 added?

The appraiser's certification # 23 is an acknowledgment by the appraiser that certain parties to a mortgage finance transaction that are not the Lender/Client and/or Intended User often rely on the appraisal report. This new certification clarifies that such other parties include the borrower, another lender at the request of the borrower, the mortgagee or its successors and assigns, mortgage insurers, government-sponsored enterprises, and other secondary market participants.

The Intended User is the party for whom the appraiser is writing the report, which is the Lender/ Client for a residential mortgage finance transaction. The revised appraisal report forms clearly identify the Intended User as defined by the Uniform Standards of Professional Appraisal Practice as the Lender/ Client. The acknowledgment of other parties that often rely on the appraisal report is not meant to expand the list of Intended Users. Instead, it is meant to clarify that others, although not Intended Users, often rely on the appraisal report as part of a mortgage finance transaction.

Our intent was to clarify through the use of this new certification that the appraiser is accountable for the quality of his or her work to those who often rely on it as part of a mortgage finance transaction. The appraiser's accountability for the quality of his or her appraisal should not be limited to the Lender/Client and/or Intended User identified in the appraisal report. Fannie Mae believes that parties to a mortgage finance transaction that are not the Lender/Client or Intender User should be able to rely on the accuracy of an appraisal report prepared by a state-licensed or state-certified appraiser and the appraiser should be held accountable for the quality of that appraisal because their reliance is customary and reasonable. We are committed to overcome the prevailing feeling in the appraisal and lending communities that appraisers are too often not held accountable for the quality of their appraisals.

7. What is Fannie Mae's perspective on Intended Users as defined by the Uniform Standards of Professional Appraisal Practice (USPAP) and the other parties to a mortgage finance transaction that often rely on the accuracy of an appraisal?

The Intended User, as defined by the USPAP, in a mortgage finance transaction is the Lender/Client and any other party identified by the appraiser (by name or type) as a user of the appraisal report based on communication with the Lender/Client when the appraisal assignment is accepted. The Intended User is the party for whom the appraiser is writing the report, which is clearly defined on the revised appraisal report forms as the Lender/Client. Although the other parties to a mortgage finance transaction that are identified in certification # 23 generally do not "use" the appraisal report like the Lender/Client, they often rely on the accuracy of the appraisal report. For instance:

• A borrower's contract to purchase a home often is contingent on an appraisal report confirming that the market value of the property is at least as much as the sale price for the purchase transaction. In fact, this may be a standard requirement for some mortgage lending programs and/or traditional practice in some geographic locations.

• It also is common for mortgage lenders to disclose any physical deficiencies or adverse conditions reported by the appraiser to the borrower for both purchase money and refinance transactions. For example, Fannie Mae recommends that lenders disclose all known property condition issues to the borrower so that the borrower may take any necessary actions to address such issues.

• Similarly, lenders (other than the Lender/Client), investors, and mortgage insurers routinely rely on the appraisal report obtained by the Lender/Client when mortgage loans are assigned, sold, or insured.

Frequently Asked Questions

These parties to a mortgage finance transaction that may rely on the quality of an appraisal report that was prepared for another as the Lender/Client and Intended User clearly do not use the appraisal report like the Lender/Client. Such parties often may not even receive or read the appraisal report, although they rely on the appraisal report conclusions as part of the normal course of business for a mortgage finance transaction. In addition, their reliance on the appraisal report is subject to the stated Intended Use, Scope of Work, purpose of the appraisal, and Definition of Market Value, which are included on each of the revised appraisal report forms.

8. Why not treat all parties that may rely on an appraisal report as part of a mortgage finance transaction as users of the appraisal and identify them as Intended Users?

The revised appraisal report forms clearly identify the Intended User as defined by the Uniform Standards of Professional Appraisal Practice as the Lender/Client. Therefore, it is Fannie Mae's position that the other parties to the mortgage finance transaction that often rely on the accuracy of an appraisal ordinarily are not Intended Users. Our rationale is simply that identifying these other parties in certification # 23 as Intended Users is neither practical nor appropriate.

• It is not practical because the Lender/Client in a mortgage finance transaction generally cannot identify, when it engages the appraiser for the assignment, all the other parties that might rely on the appraisal. For example, the lender will not know whether a mortgage insurer will be involved until after the appraisal is completed, because only then can the loan-to-value ratio be calculated. In addition, the lender may not know at the time of loan origination whether it will hold the loan in its portfolio or sell it in the secondary market. And if it plans to sell the loan in the secondary market, it may not know who the secondary market investor will be.

• It is not appropriate because the appraisal ordinarily is not prepared to address the specific needs of these other parties that often rely on the appraisal. In such cases, none of them should be named as an Intended User, and the fact that they are not named provides clear notice that the appraisal was not prepared to address their specific needs, but rather to address the specific needs of the Lender/Client as the Intended User based on the stated Intended Use, Scope of Work, purpose of the appraisal, Definition of Market Value, and the reporting requirements of the appraisal report form.

9. Why are appraisers concerned about the revised certifications on the appraisal report forms?

Some appraisers believe that these new certifications have increased their professional accountability and liability. For instance, in new certification # 23, the appraiser acknowledges that parties, other than the Lender/Client, often rely on the appraisal report as part of a mortgage finance transaction. This is simply an acknowledgement by the appraiser of the reality of a mortgage finance transaction. It clarifies that the parties to a mortgage finance transaction, such as the borrower, another lender at the request of the borrower, the mortgagee or its successors and assigns, mortgage insurers, government-sponsored enterprises, and other secondary market participants, often rely on the appraisal report. In addition, new certification # 25 was developed for the appraiser to acknowledge that any intentional or negligent misrepresentation may result in civil liability and/or criminal penalties including, but not limited to, fine or imprisonment or both.

Many in the appraisal community have made it clear to us that they would prefer to be accountable only to the Lender/Client. Fannie Mae believes that the appraiser's accountability for the quality of his or her appraisal for a mortgage finance transaction must not be limited to the Lender/Client because such limitations undermine our secondary market activity.

Frequently Asked Questions

10. Why is there confusion in the appraisal community regarding certification # 23?

The Appraisal Standards Board of The Appraisal Foundation has stated that they see little distinction between parties that "use" an appraisal report and parties that "rely" on an appraisal report. Therefore, they believe that appraisers must clarify in their appraisal reports whether the parties listed in certification # 23 are Intended Users as defined by the Uniform Standards of Professional Appraisal Practice. Although this position was communicated as an informal Q and A, which does not establish new standards or interpret existing standards, it has created confusion in the appraisal community.

11. What additional notices or statements will Fannie Mae accept on the revised appraisal report forms to eliminate any confusion regarding certification # 23?

Appraisers traditionally have not identified the other parties to a mortgage finance transaction that often rely on the accuracy of the appraisal report as Intended Users based on the current definition of an Intended User in the Uniform Standards of Professional Appraisal Practice. However, if the appraiser believes that any of these parties should be identified as additional Intended Users based on information provided by the Lender/Client or from other sources, he or she should identify them as such in the appraisal report. Fannie Mae will accept such appraisals.

We recognize, however, that there may be confusion in the appraisal community about the distinction between parties who "use" and parties who "rely" on appraisal reports. In view of this, we will accept the following additional notice or statement when the appraiser believes the Lender/Client is the only Intended User:

> "The Intended User of this appraisal report is the Lender/Client. The Intended Use is to evaluate the property that is the subject of this appraisal for a mortgage finance transaction, subject to the stated Scope of Work, purpose of the appraisal, reporting requirements of this appraisal report form, and Definition of Market Value. No additional Intended Users are identified by the appraiser."

The use of this additional notice or statement may help to clarify the identification of the Intended User as addressed in the Uniform Standards of Professional Appraisal Practice and on the revised appraisal report forms. Fannie Mae will not accept appraisals with additional notices or statements that may conflict with certification # 23, which is simply an acknowledgment by the appraiser that parties to the mortgage finance transaction that are not the Lender/Client or Intended User often rely on the appraisal report. In particular, the appraiser's accountability for the quality of his or her appraisal for a mortgage finance transaction must not be explicitly limited to the Lender/Client. In certification # 23, the appraiser acknowledges the reality of a mortgage finance transaction that reliance by these other parties is customary and reasonable.

12. How can appraisers assist lenders in determining an appropriate level of hazard insurance coverage for loans to be delivered to Fannie Mae?

Fannie Mae requires property insurance for first mortgages that protects against loss or damage from fire and other hazards. The hazard insurance coverage should provide for claims to be settled on a replacement cost basis. We prefer lenders to rely on a replacement cost estimate for the property that is made by the insurer. However, we are generally hearing from insurers that although they may provide some guidance about what the replacement cost should be, they consider it to be the responsibility of the consumer to determine his or her level of coverage. The fact that insurers appear to be reluctant to determine the replacement cost for a dwelling has become even more significant due to the general lack of guaranteed replacement cost policy endorsements. In addition, some states prohibit lenders from requiring levels of hazard insurance that exceeds replacement cost for the property.

Lenders that choose to rely on the appraiser to provide a replacement cost estimate to determine the level of hazard insurance coverage required for a one-unit property should request that the appraiser provide the information in the "Cost Approach To Value" part of either the revised Uniform Residential Appraisal Report (Fannie Mae Form 1004 dated March 2005) or the Exterior-Only Inspection Residential Appraisal Report (Fannie Mae Form 2055 dated March 2005) or to report the information as an attachment to the appraisal report form. In such cases, lenders should rely on the appraiser's estimate of the replacement cost of the improvements, which is reported as the "Total Estimate of Cost New" on the revised forms. This estimate does not include any form of depreciation or obsolescence. It is not appropriate for the lender simply to subtract the reported site or land value from the appraised value of the property to make that determination because that result is an estimate of the depreciated value of the improvements, not an estimate of their replacement cost.

13. What is expected with regard to the appraiser's reporting on the Scope of Work for an appraisal?

The Scope of Work for an appraisal based on an interior and exterior property inspection reported on the revised appraisal report forms is based on the complexity of the appraisal assignment and the reporting requirements of the appraisal report form, including the stated Definition of Market Value, Statement of Assumptions and Limiting Conditions, and Certifications. The appraiser is required, at a minimum, to:
• perform a complete visual inspection of the interior and exterior areas of the subject property;
• inspect the neighborhood;
• inspect each of the comparable sales, at least from the street;
• research, verify, and analyze data from reliable public and/or private sources; and
• report his or her analysis, opinions, and conclusions in the appraisal report.

The stated Scope of Work on the appraisal report forms reflects the minimum level of research and analysis required. The appraiser can expand the minimum Scope of Work for the appraisal and report on any additional research or analysis that was necessary and performed based on the complexity of the appraisal assignment. The need for an expanded Scope of Work is specific to the particular appraisal assignment and should be the exception, not the norm, for appraisals on typical one-unit properties.

Notes

Notes

Made in the USA
Coppell, TX
18 July 2023

19333633R00275